America in Vietnam

AMERICA IN VIETNAM

Guenter Lewy

NEW YORK
OXFORD UNIVERSITY PRESS
1978

Copyright © 1978 by Guenter Lewy

Library of Congress Cataloging in Publication Data

Lewy, Guenter, 1923–
  America in Vietnam.

  Includes index.
  1. Vietnamese Conflict, 1961–1975. 2. United
States—History—1945–   I.   Title.
DS558.L48   959.704′3373   77-26204
ISBN 0-19-502391-9

Part of this book appeared in slightly different form
in *Commentary* magazine.

Second printing, 1979

Printed in the United States of America

Preface

This book began as an effort to find answers to some of the factual uncertainties and moral ambiguities created by the war in Vietnam. It was completed some five years later amid reports of a new human tragedy in the making—uncounted hapless refugees drowning on the high seas and thousands of others seeking a new home in a world all too indifferent to their suffering.

The desirability of bringing to bear more light, rather than heat, on the discussion of the American involvement in Vietnam has been apparent for a long time, but somewhat paradoxically serious interest in this emotion-laden subject appears to have declined just as reliable information on events in Indochina is finally becoming available. Under provisions of Executive Orders 10501 and 10816, promulgated by President Eisenhower, and Executive Order 11652, issued by President Nixon on 8 March 1972, the secretaries of the military services have discretionary authority to permit qualified researchers from outside the executive department access to classified defense information.* Whether out of unacquaintance with this provision of the law or for lack of interest in a subject many Americans would prefer to forget, no scholar until now has availed himself of this rich, and indeed indispensable, source.

This book is the first work dealing with the Vietnam war which, in addition to standard sources, makes use of the classified records of the U.S. Army, Air Force and Marine Corps—after-action reports of military operations, field reports and staff studies of the pacification effort and the Phoenix program, intelligence reports, investigations of war crimes, and the like. As one would expect, the picture that emerges is novel and occasionally startling in both fact and significance.

---

* New regulations on national security information are currently being drafted by the Carter administration. It is expected that the principle of access by historical researchers will be preserved.

The first six chapters seek to provide a reliable empirical record of American actions in Vietnam and, in the process, to clear away the cobwebs of mythology that inhibit the correct understanding of what went on—and what went wrong—in Vietnam. In the interest of a treatment in depth, the scope of this study has been limited to Vietnam proper. The complex story of the growing involvement of Laos and Cambodia in the Indochina conflict requires a separate, detailed account and is therefore touched upon here only insofar as it relates most directly to developments in Vietnam.

It is among actions taken—or not taken—by the U.S. and its allies *in Vietnam* that the explanation for the course of events and the final outcome of the war has to be found. Back in 1962 President Kennedy is supposed to have called the infiltration of communist cadres from the North a built-in excuse for failure in the South. In the same way, the collapse of the South Vietnamese army in the face of still another large-scale invasion from the North, preceded by drastic cuts in aid to South Vietnam imposed by the U.S. Congress after the Paris Agreement of 1973, has tempted both the last leaders of South Vietnam and most of the U.S. military to avoid facing the fundamental reasons for this defeat. The South Vietnamese, and indeed American soldiers earlier, it is argued, could have won the war had they not been frustrated by political constraints in the U.S. and the collapse of the home front. There is no denying that the reductions in U.S. aid did weaken South Vietnam's ability to resist the well-equipped northern divisions, and war-weariness and antiwar sentiment in America were widespread. However, the nonachievement of U.S. goals in Vietnam had other and deeper causes, prominently including a failure to understand the political and social dynamics of a revolutionary war. To ignore these basic causes in favor of a facile stab-in-the-back legend will give rise to more illusions and prevent the learning of the necessary and correct lessons of the Vietnam debacle.

To a large number of Americans the Vietnam war represents not only a political mistake and national defeat but also a major moral failure. The catalog of evils with which the United States is burdened includes the indiscriminate killing of civilians, the assassination and torture of political adversaries, the terror-bombing of North Vietnam, duplicity about it all in high places and much else. For many younger people, in particular, America in Vietnam stands as the epitome of evil in the modern world; this view of the American role in Vietnam has contributed significantly to the impairment of national pride and self-confidence that has beset this country since the fall of Vietnam.

It is the reasoned conclusion of this study, developed especially in chapters 7–11, that the sense of guilt created by the Vietnam war in the minds of many Americans is not warranted and that the charges of *officially condoned* illegal and grossly immoral conduct are without substance. Indeed, detailed examination of battlefield practices reveals that the loss of civilian life in Vietnam was less great than in World War II and Korea and that concern with minimizing the ravages of war was strong. To measure and compare the devastation and loss of human life caused by different wars will be objectionable to those who repudiate all resort to military force as an instrument of foreign policy and may be construed as callousness. Yet as long as wars do take place at all it remains a moral duty to seek to reduce the agony caused by war, and the fulfillment of this obligation should not be disdained. I hope that this book may help demonstrate that moral convictions are not the exclusive possession of persons in conscience opposed to war, and that those who in certain circumstances accept the necessity and ethical justification of armed conflict also do care about human suffering.

The Vietnam experience was always more complex than ideologues on either side could allow. The reality of the Vietnam war was composed of myriad events; the intricacy and variety of the scene was such that visiting "hawks" and "doves" could each observe, investigate and leave, assured of the wisdom of the view each held upon arrival. Like pieces in a kaleidoscope, the "facts" of the Vietnam war could, and still can, be put together in a multitude of configurations which in turn lead to different political and moral judgments and conclusions. I make no claim to have overcome all of the difficulties which confront the search for "the truth" about Vietnam. I do assert that the previously untapped sources at my disposal have enabled me to clarify some of the most important, hitherto contested, issues of the war, and that my major findings are supported by evidence which stands up under critical scrutiny. Sections of the epilogue, I should acknowledge, dealing with such questions as whether the U.S. could have won in Vietnam, are necessarily in large measure speculative. That part of the book will have to be judged by different criteria, and I shall not be displeased if future events were to prove my reflections to have been unduly pessimistic—especially my observations concerning the political impact of the Vietnam disaster at home and abroad.

One of the by-products of the Vietnam war and the Watergate events has been the creation of a major credibility gap regarding official sources and a general distrust of facts and figures issued by the American government. At the same time, the most implausible and unsubstantiated allegations are often believed if in line with the conventional wisdom—widely held views and prejudices. Some of these allegations have been repeated and reprinted so many times as to supply, as it were, their own confirmation and verification. It is symptomatic of the ideological fervor which has characterized much writing on the Vietnam war that many authors have accepted as fact those portions of the *Pentagon Papers*, the Defense Department's history of the Vietnam conflict, which served the particular axe they were grinding but have rejected as tainted and unreliable documents from the same source which they deemed inconvenient and out of line with their political views.

In this book I have relied upon standard methods of historical inquiry such as cross-checking of sources and testing for consistency, and I am satisfied that the evidence derived from the official documents utilized is reliable. Not meant for public consumption, many of these documents are highly critical of various aspects of U.S. actions in Vietnam, a fact which enhances both their credibility and usefulness. Reports by American military and civilian officials in the countryside provide an important supplement and corrective to the command histories and after-combat reports of American military units. The most valuable of these original sources are the monthly and end-of-tour reports by province and district advisers and the findings of special teams of trouble-shooters, called the Pacification Studies Group, which operated outside the regular chain of command and therefore were unaffected by the prevailing pressures to report progress and success. Other important sources are recorded interviews with high-ranking communist defectors and captured documents as well as the investigative reports and transcripts of courts-martial involving war crimes. The adversary process in the interplay of prosecution and defense here provides unusual insights into the reality of the war. Specific problems of reliability, as for example the notorious exaggeration of enemy body count, are discussed in the appropriate chapters below.

New sources will undoubtedly become available in the future which will throw additional light on this topic. But the Vietnam war is too important a subject and the national trauma too deep to allow the postponement of a searching and disinterested study until the last archives everywhere have been opened. Mythology, half-truth and falsehood concerning events in Vietnam abound and, unless corrected, will enter the textbooks for the miseducation of our children. Moreover, waiting carries its own price tag. The writer loses familiarity with the spirit of the times he is describing; as some of the recent works on World War II demonstrate, the passage of time does not necessarily deepen and improve perspective. More importantly, crucial participants die and memories fade. Hence analysts in the future will have to be content with the written record, which is never complete or conclusive. Within any governmental bureaucracy, civilian or military, many memoranda, cables, directives and rules are drafted and issued to safeguard careers or for public consumption or for the eyes of the historian. It is therefore important to supplement and check the formal record through interviews with key decision-makers. In this study I have benefited greatly from discussions with several major and numerous lower-ranking participants in the events I am describing. Their number is far too large to permit listing them by name; many of them preferred to talk not for attribution. Interviews with Vietnamese refugees now in the United States have further helped clarify significant details.

I agree with the saying, attributed to Disraeli, that there are lies, damned lies and statistics; but the statistical data adduced here are merely one type of evidence. No major conclusion of this study depends on the accuracy of any particular set of figures. On the other hand, treated with the necessary circumspection and correctly interpreted, these statistical data are often highly illuminating. General readers, interested in the overall picture, can safely skip my tables, just as they can ignore my notes which generally contain only citations of sources. Scholars interested in the archival location of particular documents should consult the Note on Military Records at the back of the book.

Lastly, I wish to acknowledge my gratitude to the persons and organizations which have aided me in the preparation of this work. A grant from the research council of the University of Massachusetts/Amherst helped make possible several months of archival research in Washington, D.C. A Rockefeller Foundation Humanities Fellowship, awarded for the academic year 1976–77, provided the leisure to work through the large quantity of documentary materials obtained there and actually write the book.

I am appreciative of the cooperation of various bureaus and officials in the Departments of State and Defense; the Agency for International Development; the Offices of the Judge Advocates General of the military services; the staff of the Judge Advocate General's School at Charlottesville, Virginia (in particular Major W. Hays Parks, formerly Marine Corps representative at the school); the Records Management Division, Office of the Adjutant General, U.S. Army; the Office of Air Force History; and the History and Museums Division of the Marine Corps. I am especially thankful to Dr. Charles B. MacDonald, Mr. Vincent Demma and the other historians in the Vietnam project of the U.S. Army Center of Military History whose hospitality and assistance I enjoyed during many months in Washington. I owe a special debt to Dr. John Henry Hatcher, formerly chief archivist of Vietnam records, U.S. Army, whose unfailing willingness to be helpful cut through numerous, seemingly insurmountable bureaucratic knots and without whom this study could not have been completed in the form it finally took.

Many of those named or referred to anonymously in the preceding paragraphs have read the first draft of this book; so did my friends Abraham Ascher, Peter Berger, Stanley Elkins, Robert Gessert, William V. O'Brien, Stanley Rothman and David H. Scott. I thank them all for their thoughtful and constructive criticism. Needless to say, none of the above individuals, organizations and agencies are responsible for the opinions and conclusions reached here, which remain for better or for worse my own responsibility.

A final word of gratitude is due my wife, as always an indispensable source of encouragement and wise counsel.

Northampton, Mass.
December 1977   G.L.

Contents

Tables,
Maps,
Charts

Tables

Maps

Charts

America in Vietnam

1

The Roots of Involvement

Assistance to the French

The decision of the Truman administration in early 1950 to provide financial aid to the French military effort in Indochina was taken against the background of the fall of Nationalist China and the arrival of Communist Chinese troops on the Indochina border in December 1949. The Ho Chi Minh regime had just been recognized as the government of Vietnam by the Soviet Union and Communist China. Mao's government provided sanctuary, training and heavy arms to the Viet Minh (Revolutionary League for the Independence of Vietnam) which, despite the trappings of a mere nationalist movement, was increasingly evolving into a party openly committed by organization and ideology to the communist sphere. On 6 March 1950 the U.S. secretary of defense informed the president: "The choice confronting the United States is to support the legal government in Indochina or to face the extension of Communism over the remainder of the continental area of Southeast Asia and possibly westward. . . ."[1]

American assistance was accompanied by pressure upon the French to complete the independence of Vietnam, Laos and Cambodia, since January 1950 part of the French Union. American policy-makers were fully aware that only the complete decolonization of Indochina would lead to the establishment of a stable noncommunist force in the areas adjacent to Communist China. But American leverage was weak. The French were sensitive over what they regarded as American interference in their internal affairs and they suspected the U.S. of seeking to supplant them, economically and politically, in Indochina. Moreover, America was anxious to obtain French support for the creation of a European Defense Community (EDC). The U.S. was seriously concerned about a Soviet threat to a Western Europe made destitute by World War II—through overt aggression or internal subversion by Communist parties steadily gaining in strength. EDC therefore had high priority in American planning and this led to reluctance to antagonize the French over the issue of Indochina. France, consequently, could ignore American proddings to grant meaningful authority to the formally independent Government of Vietnam (GVN), headed by the emperor Bao Dai.

The outbreak of the Korean War on 25 June 1950 confirmed the U.S. in its view that the issues in Vietnam were far greater than those of a mere colonial war and that French resistance to the Chinese-supported Viet Minh was a crucial link in the containment of communism. Given the extensive influence exerted by the Soviet Union over other communist nations, it was natural for the U.S. to see the attempt of the communist Ho Chi Minh regime to expel the French from Indochina as part of communist worldwide aggressive designs. Accused by Senator Joseph McCarthy of being soft on communism, the Truman administration did not want the loss of Indochina to be added to the charge that it had caused the "loss" of China. On 27 June 1950 President Truman announced that the U.S., following the call of the UN Security Council, was sending troops to the aid of the attacked South Koreans. "The attack upon Korea makes it plain beyond all doubt that Communism has passed beyond the use of subversion to conquer independent nations and will now use armed invasion and war." The Seventh Fleet was ordered to protect Formosa, and U.S. forces in the Philippines were strengthened. "I have similarly directed acceleration in the furnishing of military assistance to the forces of France and the Associated States in Indo China and the dispatch of a military mission to provide close working relations with those forces."[2]

The Indochinese and Korean theaters of war were now interdependent battlefields, for in each case China was the major source of support for the communist armies involved in the fighting. Help for the French could weaken Communist China's ability to assist the North Koreans. U.S. military supplies began to arrive in Saigon and a Military Assistance Advisory Group (MAAG) was established to administer the support program. As Ho Chi Minh's forces grew in strength and the French effort lagged, American aid was stepped up. U.S. assistance, which began with the modest sum of $10 million in 1950, in fiscal year 1954 reached $1.063

billion, at which time it accounted for 78 percent of the French war burden.[3]

The increase in American aid was accompanied by an escalation in explanatory rhetoric and in the importance attributed to a noncommunist Indochina. A statement of policy, approved by President Truman and the National Security Council (NSC) on 25 June 1952, asserted that "the loss of any of the countries of Southeast Asia to Communist control as a consequence of overt or covert Chinese Communist aggression would have critical psychological, political and economic consequences." All of Southeast Asia and the Middle East would probably follow. "Such widespread alignment would endanger the stability and security of Europe. Communist control of all of Southeast Asia would render the U.S. position in the Pacific offshore islands precarious and would seriously jeopardize fundamental U.S. security interests in the Far East." The area also was the principal world source of natural rubber and tin. Its loss could result in economic and political pressures on Japan that would make it extremely difficult to prevent Japan's eventual accommodation to communism. It was, therefore, imperative to prevent a Viet Minh victory in Indochina. The French were to be assured that the U.S. regarded the successful French military effort there "as essential to the security of the free world, not only in the Far East but in the Middle East and Europe as well."[4]

No serious discussion or questioning appears to have taken place of the importance of Southeast Asia to American security interests, of the correctness of the dire predictions regarding the consequences of the loss of the area, of the probability of success in the military struggle, or of the costs of winning the war in Indochina. It was recognized, as an NSC staff study in February 1952 put it, that "in the long run, the security of Indochina against communism will depend upon the development of native governments able to command the support of the masses of the people and national armed forces capable of relieving the French of the major burden of maintaining internal security."[5] But just as during the subsequent direct American involvement and the failure of successive Vietnamese governments to heed U.S. proddings for social and economic reforms, the refusal of the French to move aggressively in the direction of full independence for Indochina did not lead to any diminution of American assistance. The authors of the *Pentagon Papers*, the Defense Department history of the Vietnam conflict, comment correctly: "The U.S. became virtually a prisoner of its own policy. Containment of communism, concern for the French in relation to the postwar Europe of NATO, EDC, and the Soviet threat in the West, . . . all compelled the U.S. to continue aid."[6] The overriding fear seemed to be that in the event of too much American pressure the French would pull out of Indochina and put before the U.S. the extremely undesirable choice of either abandoning Indochina or dispatching American ground forces.[7]

The Eisenhower administration, which came into office in January 1953, inherited this policy and saw no reason to modify it. The idea of a communist monolith that threatened the noncommunist world and had to be contained still had considerable plausibility and commanded wide adherence. If communist forces won control over Indochina or any substantial part thereof, Secretary of State John Foster Dulles declared before the Overseas Press Club on 29 March 1954, "they would surely resume the same pattern of aggression against other free people in the area." Southeast Asia, the rice bowl of the Far East and an area of great strategic value, was of transcendent importance to the entire free world and its loss had to be prevented.[8] In his press conference on 7 April 1954, President Eisenhower compared the effects of the loss of Indochina upon the rest of Southeast Asia to that of falling dominoes: "You have a row of dominoes set up, you knock over the first one, and what will happen to the last one is the certainty that it will go over very quickly." Asia had already lost some 450 million of its people to communism, "and we simply can't afford greater losses."[9]

Meanwhile time was running out for the French, and the government in Paris was under mounting domestic pressure to end the bloodletting, which showed no sign of a successful conclusion. At the meeting of the Big Four foreign ministers in Berlin in February 1954 the French succeeded in having the Indochina problem placed on the agenda of an upcoming international conference at Geneva which was to discuss a settlement of the Korean War. In anticipation of this conference the Viet Minh launched a major effort to turn the tide of battle in their favor. On 13 March forces under the command of General Vo Nguyen Giap began an assault upon the French fortress of Dien Bien Phu where General Henri Navarre had concentrated 10,000 of his men. Navarre had hoped that French superior firepower would enable him to smash such an attack and score a decisive victory. Instead, the Viet Minh, greatly helped by a substantial increase in Chinese aid, including artillery and radar, showed themselves the stronger by far and by early April the fortress was in serious danger of falling.[10] A proposal by Admiral Arthur W. Radford, chairman of the Joint Chiefs of Staff (JCS), to launch a massive American air strike for the relief of the besieged garrison was opposed by eight congressional leaders who were consulted on 3 April. The next day President Eisenhower, unwilling to intervene militarily without the support of Great Britain and congressional approval, rejected the proposed strike.[11] Attempts on the part of Secretary of State Dulles to obtain British and French commitments for a program of collective military action failed, and on 7 May 1954 Dien Bien Phu fell. The French military effort in Indochina, for all practical purposes, had collapsed.

The 1954 Geneva Conference

The discussion of the Indochina problem at the Geneva Conference began on 8 May. Buoyed by their victory at Dien Bien Phu, spokesmen for the Democratic Republic of Vietnam (DRV) demanded the withdrawal of all foreign troops and immediate free elections. But the Russians and Chinese Communists convinced Ho Chi Minh to settle for the partition of Vietnam along the 17th parallel and elections after two years. The two senior communist powers were courting the new nations of Asia and Africa with the slogan of peaceful coexistence and support for their anticolonial aspirations. There was fear that a continuation of the war would bring in the United States after all and establish it as a military power on the Asian continent. The possibility of a deal between Mendès-France and Molotov to trade off France's rejection of the EDC for Russian intervention in support of a compromise in Indochina can also not be excluded.[12]

The final outcome of the 1954 Geneva Conference has been the subject of much misunderstanding. The so-called Geneva accords in fact comprised six unilateral declarations, three cease-fire agreements, an unsigned final declaration, and the minutes of the last plenary session on 21 July. Only the cease-fire agreements, signed by the respective military commands, can be considered formally binding accords. The language of most of the documents was ambiguous and reflected the absence of consensus at the conference. Calls to "observe the Geneva accords," often heard in later years, thus were necessarily devoid of concrete meaning.

The failure of the South Vietnamese government, since 16 June 1954 headed by Ngo Dinh Diem, to accept national elections in 1956 as provided by the final declaration of the Geneva Conference has been held a justification of North Vietnam's support for the insurgency in the South. Once "it became clear that the election provision would not be carried out recourse to coercion by Hanoi was both predictable and permissible. . . ."[13] Two other students of the subject argue similarly that "when a military struggle for power ends on the agreed condition that the competition will be transferred to the political plane, the side that violates the agreed condition cannot legitimately expect that the military struggle will not be resumed."[14] But was there such an "agreed condition?"

The "Final Declaration of the Geneva Conference on the Problem of Restoring Peace in Indo-China" noted that "the essential purpose of the Agreement relating to Viet Nam is to settle military questions with a view to ending hostilities and that the military demarcation line is provisional and should not in any way be interpreted as constituting a political or territorial boundary." Free general elections by secret ballot, supervised by an international commission, were to be held in July 1956 in order to bring about a final political settlement. Meanwhile everyone was to be allowed to decide freely in which zone he wished to live.[15] And yet there are strong indications that nobody at the conference took the idea of an early unification through free elections seriously. Why have a massive exchange of population if the two zones were to be unified within 700 days or so? Why was the machinery for settling future disagreements on the implementation of this agreement so haphazard? "The provision for free elections which would solve ultimately the problem of Vietnam," wrote Prof. Hans J. Morgenthau in 1956, "was a device to hide the incompatibility of the Communist and Western positions, neither of which can admit the domination of all of Vietnam by the other side. It was a device to disguise the fact that the line of military demarcation was bound to be a line of political division as well. In one word, what happened in Germany and Korea in the years immediately following 1945 has happened in Vietnam in the years following 1954."[16]

The likelihood that the provision for a political settlement in Vietnam through free elections in 1956 was indeed a hastily improvised afterthought to help save face for the Viet Minh is strengthened by the fact that the final declaration remained unsigned and was not even adopted by a formal vote. Five of the nine delegations present at the final session failed unreservedly to commit their governments to its terms. Laos, Cambodia and the DRV did not expressly associate themselves with the declaration. The South Vietnamese delegate filed a protest against the armistice agreement which he asked to have incorporated in the final declaration. South Vietnam specifically objected to the date of the elections and reserved "to itself complete freedom of action to guarantee the sacred right of the Vietnamese people to territorial unity, national independence and freedom."[17] Undersecretary of State Walter B. Smith stated that the U.S. government "is not prepared to join in a declaration by the Conference such as is submitted." The American representative insisted that elections to be free and fair had to be supervised by the United Nations. "With respect to the statement made by the representative of the State of Viet-Nam, the United States reiterates its traditional position that peoples are entitled to determine their own future and that it will not join in an arrangement which would hinder this."[18]

In the absence of either written or verbal consent by *all* of the nine participants, the most judicious study of the Geneva Conference of 1954 concludes, the final declaration created no *collective* conference obligation, and unless *all* the participating states consented to its terms and bound themselves thereto according to the procedures required by their respective constitutions, "the operative terms of the declaration were not binding upon *all* of the participants of the Geneva Conference."[19] Under certain circumstances, oral agreements may create obligations under international law. Here, however, both South Vietnam and the U.S. had stated their opposition in no uncertain terms. Neither of them, therefore, could be considered bound by the provisions for elections in 1956.

In order to refute this rather obvious conclusion it has been suggested that South Vietnam at the time of the Geneva Conference was not yet a sovereign state and therefore remained bound by the obligations assumed by France on its behalf. Article 27 of the Vietnam armistice agreement stated that "the signatories of the present Agreement and their successors in their functions shall be responsible for ensuring the observance and enforcement of the provisions thereof."[20] But the armistice agreement contained no prescriptive provisions for elections in 1956, and there is no suggestion in the record of the Geneva Conference that in accepting the final declaration France sought to bind South Vietnam. Quite the contrary, on 14 May French foreign minister Georges Bidault stated at the fourth plenary session that France considered the Government of Vietnam, recognized by 35 states, "fully and solely competent to commit Viet Nam."[21] Moreover, there is no agreement in international law on the extent to which a newly independent state must be regarded as bound by political obligations accepted prior to full independence by the state responsible for the conduct of its foreign relations.[22] Thus, whatever the degree of sovereignty possessed by the government of South Vietnam in July 1954, the refusal of the Diem government to hold elections cannot be said to have violated international law. Still less can this refusal be held a justification for the North's employment of force against the South.

Origins of the Insurgency

By July 1955, the end of the time period prescribed for a change of residence, about one million persons had left the communist regime in the North in order to settle in the South, while about 80,000 to 100,000 Viet Minh troops and supporters had gone north. Many of the regrouped Viet Minh had contracted local marriages in order to establish family connections in the South. After further training in the North, these men were subsequently sent back as leaders of the southern insurgency. The Communists also left behind several thousand of their best cadres as well as a large number of weapons caches. Five years later these units were to become the nucleus of the developing Liberation Army, as it was to be called. According to documents captured later and the testimony of a high-ranking defector, the Communists never expected the elections to take place and from early on prepared for a strategy of armed struggle to reunify the country.[23]

In its statement to the final session of the Geneva Conference the U.S. had declared that America would refrain from the threat or use of force to disturb the accords, but that it "would view any renewal of the aggression in violation of the aforesaid agreements with grave concern and as seriously threatening international peace and security."[24] Still anxious to achieve "united action" against Communist expansion and subversion in Southeast Asia, Dulles in September 1954 succeeded in getting seven nations—Britain, France, Australia, New Zealand, Pakistan, Thailand and the Philippines—to subscribe to the Southeast Asia Collective Defense Treaty which established the Southeast Asia Treaty Organization (SEATO). The declared purpose of the SEATO treaty was to help the parties "maintain and develop their individual and collective capacity to resist armed attack and to prevent and counter subversive activities directed from without against their territorial integrity and political stability" or against "any other state or territory" specifically designated and asking for assistance. A protocol attached to the treaty, also signed on 8 September 1954, extended this protection to Cambodia, Laos and "the free territory of the state of Vietnam."[25]

The SEATO treaty was ratified by the U.S. Senate on 1 February 1955 by a vote of 82–1. The Committee on Foreign Relations, in recommending approval, noted: "Since the end of World War II the threat to the free world has come more often in the form of indirect subversion than in direct aggression, and freedom lost by subversion may be as difficult to retrieve as that lost by force."[26] However, the SEATO treaty, unlike that establishing NATO, did not require an automatic response to armed attack, i.e. military action without further consideration by Congress, and instead called for each signatory "to meet the common danger in accordance with its constitutional processes."[27] It therefore would appear that despite some ambiguous claims made from time to time by the Johnson administration, the subsequent U.S. military intervention in Vietnam conformed to the spirit and purpose of the SEATO treaty but was not part of a legal obligation required by it.[28]

From the beginning of SEATO, most of the signatories of this treaty had little sense of urgency about its implementation. The French, especially, were less than enthusiastic about military action against North Vietnam. Moreover, France was not prepared to allow South Vietnam the right to leave the French Union as Premier Diem demanded. The U.S., on the other hand, insisted upon an immediate transformation of French policy in order to win the active loyalty of the people of South Vietnam. By May 1955 France to all intents and purposes was out of Vietnam and the U.S. had assumed responsibility for large-scale economic and military aid to Diem, in particular the creation and training of a strong South Vietnamese army. American assistance, Eisenhower wrote Diem on 1 October 1954, would be given "to assist the Government of Viet-Nam in developing and maintaining a strong, viable state, capable of resisting attempted subversion or aggression through military means. The Government of the United States expects that this aid will be met by performance on the part of the Government of Viet-Nam in undertaking needed reforms."[29] Diem was happy with this show of support, but, secure in the knowledge that he was regarded by the U.S. as the only alternative to a communist South Vietnam, he was slow in implementing the American call for political and economic reforms. Eisenhower's failure to spell out what would happen in the event of nonperformance, at a time when American commitment was as yet limited, laid the groundwork for the trap in which the U.S. would eventually find itself. Warnings by the JCS in November 1954 that without a stable civilian government in control and without a willingness by the Vietnamese themselves to resist communism "no amount of external pressure and assistance can long delay complete Communist victory in South Vietnam"[30] were ignored by civilian policy-makers.

By the fall of 1955 the unexpected had happened and Diem had succeeded in consolidating his regime. He had disarmed the private armies threatening his government, the refugees from the North were being settled, agricultural production was greatly increased and South Vietnam had achieved a modicum of stability. Sen. Mike Mansfield, returning from a visit to South Vietnam, reported that Diem breathed an air of self-confidence and authority. "And with good reason, for he had taken what was a lost cause of freedom and breathed new life into it."[31] In June 1956 Sen. John F. Kennedy outlined "America's stake in Vietnam" in a speech before the American Friends of Vietnam, a speech which expressed views shared then by a broad spectrum of American political opinion, including the Eisenhower administration, liberals like Arthur Schlesinger, Jr., and the socialist Norman Thomas.

Vietnam, declared Kennedy, "represents the cornerstone of the Free World in Southeast Asia, the keystone to the arch, the finger in the dike. Burma, Thailand, India, Japan, the Philippines and obviously Laos and Cambodia are among those whose security would be threatened if the red tide of Communism overflowed into Vietnam." But, Kennedy maintained, Vietnam was important to America for other reasons as well:

Secondly, Vietnam represents a proving ground for democracy in Asia. However we may choose to ignore or deprecate it, the rising prestige and influence of Communist China in Asia are unchallengeable facts. Vietnam represents the alternative to Communist dictatorship. If this democractic experience fails, if some one million refugees have fled the totalitarianism of the North only to find neither freedom nor security in the South, then weakness, not strength, will characterize the meaning of democracy in the minds of still more Asians. The United States is directly responsible for this experiment—it is playing an important role in the laboratory where it is being conducted. We cannot afford to permit that experiment to fail.

Third and in somewhat similar fashion, Vietnam represents a test of American responsibility and determination in Asia. If we are not the parents of little Vietnam, then surely we are the godparents. We presided at its birth, we gave assistance to its life, we have helped to shape its future. . . . This is our offspring—we cannot abandon it, we cannot ignore its needs. And if it falls victim to any of the perils that threaten its existence—Communism, political anarchy, poverty and the rest— then the United States, with some justification, will be held responsible; and our prestige in Asia will sink to a new low.

Fourth and finally, America's stake in Vietnam, in her strength and in her security, is a very selfish one—for it can be measured, in the last analysis, in terms of American lives and American dollars. . . . Military weakness, political instability or economic failure in the new state of Vietnam could change almost overnight the apparent security which has increasingly characterized that area under the leadership of President Diem. And the key position of Vietnam, in Southeast Asia, as already discussed, makes inevitable the involvement of this nation's security in any new outbreak of trouble.[32]

Senator Kennedy called upon the U.S. to oppose the elections provided for by the 1954 Geneva agreement. "Neither the United States nor Free Vietnam was a party to that agreement—and neither the United States nor Free Vietnam is ever going to be a party to an election obviously stacked and subverted in advance, urged upon us by those who have already broken their own pledges under the agreement they now seek to enforce." He also urged more economic and military aid to President Diem, whose government had taken "the first vital steps toward true democracy. Where once colonialism and Communism struggled for supremacy, a free and independent republic has been proclaimed, recognized by over 40 countries of the Free World."[33]

Kennedy's rhetoric not only exaggerated the importance of Vietnam to the U.S. but also glossed over serious flaws in Diem's "democracy." As time went on, Diem's dictatorial tendencies were to jeopardize the ability of South Vietnam to develop a strong national community with sufficient cohesion to withstand communist military pressure.

Ngo Dinh Diem was a man well known for his competence and integrity; he was free of the taint of being pro-French, and with American help in the years following 1954 Diem accomplished much good for his country. "When one saw the chaos in other ex-colonial areas of Asia and Africa and the high-handed corruption and inefficient standards of government in much of Latin America," a former American official has written, "South Vietnam and its leader Ngo Dinh Diem looked very good in comparison."[34] In the face of vast obstacles, wrote David Halberstam, "Diem acted forthrightly and courageously in the early years of his government."[35] Diem's regime appeared well on the way toward creating the kind of new nation that was well worth U.S. support—in terms of America's democratic ideals as well as American national interests in a highly unstable Southeast Asia.

And yet Diem's arbitrary and authoritarian methods, including wholesale suppression of newspapers critical of his regime, gradually alienated important segments of the urban population. At the same time, Diem lost ground in the countryside by replacing elected village chiefs and councils with his own appointees, who were unresponsive to the interests of the peasantry and often corrupt. A program of land reform, begun in 1956 with American support and advice, three years later was virtually inoperative. By that time, only 10 percent of the tenant farmers had received any land at all and for many of them the reform meant merely that they had to pay for land the Viet Minh had distributed to them earlier from the holdings of absentee owners.[36] So long as the government of South Vietnam was neither popular nor efficient, writes one well-informed scholar, "it seemed obvious that the Viet Minh would fill that vacuum."[37]

The Viet Minh, defending the interests of the peasants and basking in the glory of having defeated the French, not only were popular and in effective control of large parts of the South, but they also had a highly efficient organization ready to take advantage of the democratic liberties proclaimed in the final declaration of the Geneva Conference. "There is no doubt," argues Joseph Buttinger, a historian very critical of Diem, "that the strength of the Communists and their determination to unify the country under Ho Chi Minh justified temporary dictatorial measures against them if democracy was to have a chance in the South. . . . Only thus could the people have been offered the choice between Communism and the better government that the anti-Communist West expected Diem to create."[38] After describing the lack of freedom of the press and speech in South Vietnam in early 1956, Morgenthau went on to say: "Considering the enormity of the task which confronts Diem, it would be ill-advised to be squeamish about some of the methods he used."[39] But such dictatorial measures, to be justifiable, had to be temporary, limited to the communist apparatus, and accompanied by policies that would rally the population behind the new regime. Instead, Diem's heavy hand fell upon all political elements not fully backing his regime, and many of the tens of thousands arrested were innocent of any subversive activity or design. At the same time, as noted above, the Diem government failed to respond to the social grievances of the peasantry and thus deprived itself of any kind of mass support.

The massive campaign of forceful suppression against the Viet Minh carried out by the Diem regime in 1956–57 has been cited as the real cause of the southern insurgency. According to this thesis, argued in the 1960s by Jean Lacouture and Philippe Devillers in France and George McT. Kahin and John W. Lewis in the U.S., "the people were literally driven by Diem to take up arms in self-defense."[40] Eventually, in 1960, Southerners opposed to Diem formed the National Liberation Front (NLF), which "gave political articulation and leadership to the widespread reaction against the harshness and heavy-handedness of Diem's government. It gained drive under the stimulus of Southern Vietminh veterans who felt betrayed by the Geneva Conference and abandoned by Hanoi. . . . Insurrectionary activity against the Saigon government began in the South under Southern leadership not as a consequence of any dictate from Hanoi, but contrary to Hanoi's injunctions."[41]

Evidence available today—based on captured documents and the testimony of defectors familiar with internal party directives—contradicts almost all of this thesis. It is correct that the repressiveness of the Diem regime in the years 1956–59 created pressure for armed action in the South, but the rest of the argument is false. The decision to begin the armed struggle in the South was made by the Central Committee of the Vietnamese Workers' (*Lao Dong*) party (VWP), the communist party of Vietnam, in Hanoi in 1959. "The view that a coordinated policy of armed activity was initiated in the South by a militant group outside the Party, or by a militant southern faction breaking with the national leadership," writes the well-informed Jeffrey Race, a critic of the subsequent American intervention, "is not supported by historical evidence—except that planted by the Party. . . ." Two defectors separately interviewed by him, Race relates, "found very amusing several quotations from Western publications espousing this view. They both commented humorously that the Party had apparently been more successful than was expected in concealing its role."[42] The NLF, the evidence clearly shows, was formed at the instigation of the party in Hanoi; it was established as a typical communist front organization to hide the direction of the insurgency by the Communists. "The Central Committee," one defector stated, "could hardly permit the International Control Commission to say that there was an invasion from the North, so it was necessary to have some name . . . to clothe these forces with some political organization."[43]

Why did the party wait until 1959 before launching the armed phase of the revolution? First, in the years immediately following the Geneva Conference the Communists in the North had severe problems with their own "counterrevolutionaries." In 1955–56 perhaps as many as 50,000 were executed in connection with the land reform law of 1953 and at least twice as many were arrested and sent to forced labor camps.[44] A North Vietnamese exile puts the number of victims at one-half million.[45] These domestic difficulties dictated a policy of waiting. Ho Chi Minh told the Fatherland Front Congress in 1955 that "the North is the foundation, the root of our people's struggle. . . . Only when the foundation is firm, does the house stand firm."[46]

Secondly, the Central Committee felt that the revolutionary situation in the South was not yet "ripe," the masses had not yet become convinced that armed struggle was really necessary. During the years 1956–59 the party contributed to the development of a revolutionary situation by assassinating the most effective local administrators, schoolteachers, medical personnel and social workers who tried to improve the lives of the peasants. This program of systematic terror, known as "the extermination of traitors," predictably goaded the Diem regime into stepping up its clumsily pursued and often brutal antiterrorist campaign, creating an air of capricious lawlessness. "But the more the people were terrorized," recalls a prominent defector, "the more they reacted in opposition, yet the more they reacted, the more violently they were terrorized. Continue this until the situation is truly ripe, and it will explode . . . we had to make the people suffer, suffer until they could no longer endure it. Only then would they carry out the party's armed policy. That is why the Party waited until it did."[47]

As a result of Diem's anticommunist campaign, by late 1958 the party apparatus in the South had incurred severe losses, but the revolutionary potential was increasing. The southern branch of the party increasingly now demanded a change in policy. The decision to form armed units throughout the South in order to smash the GVN was made by the Fifteenth Conference of the Central Committee, meeting in Hanoi in January 1959, though the new policy directive was not issued until May 1959.[48] July 1959 saw the beginning of large-scale infiltration of armed cadres trained to raise and lead insurgent forces; it is estimated that during 1959–60 some 4,000 Southerners who had gone north in 1954 returned to South Vietnam.[49] In January 1960 General Giap declared that "the North has become a large rear echelon of our army. The North is the revolutionary base for the whole country."[50]

The commitment of the DRV to support the southern insurgency was made public at the Third Congress of the VWP, which convened in Hanoi in September 1960. According to Secretary-General Le Duan, the party faced the task of promoting the socialist construction in the North, making it "an ever more solid base for the struggle for national reunification," as well as the task of liberating "the South from the atrocious rule of the U.S. imperialists and their henchmen." To this end, the congress resolved that "to ensure the complete success of the revolutionary struggle in south Vietnam, our people there must strive to . . . bring into being a broad National United Front directed against the U.S. and Diem and based upon the worker-peasant alliance."[51] The formation of the NLF was reported by the news media in Saigon in December 1960.

The 10-point program of the NLF borrowed extensively from Le Duan's speech at the third party congress, but otherwise North Vietnam made great efforts to show its noninvolvement in the formation of the NLF, probably at least in part to deny the U.S. the excuse to expand the war to North Vietnam. Not until the end of January 1961 did Radio Hanoi announce that various forces opposed to the fascist Diem regime on 20 December 1960 had formed the National Front for the Liberation of South Vietnam and had issued a manifesto and program. Also designed to conceal the party's role in the revolutionary movement in the South was a "Declaration of the Veterans of the Resistance," issued in March 1960, which called for armed struggle against Diem and the formation of a government of national union. As defectors told Jeffrey Race, the declaration "was simply the product of a meeting called in accord with Central Committee policy, with the dual purpose of arousing internal support for the new phase of the revolution and of misleading public opinion about the true leadership of the revolution."[52]

The NLF as well as the People's Liberation Armed Forces (PLAF) established on 15 February 1961 undoubtedly included non-Communists opposed to Diem's autocratic rule; however all key positions were in the hands of party members. For tactical reasons NLF spokesmen occasionally took positions that differed slightly from the Hanoi line; from time to time there also may have developed tensions between what in effect was Hanoi's field command in the South and its parent headquarters in the North.[53] But the ultimate control of the NLF by the VWP was never in doubt. "Although welcoming support from all quarters," agree Kahin and Lewis, "from its inception the organization seems to have been dominated by the communists."[54] Despite an elaborate worldwide propaganda effort designed to demonstrate that the NLF was an independent and indigenous southern political entity with a policy of its own, the fact of control by Hanoi was eventually accepted by most knowledgeable observers. The impotence of the NLF was revealed after the collapse of South Vietnam in 1975 when all important positions in the temporary administration of the South and later in the government of the united Vietnam were given to Northerners. In August 1976 Jean Lacouture finally conceded that he had overestimated the autonomy of the NLF which, he now acknowledged, was "piloted, directed and inspired by the political bureau of the Lao Dong Party, whose chief was and remains in Hanoi."[55]

The same tactical considerations which dictated the formation of the NLF led to the establishment of the People's Revolutionary party (PRP) in January 1962, allegedly an independent organization without ties to the VWP in the North. In point of fact, the PRP was simply the southern branch of the VWP, set up to constitute the "vanguard" of the NLF and to overcome the ideological isolation of communist cadres in the South. For the rural population in South Vietnam all these maneuvers meant nothing new. As one defector told Jeffrey Race: "The formation of the People's Revolutionary Party had no significance to the peasantry. They live in intimate contact with the Party and thus were aware that it was still the communists. The People's Revolutionary Party was useful only in dealing with city people, intellectuals, and foreigners."[56]

The Period of "Sink or Swim with Diem"

By the time John F. Kennedy assumed the presidency on 20 January 1961, the situation in Vietnam had deteriorated considerably; the Vietnamese Communists or Viet Cong (VC) for short, as the Americans began to call them, dominated large sections of the country. Diem talked about the need for social and political reforms, but at the same time argued that these measures could be carried out only after the communist threat had been destroyed. In practice this meant that while the VC increased their strength in the countryside by redistributing wealth and status, as well as through the use of terror, the government relied for its survival on force alone.

A manifesto issued by 18 old-time political figures in April 1960, known as the "Caravelle Manifesto," urged Diem to "guarantee minimum civil rights" so that the people of South Vietnam would appreciate the value of liberty. "It is only at that time that the people will make all the necessary efforts and sacrifices to defend that liberty and democracy."[57] But Diem, increasingly isolated and turning inward, rejected this counsel and after an attempted military coup in November 1960 most of the signers of the manifesto were jailed. Personal loyalty to Diem, rather than ability, became the criterion for promotion in the army. As a precaution against the formation of cliques in the armed forces, troop commanders were rotated constantly. Cautious generals, fearful of casualties, conducted operations in areas where the VC were known not to be. Frustrated by a ubiquitous enemy, the troops often behaved brutally toward prisoners and the rural population.

Kennedy's belief in the importance of Indochina and Southeast Asia to the free world went back as far as 1954. His conviction that the U.S had to stand by its commitment to the area was reinforced by Nikita Khrushchev's speech on 6 January 1961, promising support to "wars of national liberation" in the developing world, including Vietnam, and by the Russian leader's bellicose threats to renew the blockade of Berlin made during his meeting with Kennedy in Vienna in June 1961. After the failure of the American-backed invasion of Cuba in April 1961, the prestige of the U.S. seemed seriously eroded. The need to make American power credible thus was seen as urgent. Moreover, a demonstration of American resolve in the one place where there existed an open communist challenge to declared American interests, i.e. Southeast Asia, would prove the new president's toughness not only to the Russians and Chinese but also to conservative critics at home. Charges that the Truman administration had given away China by holding back aid to Chiang Kai-shek were still fresh in everyone's memory.

In April 1961 the new administration established an interagency Vietnam task force; a counterinsurgency plan prepared by the Eisenhower administration now became the basis for a series of recommended actions to be taken by both the U.S. and GVN. The recommendations of the task force were strongly influenced by one of its members, the CIA operative Col. Edward Lansdale, who had had great success in helping President Ramon Magsaysay of the Philippines defeat a communist insurgency in that country. The prevention of communist domination, the report argued, required the creation of "a viable and increasingly democratic society in South Vietnam. . . ."[58] The president's response to this report also reflected Lansdale's strongly held view that Diem was the only effective leader in South Vietnam and should be won over to American ways of thinking through persuasion and trust rather than pressure. To be sure, in return for the dispatch of about 100 additional American military advisers, who were to help train another 20,000 men for the GVN armed forces,[59] Diem was to make reforms in his chain of command and reorganize his intelligence capacity. But then as later, Diem knew how to stall on the implementation of reforms recommended to him by the Americans while U.S. aid continued to flow.

The weakness of the American leverage was primarily the result of America's strong commitment to the defense of Vietnam. In order to deter Hanoi's drive against the South and to reassure the leaders of Southeast Asia, the U.S. repeatedly stated that America was determined to help South Vietnam preserve its independence and would not allow the country to be taken over by the Communists. But while these shows of resolve had little if any effect on the Communists, they did indicate to Diem that there was no danger of the U.S. suddenly abandoning South Vietnam and that he could therefore safely spurn American demands for reform. The only effective way of putting pressure on Diem would have been to threaten him with a withdrawal of U.S. support, but in view of the often-proclaimed vital importance of Southeast Asia to the West and America's commitment to the defense of the area as well as to Diem's leadership role, this threat was just not credible and therefore was never invoked.

All through the summer of 1961 Kennedy temporized. There was talk of sending American combat troops to Southeast Asia, if the situation deteriorated, but no firm decisions were made. In line with the importance attached by the president to counterinsurgency and unconventional warfare, a group of Special Forces personnel were sent to Vietnam to train their Vietnamese counterparts.[60] In October Kennedy sent his military adviser, Gen. Maxwell D. Taylor, on a fact-finding tour to Vietnam. Taylor returned to Washington on 3 November and, among other measures, proposed the dispatch of a military task force of 6,000–8,000 men in order to raise South Vietnamese morale and demonstrate the seriousness of U.S. intent to resist a communist take-over. The introduction of this force was to be related to flood relief; it was to consist of engineering and logistical units. The military advisory effort, Taylor recommended, should be shifted "to something nearer—but not quite—an operational headquarters in a theater of war. . . . The U.S. should become a limited partner in the war, avoiding formalized advice on the one hand, trying to run the war on the other."[61]

A joint memorandum by Secretary of State Dean Rusk and Secretary of Defense Robert McNamara, dated 11 November 1961, supported Taylor's recommendation that the U.S. commit itself to the clear objective of preventing the fall of South Vietnam to communism:

> The basic means for accomplishing this objective must be to put the Government of South Vietnam into a position to win its own war against the guerillas. We must insist that the Government itself take the measures necessary for that purpose in exchange for large-scale United States assistance in the military, economic and political fields. At the same time we must recognize that it will probably not be possible for the GVN to win this war as long as the flow of men and supplies from North Viet-Nam continues unchecked and the guerillas enjoy a safe sanctuary in neighboring territory. We should be prepared to introduce United States combat forces if that should become necessary for success. Dependent upon the circumstances, it may also be necessary for United States forces to strike at the source of the aggression in North Viet-Nam.[62]

The president approved the Rusk-McNamara recommendations for contingency planning and rejected Taylor's logistical task force proposal. The decision not to send troops appears to have been taken in part as a result of reports on the extreme administrative weakness and unpopularity of the Diem regime conveyed to the White House by State Department personnel who had accompanied Taylor to Vietnam. This pessimistic political appraisal was shared by John Kenneth Galbraith, U.S. ambassador to India, whom Kennedy had asked to make a brief visit to Saigon. There also was fear of complicating the delicate negotiations over the future of Laos which had begun in Geneva. The president did approve a substantial increase in the number of American advisers, who were now allowed to participate in combat missions, as well as the dispatch of two helicopter companies with their crews. Under rules of engagement (ROE) receiving the code name FARMGATE, American helicopters were authorized to engage in combat and combat support flights; a Vietnamese was to be on board so that in case of need these missions could be explained away as part of the American training effort.[63]

Until 1961 the U.S. military presence in South Vietnam had remained within the limits set by the Geneva accords. Before the French evacuated Hanoi on 9 October 1954, a CIA team contaminated the oil supply of a local bus company and by early 1955 the Americans, under the overall command of Colonel Lansdale, had succeeded in establishing and equipping a South Vietnamese paramilitary group in the North.[64] But these actions were obviously mere pinpricks. The American military advisory group (MAAG) in Saigon had existed before the Geneva Conference of 1954 and therefore could legitimately be continued. In 1955 this group took over from the French the job of training the South Vietnamese armed forces and this activity, too, was within the provisions of the Geneva accords. Articles 16 and 17 of the cease-fire agreement for Vietnam forbade the introduction into Vietnam of additional military personnel and armaments, but they did not prohibit the building of indigenous military forces. With the permission of the International Control Commission (ICC), the size of MAAG in May 1960 had been increased to 685 men. This was still below what the U.S. regarded as the authorized figure of 888, the total number of French and American advisers in South Vietnam at the time of the armistice.[65]

During the year 1961 the Kennedy administration debated the question whether the U.S. should finally renounce these restrictions and openly assume military assistance to the GVN. The ICC, operating on the unanimity principle and limited in its travels, had been unable to prevent substantial shipments of Chinese arms to the DRV armed forces or stem the infiltration of men into the South, estimated at 500–700 a month by 1961. But the Geneva accords were held to have some residual deterrent value and it was therefore decided to introduce additional personnel covertly. Members of the Special Forces arrived in civilian clothes.[66] As late as November 1961, total U.S. military strength in South Vietnam was only about 900 men,[67] but the increases in personnel and equipment decided upon after the Taylor mission, it was felt, could no longer be hidden. There also was need to lay the legal groundwork for the possible introduction of U.S. combat forces, for which contingency plans were now under way. In December 1961 the State Department, therefore, released a study by a member of the Policy Planning Council, William J. Jorden, which had been in preparation for several months and which was designed to document the massive violations of the Geneva accords by the DRV. Since under international law a material breach of an agreement by one party entitles the other to withhold compliance with an equivalent provision, the U.S. now felt entitled to disregard the Geneva ceilings on both U.S. personnel and the shipping of military equipment to South Vietnam.

The Jorden report was published under the title *A Threat to the Peace: North Viet-Nam's Effort to Conquer South Viet-Nam.* The publication stated that the NLF was a creation of Hanoi and that the DRV was actively supporting the southern insurgency. Infiltration of espionage agents and of "VC military forces, officers and men, sometimes in organized units, had assumed ominous proportions." Large quantities of military equipment and other supplies had also been sent.[68] While the captured documents and depositions of defectors clearly established North Vietnamese involvement, the Jorden report exaggerated the significance of this outside support. In October 1961 the CIA estimated that about 10–20 percent of the VC full-time strength of 16,000 consisted of infiltrated cadres. Despite North Vietnamese help, "the VC effort is still largely a self-supporting operation in respect to recruitment and supplies."[69] More basically, the preoccupation with infiltration from the North diverted attention from the political and social grievances on which the insurgency thrived, and it fed the illusion that mere military measures—increases in border controls and in the strength of the South Vietnamese armed forces—would be sufficient to defeat the VC. "The civilian duties of government," writes an English scholar, "came gradually to be thought of as incidental to the fighting and the civilian departments of the administration ancillary to the army; comfort was taken in battle statistics without regard for the imponderable psychological elements in popular morale."[70]

In a letter to Diem of 14 December 1961, Kennedy took note of the violations of the Geneva accords by North Vietnam and promised prompt increases in assistance. "If the Communist authorities in North Viet-Nam will stop their campaign to destroy the Republic of Viet-Nam, the measures we are taking to assist your defense efforts will no longer be necessary. We shall seek to persuade the Communists to give up their attempts of force and subversion."[71] Again, in his State of the Union Message of 11 January 1962, the president declared with regard to Vietnam: "The systematic aggression now bleeding that country is not a 'war of liberation'—for Viet-Nam is already free. It is a war of attempted subjugation and it will be resisted."[72] A few weeks later the advisory body, MAAG, became MACV—Military Assistance Command, Vietnam. By the end of 1962, U.S. military personnel in South Vietnam numbered 11,326.[73] From this point on, the growth of the American military commitment to the defense of South Vietnam was steady and seemingly irreversible (see Table 1-1).

Table 1-1 Expansion of U.S. Military Effort in South Vietnam, 1960–64

	1960	1961	1962	1963	1964
U.S. military personnel[a]	875	3,164	11,326	16,263	23,310
Deaths from hostile action	NA	1	31	77	137
USAF sorties flown[b]	NA	NA	2,334	6,929	5,362
U.S. aircraft lost to hostile action:					
Fixed-wing	NA	NA	7	14	30
Helicopters	NA	NA	4	9	22

SOURCE: OASD (Comptroller), SEA Statistical Summary, Table 103, 26 September 1973; Table 860B, 18 February 1976; Table 322, 19 April 1972; Table 350A, 5 October 1973.

[a] As of December 31.
[b] Attack, combat air patrol, escort.

During the first half of 1962 the military situation in Vietnam appeared to take a turn for the better. The influx of American advisers and equipment boosted the morale of the South Vietnamese troops; the introduction of helicopters, in particular, gave government forces a new mobility and at first terrified the VC. As of 31 December 1962, the U.S. had a total of 222 aircraft in Vietnam, 149 of them helicopters; during the year 1962 American planes flew 2,048 attack sorties,[74] officially described as training missions. There were expectations that the insurgency was being brought under control and that it would be possible gradually to withdraw American military personnel. The successful ending of the war in Vietnam became an article of faith that was beyond challenge. The failure of Hanoi and Russia to live up to the neutralization of Laos, agreed upon at Geneva in July 1962, angered the president and precluded the possibility of still another retreat in Southeast Asia.

Optimism about developments in Vietnam in 1962 was related to the strategic hamlet program that was begun in February 1962 and at first showed signs of success. The idea was to concentrate the rural population in fortified villages so as to provide them with physical security against the VC; social programs to develop popular allegiance to the government were to follow. In practice, the strategic hamlets became instruments of control rather than pacification. The peasants resented having to leave their homes and gardens and being herded into fortified stockades which the government forced them to build without compensation for their labor. Instead of receiving social services and economic aid that would improve village life, the rural population, in line with Diem's philosophy of personalism, was exhorted to concentrate on self-improvement and their personal virtue. Support of the government was seen as a duty.[75] By the summer of 1962 the GVN claimed to have established 3,225 strategic hamlets which were said to hold over 4 million people, one-third of the population of the country.[76] Only after the collapse of the Diem regime in October 1963 did it become clear that many of these hamlets existed on paper only and were part of the misinformation the GVN was feeding the Americans.

Areas which could not be penetrated by government forces were declared "open zones," and villages in them were subjected to random bombardment by artillery and aircraft so as to drive the inhabitants into the safety of the strategic hamlets. The resultant flow of tens of thousands of refugees was welcomed by Diem as a show of political support: people were voting for him with their feet.[77] Actually, as was to be expected, these measures of coercion further alienated the population. The strategic hamlet program, like its predecessor the agroville idea in 1959, thus drove a wedge not between the insurgents and the peasants, but between the rural population and the government. The final result was less rather than more security in the countryside.

Senator Mansfield, who was back in Vietnam at the end of 1962 for the first time since 1955, upon his return expressed his deep concern over the trend of events. The U.S. had provided South Vietnam with over $2 billion in various aid programs. Since 1961 more than 10,000 American military personnel had been sent to Vietnam to provide advice and assistance. These forces had not been intended for combat, but in fact had been in combat and more than 50 of them had lost their lives, about half in battle. Despite all this, the strength of the VC had increased steadily and large parts of South Vietnam were unsafe a short distance outside the cities. "It is most disturbing to find that after 7 years of the Republic, South Vietnam appears less, not more stable than it was at the outset, that it appears more removed from, rather than closer to, the achievement of popularly responsible and responsive government."[78]

The indicators of deterioration were indeed many, though the optimistic reports coming out of Saigon tended to downplay them. Correspondents like David Halberstam and Neil Sheehan reported that GVN troops, poorly led by officers appointed for political reasons, avoided combat whenever possible. It was common practice, recalls the head of the USIA in Saigon during the years 1962–64, for government forces to break off battle at nightfall even when they appeared to be winning. Diem insisted on maintaining outposts even in VC-dominated areas, and the VC overran these posts so regularly and easily that American advisers began calling them "Viet Cong PXs"; the guerillas were able to use them for supplies and weapons with almost the same ease as an embassy wife shopped at the Saigon post exchange. The inability of the GVN to protect people in the hamlets at night meant that the latter found it suicidal to cooperate with the authorities.[79]

Support for Diem meanwhile became increasingly support for the Ngo Dinh family, which concentrated all authority in its hands: Diem as president and minister of national defense; brother Nhu as his chief political counselor and confidant; brother Can as proconsul in central Vietnam; brother Thuc, an archbishop, as leader of the country's two million Roman Catholics; Mme. Nhu as "First Lady" and leader of the Woman's Solidarity Movement. The Nhus, in particular, were widely hated and were the target of an unsuccessful attack by air force pilots on the presidential palace in February 1962. The U.S. over several years tried to persuade Diem to get rid of Nhu, but these moves only seemed to consolidate his influence.[80]

The crisis leading to the downfall of Diem began with a badly handled Buddhist protest demonstration in Hue on 8 May 1963 in which nine people were killed. There followed a series of well-publicized self-immolations by Buddhist monks which shocked Western opinion. Charges that the Buddhists were oppressed or persecuted were largely baseless, though Catholics did receive preferential treatment in the army and bureaucracy. Moreover, the Buddhist struggle movement quickly became the rallying point of opposition to Diem's autocratic and repressive rule.

American suggestions that the crisis be handled with more flexibility floundered on Diem's mandarin character, which would not permit the loss of face. On 21 August Nhu carried out raids on twelve Buddhist pagodas which damaged many of them and resulted in the arrest of over 1,400 Buddhists. In a hastily issued statement, improperly cleared by the required echelons, the U.S. publicly dissociated itself from these actions; two days later two Vietnamese generals planning a coup against Diem made their first contact with an American representative.

The events of the summer of 1963 revived discussions among Washington policy-makers about the desirability of finding a replacement for Diem. The new U.S. ambassador in Saigon, Henry Cabot Lodge, on 29 August cabled Rusk that in his view the war could not be won under a Diem administration and that the U.S. therefore should support the ouster of Diem.[81] But the plotting generals in Saigon did not feel sufficiently strong and feared abandonment by Washington at the crucial moment; nothing therefore came of the plans for a coup.

Differences of opinion over a new policy in Vietnam remained unresolved during the following weeks. The State Department argued for a program of pressure against Diem and favored support of a coup; the military were fearful of a possible power vacuum that would endanger the military effort against the VC. The Diem regime meanwhile continued arrests of Buddhists and students. Following another fact-finding mission by McNamara and Taylor, Kennedy on 5 October approved their recommendations for selective suspensions of aid. The purpose of these actions was described in a cable to Lodge: "Actions are designed to indicate to Diem Government our displeasure at its political policies and activities and to create significant uncertainty in that government and in key Vietnamese groups as to future intentions of United States."[82] No initiative was to be taken to actively encourage a new coup attempt, but contacts with possible alternative leaders were to be pursued. After a request by one of the plotters, General Duong Van ("Big") Minh, for clarification of the American position, Lodge was told on 6 October: "While we do not wish to stimulate coup, we also do not wish to leave impression that U.S. would thwart a change of government or deny economic and military assistance to a new regime if it appeared capable of increasing effectiveness of military effort, ensuring popular support to win war and improving working relations with U.S."[83]

The complicated and fast-moving events of October cannot be described here in detail; the 6 October message to Lodge can stand as a correct and summary description of the American posture during that crucial month. The overthrow of Diem, when it finally came on 1 November, was carried out by Vietnamese, but the U.S. had encouraged the plotters and therefore shared responsibility for the coup. It is equally clear that no American policy maker had favored the killing of Diem and Nhu; President Kennedy is said to have been stunned by the news of the brutal murders.[84]

An editorial in the *New York Times* of 3 November 1963 hailed the new rulers of South Vietnam as a group of dedicated anticommunists, saying that if the new regime identified itself with the aspirations of the people, it would have "taken a long step toward repulsing further Communist inroads throughout Southeast Asia."[85] In fact, the overthrow of Diem did not lead to a regime more responsive to the needs of the people of South Vietnam and it brought with it a dangerous degree of political instability. During 1964 there were seven governments in Saigon, none of them genuinely popular or competent. There are many, therefore, then and today, who regard American support of the coup as a fatal mistake. Diem's assassination, wrote the Vietnam scholar Ellen J. Hammer, "ended an earnest attempt to bring to the side of the Saigon government some of the nationalist fervor that the Communists regarded as their own monopoly."[86] The fast-changing successor regimes, argues another expert, did not reform any of the faults of Diem's patriarchy: "Instead whatever was already bad became worse—patronage, corruption, detention without trial or review." From then on, "the question was not going to be how to encourage a regime in South Vietnam that America could support, but of finding one that would support her in keeping up the struggle against the jubilant Communists."[87]

In some ways, it would appear, both sides in this basically unresolvable argument are right. As it turned out, we did not win with Diem's successors, who shared most of Diem's shortcomings, while in addition they lacked his prestige as a nationalist and mandarin-father figure, and therefore never enjoyed the respect and support of either the country's educated elite or the common people. And yet we probably could not have won with Diem either. Indeed, only after his downfall did the deepness of the rot become apparent as most of the statistics of progress, on which the U.S. had relied in its optimistic appraisals, turned out to have been manipulated and false.

President Johnson Inherits the Vietnam Albatross

On 22 November 1963, less than a month after the murder of Diem, President John F. Kennedy was assassinated; Lyndon B. Johnson assumed the burden of our Vietnam involvement without questioning its importance for the U.S. On 21 December McNamara reported to the new president that the situation in Vietnam was "very disturbing." In the countryside it had in fact been deteriorating "since July to a far greater extent than we realized because of our dependence on distorted Vietnamese reporting. The Viet Cong now control very high proportions of the people in certain key provinces, particularly those directly south and west of Saigon." The new government "is indecisive and drifting." Unless reversed, current trends, "in the next 2–3 months, will lead to neutralization at best and more likely to a Communist-controlled state."[88]

Against the background of a chaotic political situation in the South, the central committee of the VWP met in Hanoi in December 1963 and ordered an offensive strategy for the southern insurgency. The key task at that time was "to make outstanding efforts to rapidly strengthen our military forces in order to create a basic change in the balance of forces between the enemy and us in South Viet-Nam." Efforts must be made to increase main force units: "It is time for the North to increase aid to the South, the North must bring into further play its role as the revolutionary base for the whole nation."[89] The text of this resolution did not fall into American hands until years later, but evidence of a new aggressiveness on the part of the VC was all too apparent in early 1964. Government control of rural territory was shrinking while South Vietnamese morale was sagging. Frustrated over lack of progress in the South, decision-makers in Washington became increasingly more sympathetic to the idea of attacking what appeared to be the source of the trouble, North Vietnam.

Pressure for hitting North Vietnam with air power came primarily from the JCS. In a memo of 22 January 1964, addressed to McNamara, Chairman Maxwell D. Taylor endorsed the covert operations against North Vietnam, consisting of intelligence-gathering and harassing attacks on the coast by South Vietnamese forces, which the president had approved on 16 January.[90] But Taylor argued that these actions would have to be expanded and he urged the U.S. to make ready for aerial bombing of key targets in North Vietnam and the mining of the sea approaches to that country.[91] The interim report of an interagency group, headed by Robert

Johnson of the State Department's Policy Planning Council, issued on 1 March 1964, similarly suggested a blockade of the port of Haiphong and air strikes on North Vietnamese lines of communication (LOCs), POL (petroleum, oil and lubricants) storage areas, and key industrial complexes.[92] Underlying these recommendations was the widely held view that a poor country like North Vietnam would not want to lose its small industrial plant, achieved at great cost and sacrifice. The Vietnam expert Bernard Fall in 1962 had had a conversation with Premier Pham Van Dong in which the latter had acknowledged the extreme vulnerability of North Vietnamese factories to American air power and had expressed great fear of U.S. air attacks upon the North.[93]

The idea that destroying or threatening to destroy North Vietnam's tiny industry would pressure Hanoi into calling off its support of the VC was rejected by Roger Hilsman, assistant secretary of state for Far Eastern affairs, who resigned from the Johnson administration in early 1964. "In my judgment," Hilsman wrote Rusk on 14 March 1964, "significant action against North Vietnam that is taken before we demonstrated success in our counter-insurgency program will be interpreted by the Communists as an act of desperation, and will, therefore, not be effective in persuading the North Vietnamese to cease and desist."[94] Subsequent events were to prove that the U.S. indeed had seriously underestimated the strength of Hanoi's commitment to victory in the South and had overestimated the possible effectiveness of U.S. bombing as a way of weakening that resolve. Yet, however farsighted and correct, Hilsman's position lost out because the U.S. had a major unused air capability and because President Johnson, aware of the strong faith in air power among many influential members of Congress, was unwilling to invest American lives in a ground war before he had tried to use air power as a mode of pressure.

On 17 March 1964 the president approved a series of recommendations made to him by McNamara which became National Security Action Memorandum (NSAM) 288. The new policy statement stressed the importance of stable political leadership in South Vietnam, the development of policies that would provide economic progress to the rural population, the training of an offensive guerilla force to supplement the conventionally organized South Vietnamese army, and other measures. The South Vietnamese, it was stated, must win their own fight. However, if the Khanh government took hold vigorously or if hard information was received of significantly stepped-up arms supplies from the North, the U.S. should have the capability to initiate with 30 days' notice a program of military pressure upon the North, including air attacks against military and possibly industrial targets.[95] A news release from the White House took note of recent setbacks in Vietnam and affirmed: "It will remain the policy of the United States to furnish assistance to the South Vietnamese for as long as it is required to bring Communist aggression and terrorism under control."[96]

The instability and inefficiency of the Kahnh regime undermined the implementation of most of the actions expected of the South Vietnamese. By the summer of 1964 the U.S. had 21,000 military personnel in Vietnam and the earlier withdrawal plans had been shelved. On 20 June Deputy Commander Gen. William C. Westmoreland became commander of the United States Military Assistance Command (COMUSMACV), replacing the overoptimistic Gen. Paul D. Harkins. Both Westmoreland and Lodge favored some new vigorous American military commitment such as air strikes against Laos or North Vietnam in order to put new confidence into the South Vietnamese leadership. Premier Khanh himself argued strongly for the bombing of the North, and the JCS, too, kept up the pressure for an early beginning of such a bombing campaign. Warnings that the U.S. would initiate air and naval actions against North Vietnam unless the Communists stopped their escalatory course were conveyed to Hanoi by the Canadian Blair Seaborn, a member of the ICC, on 18 June 1964, but brought no response.[97]

Also in June, planning moved ahead in Washington for a congressional resolution of support for U.S. policy in Southeast Asia that would demonstrate American firmness and provide backing for the president if and when he decided to entertain military action against North Vietnam.[98] "I was determined, from the time I became President," Johnson recalls in his memoirs, "to seek the fullest support of Congress for any major action that I took. . . . As we considered the possibility of having to expand our efforts in Vietnam, proposals for seeking a congressional resolution became part of the normal contingency planning effort. But I never adopted these proposals, for I continued to hope that we could keep our role in Vietnam limited."[99] The events in the Gulf of Tonkin in August 1964 pushed the U.S. one crucial step closer to full military involvement.

The Gulf of Tonkin Crisis

Covert operations against North Vietnam, first approved by President Kennedy in 1961, by 1964 proceeded on two tracks. First, a program known as Operations Plan (OPLAN) 34A, carried out by the South Vietnamese with U.S. advice and logistical support, involved raids on the North Vietnamese coast and was part of the concept of gradually increasing pressure upon North Vietnam. Secondly, a program with the code name DE SOTO, run by the U.S. Pacific Command, used U.S. destroyers to observe North Vietnamese naval activity in support of the VC and to locate and estimate the range capabilities of North Vietnamese radar transmitters.[100] The belief of the North Vietnamese that these two independent programs were interrelated was probably one of the reasons for the Gulf of Tonkin incidents in early August 1964.

On 2 August 1964 the American destroyer *Maddox* was on a DE SOTO patrol 28 miles from the North Vietnamese coast, heading away from it, when it was attacked by three North Vietnamese torpedo boats. The attack took place on the high seas, but the administration decided to write off the incident as a mistake or unauthorized action of an overeager commander. The president did order a continuation of the patrols, doubled the force by adding the destroyer *Turner Joy,* provided air cover and authorized the aircraft and destroyers to attack and destroy any forces which attacked them in international waters. On this patrol the *Maddox* had been permitted to approach to within eight nautical miles from the North Vietnamese coast and the Communists had made no claim that it had come within their three-mile territorial zone. Still, to prevent a misunderstanding and incident the *Maddox* and *Turner Joy* were now ordered to go no closer than 11 miles off the mainland. Unknown to the commander of the *Maddox* or the task group commander, a South Vietnamese OPLAN 34A attack had taken place during the night of 31 July against a group of islands off the North Vietnamese coast some 130 miles from the position of the *Maddox*. To make clear that the American patrol was not connected with these 34A activities, the cruising track of the two ships was moved farther north and away from the scene of the South Vietnamese operations.[101]

On their own initiative, the two American ships went no closer than 16 miles from the coastline, well outside the extended 12-mile territorial zone which the North Vietnamese began to claim about a month after the incidents in the gulf. During the night of 4 August (9:20 A.M., Washington time), the ships reported that they had received intelligence to the effect that North Vietnamese naval forces had been ordered to attack them. About two hours later the *Maddox* radioed that the destroyers, then about 60 miles from the shore, were under attack. Due to freak weather conditions and the nervousness of a sonar technician, initial reports from the patrol commander about the details of the engagement were less than clear, but, as Secretary of Defense McNamara testified in 1968 at a congressional hearing, the fact of the attack itself was never seriously in doubt.[102] At a noon meeting of the NSC the president therefore approved an air strike on North Vietnamese naval bases in retaliation for this attack on the high seas. McNamara waited until further reports had come in, clearing up some earlier ambiguities, before at 6:07P.M. he released the final authorization for this strike. The attacks, consisting of 64 sorties launched from American aircraft carriers against North Vietnamese torpedo boat bases and a nearby oil storage area, took place in the early hours of 5 August.[103]

Shortly after the order for the air strikes had been issued, at 6:45 P.M. on 4 August, the president met with 18 congressional leaders from both parties, explained his reasons for the reprisal strikes and informed the legislators of his intention to request a statement of congressional support for his Southeast Asia policy. A formal message to this effect reached Congress on 5 August; draft resolutions introduced by Sen. J. William Fulbright and Rep. Thomas E. Morgan were discussed and approved by the Senate Foreign Relations and the House Armed Services committees on 6 August. On the following day, 7 August 1964, the resolution was approved by a unanimous House and in the Senate by a vote of 88 to 2.

The so-called Gulf of Tonkin resolution of 7 August, some phrases of which were borrowed from a draft resolution dated 25 May 1964, noted that the repeated illegal attacks on the American ships were "part of a deliberate and systematic campaign of aggression that the Communist regime in North Vietnam has been waging against its neighbors and the nations joined with them in the collective defense of their freedom." It was therefore resolved "that the Congress approve and support the determination of the President, as Commander in Chief, to take all necessary measures to repel any armed attack against the forces of the United States and to prevent further aggression." The United States regarded the maintenance of international peace and security in Southeast Asia as "vital to its national interest and to world peace" and "is, therefore, prepared, as the President determines, to take all necessary steps, including the use of armed force, to assist any member or protocol state of the Southeast Asia Collective Defense Treaty requesting assistance in defense of its freedom."[104]

This important statement of policy, it has been argued by many writers, was rushed through the Congress without the latter having a real chance to understand the implications of this grant of power to the president. There is little justification for this complaint. Debate in the House, lasting 40 minutes, was indeed perfunctory, but the Senate discussed the resolution for eight hours and Senator Fulbright, who as chairman of the Foreign Relations Committee steered the resolution through the Senate, took pains to explain what was involved in this far-reaching authorization. For example, in response to a question from Senator Brewster, who was concerned about a land war on the Asian continent and who asked whether the resolution would authorize "the landing of large American armies in Vietnam or in China," Fulbright answered: "There is nothing in the resolution, as I read it, that contemplates it. . . . However, the language of the resolution would not prevent it. It would authorize whatever the Commander in Chief feels is necessary. . . . Whether or not that should ever be done is a matter of wisdom under the circumstances that exist at the particular time it is contemplated." Fulbright expressed the hope that American sea and air power would "deter the Chinese Communists and the North Vietnamese from spreading the war."[105]

Again, when Senator Nelson expressed concern that the resolution in effect gave the president advance authority to land as many divisions as he deemed necessary and even to engage in a direct military assault upon North Vietnam, Fulbright answered that he would deplore this but he could not give Nelson "an absolute assurance that large numbers of troops would not be put ashore."[106] And when Senator Cooper asked: "Then, looking ahead, if the President decided that it was necessary to use such force as could lead into war, we will give that authority by this resolution?" Fulbright replied: "That is the way I would interpret it." In the old days, he pointed out, war usually resulted from a formal declaration of war and there was time for Congress to participate in such decisions. However, under modern conditions of warfare, "it is necessary to anticipate what may occur. . . . That is why this provision is necessary or important."[107]

Senator Fulbright's unequivocal support of the president was shared by practically all members of Congress. Senator Church was one of many who commended President Johnson for his "restraint, as well as for the promptness and effectiveness of the American retaliation," and he added: "There is a time to question the route of the flag, and there is a time to rally around it, lest it be routed. This is the time for the latter course, and in our pursuit of it, a time for all of us to unify."[108] There was the hope that this show of unity would deter North Vietnam from further escalation. Only when the price of halting this aggression had risen considerably and when a successful conclusion of the American intervention had become an increasingly distant "light at the end of the tunnel," did many of these same senators begin to have second thoughts; some of them, including Fulbright, went so far as to allege that the Gulf of Tonkin resolution had been extorted from the Congress through misrepresentation and deception.

The charge of duplicity involves the second attack on the *Maddox* on 4 August which allegedly never took place and is said to have been manufactured by the administration in order to have an excuse to expand the war and obtain congressional approval for it.[109] It is true that the president seized upon the incident in order to approve and carry out measures that had been recommended to him earlier, but this does not establish that the attack was deliberately provoked, let alone that it rests on a fabrication. While the sonar and radar readings and the visual sightings of torpedoes can be questioned as unreliable and inconclusive, there is other unambiguous evidence which leaves no doubt of the fact of an attack. As McNamara told the Senate Foreign Relations Committee in closed session in February 1968, the *Maddox* was able to intercept uncoded North Vietnamese orders to patrol boats to attack the American ships as well as transmissions from the North Vietnamese boats to their headquarters reporting on the progress of the sea battle.[110] At the time of that hearing in early 1968, most members of the committee, including Senators Mansfield and Gore, accepted McNamara's account as honest and consistent with his testimony before them in August 1964. Even Fulbright assured the secretary, "I never meant to leave the impression that I thought you were deliberately trying to deceive us. . . ."[111] Three years later into the war and a good deal more embittered, Fulbright charged just such deception.[112] By then the Gulf of Tonkin affair had become the symbol and outstanding example of the duplicity for which the Johnson administration was being condemned.

The allegation that the second attack was provoked is no more substantiated. As the authors of the *Pentagon Papers* point out in their account, not meant for public consumption, the modification of the course of the destroyers and the extension of the distance from the coast they were to observe indicate an intention to avoid—not provoke—further contact. During the two days between 2 and 4 August there is no record of staff meetings or task assignments which typically accompany preparations for a military operation. The U.S.S. *Constellation*, one of the carriers from which the retaliatory air strikes were launched, remained well outside the patrol's operating area and the mission against the North Vietnamese targets had to be delayed for several hours in order to permit the *Constellation* to approach within reasonable range.[113] The North Vietnamese conceivably may have connected the presence of the American ships with another South Vietnamese 34A operation some 70 miles away, or they may have sought to avenge their losses suffered on 2 August. Whatever their reasons, there is no evidence to show that the events of the second Gulf of Tonkin incident were the result of a deliberate provocation which would provide the U.S. an opportunity for reprisals.

The Options Narrow

During the fall of 1964 political instability in South Vietnam reached a dangerous new high, and GVN military activities against the VC all but ground to a halt. In view of the game of musical chairs at the top, efforts to develop an efficient administration made no progress at all. VC control of real estate and population was increasing steadily and by the end of the year a final South Vietnamese collapse had become a distinct possibility.

President Johnson's public posture during this period, which coincided with the presidential election, reflected his hesitation to be drawn into a wider war. American boys, he stated several times, should not be sent to Asia to do the fighting which Asian boys, with American advice and equipment, should be doing for themselves. "That is the course we are following. So we are not going north and drop bombs at this stage of the game, and we are not going south and run out and leave it for the Communists to take over."[114] Selective quotations from the *Pentagon Papers*, including the edited version published by the *New York Times*, have made it appear that while Johnson projected himself as the peace candidate, the administration in 1964 had decided to wage overt war in Vietnam and was merely holding back with this escalation until after the election in November. "Congress and the American people," charges one writer, "were led to believe that the administration was seeking a moderate solution to the Vietnam problem when, in fact, it was carefully preparing to involve the United States in a major war after the November election."[115] The record available to date does not substantiate this second charge of duplicity against Johnson.

During the latter part of 1964 various elements of the national security hierarchy urged the president to demonstrate U.S. resolve and lift South Vietnamese morale through some new military moves. Maxwell Taylor, since July U.S. ambassador in Saigon, at the end of November recommended resort to the long-debated use of air power against targets in North Vietnam and the infiltration routes in Laos, but the president rejected this counsel. "My audience in Washington," recalls Taylor, "was generally sympathetic to such ideas but still not ready to bite the bullet and face the inevitability of either taking military action against North Vietnam or running the very real risk of failing disastrously in Southeast Asia. No one was yet prepared to abandon the dictum that stable government in the south must precede military action in the north despite the improbability of ever getting stable government without the lift to the national spirit which military action against the homeland of the enemy could provide."[116] There were suggestions from the JCS and Assistant Secretary of Defense John T. McNaughton to provoke the DRV into actions which could then be answered by an air campaign against the North, but the principal decision-makers, including the president, vetoed these proposals as well.[117] A list of 94 targets for such a campaign had been ready for some time, but no decision was made to implement these contingency plans.

The president made no commitment to expand the war through air operations against North Vietnam until early February 1965, three full months after the election, and the decision to send U.S. combat forces came later still (see chap. 2). By the end of January most of Johnson's advisers had concluded that the situation in the South had become critical and, in the absence of a change of American policy, would shortly lead to a calamitous defeat. Under Secretary of State George W. Ball appears to have been the only important official to oppose a bombing of North Vietnam and to urge a compromise settlement.[118] Meanwhile, both Peking and the new leaders of Russia who had toppled Khrushchev in October 1964 were making bellicose noises. In January 1965 President Sukarno of

Indonesia, increasingly relying upon the Communists, pulled his country out of the United Nations and stepped up his campaign to destroy the new Malaysian Federation. The need for the U.S. to act in some new and decisive manner appeared to be compelling.

On 6 February the VC attacked the American base in Pleiku and killed and wounded a large number of U.S. servicemen. By now the president was ready to respond and the decision was taken to strike back with bombing attacks against North Vietnam. Another VC assault on 10 February, which caused even larger American casualties, was followed by another series of bombing raids; by early March air action against the North, codenamed ROLLING THUNDER, had become a regular and sustained effort which I will discuss further in chapter 11. Public statements tied the bombing offensive to the "larger pattern of aggression" from the North. The U.S. had now openly become a co-belligerent in the war.

Over the weekend of 12 February serious work began in the State Department on a white paper that would document the infiltration of men and supplies from the North and thus justify the bombing of North Vietnam. Work on such a document had been under way for some time and on 27 February 1965 the white paper, entitled *Aggression from the North: The Record of North Viet-Nam's Campaign to Conquer South Viet-Nam,* was ready for release. The campaign of terror and armed attack upon South Vietnam, the white paper stated, was "inspired, directed, supplied and controlled by the Communist regime in Hanoi. This flagrant aggression has been going on for years, but recently the pace has quickened and the threat has now become acute." According to incomplete evidence, during 1964, 4,400 infiltrators had entered the South and, unlike in earlier years when practically all of the infiltrators had been regrouped Southerners, 75 percent of these men now were natives of North Vietnam. Increasingly the VC relied on weapons produced in Communist China and other communist countries and most of these arms entered South Vietnam from the North. On 16 February a North Vietnamese cargo ship had been sunk in shallow waters off the coast of Phu Yen province and more than 100 tons of arms, ammunition and supplies had been seized. The white paper concluded that North Vietnam's "carefully conceived plan of aggression against the South," in violation of the Geneva accords and the U.N. charter, had been established beyond question. The U.S. would help South Vietnam repel this aggression. "The choice now between peace and continued and increasingly destructive conflict is one for the authorities in Hanoi to make."[119]

The 1965 white paper did not make as good a case for aggression from the North as would have been desirable. The presence in South Vietnam of an enemy unit had to be confirmed through prisoner interrogation or analysis of captured documents and this meant that such confirmation usually did not become available until six to nine months after the unit had infiltrated. Moreover, the most persuasive evidence on the infiltration of men and supplies was derived from intelligence sources which could not be revealed publicly without compromising their future usefulness. The white paper, therefore, was criticized as being inconclusive. I. F. Stone, the author of a widely discussed reply, found it strange that after five years of fighting the white paper could include in the case histories of infiltration only six men who actually were born in the North. The number of weapons originating in the North he described as surprisingly small.[120]

The weakness of the white paper has given support to the argument that the sharp escalation of the fighting in the South during the year 1965 was the result of the American decision to bomb the North which in turn prompted Hanoi to begin to send its own regulars into South Vietnam. The evidence indicated, claimed Roger Hilsman in 1967, "that Hanoi did not send any North Vietnamese regular units south until 1965, after the United States had decided itself to escalate the war by bombing the North."[121] Theodore Draper alleges that at the time the bombing of North Vietnam started, Hanoi had only 400 regular soldiers in the South. The U.S. converted this into an "invasion" in order to have a justification for its own escalation.[122]

More complete evidence than that available in 1965 and 1966 contradicts Hilsman and Draper and confirms the basic argument of the 1965 white paper. As I mentioned earlier, the decision to assume the offensive was taken by the VWP in Hanoi in December 1963. As the level of the fighting increased during 1964 and an early South Vietnamese collapse became likely, North Vietnam decided to send in reinforcements in order to hasten victory and guarantee Hanoi's political control after the triumph. The supply of Southerners having been exhausted, elements of the 325th People's Army of Vietnam (PAVN) Division began to prepare in April 1964 for the move south. The first regular North Vietnamese infantry regiment departed the North in September or October 1964; another followed in October and a third in December. By March 1965 three North Vietnamese regiments had joined the fighting and Hanoi had not 400 but 5,800 men in the South.[123] When the former CIA analyst Samuel A. Adams was asked in 1975 by the House Select Committee on Intelligence whether the figures of the infiltration of North Vietnamese troops had been manipulated to justify the bombing of the North, he replied that in his experience the number of North Vietnamese regulars was generally "underestimated, in fact by a good deal. . . ."[124] The initial escalation, through the introduction of North Vietnamese combat forces, thus was carried out by the Communists, well before the American decision to bomb North Vietnam. The North Vietnamese themselves until the end denied the very presence of their forces in the South. At the same time, and somewhat contradictorily, they defended their participation in the fighting with the argument that Vietnam was one single nation and the Vietnamese people therefore entitled to defend their country wherever it was being invaded by foreign imperialists.

More basically, the argument over the issue of North Vietnamese regulars in the South diverts attention from the larger pattern of North Vietnamese intervention, which, as we have seen, goes back at least to 1959. Contrary to communist propaganda, the southern insurgency was never a spontaneous uprising but from the beginning was a deliberate campaign, directed and supported from Hanoi. In view of the extensive involvement of North Vietnam, it was also misplaced to regard the conflict as simply a "civil war." North Vietnamese assistance, conveyed via an elaborate trail system through Laos and Cambodia, consisted of the dispatch of war materiel and the infiltration of regrouped Southerners who replaced battlefield casualties and often assumed command positions in the NLF. Many of these men were carefully trained cadres who became political or military officers, weapons and communications specialists, and who built the VC into a highly disciplined and effective military force. Confirmed counts put the number of personnel sent south between 1959 and 1964 at over 28,000,[125] and this is a very conservative figure.

The assertion of the Committee of Concerned Asian Scholars that "the largely peasant forces of South Vietnam received meaningful support from North Vietnam only when the American assault intensified beyond where they could resist by their own means"[126] thus represents a reversal of the real sequence of events. American support for the South Vietnamese

armed forces was stepped up in 1961 because the VC, beefed up by infiltrators from the North, were winning and threatened to take over South
Vietnam. Back in 1962 Roger Hilsman argued that the introduction of a
large number of American advisers, their involvement in combat and the
supply of equipment, formally in violation of the Geneva accords, were
"fully justified by Communist aggression,"[127] and in view of what we
know today about the methodical expansion of northern support for the
insurgency it is difficult to fault this conclusion. With regard to the years
1965–67 it is possible to maintain that the North Vietnamese merely
matched the massive American buildup, until by March 1968 North Vietnamese forces were estimated to constitute 71 percent of total communist
combat strength in the South.[128] But such a difficulty of deciding who was
initiating and who was responding does not arise for the years prior to the
full commitment of American combat forces in 1965.

Critics like Draper are on more solid ground with the argument that
the main reason for the beginning of the bombing campaign against North
Vietnam was not the need to counter the introduction of North Vietnamese regulars or the sharp increase in sophisticated communist-bloc
weapons sent south but rather the drastic deterioration of both the political and military posture of the GVN, which threatened a complete South
Vietnamese collapse.[129] While for purposes of public relations it might be
asserted by the U.S. government that massive intervention by the DRV
was responsible for the growing VC domination of the countryside, in fact
it was the weakness of the GVN which put the VC in a position to receive,
conceal, feed and deploy the professional reinforcements sent by General
Giap from the North.[130] The notion of "foreign aggression"—in itelf perfectly justified and supported by the facts—for a while enabled the U.S. to
take flight from the intractable problems of the South and it fostered the
illusion that the solution to the whole war was located in the North. The
relatively low cost and risk of an air campaign against North Vietnam,
compared with the commitment of U.S. ground forces, were another inducement to hit the North. Some American policy-makers in the spring of
1965 appear really to have believed that the bombing of selected North
Vietnamese targets would compel the leaders of Hanoi to order a stand-
down of VC violence. When this expectation proved false, the U.S. chose
the only remaining option other than a withdrawal and acknowledgment
of defeat—the introduction of American ground combat forces.

2

The Big-Unit War

The Enclave Phase

On the morning of 8 March 1965, the U.S. Marine Corps Battalion Landing Team 3/9 went ashore on the beaches just north of Danang. Its companion battalion 1/3 landed by air later that same day. The first American ground combat units had entered Vietnam.

The dispatch of the marines had been requested by COMUSMACV, General Westmoreland, on 22 February in order to help protect the Danang installations, the most important American base in the northern provinces, against VC raids, sabotage and mortar attacks. The mission assigned the two marine battalions, numbering some 3,500 men, was just that—"to occupy and defend critical terrain features in order to secure the airfield and, as directed, communications facilities, U.S. supporting installations, port facilities, landing beaches and other U.S. installations against attack. The U.S. Marine Forces will not, repeat will not, engage in day to day actions against the Viet Cong."[1]

In light of the subsequent buildup of American combat forces in Vietnam, which by the end of 1965 was to exceed 180,000 men, it is tempting to regard this language and the limitation imposed on the marines' task as mere camouflage of bigger things to come. Secretary of State Dean Rusk's assurances on "Face the Nation" one day before the landing of the American force that the marines would not engage in operations against the VC have been called "misleading" and are regarded as typical of the deception of which the Johnson administration has been accused by many critics.[2] In point of fact, it would appear that this major decision, a watershed in the history of the American involvement in Vietnam, was made without very much discussion and planning and that the sending of the marines was seen by official Washington "as a one shot affair to meet a specific situation."[3] As the internal record makes clear, the attention of the major decision-makers was still focused on the impending air war against North Vietnam, which was expected to yield an early North Vietnamese response.

General Westmoreland and his staff out in the field, on the other hand, welcomed the deployment of the marines as a first step in the implementation of contingency plans made by the American Pacific command which called for the dispatch to Vietnam of American troop units. Westmoreland had concluded that the armed forces of South Vietnam did not have the capability of defeating the VC by themselves; to him, therefore, the arrival of the marines was an important stage in the buildup of outside forces which he was seeking. Westmoreland found an ally in the Army chief of staff, General Harold K. Johnson, who visited Vietnam from 5 to 12 March. Upon his return to Washington, Johnson stressed the gravity of the situation in South Vietnam and proposed the deployment of a U.S. division. This recommendation, Westmoreland confirms in his memoirs, reflected his own thinking. While awaiting results from the bombing of North Vietnam and pending an expansion of the South Vietnamese army (ARVN), Westmoreland felt we had no choice but "to put our own finger in the dike."[4]

On 1 April the NSC met to discuss strategy for Vietnam. Ambassador Taylor had been recalled to Washington for consultations, and he met with Defense Secretary McNamara and the JCS just prior to the NSC meeting. He now learned that the JCS proposed the deployment of one Korean and two American divisions for active operations against the VC. Taylor had repeatedly questioned the wisdom of using American ground forces in a direct counterinsurgency role and he reacted negatively to this idea. Also before the conferees was Westmoreland's "Commander's Estimate of the Situation," prepared during the early weeks of March, which emphasized the need for reinforcements to offset the enemy's buildup. Westmoreland, too, wanted the equivalent of two U.S. divisions by June 1965 and possibly more thereafter if the bombing failed to halt North Vietnam's support of the southern insurgency. Whereas Taylor, if American forces were to be committed to combat, favored the restriction of these troops to key enclaves along the coast, Westmoreland wanted an offensive strategy, with U.S. troops pursuing the enemy concentrations in the central highlands. The commitment of American troops was defensive in the sense of seeking to forestall a South Vietnamese defeat, he recalls, but "the adage that a good offense is the best defense was as applicable in

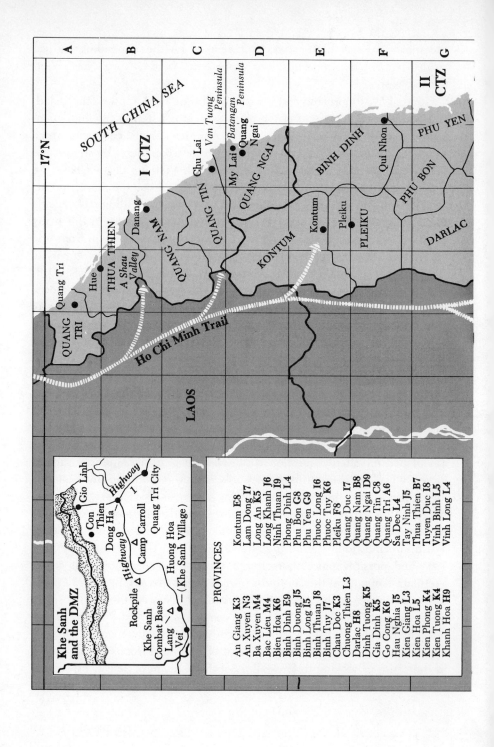

SOUTH CHINA SEA

17°N

I CTZ

II CTZ

Van Tuong Peninsula
Batangan Peninsula

Chu Lai
My Lai • Quang Ngai

QUANG NGAI

QUANG TIN

Danang
QUANG NAM

A Shau Valley
Hue
THUA THIEN

Quang Tri
QUANG TRI

KONTUM

Kontum

Pleiku
PLEIKU

BINH DINH

Qui Nhon

PHU YEN

PHU BON

DARLAC

Ho Chi Minh Trail

LAOS

Khe Sanh and the DMZ

Gio Linh
Con Thien
Dong Ha
Highway 1
Quang Tri City
Camp Carroll
Rockpile
Highway 9
Khe Sanh Combat Base
Lang Vei
Huong Hoa
—(Khe Sanh Village)

PROVINCES

An Giang **K3**	Kontum **E8**
An Xuyen **N3**	Lam Dong **I7**
Ba Xuyen **M4**	Long An **K5**
Bac Lieu **M4**	Long Khanh **J6**
Bien Hoa **K6**	Ninh Thuan **I9**
Binh Dinh **E9**	Phong Dinh **L4**
Binh Duong **J5**	Phu Bon **G8**
Binh Long **I5**	Phu Yen **G9**
Binh Thuan **J8**	Phuoc Long **I6**
Binh Tuy **J7**	Phuoc Tuy **K6**
Chau Doc **K3**	Pleiku **F8**
Chuong Thien **L3**	Quang Duc **I7**
Darlac **H8**	Quang Nam **B8**
Dinh Tuong **K5**	Quang Ngai **D9**
Gia Dinh **K5**	Quang Tin **C8**
Go Cong **K6**	Quang Tri **A6**
Hau Nghia **J5**	Sa Dec **L4**
Kien Giang **L3**	Tay Ninh **J5**
Kien Hoa **L5**	Thua Thien **B7**
Kien Phong **K4**	Tuyen Duc **I8**
Kien Tuong **K4**	Vinh Binh **L5**
Khanh Hoa **H9**	Vinh Long **L4**

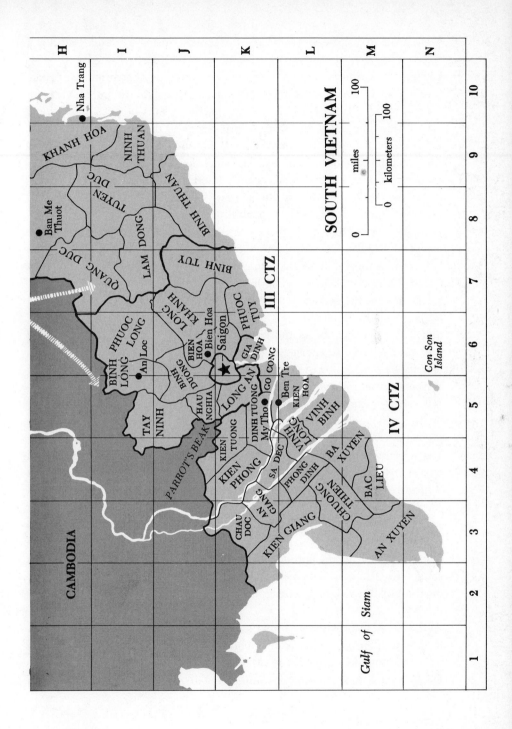

Vietnam as it has been elsewhere throughout history."[5] This traditional attack mission of the infantry—to find, fight and destroy enemy forces— became the cornerstone of Westmoreland's strategy of attrition. But since the setting of a counterinsurgency war in the environment of Vietnam posed anything but traditional problems, the results of this conventional way of thinking and acting were to prove a great disappointment.

President Johnson was not yet ready for such a drastic increase in the American involvement. NSAM 328, which formalized the president's decisions made on 1 April, instead authorized the deployment of two additional marine battalions and an increase of 18,000–20,000 men in U.S. military support forces. The possibility of introducing combat elements from the armed forces of Korea, Australia and New Zealand was to be explored. NSAM 328 also approved "a change of mission for all marine battalions deployed in Vietnam to permit their more active use under conditions to be established and approved by the secretary of defense in consultation with the secretary of state."[6] Approval of these measures by the GVN was to be obtained by Ambassador Taylor, who described the new, more offensive mission of the marines to the GVN in the following way: the marines would engage in a mobile counterinsurgency role in the vicinity of Danang for the improved protection of that base and, following the acquisition of experience in such missions, would be available as a reserve force in support of ARVN operations within 50 miles of the base.

The authors of the *Pentagon Papers* correctly describe NSAM 328 as "a pivotal document. It marks the acceptance by the President of the United States of the concept that U.S. troops would engage in offensive ground operations against Asian insurgents."[7] At the same time, the president's actions reflected his caution. Johnson shared the reservations Taylor had cited concerning the ability of Western troops to fight successfully against an Asian guerilla enemy. By approving a limited combat role for troops operating from secure enclaves he would be able to evaluate the performance of these forces and withdraw them with ease should the situation so dictate. The marines enlarged their patrol perimeters, but for the next few months they did not engage in any offensive operations in support of the ARVN.

The delay in providing combat support for ARVN was due in large part to the problems encountered in working out an appropriate structure of command for such cooperation. McNamara urged Westmoreland and Taylor to establish a combined command with the Vietnamese, but both

Westmoreland and the GVN were opposed to the idea. The knowledge that it would take time to find a mutually acceptable solution to this problem was probably one of the reasons for the insistence of NSAM 328 that premature publicity with regard to the decisions taken was to "be avoided by all possible precautions." The troop movements and changes in mission were to be described as being "wholly consistent with existing policy."[8] It is possible also that Johnson wanted to retain a free hand to change course should the experiment of an active American role in counterinsurgency fail. There was furthermore the hope that the bombing of North Vietnam would soon have the desired deterrent effect and that further escalation in the South, therefore, would not be necessary. Why, then, raise an issue which, if criticized, might weaken the impact on Hanoi of this show of resolve? On 31 March, after meeting with Taylor and other officials, the president assured reporters: "I know of no far-reaching strategy that is being suggested or promulgated."[9] Needless to say, Johnson here was being less than candid. Inevitably, word about the increased American role eventually got out and the administration stood accused of calculated deceit. The credibility gap was beginning to open up.

The president's deliberate pace was not being shared by Westmoreland and the JCS. They chose to interpret the increase in support troops as a logistical preparation for an early introduction of the two to three additional divisions they had asked for earlier. During the two weeks following NSAM 328 Taylor was bombarded with messages and instructions from Washington which indicated an eagerness to speed up the deployment of U.S. and Third Country* combat forces well beyond what had been authorized on 1 April. In the face of Taylor's annoyance and in order to restore a sense of common purpose, McNamara convened a conference of several military and civilian decision-makers in Honolulu for 20 April. After much discussion it was agreed to recommend the dispatch of about nine additional battalions, bringing total American strength to 82,000. While the thinking of the conferees seemingly still operated within the framework of the coastal enclave strategy, a JCS memorandum (JCSM) issued only 10 days later again spoke of the introduction of a division into the highlands. "From the thrust of this JCSM it is apparent," conclude the *Pentagon Papers*, "that the enclave strategy was no stopping place as

---

* Other than American or South Vietnamese—e.g. Korean and Australian units.

far as the Chiefs were concerned. They continued to push hard for the earliest possible input of three full divisions of troops. They were well ahead of the pack in that regard."[10] McNamara deferred action on the three-division plan.

The debate over the wisdom of the enclave strategy continued during a relative lull in combat. Taylor wanted to give the South Vietnamese maximum opportunity to save themselves and favored moving slowly on foreign troop deployments. Denying the enemy certain critical areas would buy time and enable the ARVN to expand at a controlled rate. Westmoreland, on the other hand, supported by Admiral U. S. G. Sharp, commander in chief, Pacific (CINCPAC), expected an enemy offensive in the highlands during the summer monsoon season which could lead to the establishment of a front government there and might cut South Vietnam in half along a line from Pleiku to Qui Nhon on the central coast. The war would be lost if allied forces were to stay in coastal enclaves.

These questions became moot in the heat of the VC monsoon offensive, which began with a series of regiment-sized attacks in May. An action in Quang Ngai province, which left two ARVN battalions decimated, and a similarly disastrous defeat at Dong Xoai in War Zone C northwest of Saigon made American observers on the scene conclude that the South Vietnamese forces were close to collapse. Tactical ineptness and lack of leadership were blatantly evident. The violence of the clashes and the level of ARVN casualties were both unprecedented. Desertion rates were inordinately high. Personnel being trained for new battalions now had to be used as fillers for heavily attrited units, and this meant that until the end of the year at least no new ARVN battalions would become available. The GVN/VC force ratio, upon which estimates of the situation in March had been based, had taken an adverse trend, Westmoreland informed CINCPAC in early June:

> In order to cope with the situation outlined above, I see no course of action open to us except to reinforce our efforts in SVN with additional U.S. or Third Country forces as rapidly as is practical during the critical weeks ahead. Additional studies must continue and plans develop to deploy even greater forces, if and when required, to attain our objectives or counter enemy initiatives. Ground forces deployed to selected areas along the coast and inland will be used both offensively and defensively. U.S. ground troops are gaining experience and thus far have performed well. Although they have not yet engaged the enemy

in strength, I am convinced that U.S. troops with their energy, mobility, and firepower can successfully take the fight to the VC. The basic purpose of the additional deployments recommended below is to give us a substantial and hard hitting offensive capability on the ground to convince the VC that they cannot win.[11]

By mid-June 1965 the VC summer offensive was in full stride, and, as Westmoreland had expected, it included the central highlands. The near-catastrophic defeats of ARVN meant that the occasional assist from allied forces envisaged by Taylor's enclave strategy was no longer sufficient to deny the enemy victory. On 12 June, Nguyen Cao Ky, commander of the Vietnamese Air Force, together with other officers overthrew the civilian government of Prime Minister Quat, an event which represented the high point of a period of political instability marked by riots, coups and attempted coups. On 26 June Westmoreland was given permission to "commit U.S. troops to combat independent of or in conjunction with GVN forces in any situation in which the use of such troops is required by an appropriate GVN commander and when, in COMUSMACV's judgment, their use is necessary to strengthen the relative position of GVN forces."[12] A day later U.S. forces began their first major ground combat action in the Vietnam war, a search-and-destroy operation together with ARVN and Australian units into VC base areas in War Zone D northeast of Saigon.

With decisions in Washington seemingly dictated by the threatening collapse of South Vietnamese resistance, Undersecretary of State George Ball once again warned against a further deepening of the American involvement. In two memoranda dated 29 June and 1 July, addressed to the president, Rusk, McNamara and other officials, Ball urged that the United States should cut its losses before large numbers of American troops were committed to direct combat and "begin to take heavy casualties in a war they are ill-equipped to fight in a non-cooperative if not outright hostile countryside."[13] On 30 June Ball's colleague in the State Department, William P. Bundy, while opposing a withdrawal which "would create an immediate and maximum shock wave for Thailand and the rest of Asia," also warned that unless the performance of the South Vietnamese improved substantially our intervention in force "would appear to be turning the conflict into a white man's war with the U.S. in the shoes of the French."[14]

The Emergence of the Tactic
of Search-and-Destroy

Before making a final commitment to a greatly enlarged American role in the war, President Johnson sent McNamara to Vietnam to confer with the Vietnamese leaders and American military and civilian officials. The secretary returned to Washington on 20 July and there followed another round of meetings in the White House. Freedom of action by now had narrowed considerably. The 75,000 Americans in Vietnam in a sense had become a hostage which could not be pulled out without a great loss of prestige. Repeatedly during the preceding months the president, seeking to deter Hanoi by a show of American determination, had stated that the United States would not be defeated, would not tire or withdraw. "We will remain as long as is necessary," he had said on 17 April, "with the might that is required, whatever the risk and whatever the cost."[15] The bill for this commitment now had to be paid. A substantial buildup of American forces would be required in order to defeat the Communists' concerted drive for a complete take-over. McNamara, reporting on a dangerously deteriorating situation, recommended the deployment of 100,000 men by October, which would bring American strength in Vietnam to 175,000. Depending on developments, an additional 100,000 might be needed in early 1966. He also suggested that the president ask Congress for authority to call up 235,000 men in the reserves and National Guard.

The president accepted the recommendation of building up to 175,000 men, but he disapproved the call-up of reserves. In his memoirs Johnson explains that he had wanted to avoid "making threatening noises to the Chinese and Russians by calling up reserves in large numbers." If America went on a war footing, Hanoi would ask China and Russia for help which they would not be able to refuse.[16] But this is probably not the entire story. As one knowledgeable member of the White House staff recalls, "Johnson was determined to fight the war with minimum disruption at home. . . . Doling out additional forces with a view to balancing off military requirements in Vietnam and political consequences at home typified the President's approach."[17]

On 27 July Johnson briefed selected members of Congress on his decision. Only Senator Mansfield expressed serious doubts and opposition, but he promised to support the president. A day later Johnson addressed a nationally televised press conference and told the American people that a difficult and long road lay ahead. To finally defeat the Communists and achieve an independent South Vietnam might take "months or years or decades." He had asked General Westmoreland what additional troops he needed now to meet the mounting aggression and the commanding general's needs would be met. "Additional forces will be needed later, and they will be sent as requested."[18] The president thus signed a blank check, payment of which was to become increasingly more difficult in the days ahead. This open-ended commitment would also make it later politically hazardous to oppose the ever-growing requests of the military for more American troops.

During the question period which followed the president's prepared statement Johnson was asked whether the sending of additional American forces to Vietnam implied any change in the policy of relying mainly on the South Vietnamese to carry out offensive operations while American troops guarded installations and acted as an emergency backup. The president replied: "It does not imply any change in policy whatever. It does not imply change of objective."[19] In his memoirs, published six years later, Johnson assesses the significance of his July 1965 decisions more accurately: "Now we were committed to major combat in Vietnam."[20] Indeed, Westmoreland, backed by CINCPAC and the JCS, had never accepted the passive enclave strategy embraced by the president's reply to the newsman; he had sought a free hand to move troops around inside the country, and he had wanted to get as quickly as possible into an offensive posture. A month earlier, on 27 June, his troops had gone on their first search-and-destroy operation. A JCS study group, in a report given to McNamara on 14 July, similarly affirmed that after securing their bases U.S. and allied forces would "seek out and destroy major Viet Cong units, bases and other facilities." The cumulative effect of such offensive land and air action, "coupled with the interdiction of DRV efforts to provide the higher level of support required in such a combat environment, should lead to progressive destruction of the VC/DRV main force battalions."[21] This was a succinct statement of the strategy of attrition which was to govern the American conduct of the war until well into 1968.

As later developments were to show, the search-and-destroy tactic, which aimed at the gradual attrition of the enemy, badly underestimated the ability of the other side to escalate in response to the American buildup. U.S. force levels consequently had to rise constantly. By the end of 1965 American strength in Vietnam stood at 184,314, and the end was nowhere in sight. The strategy of attrition also devoted insufficient attention to pacification—the complex task of achieving a politically and economically viable society within the framework of an effective government which enjoyed the support of the people. This difficult undertaking required, most basically, the creation of sustained and credible territorial security and the destruction of the communist underground apparatus in the countryside. Yet Westmoreland was critical of the mode of operation of the marines in the northern provinces who had established beachheads at Danang and Chu Lai and who insisted on gaining firm control in hamlets and villages before enlarging the perimeters of their tactical area of responsibility (TAOR). According to Westmoreland, this way of fighting a counterinsurgency war left the VC free to expand their main force battalions and to operate in the hills with impunity.[22] Several years were to pass before the American command began to accept the crucial role of population security.

In pressing for his plan to put American forces into the highlands, Westmoreland had stressed the importance of keeping U.S. forces away from major population concentrations on which, he feared, they would have an abrasive effect. By fighting in the sparsely populated highlands U.S. firepower could also be employed more freely. That Westmoreland's concerns about the effect of heavily armed American troops fighting in the densely settled coastal plain were not unfounded was demonstrated by an incident involving the marines near Danang.

On 3 August, a reinforced marine rifle company was sent on a search-and-destroy operation against a complex of six hamlets named Cam Ne (4) south-southwest of the Danang air base. It was from this direction that on 1 July a VC demolition squad had penetrated the base, destroying several aircraft, killing one airman and wounding three marines. The area had long been controlled and occupied by the VC, and spread throughout the villages were trenches, fighting holes, tactical caves and tunnels. Almost impenetrable thorny hedgerows around the villages and hamlets were often mined and booby-trapped. On 12 July another marine company had made a sweep through Cam Ne (4); three marines had been killed and four wounded in an action in which heavy fire had been encountered from both men and women. The instructions of Company D for their operation in the same area on 3 August were to destroy the enemy and his positions and fortifications.

Approaching the village, the third platoon on the right flank drew sustained sniper and automatic-weapon fire. After a while, the VC, estimated at over 30, withdrew, but progress in penetrating the hamlet, checking civilians and huts, and in searching for booby traps and mines was nevertheless slow. Some houses were burned as a result of being hit by infantry weapons in reply to enemy fire; others, after the villagers had been called together outside the dwellings, were set afire or blown up in order to ensure that the firing positions and tunnels around the houses would not again become military installations. In one of the huts, fired upon when a VC had taken cover in it, a dead Vietnamese boy of about 10 years of age was found. Several other civilians were wounded and so were four marines.[23]

The search-and-destroy operation described here was typical of many such actions that were to take place throughout the war. When the VC converted villages into fortified places and fighting ensued, civilians inevitably suffered and property was destroyed. What marked this particular operation was the fact that parts of it were filmed by a CBS television crew, and on 5 August 1965 American viewers of the CBS evening news were exposed to the spectacle of American marines using their cigarette lighters to set fire to thatched huts in a Vietnamese village. The commentary by Morley Safer did not make reference to the action in Cam Ne (4) in July, in which several marines had been killed and wounded, nor did he mention the existence of trenches, mines and booby traps and the fact of hostile fire. Where the marine unit's after-action report spoke of 51 structures and 38 trenches, tunnels and prepared positions destroyed, Safer reported the burning of from 120 to 150 houses and the leveling of a village. The impression left with the television audience was of senseless and wanton destruction of ancestral homes and disregard for innocent civilian life.

The Cam Ne episode conveys the reality of counterinsurgency warfare in Vietnam and the difficulty encountered in making the American public understand the true nature of this conflict. Westmoreland's hesitation in placing American troops into this kind of environment is understandable. Unfortunately, as experience was to demonstrate, no headway could be made against the insurgents until their presence in the populated areas was effectively challenged. The employment of U.S. forces in offensive operations against enemy main force units in remote war zones and base areas was to exact a heavy toll in American casualties with little concomitant benefits in permanent security for the populated countryside.

South Vietnam was divided into four regions known as Corps Tactical Zones (CTZ), representing both military and civilian/political units of administration. At the end of July, Maj. Gen. Lewis W. Walt, commander of the marines in Vietnam, the III Marine Amphibious Force (III MAF), was put in charge of all U.S. ground elements in I CTZ, including the five northernmost provinces, and in early August Walt was given authority to undertake offensive operations not directly linked to the defense of the marines' base areas. There followed on 17 August Operation STARLIGHT, the first regimental-sized U.S. battle since the Korean War.

A few days earlier hard intelligence had been received that a VC main force regiment, some 2,000 strong, had moved into prepared positions on the Van Tuong Peninsula, a VC stronghold with many fortified hamlets 15 miles south of the Chu Lai airstrip. The marines had constructed this field on a bare stretch of beach 55 miles southeast of Danang in order to relieve some of the congestion at Danang. Operation STARLIGHT was designed to blunt any impending attack on the developing base; the operation utilized an amphibious landing and a helicopter lift of blocking forces inland. The marines were assisted by ARVN units and by extensive air support, beginning with a protective cover of the landing zone (LZ). Amphibious tractors and tanks provided close-in fire support, while a U.S. cruiser offshore delivered fire from its six-inch guns. When the operation ended on 24 August after a week of often bitter fighting the marines reported having killed 688 VC. The marines had encountered extensive tunnel and cave complexes which they sealed by means of demolition charges. An undetermined number of persons were caught in these caves, as was indicated by the odor pervading the area in the weeks following the operation. The marines' own casualties were 45 killed in action (KIA) and 204 wounded (WIA).[24]

In some ways Operation STARLIGHT was one of the more successful actions of its kind. The VC were known for their ability to slip out of traps, and they were rarely caught in such large maneuvers. Here they had been made to stand and fight. Yet the operation apparently had also exacted a heavy toll among the villagers of the area. The guerillas were adept at hiding and carrying away the weapons of their dead. Still, a comparison of the number of VC reported killed with the number of weapons captured could give an indication of the loss of life among those not armed. In Operation STARLIGHT 109 weapons were captured and 688 VC reported killed, a ratio of 1:6.31. This was a rather poor showing; in large operations the ratio averaged 1:3.[25] Given this low ratio and bearing in mind that the fighting had taken place in and around several fortified hamlets, it is a safe assumption that, as in most operations of this nature, a considerable number of villagers had been killed along with the men of the VC regiment. The First Battalion reported on 23 August that Van Tuong village #4 had been totally destroyed in the fighting and that a large number of villagers required medical aid.[26] Whether these casualties are to be considered innocent noncombatants is a difficult question to which we will return. Villagers in VC strongholds often assisted as porters and in other support functions, and in view of the impossibility of establishing who had volunteered and who had been impressed into such services, any black-clad dead found on the battlefield were routinely classed as VC.[27] At least some villagers undoubtedly died as a result of the lavish use of American firepower. Almost half the VC reported killed by the Second Battalion of the Fourth Marines in Operation STARLIGHT— 150 out of 342—were killed by either air strikes or artillery. In his commentary on the battle just concluded the commanding officer of another battalion stated: "More concern must be given to the safety of villages. Instances were noted where villages were severely damaged or destroyed by napalm or naval gunfire, wherein the military necessity of doing so was dubious."[28]

The significance of these considerations goes beyond the legal, political or moral questions involved. If a substantial number of those reported as VC killed were in fact mere VC sympathizers or perhaps just villagers caught in a battle, all estimates of VC losses and strength and, more basically, the strategy of attrition were in difficulty. This was indeed the case.

During the remainder of 1965 the American buildup continued at a rapid pace. In the face of the grave tactical situation, Westmoreland later recalled, "I decided to accept combat troops as rapidly as they could be made available and to improvise their logistic support."[29] Facilities for receiving supplies were virtually nonexistent and the Saigon harbor soon became choked with ships and supplies. Some materiel had to be shipped two or three times because the forces in Vietnam could not find it. By December 1965 the near-chaotic supply situation forced the delay of some tactical unit deployments. In April 1966 Westmoreland informed McNamara that munitions shortages were adversely affecting air operations.[30] The other side, meanwhile, was more than matching the American buildup. Between July and November 1965 VC regimental-size units increased from 5 to 12; the infiltration of units from North Vietnam also accelerated. By 17 November, six confirmed, two probable and one possible North Vietnamese Army (NVA) regiment had been identified in South Vietnam. Total VC/NVA strength stood at 110 battalions—63,500 in combat units, 17,000 in combat support units and 53,600 in the militia.[31] The VC/NVA buildup rate, Westmoreland reported on 23 November, was double that of U.S. forces. "Whereas we will add an average of seven maneuver battalions per quarter, the enemy will add fifteen."[32]

After his return from a visit to South Vietnam, Senator Mansfield reported to the president on 17 December that the U.S. military effort had succeeded in preventing a collapse of the Saigon government, but that victory was nowhere in sight. Mansfield favored granting Westmoreland's request for 150,000 additional men, though he felt that this was probably just an installment. "It would be wise to anticipate a rapidly growing need for men because we are not confronted with an opposition whose strength is definable within fixed maximums. On the contrary, the enemy can add manpower to the conflict, as he sees fit, if not out of local resources then out of the resources of North Vietnam. . . . The fact is that we do not know how far the Communists are prepared to go in the escalation." It was "not too early to begin to contemplate the need for a total of upwards of 700,000." Mansfield concluded with a plea for a policy of restraint—to protect Saigon, the major cities and bases or perhaps just the coast "and to hold those more defensible enclaves for the indefinite future, pending negotiations."[33]

The Pursuit of Attrition

The military commander in Vietnam had long since abandoned the enclave strategy, and in November 1965 there took place the first large-scale contest with North Vietnamese regulars in the highlands. The location of this encounter was the mountainous and trackless jungle of Pleiku province near the Cambodian border, where the North Vietnamese had concentrated three regiments. As captured documents were to reveal, the enemy's plans were to capture three Special Forces camps and the province capital and then push to the sea to split the country in two. Against this concentration of enemy forces, Westmoreland on 27 October sent a brigade of the just recently arrived First Cavalry Division (Airmobile).

For the first two weeks of this search-and-destroy operation contact with the North Vietnamese was sporadic and light. The most intense fighting, much of it hand to hand, took place between 14 and 18 November in the Ia Drang Valley southwest of Pleiku after a battalion of the division's Third Brigade had landed by helicopter almost on top of two of the North Vietnamese regiments. For the first time in the war B-52 bombers were called in to provide direct tactical support to the beleaguered American troops. The fierce battle ended with the North Vietnamese retreating across the Cambodian border. They left behind over 1,300 dead; the First Cavalry Division lost 300 men killed in a month of operations around Pleiku and in the Ia Drang Valley.[34] The contest of attrition in this war without fronts had started in earnest.

Although Westmoreland preferred to find and defeat the enemy in the sparsely inhabited plateau area of Vietnam, most of his operations during the first half of 1966 took place in or near the coastal plain. Given the limited resources at his command and the pressing need to protect the populated parts of the country, Westmoreland engaged in a series of operations to defeat the VC/NVA in these critical areas. The plan was for American and other allied forces to concentrate on search-and-destroy operations against larger enemy units, while South Vietnamese troops would follow to take on the local guerillas, weed out the VC infrastructure and maintain security. Unfortunately, the generally successful operations against communist main force units did not prevent the enemy from moving back into the "liberated" areas as soon as American forces had left. Battles were being won but the end of the war was not getting any nearer.

Among the areas "cleared" over and over again in the course of repeated forays was the northern half of Binh Dinh province (II CTZ) on the central coast, a long-time VC stronghold. In Operation MASHER (later renamed WHITE WING because of President Johnson's concern over public reaction to the image portrayed by the name "Masher")[35] the U.S. First Cavalry Division in early 1966 here fought a series of pitched battles with VC and North Vietnamese troops. The troopers made effective use of their helicopter assets and great firepower; between 25 January and 6 March 1966, artillery fired 141,712 rounds.[36] After six weeks of almost continuous contact the 1st Cav reported that it had killed 1,342 of the enemy, captured 633 and detained 1,087 VC suspects.[37] Five of nine communist battalions in the area were said to have been rendered ineffective. MASHER/WHITE WING was followed by THAYER I/IRVING, the latter ending on 24 October 1966. Assisted by Korean and ARVN units, the Americans anew combed the densely populated coastal plain and pursued the enemy into the province's mountain valleys. The use of firepower was again lavish. Ships offshore fired their heavy guns, B-52s staged strikes, and U.S. Air Force fighter-bombers flew 1,126 sorties, during which they dropped a total of almost 1.5 million pounds of explosives and 292,500 pounds of napalm.[38]

While the enemy's large units generally avoided contact, well-entrenched rearguard formations put up determined resistance which often was not broken before extensive use of artillery and air strikes. Many of these battles were fought in heavily populated areas. When a Swiss newspaper in September 1966 reported that in one instance two whole villages had been put to the torch, the Army's assistant judge advocate general explained that the villages "were not burned as a reprisal for the hostile fire that came from the houses in the village. They were destroyed because the houses and tunnel networks connecting them constituted enemy fortified positions."[39] At the conclusion of Operation IRVING in late October, the 1st Cav counted 912 enemy killed with another 550 reported as possible kills. Large quantities of ammunition, foodstuffs and medical supplies had also been captured along with 1,172 suspects.[40]

The contribution of these operations to the pacification of the province was not obvious and indeed seems to have escaped any kind of systematic attention. Successful initial engagement was one thing, and eliminating the enemy and breaking up his strong political apparatus was quite another. The enemy had been driven from the coastal plain, stated the final report on Operation MASHER/WHITE WING, and "so far as is now known, the GVN intends to reestablish civil government in this area."[41] But in point of fact the GVN lacked the ability and forces to follow up the military successes scored by the American troops and security remained highly precarious. As an evaluation of the pacification effort put it, with a VC "infrastructure numbering in the thousands, and the sincere but all too often vicious and insensitive ROK [Republic of Korea] and US forces, Binh Dinh was an extremely dangerous and unpredictable place to live."[42]

The intensive military engagements also led to a tremendous increase in the refugee population. Some people moved on their own volition to escape the fighting; others were relocated by the 1st Cav Division, which added the large number of evacuees to its scorecard. As "an indication of the 1st Cavalry Division's capability," the report on MASHER/WHITE WING related, "3,491 refugees were evacuated from the An Lao valley by helicopter." In the Hoai An district the division's "operations freed over 10,000 war victims most of whom occupied vacant buildings or moved into homes of friends."[43] Operation THAYER resulted in 1,884 refugees, and 10,779 more were evacuated from areas previously under VC control during IRVING.[44] By December 1966, Binh Dinh province had 85 refugee camps with a reported population of 129,202.[45] An undetermined number of refugees—generally known to be far larger than the in-camp population—crowded into the district towns, existed as squatters along Highway 1 or found refuge with other villagers. Since the total population of Binh Dinh province in 1966 was given as 875,547 people, this meant that about one-third of the province's population had become refugees.

The struggle for control of Binh Dinh continued into 1967. The communists by now had adjusted to the helicopter sweeps of the 1st Cav and locating the enemy's forces became increasingly difficult. NVA units employed lookouts on hills and trees to watch for approaching helicopters; allied movements on the ground were reported by the ever-present VC infrastructure in the hamlets. "If NVA and VC units do not wish to make contact with US forces in an area," reported the commander of Operation THAYER II, which ended on 12 February 1967, "they will simply move aside and let the enemy [U.S. forces] move past their location. When the enemy has searched the area and moved out, the VC will move back into the area."[46]

At locations of their choice the Communists fired at American troops from within villages. The troopers, anxious to make contact with the elusive enemy, usually fell for the bait and assaulted the hamlets utilizing artillery barrages, aerial rocketry and tactical air strikes. In all, during three and a half months of fighting in the same general area worked over during the course of the 1st Cav's earlier operations in 1966, tube artillery fired 136,769 explosive shells, U.S. warships offshore lobbed 5,105 rounds of various caliber, B-52s flew 171 sorties dropping 3,078 tons of bombs, and fighter-bombers flew 2,622 sorties dropping 2.5 million pounds of explosives and 0.5 million pounds of napalm. The 1st Cav reported 1,757 enemy killed (657 of them NVA) at a cost of 242 of its own men killed and 947 wounded. Large quantities of ammunition and food and 479 weapons were captured as well as 3,200 NVA uniforms. The fighting generated

1,100 refugees, including the remaining population of the Kim Son Valley, who were evacuated; the valley was made a free-fire zone, an area where artillery fire and air strikes could be delivered without the political and tactical clearance by the South Vietnamese province chief otherwise required. Eighty percent of the population in the area of operations, the 1st Cav reported at the conclusion of Operation THAYER II, were now "free from organized Viet Cong control, at least temporarily. This is not to mean that they have been brought under government control. . . . As far as political control is concerned, the AO [area of operations] is still a power vacuum. . . ."[47] That, if anything, was an overly optimistic appraisal, as events in early 1968 were to demonstrate.

The most serious problem encountered, reported the 1st Cav at the conclusion of Operation THAYER II, had been the extreme difficulty of staging undetected and unreported movements of troop units. "Even movement at night, particularly of a force of any size, cannot be assumed to have gone unnoticed."[48] The problem arose, first, because large American infantry units, accompanied and supported by cumbersome and noisy mobile equipment, practically telegraphed their every move to the enemy. Second, American commanders were in the habit of "prepping" helicopter landing zones with air strikes or artillery fire. A study completed at CINCPAC in the spring of 1968 argued that while the sacrifice of the element of tactical surprise in order to achieve supremacy of force and firepower might have been appropriate operating doctrine in earlier conflicts, "this doctrine may be unsuitable against an enemy that withdraws in the presence of force, ambushes and interdicts in situations of its own choosing, and then melts into the jungle where it is indistinguishable from the native population. To provide this kind of enemy with tip-offs is to ensure that we will plunge full force into a vacuum. Subsequent contacts with the enemy will be at best fortuitous, at worst the result of enemy counter-attack and ambush."[49] There are indications that officers in the field, anxious to protect helicopter landing operations against enemy fire, found this suggestion less than persuasive.

Another factor working against successful tactical surprise was the lack of appreciation for the enemy's highly effective intelligence capability; VC agents over the course of many years had succeeded in working their way to the highest levels of the Vietnamese government and military services. The work of these agents was simplified by the extreme carelessness which for a long time characterized the planning and preparation of large

American operations. The requisitioning of supplies, submitted weeks in advance, commonly utilized indigenous personnel; Vietnamese air traffic controllers were informed of preparatory air strikes; areas of planned operations were surveyed by aerial reconnaissance; and the intensive American communications traffic was easily monitored by the VC/NVA. Amphibious landing operations usually followed a standard pattern—a hospital ship was stationed offshore, naval gunfire was directed on the objective area prior to the assault, and the actual landing from the previously assembled flotilla commonly took place at the same early morning hours. All this enabled the enemy much of the time to avoid large American sweep operations and to fight at places of his own choosing.

The more elaborate an American operation the greater, obviously, was the chance of its being compromised. This was demonstrated by Operation DOUBLE EAGLE in early 1966, the largest amphibious operation of the war up to that time. The target of this ambitious undertaking was the 325A NVA Division which confirmed intelligence had placed operating on the border of Binh Dinh and Quang Ngai provinces. On 28 January 1966 two battalions of marines went ashore some 20 miles south of the town of Quang Ngai from a Task Force Delta flotilla which included two attack transports, an attack cargo ship, a cruiser, a destroyer and several smaller ships. On D day plus one, a third battalion was helilifted to an objective five miles west of the landing beaches, on D plus four another battalion of marines moved southward from the Quang Ngai airstrip into the mountains northwest of the beach. A fifth battalion remained in floating reserve aboard three other ships offshore. Despite the carefully orchestrated maneuver, the North Vietnamese division was nowhere to be found. When the operation was ended on 16 February the only enemy encountered had been VC sniper teams. "In analysis of DOUBLE EAGLE operations," stated the after-action report of Task Force Delta, "the single factor of most significance was the complete lack of contact with main force VC elements."[50] Interrogation of prisoners indicated that the enemy had had prior knowledge of the time and place of attack of the elaborately planned operation.

The lesson that multibattalion search-and-destroy operations could not achieve surprise and therefore enabled the enemy to choose whether to stand and fight or evade was resisted by MACV planners. Westmoreland was anxious to move into Phase Two of his strategy, which called for seizing the offensive by invading the enemy's sanctuaries and base camps and taking on his main forces. Back in Washington, on the other hand, voices began to be heard that urged greater attention to the task of providing permanent security for the populated countryside. After careful study a group of officers in the Army staff in March 1966 recommended a revision of priorities and stressed the crucial importance of pacification. By the summer of 1966 there were indications that MACV was beginning to feel the need to respond to these pressures. Westmoreland's "Concept of Military Operations in South Vietnam" of 24 August 1966 projected his strategy over the period until 1 May 1967 as "a general offensive with maximum practical support to area and population security." A significant number of U.S. battalions was to be committed to tactical areas of responsibility where they would support pacification by spreading security radially from their bases.[51] The operations of the U.S. Twenty-fifth Infantry Division, commanded by Gen. Frederick C. Weyand, for a time conformed to and implemented this new mission.

On its arrival in Vietnam in early 1966 the Twenty-fifth Division had established its base camp in Hau Nghia, an important province northeast of Saigon and bordering on a major enemy base area in a region of Cambodia known as the Parrot's Beak. Operation LANIKAI by the Fourth Battalion, Ninth Infantry, in neighboring Long An province from the middle of September to early November 1966 can serve as an example of how the division carried out its pacification mission. The battalion emphasized integrated U.S.-Vietnamese operations in order to take advantage of the natives' knowledge of the area and to upgrade the performance of the Vietnamese forces. Since the mission of the battalion was to provide security for the people of a very densely populated district, the movement of refugees was discouraged and the Americans operated under restrictive rules of engagement designed to limit the use of their great firepower. Helicopters were not to fire when going into a landing zone unless they themselves were fired upon from a clearly identified source. Gunships flying cover in other than landing operations were not to fire into a village from which two or three shots were being fired even if they could see the target. Air strikes were not to be directed against hamlets except in emergencies, and when there was doubt as to whether artillery and mortar fire might cause casualties among noncombatants artillery and mortar fire was not to be used. Fleeing males were to be warned by warning shots, and much more.[52]

During the course of Operation LANIKAI the American battalion learned several important lessons. Its units encountered only hit-and-run snipers, but it was realized that this did not necessarily mean a weakening of enemy strength. The VC's normal mode of operations was to disperse into platoon-size units and consolidate only for carefully planned attacks. The success of a pacification operation, the battalion reported, could not be measured in terms of VC body count. Indeed, the battalion achieved a higher number of defectors (105) than enemy dead (26). Most importantly, the battalion's final report stressed, U.S. units on pacification missions "must be prepared to live in the pacification area until the people have been made to feel secure and their cooperation has been won." Provision must be made for some form of permanent security by local forces or ARVN units. "The full benefits of pacification type operations in an area can only be realized through vigorous and constant efforts to sustain the favorable conditions created until such time as the local Vietnamese officials and military leaders are prepared to accept the full gamut of civil and military responsibilities."[53]

The kind of familiarity with an area of operations required for successful pacification could not be achieved overnight. Yet the battalions of the Twenty-fifth Division rarely were given the chance to sink real roots. The Fourth Battalion was pulled out of Long An in early November to join Operation FAIRFAX in Gia Dinh province near Saigon, and the pacification mission of other units of the Twenty-fifth Division was similarly disrupted repeatedly in the following year. When the Americans left an area, control usually reverted to the VC. While Westmoreland had made verbal commitments to pacification, his main interest remained in seeking engagements with the enemy's main force units in order to attrite them and keep them away from the populated areas. During the last five months of 1966 MACV invested 95 percent of all combat battalions in search-and-destroy operations.[54] In a situation of limited manpower resources, this meant that Westmoreland had to strip forces from pacification missions and rely upon the poorly performing ARVN and local force units for the major part of pacification security. With U.S. forces preoccupied with hunting the enemy's large units, the VC infrastructure much of the time had a free run in the villages and hamlets of Vietnam. The "shield" which Westmorland was seeking to create for the protection of pacification remained a shield behind which pacification made little or no progress.

Attacks on the Enemy's Supply System

One of the most ambitious and largest operations of the war began on 8 January 1967 in the so-called Iron Triangle northwest of Saigon. This jungle-covered area was for years a major communist base; it was considered impregnable and served as the headquarters sanctuary of the VC's Military Region IV, which directed communist activities in and around Saigon. Operation CEDAR FALLS was designed to scour the triangle for enemy installations and clear it of all civilians so that it could be declared a specified strike zone (previously called a free-fire zone). The 19-day-long operation employed two U.S. infantry divisions, reinforced with ARVN units, but enemy forces known to be in the triangle managed to evade the trap and did not conduct an organized defense. Nevertheless, American casualties were substantial—72 killed and 337 wounded. Enemy losses were 720 confirmed dead and 280 taken prisoner. Six hundred thirteen weapons along with very large quantities of ammunition, uniforms, documents and rice were captured.[55]

All civilians in the operational area were presumed to be either members of VC families or VC laborers, and they were removed in a carefully organized mass evacuation—6,106 people with their belongings and livestock. The very large number of tunnels and bunkers that had been discovered were then blown up; bulldozers and Rome plows (bulldozers equipped with a sharp blade capable of felling trees) completed the leveling of all fortifications, structures and houses and cut roads through the forest. One major tunnel complex was found in the village of Ben Suc, a VC-controlled and fortified supply center, which provided the title for a book by the American writer Jonathan Schell describing parts of the operation.[56] A majority of the 7,642 uniforms captured during Operation CEDAR FALLS were found at Ben Suc.

The removal of the civilian inhabitants of the Iron Triangle was intended to deny the enemy manpower, food, revenue, transportation and intelligence. Since the guerillas moved among the people—in the words of communist terminology, like fish in the water—it was believed that a serious blow could be struck at them by relocating the people out of VC-dominated areas and thus depriving the fish of the water upon which they depended for their survival. Moving civilians out of the way of hostilities would also make possible the more effective employment of American firepower. "All military planning," declared MACV Directive 5-66 dealing with refugees dated 7 November 1966, "should include measures to ensure that the local population does not interfere with military operations." In the eyes of some officials the movement of refugees into GVN-controlled areas also represented a political victory—people were "voting with their feet."

Plans for the relocation of noncombatants had been developed by MACV since the summer of 1966, and in the course of the year 1967 what amounted to the encouragement and creation of refugees became accepted policy. In view of the great difficulties experienced in bringing security to the people it was considered easier to bring the people to security, and until late 1968 the prevalent but uncodified policy was that of compulsory relocations and displacement by military pressure through combat operations, crop destruction and the creation of specified strike zones. During 1967 the total number of refugees almost doubled. It reached close to one million by the end of 1967 and the increase was sharpest in areas of heavy military activity. The special assistant to the JCS for counterinsurgency and special activities (SACSA) reported in December 1967 after a field trip to Vietnam: "Although the policy to create refugees for military purposes does not, in so many words, appear in any MACV document, the necessity is openly recognized as a realistic requirement which will be acted upon a case-by-case basis." In point of fact, he added, this policy could become a much more productive strategy, and he recommended the creation of two million refugees for 1968, primarily in the Delta.[57] Fortunately for the progress of pacification, this scheme was never approved though compulsory relocations on a smaller scale continued.

General Westmoreland considered the enemy's supply system his "Achilles heel" and the campaign plans for 1967 devoted special attention to the destruction of base areas like the Iron Triangle. "If we can neutralize the enemy base areas and prevent replenishment of the material captured or destroyed, we will have taken a long stride toward ultimate victory."[58] Unfortunately, after allied troops completed their sweeps, the enemy usually returned and continued use of these hideouts. Less than two weeks after the conclusion of Operation CEDAR FALLS, recalls an officer who participated in the operation as assistant division commander, "the Iron Triangle was again literally crawling with what appeared to be Viet Cong,"[59] and this was by no means an isolated case. The situation was similarly unsatisfactory with regard to the interdiction of reinforcements from the North. Despite the stepped-up bombing of the southern panhandle of North Vietnam and Laos, infiltration was still increasing (see Table 2-1). The fact that much of this infiltration was coming through the Demilitarized Zone (DMZ), the border between North and South Vietnam, led to plans for the construction of an anti-infiltration barrier.

Table 2-1 Estimated Infiltration from North Vietnam, 1964–67

1964	1965	1966	1967
12,400	36,300	92,287	101,263

SOURCE: OASD (Comptroller), SEA Statistical Summary, Table 5, 18 January 1972.

In the summer of 1966 a group of scientists known as the Jason Committee had proposed an air-supported barrier south of the DMZ and extending into Laos which would utilize minefields and electronic sensors. In September of that year McNamara ordered the implementation of this plan, which soon came to be known as the McNamara Line. Both Westmoreland and CINCPAC were skeptical that the time, effort and resources invested in a barrier project were worth the limited results that could be expected. No fence, they felt, electronic or otherwise, could work without ground forces tending it, and this raised the specter of tying down sparse and precious manpower in static positions.[60] Despite these misgivings of the military command, planning and the assembly of components proceeded. It was estimated that construction of the barrier would necessitate the removal of 4,379 families, affecting 23,735 people, but the embassy informed Washington on 24 April 1967 that this relocation program was feasible providing it enjoyed equal priority for labor, supplies and transport with the actual construction.[61] Work on the project was begun the same month, but it soon had to be halted because of the intensity of the enemy's mortar, artillery and rocket fire coming from within and north of the DMZ. Although the barrier was never completed, certain portions of it were sufficiently developed to permit their use; they became part of the fire-support and patrol bases which Westmoreland had begun to construct just south of the DMZ. The aim of this strongpoint obstacle system was to force enemy infiltration into well-defined corridors where it could be hit with air, artillery and mobile ground reserves.

The War Near the DMZ

The North Vietnamese buildup in Quang Tri, South Vietnam's northern-most province, had been proceeding steadily since the summer of 1966 and resulted in a series of major clashes between North Vietnamese regulars and the marines. In the course of these operations in the DMZ region between 1 July 1966 and 31 March 1967, 541 marines were killed and 2,732 wounded,[62] but the bitterest fighting occurred in late April and early May 1967 near Khe Sanh in western Quang Tri province. In order to control key terrain dominating infiltration routes the marines were ordered to take three hills held by the enemy. Despite heavy air and artillery support the seizure of the peaks was costly and resembled the bloody hill battles in the last stages of the Korean War. At the end of what became known as the First Battle of Khe Sanh, the marines had lost 155 killed and 424 wounded; enemy losses were reported as 940 killed and 2 prisoners.[63]

The communist strategists were pleased with the heavy casualties they had forced upon the marines, and there is evidence to indicate that they welcomed the deployment of most marine combat strength to the two northernmost provinces. In a series of articles published in September 1967 in *Nhan Dan,* organ of the North Vietnamese Communist party, and in the North Vietnamese armed forces newspaper *Quan Doi Nhan Dan,* General Vo Nguyen Giap stated that the purpose of the battles along the frontiers was to draw American forces away from the populated areas and thus frustrate efforts at pacification. The marines, he wrote, "are being stretched as taut as a bowstring over hundreds of kilometers. . . ."[64] Westmoreland considered the article "planned deception,"[65] and he continued to seek battle with NVA/VC main force units in the border areas.

Most of these operations required large numbers of allied troops, and while they often inflicted heavy casualties on the enemy and captured much war materiel, they also led to significant American losses. Operation ATTLEBORO in the jungles of Tay Ninh province, an area known as War Zone C, in the previous November had involved over 22,000 American troops and, according to incomplete records, cost 155 killed and over 800 wounded. Operation JUNCTION CITY in February–May 1967 in the same general part of III CTZ occupied 22 American and 4 South Vietnamese battalions and exacted 282 killed and 1,576 wounded. In the fierce fighting southwest of Dak To in Kontum province near the Cambodian border in November 1967, engaging 16 American and South Vietnamese battalions, the Americans lost 289 killed. Communist losses in all of these battles were far higher than those suffered by the Americans, but Giap regarded these efforts as worth the price. "His is not an army that sends coffins north," wrote a former American intelligence officer in 1968; "it is by the traffic in homebound American coffins that Giap measures his success."[66]

In January 1968, Westmoreland, concerned about North Vietnamese pressure on Khe Sanh and expecting a major enemy effort in the two northern provinces, deployed two additional brigades belonging to the First Cavalry Division to I CTZ, a move which significantly weakened allied strength in the populated areas just prior to the enemy's Tet assault. Whether the enemy buildup around Khe Sanh was a feint designed to draw U.S. forces away from the populous coastal plain or whether Giap really planned to stage there another Dien Bien Phu and seize the two northern provinces of South Vietnam cannot be established at this time. What is uncontested is that the bloody battles in the rough terrain along the DMZ and in the jungles of the highlands soaked up precious combat manpower and exacted a heavy price in American lives, a fact which contributed to the further weakening of the home front.

A Marine Corps study in late 1967 pointed out that these engagements provided the enemy with a double bonus: they took allied forces away from the pacification effort and, in addition, involved them in combat under conditions favorable to the enemy. The NVA/VC benefited from short supply lines and nearby havens across the border which enabled them to ambush, defend briefly and withdraw. They also could fight under the protective cover of thick jungle which created low visibility and weakened the effectiveness of allied air power and other heavy support weapons.[67] Westmoreland was aware of these problems, but downgraded their importance. In the words of the authors of the *Pentagon Papers,* "the important thing was to fight—to engage the enemy and create casualties. It mattered little that you accepted combat in regions with certain advantages for the enemy—the prime objective was to engage and kill him."[68]

Combat amid the Hamlets

The fighting with North Vietnamese regulars around Khe Sanh represented conventional warfare with friend and foe clearly defined and no civilians in the way to clutter up the battlefield. A quite different kind of war was fought in the populated coastal provinces, as during Operation MALHEUR, a search-and-destroy operation staged by the First Brigade of the newly formed Task Force Oregon (later reinforced and redesignated the Twenty-third Infantry or "Americal" Division) in southern Quang Ngai province. In its destructive impact MALHEUR resembled the operations of the 1st Cav in neighboring Binh Dinh province discussed earlier.

Operation MALHEUR began on 11 May 1967 and continued until 2 August 1967. The area of operations was in the Duc Pho district which, like much of the rest of the province, had been dominated by the VC for a long time; many hamlets were heavily fortified. The enemy often would allow patrolling American forces to enter a village before opening fire and in the ensuing fighting with U.S. forces, who would call on naval gunfire, artillery and tactical air support, many of the houses next to the spider holes and fortified bunkers would be destroyed. In other cases, after repeated warnings to the population had failed to prevent the use of a hamlet as a base for sniping and mining, the hamlet would be surrounded and searched and the inhabitants screened for VC suspects. The conclusion of such operations is described by a pacification evaluator: the inhabitants "are allowed time to pack their belongings and collect their livestock and then are moved to one of the sixty-five refugee camps in the province. Shortly thereafter, the hamlet is destroyed. Notwithstanding this type of operation, friendly forces still continue to receive fire from such hamlets and encounter mines, but they no longer are inhibited from returning fire and calling in artillery and air strikes." [69]

The First Brigade of Task Force Oregon during Operation MALHEUR distributed more than 23 million leaflets to the population. "The VC claim that they are concerned for the welfare of the Vietnamese people. Why do they use your villages as a base to fight the forces of your government, the Republic of Vietnam?" asked one of these leaflets. "Why do the VC always hide in the midst of the people and refuse to meet the government's forces on the battlefield? The VC say they are strong, why must they continue to use defenseless women and children as shields and your villages for their protection? Refuse the VC demands and tell him to do battle in the fields, rice paddies, and woods away from your village and you. The GVN forces have no design to harm innocent civilians but we will destroy the VC and NVA where we find them." [70] Such appeals, unfortunately, had only meager results. While many villagers belonged to VC associations and voluntarily helped the VC, many others were forced to assist the VC out of fear for themselves or their families. Since allied forces were not numerous enough to leave detachments in the villages they searched, the VC would often return within 48 hours after U.S. troops had departed. As long as allied troops could not guarantee the safety of villagers who wanted to help the GVN, the latter had little choice but to seek an accommodation with the VC.

At the end of Operation MALHEUR the First Brigade, Task Force Oregon, reported having killed 869 VC/NVA at a cost of 81 Americans—a kill ratio of 10.73:1. The brigade also reported evacuating 8,885 villagers and burning their houses in order to deny the use of these facilities to VC/NVA forces in the area and to discourage the villagers from returning to their homes.[71] The picture of desolation was much the same in the northern part of the province, the scene of intense fighting between U.S. Marines and VC and NVA units in 1966 and early 1967, much of it in and around heavily fortified hamlets. The extensive use of artillery and air strikes with high explosives and napalm had helped keep down American casualties but had also resulted in large-scale destruction and the deaths of villagers and many refugees.[72]

In the summer of 1967 the fighting in northern Quang Ngai province was taken over by units of Task Force Oregon and the Second Korean Marine Brigade—with similar results. In Operation DRAGON HEAD V, carried out by the ROK brigade in the first week of August, 3,000 villagers were removed on short notice. The pacification evaluator who reported this action estimated that in September 1967, 160,000 of the province's estimated 712,000 inhabitants, almost a fifth of the population, were refugees.[73] While some refugees moved voluntarily because they no longer wanted to live under VC control or because they sought to escape the intense military activity in and around their villages, others were the result of "forced evacuation of the inhabitants by Allied Forces for purposes of their safety and for population and resource control."[74] About half of the northernmost district of Binh Sonh was now unpopulated and about 40,000 persons, one-third of the inhabitants, lived as refugees in camps or as squatters. "The situation," reported the American district adviser, "had been caused by floods originally, and then methodical 'Search and Destroy' operations, the relocation of people to government-controlled areas, and the retention of large FWF [Free World Forces] 'Free Fire Zones.' "[75]

The operations of Task Force Oregon (Americal Division) in Quang Ngai province in the course of 1967 destroyed or drove away the enemy's main force units, though in the process the American forces contributed materially to the depopulation and destruction of large sections of the province. In the fall of 1967, Jonathan Schell flew for several weeks with American forward air controllers (FACs), the men who directed air strikes in support of ground operations, in Quang Ngai. He acknowledged seeing from the air trenches running down the center of many villages as well as entrances to caves and networks of tunnels, yet this information was overshadowed by his report of the grisly banter of the FACs and the widespread destruction he had observed.[76] Pressed from Washington for comment, the Saigon embassy ordered an American officer to conduct a similar low-level visual reconnaissance flight over Quang Ngai and Quang Tin provinces. His report stressed the extent to which many hamlets in Quang Ngai were in fact fortified places. Villagers built bomb shelters, he said, but innocent villagers do not construct fighting positions around their bunkers. He nevertheless confirmed that the destruction of dwellings was extensive. He estimated that in the two southern districts of Quang Ngai province, Mo Duc and Duc Pho, about 30 to 40 percent of the houses were destroyed.[77] During the year 1967, according to AID figures, 6,400 civilian war casualties were admitted to the Quang Ngai hospital, about half of them women and children.[78]

Military operations of the First Cavalry Division in Binh Dinh province in 1966 and early 1967 had led to similarly destructive results and this pattern continued there during the rest of 1967. At least some of this destruction and loss of life among the rural population was again the consequence of the enemy's tactic of entering villages and succeeding in provoking allied forces into attacks on built-up areas. "With increasing frequency," wrote a pacification official in early 1968, "VC and NVA forces enter a hamlet, raise their flag and announce that they are staying. In order to root them out, we often have to destroy the hamlet. Since December 5, a total of 13 hamlets have been destroyed in An Nhon district alone."[79] Repeatedly during Operations PERSHING and PERSHING II, the latter ending on 29 February 1968, 1st Cav units attacked VC-occupied hamlets after heavy barrages of artillery, aerial rocket artillery and air strikes had softened the objective. In many instances the enemy's main force escaped before the final assault. "Even under artillery fire," noted the after-action report on Operation PERSHING, "the enemy can reorganize and attempt an escape with his main force through many avenues such as hedgerows, tunnels, stream beds, paddies, or sugar cane before the encirclement can be completed. In attempting escape, the enemy will generally leave a small covering force in the village with the mission of directing enough fire at our elements so that we will not assume a breakout maneuver."[80] The hamlet and its people, if any, meanwhile took the brunt of the attacking Americans' vast firepower.

Another favorite tactic of the VC was to snipe at American convoys from within hamlets situated along major roads in order to get the Americans to fire back with their heavy weapons. A study of the pacification mission of the U.S. Twenty-fifth Infantry Division in the Cu Chi district of Hau Nghia province (III CTZ) reported that in the autumn of 1967 such sniping incidents were frequent along Route 1 and that American armor and mechanized infantry responded as the VC desired. After one such incident, the report related, in which numerous houses in Bau Tre hamlet had been destroyed and several civilians wounded, a pacification adviser asked whether such destruction was really necessary in response to sniper fire. A spokesman for the unit replied that if the people did not wish to suffer such destruction they could avoid it by warning U.S. troops of the presence of VC in their hamlets.

On 28 February 1968 troops of an armored unit were warned by villagers of the presence of VC in this same hamlet of Bau Tre. Subsequently one armed personnel carrier (APC) was hit by a rocket and knocked out. The remaining armored vehicles then deployed themselves along one side of the hamlet and requested reinforcements, which deployed along the other side. In the interim, most of the VC force had withdrawn, leaving behind a covering force. The APCs fired into the hamlet with their guns and called for helicopter gunships which flew down the axis of the hamlet, strafing the most densely populated portion. When the battle was over, there were no VC bodies available for counting, but 58 houses had been destroyed, 10 villagers killed and 12 wounded. Next time, the report concluded, the villagers would think twice before reporting VC infiltrators. The impact on pacification, of course, was also highly negative. "It becomes relatively easy for the VC to replace losses from a population resentful and disgruntled at the destruction of their lives and property and therefore hostile to the GVN and its allies."[81]

The End of the American Buildup

Westmoreland was pleased with the military gains he felt a relatively small number of American troops had achieved in Vietnam, and he believed that his strategy of attrition was working. Battle plans, he told the press on 14 April 1967, remained unchanged: "We'll just go on bleeding them until Hanoi wakes up to the fact that they have bled their country to the point of national disaster for generations. Then they will have to reassess their position."[82] In the eyes of many Washington officials, on the other hand, Hanoi's own strategy was perhaps working even better. American casualties had been steadily rising, reaching an average of 816 killed in action per month during the first half of 1967—compared with a monthly average of 477 in 1966—and in the face of this steadily growing human toll to which no end was in sight, public support for the war was gradually eroding. These considerations played an important role in the deliberations about future force levels that took place in Washington from April through July 1967.

On 18 March Westmoreland had submitted his troop requirements through fiscal year 1968. American forces, he argued, had gained the tactical initiative and by employing additional troops his command could build upon these successes and speed up the end of the American role. He proposed two plans: the first called for a "minimum essential force" of 80,500 men which would raise American strength to 550,000. With these forces "we shall be able to complete more quickly the destruction and neutralization of the enemy main forces and bases and, by continued presence, deny to him those areas in RVN [Republic of Vietnam] long considered safe havens. As the enemy main forces are destroyed or broken up, increasingly greater efforts can be devoted to rooting out and destroying the VC guerrilla and communist infrastructure." The second plan involved an "optimum force" of 201,250 additional men, for a total strength of 671,616.[83] This force would make possible an even greater step-up in operations and create an ability to take the war to the enemy in Laos and Cambodia and to stage an amphibious landing north of the DMZ.[84] Only presidential adviser Walt W. Rostow supported the idea of operations outside of South Vietnam, and in the end Westmoreland reluctantly agreed to receiving even less than his "minimum essential force"—just over 47,000 men, creating a troop ceiling of 525,000. A major factor in this decision was Johnson's desire to avoid having to call up the reserves. "Domestic resource constraints with all of their political and social repercussions, not strategic or tactical military considerations in Vietnam," the *Pentagon Papers* point out, "were to dictate American war policy from that time on."[85]

In his assessment of the military situation at the end of 1967 Westmoreland struck an optimistic note: "During 1967, the enemy lost control of large sectors of the population. He faces significant problems in the areas of indigenous recruiting, morale, health and resources control." In many areas the enemy had been compelled to disperse and avoid contact.[86] Earlier in the year MACV officials had surmised that they had reached the "cross-over point" when American forces put out of action more men than the enemy could infiltrate or recruit for that month. At year's end, allied forces in I CTZ reported that during 1967 they had killed, disabled or captured 59,418 VC/NVA while the total enemy input from infiltration and recruitment was estimated at 28,800. This amounted to a net loss to the enemy of 30,618 and meant that the goal of inflicting losses on VC/NVA in excess of their gains from infiltration and recruitment had been more than fulfilled. The strategy of attrition was seemingly bearing fruit. And yet, the same report admitted, according to valid intelligence estimates total enemy strength in I CTZ and the DMZ region had risen from some 32,800 troops in January 1967 to 43,100 by year's end, an increase of 10,300 men. Acknowledging its inability to resolve this contradiction, the report reaffirmed the decisiveness of the enemy's casualty figure—"the hard fact remains that the marine and army units of III MAF left 25,564 confirmed enemy dead on the battlefields of I CTZ and the DMZ region during 1967." The goal of attrition, it was "reasonable to conclude," had "in good measure, been achieved."[87]

The American commander in I CTZ may have believed his own wishful thinking, but back in the U.S. disillusionment and criticism were growing. In November 1967 Johnson summoned Westmoreland to Washington, ostensibly for consultations, but in reality, as the latter recalls, "for public relations purposes."[88] During his visit Westmoreland cited as evidence of progress in Vietnam the decline in enemy armed strength from 285,000 in the fall of 1966 to 242,000 in November 1967. Actually, the general was playing the numbers game. As officials soon acknowledged, this decline was due to the deletion from enemy strength figures of the VC infrastructure and of two categories of VC irregulars—the Self-Defense and Secret Self-Defense forces engaged in propaganda, sabotage and the construction of fortifications as well as the defense of hamlets and villages in VC-controlled areas.[89] The exclusion of these elements from the enemy order of battle* may have been perfectly justified. The debate over whether these groups, few of them adequately armed, should be counted as part of the enemy's military force had been going on for many months and it was finally resolved in October 1967 with the decision to exclude them. Still, the fact remains that without this statistical revision enemy strength would have shown a substantial expansion; the revised order of battle listed 55,960 more men in the categories of administrative service and guerilla personnel than previous estimates.[90]

In 1968 and again during the hearings of the House Select Committee on Intelligence in the fall of 1975, it was charged that MACV in 1967 had underreported enemy strength in order to show light at the end of the tunnel. The former CIA official Samuel A. Adams testified on 18 September 1975 that "corruption in the intelligence process" had been one of the main reasons for our surprise by and lack of preparedness for the Tet offensive.[91] This charge is unfounded if only because enemy elements excluded from the revised order of battle played no part in the assault on the cities in February 1968. There also is no proof for Adams' charge that this revision was undertaken in order to help demonstrate progress in grinding down the enemy. The argument over enemy strength may indeed have involved no more than what the former chief of pacification, Robert W. Komer, has called "a highly esoteric and complex dispute" in the intelligence community.[92] And yet the timing of this adjustment was felicitous. Intended for this purpose or not, the revision of the figures enabled Westmoreland to claim success in his strategy of attrition while in fact enemy strength had not been eroded. Indeed, subsequent and more complete intelligence revealed that North Vietnamese forces in South Vietnam, too, had greatly increased—from 58,600 in December 1966 to 79,900 by December 1967.[93]

In his 1967 year-end assessment Westmoreland stated: "The friendly picture gives rise to optimism for increased success in 1968."[94] The enemy's Tet offensive, which involved offensive operations throughout

* Information on strength, disposition and combat effectiveness.

South Vietnam and included an extensively publicized attack on the U.S. embassy in Saigon on 31 January 1968, caused a rude awakening from these optimistic appraisals. As of 11 February, MACV reported, attacks had taken place on 34 provincial towns, 64 district towns, and all of the autonomous cities. To be sure, from a strictly military point of view, the Tet offensive was a defeat for the VC. The general uprising on which they had counted failed to materialize and only in the case of Hue was the enemy able to hold on to an objective for any appreciable length of time. By the end of February enemy losses had reached 37,000 killed. But in a guerilla war, as Henry Kissinger has pointed out, purely military considerations are not decisive, and psychological and political factors are at least as important. "On that level the Tet offensive was a political defeat in the countryside for Saigon and the United States." The VC had demonstrated that despite allied claims to be able to protect an ever-larger part of the population, there still were no secure areas for Vietnamese civilians.[95]

Back at home the psychological and political impact was equally damaging. Television viewers saw house-to-house fighting in the midst of ruined and smoking cities which seemed to belie the assurances of victory given out by military and civilian officials. After almost three years of a contest in which the U.S. had claimed steady progress, the VC were still strong enough to launch a devastating countrywide effort. In the wake of this blow American strategy was subjected to a new and searching re-examination. Dissatisfaction with Westmoreland's conduct of the war had been building up for some time. The reasons for this mounting critique, which was not limited to civilian policy-makers, will occupy us next.

3

The Failure of Attrition
and Pacification

The big-unit war had been going on for over a year when Defense Secretary McNamara, following another visit to Vietnam, communicated to the president his realization that American strategy was seriously flawed. In a memorandum dated 14 October 1966, McNamara noted that while American forces had succeeded in preventing a North Vietnamese military victory they had failed to translate their successes into the "end products" that counted—broken enemy morale and the ability of the GVN to win the allegiance of its people. Large-size military operations had inflicted heavy casualties on the enemy. "Allowing for possible exaggeration in reports, the enemy must be taking losses—deaths in and after battle—at the rate of more than 60,000 a year. The infiltration routes would seem to be one-way trails to death for the North Vietnamese. Yet there is no sign of an impending break in enemy morale and it appears that he can more than replace his losses by infiltration from North Vietnam and recuitment in South Vietnam."

Moreover, the secretary continued, the large-unit war in which we had had our successes was "largely irrelevant to pacification as long as we do not lose it." Pacification was a bad disappointment and, if anything, had gone backward:

As compared with two, or four, years ago, enemy full-time regional forces and part-time guerilla forces are larger; attacks, terrorism and sabotage have increased in scope and intensity; more railroads are closed and highways cut; the rice crop expected to come to market is smaller; we control little, if any, more of the population; the VC political infrastructure thrives in most of the country, continuing to give the enemy his enormous intelligence advantage; full security exists nowhere (not even behind the US Marines' lines and in Saigon); in the countryside, the enemy almost completely controls the night.[1]

In other words, the strategy of attrition was not attriting and, more importantly, had failed to achieve greater security for the people of Vietnam.

The MACV Strategic Objectives Plan, approved by Westmoreland's successor, General Abrams, in the spring of 1969, evaluated the 1965–68 period of the war in a similar way. The extensive and massive operations against VC/NVA forces, reflecting classic military emphasis on offensive action and destruction of the enemy, caused us to lose sight of the real purpose of providing a shield of containment for the people of South Vietnam. "In single-mindedly attempting to achieve the destruction of the VC/NVA forces . . . we have failed to do what was urgently required: Steadily provide genuine security to increasingly large numbers of people. . . ." The "shield of containment" had not really provided protection.[2] The evidence for these harsh criticisms deserves further examination.

Body Count

The indicators that measured progress in the war included the security conditions of roads and hamlets and the percentage of population under GVN control. But in view of the emphasis placed by Westmoreland on attriting the enemy's armed strength it was inevitable that enemy casualty figures would assume a crucial importance. Since Vietnamese troops had been known to exaggerate the number of enemy killed and since Washington officials insisted on accurate casualty data in order to have a reliable basis for evaluation and planning, the system of "body count" had come into use. The regulations required that the number of enemy killed in action, before being considered "confirmed," be substantiated by counting the bodies of "males of fighting age and others, male or female, known to have carried arms. Body count made from the air will be based upon debriefings of pilots or observers which substantiate beyond a reasonable doubt of the debriefing officer that the body count was, in fact, KIA."[3] In the early years of the conflict, units also reported "probable kills," but by the spring of 1968 this category had been abolished. "Possible kills" were reported by U.S. and allied forces but were not counted as confirmed enemy losses.

The reliability of the body count as an accurate measure of enemy losses soon came to be subject to considerable questioning, some of it from within the military community, but Westmoreland's intelligence officers rejected these criticisms. A fact sheet issued by the MACV intelligence staff in 1968 acknowledged that several factors tended to have an inflationary effect on enemy loss statistics: combat conditions which precluded a search of the battlefield and led to resort to estimates; body counts reported by aerial observers; duplication of count; the counting of porters and other villagers aiding the VC who, when found killed in the battle area, were counted as VC or NVA; illiterate people wandering into free-fire zones who were killed and became part of the body count. "The problem of identifying innocents from VC and VC sympathizers but counting all as VC will have to a certain degree an inflationary effect on enemy body count." On the other hand, the fact sheet stated, there were several deflationary factors at work: the high priority placed by the enemy on reclaiming bodies from the battlefield; the difficulty of finding bodies in jungles and swamps; nonbattle casualties due to injury and disease. On balance, the MACV intelligence officers concluded, exaggerations were "more than offset by casualties from actions in which no bodies are recovered." An analysis of captured documents conducted in late 1966 and early 1967 showed "a clear corollary between KIA as reported by the enemy and as reflected in our statistics." Lastly, it was estimated that for every 100 enemy KIA there were 35 enemy soldiers who died of their wounds or became permanently disabled.[4]

MACV estimates of enemy wounded put out of action can be considered acceptable.[5] The body count figures, on the other hand, were received in Washington with some skepticism, and this attitude of doubt was not allayed by the assurances conveyed in a report of the MACV inspector general of April 1968 to the Army chief of staff that "personnel at all echelons visited were performing body count in a manner characterized by professional integrity."[6] A review and reanalysis by the Systems Analysis Office in the Department of Defense (DOD) of the captured documents, upon which the MACV intelligence staff had relied to corroborate the body count figures, concluded that the enemy body count in fact was overstated by at least 30 percent.[7] Ambassador Ellsworth Bunker, too, informed the State Department that MACV had "serious doubts" about the methods of analysis employed in that study.[8] Another study, based on a larger number of documents and further refinements in the method of analysis, concluded that both the number of VC/NVA killed on the battlefield and total losses (including disease) amounted to about half of the official estimates.[9] General Giap, in an interview with the Italian journalist Oriana Fallaci in 1968, is reported to have acknowledged the loss of 500,000 men (the official count stood at 435,000 at the end of 1968),[10] but the importance to be attached to this casual remark is open to question.

The body count was regarded as unreliable for many reasons. There were, first, the errors acknowledged even by the MACV intelligence staff such as duplication of count. A pacification official reported in 1969, "Whenever several agencies combined in a single operation, it appears to be common practice for each to claim 100 percent of the results."[11] To prevent such duplication and, at the same time, to demoralize and terrorize the enemy, a battalion of the 101st Airborne Division in 1968 placed cards with the inscription "Compliments of the Strike Force Widow Makers" into the mouths of dead VC/NVA.[12] In order to find enemy weapons buried in underground caches as well as in order to check out the number of dead buried by the VC, American troops, when time and conditions permitted it, would dig at any site of freshly disturbed earth. This also led to double counting. In a message to all commanders COM-USMACV in 1967 ordered that only bodies found in fresh graves in the area of contact be included in the body count. Others could not reasonably be associated with a specific action and were to be presumed to have been counted previously.[13] Of course, the difficulty of distinguishing dead combatants from innocent bystanders caught and killed in a battle was compounded in the case of bodies dug up from graves.

An exact appraisal of the frequency of exaggerated body counts that took place as a result of command pressure is impossible to provide, but that such pressures to produce results did exist cannot be doubted. "The incentives for field commanders clearly lay in the direction of claiming a high body count," writes the former assistant secretary of defense for systems analysis, Alain C. Enthoven. "Padded claims kept everyone happy; there were no penalties for overstating enemy losses, but an understatement could lead to sharp questions as to why U.S. casualties were so high compared with the results achieved. Few commanders were bold enough to volunteer the information that they had lost as many men in an engagement as the enemy—or more."[14]

Two surveys of officers who had commanded combat units in Vietnam tend to support these findings. In November 1968 Lt. Col. Richard A. McMahon surveyed 65 such officers at the Army War College (43 had commanded battalions, 5 had commanded brigades). Forty officers (slightly over 60 percent) responded that enemy casualties they reported were based on a combination of body counting and estimates. Body counts were usually "upped," sometimes honestly and sometimes with great license. Several officers in this group reported various kinds of pressure from their headquarters to turn in high body counts, and this pressure was especially pronounced when the actual score was in the enemy's favor.[15] The second survey was made in 1974 by Douglas Kinnard, a former general officer in Vietnam, and included 173 fellow general officers with service in Vietnam. Sixty-one percent of those responding (108 in all) agreed that the body count was "often inflated," while 26 percent felt that the count was "within reason accurate." A frequent added comment was that the veracity of the body count depended completely upon the commander. The implication was, comments Kinnard, "that some commanders, particularly at lower levels, resorted to false reporting to 'look good' and perhaps in some cases to prevent their own relief."[16]

The body count of one division commander was singled out in the Kinnard survey as especially suspect by respondents who included both his immediate commander and an adjacent division commander. Kinnard does not mention the name of this division commander, but information derived from other sources points to Maj. Gen. Julian J. Ewell, the commanding officer of the Ninth Infantry Division in 1968–69, which amassed an unsurpassed record of enemy casualties. Ewell acquired a reputation of being obsessed with body count, and he is said to have set up quotas for his subordinate commanders. Threatened with relief if they did not fulfill their quotas, many company commanders lied rather than shoot innocents.[17]

Command pressure for a high body count appears to have continued in the Ninth Division even after General Ewell relinquished command on 5 April 1969. At the court-martial of Lt. James B. Duffy, an officer in the Ninth Division who was convicted in March 1970 of ordering the killing of a prisoner in September 1969, there was much testimony about emphasis on attaining a high body count. Several officers of Duffy's battalion testified that a unit's effectiveness was measured by its body count and that there was competition between battalions and companies for the highest monthly count. Duffy himself was said to have worried about his efficiency report.[18]

Command pressure for a high body count and the frequent inclusion in the count of villagers found dead on the battlefield probably had other deleterious consequences for professional ethics. After witnessing the inclusion of all Vietnamese bodies in the body count, "combat soldiers might understandably lack the ability or disposition to agonize over distinctions between combatants and noncombatants."[19] More fundamentally, both the widespread exaggeration of body count figures and the counting of unarmed killed bystanders may help explain why the high enemy casualty count did not translate into a reduction of enemy combat forces. It is possible, wrote McNamara in a November 1966 draft memorandum for the president, "that our attrition estimates substantially overstate actual VC/NVA losses. For example, the VC/NVA apparently lose only about one-sixth as many weapons as people, suggesting the possibility that many of the killed are unarmed porters or bystanders."[20]

Regulations required that only the bodies of those "known to have carried arms" be counted, but in view of the guerillas' practice of carrying away and hiding their weapons and the ambiguous status of villagers assisting the VC, this rule was never strictly applied. Needless to say, once allowance was made for the disappearance of weapons and once it became common to count all black-clad bodies as enemy dead, a precise count of enemy combatants became quite impossible. The magnitude of the distortion thus introduced can only be guessed. The fact that the discrepancy between the number of weapons captured and the number of VC/NVA reported killed was generally most pronounced in areas of combat with a high population density such as the coastal provinces and the Delta suggests that the number of villagers included in the body count was indeed substantial.

The Futile Pursuit of Attrition

The strategy of attrition failed for several other even more important reasons. First, studies undertaken in 1967 in the DOD Systems Analysis Office showed that the enemy, within some limits, had control over his own losses by controlling the pace of the action—the number, size and intensity of combat engagements. "The VC/NVA started the shooting in over 90% of the company-sized fire fights," Enthoven informed Mc-Namara in May 1967. "Over 80% began with a well-organized enemy attack. Since their losses rise (as in the first quarter of 1967) and fall (as they have done since) with their choice of whether or not to fight, they can probably hold their losses to about 2,000 a week regardless of our force levels. If, as I believe, their strategy is to wait us out, they will control their losses to a level low enough to be sustained indefinitely, but high enough to tempt us to increase our forces to the point of U.S. public rejection of the war."[21]

The great majority of all ground battles were at the enemy's choice of time, place, type and duration. For example, less than one percent of nearly two million allied small-unit operations conducted in Vietnam during 1967 and 1968, the CIA reported in early 1969, resulted in contact with the enemy and in the case of ARVN it dropped to one-tenth of one percent.[22] During the year 1966 the military activity of allied forces had increased greatly, McNamara stated in his November 1966 draft memorandum for the president. Battalion days of operation had increased by 44 percent and small-unit operations by 28 percent. Armed helicopter sorties more than doubled from 14,000 to 29,000 per month and attack sorties rose from 12,800 to 14,000 per month. Yet the enemy loss rate was not significantly affected by this stepped-up allied activity.[23] Correlations between enemy attacks and enemy losses were high; the correlations between allied force activity and enemy losses, on the other hand, were insignificant. The JCS therefore concluded: "The enemy, by the type of action he adopts, has the predominant share in determining enemy attrition rates."[24]

A review of enemy strength figures during the years 1965–67 reveals, second, that Westmoreland's eagerly sought "cross-over point"—when the allies would be able to put out of action more soldiers than the enemy could replace through recruitment or infiltration—was in fact never reached. Reported enemy deaths went up from 35,436 in 1965 to 88,104 in 1967; in all, from January 1965 through December 1967 the enemy was said to have lost 179,064 killed. During the same period (using the MACV ratio of 100:35 discussed earlier) another 62,650 VC/NVA died of their wounds or were permanently disabled, 18,270 were taken prisoner and some 83,759 defected or deserted.[25] This meant that during three years of combat the enemy had apparently lost about 344,000 of his combat troops. Despite these huge losses enemy strength continued to increase.

In December 1964 total enemy strength was estimated to be 180,700; by December 1967 it stood at 261,500.[26] In other words, assuming the broad accuracy of the above figures, the VC/NVA had successfully replaced their losses and, in addition, had increased their strength by 80,800 men—requiring and achieving a total input through infiltration and recruitment of 424,800 men in three years. The enemy had also matched the allied force buildup—the ratio of friendly to enemy maneuver (combat) battalions had remained relatively constant since mid-1965.[27] Meaningful attrition had not been accomplished.

The outlook for the future was no better. At the beginning of 1967 Westmoreland estimated that despite the bombing of the infiltration routes and the naval blockade of the South Vietnamese coast the North Vietnamese could infiltrate personnel at the rate of about 8,400 per month and the VC could recruit about 3,500 men per month in South Vietnam for their main and local forces.[28] This gave the enemy a yearly input of 142,800 men, more than enough than was needed to replace his losses, which in October 1966 were running at the yearly rate of 115,960. An even more pessimistic Secretary McNamara, using higher recruitment figures provided by the U.S. Intelligence Board, concluded in November 1966 that the enemy "can replace current losses solely from within South Vietnam if necessary."[29] By late 1968 MACV had raised its estimate of enemy infiltration and recruitment for the year 1968 to 300,000. Thus even at the extremely high casualty rate of 291,000 which the enemy was said to have suffered as a result of his offensive tactics in 1968, no attrition was taking place.

If one looked at the manpower pool available to the enemy the picture was still bleaker. North Vietnam had about 1.8 million males aged 15 to 34; in 1968 only 45 percent of these were serving in the armed forces, and approximately 120,000 new physically fit males reached the draft age each year. The total VC/NVA able-bodied manpower pool was estimated at 2.3 million. Even at the unusually high loss rate incurred by the enemy during the first half of 1968, which nobody expected to continue, it would take 13 years to exhaust this manpower pool. With more normal casualty rates, a National Security Council study of early 1969 concluded, the enemy's manpower pool and infiltration capabilities could outlast allied attrition efforts indefinitely.[30] The hope of defeating the enemy through a war of attrition could not be sustained.

The Neglect of Population Security

"Modern wars are not internecine wars in which the killing of the enemy is the object," reads U.S. War Department General Order No. 160, dated 24 April 1863. "The destruction of the enemy in modern wars, and, indeed modern war itself, are means to obtain that object of the belligerent which lies beyond the war." These sentences were chosen by a group of officers as the motto for a study of the problems faced in Vietnam which they had been commissioned to undertake by the Army chief of staff; the lengthy study, known as PROVN, was completed after eight months' work in March of 1966. In Vietnam "the object . . . which lies beyond the war," the PROVN study argued, was the allegiance of the people of South Vietnam to their government, yet this basic insight all too often was being ignored.[31] Military engagements were being fought without regard to their impact on the long-range goals of the war.

The same basic criticism has been made by a British expert. "The American forces," Sir Robert Thompson has written, "fought a separate war which ignored its political and other aspects, and were not on a collision course with the Vietcong and North Vietnamese, who therefore had a free run in the real war."[32] There was much talk about the significance of the "other war," about winning the hearts and minds of the people, the importance of defeating the enemy's insurgency through political and social reform and so forth, but in reality pacification took a back seat and the efficacy of psychological operations was commonly measured by the number of leaflets dropped and the number of loudspeaker broadcasts made.

The Kennedy administration had tried hard to get the military to develop an understanding of and capacity for counterinsurgency. The nature of guerilla warfare and the measures necessary to meet this challenge were studied at the Special Forces School at Fort Bragg and the war colleges, but the military never developed counterinsurgency capabilities on any major scale. The Army's Green Berets and similar units in the other services remained small-scale efforts outside the main career stream; the importance of attacking the social and political roots of insurgency was never fully appreciated and accepted. "It is fashionable in some quarters to say that the problems in Southeast Asia are primarily political and economic rather than military," declared Gen. Earle G. Wheeler, soon to become Army chief of staff, in a speech at Fordham University on 7 November 1962. "I do not agree. The essence of the problem in Vietnam is military."[33] General Walt, who came to Vietnam in March 1965 as commander of the marines, recalls candidly: "Soon after I arrived in Vietnam it became obvious to me that I had neither a real understanding of the nature of the war nor any clear idea as to how to win it."[34]

Bureaucracies, whether civilian or military, tend to do what they are trained and equipped to do, the former chief of pacification, Robert Komer, has noted in a monograph dealing with institutional constraints on U.S. performance in Vietnam, appropriately entitled *Bureaucracy Does Its Thing*. The military establishments "knew how to mobilize resources, provide logistic support, deploy assets, manage large efforts. So they employed all these skills to develop irresistible momentum toward fighting their kind of war"[35]—a war which followed the classic Army doctrine of finding, engaging and destroying the enemy with the fewest friendly casualties. The rival strategy of protecting the population was rejected as unduly defensive. Instead, American forces, committed to aggressiveness and offensive tactics, went after the enemy's main forces, and there followed the big-unit war which I have described in the previous chapter. The employment of helicopters, making for mobility and fast reaction, and the fighting quality of the American soldier resulted in many successful battles, though the contribution of these victories to the goal of defeating the VC insurgency was not always clear.

In 1965 and 1966, when newly created VC main force units and North Vietnamese regulars threatened the collapse of the South Vietnamese army, a major quasi-conventional military response was probably unavoidable. Large operations against the enemy's main force units were necessary to provide a shield behind which pacification and the struggle against the guerillas in the villages could proceed. However, these large search-and-destroy operations soon became an end in themselves, and the tautology that "the destruction of the enemy would bring security to the countryside" obscured the more basic question of who and where the enemy really was. As Francis J. West, Jr., a former Marine Corps officer and an astute analyst of American strategy and tactics in Vietnam, has written: "The rationale that ceaseless U.S. operations in the hills could keep the enemy from the people was an operational denial of the fact that in large measure the war was a revolution which started in the hamlets and that therefore the Viet Cong were already among the people when we went to the hills. The belief that American units would provide a shield ('support for pacification') behind which the rural GVN structure could rebuild itself assumed that the hills threatened the hamlets." West illustrates the irrelevance to pacification of much of the big-unit war by this episode:

> In November of 1967 two officers from an American division visited the senior adviser to the district which abutted their division headquarters in order to be briefed on the local situation. The adviser said the situation was terrible, with the VC in control and the GVN unsure even of the district town. So bitter was the adviser that the visiting officers grumbled about his "negativism," pointing out that their division had the NVA units in the hills on the run and had killed over 500 of them in the past month. . . .
> The officers returned to their headquarters for dinner and that same night a team of enemy sappers from a local force unit leveled the district headquarters and killed the adviser.
> In October of 1968 I revisited that district and both the assistant district chief for security and the senior subsector adviser told me that the situation had not improved, that the VC still controlled the district, and that the division was still out in the hills bringing them security.[36]

While American large units prowled around to thwart enemy main force units, the pacification of the countryside became a sideshow. After American troops had cleared an area of enemy main force units, Vietnamese troops, police and pacification cadres were supposed to move in to root out the VC infrastructure and provide permanent security and development help to the hamlets. Unfortunately, this plan was rarely implemented. Not enough ARVN and paramilitary forces were available for this assignment and, where and when available, they usually settled into fixed installations from which they ventured out only during daylight hours. All too often ARVN operations were in the nature of "search-and-avoid"; ARVN conduct toward the rural population was arrogant and abusive.

A South Vietnamese division cost roughly one-twentieth as much to establish and operate as a U.S. division, yet the program to re-equip and improve the effectiveness of ARVN did not really get under way until 1968. The ARVN, McNamara complained in October 1966, did not understand the importance (or respectability) of pacification; it was weak in dedication, direction and discipline. The image of the government could not improve unless and until the ARVN improved markedly. "Success in pacification depends on the interrelated functions of providing physical security, destroying the VC apparatus, motivating the people to cooperate and establishing responsive local government." An essential precondition for the success of this process was "vigorously conducted and adequately prolonged clearing operations by military troops, who will 'stay' in the area, who behave themselves decently and who show some respect for the people. This elemental requirement of pacification has been missing."[37]

Precise statistics on VC terrorism do not exist, but reliable estimates put the number of government officials assassinated during the years 1964–67 at more than 6,000.[38] Many more were kidnapped and their fate remains unknown. These were the hamlet chiefs, schoolteachers and social workers—the natural leaders of the community. For every Vietnamese official assassinated or abducted several villagers were murdered or seized. To thwart this program of intimidation, designed to discourage cooperation with the Saigon government, a permanent presence of security forces was essential. Government control of territory during the daytime was irrelevant. If Saigon officials and pacification cadres withdrew after dark into the district and province capitals, the villagers could not be expected to resist the VC or provide the intelligence needed to root out the VC infrastructure in the hamlets. "In almost no contested area designated for pacification in recent years," McNamara wrote in October 1966, "have ARVN forces actually 'cleared and stayed' to a point where cadre teams, if available, could have stayed overnight in hamlets and survived, let alone accomplish their mission. VC units of company and even battalion size remain in operation, and they are more than large enough to overrun anything the local security forces can put up."[39]

The theory of successful pacification was well known. From both military and political points of view, stated a MACV pamphlet issued in early 1964, "clear-and-hold" operations are the most effective, while sweeps are generally a waste of time. "The people will not cooperate with friendly forces when they know that several days later they will be abandoned to the mercy of the VC."[40] But the gap between theory and practice remained wide. Westmoreland has argued that the shortage of allied troops was the main reason for his inability to pursue a clear-and-hold strategy. "Had I had at my disposal virtually unlimited manpower, I could have stationed troops permanently in every district or province and thus provided an alternative strategy. That would have enabled the troops to get to know the people intimately, facilitating the task of identifying the subversives and protecting the others against intimidation."[41] The point is partially valid, yet Westmoreland, had he decided on different priorities, could have made more manpower available for pacification.

"Now that the threat of a Communist main-force military victory has been thwarted by our emergency efforts," McNamara urged in November 1966, "we must allocate far more attention and a portion of the regular military force (at least half of the ARVN and perhaps a portion of the US forces) to the task of providing an active and permanent security screen behind which the Revolutionary Development teams and police can operate and behind which the political struggle with the VC infrastructure can take place."[42] The PROVN study of March 1966 similarly suggested a substantial revision of priorities and argued that pacification should be designated unequivocally as the major US/GVN effort. "Victory" could be achieved only through bringing the individual Vietnamese, typically a rural peasant, to support the GVN willingly. The critical actions, the PROVN study argued, were those that occurred at the village, district and province levels. This was where the war had to be fought and won. The military destruction of the communist regiments was not the solution to the complex challenge presented by the Vietnam conflict. "Present US military actions are inconsistent with that fundamental of counterinsurgency doctrine which establishes winning popular allegiance as the ultimate goal."[43] Westmoreland failed to heed these pleas and the emphasis remained on the big-unit war of attrition. In fiscal year 1968 almost $14 billion was spent for bombing and offensive operations but only $850 million for pacification and various aid programs.[44] McNamara, already fighting with the JCS over the bombing of North Vietnam, apparently was unwilling to pay the additional political costs in terms of friction with the military to insist on a change in ground strategy.[45]

Until 1967, if not 1968, most of the pacification programs were little more than ill-planned and badly executed social control and welfare efforts. The names of the programs, as one analyst has pointed out, suggest their trial-and-error nature: Reconstruction, Civic Action, Land Development Centers, Agglomeration Camps, Agrovilles, Strategic Hamlets, New Life Hamlets, Hoc Tap (Cooperation), Chien Thang (Victory), Rural Construction, Rural Reconstruction, and Revolutionary Development.[46] All of these stop-and-start efforts failed because of the lack of a secure environment in which they could thrive, the result of a faulty strategic concept; but there were many other serious shortcomings.

One of these was the failure to expand the police and the locally recruited Regional and Popular Forces. The Popular Forces program, wrote an adviser in Quang Ngai province (I CTZ) in early 1968, was the closest thing to grass-roots security and yet it was the worst supported. "Unless drastic changes are made to upgrade these forces, across the board, we can forget about winning." Allied forces, he suggested, should be broken down into small units and used to provide security in the hamlets. "The problem is within the hamlets. The VC operate there, not out in the paddies and boonies."[47]

Corruption and Unpopularity of the GVN

The widespread corruption within all levels of the GVN was another problem which did not receive timely effective attention. For example, it was soon learned that one of the factors contributing to corruption was the low salaries paid to both civilian and military officials, yet the program of providing the GVN and ARVN with better pay, eventually given priority, was another late starter.

In most traditional societies the family is the only unit of permanence and stability and the only real claimant of a man's enduring loyalty. To a considerable extent, therefore, the appropriation of public property and the use of official status for the benefit of one's kin were part of a time-honored tradition which was accepted in Vietnam provided it was kept within certain traditionally defined bounds of propriety. In a society where most people had little contact with government and where no premium was placed on action, bribery had the characteristic of a user's tax which had to be paid by those few who came to trouble officialdom with a request for action. Still, the large and often poorly managed aid programs introduced by the Americans created pressures and opportunities to exceed the traditional limitations on the use of public office for private gain. Graft and bribery soon went beyond reasonable limits and became exposed to public view; ostentatious high living demonstrated a lack of style. In this new situation the fact that government officials used and subverted the war effort for personal enrichment began to alienate and embitter the population and corruption became a significant deterrent to victory.

That the "corrupt" Saigon government was a major cause of the VC insurgency has often been argued by critics of American policy in Vietnam. This idea is surely too simplistic: honest governments are not necessarily immune to guerilla insurgency. There has also been much self-righteous finger-pointing which has ignored the systemic corruption built into communist societies, on one hand, and has failed to acknowledge the continued existence of corruption in our own country, on the other. It is often forgotten that endeavors to control waste and corruption through various methods of accountability are a fairly recent development in America, and that to this day the application of these remedies in many state and local governments has been uncertain at best. Still, there is no denying that GVN corruption was a major cause of the slowness and ineptness with which the government in Saigon and in the provinces responded to the VC threat. The improper conduct of GVN officials and the continuation of unworthy men in power, a study conducted in 1968 by the Rand Corporation found, "may well overshadow the complaints against the hardships that society imposes on the poor."[48] Without good government the GVN could not hope to attract the voluntary support of its people, and without this support no purely military measures could hope to end the insurgency.

Corruption meant not only that a sizable percentage of U.S. aid to the war-stricken countryside found its way to the VC or into the pockets of government officials; it also undermined important programs which the American command regarded as barometers of progress in the war. The fate of the so-called Third Party Inducement Program, part of the Chieu Hoi (Open Arms) program for returnees to GVN control, can serve as an example. Begun in 1963, the Open Arms Program by the end of 1967 had resulted in the defection of over 75,000 VC and NVA soldiers.[49] Most of them were of low rank, yet the ralliers (defectors) bit into the enemy's manpower and many of them volunteered for the South Vietnamese military and paramilitary forces. Some became scouts for American units and their knowledge of communist tactics proved highly useful.

Starting in September 1964 a special reward was given to those who surrendered with a weapon or who led government forces to weapons caches, and many substantial arsenals were found in this manner. Another reward program was started in the summer of 1967 in IV CTZ and in November of 1968 was implemented countrywide. Under it people who induced a VC/NVA to surrender received a reward which varied with the rank of the defector. At first this program appeared to be highly successful. The number of ralliers shot up from 17,836 in 1968 to 47,088 in 1969. Yet it gradually became evident that many of the alleged ralliers were not

VC at all and that the program had turned into a profitable source of monetary gain for government officials and officers who organized groups of alleged ralliers in order to collect the inducement rewards. Far fewer ralliers now turned in weapons and most of them claimed to be induced by a third party with whom they apparently split the reward. It was estimated in early 1969 that in some areas as many as one-half of the ralliers brought in through a third party were not true ralliers at all.[50]

By August 1969 the American senior adviser in IV CTZ reported that the program had turned into a "big money-making business" with thousands of false claims being discovered. There were cases of upgrading the ranks of returnees in order to increase the inducement reward.[51] He recommended that the Third Party Inducement Program be terminated as soon as practicable and this was indeed done at the end of 1969. As was to be expected, the number of ralliers promptly dropped significantly. During the last six months of 1969 there were 25,865 ralliers; during the first six months of 1970 the number was down to 16,415.[52] The senior American adviser in Quang Nam province reported that the number of ralliers in January 1970 was 63 percent of what it had been in December 1969, a decline he attributed mainly to the termination of the Third Party Inducement Program.[53] The end had come to a program which had been designed to strengthen the GVN and which instead had turned into a source of fraud and corruption.

The Open Arms program aimed at convincing the guerillas that they should return to the fold of the GVN because that government would provide for them a better life than they could expect under VC rule. To this end the allies used family contacts, radio and loudspeaker broadcasts, and they dropped millions of leaflets that focused on the prospective rallier's grievances and aspirations. But actions speak louder than words and it was here, in the area of deeds which could have persuaded the people that the Saigon government deserved their support, that the pacification program prior to the Tet offensive failed badly.

In order to improve the living conditions of the Vietnamese people, and thus indirectly make life under the GVN more attractive, the U.S. during the fiscal years 1961–68 provided economic aid to South Vietnam in the amount of $2,934,900,000, almost three billion dollars.[54] In addition, the allied military forces engaged in an extensive "civic action" program designed to assist the people living in the vicinity of their base areas. In order to reduce the hardships of the war and raise the living standards of the people, the troops distributed food, clothing, building materials and fertilizer; they constructed and repaired bridges, built schools and medical dispensaries, provided medical examinations and immunizations, and drained and sprayed swamps. It is almost touching to read in a MACV report on civic action during 1967 that U.S. and other allied forces in one year had distributed 572,121 cakes of soap, conducted personal hygiene classes for 212,372 people, provided 69,652 haircuts and bathed 7,555 children.[55] Yet the expenditure of so much goodwill and massive resources did not translate into the genuinely voluntary involvement of the people on the side of their legitimate government.

An important reason for this failure to win the loyalty of the people was the inability of the allies to understand the real stakes in a revolutionary war. The measures taken by the GVN with U.S. support here failed in two basic ways. First, the attack on economic hardships and poverty did not address the conflicts in Vietnamese society which the revolutionary movement exploited and used to motivate its forces. Aid measures like building roads and schools, digging wells, medical care, etc., were incremental rather than distributive. While the VC offered to redistribute status, wealth and income, the GVN's efforts were perceived as the preservation of the social status quo, albeit on a higher level.[56] One of the main lessons of the successful defeat of the communist insurrection in Malaya and the Philippines, Edward G. Lansdale wrote in a 1964 article entitled "Vietnam: Do We Understand Revolution?" was that "there must be a heartfelt *cause* to which the legitimate government is pledged, a cause which makes a stronger appeal to the people than the Communist cause. . . ."[57] Unfortunately, this insight was ignored. It was not until the 1970s that redistributive measures like land reform, for example, aiming at the building of a more equitable society, got under way in earnest.

Much the same point was made in July 1966 by the Priorities Task Force formed in Saigon by Deputy Ambassador William J. Porter. The pressure for success and the desire for immediately visible statistical results and progress had led to excessive stress on the material and easily measurable aspects of pacification and had "failed to emphasize the political, social and psychological aspects of organizing the people and thus eliciting their active cooperation."[58] In 1966 only one in seven Vietnamese ordered to report for induction actually complied with the call to arms. The very fact that the GVN was unable to raise sufficient troops and had to rely on foreign assistance should have served as a warning that the existing social organization was unable to motivate enough forces to defend itself and that remedial social change was needed.

It is significant that the villages and districts best able to resist communist pressure were those populated by religious minorities where strong community leadership was closely linked to the local population by ties of critical interest. An Giang province in the Delta, the home of the Hoa Hao sect, consistently had the highest security rating even though it was only 30 miles from the Cambodian border and nearby communist base areas. No ARVN division had to operate there because the people were motivated to defend themselves. The same situation prevailed in villages like Luong Hoa in Long An province, whose Catholic population was united behind its local leadership because of the perceived common interest of protecting the Catholic faith.[59] Policies and programs serving the practical interests of the peasant population could have gone a long way toward obtaining a similar commitment from the mass of the rural population. As a veteran student of Vietnamese society, Charles A. Joiner, wrote in 1967: "It is not possible to fight something with nothing."[60]

A second and related failure involved the inability to create a machinery of government with a broad popular base. Between November 1963 and the end of 1969 there were 11 cabinet changes, but no real change in the character of the top officeholders. The main support of the Saigon government remained the military officer corps: instead of the social revolution promised repeatedly in high-sounding declarations drawn up by Americans, the government continued to protect a power structure based on the wealthy urban elements of society. National elections, held in 1966 and 1967 and generally conducted more honestly than many critics allowed, were alien to Vietnamese tradition which emphasized the accountability of local officials rather than of a national government.

As a result of American pressure, in April 1967 elections had taken place to village councils and the authority of village chiefs had been upgraded. But all too often GNV officials, usually drawn from the urban elite of the country, displayed a contemptuous attitude toward the people they governed. A study undertaken by the Rand Corporation in 1968 noted that the VC "have as supreme leader a mild and modest uncle whom they temperately revere . . . and they exert themselves—with some success— to avoid, in their conduct, the manners traditionally associated with superiors." GVN officials, on the other hand, usually behaved like disagreeable fathers to their children. Beatings by GVN agents—in drunkenness or in anger—were frequent.[61] Abuse of the population by police and prison officials reinforced the image of a lawless and repressive regime.

The deep-seated corruption, mentioned earlier, increased disgruntlement. "One reason the South Vietnamese Government does not receive the support of the people," wrote an American adviser in April 1967, "is that it doesn't operate correctly toward these people. Too often its administrative machinery is disorganized and inefficient. It dispenses graft, corruption, and favoritism. It does not receive the support of the people because only a small minority of these people feel any identification with it." There was no upward mobility because the secondary education that was essential for entry and advancement in the civil service and the army officer corps was available only to the sons of the prosperous. Peasant boys who were sent to primary school but then could not go on to secondary school understandably developed discontent and resentments. Frustrated in their ambitions, many joined the VC, who promised advancement and rewarded outstanding performance. By contrast, complained the American adviser, in the Vietnamese government, which seeks victory in a revolutionary war for the allegiance of the people, the privileged elite reigned supreme. In Kien Hoa province, for example, the province chief's most valuable assistant, the deputy for pacification, was carried on the rolls as a private in the Regional Forces for, lacking the baccalaureate degree, he could not get a regular appointment in the bureaucracy. What all this amounted to, the adviser concluded, was that natural leaders were ignored, good men were not promoted, and cowards and buffoons with connections rose to positions of power.[62]

Damage to Civilian Life and Property

The damage done to Vietnamese society by allied military operations was another handicap to pacification. It was difficult to convince villagers that the Americans had come as their protectors if in the process of liberating them from the Communists allied troops caused extensive harm to Vietnamese civilian life and property. The American command from the very beginning realized the potentially damaging effect of the great firepower of American combat forces and it therefore issued ROE governing ground and air operations which were designed to minimize the destruction of property and the loss of life among noncombatants. In addition, Westmoreland repeatedly reminded his commanders that "the utmost in discretion and judgment must be used in the application of firepower" and that noncombatant casualties resulting from the application of air power and artillery had "an adverse effect on the rural reconstruction effort and the attainment of the GVN national goals."[63] In a statement to the press, handed out on 26 August 1966, Westmoreland acknowledged the special nature of the war in Vietnam, a conflict "fought among the people, many of whom are not participants in, or even closely identified with the struggle. People, more than terrain, are the objectives in this war, and we will not and cannot be callous about those people."[64]

And yet, these sensible ideas ran head on against the mind-set of the conventionally trained officer, who, seeing the war in the perspective of his own expertise, concentrated on "zapping the Cong" with the weapons he had been trained to use. There also was the understandable endeavor of commanders to minimize casualties among their troops. Ever since the huge losses of life caused by the human wave assaults of World War I, the military had embraced the motto "Expend Shells Not Men." Hence when American troops encountered a VC company dug into a Vietnamese hamlet, or in the fighting in Saigon and Hue during the Tet offensive of 1968, the tempting thing to do was to employ all of the powerful military instruments developed by the leading industrial, technology-conscious nation of the world—artillery, tactical air power, naval gunfire, aerial rocket artillery, helicopter gunships. "The unparalleled, lavish use of firepower as a substitute for manpower," wrote an American officer in early 1968, "is an outstanding characteristic of U.S. military tactics in the Vietnam war."[65]

That some American military techniques were counterproductive in terms of "winning hearts and minds" was recognized by many civilian and military officials from the earliest days of our involvement. A military analyst of air operations in the populated Delta area pointed out in January 1963 that less than highly accurate and discriminating air strikes took a heavy toll of essentially innocent men, women and children. "It is possible that an analysis of past performance might show that air strikes have rarely been justified in terms of enemy casualties. Such an analysis might well show that more noncombatants than fighters have been killed and that other noncombatants were driven into insurgency through resentment. Indiscriminate killing gives the VC a propaganda and recruiting tool, loses support for the GVN, and dries up sources of intelligence at the 'rice roots' level."[66] After Roger Hilsman, head of the State Department's

Bureau of Intelligence and Research, had visited Vietnam in January 1963 he reported to President Kennedy that despite excellent controls on air strikes it was difficult to be sure that air power was being used in a way that minimized its adverse political effects.[67] COMUSMACV, Gen. Paul D. Harkins, responded that he was aware of the problem, but that until the VC were more effectively isolated no real solution was possible. "Improving intelligence and common sense controls are the only known ways to minimize the problem and still use an important military capability, without which victory would be difficult to perceive."[68]

Unwillingness to forego tools that appeared to be militarily useful, insensitivity to the political and human costs involved, and lack of awareness of the counterproductive consequences of many of these tools were even more pronounced among South Vietnamese and Korean forces in Vietnam, trained in American military doctrine. It was commonly observed that ARVN commanders had a penchant for calling in artillery and air support at the slightest sign of enemy resistance, using air strikes in particular as a substitute for rather than in support of infantry forces, and much of the time they seemed quite oblivious of the destruction and suffering these weapons inflicted on the civilian population. Because of a dictum from President Park, Westmoreland recalls, all Korean units "were sensitive about keeping casualties down, which resulted in a deliberate approach to operations involving lengthy preparations and heavy preliminary fire."[69] At a meeting with American officials held in February 1966, the South Vietnamese Minister for Rural Construction, General Thang, complained that ROK units operating in Binh Dinh province had lobbed 2,000 artillery shells into a hamlet as preparatory fire before an attack and had almost completely destroyed it. He stressed the need to minimize civilian casualties in priority pacification areas and urged stricter adherence to the rules of engagement.[70]

This is not to say that the employment of artillery and air power always hurt pacification efforts. Some of the heaviest fighting of the war took place in unpopulated jungle areas where American superiority in firepower could be put to good advantage without adverse effects. In a situation where the enemy usually chose the time and place of battle, close air support often provided the saving factor for ambushed or besieged units, and it was not uncommon for forward air controllers to direct supporting air strikes within 50 yards of the American lines. A correspondent who in 1967 stayed with the marines on the frequently shelled hilltop positions south of the DMZ wrote of the appreciation the troops had for this support. "When B-52 bombs fell on the DMZ a mile in front of their lines and Observation Post One, shaking the bunker, a voice came from the darkness: 'That's the most beautiful sound on this earth.' "[71] Moreover, there were instances when allied units voluntarily refrained from using their big weapons. Ward S. Just, correspondent for the *Washington Post*, described an engagement in which an American officer decided against shelling a village in order not to hurt noncombatants. The village was taken by assault, 15 American soldiers were wounded, but no civilians were hurt.[72] We do not know how many other commanders acted the same way. The heavy toll of civilian war casualties, discussed in more detail in Appendix I, suggests that the lavish use of artillery and air power was widespread.

The very availability of highly sophisticated military hardware, Robert Komer has argued, to some extent at least provided a powerful incentive for its use. For example, the marines were anxious to prove the need for and the usefulness of their Special Landing Forces, and even though these amphibious operations trapped few enemy forces—Operation DOUBLE EAGLE discussed in the previous chapter is a good case in point—there were 62 such landings on the Vietnamese coast between 1965 and 1969. As a marine historian explains: These "landings not only kept the amphibious art alive, but also actually advanced it by providing testing and training in a combat environment. A large number of Marines and Navy men were exposed to the doctrines, procedures, and techniques of amphibious operations which they otherwise would have missed."[73] Again, analysis of air operations in South Vietnam had revealed that the slower-flying propeller-driven aircraft were almost three times as efficient per target destroyed than jets and that it cost only 20 percent as much to destroy a target with them. At night, the destruction of a target by a jet cost about 13 times more than with a propeller aircraft. Even though the fast-moving jets made a more difficult target than their slower and older cousins, aircraft and crew losses per target destroyed with propeller aircraft were about the same, if not fewer. Yet over 90 percent of all sorties in Southeast Asia were flown by expensive high-performance jets.[74] These were the planes the Air Force had and wanted in its arsenal, geared for a Russian or Chinese threat, and these were the planes the pilots were to learn to fly well.

The "availability" thesis, Komer thinks, explains the tremendous increase in the expenditure of munitions over any previous war. During the month of January 1967, for example, when air operations had still not reached their highest degree of intensity, American aircraft delivered 63,000 tons of ordnance, 2½ times the quantity delivered during the peak month of the Korean War.[75] In the years 1966–68 allied air munition expenditures in Southeast Asia were 2,865,808 tons, while the total tonnage of bombs dropped in World War II, in both the European and Pacific theaters, was 2,057,244 tons.[76] Since one of the problems in the Vietnam war was that of finding and fixing the highly elusive enemy, it is not likely that a higher number of lucrative targets explains this increase. Rather, as the Joint Logistic Review Board has stated, the extraordinary increase in the expenditure of air munitions stemmed from the availability and employment of high-performance jets capable of delivering large quantities of munitions at high sortie rates.[77] Availability rather than need probably also accounts for the equally immense artillery ammunition outlays, and this proclivity toward the lavish use of firepower was further reinforced by what Komer calls "organizational incentives." He writes: "In the absence of sufficient hard intelligence on the results of their activities, artillery and air unit commanders tended to be evaluated largely on the ammo expenditures or sortie rates of their units."[78]

That some of the tremendous firepower had questionable consequences for both pacification and allied casualty rates is demonstrated by the experience with harassment and interdiction (H&I) fire. This program was designed to bring and keep under fire "major base areas, known or suspected unit locations, supply areas, command and control installations, and infiltration routes within SVN."[79] The purpose of the program—employing strategic and tactical air resources, naval gunfire and artillery without ground or air controllers directing or observing the strikes—was to harass, interdict and disrupt enemy activities and movement. In 1966 some 65 percent of the total tonnage of bombs and artillery rounds used in Vietnam involved such unobserved fire; in the first six months of 1967, 45 percent of all artillery ordnance was expended on H&I missions.[80] H&I fire required the approval of Vietnamese authorites—generally given routinely. The U.S. military, reported an embassy official in December 1967, was more concerned about the safety of the population than GVN officials.[81] Targets were to be developed in such a manner as to minimize noncombatant casualties and damage to civilian property, and most of this unobserved fire was indeed directed at lightly populated areas under VC control. Still, innocent civilians were known to get killed and wounded. These were primarily people returning to zones cleared for H&I fire or violating night curfew regulations.

While hard evidence on the effect of this fire on the population is sparse, some observers in the field reported a damaging impact on pacification. An AID adviser in Quang Nam province in a report in early April 1966 suggested that a study be made of "the H&I artillery fire which may interdict a trail for a few minutes but the effect of unobserved H&I is to cause needless casualties and harassment of people who could be won over—rather than hurting the Viet Cong."[82] A study made by the Systems Analysis Office in July 1967 concluded that "the huge expenditure of ordnance on unobserved strikes affects our relationship to the civilian population. To them it is a constant, noisy menace, creating an image of indiscriminate, unthinking use of force. Every new visitor to a U.S. base camp is startled by the constant roar of artillery, day and night. It is bound to be frightening to Vietnamese, many of whom have been hurt by the careless and incompetent use of artillery by their own army."[83] Another study suggested that "we can assume our unobserved fire alienates the local peasants in most cases, thus harming our efforts to break down their loyalty to and support for the Viet Cong."[84] In 1969, two Rand researchers argued that damage which is perceived as "unintelligible and unpredictable" was apt to create in the population a belief in the government's "incompetence and destructiveness," making it appear contemptible as well as hateful.[85]

Enemy casualties from H&I fire were hard to determine. Before the introduction of electronic sensors most H&I fire was based on what one Marine Corps intelligence officer, testifying before the Senate Armed Services Committee in 1970, called "yesterday's intelligence." The former commanding general of the Third Marine Division in Vietnam, Maj. Gen. R. McC. Tompkins, told the same committee that in his view "most H. and I. fire is utterly worthless. . . . It is a great waste of ammunition."[86] And Lt. Gen. Frank T. Mildren, Deputy Commanding General, U.S. Army Vietnam from 1968 to 1970, is on record as stating that "pure H&I fires in Vietnam environment have little, if any, value while doing practically no damage to the enemy."[87] Not all officers associated with the H&I program may have agreed with these negative appraisals, but it was generally conceded that the actual number of enemy soldiers killed by H&I fire was very small.

There was evidence to show that B-52 strikes had a substantial psychological effect. The giant bombers, which in the first half of 1967 dropped 41 percent of all H&I bomb tonnage, approached at altitudes which made them noiseless and unobservable to the naked eye, and they then dropped the 58,000 pounds of bombs they carried on the unsuspecting enemy. Russian trawlers or other intelligence leaks often provided the VC/NVA with advance warning of an approaching B-52 strike, but when the B-52s found their target, reports from defectors and captives indicated that the noise and destruction caused resulted in intense fear, shock and a sense of helplessness. The bombers also were highly effective in destroying tunnel complexes and ammunition caches hidden in remote jungle terrain.

Against these accomplishments of H&I fire one had nevertheless to balance not only the above mentioned negative impact on the civilian population but also the fact that a considerable number of allied troops and noncombatants were killed by mines and booby traps built from explosive material extracted from American dud (unexploded) bombs. During the first six months of 1967, 17 percent of all U.S. casualties were caused by mines and booby traps—539 killed and 5,532 wounded; in some units and during some operations more than half of all casualties were from this source. No precise statistics were available to indicate how many of these deadly devices contained U.S. explosives, but the percentage was known to be high. The dud rate of artillery ordnance fired was 2 percent, that of the bombs dropped by B-52s 5 percent. This provided the enemy with more than 800 tons of explosives per month, more than enough for every mine and booby trap they were willing to make.[88] Here, then, was a program costing an estimated $2 billion a year, which, along with some positive results, had an often undesirable effect on civilians and in addition took care of a significant part of the enemy's logistic effort.

The VC/NVA's practice of "clutching the people to their breast" added to the difficulty of protecting the civilian population. The enemy liked to make the villages and hamlets a battlefield because in the open valleys and coastal lowlands the villages contained much natural cover and concealment. The hamlets also offered the VC a source of labor for the building of fortifications, their spread-out arrangment afforded avenues of escape, and, lastly, the VC knew that the Americans did not like to fire upon populated areas. It was the decision of the VC to dig in among the people which led to the much-criticized destructive use of American firepower, and it was therefore not really fair, argued Neil Sheehan in October 1966, to place all the blame on American troops. "The Vietcong and the NVA regulars habitually fortify hamlets with elaborate trenchwork and bunker systems," Sheehan pointed out. "Infantry attacking in classic style across open paddy fields would suffer prohibitive casualties. Under these circumstances, military commanders can only be expected to use whatever force is at their disposal."[89] It also was far from easy to distinguish the tunnels and bunkers constructed by the VC from the shelters, often with multiple exits, built by villagers for their protection, or to establish whether a hamlet was "friendly" or "unfriendly." To add to the problem, the VC often deliberately drew fire on a hamlet by sniping from it at allied troops or planes and goading them into overreactions.

Supporting fire on populated areas by artillery, naval gunfire or air strikes was authorized by the ROE only when organized resistance was encountered, and sniping was not so regarded. In a message dated 7 October 1966, Westmoreland pointed out that the VC by sniping from hamlets or fields in which large numbers of Vietnamese were working sought to provoke U.S. troops into inflicting casualties upon innocent civilians and thus gain a propaganda advantage. Commanders were urged to insure that their troops practiced "the utmost of fire discipline. We must become the masters and not the victims of this VC tactic."[90] Yet the distinction between sniping and more sustained fire was a matter of judgment and in many instances, as during Operation MALHEUR in Quang Ngai province described in the previous chapter, repeated sniper fire led to a decision to destroy the offending hamlet.

Even when troops were attacking a hamlet known to contain VC forces the population was to be warned by leaflets and loudspeaker announcements of impending air strikes and ground operations. In the latter case, however, the ROE qualified this requirement with the words "whenever possible" and "with due regard to security and success of the mission," and in many cases to issue such a warning would indeed have jeopardized the success of operations designed to entrap and destroy enemy forces. Consequently, warnings were often dispensed with.

The ROE also required "the proper selection of landing zones, the careful planning and execution of air strikes and the proper employment of artillery and armed helicopters" so as "to avoid unnecessary damage to lives and property of non-combatants." Prestrikes in populated areas, it was pointed out, were "counterproductive in the long run."[91] The assault on My Lai (4) on 16 March 1968 made use of an artillery preparation intended to land on the edge of the hamlet, and, as the Peers Inquiry, the Army's probe of the My Lai massacre, pointed out, even though this pre-strike clearly violated the spirit of the applicable ROE, it was technically within the legal limits of these directives.[92] After the conclusion of a year of operations in Binh Dinh province (II CTZ) in early 1968, the First Cavalry Division's combat after-action report recommended that all landing zones be "prepped." "Experience has shown that detailed visual reconnaissance is insufficient to insure the absence of enemy pressure or activity."[93] No data are available to indicate to what extent this practice was followed by other American units as well, but it would appear that artillery fire, aerial rocket artillery or tactical air strikes, though they compromised the element of surprise, were generally employed to prepare landing zones for the assaulting infantry, often indeed just as a precautionary measure.

The frequent result of the use of preparatory fire was the loss of civilian life and a setback to pacification. According to information gleaned from ralliers and captives, bombed villagers sometimes blamed the VC, but more often found fault with the Americans and ARVN who caused most of this destruction. A VC propaganda cadre who defected in February 1969 told interrogators that the effect of air strikes in Vinh Binh province (IV CTZ) had been to drive many villagers to join the VC. He himself had never heard a warning prior to air strikes.[94]

Most military commanders during Westmoreland's tenure as COMUS-MACV felt that they had no choice but to meet the enemy head-on wherever they encountered him. In a message to Washington, written on 30 December 1967 and addressing the problem of civilian war casualties, Ambassador Bunker expressed the same idea. The savage fighting in the villages was unavoidable, he wrote. We had to combat the enemy where we found him—in the houses and hamlets—the terrain which the VC had chosen for battle.[95] Yet there were knowledgeable and responsible critics who challenged this point of view.

A few American commanders in Vietnam realized the provocative nature of these VC maneuvers and argued against using allied weapons to accommodate the enemy. "I have witnessed the enemy's employment of this tactic for the past 10 years," wrote John Paul Vann, then (in 1972) senior American adviser in II CTZ, a man generally acknowledged to have been one of the most experienced and effective Americans to serve in Vietnam. He continued:

> His specific objective is to get our friendly forces to engage in suicidal destruction of hard-won pacification gains. Invariably, he is successful since in the heat of battle rational thinking and long term effects usually play second fiddle to short term objectives.
>
> In the last decade, I have walked through hundreds of hamlets that have been destroyed in the course of a battle, the majority as the result of the heavier friendly fires. The overwhelming majority of hamlets thus destroyed failed to yield sufficient evidence of damage to the enemy to justify the destruction of the hamlet. Indeed, it has not been unusual to have a hamlet destroyed and find absolutely no evidence of damage to the enemy. I recall in May 1969 the destruction and burning by air strike of 900 houses in a hamlet in Chau Doc Province without evidence of a single enemy being killed. . . . The destruction of a hamlet by friendly firepower is an event that will always be remembered and practically never forgiven by those members of the population who lost their homes.

In view of the fact that the occupation of few places in Vietnam was truly essential to allied objectives, Vann argued, much the best move in a situation where all courses of conduct were unsatisfactory was to leave the enemy force in possession of the hamlet until it left again of its own accord. "While this course of action does not satisfy most natural emotions, it is a course of action which does not aid and abet the enemy in accomplishing his objectives." [96] Vann's counsel was seldom followed.

The same argument was pressed by some outside observers. In a war fought for the allegiance of the people, Sir Robert Thompson urged, property damage and civilian casualties must be severely limited and the use of destructive weapons in inhabited areas must be carefully controlled. [97] The U.S., suggested the defense specialist Herman Kahn, should realize the enormous political value of fighting a "just war," of being on the side of justice and correct behavior. If the VC deliberately used civilians as a shield the U.S. had to "accept the disabilities incurred in much the same way that police accept such disabilities when chasing a criminal. No police department permits indiscriminate fire in a crowded city street, however desperately the criminal may be sought—and especially not if the criminal deliberately uses bystanders to shield himself." The minimizing of casualties among American troops should not be the only consideration. "The United States must adopt as its working position that the lives of Vietnamese civilians are just as valuable as American lives."[98]

The position verbalized by Kahn was never fully accepted by American policy-makers; the growing disdain for the Vietnamese people among U.S. military personnel in Vietnam (soon to be discussed in more detail) further undercut appreciation of the value of Vietnamese lives. A MACV directive, issued 14 October 1966, pointed out that the battle of Vietnam flowed backward and forward across the homes and fields of the hapless rice farmers who had little control over whether they lived in a VC- or GVN-controlled hamlet. Noncombatant casualties embittered the population and made the goal of pacification more difficult and more costly. These circumstances called "for the exercise of restraint not normally required of soldiers on the battlefield. Commanders at all echelons must strike a balance between the force necessary to accomplish their missions with due regard to the safety of their commands, and the high importance of reducing to a minimum the casualties inflicted on the noncombatant populace."[99] To find this balance remained an elusive goal, and during the days of the war of attrition it may well have involved incompatible demands. Many American officers were quite aware of the dilemmas created by counterinsurgency warfare. After the destruction of the hamlet of Cam Ne (4) in August 1965, described in the previous chapter, the commanding officer of the marine unit involved wrote in his after-action report: "It is extremely difficult for a ground commander to reconcile his tactical mission and a people-to-people program."[100]

Free-Fire Zones

American search-and-destroy operations were not tantamount to a scorched-earth policy, Westmoreland has written, though he acknowledges that "it was necessary on some occasions intentionally to raze evacuated villages or hamlets." The only way to establish control over certain VC-dominated parts of the country "was to remove the people and destroy the village." In such an area, designated a "free-fire zone," anyone who remained was considered an enemy combatant and "operations to find the enemy could be conducted without fear of civilian casualties."[101] Unfortunately, this assumption often did not correspond to reality.

Because the term "free-fire zone" conveyed the connotation of uncontrolled and indiscriminate firing, MACV Directive 95-2 of 20 December 1965 changed the name to "specified strike zone" (SSZ). In these zones, established by a Vietnamese province chief for a specified time, artillery fire and air strikes could be launched without prior approval by GVN authorities which otherwise was required for all fire missions except artillery, mortar and naval gunfire against VC/NVA forces in uninhabited areas. SSZs were to be "configured to eliminate populated areas except those in accepted VC bases"[102] and were presumed to contain no friendly forces or friendly populace.

Still, the conduct of fire in SSZs had to be in conformity with established ROE (and, implicitly, with the law of war). Thus, the often-repeated instructions regarding the protection of civilian life and property governed fire missions in SSZs just as everywhere else. Whenever possible, air strikes in SSZs were to be controlled by forward air controllers (FACs), and these men, piloting slow, low-flying light planes, became so familiar with their assigned geographical area of responsibility that they could easily recognize any man-made changes in the terrain and became rather adept at telling friend from foe. On the other hand, since the definition of an SSZ included the assumption that it contained no friendly civilians the implementation of command concern for noncombatants clearly was difficult. Westmoreland had exhorted his commanders that "the Vietnamese populace must be presumed to be friendly until it demonstrates otherwise,"[103] yet in the SSZ this presumption was reversed. It was therefore faultless logic which made the commanding general of U.S. Army units in Vietnam in 1969 conclude that the probability of killing or injuring innocent civilians in hamlets situated in SSZs is zero, by definition.[104]

There were other problems. The designation of SSZs changed frequently, which made it difficult for the population to know and avoid such areas. Because of the dismal conditions in most refugee camps many refugees drifted back to their homes, and this occurred especially in the case of those relocated by allied forces. Others refused to leave hamlets situated in combat zones even though repeatedly urged to do so. Many persons, the Peers Inquiry pointed out, "elected or were forced to accept the risks attendant in remaining and thus there were villages and hamlets such as My Lai (4) where relatively large numbers of persons, both willingly and unwillingly, lived in VC-controlled areas."[105] Being in areas which had been declared an SSZ, they were subject to unannounced artillery and air strikes, and anyone who took evasive action became a suspect and potential target.

In March 1968 a group of rice merchants from the Delta complained to the Ministry of Economy that four of their junks transporting unmilled rice from outlying villages to the provincial centers had been strafed and sunk by American helicopters. The American AID adviser who brought this incident to the attention of the American command stated that this was only one example of numerous similar incidents. Junk operators were so frightened of the helicopters that they jumped into the water whenever they heard them coming. The choppers apparently viewed this behavior as *prima facie* evidence of guilt and proceeded to attack. "The actions of both the pilots and the junk operators seem to have created a vicious circle." The adviser recommended that the practice of attacking these boats be stopped because the costs of trying to deny rice to the enemy in the Delta by such measures considerably outweighed the benefits. His request drew opposition. An investigation had shown that the attack in question had taken place in or near an SSZ, and in such an area all canal traffic had to be considered hostile and subject to attack unless women and children were observed to be present. The establishment of SSZs, argued the senior adviser in IV CTZ, was "an essential element to our VC interdiction program" and could not be abandoned. "Although there have been incidents whereby gunships have inflicted casualties on friendly civilian and military personnel, subsequent investigations have failed to disclose any laxity in adherence to the established rules of engagement."[106]

In other words, civilian casualties in an SSZ could not really be prevented and were regarded as the price tag of an essential military activity. Many American advisers looking at some of the consequences of this program from the point of view of pacification, on the other hand, were less than happy with the cost-benefit equation.

The Refugee Problem

Another challenge to pacification was the tremendous increase in the number of refugees during 1965, 1966 and 1967. At least some of this deluge could have been prevented by different U.S. policies. No reliable statistics on the number of refugees are available until 1968, but it was estimated that between December 1965 and June 1967 there were 1.2

million officially recorded refugees and a far larger number who blended in with the general population as best they could and received no government assistance whatever. During the first eight months of 1966 alone the number of refugees officially processed was more than half a million. Between 1964 and 1969, as many as 3.5 million South Vietnamese, over 20 percent of the population, had been refugees at one time or another. This figure did not include people only temporarily displaced by acts of war, such as the almost 1 million persons whose houses were destroyed during the enemy's Tet and post-Tet offensives in 1968.[107]

For a long time the response of the GVN to this uprooted mass of humanity was grossly inadequate and reflected a feeling of indifference at best. An American official, investigating conditions in Quang Ngai and Quang Tin provinces (I CTZ) in December 1967 found that "many Vietnamese officials do look upon refugees as a cursed nuisance and feel that if the Americans are so concerned let the Americans care for them."[108] Despite large sums of money provided by various American government and voluntary agencies most refugee sites were bleak camps which fell short of minimum standards for physical facilities, economic viability and opportunities for employment. A pacification program report of September 1967 on refugee handling in Quang Ngai, a province which had more than half of the total refugee population of South Vietnam, stated: "Refugee camps are generally dirty, crowded and unpleasant; languishing in such places leads to despair or discontent."[109] After a long stay, people in the camps developed a dependent mentality and lost the will to work. Only in terms of medical care and security from the hazards of war did the camps present an improvement over conditions in the war-torn countryside; the majority of the refugees longed to go back to their former homes. The GVN provided limited assistance for refugees to be resettled and for those who, as a result of improved security, were able to return to their villages; a steady trickle found their way back even to areas still under VC control.

The continuing flow of refugees had several causes, often working in combination. The problem began with the most devastating flood in modern Vietnamese history, which in the fall of 1964 inundated vast areas in the northern coastal provinces and left about 100,000 persons homeless. The intensification of fighting in 1965 quickly increased the refugee population. The GVN referred to all refugees as "compatriots who have fled from communism," and many of those who left their homes did so indeed to escape the repressive hand of the VC. A certain part of the population movement involved job-seekers who moved to the cities or near American bases to take advantage of employment opportunities provided by the new American presence. But the largest single factor explaining the influx of refugees was the stepped-up tempo and intensity of the war. "US-RV-NAF bombing and artillery fire, in conjunction with ground operations," concluded the Army chief of staff's PROVN study in 1966, "are the immediate and prime causes of refugee movement into GVN-controlled urban and coastal areas."[110]

The conclusion of the PROVN study was substantiated in a study of the refugee situation in the Delta province of Dinh Tuong in the summer of 1966. The most frequently cited reason for moving expressed (53.7 percent of the citations) was artillery and bombardment, and not unexpectedly the GVN and the Americans were seen as the causal agents associated with this military activity.[111] In another study, carried out a year later, 65 percent of the refugees surveyed in IV CTZ gave GVN/U.S. bombing and shelling as the reason for moving; in I CTZ this factor was cited by 31 percent.[112] It was difficult to ascertain the destruction caused by the war with any precision, an NSC study found in early 1969, if only because the information available did not discriminate between lasting damage and accidental property destruction. "Even under the most generous interpretation of the available data, however, it must be admitted that the rural hamlets take a tremendous beating by both friendly and enemy forces. This aspect of the war is borne out by the flow of refugees and migrants to the urban areas of South Vietnam."[113]

Other frequent complaints cited by the refugees were increased conscription, forced labor and high taxes in communist-controlled areas. For these they blamed the VC. Responsibility for the destruction of crops in VC-controlled regions by chemical spraying was laid at the door of both the GVN/U.S. and the VC, the latter having caused the crop destruction by their presence in the area. One rallier reported: "The truth is, if these people moved to GVN-controlled areas, it was not only because their crops had been sprayed with chemicals; because since their areas had been hit by bombs and mortars, they had already had the intention to leave, and they would probably have done so, had it not been for the fact they could not decide to part with their crops. Now that their crops were destroyed by chemicals, they no longer had any reason to be undecided. . . ."[114]

In many cases the refugees were literally created by military pressure. As allied forces stepped up their activities and began to attack the VC in their strongholds, a pacification official stated, "search and destroy operations produced tactical conditions in which the civil population could not live—and sometimes in which they could not be permitted to live. Hence the refugees."[115] H&I fire often had the same effect. Leaflets dropped on the countryside capitalized on these pressures and urged the population to move to GVN-controlled areas. Still, the hope that the flow of refugees would deprive the VC of their civilian shield and thus allow the allies to utilize their firepower without constraint was not always realized. A study of the refugee problem in heavily contested and fought over Phu Yen province (II CTZ) in 1967, for example, showed that there were still considerable numbers of civilians remaining in the villages. Only 18 (19.5 percent) of the villages had lost more than 30 percent of their residents and no village had suffered more than 60 percent depopulation. "While most of the remnant adult population may fall into the category of Viet Cong sympathizers, there are still large numbers of women, children and old people in the rural areas of Phu-Yen."[116]

Some 100,000 refugees, it is estimated, were generated by allied forces in 1967, most of them by relocation sweeps in the spring and summer of that year. The removal of some 6,000 people from Ben Suc and the Iron Triangle in the course of Operation CEDAR FALLS in January 1967 was discussed in the previous chapter, and there were other large-scale forced evacuations. In April 1967 more than 8,000 Jarai tribesmen, part of the so-called Montagnards or mountain people who inhabited the central highlands, were relocated from their hamlets in the westernmost part of Pleiku province to the Edap Enang resettlement area southwest of Pleiku city. The stated purpose of this move was to deny manpower and food to the VC, to bring more people under GVN control, and to create a free-fire zone along the Cambodian border where one of the termini of the Ho Chi Minh Trail entered South Vietnam. An even larger relocation took place in May 1967 when 13,000 people were removed from the DMZ and from the area just south of it as part of Operation HICKORY and taken to the Cam Lo resettlement area. The objective here was to clear parts of the DMZ and adjacent areas so as to permit the bombing of North Vietnamese troops and artillery located there without fear of civilian casualties. These concentrated shellings, in turn, were to facilitate the construction of the McNamara Line discussed earlier. In addition to these major relocation operations there were numerous others on a smaller scale.

These relocations, American civilian and military policy-makers expected, would accomplish several aims. A State Department message to the Saigon embassy, dated 3 September 1966, urged that the refugee flow be systematized in coordination with military plans. "This helps deny recruits, food producers, porters etc. to VC, and clears battlefield of innocent civilians. Indeed in some cases we might suggest military operations specifically designed to generate refugees—very temporary or longer term depending on local weighing of our interests and capacity to handle them well. Measures to encourage refugee flow might be targeted where they will hurt the VC most and embitter people toward US/GVN forces least."[117]

Despite some initial misgivings, the military command in Vietnam soon accepted this reasoning, and the developing increase in the number of refugees came to be regarded as a sign of progress in the war. Taking note of the fact that the number of refugees in I CTZ had increased from 165,000 in January to 282,000 in December 1966, the Marine Corps Command History commented: "The influx has had the favorable effect of denying the VC a needed labor and agricultural force, and of decreasing the manpower base from which to impress recruits."[118] By October 1967 the number of refugees in I CTZ had gone above half a million, about one-fifth of the total population. Of these an estimated 230,000 lived as displaced and homeless persons with relatives or in squatter settlements. The Marine Command History opined: "The presence of an estimated 539,000 refugees in I CTZ at the close of October is a reflection of the growing confidence of the Vietnamese people in their government."[119] It is easy to see how this attitude toward the refugee problem would lead quite logically to the intentional generating of refugees.

The relocation of the population from guerilla-dominated areas, declared a Marine Corps handbook on counterinsurgency operations issued in December 1967, helped in depriving the guerillas of local support and freed innocent civilians from terrorism. "Clearing civilians from guerilla areas also simplifies tactical operations."[120] In addition, of course, such relocations had the result of removing civilians out of harm's way. All this had considerable moral and tactical merit, and yet, as many officers connected with the pacification program pointed out repeatedly, the practice of forced relocations had several inherent weaknesses and ignored critical facets of antiguerilla warfare:

1. In most cases, forced relocations created a conglomerate mass of unhappy and unproductive humanity—discontented, inadequately controlled; a haven for the VC infrastructure which often moved along with the relocated villagers; and perfect conditions for the incipiency of a new insurgency.

2. The policy took vital, arable land out of production and thus hampered economic progress.

3. People taken off the land could no longer be a source of information regarding enemy movements; however inadequate, people were the most reliable source of intelligence.

4. People contented in their own villages were the best weapon against the insurgents and the achievement of such a state of satisfaction was the goal of pacification. At the same time, it was clear that apathetic refugees in squalid camps or squatters leading a precarious existence were decidedly unsuitable candidates for pacification, and areas could not be pacified if there were no people living in them.

5. Relocation of villagers rarely deprived the VC of a significant number of recruits, for the percentage of males of military age in the refugee population was low. Most were old people and women and children.

6. Relocation did not in fact create a battlefield cleared of civilians because a considerable number of refugees slipped away from the camps and returned to their hamlets. "As in the earlier Strategic Hamlet Program under the Diem government," Westmoreland conceded in 1968, "the separation of a rural people from their ancestral lands caused fear and resentment. Their usual reaction is to attempt to slip back as soon as the opportunity arises [and] . . . this pattern was repeated at Ben Suc and Edap Enang."[121]

7. Lastly, and perhaps most importantly, refugees dramatized failure. "Refugee movement is highly visible evidence of the failure of the government to protect the rural population from the Viet-Cong," concluded the previously cited 1967 study of the refugee problem. "For a people as pragmatic as Vietnamese peasants appear to be, the message implied in refugee movement is a clear one—'The GVN is not able to protect even its supporters from the insurgents so one had best withhold making any overt commitment to the government.' " Such an attitude was found to be present in many refugee camps.[122]

These arguments, stressing the negative impact of relocation on pacification, took a long time to be accepted. Upon his departure for Saigon to head the pacification effort, Robert Komer on 24 April 1967 still suggested to the president "to step up refugee programs deliberately aimed at depriving the VC of a recruiting base," and Undersecretary of State Katzenbach, in a memorandum dated 8 June, similarly proposed to "stimulate a greater refugee flow through psychological inducements to further decrease the enemy's manpower base."[123] Meanwhile the refugee situation, particularly in I CTZ, was getting out of hand. Large numbers of refugees, generated by military sweeps, continued to be dumped into the hands of officials quite unprepared and unable to care for them. In late July 1967, a report by an American refugee official highly critical of the handling of the refugee problem was leaked to the press and there followed a sudden new interest in the predicament of the refugees and the travail of pacification. Senator Kennedy, head of a Senate subcommittee on refugees, sent investigators to Vietnam, reporters streamed in, and a General Accounting Office (GAO) team probed the situation.[124]

Finally a decision was made to halt the further generating of refugees. The "Combined Campaign Plan for 1968," issued by MACV in December 1967, placed upon commanders the responsibility to ensure that military operations did not needlessly and heedlessly generate more refugees. Persons in VC-dominated areas were no longer to be encouraged to come to GVN-controlled regions except in conjunction with ongoing military or pacification operations and at times when the GVN was capable of caring adequately for such refugees. Whenever possible in the light of security restrictions, advance notice was to be given refugee officials of military plans which might result in refugees, so that reception areas and supplies could be prepared. Military commanders were to assist in both the initial and subsequent care of refugees.[125]

Official policy had now changed, but implementation proved difficult. In a memo dated 29 December 1967, Robert Komer drew Westmoreland's attention to the fact that junior commanders in many cases were not following the new procedures. "While I too fully recognize that we have a war on and that . . . Quang Ngai and Quang Tri were practically solid VC area which required drastic action for protection of our own troops, I nonetheless believe that we have a serious 'political problem' on our hands." Senator Kennedy's sleuths were uncovering a large amount of evidence on destruction and the deliberate generation of refugees and "are zeroing in on the way we are allegedly destroying the Vietnamese countryside and uprooting the civilian population in the name of defeating aggression." Komer suggested that Westmoreland issue a new directive restating MACV policy, for there was ground to suspect that this policy was not being fully observed at lower levels.[126] As we will see in more detail later, this problem continued to haunt the American command.

Disregard of Experience

The handling of the refugee problem exemplifies the costly delay encountered, as well as the persistent difficulty which both military and civilian policy-makers had in learning from experience. An American field commander traditionally is given maximum freedom to devise his own strategy and tactics, and Westmoreland took full advantage of this tradition. His headquarters, especially in the early stages of the war, gave officers in the field a relatively free hand to accomplish their mission—albeit within the framework of accepted military doctrine. All this meant that there was scant self-critical evaluation of policy which might call into question ongoing modes of operation. A proposal by social scientists who had conducted thousands of interviews with prisoners and defectors to undertake a field study, using interview techniques, of the ROE in order to assess the impact of air and ground operations on the rural population as well as on the VC, to assess accomplishments under the present ROE and to recommend changes was turned down by Westmoreland, who made it clear that such a subject was not open for study.[127]

Westmoreland's immediate superior, CINCPAC, and the JCS viewed their role as that of supporting COMUSMACV. The PROVN study of 1966, commissioned by the Army chief of staff, which questioned Westmoreland's strategy and urged that top priority be given to pacification, at the request of MACV was reduced to a "conceptual document." According to the *Pentagon Papers*, the study for a while was treated with such delicacy that Army officers were forbidden even to discuss its existence outside DOD.[128]

Civilian officials in Washington were deluged with statistics emanating from the field, but they had few independent sources of information which would have enabled them effectively to evaluate and challenge the ever-optimistic reports coming out of MACV. Moreover, as the American involvement deepened without a corresponding show of progress and as political support for the war eroded, a worried President Johnson increasingly limited the number of people with access to sensitive information. Those who had the necessary access came to be overwhelmed by attention to day-to-day operations and crises, and therefore had little time for contemplative and innovative analysis.[129]

Nor did President Johnson get many innovative ideas from any other quarter. Secretary of Defense McNamara in 1961 had established the DOD Systems Analysis Office to help him develop a capacity for rational budget procedures. But this office, as its former head recalls, "did not have a prominent, much less a crucial, role in the Vietnam war. Prior to June 1965 it had no role at all, and afterward it was never closely involved with the development of strategy or operations. . . . It had no policy role in determining the over-all totals of men to send to Vietnam, or in figuring out what they should do when they got there."[130] Despite the fact that the Systems Analysis Office also had no access to information independent of the military chain of command and rival service interests, it nevertheless engaged in an attempt to apply cost effectiveness analysis to the conduct of operations in Vietnam, and because of this activity it soon drew the enmity of the military command. In particular, its publication *Southeast Asia Analysis Report,* issued monthly beginning in January 1967, got a hostile reception and the JCS twice tried to stop its distribution to the military services and other government agencies.[131] The military derisively referred to "McNamara's whiz kids," those irreverent young men with advanced degrees from Harvard and Yale in the offices of the assistant secretaries of defense for systems analysis and international security affairs, who, as Westmoreland puts it, "constantly sought to alter strategy and tactics with naive, gratuitous advice."[132]

Westmoreland was equally resentful of the State Department which at times, and indeed rather timidly, sought to inject political considerations into the conduct of the war and which as early as September 1965 urged greater attention to pacification. To this day he bristles at the mention of what he calls "the self-appointed field marshals in the Vietnam Task Force" and asks: "What special audacity prompted civilian bureaucrats to deem they knew better how to run a military campaign than did military professionals? Is no special knowledge or experience needed?"[133] Unfortunately, one is driven to the conclusion that the special knowledge that Westmoreland and most of his subordinates had equipped them poorly to understand the political and social dynamics of the war in Vietnam. It was one of the tragedies of Vietnam, an American officer who had commanded a brigade in Vietnam wrote in 1968, that the services refused to recognize the realities of a people's war and clung to the illusion that this was a war which troops could win. "A political revolution is something quite different from a conventional military campaign, and yet we persist in viewing Vietnam as a war which will be won when we bring enough power and force to bear."[134]

It was not until after the Tet offensive of 1968 and the subsequent serious erosion of domestic political support for the war that civilian policy-makers finally asserted themselves. From 1969 on, under President Nixon, a greatly expanded and strengthened NSC staff became the focal point for keeping tabs on the war and trying to do for the president what the Systems Analysis Office did for the secretary of defense.

The unwillingness to try new approaches on the part of Westmoreland's command was exemplified by MACV's negative attitude to the Combined Action concept pioneered by the Marine Corps, one of the most imaginative approaches to pacification. The Combined Action program was begun in August 1965 and involved the combination of a marine rifle squad (14 men) and one navy medical corpsman—all volunteers—with a locally recruited Popular Forces (PF) platoon (38 men). The resulting Combined Action Platoon (CAP) became responsible for the security of a village, typically consisting of five hamlets spread out over four square kilometers and averaging 3,500 people. The marines lived with the PF platoon and, being an integral part of it and despite occasional friction, generally had an energizing effect. Tactically, the Americans gained in knowledge of the terrain, while the Vietnamese gained in firepower and firefight skills and discipline. Most importantly .perhaps, the presence of the marines provided assurance to the Vietnamese soldiers and villagers that they would receive help in the moment of need. The marines did not arrive by helicopter in the morning and abandon the people to the mercy of the enemy by evening. In effect they became hostages and demonstrated by their presence that the allies were there to stay. The villagers also recognized that they had acquired a shield against the excessive use of firepower by allied forces, and after gaining confidence in the CAP's capability and staying power they began to provide information on enemy movements.[135]

By 1966 the program had grown to 57 CAPs; by the end of 1967 there were 79 CAPs, all in I CTZ. While the original goal of gaining three effective PF soldiers for one marine had not been achieved and even though no PF unit had yet been brought up to the point where the marines could withdraw—indeed, CAP marines, per man, took 2.4 times the casualties of the PF in the CAP[136]—the overall results were encouraging. By July 1967, hamlets with a CAP had achieved a security score nearly twice as high as that of the average hamlet in I CTZ. Moreover, despite active patrolling the CAPs had achieved their pacification successes at a cost in American casualties substantially lower than in regular infantry units. They also had demonstrated that when properly equipped and supported the Vietnamese could successfully defend their villages. "The Vietnamese," wrote an American marine, "like being part of an organization which cares, and they respond well and bravely. . . . There are sufficient men who will fight if they know the system is competent and cares."[137]

Despite demonstrated success, Westmoreland was unwilling to adopt the CAP program. He has since explained that he "simply had not enough numbers to put a squad of Americans in every village and hamlet; that would have been fragmenting resources and exposing them to defeat in detail."[138] There is some truth to this argument, but involved here also was a sharp difference of opinion over basic strategy and a rigidity of doctrine. The CAP program, in Westmoreland's eyes, represented a static and defensive employment of forces while the traditional infantry approach was that of the aggressive pursuit and destruction of enemy forces. In the eyes of many marine commanders, on the other hand, the real enemy was in the villages. Once these had been secured, the repelling of enemy main force incursions by allied reaction forces, given their mobility and massive firepower, was not a difficult problem. Moreover, they argued, without prepositioned supplies these large enemy units could not successfully maintain their attacks and in pacified areas such caches could not easily be hidden.

As it turned out, the CAP concept was never fully put to the test. In 1967 the marines were assigned to the defense of strongpoints south of the DMZ, including the Khe Sanh base, and the commitment of U.S. manpower to the CAP program therefore had to remain limited and spread over scattered areas.

There were other obstacles to learning from experience, including the bureaucratic inertia with which all large organizations are afflicted. "Bureaucrats prefer to deal with the familiar," writes Robert Komer. "It is more comfortable and convenient to continue following tested routines, whereas to change may be to admit prior error—a cardinal bureaucratic sin. . . . Moreover, once large organizations become committed to a course of action, the ponderous wheels set in motion, vast sums allocated, and personnel selected and trained, it is difficult to alter course. Instead, programs tend to acquire a built-in momentum of their own. And if obstacles are encountered, the natural tendency is to do more of the same—to pour on more coals—rather than to rethink the problem and try to adjust response patterns."[139]

Another serious handicap to adaptation and the ability to learn was the prescribed twelve-month tour of duty for all military personnel other than general officers. While this rotation policy, also used in Korea, had a highly beneficial effect on morale, it exacted a heavy price in terms of personnel turbulence—weakening unit cohesion and effectiveness—and, most importantly, by preventing the achievement of an institutionalized memory. The continuous turnover and influx of new people, a civilian observer noted in 1968, tended "to ensure that our operations will always be vigorous, will never grow tired, but also will never grow wiser."[140] Each new generation repeated at a higher level the errors of the previous one, or, as John Paul Vann is said to have put it, "We don't have twelve years' experience in Vietnam. We have one year's experience twelve times over."

The problem of turnover was aggravated by the desire of the military services to rotate as many career officers as possible through command slots for training purposes. Since the number of command positions was in short supply, most combat commands were limited to six months, and this practice of "ticket-punching" meant that officers were pulled out just as they had acquired a degree of expertise and familiarity with the special problems of their assignment. Analysis of casualty statistics revealed that Army combat battalions under experienced commanders suffered battle deaths at only two-third the rate of units under commanders with less than six months' experience in command,[141] and eventually the tour of duty of battalion commanders was extended to one year. The fact that many officers voluntarily stayed longer or returned for another tour of duty also helped. Yet for a long time the command of all too many combat units was in the hands of officers who knew a little about a lot of things but not enough about their trade as combat leaders and the challenges presented by the uncommon and unfamiliar Vietnam environment.

As one would expect, the lack of experience and institutional memory was particularly damaging in the advisory effort and in pacification, where no quick and easy solutions were to be found. The short term of duty discouraged attention to long-term projects, and the system of efficiency reports used in the promotion process tended to disincline officers to rock the boat by pointing out weaknesses and proposing innovations. Many officers in the field discerned shortcomings and mistakes, but, as a close observer of the early pacification program pointed out, "they were blocked from communicating their insights by layer upon layer of efficiency reports." The major rating the captain might agree with the criticism of the captain, but what about the colonel rating the major, and so on. The chances of valuable criticism breaking through to the top were not very good, and those in a position to make changes were therefore often insulated from the information substantiating the need for change.[142]

Moreover, the criteria upon which officers were being judged, as they knew, were those that had emerged from World War II. These put a premium upon bringing the enemy to battle and achieving a tactical victory in a battle big enough, each officer hoped, so that he would be there on the ground and eligible to be decorated. Thus the competition for promotion institutionalized and provided an incentive for the pursuit of large search-and-destroy operations,[143] while excellence in pacification work did little to enhance a career. The most desirable slots were those in command of American forces; next came positions as tactical advisers to Vietnamese units; and last those as military advisers in pacification work. Career incentives, Komer recalls, therefore operated to the detriment of the pacification program.[144]

Ineffective Management

The lack of unified management contributed to the difficulties of the pacification effort. A bewildering variety of programs, organizations, funding sources, and reporting systems were being administered through the existing bureaucratic structure—AID, the Joint U.S. Public Affairs Office, the CIA—without any single agency pulling them together in accordance with an overall plan or in coordination with military operations. Pacification consequently was everybody's and nobody's business.[145] Formally, the ambassador in Saigon was in charge of all civilian activities, but in fact the multitude of agencies and programs were given little overall direction. As a simile describing the situation, John Mecklin, head of the U.S. Information Service in Saigon from 1962 to 1964, uses the joke circulating there during that period: the U.S. mission was "like a log floating down a stream, covered with ants, each one of whom thinks he is steering."[146] This chaotic situation remained essentially unchanged until 1967.

Part of the problem encountered by the pacification program, wrote McNamara in his memo of 14 October 1966, following a visit to Vietnam, "undoubtedly lies in bad management on the American as well as the GVN side. Here split responsibility—or 'no responsibility'—has resulted in too little hard pressure on the GVN to do its job and no really solid or realistic planning with respect to the whole effort."[147] Getting the Vietnamese military to build an effective administrative machinery and to face the challenge of pacification indeed remained until the very end the Achilles heel of the American war effort. The Vietnamese generals, wrote the authors of the *Pentagon Papers*, "promised much on this latter score, but delivered little. Knowing that we had no one else to turn to, they continued their old habits and often openly did what they pleased. . . ."[148] Alternately pressuring and coaxing, the Americans found their leverage decreasing as their involvement deepened. The stakes for the U.S. increased with each increment in the troop buildup and the credibility of an American withdrawal decreased in proportion. The Saigon government, on the other hand, gradually created for itself what Bernard Fall called an "unassailable position of total weakness" by confronting American planners with the specter of total collapse and chaos.[149] Taking maximum advantage of the U.S. fear that pressure tactics would backfire and hasten this collapse, successive Vietnamese leaders for the longest time were able to stave off most of the American attempts to impose programs and reforms they did not like. In addition, there was the ever-present American anxiety about undermining the xenophobic Vietnamese government's self-respect and its standing in the eyes of its own people.

The debate over how the U.S. in this difficult situation could most effectively exert leverage lasted as long as the war without ever leading to a full solution. American advisers with the ARVN and various Vietnamese civilian agencies kept up a steady barrage of complaints, often sounding a note of real despair. "It is my firm conviction," wrote the senior American province adviser in Kien Hoa province in the Delta in February 1968, "that this war will never be won if we permit the Vietnamese to conduct it as they have in the past. For far too long we have watched in frustration while incompetent or corrupt officials and commanders at every level have bungled, procrastinated, evaded, filled their pockets, and produced bundles of fabrications to soothe their advisors' soul."[150] Proposals for redress included insistence on the dismissal of unqualified officeholders, a selective cutting off of aid to districts run by corrupt officials, and the reduction of commodities and tactical support to units commanded by incompetent officers. All of these measures, and others, were applied at one time or another with mixed results.

Americans in the field also pointed out the lack of coordination between the different elements of the pacification effort. ARVN commanders often refused to accept the authority of the district chief; American, Korean and South Vietnamese commanders failed to coordinate their military operations with those responsible for pacification or with each other. An important road in the northern part of Quang Ngai province (I CTZ), complained an American pacification official in September 1967, could not be kept open because it lay along the tactical boundary between the American Task Force Oregon and the Second ROK Marine Brigade and consequently it was not adequately policed or guarded by either.[151] At the opposite pole from these management and planning problems was that of overlapping jurisdictions.

The one proposal which might have gone a long way toward solving most of these difficulties—the idea of a combined command—was rejected by the military commanders of the American, South Vietnamese and Korean forces fighting in Vietnam. The failure of American civilian policy-makers to insist on this or a similar solution to a steadily worsening administrative problem again evidences the predominance of the U.S. and GVN military in the direction of the war.

The advisability of some form of combined command had been brought up in Washington as early as March 1965 after Army Chief of Staff Johnson had returned from a visit to Vietnam with the recommendation for deployment of U.S. combat forces. In the eyes of McNamara and others, the close association of American and South Vietnamese troops would have helped mold the latter into an effective fighting force just as it would have enabled COMUSMACV to relieve incompetent commanders and develop coherent plans. Westmoreland opposed the idea, among other reasons on the grounds that it would offend South Vietnamese sensitivities regarding sovereignty and provide ammunition for communist propaganda, which liked to depict the South Vietnamese rulers as the "puppets of the U.S. neocolonialist imperialists." In May both Ky and Thieu publicly condemned any combined command idea in press interviews, and since the Koreans, too, had indicated their opposition, the proposal was effectively dead.

From time to time thereafter the combined command idea was resurrected, as the American buildup proceeded and difficulties in adequate management and control multiplied. Robert Komer, for example, proposed in April 1967 that "at least ARVN be put under Westy and his corps commanders,"[152] but MACV again rejected the proposition. Various proposals for encadrement which would have forced some form of unified command, such as the insertion of U.S. soldiers into South Vietnamese units or vice versa, drew the same negative response. Instead, MACV worked out and adhered to a program of informal cooperation and coordination, with the different national forces maintaining their organizational independence.

After retiring from his position as COMUSMACV in 1968, Westmoreland again justified his objections to the combined command idea: "I consistently resisted suggestions that a single, combined command could more effectively prosecute the war. I believed that subordinating the Vietnamese forces to U.S. control would stifle the growth of leadership and acceptance of responsibility essential to the development of Vietnamese Armed Forces capable eventually of defending their country. . . . I was also fully aware of the practical problems of forming and operating a headquarters with an international staff."[153] Such international staffs had, of course, operated successfully in World War II, but Westmoreland perhaps here had in mind an issue not often discussed in public—the problem of security. "The VC have penetrated Vietnamese society in depth," Westmoreland told his commanders on 24 October 1965. "It is a problem US Forces have not encountered before. If the Vietnamese are brought into U.S. operations far in advance compromise is probable."[154] Vietnamese planning staffs at all levels, warned a MACV memo to the U.S. senior adviser in IV CTZ in October 1968, "are subject to infiltration by VC, VC sympathizers, and individuals who can be bought. No plan can be considered secure."[155] In such a situation a combined command raised obvious difficulties.

The desire to operate American forces autonomously, one should add, undoubtedly also gave further impetus to Westmoreland's preference for and preoccupation with pursuing the enemy's main force units in the highlands and the rejection of the rival population security concept. The latter would have required the kind of close cooperation with Vietnamese forces MACV sought to avoid, while the strategy of attrition, as Sir Robert Thompson notes, "only required perfunctory co-ordination with corresponding Vietnamese commands. In this way the war could be fought as an American war without the previous frustrations of co-operating with the Vietnamese."[156]

In his recently published memoirs, Westmoreland has reaffirmed the view that a combined command was undesirable as well as unworkable. "In the final analysis, I had the leverage to influence the South Vietnamese and they knew it. . . ."[157] The documentary record and the recollections of other high-ranking officials fail to bear out this optimistic appraisal, especially as concerns pacification. U.S. leverage with the Saigon government really improved only after the shock of the Tet offensive; the prospect of peace negotiations and the beginning of U.S. de-escalation then finally brought about the recognition that the U.S. commitment was not unlimited and that the GVN, if it wanted to survive, would have to make a far greater effort than in the past. There followed national mobilization, considerable improvement in administrative performance and a major acceleration of the pacification effort. This change was facilitated by the first meaningful American move to organize a pacification program in full coordination with the military effort—the establishment of CORDS in May 1967.

A Coordinated Pacification Program at Last

Following the meeting with President Johnson in Honolulu in February 1966, the South Vietnamese government had decided to call the pacification program "Revolutionary Development" (RD). In November 1966, Ambassador Lodge had been forced by Washington to create the Office of Civil Operations (OCO), another reorganization designed to achieve more efficient management of the pacification effort, and the last attempt to have the program run by the U.S. mission in Saigon. The new agency created in May 1967 combined the names of these two organizations: CORDS was an acronym for "Civil Operations and Revolutionary Development Support."

In many ways, CORDS represented a unique experiment in unified civil/military organization. All parts of the pacification program were now made an integral part of the military command—MACV—but personnel for CORDS were drawn not only from the military services but also from AID, the State Department, CIA, USIA, and the White House. Thus at all levels civilians came to serve under soldiers, and vice versa. CORDS was headed by Robert W. Komer, who assumed the title of Deputy to COMUSMACV for CORDS and who held ambassadorial rank—a civilian serving as an operational deputy to a field theater commander. Back in March 1966 Komer had been appointed special assistant to the president for pacification; because of his indefatigable energy and his strenuous efforts to put life into the "other war," he soon acquired the nickname "The Blowtorch." He now assumed overall command of the U.S. pacification support program, for the first time bringing together its civil and military aspects under unified management and a single chain of command.

To those who during several years had witnessed numerous reorganizations of the pacification program, none leading to meaningful results, the formation of CORDS at first seemed but another instance of the American penchant for organizational tinkering. But it soon became apparent that this marriage of civilian with military personnel and resources was indeed the managerial key to a radically improved program. CORDS established for all the 44 provinces and 250 districts unified civilian-military advisory teams which served with each of the South Vietnamese ministries involved in pacification matters—at the hamlet, village, district, province and corps level as well as at the top of the ministry. At its peak strength at the end of 1969, CORDS had about 6,500 military and 1,100 civilians assigned to it, and these men worked at coordinating the U.S. and GVN efforts in the field. They also provided both the U.S. and GVN with periodic reports on the progress of the various programs and on the impact of military operations on pacification. These "report cards" led to the identification of incompetent and corrupt South Vietnamese officials and became an important instrument of U.S. leverage, sometimes leading to their replacement.[158]

CORDS had the full support of the new ambassador in Saigon, Ellsworth Bunker, who assumed office in late April 1967. At one of his first meetings with the mission staff Bunker declared: "I dislike the term 'The Other War.' To me this is all one war. Everything we do is an aspect of the total effort to achieve our objectives here."[159] This statement reflected the new approach to pacification, which was no longer to be relegated to a subsidiary role. Under the dynamic leadership of Komer, CORDS prevailed upon the GVN to launch a major effort to improve the Vietnamese Regional and Popular Forces, including better training and equipment, to revamp and strengthen the police, to accelerate the Chieu Hoi program, and to mount a new attack on the VC infrastructure with the soon-to-become-controversial Phoenix program. "We realistically concluded," Komer wrote some years later, "that no one of these plans—relatively inefficient and wasteful in a chaotic, corrupt Vietnamese wartime context—could itself be decisive. But together they could hope to have a major cumulative effect."[160]

CORDS' actual accomplishments in the remainder of 1967 were indeed meager. In terms of the Hamlet Evaluation System (HES), a standardized measurement tool assessing a matrix of 18 security and development indicators according to a five-letter scoring system ranging from A to E, the total population in the "relatively secure" category (A + B + C) rose by 1.3 million in 1967, but most of this increase was due to the movement of refugees into GVN-controlled areas, especially to the cities, rather than to an expansion of territory protected by allied military forces. VC-controlled hamlets (30.7 percent of the total) were still the largest single category; during 1967 only 3.8 percent of the rural population experienced an improvement in security, and in the second half of 1967 the HES reports indicated that pacification had actually lost ground.[161]

Following a visit to Vietnam, a Harvard professor, Samuel P. Huntington, in a report prepared for the State Department in December 1967, noted that "the pacification program to date has still to demonstrate that it can be successful in organizing villages to defend themselves." With rare exceptions, the only localities pacified were those organized by ethnic or religious minorities. The single most important factor accounting for the expansion of the secure population, Huntington concluded, was urbanization; during the years 1965–67 the urban population had roughly doubled.[162]

The establishment of CORDS in 1967 was thus merely a beginning, the creation of organizational tools and a period of building up and training of the weak U.S. and GVN assets available for pacification. The Tet offensive of February 1968 demonstrated the fragility of the security situation and the basic failure of Westmoreland's strategy. He had accomplished neither the attrition of the enemy nor the pacification of the countryside. It was clear that "more of the same" would no longer do. Simply to increase the effort would merely magnify the original error.

4

Disengagement

The Post-Tet Reassessment

The strength of the enemy's attacks during the Tet offensive of February 1968 caused a shock in the United States that was to have far-reaching consequences. To be sure, most urban areas except for the city of Hue were cleared of enemy forces within several days, but the fighting was heavy and destruction widespread. In Saigon the VC, up to battalion strength in some cases, had holed up in residential areas; to dislodge them ARVN and U.S. troops employed artillery and air strikes, and several sections of the city were heavily damaged. The fighting for the city of My Tho, capital of the Delta province of Dinh Tuong, lasted three days and left 5,000 houses destroyed and 25,000 people homeless. Ben Tre, capital of the Delta province of Kien Hoa, was retaken after extensive use of artillery and air strikes that caused the destruction of much of the town, killed about 550 inhabitants and wounded 1,200 others.[1] It was after the battle for Ben Tre that an American officer was said to have made the widely quoted statement "It became necessary to destroy the town to save it." MACV estimated the total number of civilian casualties incurred during the Tet offensive as 12,500 killed and 22,000 wounded.[2] There were almost one million new refugees.

Much of the doomsday atmosphere generated in the United States by the Tet offensive was caused by extremely pessimistic reporting by press and television, and official Washington was not unaffected by these gloomy reports. The impact of the Tet offensive was heightened by apprehension over Khe Sanh, where one South Vietnamese and four American marine battalions, about 6,000 men in all, were surrounded by two enemy divisions. Westmoreland had decided to hold on to the isolated outpost in order to have a western anchor for his defenses south of the DMZ. Khe Sanh also could serve as a jump-off point for eventual operations to cut the

Ho Chi Minh Trail and, as the siege developed, it tied down substantial enemy forces—15,000–20,000 men. Despite the superior American air power and other differences, the struggle for Khe Sanh inevitably raised parallels to the disastrous battle of Dien Bien Phu.

The president's concern was increased even more when he learned that General Westmoreland had established a study group to consider the employment of tactical nuclear weapons. Since the region around Khe Sanh was virtually uninhabited, civilian casualties would be minimal. "If Washington officials were so intent on 'sending a message' to Hanoi," Westmoreland recalls in his memoirs, "surely small tactical nuclear weapons would be a way to tell Hanoi something, just as two atomic bombs had spoken convincingly to Japanese officials during World War II and the threat of atomic bombs induced the North Koreans to accept meaningful negotiations during the Korean War."[3]

During the last days of January and early February 1968, Johnson repeatedly phoned the chairman of the JCS, Gen. Earle G. Wheeler, seeking reassurances about Khe Sanh and the overall situation in South Vietnam. Wheeler, sensing a willingness on the part of the civilian decision-makers to send reinforcements in excess of the troop ceiling of 525,000 men set in mid-1967, encouraged Westmoreland to ask for additional troops. The JCS were concerned about renewed tension in Korea— an attack by North Korean raiders on the presidential residence in Seoul and the capture of the American intelligence ship *Pueblo* on 23 January— and by intelligence reports of possible trouble around West Berlin. The strategic reserve left in the United States to meet any sudden crisis was less than three divisions; the opportunity finally to achieve a call-up of the reserves seemed propitious. CINCPAC, too, thought that Washington should be pressured to lift the 525,000 troop ceiling.[4]

On 9 February McNamara asked the JCS to submit plans for emergency reinforcements for Vietnam and on 12 February Westmoreland's request, submitted at the urging of Wheeler, was discussed at the White House. COMUSMACV's message asked for "reinforcements in terms of combat elements. I therefore urge that there be deployed immediately a marine regiment package and brigade package of the 82nd Airborne Division and that the remaining elements of those two divisions be prepared to follow at a later time. Time is of the essence." Qualifying this tone of urgency, Westmoreland added that the situation presented not only great risks but also great opportunities. The enemy's losses were extremely heavy. "Therefore, adequate reinforcements should permit me not only to contain his I Corps offensive but also to capitalize on his losses by seizing the initiative in other areas. Exploiting this opportunity could materially shorten the war."[5] Despite the insistence of the JCS that emergency reinforcements to Vietnam not be sent without a concomitant call-up of reserves, Johnson and McNamara approved Westmoreland's troop request and these units, almost 10,500 men, arrived in Vietnam before the end of February.[6]

Before making any decisions about further deployments or new strategies, the president sent General Wheeler to Vietnam for a fact-finding visit. Wheeler arrived in Saigon on 23 February; his outlook, Westmoreland notes, mirrored the gloom that pervaded official circles in Washington. The two generals discussed future developments in terms of the worst as well as the most promising contingencies. The worst included a collapse of the South Vietnamese government, major increases in North Vietnamese strength in the South and a withdrawal of the South Korean troops. The brightest picture envisaged continued political stability in Saigon and improvement of the ARVN, which would make possible a more offensive strategy. Contemplated under this eventuality was the implementation of previously drawn up contingency plans for attacks on the Ho Chi Minh Trail and enemy sanctuaries in Laos and Cambodia as well as an amphibious landing in North Vietnam just north of the DMZ. In order either to counter the worst contingencies or to launch new moves, Wheeler and Westmoreland agreed that there was need for additional manpower. The figure arrived at was 206,000 men, about half to be earmarked for Vietnam and the others to constitute the strategic reserve which would be sent to Vietnam in case of dire need or if the president approved a more aggressive strategy.[7]

Stopping at Honolulu on his way home on 26 February, Wheeler sent to Washington a highly pessimistic report on the situation in Vietnam. Genuinely worried or perhaps hoping to exploit the atmosphere of crisis in Washington in order to achieve a call-up of the reserves, Wheeler presented the request for the 206,000 additional troops as an emergency measure and made no mention of either Westmoreland's plans for a more offensive strategy or the rebuilding of the strategic reserves. The thrust of Wheeler's oral presentation at the White House on 28 February was similarly the urgent need for more than 200,000 new troops.[8] McNamara, who was to leave office the next day, argued against what amounted to a rise in the total troop strength to 731,756 men; the president, too, was unwilling to approve this big increase, which would have required calling up about 250,000 reserves, without further study. He therefore ordered Secretary of Defense–designate Clark Clifford to head a group with the mission to undertake a complete and searching reassessment of the entire U.S. strategy and commitment in Vietnam.

Staff studies in preparation for the report of the Clifford task force were made in the Defense, State and Treasury departments as well as by the CIA and the JCS. The most critical view of Westmoreland's conduct of the war was taken by several papers prepared in the Office of the Assistant Secretary of Defense (Systems Analysis). Search-and-destroy operations and the strategy of attrition, it was argued here, had not worked and adding 206,000 more men would not make any real difference. "We know that despite a massive influx of 500,000 US troops, 1.2 million tons of bombs a year, 400,000 attack sorties per year, 200,000 enemy KIA in three years, 20,000 US KIA, etc., our control of the countryside and the defense of the urban areas is now essentially at pre–August 1965 levels. We achieved stalemate at a high commitment. A new strategy must be sought." After discussing several alternatives, the authors suggested a population control strategy, a solid commitment to a U.S. force ceiling and returning "to the concept of a GVN war with US assistance instead of the present situation of a US war with dubious GVN assistance."[9]

An initial draft of a memorandum for the president, prepared by senior officials in the Office of International Security Affairs (ISA) of the Department of Defense, was discussed at a meeting in Clifford's office on 1 March. "The current strategy," this draft memorandum maintained, "can promise no early end to the conflict, nor any success in attriting the enemy or eroding Hanoi's will to fight." To add 200,000 men would mean a total Americanization of the war and have most unfortunate effects both on the GVN and in the United States.

> We can obtain our objective only if the GVN begins to take the steps necessary to gain the confidence of the people and to provide effective leadership for the diverse groups in the population. ARVN must also be turned into an effective fighting force. If we fail in these objectives, a military victory over the NVN/VC main forces, followed by a U.S. withdrawal, would only pave the way for an NLF takeover.
>
> Our military presence in South Viet Nam should be designed to buy the time during which ARVN and the GVN can develop effective capa-

bility. In order to do this, we must deny the enemy access to the populated areas of the country and prevent him from achieving his objectives of controlling the population and destroying the GVN.

Such a strategy of "population security," the memorandum argued, would reduce civilian casualties and the generation of refugees.[10]

The ISA draft memorandum drew vigorous objections from General Wheeler, who was appalled at the apparent repudiation of American military policy in Vietnam. Drawing upon a back-channel message from Westmoreland and an analysis of various deployment options prepared in the Plans and Policy Directorate, Joint Staff, Wheeler warned that the proposed new strategy would mean a posture of static defense and increased fighting in or near population centers.[11]

Wheeler's objections led to a redrafting of the ISA memorandum, and this less controversial version was apparently approved by Clifford and forwarded to the president on 4 March. The secretary of defense recommended the immediate deployment of 22,000 additional men to Vietnam and early approval of a call-up of reserves adequate to meet the balance of Westmoreland's request and to restore a strategic reserve in the United States. The decision on whether to meet COMUSMACV's troop request in full was made contingent upon future military developments, an improved political performance by the GVN and a more effective military contribution by ARVN. To this end, the memorandum supported an urgent effort to improve and modernize the equipment of the South Vietnamese armed forces as well as greater pressure on that country's political and military leadership to enact and carry out certain essential reform measures. A high-level mission to Saigon was to make clear that any further U.S. support would have to be matched by GVN actions and improvements. Merely to increase American forces would provide no assurance of a more favorable military position, and "in the absence of better performance by the GVN and the ARVN, the increased destruction and increased Americanization of the war could, in fact, be counterproductive." Indeed, the memorandum concluded, there was no reason to believe that even by doubling or tripling the additional 200,000 American troops sought by Westmoreland could we hope to destroy the enemy forces or expel them completely from South Vietnam. There was need, therefore, for a new strategic guidance to Westmoreland which should be the subject of a detailed interagency study over the next several weeks.[12]

The Clifford group was divided on whether to recommend a new policy for the bombing of North Vietnam. Altogether, it was clear that substantial and serious differences of opinion had emerged between the Pentagon civilians on one side and the chairman of the JCS and his officers on the other. The recommendations of the Clifford task force, therefore, represented a compromise. The report deferred a decision on the large troop request sought by Westmoreland and the JCS, but it did provide for a call-up of the reserves, and it shelved the adoption of the new "population security" strategy proposed by the ISA staff. This reduced-cost strategy, concomitant with a "Vietnamization" of the war and a deliberate policy of minimizing American casualties, was to become the policy of the Nixon administration in the following year.

While the president pondered the report of the Clifford task force, Westmoreland's request for 206,000 more American troops and details of the debate created by this request within the Johnson administration were leaked to the press. The *New York Times* story on 10 March dealing with these events was startlingly accurate, and it set off a new debate in the Congress and the press, most of it highly critical of the contemplated troop commitment. There followed the unexpected strong showing of the "peace" candidate, Senator Eugene McCarthy, in the New Hampshire primary on 12 March and the announcement by Senator Robert Kennedy on 16 March that he would seek the Democratic nomination for president. On 18 March nearly one-third of the House of Representatives joined in sponsoring a resolution which called for an immediate congressional review of U.S. policy in Southeast Asia.

Throughout these days in March 1958 the president met repeatedly with his senior advisers seeking to clarify the options before him. The news of a possible major new troop commitment and of a large call-up of reserves, expected to add an expense of many billions of dollars to an already strained budget, had set off a rush to trade dollars for gold in financial markets throughout the world. Here, then, was another weighty reason to move slowly. By 22 March the die had apparently been cast. On that day Johnson announced that Westmoreland would be recalled from Vietnam to become the new Army chief of staff, a move interpreted by many as a rejection of the Westmoreland strategy. Two days later Wheeler told Westmoreland at a meeting in the Philippines that the will of American politicians was faltering and that his request for a large additional American force and permission for a widening of the war was doomed. The president, Wheeler said, "felt he had no choice over the next few months but to try to calm the protestors lest they precipitate an abject American pull out."[13]

On his return from the East Wheeler was accompanied by Gen. Creighton Abrams, Westmoreland's deputy commander in Vietnam and rumored to become his successor as COMUSMACV. The two generals briefed Johnson on the latest developments and later repeated their assessment of the situation to a group of old friends and confidants from outside the government whom Johnson had asked to come to Washington to give him their advice. The dovish verdict which these so-called Wise Men rendered on 26 March must have reinforced Johnson's conclusion that a major conciliatory step was indeed essential. The Wise Men were as steady and balanced a group of men as could be found anywhere, Johnson later wrote in his memoirs. "If they had been so deeply influenced by the reports of the Tet offensive, what must the average citizen in the country be thinking?" The American people were deeply worried and a collapse of the home front, so eagerly awaited by Hanoi, had to be prevented.[14]

On 31 March the president told the nation that he had ordered a halt in the bombing of North Vietnam except just above the DMZ, that manpower increases in Vietnam would consist of about 13,500 support troops, that the Vietnamese henceforth would take on a larger share of combat operations, and that he himself would not be a candidate for reelection. Even though the post-Tet reassessment had not resulted in the adoption of a new ground strategy, the replacement of Westmoreland and the rejection of the request for 200,000 additional American troops spoke for themselves. The president had not referred to the additional deployment as a final installment, but, as a well-informed student of the Tet events puts it, "the decision had an air of finality about it. The limit as to how much force the American military could commit to Vietnam without a mobilization had finally been reached."[15] Moreover, whatever uncertainty Johnson's own announcement may have left was dispelled in the following weeks by Secretary of Defense Clifford, who repeatedly spoke of the new 550,000 troop level as a ceiling that was not going to be exceeded. The president did not dispute Clifford.

A New COMUSMACV

On 1 July 1968 Gen. Creighton Abrams took command of American forces in Vietnam. Abrams had been associated with the PROVN study, which as early as 1966 had recommended that top priority be assigned to pacification. Since his arrival in Vietnam in the summer of 1967 he had been devoting most of his attention to upgrading the South Vietnamese forces. Being an informal person, he had developed good rapport with the Vietnamese. Since the combat responsibility of the latter was going to be expanded, he was the natural person to succeed Westmoreland.

During the second half of 1968, correspondents on the scene began to note a decline in the number of search-and-destroy operations mounted by American forces and many of them attributed this change to a new "Abrams strategy." This was a false inference. American tactics changed to meet a changing military situation.

The enemy's Tet attacks on the cities had left a vacuum in some of the rural areas. As allied forces regrouped to defend the towns, security in the countryside at first dropped sharply. But this setback proved less severe than feared. The shock of the enemy's attack on the cities began to wear off and the offensive soon served as a kind of Pearl Harbor. The disregard for civilian life and property and the atrocities committed at Hue produced widespread revulsion and hostility toward the VC which helped to achieve a stepped-up mobilization. The GVN finally moved ahead with long-delayed plans to arm the rural population. A People's Self-Defense Force (PSDF) was created which soon was to become 1½ million strong. The territorial security forces received better weapons and additional guidance and training. By the end of June Regional and Popular Forces began to display a new vigor. The successful attack on the VC in the villages benefited from the fact that some of their infrastructure had surfaced during the Tet offensive and thus had become exposed.

On 1 November 1968 a special three-month effort got under way to take advantage of these opportunities and to expand rapidly the GVN presence in the countryside—the first Accelerated Pacification Campaign. The aim was to establish a minimum GVN presence in some 1,000 additional hamlets. Rumors that the VC at the Paris talks might demand a cease-fire in place lent urgency to this move. Greater attention to pacification and population security was facilitated by a significant decrease in enemy aggressiveness. In the first half of 1968, the number of attacks staged by enemy battalions or larger forces averaged 16 per month; in the second half it was less than 5 per month.[16] Having suffered extremely heavy casualties during the Tet offensive and the minor surges during May and August, enemy main force units dispersed or retreated to their border sanctuaries and evaded contact. As a result, more allied forces became available for pacification-type operations and territorial security improved. Many of the American forces were broken down into company, platoon, and squad-size units and engaged in patrolling and the placing of ambushes in the inhabited areas. Benefiting from improved intelligence, joint small-unit operations with Vietnamese forces, designed to ferret out the VC infrastructure, became more frequent. These small-unit operations were more effective in achieving contact and causing enemy casualties while at the same time they were less costly in allied casualties than the large battalion-size search-and-destroy sweeps.

The pacification of the Quang Dien district of Thua Thien province on the coastal plain northwest of Hue can serve as an example of how this cooperation worked. When the First Battalion, 502nd Infantry, of the 101st Airborne Division deployed to Quang Dien in April 1968, this rich riceland area was dominated almost completely by NVA/VC units. GVN forces were holding out in three beleaguered posts, controlling less than 5 percent of the district. In a series of sharp clashes the American troops defeated the enemy main force units and they then proceeded with the task of eliminating the local VC forces and infrastructure in the hamlets. In these operations the use of artillery and air strikes was limited and it was here that the effective utilization of the district's Regional and Popular Forces proved crucial, for what these local forces lacked in aggressiveness and fire discipline they made up in certain inherent skills. Operating in the vicinity of their native villages, they knew the area's trails, streams and hedges like the backs of their hands; they were also adept at detecting booby traps and hidden bunkers. Furthermore, the RF/PF knew who lived in which house, which family had relatives fighting with the VC, and what kinds of information various villagers could reasonably be expected to have. Most important, the villagers came to believe that the RF/PF would remain in the district and would protect them if they cooperated with the GVN. As a result, the people of the district increasingly volunteered information about the VC, and a considerable number of the latter, at the urging of wives, parents and other relatives, turned themselves in to district forces.

American and RF/PF at first engaged in combined operations, planned from a command post in the headquarters of the district chief. Gradually, as RF/PF competence and confidence increased, these forces conducted independent operations, and U.S. forces provided helicopter transport only. By November 1968 the district was successfully pacified and attention could be shifted to the resettlement of refugees, reconstruction of homes and schools and the rebuilding of the economy.[17] The pacification of Quang Dien district did not proceed without the destruction of some VC-dominated hamlets and the movement of some people into more secure areas, but for the most part the tactic was that of clear-and-hold . Security was being brought to the people.

The most important new factor, which eventually was significantly to change the face of the war, was the advent of the Nixon administration. Benefiting from the disenchantment of the American people with President Johnson's stewardship of the war, Richard Nixon in November 1968 defeated Johnson's vice-president, Hubert Humphrey, in a close election. During the campaign Nixon had stressed the need for a new strategy which would put greater emphasis on small-unit actions, strengthen local forces and generally help the South Vietnamese to fight their own war. These ideas were stated more systematically by Nixon's foreign policy adviser, Henry A. Kissinger, in an article published in *Foreign Affairs* in January 1969, just before Nixon took office, which severely criticized Westmoreland's strategy of attrition. American "victories," he argued, were largely empty and had been achieved at an unacceptably high price. "We fought a military war; our opponents fought a political one. We sought physical attrition; our opponents aimed for our psychological exhaustion. In the process, we lost sight of one of the cardinal maxims of guerilla war: the guerilla wins if he does not lose; the conventional army loses if it does not win. The North Vietnamese used their main forces the way a bullfighter uses his cape—to keep us lunging into areas of marginal political importance." The American people, Kissinger was convinced, would tire of this bloodletting before Hanoi did, and it was therefore essential to devise and "adopt a strategy which is plausible because it reduces casualties. It should concentrate on the protection of the population, thereby undermining Communist political assets. We should continue to strengthen the Vietnamese army to permit a gradual withdrawal of some American forces."[18]

With Kissinger assuming the post of national security adviser to the president, Vietnamization and a phased American disengagement became the official policy of the Nixon administration. According to knowledgeable insiders, the word was passed to the American commander in the field that American casualties had to be reduced lest the United States fail to last the course.

Abrams' campaign plan, approved in early 1969, acknowledged these political constraints. "The realities of the American political situation indicate a need to consider time limitations in developing a strategy to 'win.' " The American public did not see the war in Vietnam as being worth the cost. "Time then is running out." The target date for achieving a reduction in financial and personnel resources devoted to Vietnam was 30 June 1972. That date, prior to the congressional and presidential elections of 1972, "should mark the termination of major commitment of military resources in Vietnam. Additional 'time' for achieving a 'win' beyond that date cannot be reasonably expected."[19]

The new MACV plan also outlined a new strategy which has been variously described as the "area security" concept or as the "one-war" approach, blending combat operations and pacification. As stated summarily in the MACV Strategic Objectives Plan, approved by Abrams in the spring of 1969: "The key strategic thrust is to provide meaningful, continuing security for the Vietnamese people in expanding areas of increasingly effective civil authority."[20] In the past, the new plan stated, high priority had been assigned to the destruction of VC/NVA main forces in South Vietnam. Progress had been measured by the number of enemy killed. "It is important that the command move away from the over-emphasized and often irrelevant 'body count' preoccupation"; instead, the indicator of success should be the attainment of security for the population. "In order to provide security for the population our operations must succeed in neutralizing the VCI [Viet Cong infrastructure] and separating the enemy from the population. The enemy Main Forces and NVA are blind without the VCI. They cannot obtain intelligence, cannot obtain food, cannot prepare the battlefield, and cannot move 'unseen.' "

Real security also required restraints upon the use of firepower. "All too often in the past the enemy has been successful, either by himself threatening the people's security, or by provoking responses by the allied forces that have been exceptionally destructive to the people." GVN, U.S. and other forces had to operate within a "one-war" concept "which does not recognize a separate war of big battalions, war of pacification or war of territorial security." Cooperation between U.S. and GVN military and civilian officials had to be strengthened and all military elements brought into a single effort. The armed forces of South Vietnam had to be improved so that eventually the provision of security would no longer be dependent upon the presence of U.S. combat forces. The enemy's strategy of winning by weakening the resolve of the United States to continue its assistance to South Vietnam would then become irrelevant.[21]

Abrams' new campaign plan, drawn up by an imaginative Long Range Planning Task Group, represented a significant change in strategy, yet its implementation ran into serious problems. The new instructions often received token compliance while the worst features of the traditional mode of operation persisted. Despite the new emphasis on bringing security to the people and explicit orders against involuntary population movements, such relocations continued to take place. Most senior commanders in the field kept relying on the lavish use of firepower. The idea that the forces under their command, which they had worked long and hard to modernize and improve in terms of mobility and firepower, should become not more sophisticated but more primitive in order to deal effectively with the VC was simply unacceptable. "I'll be damned," one senior American officer is quoted to have said, "if I permit the United States Army, its institutions, its doctrine, and its traditions to be destroyed just to win this lousy war."[22] Abrams' position, as one of his advisers recalls, illustrated the powerlessness of the powerful. Being COMUSMACV, the ostensible theater commander, did not guarantee actual power over senior subordinates who were used to having a relatively free hand in planning and carrying out operations in their areas of responsibility.

Abrams is said to have been aware of the lack of compliance with his strategic plan but unwilling to ruin the careers of senior commanders to whom he was tied by bonds of professional background and, often, personal friendship. The relief of a combat leader is not undertaken lightly in war. To the troops it indicates dissatisfaction with their performance; removing a subordinate inevitably also reflects on the competence of the superior and on his ability to provide proper guidance. Division commanders were relieved in World War II where objectives were clearly defined and ineptitude could show itself easily. In a war without fronts like Vietnam, on the other hand, the tactical autonomy of commanders was adhered to even more strictly than is generally the case. In such a war, without visible objectives, it was difficult to call a combat leader to account without in effect making COMUSMACV take over decisions on *how* the job should be done—one of the basic taboos of military command.[23] Abrams may justifiably have feared that for such an assertion of authority he would not have received the backing of his superiors—CINCPAC and the JCS—to whom, in any event, Abrams' campaign plan may have remained as unappealing as to the commanders in the field. Moreover, even if Abrams had wanted to relieve some of these men, he could not have been sure to be able to find other commanders more in tune with the new strategy.

For all these reasons, therefore, Abrams' campaign plan, for the most part, remained a paper exercise. The doctrinal and organizational rigidities of the military institution proved just too strong. General Abrams emerges as an almost tragic figure who had to assume the thankless task of liquidating the American combat role and who was unable to impose his own solutions to the problems faced in Vietnam.

The War of Attrition Continues

BOLD MARINER/RUSSELL BEACH, a combined Marine Corps–Army multibattalion operation in Quang Ngai province in January 1969, was an action quite indistinguishable from those conducted during the days of the big-unit war under Westmoreland. The target of this largest special landing force effort of the war was the Batangan Peninsula in the northern part of the province, a few short miles from My Lai, an area symbolizing VC influence in Quang Ngai and an almost permanent VC sanctuary and base. American, Korean and ARVN forces had conducted search-and-destroy operations in the peninsula, but the VC had usually merely faded away until the termination of these sweeps and then returned in strength. On 13 January, two marine battalion landing teams landed on the northern face of the peninsula, two marine special landing forces set up blocking positions in the west, and two battalions of the Americal Division moved to cut off the southern exits. Total enemy forces were estimated at about 300; all men of military age were to be considered VC. In addition there were thought to be between 5,000–8,000 civilians—sympathetic to the VC or part of the communist infrastructure.

Making maximum use of air, artillery and naval gunfire, the Army-Marine cordon swept toward the sea, scooping up all Vietnamese civilians for screening. A large number of leaflets were dropped urging the population to come toward the cordon. Those who remained were regarded as VC. There was little organized resistance and most American casualties were caused by mines and booby traps. Numerous tunnel complexes were discovered in which both civilians and enemy soldiers were found. When the joint operation ended on 9 February, the enemy body count stood at

239 and 102 had been captured. Some 12,000 Vietnamese civilians were helilifted out of the area to a holding and interrogation center where 256 of them were identified as VC cadres.[24] The number of civilians encountered and removed was roughly double what prior intelligence had predicted.

The more than 11,000 persons who had passed the screening process were placed in a refugee camp, and preparations were made to return them to the Batangan Peninsula. By the end of April 1969 all 11,270 refugees had been resettled in four new sites on the peninsula and given material to build new houses; the entire action was regarded as a significant victory for the allied cause. A VC stronghold had been eliminated and 11,000 villagers returned to GVN control. Yet this conclusion was open to question. All these people had been uprooted and their homes systematically destroyed. Their allegiance to the GVN could not be taken for granted. VC forces in the area kept up harassment and abductions; economic sustenance was difficult. "The camps," wrote a CORDS evaluator after a visit in August, "are for the most part inaccessible by land routes and expansion outside of their camps is difficult because of the residual mines and booby-traps in the surrounding area. Although the classification may be a moot point, by any reasonable or humane criterion they are in fact 'Refugees' and should be accorded that status along with the benefits therein accruing."[25] Security on the Batangan Peninsula remained poor. Units of the Americal Division which continued operating in the area had to enforce a dusk-to-dawn curfew; 95 percent of the American casualties were caused by mines and booby traps. The after-action report stated: "A highly contested area is a poor environment for community development."[26]

Many operations of the Americal Division in the northern part of Quang Ngai province in the early part of 1969 were conducted with little awareness of the new command emphasis on minimizing damage to civilian life and property. For example, on 20 January, during a mission to locate 800 abducted villagers, four companies attacked an enemy force of undetermined size entrenched in the village of Chau Nhai. Despite air strikes and heavy artillery barrages that lasted two days and two nights, repeated assaults accompanied by armored personnel carriers were unable to dislodge the enemy from his fortified bunkers and tunnel complexes. On the morning of 23 January a final call went out for surrender which was followed by another series of extremely heavy air strikes. In all, fighters dropped 648,000 pounds of bombs, and artillery fired 2,000 rounds into the village. When the smoke lifted, ground units with tracks swept through the area without meeting further resistance. The next three days, a report stated, were spent digging through the ruins; 41 NVA, 6 VC and 21 weapons were all that could be excavated from the tons of displaced earth and collapsed tunnels.[27]

In another series of battles in late February and March in which Americal units sought to drive enemy forces from hamlets they had seized during the Tet 1969 offensive, artillery, helicopter gunships and air strikes were again used freely. Relief officials in Quang Ngai province reported that during the period from 23 February to 24 March, 306 civilians were killed and 396 wounded, and 3,132 houses were 50–100 percent destroyed. The province chief estimated that 40 percent of the civilian casualties were due to allied fire, air strikes and artillery.[28] During the months of February–March 1969 the Quang Ngai hospital admitted 2,452 civilian war casualties, the highest two-month total of the war.[29] By the end of March, 15,000 persons had been added to the province's refugee population, bringing the total number of people inhabiting refugee camps to 100,072. Another 112,000 were estimated to subsist outside the refugee centers, making do as best they could on their own. Altogether, about one-third of the population of Quang Ngai was classified as refugees.[30]

Similarly, operations of the U.S. Ninth Infantry Division in the Delta during the first half of 1969 far more resembled the war of attrition fought during the years 1965–68 than they conformed to a pacification-oriented strategy. American troops had first begun to operate in IV CTZ in January 1967. Members of the U.S. mission, in particular William Porter, Ambassador Lodge's deputy, had been wary of introducing American troops with their great firepower into the densely populated Delta provinces, but the poor performance of ARVN troops there, on one hand, and the good pacification record of the Twenty-fifth Division in neighboring Hau Nghia and Long An provinces, on the other, had led to approval of this assignment. The Ninth Infantry Division, earmarked for this mission, arrived in Vietnam in December 1966; one of its brigades was combined with two Navy river assault squadrons to form the Mekong Delta Mobile Riverine Force. Transported on Navy troop-carrier boats and supported by armored boats nicknamed "Monitors," the infantry troops were thus able to operate in a terrain of few all-weather roads, crisscrossed by numerous rivers, canals and streams. For some areas of operation, like Long An province with a very high population density, the division had special rules of engagement; the problem of preventing noncombatant casualties was acute everywhere. As one officer put it, "It is difficult for US troops to know whether they are seeing a VC or an innocent civilian."[31] During Operation SPEEDY EXPRESS in the first half of 1969 the Ninth Infantry Division appears to have been less than successful in making this distinction.

Operation SPEEDY EXPRESS lasted from 1 December 1968 until 1 June 1969 and concentrated on three densely populated provinces of the upper Delta—Dinh Tuong, Kien Hoa and Go Cong. The commander of the Ninth Infantry Division, Maj. Gen. Julian J. Ewell, had the reputation of being an officer who insisted on performance. As mentioned in chapter 3, Ewell was said to be obsessed with body count, and the results of SPEEDY EXPRESS were indeed spectacular. During six months of combat the division reported to have killed 10,883 of the enemy at a cost of only 267 Americans killed, a ratio of 40.8:1. Most engagements were small-scale and about half of the enemy kills were reportedly made by helicopter-borne air cavalry units and helicopter gunships; 40 percent were achieved in night operations.[32]

And yet there were indications that the amazing results of Operation SPEEDY EXPRESS could not be accepted at face value. The most unusual feature was the small number of weapons captured—748 in all, resulting in a ratio of enemy killed to weapons seized of 14.6:1. The normal ratio was 3:1, in other IV CTZ operations in 1969 it was 3.5:1 and in III CTZ, 4.1:1.[33] The division's after-action report attributed the low weapons count to such factors as the high percentage of kills made at night and by air cavalry and Army aviation units and to the fact that "many individuals in the VC and guerilla units are not armed with weapons."[34] This was another way of acknowledging that many of those killed were not really combatants. Ewell himself recalls: "Viet Cong units dispersed and blended very effectively with people in the numerous villages and hamlets, greatly complicating reconnaissance difficulties and problems of fire control."[35] CORDS observers on the scene at the time reported that in their view "the high body counts achieved by the 9th were not composed exclusively of active VC. The normal ratio of three or four enemy KIA for every weapon captured was raised at times to fifty to one; this leads to the suspicion that many VC supporters, willing or unwilling, and innocent bystanders were also eliminated."[36]

General Ewell, who had been a combat infantryman during his entire

Army career, continued doing in Vietnam what to an aggressive infantry commander comes naturally—searching out and killing the enemy. In his debriefing report, composed in September 1969, Ewell wrote: "I guess I basically feel that the 'hearts and minds' approach can be overdone. In the Delta the only way to overcome VC control and terror is by brute force applied against the VC."[37] The key to success, he felt, was relentless and continuous pressure on the enemy to achieve attrition—high kill ratios and low American casualties—and this translated into pressure upon subordinates to produce body count. Here, then, was another reason for the spectacular enemy casualty reports. Unable to satisfy Ewell's expectations, commanders apparently falsified body count figures. An Air Force report on U.S. operations in the Delta, issued 31 August 1969, took note of the disparity between enemy KIA and weapons captured and explained it as probably caused by inflation of KIA figures: "This supposition was supported by several Army officers of the 2nd Brigade [of the Ninth Infantry Division] who pointed out a ground commander was rated upon his body counts—the higher the body count, the greater the success of the commander."[38]

When the Ninth Infantry Division redeployed from the Delta after the conclusion of Operation SPEEDY EXPRESS, it left behind a weakened enemy but also a great deal of devastation, thousands of new refugees and much loss of innocent life. The assertion of Kevin P. Buckley of *Newsweek* that perhaps close to half of the more than 10,000 killed in Operation SPEEDY EXPRESS were noncombatants[39] remains unsubstantiated, but the free use of air strikes, artillery and helicopter gunships in the densely populated Delta undoubtedly caused considerable havoc. The generally reliable Robert Shaplen reported that upon its departure the Ninth Division "left as many enemies as friends among the South Vietnamese."[40] And the above-cited CORDS report concluded that in the opinion of several observers, the presence of the Ninth Division had been counterproductive. The security umbrella provided by the Americans had aided pacification, but this had to be counterbalanced by negative aspects such as stealing, highway accidents "and particularly incidents in which civilians had been killed by 9th Division fire [which] had a significant negative impact on the population."[41] Despite the heavy losses allegedly inflicted on the enemy, the overall security situation left much to be desired. In Dinh Tuong and Kien Hoa provinces, on which SPEEDY EXPRESS had been focused, only 45 and 37 percent of the population respectively were considered secure (residing in GVN-controlled, so-called A + B, hamlets).[42]

General Westmoreland had encouraged his commanders to seek battle with enemy main force units wherever they could find them, and this preoccupation with attacking enemy base areas and causing attrition emerged once again during the bloody fighting in the A Shau Valley in the spring of 1969. This major enemy staging and supply center in the rough terrain of Thua Thien province (I CTZ) near the Laotian border had been attacked many times before. Even though in each instance the enemy had lost large amounts of war materiel, allied forces had usually suffered heavy casualties and been unable to prevent the enemy from re-establishing himself in the valley. The most recent incursion had been Operation DELAWARE VALLEY in April–May 1968, which had cost 142 Americans killed and 731 wounded.[43] Another such costly encounter took place in May 1969, involving once again the 101st Airborne Division.

Operation APACHE SNOW began on 10 May 1969 when contingents of the 101st Airborne Division and of the First ARVN Division helicop-tered into the 30-mile-long A Shau Valley. Each landing zone was exten-sively prepped by air strikes, artillery and gunships; the enemy thus had ample notice of the allied attack. On the second day of the operation, Company B of the third battalion encountered an enemy force on Dong Ap Bia (military designation Hill 937), but was unable to dislodge it. Dur-ing the next 10 days Maj. Gen. Melvin Zais, the commander of the 101st Airborne Division, threw more and more troops into the battle for the rugged, densely forested and heavily fortified peak, which, chewing peo-ple up like meat, soon acquired the nickname "Hamburger Hill." Each as-sault was preceded by heavy air strikes and artillery preparations, but enemy forces were deeply entrenched and fought back tenaciously. In all, the Air Force flew 272 attack sorties, dropping more than one million pounds of bombs, including 152,000 pounds of napalm. Artillery fired 21,732 rounds. On 20 May the hill was finally taken in an assault involving four battalions. The fighting from bunker to bunker on that day was bitter; the noise level was so high that radios could not be used. In the 10-day battle for Hill 937 the Americans suffered 56 killed and 420 wounded. Enemy losses were given as 505 killed. After the hill had been secured and the bunker complexes searched and destroyed, allied forces aban-doned the peak.[44]

The drawn-out bloody battle for Hamburger Hill drew heavy criticism back home. Sen. Edward Kennedy called it "madness" and challenged President Nixon to issue orders forbidding such senseless and irresponsible operations. In an interview on 22 May with David Hoffman of the *Washington Post*, General Zais defended the action: "That hill was in my area of operations, that was where the enemy was, that's where I attacked him. . . . If I find him on any other hill in the A Shau, I assure you I'll attack him."[45] In a later report, written for the clarification of the record, General Zais put it thus: "It is true that Hill 937, as a particular piece of terrain, was of no tactical significance. However, the fact that the enemy force was located there was of prime significance. While Allied forces were not oriented on terrain, and had no mission to seize and hold any particular hill, obviously the enemy had to be engaged where he was found if the mission was to be accomplished."[46]

The real question was, of course, why the enemy had to be engaged wherever he was found. If the aim of American operations was the attrition of enemy forces, irrespective of U.S. casualties, then it was indeed "obvious" that charging up heavily fortified hills out in the sticks and withdrawing from them again after the conclusion of the battle was necessary. However, the strategy of attrition had supposedly been repudiated by General Abrams' campaign plan, which stressed population security. Neither Abrams nor Zais, of course, had planned or expected an action like Hamburger Hill. But once it had started, the prestige of an Army commander apparently demanded that the hill be taken. The only way to prevent such costly escapades was to limit forays into the border areas which inevitably exacted heavy casualties with little permanent benefit.

General Zais defended the incursion into the A Shau Valley as necessary in order to preempt an enemy attack on Hue and the populated coastal areas of Thua Thien province. But why was it necessary to preempt and to accept battle under conditions so overwhelmingly favorable to the enemy? Successful military strategists have always insisted on an indirect approach, avoiding the line of the enemy's toughest resistance. Moreover, such operations soaked up precious manpower which could have been employed more usefully in securing the country's populated areas. The beneficiaries were the Communists who, as in 1967, had once again succeeded in luring the Americans into the wilderness of the border regions. The battle for Hamburger Hill, wrote the *Vietnam Courier* in Hanoi on 2 June 1969, was another example of the PLAF drawing the Americans into a peripheral area and creating a vacuum in the populated rear. The tactic was similar to that which had worked so well in the case of Khe Sanh in 1967–68, continued the article, when "6,000 of Westmoreland's best troops were pinned down and 40,000 others poised in the surrounding areas to fly to the rescue of the entrenched camp, while the PLAF stormed the coastal cities and seized control of Hue for weeks."[47] The logic of this argument was difficult to fault. CORDS reports from Thua Thien province showed that while allied forces busied themselves in the far-away A Shau Valley, acts of terrorism against pacification teams in the lowlands increased and the pacification effort suffered.[48]

For the Nixon administration the domestic uproar over the battle of Hamburger Hill underscored the urgency of reducing American casualties in order to achieve an orderly disengagement from Vietnam. On 15 July 1969 Defense Secretary Laird told the Senate Foreign Relations Committee that while there had been no change in the orders of U.S. field commanders to maintain maximum pressure on the enemy, "the entire matter is under review." He confirmed that President Nixon had given orders "to make the reduction of American casualties" a primary objective of the U.S. commander in Vietnam.[49] When President Nixon visited Vietnam on 30 July, he personally emphasized the importance of this matter to General Abrams in order, conceivably, to prevent follies like Hamburger Hill. On his visit, the president later explained, he "changed General Abrams' orders so that they were consistent with the objectives of our new policies. Under the new orders, the primary mission of our troops is to enable the South Vietnamese forces to assume the full responsibility for the security of South Vietnam."[50]

What the review of ground strategy after Tet 1968 and the appointment of a new American commander in Vietnam had not accomplished was thus now being achieved through direct presidential orders. As far as the American ground combat role was concerned, the war was to be wound down; the South Vietnamese were to take on an increasing share of the fighting. This is indeed what happened. The number of American servicemen in Vietnam, which had peaked at 543,000 in April 1969, began therafter to decrease steadily; the number of American-initiated large operations was reduced and American casualties declined (see Table 4-1). A total of 222,351 U.S. servicemen were killed or wounded during the Johnson years (1964–68); during the first term of the Nixon presidency (1969–72), the corresponding number was 122,708.[51] By the time of the North Vietnamese offensive in the spring of 1972, the American ground

Table 4-1 Decline of U.S. Combat Role, 1968–72

	U.S. Troop Strength	Ground Operations (bn or larger)	Deaths from Hostile Action	Deaths per 1,000 Strength
January 1968	498,000	NA	1,202	2.4
July 1968	537,000	71	813	1.5
January 1969	542,000	56	795	1.5
July 1969	537,000	89	638	1.9
January 1970	473,000	58	343	0.7
July 1970	404,000	64	332	0.8
January 1971	336,000	64	140	0.4
July 1971	225,000	40	65	0.3
January 1972	133,200	9	16	0.1
July 1972	45,600	0	36	0.8

SOURCE: OASD (Comptroller), SEA Statistical Summary, Table 6, 18 August 1973; Table 9, 7 November 1973.

combat role had effectively ended. American air support still played an important role in repelling the 1972 Easter invasion, but after the January 1973 Paris agreement the South Vietnamese were on their own. The process of Vietnamization, discussed in more detail in chapters 5 and 6, had run its course.

The U.S. Marines' Battle for Quang Nam Province

In 1969 the province with the largest American casualty toll was Tay Ninh in III CTZ; the heavy fighting there, involving some 50,000 North Vietnamese regulars who shuttled back and forth across the Cambodian border, provides the background for the secret bombing of communist sanctuaries in Cambodia which began in March 1969, as well as for the April 1970 incursion into that country. But during the last two years of U.S. ground combat involvement overall, as during most of the Vietnam war, the most intense fighting took place in I CTZ (from 1 July 1970 on called Military Region 1 [MR 1]). Quang Nam province, west and south of Danang, in particular, exacted a heavy price in American casualties and defied meaningful pacification. Here, between 1965 and 1969, the First

U.S. Marine Division, which was assigned to this area, lost more than 6,000 killed, representing almost half of all marine deaths from hostile action during the entire war.[52] Yet when the marines left the province in the spring of 1971, the security situation in most areas was still precarious, the result, primarily, of a deeply rooted VC presence. Many of the marine operations in this province again bore little resemblance to the strategic blueprint laid out in General Abrams' overall campaign plan. The use of firepower was as lavish as before, and instead of bringing security to the people, American forces continued to relocate sizable segments of the population and generated new refugees.

The objective of Operation PIPESTONE CANYON, which began on 26 May 1969 and involved four marine battalions as well as ARVN and Korean units, was to destroy the Thirty-sixth NVA regiment on Go Noi Island, a delta formed by the Ky Lam River and located about 12 miles south of Danang. This densely populated area had been fought over many times before. Operation ALLEN BROOK in the summer of 1968 was said to have killed 1,017 of the enemy. Most of the hamlets had been fortified and were taken only after heavy air strikes, artillery bombardment and the employment of tanks. Only 129 weapons were captured, a ratio of 1:7.88 KIA and probably indicative of extensive loss of life among the local population, which was known to support the VC/NVA. Following the withdrawal of the marines, large parts of the island were cleared by Rome plows of vegetation, bunkers and fortifications.[53] But a year later the VC/NVA were back on the island in force and another attempt was under way to secure the area for the GVN.

The attacking marines were preceded by heavy artillery and naval gunfire, and the assault itself was supported by numerous air strikes. During the first two phases of Operation PIPESTONE CANYON, which lasted from 26 May to 10 June, the island, roughly five miles long and two miles wide, was hit by 750,000 pounds of bombs. No organized resistance was encountered and most American casualties were from mines and booby traps. Several hundred villagers were again removed for screening, and then the Rome plows returned. By 25 July, 8,039 acres had been plowed and the after-action report stated that "Go Noi Island had been converted from a densely populated, heavily wooded area into a barren wasteland, a plowed field. In that, the operation was a success."[54]

PIPESTONE CANYON then was expanded into an area three miles closer to Danang which the troops called "Dodge City" because of its

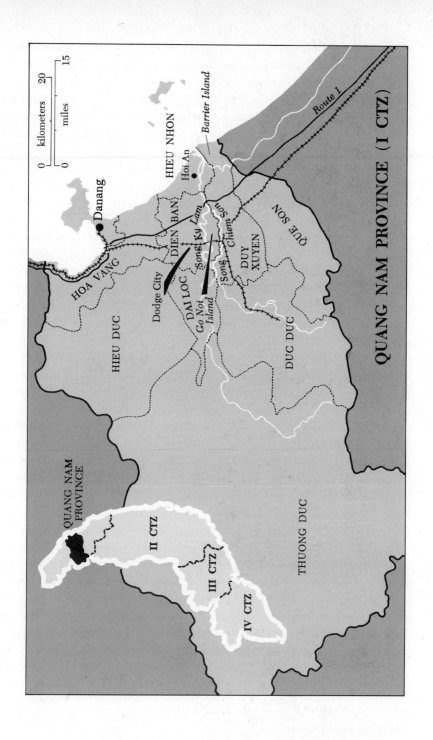

QUANG NAM PROVINCE (I CTZ)

shoot-'em-up characteristics. "It was low ground," writes a marine historian, "criss-crossed with rivers and streams, honeycombed with caves and tunnels; each hamlet, with its bamboo and thorn hedges and its drainage ditches indistinguishable from fighting trenches, was a potential fortified position."[55] This area, too, had been fought through many times before, most recently during Operation MEADE RIVER in November–December 1968, when the marines had reported killing 1,210 of the enemy and seizing 182 weapons (a ratio of 6.65:1).[56] The most important part of the action this time focused on the hamlet complex of La Huan and Giang La. On 18 October the hamlets were surrounded and searched, 813 villagers were removed for screening and on orders of the province chief all houses in the complex were burned. At the conclusion of Operation PIPESTONE CANYON the number of enemy killed was listed as 852, air strikes accounting for 55 of these; the number of weapons captured was 420. Marine casualties were 54 killed and 541 wounded.[57] The CORDS province report for January 1970 stated that 38,000 refugees from Go Noi Island were still not resettled. By late May the resettlement of 17,000 refugees on Go Noi Island had begun.[58]

Troops of the First Marine Division launched two similar operations on Barrier Island, about 20 miles south of Danang. This barren, sandy area of fishing villages had been under VC control for years. Many of the hamlets were fortified. The island had been swept repeatedly by allied forces without eradicating the presence of the VC. On 5 May 1969, in Operation DARING REBEL, the island was cordoned off by a marine landing force and elements of ARVN, Korean and Americal Division units. Most of the island for some time had been treated as a free-fire zone and the attackers did not hold back in the use of firepower. Four destroyers and one rocket-firing ship lobbed 5,236 shells and rockets from offshore, marine planes dropped 73 tons of bombs and almost 15 tons of napalm, howitzers and mortars fired 6,707 rounds. As usual in these big operations, no organized resistance was encountered. The NVA regiment supposed to be there had melted away; the attackers were met only by sporadic sniper fire and an occasional mortar round. The civilian population had been removed in earlier operations, but the villagers had always returned to the island and built new homes. Nearly 7,000 of them were now collected and removed by helicopter in order to deny the enemy a source of food and taxes. At the end of the 20-day operation, the marines reported that they had killed

400 of the enemy, captured 328 and seized 118 weapons. Marine casualties were 2 killed and 51 wounded.[59]

Three months later the marines returned to Barrier Island for still another sweep. Operation DEFIANT STAND, assisted by Korean marines, began on 7 September 1969; it was to be the last special landing force operation of the war. As a result of preparatory naval gunfire and air strikes the landing was unopposed. After 12 days of combing the hamlets and their tunnels and bunkers the allied forces reported that they had killed 298 of the enemy and seized 118 weapons at a cost of 4 Americans and 1 Korean killed. They removed 2,549 civilians for screening, of whom 11 were found to belong to the VC infrastructure.[60]

Apart from keeping the VC/NVA on the move, it is difficult to see what these sweeps—the marines referred to them as "scrubbings"—accomplished. In view of the absence of organized resistance, the low number of American casualties and the lavish use of firepower, it is a safe assumption that many of those reported as killed were not combatants but villagers, willing or unwilling helpers of the VC. The two Vietnamese hospitals in the area, located in Hoi An and Danang, during the course of the year 1969 admitted 8,030 civilian war casualties[61] and a sizable percentage of these undoubtedly were the victims of the "scrubbing" of the densely populated villages and hamlets south of Danang. This figure was the highest in the country, surpassing the number of such casualties admitted in Dinh Tuong and Kien Hoa provinces, the scene of Operation SPEEDY EXPRESS in the Delta.[62] In a study of air strike locations in 1969, the operations of both the Ninth Infantry Division in the Delta and the First Marine Division in Quang Nam province stood out, with fixed-wing attack aircraft in those areas dropping their ordnance particularly close to population centers.[63]

In December 1969 CORDS officials in Quang Nam province reported that during the course of that year they had received compensation claims for 6,091 houses destroyed more than 50 percent and 2,407 houses destroyed 20–50 percent, involving a total of 52,608 persons.[64] How many of these people were made homeless by allied military operations cannot be determined. We do know that these operations generated many thousands of new refugees. As of 20 December 1969, Quang Nam province had 169,103 registered refugees out of a total population of about 600,000, by far the highest percentage in the country. Another 100,000 or so were living outside the camps without receiving any assistance. Since the generating of refugees was contrary to long-standing orders, Vietnamese officials did not recognize the newly displaced persons as refugees. "The GVN authorities," reported CORDS refugee officials in December 1969, "have gotten themselves into a box on this matter. On the one hand, their forces and Province authorities evacuate people and approve FWMAF [Free World Military Assistance Forces] evacuations in violation of their Government's instructions. On the other hand, they then cite these same instructions as authority for denying the evacuees refugee status and benefits." Moreover, the CORDS officials pointed out, the forceful relocation of people was counterproductive. "Many people in VC or contested areas hate the VC and can be enlisted if given the right approach to give intelligence and otherwise assist in driving the VC out of their areas. Bringing them in against their will leaves our side blind in their former home areas, causes the people to resent the GVN and FWMAF and may in some cases bring the enemy into our midst."[65]

A regional CORDS refugee director who visited the area in May—June 1969 described these so-called temporary refugees as the most deprived group of any in Vietnam "in terms of standard of living and education and medical services" and he urged an end to these "cruel, counterproductive and heavy-handed operations . . . [which] continue to dump thousands of utterly hopeless, destitute people into the laps of province services that are already overwhelmed by their workload. . . ."[66] The same official called the cordon-and-search operations producing these refugees detrimental to the pacification effort and he questioned the "propriety of associating U.S. forces with operations which lead to the detention and immiseration of Vietnamese citizens (the preponderant majority being women and young children)." Both military and civilian CORDS advisers, he reported, severely criticized such operations and felt "that the net return to Pacification represented by low level Hoi Chanh ralliers and neutralized VCI scarcely compensate for some of the negative effects mentioned above, to say nothing of the heavy U.S. casualties that are taken, largely from booby-traps, on these operations."[67]

Such criticisms apparently had little effect. An end to these heavy-handed tactics finally came about as a result of the steady troop withdrawals imposed by the Nixon administration. U.S. Marine Corps strength in Vietnam, which had been 81,377 on 31 December 1968, a year later stood at 55,089 and by 31 December 1970 was down to

25,139.[68] Large multibattalion operations thus were no longer possible. More than ever, marine manpower now was employed in small-unit patrolling. Periodically company-size sweeps would try to make contact with the elusive enemy, but the initiative for the most part remained with the VC. One of the most difficult terrains was in the Que Son district in the southernmost part of Quang Nam province. The VC/NVA here hid out in the numerous caves in the hills surrounding the Que Son Valley; most marine casualties were from snipers and booby traps. The frustrations produced by this kind of war, in which enemy combatants were rarely seen while women and children planted and detonated mines and traps, led to several atrocity killings by the marines (related in a later chapter).[69]

The last marine combat forces deployed from Quang Nam province in April 1971. They left behind a weakened enemy but also a war-weary population without firm commitment to the GVN. An in-depth study of the province in February 1972 found between two-thirds and three-fourths of the people displaced from their original homes and 279 of the province's hamlets (46 percent) abandoned. Major enemy units were back in the Que Son Mountains. At the end of 1971, 69 percent of the population was said to be residing in GVN-controlled (A + B) hamlets; but this figure, the study noted, was inflated by the inclusion of the largely urban populations living in the two districts around the city of Danang. The departure of U.S. forces had left two-thirds of the province's land area free of security forces and in effect abandoned to enemy movement and control. Vietnamese forces devoted much of their time to static, defensive-type operations and lacked aggressiveness. Terrorist incidents against GVN officials and civilians were on the increase.[70] In sum, during years of intense fighting in Quang Nam province the U.S. Marines had won most of the battles, but they had been unable to achieve what the PROVN study of 1966 had called the object which lay beyond the war—the allegiance of the people of South Vietnam to their own government, which alone could guarantee final victory.

The Crisis in Discipline

During the final years of the American ground combat involvement in Vietnam, there developed a serious decline in discipline and morale; by 1971 this problem appeared to have reached crisis proportions. In a widely discussed article published in June 1971, Robert D. Heinl, a retired officer and military analyst for the *Detroit News*, noted: "By every conceivable indicator, our army that now remains in Vietnam is in a state of approaching collapse, with individual units avoiding or having refused combat, murdering their officers and noncommissioned officers, drug-ridden, and dispirited where not near-mutinous."[71] Secretary of Defense Laird, in a letter to the chairman of the House Armed Services Committee, called Heinl's sweeping indictment not justified,[72] but the Army itself was deeply concerned. In a lengthy report on the situation, dated 19 July 1971, Lt. Gen. W. J. McCaffrey, commanding general, U.S. Army Vietnam, acknowledged that since 1969 "discipline within the command as a whole has eroded to a serious but not critical degree" and that "mission accomplishment has undergone degradation in some units, primarily in terms of lowered quality of performance."[73] Given the magnitude of the crisis, this was indeed an understatement.

The objective indices of trouble were not in dispute. One of the most visible and widely publicized problems was drug abuse. Correspondents reported encountering goggle-eyed sentries and attending pot parties at fire bases in the field. Hard drugs, too, were said to be in wide use. Available statistics bear out the gravity of the drug problem in Vietnam. A DOD-sponsored survey showed that during the year 1971, 50.9 percent of Army personnel in Vietnam had smoked marijuana, 28.5 percent had used narcotics such as heroin and opium, and 30.8 percent had used other psychedelic drugs.[74] The facts that despite the easy availability of cheap drugs in Vietnam the percentages of drug users there were not much higher than in other theaters of command, and that the majority of these men had used drugs before coming to Vietnam provided small comfort. Marijuana and other drugs, most observers agreed, were rarely used during combat operations, and there was dispute over whether drug abuse was a cause or consequence of disciplinary breakdown. However, the situation obviously was indicative of a serious erosion of discipline.

Another problem brought into the military services from the larger society back home was racial tension. The racial situation was not helped by the charge, made by Martin Luther King, Jr., and others, that young blacks in Vietnam "fight and die in extraordinarily high proportions relative to the rest of the population."[75] This allegation was false. In 1973 the percentage of blacks of military age was 13.5 percent of the total population; the proportion of blacks among American servicemen in Vietnam was 9.8 percent in 1967 and throughout the war was never higher than

12.5 percent. Through March 1973, blacks accounted for 12.3 percent of all combat deaths.[76] A disproportionate number of blacks were found in ground combat units, and significantly fewer blacks than whites were officers, but this was the result of social class and educational differentials and not racial discrimination on the part of the military.[77] Altogether, soldiers in combat reported a generally positive racial climate, for survival tended to transcend all other problems.[78] Racial polarization and racial incidents were most frequent among support troops and in rear areas.

The growing self-consciousness among blacks in the U.S. had its counterpart among black servicemen in Vietnam who gave the black power salute and typically associated closely with each other. By 1969 there were numerous incidents with racial overtones, with blacks being the aggressors in a high proportion of cases. Among Army personnel in Vietnam during the period 1 October 1968 to 30 September 1969, a pattern of black subject and white victim was found in 19.2 percent of all murders, 50 percent of cases of attempted murder, 43 percent of aggravated assaults and 71 percent of cases of robbery. The data do not show how many of these acts of violence were racially motivated and how many were ordinary crimes. During that time, blacks comprised 9.1 percent of total U.S. Army Vietnam strength, but the stockade population on the average was 58 percent black.[79] On the other hand, a review of court-martial decisions in the Twenty-fifth Infantry Division revealed no discernible pattern of racial discrimination in the administration of justice. In 272 cases of special courts-martial where the race of the accused could be determined, for example, 6.3 percent of whites were acquitted and 6.7 percent of blacks.[80]

A racial motive appeared in some cases of violence involving the use of fragmentation grenades or other explosives against officers and NCOs, incidents known as "fraggings," but most of these were aimed at intimidating or punishing persons in authority irrespective of race. Enlisted men at times would seek to enforce the avoidance of combat, and fraggings were attempts to kill or injure those of their leaders who refused to go along with these practices. From 1969 on, such incidents showed a sharp increase (see Table 4-2). Officers and NCOs, it appears, were the known intended victims in 52.3 percent of the incidents. The attacks on enlisted men represented instances of "counterfragging" against troublemakers or acts of private violence.

In 1971 and 1972 there were several incidents of troops refusing to go into battle. However, the more typical occurrence apparently was a nego-

Table 4-2 Fragging Incidents, U.S. Army Vietnam, 1969–71

	1969	1970	1971
Total incidents	126	271	333
Actual assaults [a]	(96)	(209)	(222)
Possible assaults [b]	(30)	(62)	(111)
Total incidents per 1,000 strength at midyear	0.35	0.91	1.75
Deaths	37	34	12
Intended victim:			
Officer/NCO	70	154	158
Enlisted man	17	40	43
Vietnamese	7	20	28
Unknown	32	57	104

SOURCES: U.S. House, Committee on Appropriations, Subcommittee on Department of Defense, *DOD Appropriations for 1972,* Hearings, 92nd Congress, 1st sess., part 9, 17 May–23 September 1971, p. 585 (updated later); OASD (Comptroller), *Selected Manpower Statistics,* May 1975, p. 63.

[a] Actual assaults: Intent to kill, do bodily harm or intimidate is the determined motive.

[b] Possible assaults: Intent to kill, do bodily harm or intimidate is a possible motive.

tiated agreement to undertake a "search-and-evade" operation. No statistics on cases of mutiny only are available. We do have figures on cases of insubordination, mutiny and willful refusals to obey orders among Army personnel (see Table 4-3). The figures do not reveal what portion of these incidents were politically motivated, and similar incidents occurred in other theaters of command as well. Still, the sharp increase between 1968 and 1970, indicative of the overall weakening of discipline, was again bound to have a particularly damaging effect in a combat zone.

Other indices of indiscipline were an increase in the rate of servicemen absent without leave (AWOL) and of desertions, which in the case of the Army by 1971 approached or surpassed previous highs set toward the end of World War II and in Korea (see Table 4-4). The vast majority of those going AWOL and most deserters during the Vietnam era, as in previous wars, absented themselves not for political reasons but because of per-

Table 4-3 Insubordination, Mutiny and Other Acts Involving Willful Refusal to Perform a Lawful Order, U.S. Army Vietnam, 1968–70

	1968	1969	1970
Tried	94	128	152
Convicted	82	117	131
Convicted per 1,000 strength at midyear	0.28	0.32	0.44

SOURCES: U.S. House, Committee on Internal Security, *Investigation of Attempts to Subvert the U.S. Armed Services,* Hearings, 92nd Cong., 2nd sess., 1972, p. 7057; OASD (Comptroller), *Selected Manpower Statistics,* May 1975, p. 63.

Table 4-4 Worldwide AWOL and Desertion Rates—World War II, Korea and Vietnam (Per 1,000 Average Enlisted Monthly Strength)

	Army		Marine Corps	
	AWOL	Desertion	AWOL	Desertion
World War II				
CY 1943	*	*	*	FY 8.8
CY 1944	*	63.0	*	FY 6.9
CY 1945	*	45.2	*	FY 5.4
Korean War				
FY 1951	*	CY 14.3	*	10.1
FY 1952	181.0	22.0	*	19.7
FY 1953	158.0	22.3	*	29.6
Vietnam War				
FY 1965	60.1	15.7	*	18.8
FY 1966	57.2	14.7	*	16.1
FY 1967	78.0	21.4	*	26.8
FY 1968	89.7	29.1	*	30.7
FY 1969	112.3	42.4	*	40.2
FY 1970	132.5	52.3	174.3	59.6
FY 1971	176.9	73.5	166.6	56.2
FY 1972	166.4	62.0	170.0	65.3
FY 1973	159.0	52.0	234.3	63.2

SOURCE: Data provided by OASD (Manpower and Reserve Affairs).

*Data not available.

DISENGAGEMENT

sonal or financial problems or inability to adjust to military life. The increases experienced toward the end of the war were again, as in World War II and Korea, primarily the result of lowered induction standards and a greater number of inexperienced leaders.[81] Whatever the reasons, the high rates of AWOL and desertion were disruptive and another symptom of disorder.

The decline in discipline in Vietnam also manifested itself in worsened relations with the local civilian population. By 1970–71 anti-Americanism was on the upswing and several cities saw student-led demonstrations against the American presence. Two particularly violent demonstrations took place in Qui Nhon, the capital city of Binh Dinh province (MR 2), in December 1970 and February 1971. A study of the causes of these anti-American outbursts noted that there existed "widespread popular grievances against the Americans" and that "it would be an error for Americans to assume that the typical anti-American incident is necessarily Viet Cong instigated."[82]

An investigation of the situation in Binh Dinh province undertaken in March 1971 concluded that the long-existent anti-American sentiment there was "stimulated by an American record of several years of overt disrespect shown to all strata of Vietnam society." The record of "dramatic misconduct" included running Vietnamese cyclists and pedestrians off the road; hitting Vietnamese with rocks and cans; firing into hamlets from convoys without cause on pretext of having heard sniper fire; joy-killing of water buffalo and cattle; raping Vietnamese girls; being drunk, disorderly and obnoxious; and much more. "Relating that he could see the recent demonstrations building up two years ago as incident after incident occurred, the Binh Dinh police adviser explained how frustrating and futile it had been to try to follow-up on the incident reports. Over the past years, there had been minimal disciplinary action taken and this only in a few cases." The large concentration in the Qui Nhon area of support troops, "notoriously difficult to control and discipline," was a complicating factor, but there also prevailed a relaxation of discipline coupled with leadership, racial and drug problems.[83]

What were the causes of this erosion of discipline? The impact of the antiwar movement within the military was relatively small. Between 1967 and 1972 there appeared a total of 245 so-called GI underground newspapers,[84] some of them published overseas, but many disappeared after one issue and their readership remained limited. Organizations like GIs

United Against the War in Vietnam, the American Servicemen's Union and the Movement for a Democratic Military never became mass organizations and, as one student of the phenomenon of troop dissent concludes, "failed to crystallize the inchoate resentments of many of the lower ranks into a mass antiwar force."[85] Between 1965 and 1970, the Navy experienced a growing number of cases of sabotage and arson on its ships, but no evidence could be found that antiwar activists had directly participated in a sabotage attempt on a Navy vessel.[86] Cases of fragging and avoidance of combat may well have been instigated at times by antiwar militants, though no hard evidence of organized subversion was ever discovered. Greater damage to morale than that caused by the antiwar movement probably resulted from the feeling among many servicemen that people at home did not appreciate their sacrifices. Disenchantment with the Vietnam war on the part of the media, "peace" demonstrations and antiwar statements on the part of prominent public officials could not but create a climate of doubt and lack of sense of purpose which posed a severe challenge to dedication and discipline.

Growing permissiveness in American society and an increase in social pathology, such as a rising crime rate and widespread attitudes of disrespect toward authority and law enforcement, undoubtedly played an important role. The crisis in military discipline, it should be stressed, was worldwide and not limited to Vietnam. The highest desertion and AWOL rates on record to date were reached in the Marine Corps in fiscal year 1975, and the Navy had its highest desertion rate in fiscal year 1976[87]—all well after the conclusion of the American involvement in Southeast Asia. These trends point to more basic problems transcending the unpopularity of the Vietnam war.

The winding down of the war did have a damaging effect on performance. The combat efficiency of individual American servicemen in Vietnam, it was observed, generally declined during the last two months of the one-year tour of duty. As the soldier approached the date at which he was eligible for return from overseas (DEROS), he became more cautious, not wanting to die during the last few remaining days of his exposure to the hazards of combat. Something similar to this experience took place on a larger scale as the combat involvement of U.S. forces in Vietnam drew to a close. During the years 1970–72 the feeling of not wanting to be the last man killed in a war that was closing down appeared to have a detrimental effect on morale and discipline.[88]

Related to the winding-down of the American combat role was discontent resulting from idleness. "The most persistent enemy a U.S. soldier faces in South Vietnam these days," wrote an American correspondent visiting troops in the field in January 1971, "is not the Communists—it seems to be boredom. . . . In this strange state of listlessness, commanders face new problems: a sharp drop in troop morale, increased use of drugs and alcohol, touchy relations between black soldiers and white."[89] Similar problems of discipline had cropped up among troops waiting for transportation home from overseas after World Wars I and II.

The decline in the frequency of combat may have been one of the reasons for the sharp increase in the neuropsychiatric disease rate, for neuropsychiatric casualties are known to occur predominantly when the lines of battle are static.[90] Between 1965 and 1970, the rate of admissions to hospitals and quarters for neuropsychiatric cases among Army personnel more than doubled; in 1970 the overall rate for psychiatric conditions in Vietnam was 24.0 per 1,000 average annual strength as against 15.4 in the Army worldwide. A growing identification with a rival peer group such as one based on race, political affiliation, or drug use may have undermined the integrity of the squad, which traditionally has provided the infantryman with certainty and support during the stress of combat.[91]

Personnel turbulence, resulting from the one-year tour of duty, not only led to lack of unit cohesion, but also meant that leaders did not stay long enough with their units to have any lasting influence on the severe problems that existed. The military services, through "Project 100,000," a program to help disadvantaged youths, had to fill a certain percentage of their strength from men of lower intelligence ratings. These enlistees had disciplinary problems and court-martial convictions at about double the rate of other men.[92] Moreover, military justice, as noted in the report dealing with the Qui Nhon disturbances, was "neither swift nor certain, and transgressors have been comparatively free to repeat their acts with impunity."[93] Many commanders felt that the system of military justice was too permissive and over-zealous in guarding the rights of individuals, and was thus more of an antagonist than an ally of their efforts to control the deterioration in discipline.[94]

Last but not least, there was the decline in leadership quality. The quick expansion of the armed forces to meet the demands of Vietnam had taken place without mobilizing the reserves and tapping experienced reserve and National Guard officers. As a result of growing antiwar sentiments on the campuses, the number of officers coming through the Reserve Officers Training Corps (ROTC) program had declined sharply. Hence many of the junior officers and noncommissioned officers were hastily promoted, green young men whose desire to have good relations with younger enlisted personnel resulted in permissiveness and a failure to recognize the symptoms of poor or crumbling discipline and to take corrective action. On the other hand, noted General McCaffrey in July 1971, many men in positions of leadership were "more interested in advancing their careers than in caring for those placed under their charge. . . . Some commanders harbor the view that the authority they require to maintain discipline has been passed to judge advocates, personnel managers and doctors; that control of personnel has been denied them by action to centralize control at higher levels."[95] A more recent study has related the decline in discipline to the replacement of the traditional "gladiatorial" officer type with the managerial nonparticipant in combat for whom efficency and career advancement take the place of the ethic of the professional soldier—Duty, Honor, Country.[96]

The crisis in discipline occurred at a time when American forces disengaged from Vietnam and when the responsibility for combat was increasingly assumed by the South Vietnamese. Consequently, the impact of the deterioration in discipline on the conduct of the war is difficult to assess. More and more, the outcome of the military contest was now being determined by the performance of the South Vietnamese armed forces. We will turn next, therefore, to a discussion of this important change in the military scene, a process known as "Vietnamization."

5

The Travail of
Vietnamization

Throughout the years of the American involvement in Vietnam American policy-makers repeatedly emphasized that the purpose of U.S. intervention was to help South Vietnam defend itself, and that eventually South Vietnam would have to take over and carry on alone its struggle for independence from the North. "In the final analysis," insisted President Kennedy in September 1963, "it is their war. They are the ones who have to win or lose it."[1] President Johnson stessed the same point once again in the spring of 1968: "We and our allies can only help to provide a shield behind which the people of South Vietnam can survive and can grow and develop. On their efforts—on their determination and resourcefulness—the outcome will ultimately depend."[2] And yet for well over two years this basic insight was largely ignored and the war was fought essentially as an American war with the South Vietnamese increasingly watching from the sidelines. The effort to turn the war back over to the Vietnamese—a program which eventually became known as "Vietnamization"—did not get under way in earnest until after the Tet offensive of 1968, and it did not begin to show real results until even later.

Americanizing the War

The reasons for the Americanization of the war were manifold. An important factor was the years of frustration experienced by the members of the American advisory program, which eventually led the military to conclude that by doing the job themselves they would save much irritation and seemingly wasted effort. Moreover, by the summer of 1965 the South Vietnamese army was near collapse and a major American military effort was obviously necessary to stave off a communist victory. Although both civilian and military decision-makers thereafter continually talked of merely helping the South Vietnamese to help themselves, the war in fact was increasingly fought by the Americans.

The South Vietnamese participation, in terms of men under arms, grew by about 100,000 between 1965 and 1967, reaching close to 650,000 by 1967, yet these forces all too often practiced the strategy of search-and-avoid, moving where the enemy was known *not* to be. During the first nine months of 1966, only 46 percent of ARVN's large operations (battalion or larger) resulted in contact with the enemy while the corresponding figure for U.S. forces was 90 percent. During that same period the number of VC/NVA killed by ARVN dropped from a weekly average of 356 to 238 while the U.S. average rose from 476 to 557. In terms of enemy killed per battalion per week the figures showed that an ARVN battalion averaged 1.8 compared to 8.6 for American combat battalions. For small-unit operations (company or smaller) the picture was even more disheartening and the failure to carry the war to the enemy still more pronounced. It would appear that as the number of American combat units in Vietnam increased and as these forces began to take heavier and heavier casualties, ARVN's distaste for combat grew correspondingly. Over 115,700 South Vietnamese military personnel (19 percent of total strength) deserted during 1965; in the first nine months of 1966 desertions were running at the annual rate of 130,000 (21 percent). The performance of the South Vietnamese, wrote Assistant Secretary of State William P. Bundy in a memo dated 2 June 1967, "appears to confirm that the massive US intervention has in fact had a significant adverse effect in that South Vietnamese tend to think that Uncle Sam will do the job for them."[3]

During the first nine months of 1966, U.S. advisers rated 32 percent of all ARVN units as having unsatisfactory or marginal combat effectiveness.[4] Poor leadership, the result of the GVN's practice of appointing and promoting officers for their political loyalty, family connections and formal education rather than for military ability, was cited as one of the main reasons for this low level of performance. On the other hand, at least some of the superior combat effectiveness of U.S. forces was due to their firepower, the availability of artillery and air support, and their better mobility. Whereas increasing numbers of enemy troops were equipped with the powerful automatic AK-47 assault rifle, most South Vietnamese troops until 1968 were armed with the semiautomatic M-1 rifle of World War II vintage whose strong recoil, moreover, was most unsuitable for the small Vietnamese soldier. A study carried out in the fall of 1968 revealed that the U.S. soldier, per man in a combat battalion, was supported by 10 times as many rounds of artillery and air attack sorties as a Vietnamese in an ARVN unit.[5] The number of helicopters available to U.S. troops was similarly disparate.

The failure to upgrade the equipment of the South Vietnamese armed forces (RVNAF) was due in part to American production shortages. Under President Johnson's "policy of guns and butter—but mostly butter," Westmoreland recalls, "M-16 rifles, machine guns, mortars, radios, trucks, recoilless rifles, artillery pieces all were hard to get." Not until well into 1968 did these items become available in any quantity for other than American troops.[6] On the other hand, it was the impression of some Washington officials that Westmoreland until 1967 was reluctant to make the RVNAF a more equal and trusted partner in the war or to put a greater part of the combat burden upon it. "There is no indication," wrote the assistant secretary of defense (SA) in a memo dated 1 May 1967, "MACV has the same sense of urgency about increasing ARVN effectiveness as it has about increasing the number of U.S. forces."[7] More recently, former premier Nguyen Cao Ky has made the same point. The U.S., he said, delayed in preparing the Vietnamese to fight on their own because U.S. officials felt the superior American firepower would assure a swift victory. Vietnamization, according to Ky, should have begun in 1965 instead of in 1969.[8]

The Beginning of Vietnamization

The process of upgrading the Vietnamese forces, it is generally agreed, began in the summer of 1967—after the establishment of CORDS under Komer and the new emphasis on pacification and after President Johnson in July had decided to limit the further input of American troops. All the military ever want is more of the same, Johnson told his "intellectual-in-residence," John P. Roche, later that year, but "I'm not going to give it to them. They're going to have to live with what they got . . . and waste some of their valuable time training Viets."[9] Westmoreland's new deputy commander, Gen. Creighton Abrams, now was given specific responsibility for improving the performance of the RVNAF. During his visit to Washington in November 1967, Westmoreland told the National Press

Club that within two years or less it might be possible to phase down the American level of commitment and turn more of the burden of the war over to the Vietnamese, whose army was being modernized.[10] This forecast proved accurate, though the shakeup produced by the enemy's Tet offensive undoubtedly was a crucial factor in maintaining if not accelerating the pace of Vietnamization.

The report of the Clifford task force, delivered to President Johnson in early March 1968, proposed an urgent effort to improve and modernize the equipment of the RVNAF, and this recommendation was acted upon by the president almost immediately. On 5 March he told the new secretary of defense to take whatever steps were necessary to increase the effectiveness of ARVN by providing more helicopters, additional M-16 rifles and other needed equipment. The following day orders went out to accelerate the production of the M-16 rifle, which had been lagging badly.[11] Hanoi's agreement to President Johnson's proposal to begin peace talks and the prospect of a negotiated withdrawal of U.S. troops gave further urgency to these moves. On 16 April Clifford ordered the development of a program to gradually shift the burden of the war to the South Vietnamese and to support as quickly as possible the modernization of their armed forces. Plans for Phase I of this effort, providing for the improvement of Vietnamese ground combat forces through the addition of more artillery, armor and helicopters, were ready by late August and were approved on 23 October 1968. On 31 October the president announced a complete halt of the bombing of North Vietnam and there was great expectation of quick progress at the peace talks, held in Paris. On 9 November the new MACV commander, General Abrams, requested permission to move rapidly toward Phase II of the Vietnamization plan, which called for the creation of a self-sufficient RVNAF capable of coping with the internal insurgency after a U.S.–North Vietnamese withdrawal. The JCS concurred, and the outgoing deputy secretary of defense approved the Phase II plan on 18 December.[12]

The higher Vietnamese force levels called for by these plans became possible as a result of a new willingness on the part of the GVN to assume a greater share of the fighting. Jarred by the Tet attacks and disturbed by the evident hesitancy of the Johnson administration to rush in more American troops, Saigon ordered a recall of reservists and the drafting of nineteen-and eighteen-year-olds. On 19 June a new general mobilization was announced which provided for the conscription of all males between the ages of 16 and 50. Those between 18 and 38 were to serve in the armed forces; the others were to form the new People's Self-Defense Force, a part-time local militia. The new mobilization by the end of 1968 succeeded in producing 99,145 conscripts for the armed forces (as against 48,545 in 1967); under pressure of the draft 215,336 men volunteered for units and stations of their own choosing (as against 115,769 in 1967). While the RVNAF lost 116,000 men through desertions in 1968, the year ended with the armed forces at the all-time high of 819,200, up 176,000 from 1967.[13]

The Nixon Phase

The Vietnamization program initiated by Clifford went into high gear under the Nixon administration, which assumed office in January 1969; it now became an essential ingredient of the policy of lightening the American combat burden while the U.S. gradually disengaged from Vietnam. By preparing the South Vietnamese to take over the fighting the new administration developed a back-up position in case the Paris negotiations failed to result in a peace agreement. At the same time, the increase in the armed strength and capability of the RVNAF could exert pressure on Hanoi to come to terms.

On 8 June 1969, Presidents Nixon and Thieu, accompanied by other major military and civilian officials, met on Midway Island. After conferring with Thieu for several hours, Nixon announced that 25,000 American troops would be withdrawn from South Vietnam by 31 August. Further troop pullbacks would be made as the South Vietnamese assumed more of the fighting. Subsequent administration statements spoke of withdrawing 100,000 men during 1969 and an additional 100,000–150,000 during 1970. In a nationally televised speech on 3 November, Nixon declared that while previous administrations had Americanized the war, it was now being Vietnamized and the way prepared for the eventual complete withdrawal of all U.S. combat forces. The rate of withdrawal would depend on the status of the Paris talks, the level of enemy activity and progress in improving the strength of the armed forces of South Vietnam.

The program of enlarging and upgrading the RVNAF continued during the next three years. By April 1969 all ARVN units were equipped with the M-16 rifle, and by February 1970, 95 percent of the Regional and

Popular Forces had also received this automatic weapon. At the beginning of 1972 South Vietnamese combat strength was indeed formidable, and the RVNAF had taken over completely the combat on the ground. There were 120 infantry battalions in 11 divisions supported by 58 artillery battalions and 19 battalion-size armored units—all equipped with highly sophisticated military hardware. In addition to these almost 429,000 men in the South Vietnamese army and marine corps there were 43,000 sailors operating 1,680 naval craft, and 51,000 airmen flying well over 1,000 planes, including about 500 helicopters. The territorial forces had become stabilized at 300,000 Regional Forces (RF) and 250,000 Popular Forces (PF), while the PSDF was said to have reached more than four million, equipped with about half a million weapons.[14]

There is general agreement that during these years of American disengagement the effectiveness of RVNAF increased significantly. It began with the Tet offensive, during which ARVN held up better than anyone had expected. Thereafter, measurable progress continued—whether judged according to the number of operations with contact, the number of enemy killed or other indices. By 1970–71 the South Vietnamese carried out almost three times as many large operations as in 1966–67 and they were suffering about double the number killed.[15] There was an increase in combined operations with American forces which not only served as training vehicles but also provided a transitional period during which Vietnamese commanders could gradually assume their new responsibilities.

ARVN forces, it was reported, performed well during the operations in April–May 1970 against communist sanctuaries in Cambodia and demonstrated increasing ability to conduct operations with a diminishing reliance on U.S. logistical support. Some of the enhanced troop morale generated by these Cambodian operations was lost during the incursion into Laos in February 1971, carried out without American advisers, during which ARVN took heavy casualties and lost or had to abandon large quantities of equipment in a less than orderly withdrawal. Still, on the whole, Vietnamization seemed to be working. ARVN forces, wrote a highly placed MACV officer in late 1971, "have demonstrated their ability to work without U.S. advisory assistance and have done remarkably well." Military competence was high and the future could be faced "with confidence."[16]

The Advisory System

At least some of the optimism about Vietnamization probably was the result of a long-standing tendency on the part of most American advisers in the field to report ever-steady progress. Advisers, whether serving with Vietnamese civilian officials or military commanders, aimed at building rapport so as to maximize their influence; they sought to encourage their counterparts to bolder action by stressing the positive. But this emphasis on building morale also inhibited criticism and all too frequently resulted in a situation where the adviser, sometimes quite unconsciously, gradually tempered his professional judgment and no longer asserted himself sufficiently. Frustrated and disillusioned by the slow pace of improvement, many an American adviser eventually resigned himself to the truth of Rudyard Kipling's saying:

> It is not good for the Christian's health
> to hustle the Asian brown,
> for the Christian riles and the Asian smiles
> and he weareth the Christian down.

These problems were compounded by the Americans' unfamiliarity with an oriental culture, their reliance on interpreters which further discouraged a frank, face-to-face exchange of ideas, and the short terms of duty. The Vietnamese soon learned to manipulate the ever-changing, inexperienced American officers who were impressed by Vietnamese speaking English and whose desire for "rapport" could be played upon. Writes Westmoreland: "Many a wily South Vietnamese officer tried to compromise his adviser, usually with women, to afford a fulcrum for assuring good reports on his unit or for avoiding interference with his corrupt manipulations."[17] The fact that promotions were achieved through assignments with U.S. units rather than through advisory service meant that ambitious officers sought to avoid such duty and that the quality of the advisory personnel suffered. Last but not least, advisers were concerned that by reporting too critically on their counterparts they would damage their own careers. The official spirit was one of optimism; "negativism" was frowned upon. Too much criticism could show lack of progress and result in a poor efficiency report.

A MACV study in early 1969 emphasized the importance of making clear "to the adviser-rater that the measurement system will in no way be used to judge the rater. In fact, it may be advisable to encourage slightly pessimistic ratings in order that the exaggerations may be cut down, and that false indicators of success do not show a false quick mission accomplishment."[18] Yet career incentives and other institutional constraints generally proved stronger than such attempts at reform. The author of a recent Department of the Army monograph on the training of the South Vietnamese armed forces, Brig. Gen. James L. Collins, Jr., writes in his conclusion: "To often advisers did not take firm stands with their counterparts on key issues nor recommend the relief of unsatisfactory commanders for fear that such recommendations would reflect badly on their own abilities. . . . In any future situation where advisers are deployed under hostile conditions, the emphasis should be on getting the job done, not on merely getting along with the individual being advised."[19] The distortions introduced by all of these problems into the advisory reporting and rating system can only be guessed at. Knowledgeable insiders like John Paul Vann complained that the system seriously underplayed or concealed the often harsh facts of RVNAF incompetence.[20]

All hierarchical organizations are conducive to the concealment and misrepresentation of information which could reflect unfavorably on those reporting it, and the military hierarchy in Vietnam was no exception to this rule. Still, there were some advisers who reported shortcomings and took a more searching view. The Vietnamese armed forces, wrote the Phu Yen province senior adviser in September 1970, had attained the experience, training and necessary equipment required for victory. "The real question, however, is whether or not the Vietnamese have the *will* to bring the war to a successful conclusion. The problems presently facing the GVN and its armed forces are not significantly different than they were in 1963; corruption is rampant; public officials are indifferent to the problems at hand; the logistics system is bogged down in bureaucracy; the troops are undisciplined; and the list could go on and on."[21]

Problems of Leadership

A recurrent theme of complaints was poor RVNAF leadership; the seriousness of this crucial problem was well known to the MACV staff. "The greatest obstacle in improving and training the armed forces," writes General Collins, "was the lack of qualified leadership at all levels, both officer and noncommissioned officer. . . . Battalion and company commanders were often inexperienced and lacked initiative, few operations were conducted in the absence of detailed orders. Senior commanders issued directives, but failed to supervise their execution, and results were usually negligible. U.S. advisers continually cited poor leadership as the foremost reason for unit ineffectiveness. But with the lack of replacements, unsatisfactory commanders were seldom relieved."[22] The commissioning system heavily emphasized formal education, which meant that the great majority of the population, who had no access to secondary schools, could not rise to officer rank. The potential leadership ability in the army's enlisted ranks thus remained largely unexploited. "True leaders," wrote John Paul Vann in late 1967, "are motivated to seek an environment wherein their potential can be manifested. Being denied the opportunity on the side of the government, a disproportionate large number of the rural leaders turn to the VC for their leadership opportunity."[23]

The ARVN officer corps, by and large, came from the middle and upper classes of South Vietnam's urban society and had great difficulty in relating to their own soldiers, who were primarily of peasant origin. While there were notable exceptions, many of the officers lacked aggressiveness and leadership ability, and they preferred rear area staff positions to combat commands. Until late in the war, battlefield promotions were very rare—in the years 1966–68 less than 2 percent of all promotions were due to combat victories[24]—and this added to the incentive to avoid combat assignments.

MACV repeatedly urged the commissioning of qualified individuals from the ranks and other related reforms, but Vietnamese response was all too slow. The appointment and promotion of the top-ranking officers, in particular, always remained closely linked to President Thieu's endeavor to protect the base of his political support within the officer corps; most of his general officers, therefore, owed their position more to their political dependability than to battlefield performance. Because of family and political ties, the removal of incompetent officers was extremely difficult. CORDS had a system of keeping dossiers on province and district chiefs, and this information could be used to put pressure on the GVN to achieve needed changes; by 1970 almost all of the worst province and district chiefs had been replaced. MACV, on the other hand, never managed to put enough pressure on the South Vietnamese to get rid of the poorest military commanders.[25]

Between 1967 and 1970 the RVNAF grew by 60 percent, creating a steady demand for leaders, but qualified officers remained in short supply. Despite accelerated promotions, by May 1971, 46 of the 133 infantry maneuver battalions (35 percent) were still commanded by captains; 80 of them had been in command one year or less and 52 of these for less than six months. Writes Collins: "The occupation was simply too dangerous and combat operations often eliminated the best commanders."[26] Many of the rich and powerful were sending their sons abroad or placing them in safe positions in the Saigon bureaucracy, thus further diminishing the pool of available talent. Given the shortage of combat leaders and the centralization of authority in the Vietnamese army, when a commander was killed the unit sometimes fell apart immediately. The dead commander's subordinates had simply not been trained to take any initiative without his lead. In late 1967 John Paul Vann had written: "Coupled with the corruption that exists in the form of padded payrolls, the hiring out of troop labor, the theft and/or sale of material resources, the selling of jobs and promotions, the rental of military vehicles to smugglers or worse, the illegal taxation of farmers and travellers, it is surprising that the GVN armed forces perform as well as they do."[27] Some four years later, according to all accounts, this evaluation was still essentially valid.

Poor leadership was undoubtedly the key problem besetting the RVNAF and it affected everything else, for the foundation of any army is its officer corps. The building of an effective combat force, wrote General Matthew B. Ridgeway, formerly U.S. commander in Korea, in 1971, requires "leadership, weapons, and training, and in that order of importance, for without leadership from the top down the other two factors will be nullified."[28] Experience at all levels and in all branches of the armed forces of South Vietnam fully confirmed Ridgeway's view. Generally speaking, observed the senior adviser of territorial forces in II CTZ at a briefing on 23 April 1971,

> RF and PF units are well trained, and certainly better equipped than the VC. The problem is still the lack of leadership. . . . When we mention a deficiency and ask what's been done about it we get the indignant answer, "I give order." And so he has, but no one ever follows up to see if the order was carried out. Few Vietnamese leaders ever get out to the company and platoon to see what's going on; they are content to listen to bullshit briefings at sector or subsector and consume lei-

surely lunches. . . . We have a few energetic province chiefs, and a number of effective unit commanders, but good leadership at any level is only one-deep. The commander who is aggressive and effective doesn't last long, because he makes too many enemies on both sides. . . . These people don't need advisers; or, if they do, then we have already failed. Charlie [VC] doesn't need advisers when he conducts a sapper attack. He doesn't need Tac air or gunships or artillery. He's hungry and he's got a cause and he's motivated. Therein lies the difference. On our side nobody is hungry and few are motivated because leadership is lacking.[29]

Desertions and Morale

Another danger signal was the large number of desertions from the RVNAF, which continued at an alarmingly high rate throughout the years of Vietnamization and remained the biggest single cause of manpower loss. The figures presented in Table 5-1 tell much of the story. The problem was most acute in ARVN combat units, where desertion rates tended to rise after major operations with substantial casualties, thus casting doubt on the ability and willingness of these forces to stand their ground. Men in ARVN combat units were deserting at about 2.5 times the overall RVNAF rate and ARVN was losing about one-third of its strength each year through desertions. To be sure, defection to the enemy

Table 5-1 RVNAF Desertions, 1968–71

	1968	1969	1970	1971
Net desertions[a]	116,064	107,942	126,753	140,177
Net desertions per 1,000 per month	11.8	9.2	10.1	11.2
Gross desertions per 1,000 per month	—	11.5	12.3	13.2[b]
ARVN combat units	—	28.2	32.2	35.6[b]
ARVN noncombat units	—	5.4	5.9	7.0[b]
Regional Forces	—	11.9	10.9	10.7[b]
Popular Forces	—	6.1	7.4	7.9[b]

SOURCES: OASD (Comptroller), SEA Statistical Summary, Table 3, 26 September 1973, and Table 7, 9 February 1972. OASD (SA), *SEA Analysis Report*, June/July 1971.

[a] Adjusted for the approximately 14 percent of deserters who returned or were returned to their units.

[b] Through April 1971.

was rare. Many ARVN deserters, it would seem, objected more to fighting away from home than to fighting itself; a steady number (no precise count was available) joined territorial forces (RF and PF) nearer home. Still, the ARVN deserters were a source of serious disruption and represented a major manpower drain on the regular combat units.

The territorial forces contained about 50 percent of the military manpower and sustained close to 50 percent of all RVNAF combat deaths.[30] Service in the RF and PF thus was no less dangerous than service with ARVN, yet the desertion rate of the RF, whose soldiers served in their own province, was considerably lower than that of the regular army, and the desertion rate of the PF, whose soldiers served in their own villages, was lower yet. Villagers able to afford the price often paid a bribe in order to be able to join the RF or PF and thus escape ARVN. Studies showed that a major factor in the high desertion rate of ARVN combat units was homesickness, concern for the poor living conditions of families left behind, and the failure of officers to pay attention to the welfare of their men.[31] Medical care of the wounded in the generally overcrowded hospitals was poor; leave was difficult to obtain. The soldiers' low pay, which never caught up with the rampant inflation, contrasted sharply with the pay and life style of their higher officers and with the riches which the more corrupt among these officers were amassing. Men were in ARVN "for the duration"; death, disability or desertion were the only means of exit. In these circumstances many of the soldiers saw little point in risking their lives for a poorly understood or appreciated national cause. Instead they went home to take care of their families, the traditional primary object of loyalty in Vietnam.

The Communists, too, had a desertion problem, though its magnitude was hardly comparable to that of the government forces (see Table 5-2). Moreover, by late 1970 and early 1971, recurring evidence indicated a concerted enemy effort to use the Chieu Hoi (Open Arms) program to infiltrate VC cadres into the GVN's territorial forces. In the spring of 1971, 31 RF/PF outposts were overrun amid indications of collusion between false ralliers in the outposts and the attacking VC/NVA outside. [32] The mere number of communist defectors thus did not tell the entire story.

The question of why "their" Vietnamese seemingly had so much more stamina than "our" Vietnamese was a frequent subject of discussion in Vietnam. American soldiers had a healthy respect for the tenacious enemy they were facing and there was probably general agreement with the view

Table 5-2 RVNAF Desertions (Net) vs. NVA/VC Defections (Military), 1967–71

	1967	1968	1969	1970	1971
RVNAF deserters	77,714	116,064	107,942	126,753	140,177
NVA/VC defectors	17,672	12,569	28,405[a]	17,145	10,914

SOURCE: OASD (Comptroller), SEA Statistical Summary, Table 6, 18 April 1973, and Table 7, 9 February 1972.

[a] Year of Third-Party Inducement Program (see chap. 3).

expressed by the veteran Marine Corps combat correspondent, Keyes Beech, in his last report upon leaving Vietnam: "In closing I would like to offer a salute to that skinny little Viet Cong somewhere in the jungle shivering in the monsoon rains. . . . He is one hell of a fighting man."[33] Even though there existed some crack South Vietnamese units, few Americans were talking in such terms about the RVNAF. The generally high combat efficiency of the North Vietnamese could be explained by the ability of a totalitarian regime to indoctrinate its people. Some captured soldiers had tattoos on their bodies bearing the slogan, "Born in the north, to die in the south" and they told of funeral ceremonies in their honor before they left their villages.[34] But what about the morale of the VC? After all, both the RVNAF and the VC were recruited from the same population base, indeed frequently from the same families.

To put this discussion in its proper perspective it is necessary first to recognize that in any military conflict the attacker has an inherent advantage, and this advantage is magnified in an insurgency which puts a premium on "hit-and-run" type attacks by small rebel units. Moreover, in the Vietnam conflict the insurgents enjoyed the benefit of relatively secure bases which, for the most part, remained beyond the effective reach of allied forces. According to the nearly unanimous consensus of legal authorities expounding customary international law, the failure of a neutral state to prevent the use of its territory by a belligerent entitles the injured belligerent to resort to force to stop the hostile use of the neutral's territory.[35] However, in the case of the Vietnam war the pursuit of such measures of redress was made difficult by political constraints—domestic and international; the short-lived incursions into Cambodia and Laos in 1970 and 1971 could not permanently neutralize the value of these sanctuaries. Attempts to interdict the flow of men and supplies by air floundered primarily on the hard facts of geography—the great length of a border running through mountainous jungle terrain.

In the face of an opponent who held the tactical initiative the allies had to assign a substantial part of their armed manpower to the defense of military bases, lines of communications (roads, canals, etc.) and the politically important centers of population like district and province capitals as well as Saigon itself. In this way the enemy tied down a large number of allied units in static, defensive positions which, nevertheless, remained vulnerable to random shelling and night attacks. Such a situation created the image of an ever-present, elusive enemy who could strike any target at will. The ability of the Communists to achieve a superiority of numbers at chosen points of attack undoubtedly contributed to VC morale. At the same time it undermined to a considerable extent the allies' overwhelming superiority in firepower, logistical support and mobility as well as the value of their greater total manpower. In January 1968, for example, only 40 percent of allied infantry maneuver forces were available for offensive actions.[36] All this is, of course, related to the often-mentioned force ratio of 10 to 1 which is said to be necessary to defeat an insurgency.

There were other important factors impinging on the overall military balance. The allies had a substantial advantage in total military manpower and always outnumbered the VC/NVA by at least three to one. Yet, the allies' "foxhole strength"—the number of rifle-carrying infantrymen—was much lower. American forces, and the South Vietnamese organized and operating in accordance with the American model, relied heavily on armor, artillery, air support, all manner of sophisticated equipment, and the lavish use of firepower; this absorbed much manpower and required a big logistical tail. Of the total allied military manpower of 1,593,300 men in August 1968, for example, no more than 222,800 (14 percent) were in main force infantry units. Even with the addition of a fourth rifle company to U.S. Army and Marine Corps battalions, these battalions were estimated to have only 54 percent of their men in rifle platoons. In view of the before-mentioned need to defend bases, cities and lines of communications, the allies' offensive capability in 1968 was not decisively larger than that of their opponent—88,400 allied soldiers to 70,000 VC/NVA. In the following years,, the growth of the Regional and Popular Forces improved the allied position, even as U.S. forces were disengaging, but in terms of regular infantry battalions—the cutting edge of any army—by 1972 the force ratio had actually shifted to an allied disadvantage of 0.8 to 1.[37]

The question of morale must be examined in this overall context, for it is well known that perceptions of strength or weakness and expectations of victory or defeat can have a substantial impact on military *esprit de corps.* For example, examination of captured documents and interrogation of VC defectors and captives showed that VC morale suffered in the wake of the failure of the 1968 Tet and summer offensives to deliver the expected victory; the redefinition of the concept of the "general uprising" as a "prolonged strategic offensive"[38] with no terminal date apparently was less than convincing. Based on a careful study of all available evidence, the political scientist Paul Berman concludes that for most rank-and-file members of the insurgent forces, severe combat stress and a perception of loss undermined the legitimacy of the revolutionary cause, weakened unit cohesion and led to defections.[39]

There was reason to believe that a minority of the VC had actually sought out and voluntarily joined the National Liberation Front—to satisfy a sense of adventure and excitement, out of a desire for social advancement and status, to get even with an arrogant or abusive GVN official or officer, because of resentment over lost land, to drive out the American imperialists. Most of them had either been gradually and skillfully drawn into the NLF village organization and later recruited for fulltime military service or had been coerced through threats against their families or themselves.[40] Despite the cadres' use of rewards and penalties and frequent criticism and self-criticism sessions, the villagers' belief in the legitimacy of the revolutionary organization they belonged to was not firm and could be shaken by severe adversity. Yet feelings of pessimism regarding a final triumph, as studies of the German Wehrmacht in World War II have shown, can be counterbalanced by the psychological support provided by a closely integrated primary group and forceful leadership by respected officers.[41] These morale-sustaining factors were completely absent from the RVNAF, and this fact should go on a long way toward accounting for their weaker spirit and poorer fighting behavior.

The South Vietnamese officer corps, as I noted earlier, did not relate well to the enlisted men. Vietnamese villagers were known to be very sensitive to arrogance and rudeness, and while the VC made a considerable effort to get their cadres to control these traits and to act as fathers to their soldiers, the RVNAF was content in this regard with pious aspirations and admonitions. The impressment of recruits was often done with brutality and, unlike that of the VC, who also used force to recruit soldiers, was never accompanied by explanations.[42] The professional ability of the officers was often poor and many of them were not respected as strong leaders. Their lack of concern for the welfare of their men and callousness further damaged the unit cohesion and team spirit so important for a well-functioning military organization.

Professional competence and pride in belonging to a superior military outfit can probably be more important than dedication to an ideological cause. Mercenaries like the French foreign legionnaires fought extremely well despite heavy adverse odds and the lack of common political sentiments. But the legionnaires were led by able and respected officers; and they lived the mystique of the legion, for they had nothing else and no other place to go. The ARVN soldier, on the other hand, could easily return to his family and village, and his ineffective government rarely caught up with deserters. Lastly, in addition to primary-group ties, the average soldier's effectiveness and combat motivation are sustained by his belief in the legitimacy of the military organization and the political society of which he is a member and which he serves.[43] Despite all attempts to clothe the Thieu regime in the mantle of nationalism and social revolution, the South Vietnamese soldier's commitment to the worth of the larger political and social system for which he was to risk his life remained weak. It should be stressed that I am speaking here of the way both the VC and RVNAF soldiers *perceived* their respective military organizations and societies. As history demonstrates abundantly, there is, of course, no necessary connection between the efficiency of an army and the absolute value of the political ideas it serves. The outcome of a military contest has no moral significance. Virtuous governments may lose to evil rebellions and evil governments may quell virtuous rebellions.[44]

Damage to Pacification

High on the list of the shortcomings in ARVN's performance which had an especially adverse effect on pacification was ARVN's attitude toward the rural population. This problem had been a source of American concern since the earliest days of the U.S. involvement. An Army Civil Affairs Team, following a visit to Vietnam in the fall of 1961, urged that something be done to improve the behavior of the South Vietnamese army toward the civilian population. Army drivers, like the French before them, were accustomed to drive at top speed through towns and villages. "The army steals, rapes, and generally treats the population in a very callous fashion. . . . The army is particularly bad in its treatment of minority groups like the Montagnards."[45] In October 1965, at the request of COMUSMACV, the chief of the Vietnamese Joint General Staff (JGS) agreed to initiate a program of orienting senior officers and troops regarding their attitude toward the people and the necessity of gaining popular support,[46] but as with so many programs launched in response to American prodding the results were meager. The report of the "Roles and Missions" study group, formed by Deputy Ambassador Porter in July 1966, recommended that the Rangers (units with special training in counterinsurgency) be disbanded "because of their frequently intolerable conduct toward the populace"; MACV opposed this move on the grounds that it would seriously reduce ARVN combat strength.[47]

From 1967 on, in order to cut down on RVNAF stealing from the population, the cost of the soldiers' field rations was no longer deducted from their low pay, yet reports on ARVN misconduct continued unabated. In the fighting for Can Tho during the 1968 Tet offensive, reported the CORDS senior adviser in Phong Dinh province in the Delta, Vietnamese dive bombers caused much destruction which was followed by large-scale looting by ARVN troops. Many people "found it difficult to consider the soldiers as their protectors."[48] An NSC study in early 1969 reported that RVNAF caused major and minor incidents affecting the civilian population—ranging from drunkenness and chicken stealing to murder and rape—in 42 percent of all hamlets. Officers tolerated looting in the belief that it "makes soldiers fierce" and "unites them with a tradition of soldiering associated with the legendary and successful armies of Vietnam's past."[49] The Ninth ARVN Division, operating in the Delta, in 1971 was widely known as the "chicken division" because its soldiers made a habit of stealing chickens. The Vinh Binh province chief had the Second Battalion of the Fourteenth Regiment thrown out of his province after he caught them stealing not only chickens but cattle, and shipping them off in barges.[50] Acts of RVNAF depredation, including the "taxing" of traffic on interprovincial highways, failure to pay for goods and services, armed robbery and assaults, were, concluded a special CORDS study in December 1971, "widespread and detrimental to the pacification program."[51]

Some of these illegal acts against the civilian population were carried out by deserters and other bandits and, because of the uniforms used, were blamed on RVNAF forces. This exculpation was not available for certain other ARVN actions undermining the pacification effort, such as the continuing use of forced population transfers. Instructions issued in 1967 and expanded in 1969 required military operations to be conducted in such a manner as to minimize the destruction of property and the generation of refugees. The basic principle of this policy, it was said, was to bring security to the people, not the people to security. Exceptions to this rule required the approval of the GVN's Central Pacification and Development Council (CPDC), yet despite these regulations forcible relocations continued, especially in I CTZ.

In 1969 about 25,000 refugees were generated in Quang Nam province; between November 1969 and May 1970, military operations in Quang Ngai province resulted in the relocation of 22,500 people. The time allowed for evacuation was often very short; crops, animals and houses were destroyed after the people had been moved out. Since GVN instructions forbade the generating of refugees, these people were not recognized by the province chiefs as refugees, received no assistance and were described in a February 1970 CORDS report as "living in deplorable conditions." Vietnamese authorities defended the relocations as necessary to prevent the crops of these people from being used by the VC; but the real reason appeared to be the desire to upgrade the rating of the provinces in the Hamlet Evaluation System by eliminating VC-dominated hamlets so that it could be claimed that 100 percent of the population lived in A+B+C hamlets under GVN control, as envisaged by the 1970 pacification plan. In a letter to the prime minister in early 1970, CORDS chief William E. Colby suggested informing province chiefs that a failure to meet the 100-percent goal attributable to a disapproved proposal to relocate people would be accepted by the CPDC.[52]

During the years 1970–71, two large-scale relocations were carried out with the approval of the CPDC though against the wishes of at least some CORDS officials. In late 1970 ARVN troops began a major military campaign in the U-Minh Forest, a long-time communist stronghold in the southern Delta. People were instructed by loudspeakers and leaflets to leave the area, and by May 1971 this operation had resulted in 63,800 refugees. In a survey carried out in the following month, air strikes and artillery fire by GVN forces were cited as the major cause of this movement. Even though the relocations were planned in advance, government assistance was late and inadequate. An overwhelming majority of those questioned (93 percent) indicated a desire to go back to their villages, and about one-third indeed resettled at or near their original homesites.[53]

The second major relocation took place between May 1970 and August 1971 in the highlands of II CTZ and resulted in the displacement of over 60,000 Montagnards, many of them relocated against their will and with inadequate notice. Some of these people had been moved already several times—in 1967, 1968 and 1969—but they had always abandoned the resettlement sites and returned to their homes. Living conditions at the new sites were again bad. There was a shortage of water, food and relief supplies; several hundred tribesmen died of exposure and malnutrition. A CORDS study carried out in May 1971 concluded that the new relocations

> on the whole . . . were ill-planned, ill-conceived, and ill-executed. These security-directed relocations have been responsible for pinning down Territorial Forces in static positions. As many as 300 persons out of the 1,900 resettled at Ko Tu, in Pleiku, died at the relocation site in the first 100 days. Countless other thousands are literally wards of the highland province social welfare services and various volunteer agencies. Some relocation sites have been evacuated in *toto*. Some have come under attack because of the new threat or opportunity they presented to the enemy. The enemy has also enjoyed a new freedom of movement. Intelligence nets have been destroyed or disrupted. The enemy has reacted to his losses in taxation, recruiting, and labor force losses by taxation at the new site or in the fields, by kidnapping, and by recruitment of disillusioned evacuees and residents of the new settlement sites.

Because of a shortage of arable land many of the Montagnards once again were returning to their mountain villages. In all, these relocations "are counterproductive" and "have not succeeded in their denial of resource intent."[54]

Not surprisingly, attitude surveys showed a high degree of correlation between forcible evacuation and procommunist attitudes. As a team of CORDS evaluators in Binh Dinh province stated: "Putting the people behind barbed wire against their will is not the first step towards earning their loyalty and support, especially if there is no concentrated effort at political education and village development."[55] These relocations, even when voluntary, created mammoth welfare problems which seriously impaired the GVN's ability to pursue its pacification and development goals. Fundamentally, people who had to be removed from contact with the VC and who needed protection were people who were unwilling to defend themselves against the VC. Their relocation signified the GVN's confession of failure in the drive to bring them over to its side. On 12 May 1971 the CPDC issued a new communiqué on relocations which once again restated the need to minimize such population transfers and ordered a halt to all unauthorized relocations.[56] It appears that at least major relocations ceased after this date.

The low regard for human life and suffering which characterized the general mode of operation of RVNAF was reinforced and aggravated by the reliance on heavy weapons supplied by the Americans. At issue was not the need for a regular army, armed with heavy equipment, that could withstand an attack by large enemy forces. The question was the use in a counterinsurgency war of conventional tactics, induced by the availability of conventional weapons. American advisers were told to "make every effort to convince Vietnamese counterparts of the necessity for preservation of the lives and property of noncombatants."[57] After the destructive fighting in the heavily populated urban areas during the 1968 Tet offensive, the Vietnamese JGS issued instructions to all commanders to lower civilian casualties by avoiding unnecessary use of air, artillery and armor support,[58] yet saturation bombing by artillery and air strikes remained an accepted and widely used tactic.

A 1971 Rand Corporation study pointed out that the "addiction to the opium of heavy weapons" increased ARVN's alienation from the people:

> When soldiers have helicopters they seem to worry less about the disposition of the population along the roads they would otherwise have to travel. When they have armor, the attitudes of villagers seem less important. The indifference is reciprocated. Some people in South Vietnam have come to regard their own army as a foreign army, fighting according to an imported doctrine and entirely dependent on foreign support, or, according to the propaganda from Hanoi, as "puppets." Its destructive style of fighting coupled with the bad behavior of many of its soldiers cause the people to fear the army that is supposed to be

defending them as a bigger threat to their own security than the enemy.[59]

ARVN had become so dependent on massive fire support and airmobility, noted an American province senior adviser in 1972, that it no longer was prepared to fight like infantry. Since the number of operational helicopters was not sufficient to support airmobile operations except in a few divisions, the lack of aircraft usually resulted in immobility. Reliance on massive firepower was substituted for envelopment or flanking maneuvers on the ground. "ARVN battalions appear to be completely dependent on outside fire support which is a tragic situation because much of this outside fire support will eventually be gone."[60]

The Territorial Forces

By 1971 ARVN had taken over from the disengaging Americans much of the shield function against enemy main force units, and responsibility for local population security in the main had devolved upon the territorial security forces, the RF and PF, who were recruited from the same population they were assigned to protect. Table 5-3 (Appendix II, p. 455) shows the expansion which these units had undergone since the beginning of Vietnamization; by 1971 they represented 51 percent of South Vietnam's national military strength. Even though the territorial forces received less than 20 percent of the total RVNAF budget, lacked heavy equipment and enjoyed low priority for air and logistical support, they carried a major part of the total combat burden: in 1971 they contributed nearly 40 percent of enemy KIA in the country.[61] Their performance in battle differed greatly from province to province and district to district, depending, first, upon the strength and number of enemy attacks, and, second, upon the caliber of their officers. The RF/PF were rated as poor in provinces like Binh Dinh (II CTZ) and considered a real success story in Quang Tin (I CTZ). They sought, and in most provinces gradually achieved, improved security for the rural population. They helped inhibit VC terrorism, recruiting, taxation and propaganda.

To provide local defense against infiltration by small enemy units was the task of the People's Self-Defense Force, an unpaid part-time militia, which by 1971 was said to be more than four million strong. The PSDF was divided into combat members, trained to use weapons, and support members providing runners, first aid, etc. Membership was compulsory for all males between the ages of 16 and 17 and 39 and 50, i.e. below or above draft age; it was also often obtained through bribery—the purchase of deferment from service in the armed forces. The commitment to the GVN of these daytime farmers, carpenters, barbers who became armed defenders of their hamlets at night was uncertain. In some provinces the VC had tried to introduce their cadres into the PSDF and this had led to purges and the withdrawal of weapons.

Field surveys and observations by advisers indicated that PSDF strength, as reported through GVN channels, was grossly inflated. Their most useful function could have been to engage the population in anti-VC activity and thus prevent a pattern of local accommodation. Just as in the Combined Action Platoons in I CTZ, once villagers actively fought the VC they became the VC's enemy and thus presumably had no choice but to continue to throw in their lot with the GVN. Yet this, it appears, was not always the case. A province senior adviser in Binh Duong (III CTZ) reported in November 1970, at a time when that province had received a well-above-average HES rating of over 90 percent: "Considering that most villagers (PSDF members) believe that they can be assassinated—but that they won't be as long as they don't really do anything to hurt the VC, then it's not too difficult to understand why the majority remain uncommitted. In general, they hope and believe that the VC won't terrorize their families as long as they behave themselves."[62] If this was the situation in a province considered among the best pacified, not too much could be expected from the PSDF in less secure parts of the country.

The PSDF also had the undesirable side effects of encouraging the establishment of a new generation of strategic hamlets and of reinforcing the tendency of many local defense forces to assume a static role instead of engaging in active and aggressive patrolling. Since it was often difficult to defend villages with widely dispersed hamlets and subhamlets, the temptation arose to consolidate people in more concentrated locations, surrounded by bamboo fences or barbed wire. Yet these new hamlets generally provided only an illusion of security. The VC usually found little difficulty in entering them at night, and the barriers and fortifications were not sufficient to stop a large daytime attack. The frequent result was to keep the local defenders holed up in their fortified outposts and to create bad feelings against the GVN among the villagers who were forced to walk long distances to their fields and were subjected to many other inconveniences.

A team of CORDS evaluators reported about one such relocation effort, involving nearly 900 families in southeastern Binh Dinh province, that it had failed to separate the people from the influence of the VC, had provided the VC with new issues to exploit and thus was in effect counterproductive. "The program seems to be a stop-gap effort at pacification avoiding the real problems in implementing a pacification plan—a gimmick. It circumvents the real problems bothering the people just as the old Strategic Hamlet Program did. . . ."[63] Some critics suggested that the PSDF should not "defend" hamlets in the conventional sense but should organize the people politically against the VC—"to resist the enemy when he is few, to undermine his morale when he is many, and most of all constantly to show the enemy that the people are bitterly opposed to him."[64] This, of course, presupposed the kind of strong anticommunist conviction which unfortunately existed all too rarely.

The total number of men under arms in South Vietnam was considerable, but their effectiveness was diminished by a lack of unity of command. ARVN was less a national army than a federation of semiautonomous corps; there was little flexibility in deployment and the dispatch of a division from one region to another could create major problems. Each division commander believed that only he knew how to fight the war and resisted outside direction. New concepts like "area security" were difficult to implement for the same reason.[65] Close cooperation of all forces in a given area—ARVN, RF and PF—was rarely achieved; the *de facto* RVNAF chain of command was generally more a function of force of personality than of flow charts. The result was that responsibility was hard to fix, efforts at coordination were slow and cumbersome, and forces were ineffectively utilized. The enemy took advantage of this lack of unity of command, a basic principle of war, by maximum use of boundaries where the authority of one force ceased and that of another began.

The National Police

Serious efforts to enlarge and upgrade the police began in 1967. The goal was to create a system of law enforcement with more local roots, especially for the rural population. It was believed that civilian police could fulfill this function more efficiently than military forces. To achieve a more professional police competence which would also be more humane was the purpose of the American advisory effort, handled by AID's Office of Public Safety and operating through CORDS.

Total police strength rose from 52,300 in 1965 to 120,700 in 1972,[66] a statistic often cited by critics of American policy in Vietnam as an indication of the repressive character of the Thieu regime. Actually, only slightly more than half of this total force was assigned to duty as uniformed police in towns and villages, like their American counterparts; the rest belonged to paramilitary formations such as the National Police Field Forces and the Provincial Reconnaissance Units, engaged primarily in fighting the insurgency. The objection to South Vietnam's large police force thus was, at least in part, a disguised objection to the fight against the communist insurgency.

As with all American-assisted programs in Vietnam, implementation of the plans to improve police competence could never match conception. The 225 or so American police specialists training the Vietnamese police soon ran into problems for which they were not professionally prepared and which remained beyond their control. The mobilization law which gave priority to the armed forces, prevented the police from recruiting supervisory personnel with the required educational background, and extremely low salaries made the retention of qualified people very difficult. For a time, it was hoped that the needed additional police could be recruited through volunteers and that it would not be necessary to draft ARVN personnel. It was feared that if commanders were forced to transfer troops they would unload all their worst personnel and the police would end up with army rejects. Yet such transfers finally could not be avoided and the quality of the expanded police force suffered accordingly.

Corruption of all sorts flourished more than ever. Promotions were bought, money extorted on the threat of denouncing or arresting people as VCI suspects, and police checkpoints exacted tribute from villagers and merchants taking their goods to market. VC purchasing agents who regularly came into Saigon and other cities to buy supplies which were shipped back on trucks to VC base areas avoided detection at checkpoints by paying the prescribed bribe. Little improved security could be expected from such programs as the issuing of tamper-proof identity cards to all Vietnamese 15 years and older if the personnel administering and enforcing the program could be bought almost at will. So bad was the reputation of the police and so low their standing in the community that some

American province advisers opposed the establishment of police stations in their villages.

Singled out as the prime causes of this sorry state of affairs were low pay—aggravated by inflation—and bad living conditions. "If you talk about corruption, laziness, inefficiency, dishonesty, disinterest or any of the myriad faults that can be found with the Police as a whole or with groups or individuals," wrote an American province senior adviser in 1972, "you are talking basically of substandard working and living conditions." [67] Gradually certain changes were made, some as a result of a thorough inspection visit by Sir Robert Thompson and his police associates from Great Britain in the spring of 1971 which led to a report listing no less than 157 recommendations for reforms. Police officers were given equivalent army rank and status, the command structure was improved so that police chiefs could fire corrupt officers, an Internal Security Bureau was established to prosecute corrupt practices. The treatment of detainees improved. Unfortunately, the time for these reforms to have their expected long-range effects was not available. The same goes for another important program designed to alleviate popular grievances and to boost the image of the GVN, the Land-to-the-Tiller law of March 1970.

Land Reform

In 1967–68 the Stanford Research Institute conducted a survey of the farming population in the Delta region of South Vietnam, most of them rice farmers and constituting about half of the country's population. The survey revealed that the vast majority of these farmers had an extraordinary desire to own or acquire more land.

Official statistics indicated that about two-thirds of the rural population of South Vietnam was comprised of tenants. In the Delta, nearly 50 percent of the population owned no land at all and 77 percent had either none or less than two acres, which was not enough to make a living. Tenants paid an average of 34 percent of their crop as rent (the legal maximum was 25 percent), and being in debt was a way of life for a majority. The Viet Minh, who had controlled a substantial part of this area at the time of the Geneva accords, had distributed land owned by absentee landlords, but concomitant with the consolidation of the Diem regime both large and small landlords returned to reclaim their land. This led to another cycle of communist land reform in which the Diem regime was denounced as the tool of the landlords. While poverty itself is never a sufficient cause of rebellion, agitation here by the Viet Minh, and later the VC, had created a volatile situation in which inequities in land ownership, illegally high rents and the burden of debt based on exorbitantly high interest rates had come to be seen as indicative of an exploitative and unjust society. The demand for land ownership became a demand for an end to peonage and for personal freedom, and those supporting this demand would stand to gain the support of the mass of the rural population.[68]

The failure of successive South Vietnamese governments to address the distributive conflicts in Vietnamese society in a meaningful way helped isolate these governments from a majority of the people. The attempted land reform under the Diem government was mentioned earlier. By 1961 the distribution of land had come to a near halt while the VC continued to make political headway by distributing land and pressing for a lowering of rents and an increase in rural wages. During the period 1965 through 1968, allied support for land reform was uncertain at best. Although some Americans realized the political potential of the land issue, official policy was one of going along with the GVN's adherence to the status quo. The Ky government was afraid of antagonizing the landlords and the army officers belonging to the land-owning class on whose support the shaky regime depended. In March 1967, in a move publicized as part of the "social revolution" repeatedly promised the Americans, Ky issued permanent land titles to replace the temporary ones granted during the Diem land reform. But this was an empty gesture, substituting one piece of paper for another to farmers who had tilled the land involved for a decade.

The GVN could have exploited the fact that the distribution of land by the VC was explicitly provisional and that grantees retained their land only as long as they cooperated with the VC. From 1964 on, the beneficiaries of this distribution became subject to increasingly heavy taxation and military service, and this may have cost the VC some of the support their land reform had gained for them earlier.[69] Yet the GVN failed to capitalize on this development.

The distribution of the choice lands seized by Diem but never distributed began at last after Thieu became president in October 1967. Between January 1968 and December 1969, some 50,000 families received government-owned land. In a series of decrees Thieu prohibited officials or soldiers in newly secured villages from reinstalling landlords or helping to collect rents; landlords were forbidden to evict tenants or to collect back rents, and rents themselves were frozen. Observers reported that the occupancy "freeze" was being widely adhered to, while the rent "freeze" appeared to be only spottily effective.[70] Finally, Thieu helped push through the lower house and over strong landlord opposition a sweeping land reform bill, which became law on 26 March 1970 and is known as the Land-to-the-Tiller Law (Law 003/70). The slogan "Land to the Tillers" was part of the 1967 NLF program, and there can be little doubt that this new law stole much of the enemy's thunder. It provided for an immediate cessation of rent payments and for the transfer of ownership to the present tillers of the land, the landlords to be compensated by the government. The amount of rice land that any landowner could retain was curtailed from the 250 acres under the Diem land reform to 37 acres and then only if the owner and his family themselves cultivated the land. The law also set goals for the distribution of government-owned land. The elimination of tenancy alone was expected to benefit some 800,000 tenant families.[71]

A notable feature of Law 003/70 was the enhancement of the village governments, which were given a major role in carrying out the program; tenant farmers obtained the cancellation of rent payments by submitting an application to the village councils. This new function, coupled with the recently granted decision-making authority over local development funds and control over military and paramilitary forces in the village, strengthened local government. By 1970 well over 90 percent of all hamlets had elected councils and chiefs; a new relationship between the rural population and government was slowly being created. To be sure, appointed officeholders jealously guarded their prerogatives. Race reports on Long An (III CTZ): "Despite considerable 'command emphasis' from Saigon that district and provincial officials 'pay attention to the wishes' of their village chiefs, the haughty and sometimes contemptuous attitudes of earlier days persisted in Long An in 1970."[72] There was still no upward mobility for village officials such as was provided by the VC with promotion to district and higher levels; the village was not integrated into the national political structure, which continued to be dominated by urban elite social groups. Still, the power of the landlords over rural life had been seriously weakened and a beginning made in changing the perception of government as simply the protector of the rich and powerful. This was no small achievement.

Despite wartime conditions and a creaky administrative apparatus, the implementation of the Land-to-the-Tiller Law proceeded more or less on schedule. By May 1972, titles of ownership had been issued to almost 400,000 farmers, involving more than 1.5 million acres of land, and tenancy had been reduced from 60 to 34 percent.[73] The goal of decreasing it to less than 7 percent no longer seemed visionary (and indeed was reached in 1973). Apart from reducing social inequality, the law also brought increasing economic benefits. Money once paid as rent to the landlords could now be spent on fertilizer, improved irrigation and better farming utensils. Agricultural production increased and many farmers experienced a new wave of prosperity. One of the most divisive issues, a class conflict which the VC had exploited for years, had been largely neutralized. Occasional acts of enrichment by highly placed GVN officials continued to take place, but this did not change the fact that a substantial number of previously disgruntled farmers had been given a stake in their society. A shift of political allegiance toward the GVN on the part of the rural population seemed to be in the making.

6

Vietnamization on Trial: The Collapse of South Vietnam

Improved Security

Despite many weaknesses, both structural and operational, on the part of the Vietnamese forces fighting the communist enemy and in the pacification program, by 1971 overall security in the country had greatly improved and the war had become largely localized. Insurgency activity and VC incursions into populated areas were now for the most part concentrated in two provinces of I CTZ (Quang Nam and Quang Ngai), three provinces in northern II CTZ (Binh Dinh, Phu Yen and Pleiku), Hau Nghia province in III CTZ, and four provinces in the Delta (Kien Hoa, Vinh Binh, Chuong Thien and An Xuyen). These 10 provinces included somewhat more than one-quarter of South Vietnam's population.[1]

In the rest of the country, the intensity of the conflict had declined drastically. The GVN had established a strong presence in many areas previously under VC control, and the VC appeared to be on the defensive. In an article appropriately entitled "South Vietnam and the New Security," a long-time American observer, comparing the situation in the Delta in 1971 with that of 1967, wrote: "What were isolated enclaves of population in insecure territory, then, by 1971 had become major centers as the locus of the war shifted. The VC by 1971 occupied roughly the position that the GVN had in 1967."[2] In much of the country, tractors and Hondas were ubiquitous and marketplaces were bustling. By 1970, nationwide, 82 percent of the primary-school-age population were attending school, and secondary schools in the rural areas had expanded significantly. A substantial number of refugees had been resettled in new vil-

Table 6-1 Enemy Strength in South Vietnam and Enemy-Initiated Attacks-Assassinations, 1968–71

	1968	1969	1970	1971
Estimated enemy strength[a]	250,300	236,800	213,800	197,700
Ground attacks[b]	3,921	3,821	3,539	2,244
Battalion size	126	34	13	NA
Other	3,795	3,787	3,526	NA
Monthly average	327	318	295	187
Civilians assassinated	5,389	6,202	5,947	3,537

SOURCES: OASD (Comptroller), SEA Statistical Summary, Table 105, 10 January 1973, and Table 6, 18 April 1973; OASD (SA), *SEA Analysis Report*, November 1971–January 1972, p. 4.

[a] Includes VC/NVA combat battalions, administrative service and guerillas (at end of year).
[b] Includes ground attacks, ambushes, attacks by fire (more than 20 rounds).

lages and hamlets; during the years 1969–71, more than one million refugees had returned to their original homes.

To be sure, many of these gains were due primarily to a lack of enemy activity. Whether as the effect of losses inflicted by the allies and consequent weakened overall strength, or whether as the result of a decision to await the end of the American combat role, the number of enemy attacks and acts of terrorism in 1971 were lower than at any previous time (see Table 6-1). On the other hand, at least some of this progress can probably be attributed to the pacification program. "Like most things in Vietnam," Robert Komer wrote in 1971, "it has been cumbersome, wasteful, poorly executed, and only spottily effective in many respects."[3] Yet the pacification program, far better funded during 1968–71 than in the earlier period of the war, had had a cumulative effect and some parts of it by 1971 had produced an impact on VC prospects in the countryside.

The overall improved situation of the GVN was mirrored in the HES statistics (see Table 6-2) and other data reporting systems on matters such as the security condition of roads and waterways. But, as Komer correctly noted, the real question, of course, was

> the impact of these changes on—to use the once fashionable cliché—the hearts and minds of Vietnam's peasants. In terms of popular reactions, to what extent are any positive effects of pacification (improved security, economic revival, etc.) offset by the negative effects of how

Table 6-2 Population Control in South Vietnam, End of Year 1968–71 (By Percentage)

Section of Population	1968	1969	1970	1971
Secure (A + B)	47	71	75	84
Relatively secure (C)	30	21	20	13
Contested (D + E)	11	5	5	3
VC/NVA control	12	2	0	0

SOURCE: Hamlet Evaluation System Computer Tapes.

the GVN and U.S. have conducted the war? To what extent has coercion, corruption, or arbitrary use of power by GVN administrators taken the bloom off the rose? Is peasant alienation from VC terror and exactions significantly greater than his alienation from similar GVN actions in many cases? Is the farmer fatalistic about all the destruction, or would he rather have a harsh peace even under VC control than the continued destructiveness of the U.S. style of war? One can only pose these questions.[4]

Retrospective studies of the HES system have since confirmed what many Americans in Vietnam suspected all along, namely, that HES figures suffered from inflation, the main reason being command pressure for results.[5] In a revised version called HES/70, which had come into use in 1970, advisers no longer did the rating and all scoring was done in Saigon by a weighting formula not known in the field. But it probably was not very difficult to figure out what kinds of conditions in the hamlets would result in a high rating, and advisers, in effect, were still rating their own success in achieving pacification. The system still depended on correct local data, and this correctness could not always be taken for granted. The Phu Yen (II CTZ) province senior adviser reported in November 1970 that "the previously suspected concealment of incidents and abductions in 'pacified' Hieu Xuong District is becoming more of a fact than a suspicion. The efforts by local officials to keep the District looking good in the HES rating by not reporting all incidents has long been suspect. Between 1–18 November 1970, 12 persons were found to be abducted but had not been reported."[6] More importantly, even though HES was supposed to be no more than a management tool, designed mainly to facilitate the identification of problems and their analysis, and not a measuring rod of popular attitudes, it inevitably came to be seen as just that—an indicator of overall progress in the pacification effort and of GVN strength. Yet this was precisely what always remained beyond measurement. HES measured control and the suppression of opposition; it could not measure popular allegiance and the strength of commitment to the GVN.

Weakness of Commitment

The peasants, it was generally agreed, loved a winner; considerations of self-interest were more important than abstract ideology. The turning point here appeared to have been the 1968 Tet offensive. The VC had lost, and VC terror and the destructiveness of fighting had stood in sharp contrast to communist promises of a secure and happy future for every Vietnamese. By calling the prospect of victory into question and betraying the promise of a better future, the Tet offensive had stripped away the VC's two most alluring claims to popular support and compromised the integrity of their propaganda. With the GVN expanding its area of control, life with the VC gradually became more and more hazardous while increased security and growing economic prosperity in government-controlled zones made adherence to the GVN the sensible and rational behavior. But did these calculations of gains and losses (mind) also lead to a permanent shift of allegiance and sentiments (heart)?

While Americans in the field were reporting gains based on "mind," they were more pessimistic on the crucial matter of "heart." For example, at a time in 1970 when the province HES score indicated that 80.2 percent of the population of Binh Duong (III CTZ) lived in secure (A+B) hamlets, an American official wrote:

> The VC's loss has not been the GVN's permanent gain. People follow the GVN now because it is strong and offers a chance to make a living. Should it be unable to maintain both security and a reasonable livelihood for individuals, it will be deserted as was Macbeth by his thanes. In no conversation during these last few days was there mention of a loyalty transcending self-interest or participation in an organization out of belief in some cause or principle. The RF privates chose the GVN over the VC because it was an easier life with greater likelihood of "arranging" profitable moonlighting. The Hoi Chanh [ralliers] were impressed with GVN security, not its righteous cause. Villagers all readily acknowledged that if the VC came back in force, recalculation of behavior would be in order. In fact, the GVN is surrounded by fair-weather friends.[7]

Reports from other, less secure, provinces spoke of accommodation and defections-in-place (a phrase coined by Robert Thompson)—patterns of neutralism and inaction or doing just enough for the enemy so as to secure one's future in case the other side came out on top. Again, HES ratings seemed incapable of detecting these signs of weakness. American advisers, warned a Foreign Service officer serving as deputy province senior adviser in August 1971, were "abysmally insensitive" to political factors and completely ignored the psychological atmosphere. In Vinh Binh province (IV CTZ), he wrote, there was a hamlet which

> contains a cluster of people rated as "B" on the HES *and* the 312 Main Force VC Battalion. The VC and the local Government forces have reached a tacit accommodation; they avoid each other without openly recognizing these arrangements. When the VC do come into the populated area to collect taxes, propagandize or otherwise terrorize the people, the people do not report to the authorities: they are frightened. The paddies farmed by the people are next to the VC area. The people paint the Government flag on their doorposts, participate in PSDF (in an accommodating manner) and their children learn the National Anthem. The VC, however, still hold a veto power over the life and death issues in this hamlet. With no reported incidents and overt pro-Government responses by the people, the HES marks this a "B" hamlet.[8]

A similar situation was reported from Binh Dinh province (II CTZ). Those who are only concerned with statistics and meeting goals, argued the province senior adviser in September 1971, should spend some time in the hamlets with the existing security forces. "Nowhere in the HES is it asked if RF/PF are carrying out their missions." These units, responsible for providing security for the population, "receive good intelligence and utilize it effectively; when they know the enemy is coming to a hamlet they simply avoid them by withdrawing or defending in the wrong direction."[9] Local government in Binh Dinh, stated an in-depth study of the province in June 1971, "can be generally characterized as compromised and ineffectual. There is ample evidence of accommodation between local officials and the enemy." Village government "seems to be an 0900–1400 affair with officials migrating *en masse* out of the villages in the early afternoon. Underneath this smattering of government is a society basically in enemy hands." The GVN maintained military superiority—the province had two ARVN battalions and 27,000 RF/PF troops as against an estimated 12,000 VC/NVA—but its political situation was internally weak. Compared with the VC the GVN troops were "poorly disciplined, ill-led, and lacking in inter-unit cooperation."[10]

The same general picture emerged from an assessment of the overall situation in MR 2 prepared in April 1971 by the senior adviser of territorial forces, from which I have quoted earlier in regard to RVNAF leadership problems. According to HES statistics for that month, 62 percent of the population in MR 2 lived in secure (A + B) hamlets, 89 percent in secure and relatively secure hamlets (A + B + C), and only 10 percent in contested territory (D + E). Yet the evaluation of the forces available to provide security for this region, covering 49 percent of the total land area of South Vietnam, resulted in a quite different and far more pessimistic appraisal. The American officer began by saying that it was "time for a note of realism in all the euphoria of Vietnamization and withdrawal." In the previous month, he related, full-scale battles lasting four days had been fought in southern Pleiku in which a district headquarters and nine hamlets were destroyed; 2,800 people, a majority of them resettled Montagnards, had abandoned the area, the number of killed and wounded was as yet undetermined and pacification was probably set back by a year. "In these two battles the enemy were first-class NVA regiments, for which the RF/PF are surely no match. There is considerable doubt in my mind that the ARVN we have in MR 2 are a real match, either, without the overwhelming power of US air, artillery, and gunships." The territorial forces were plagued by "understrength units, desertion and casualty rates which exceed recruitment, indefensible compounds, ambushes which are reported but not conducted, and many search and avoid mobile operations." People, including the soldiers, were tired of the war and therefore "there is a reluctance to go out and fight, as well as aversion to volunteering for service with the RF and PF. There are many others who are not sure which way the war is going to end, including military officers. They don't want to be the first to die if it ends the wrong way, so they practice a 'Live and let live' philosophy. This attitude is more widespread than we think, but extremely difficult to identify or prove. On the other hand, how else account for repeated failure to find and destroy the enemy?"[11]

The 1972 Easter Invasion

An important test of Vietnamization was not far off. Exactly when Hanoi made the decision to stage a full-scale invasion of South Vietnam, we do not know; it may have been as early as the end of 1970 or in the early part of 1971. In the spring of 1971, Le Duan, first secretary of the Lao Dong party, paid a prolonged visit to Moscow; at that time he probably arranged for the supply of heavy offensive weapons which would be needed for such an onslaught. The war in the South had become a stalemate. Pacification and Vietnamization were moving ahead and communist prospects were not at all promising. As we have seen, in most of the country the VC were now on the defensive, and guerilla units had to be strengthened by fillers from North Vietnam. Hence the decision was made to abandon the strategy of protracted war and to force a decision by a conventional invasion. By 1972, the Politburo concluded, American ground combat units would no longer be available to support and bail out the South Vietnamese; the RVNAF alone would be no match for North Vietnam's heavily armed divisions. Moreover, a decisive defeat of the GVN in early 1972 might succeed in thwarting Nixon's bid for re-election in the fall of that year and lead to the election of a more dovish president. Just as the Tet offensive in 1968 had led to the American decision to disengage, a decisive victory in 1972 could strike the final blow at U.S. will and resolve and thus at long last achieve a surrender at the conference table in Paris.

For Russia an American defeat in Vietnam was, of course, a no less attractive prospect. It would strengthen Russia's position vis-á-vis the United States and would lead to a strong and united Indochina on China's southern border which would be indebted to its Russian protector and chief supplier. The hardware for the planned invasion—trucks, heavy tanks and artillery, SAM missiles, etc.—was delivered during the course of the year 1971. By early 1972, allied intelligence knew that a major invasion from the North was in preparation.[12]

The main attack began in the north. In the early hours of 30 March 1972, three North Vietnamese divisions sliced into MR 1—southward across the DMZ and eastward along Highway 9 from Laos and through the A Shau Valley toward Hue. Supported by 200 Russian T-54 tanks and large numbers of 130-mm guns, the attackers rapidly overran outgunned firebases like The Rockpile and Camp Carroll and within a week had captured the 10-mile strip between the DMZ and the Cua Viet River. Next came an attack in Binh Long province (MR 3), where three NVA divisions captured the town of Loc Ninh near the Cambodian border and then moved on toward An Loc, a town situated on Highway 13 leading to Saigon. By 13 April, An Loc was surrounded and the defenders had to be supplied by parachute drops. On 23 April, finally, came the long-awaited assault on Kontum in the central highlands. The defending Twenty-second ARVN Division fell back in disarray, but Kontum was reinforced by the Twenty-third Division and was able to hold. In Binh Dinh province, meanwhile, another NVA division had captured three coastal districts and threatened to cut the country in two. The situation looked ominous.[13]

On 6 April President Nixon ordered the resumption of full-scale bombing of North Vietnam; heavy air strikes and naval gunfire support for the beleaguered South Vietnamese also helped shore up morale. But the real trial was still to come. On 27 April the North Vietnamese renewed their offensive on the northern front and this time the newly formed ARVN Third Division, which had withstood heavy pounding for almost a month, broke. Lack of unity of command aggravated the difficulties of the defenders: the commander of the Third Division, an experienced officer, had no control over ARVN tanks and the marines fighting in the same sector. Dong Ha fell on 29 April, Quang Tri city on 1 May, and three days later practically all of Quang Tri province was lost. Rout and panic characterized the flight south. No orderly withdrawal plan had been prepared and, deserted by their officers, leaderless South Vietnamese soldiers and thousands of fleeing civilians clogged Highway 1, moving like a tidal wave toward Hue. North Vietnamese artillery pounded this frightened mass of humanity and as many as 20,000 may have been killed or wounded, a large number of them civilian refugees.

On 2 May President Thieu dismissed the commander of the Third ARVN division as well as the regional commander and put Gen. Ngo Quang Truong in command of all forces on the northern front. Known as South Vietnam's best general officer, Truong quickly proved his reputation. Orders were issued for the execution of deserters and looters and within two days a new defensive line had been established some 25 miles north of Hue. Further south, Kontum and An Loc, though completely surrounded, also were holding. Fierce house-to-house fighting continued there throughout the month of May, but the defenders stood their ground. By the end of May the siege of both cities had been lifted. On 8 May Nixon had ordered the mining of Haiphong harbor and other North

Vietnamese ports, and even though this blockade could have no immediate effect on the fighting in the South, it buoyed the spirits of the South Vietnamese. By 28 June, ARVN forces north of Hue were able to begin a counteroffensive. On 19 July, operations began in Binh Dinh province to regain the three northern districts, and by the end of the month the district capitals had been taken. The drive to recapture Quang Tri city encountered fierce North Vietnamese resistance and in the heavy fighting that city, like An Loc earlier, was reduced to rubble. On 15 September, South Vietnamese marines finally hoisted the flag over the citadel of Quang Tri city. The northern part of the province remained in communist hands.

By the end of September ground fighting in South Vietnam had decreased to its lowest level since the start of the offensive on 30 March. The North Vietnamese had thrown into the battle 14 divisions and 26 independent regiments, practically all of their armed might, but the invasion had failed to accomplish its goal. The South Vietnamese army had not been put out of action; North Vietnamese losses were heavy—they were listed as close to 100,000 killed. To be sure, the enemy had been able to take advantage of the preoccupation of ARVN with the invading NVA divisions, and pacification in most of South Vietnam had been set back severely. The percentage of the population under enemy control had risen from 3.7 in February to 9.7 at the end of July. Hardest hit were MR 1 and 2 in the north, where whole districts had been lost, but there were substantial reverses in other parts of the country as well. By the end of August, the enemy offensive had generated over 970,000 new refugees of whom 600,000 were living in camps. Many of them faced an uncertain future since the chance of returning to their villages was very slim. Still, the overall situation was rated better than after the Tet 1968 offensive. In March 1968 there had been 4,093 hamlets under VC control, in July 1972 the corresponding figure was given as 963.[14] With all allowance made for the softness of HES statistics, this general picture can probably be considered reliable.

The Failure of the 1972 Offensive

What did the outcome of the 1972 Easter invasion signify for the status of Vietnamization? As was to be expected, the performance of ARVN varied greatly. Some divisions like the Twenty-third defending Kontum and elements of the Fifth holding An Loc against superior forces acquitted themselves well. Elite units like the Rangers and marines also generally fought tenaciously. Other divisions, like the Third and Twenty-second, on the other hand revealed glaring weaknesses in discipline and effectiveness. The performance of the territorial forces also was very uneven and was rated as ranging "from outstanding to poor." The contribution of the PSDF was evaluated as "marginal";[15] one of the few exceptions was An Loc where the PSDF had successfully held a portion of the perimeter during the siege. In most cases and not surprisingly, the effectiveness of RVNAF units seemed to depend on the caliber of their officers. Some well-led troops, like the defenders of An Loc and Kontum, performed admirably; others, abandoned by their commanders, fell apart.

The defeat of the invasion was helped by the many serious mistakes made by the North Vietnamese. Instead of concentrating all his forces for one overwhelming thrust, General Giap attacked on three fronts simultaneously. If one or more of the divisions employed in the drives on An Loc and Kontum had been available in the north, the NVA probably would have been able to maintain the momentum of their original attack until at least the capture of Hue, causing possibly a serious collapse of RVNAF morale. Instead, after reaching the Cua Viet River, the NVA divisions paused for three weeks and this delay in pressing their attack gave the South Vietnamese time to move up reinforcements. In this way, the defenders were able to reverse the NVA's initial advantage and eventually to turn the tide.[16]

The mistakes made by the strategist, Giap, were compounded by his field commanders. First, they lacked the experience of coordinating attacks employing artillery, tanks and infantry. Tanks were used in the battles for An Loc and Kontum, where they bogged down in the rubble created by NVA artillery and became vulnerable to the defenders dug into this same rubble and using efficient antitank weapons. Tanks often were sent into the attack without supporting infantry, and they were wasted in quasi-static battles instead of bypassing towns like An Loc and driving on Saigon. Secondly, NVA commanders threw away the numerical superiority gained as a result of concentrating their troops at chosen points of attack by repeated shock assaults which caused extremely heavy casualties and soon resulted in a manpower balance favoring the RVNAF.[17]

Last but not least, one must mention the crucial role played by American fire support, in particular the tremendous volume of U.S. air activity.

On several occasions, large bodies of enemy troops were caught by B-52 strikes, with devastating results. At both An Loc and Kontum the besieged RVNAF troops had no artillery support, and there is general agreement that without the enormous quantity of bombs dropped in relatively compact areas the vastly outnumbered and outgunned defenders could not have withstood the siege. Similarly, on the northern front, it was air power which broke the back of NVA armor, and only aircraft could get at the NVA's 130-mm guns, which outranged the American-supplied howitzers of ARVN by several miles.[18] It was estimated that half of the enemy tanks destroyed and half of his personnel casualties were the result of tactical air support. Of all sorties flown during these six months, 74 percent were by American aircraft,[19] making the role of American airpower indeed decisive. Lastly, every available ship of the Seventh Fleet was pressed into service. Two cruisers and five destroyers pounded enemy targets on the northern front from offshore. The volume of ordnance delivered by the big naval guns from April through September 1972 was 16,100 tons, a quantity higher than at any time since the heavy fighting of 1969.[20]

To the impact of fire support provided at the South Vietnamese battle fronts one must add the effect of the resumed bombing of North Vietnam, which in 1972 was far more effective than the attacks staged during the ROLLING THUNDER campaign of 1965–68. Not only did the Air Force now have an arsenal of laser- and television-guided "smart bombs," but the heavily armed NVA divisions of 1972 were far more vulnerable to the interdiction of their lines of supply than had been the guerilla-type forces linked to secure sanctuaries in Cambodia. The consumption of ammunition and gasoline alone was estimated to be running at several thousand tons a day. The heavy bombing of supply dumps and lines of communications could not choke off all supplies moving south, but it destroyed a substantial part; there were recurring reports of NVA tanks running out of gas.[21]

In all, then, one must agree with the judgment of Robert Thompson that while "it is untrue to say that the battles were won solely by American air power, it would be true to say that they could not have been won without it."[22] After initial defeat, the South Vietnamese had acquitted themselves well. But, as an American officer who knew the RVNAF well told Congress in 1975, this success "was accomplished under the protective umbrella of a powerful U.S. air arm, superior artillery, and a functioning, efficient and sufficient U.S.-run logistics system. Further, the North Vietnamese were acutely aware of the threat posed by a considerable U.S. ground presence still in the country."[23] All this means, of course, that the 1972 offensive did not really constitute a conclusive test of Vietnamization. That would come only in a situation where the RVNAF were fighting completely on their own. Three more years were to pass before such a decisive trial of strength.

Even though the 1972 offensive had failed to bring about a South Vietnamese collapse, the Communists now controlled much additional territory and they considered themselves to be in a stronger position for accepting the American peace proposals secretly handed their representatives in Paris in October 1971. South Vietnam on the other hand, had barely escaped a complete defeat and this fact was not lost on its people. "Until the current offensive," wrote the Quang Tin province senior adviser in June 1972, "the people became more and more committed to the GVN. Now, many are measuring sides and their commitments waiting for the winner."[24] The invasion had not been accompanied by any substantial VC terrorist support, but there were new reports of acts of accommodation between VC and territorial forces.

In order to create a sense of urgency, President Thieu on 10 May had proclaimed martial law, and a day later a decree announced a lowering of the draft age to 17, a curbing of draft deferments and other measures aimed at rebuilding RVNAF strength. This mobilization, however, enacted in an hour of grave national crisis, met less than wholehearted popular support. CORDS officials in the Delta reported "increased corruption at the village/hamlet level in connection with the administration of this campaign. Officials allegedly will provide documentation for the purpose of avoiding the draft for 10–20,000 piasters. Draft dodgers and deserters arrested in the numerous police operations allegedly can 'for a sum' obtain release. In Can Tho it is reported that legal requests for a draft exemption are approved only after the payment of 30,000 piasters while illegal deferments cost in excess of 100,000 piasters."[25] In Vinh Long "some families prefer to have their sons join VC forces rather than the ARVN since they remain in the vicinity and are on occasion permitted to return home. Other youths may be dodging the draft, while the families claim VC abduction."[26]

The Situation after
the 1973 Paris Agreement

Meanwhile, the stalemate in the peace negotiations in Paris had been broken and after several false starts a cease-fire agreement was finally signed on 27 January 1973. Crucially affecting South Vietnam's chances for survival were two key provisions: the implicit legitimation of the presence of NVA forces in the South and the unanimity principle adopted for the new International Commission on Control and Supervision, which virtually guaranteed that the supervision of adherence to the accords would be ineffective. Yet these were the best terms Kissinger had been able to obtain. It was a less than perfect or happy ending to the process of Vietnamization begun some four years earlier—an ending, like the original decision to disengage, strongly influenced by domestic considerations. It was hoped that the agreement would at last put an end to the festering wound of divisiveness in the U.S. created by the Vietnam conflict. As Kissinger was later to explain—"we believed that those who opposed the war in Vietnam would be satisfied with our withdrawal, and those who favored an honorable ending would be satisfied if the United States would not destroy an ally."[27]

On the face of it, the agreement did look like an abandonment of South Vietnam by its American ally. The commander of the Australian army advisory team in Vietnam called it "a shameless bug-out," and Robert Thompson concluded that after Hanoi had failed in the Easter invasion, the Paris accords "restored its chance of winning the war in Indochina and practically eliminated the risk of losing it."[28] President Thieu in vain had opposed the agreement for the same reasons. Yet there was another side to it. Unknown to all but top policy-makers, the Nixon administration had assured the GVN that in case of any major violation of the accords by Hanoi, the U.S. would react forcefully, presumably by resuming the bombing of North Vietnam. These assurances were contained in two personal letters addressed by President Nixon to President Thieu before the signing of the Paris agreements. "You have my absolute assurance," Nixon wrote on 14 November 1972, "that if Hanoi fails to abide by the terms of this agreement it is my intention to take swift and severe retaliatory action." Enforcement of the agreement would not depend on any of its clauses but on the joint willingness of South Vietnam and the U.S. to maintain it. "I repeat my personal assurances to you that the United

States will react very strongly and rapidly to any violation of the agreement." When Thieu continued to express his concern about the presence of NVA troops in the South, Nixon told him on 5 January 1973, "you have my assurance of continued assistance in the post-settlement period and that we will respond with full force should the settlement be violated by North Vietnam."[29]

Prompted by these assurances of future support and by threats that the U.S. would sign the cease-fire without South Vietnam, Thieu finally swallowed his reservations and agreed to the Paris agreement. There was, of course, no reason why he should doubt Nixon's word. The American president had just been re-elected by an overwhelming majority and his power was at an all-time high. The Watergate break-in seemed all but forgotten and, in any event, did not appear to involve the president. On 23 January Nixon announced the conclusion of the cease-fire agreement to a nationwide radio and television audience and he publicly repeated his promises of support for South Vietnam: "The United States will continue to recognize the government of the Republic of Vietnam as the sole legitimate government of South Vietnam. We shall continue to aid South Vietnam within the terms of the agreement. . . . We shall do everything the agreement requires of us, and we shall expect the other parties to do everything it requires of them."[30]

No sooner had the agreement been signed than North Vietnam started violating its provisions. Large numbers of NVA troops were infiltrated into South Vietnam via Laos and Cambodia and SAM-2 missiles were installed at the rebuilt airstrip of Khe Sanh. During a visit to Hanoi in early February, Kissinger appealed to Hanoi to stop these violations, but intelligence reports showed that they continued. At a news conference on 15 March Nixon stated that while truce violations by both sides were to be expected, the infiltration of men and equipment exceeding the replacement provisions of the Paris agreement was a more serious matter. Using his strongest language yet, Nixon went on to say, "we have informed the North Vietnamese of our concern about this infiltration . . . and I would only suggest that based on my actions over the past four years, that the North Vietnamese should not lightly disregard such expressions of concern, when they are made with regard to a violation."[31] Weight was added to this threat by the resumption of American reconnaissance flights over North Vietnam.

On 29 March the last American prisoners were released in Hanoi and the final installment of American troops left South Vietnam. Also on that day, in a nationwide address, Nixon hailed the completion of the American withdrawal from Vietnam. Some problems such as continued infiltration remained, and he warned that "we shall insist that North Vietnam comply with the agreement and the leaders of North Vietnam should have no doubt as to the consequences if they fail to comply with the agreement."[32] Less than a month later, according to reliable sources, the president had just about decided to follow through on these threats and resume the bombing of North Vietnam when the floodgates of Watergate opened up: Nixon learned that his counsel, John Dean, had begun to talk to the Watergate prosecutors. Realizing that the renewed bombing would spur violent criticism and knowing that Dean's testimony could tie him directly to the Watergate scandal, Nixon refrained from approving the raids.[33]

Reports of the continuing North Vietnamese buildup persisted during the following months, but Nixon, preoccupied with fighting for his political life, failed to respond. The possibility of sending the bombers back disappeared when Congress, worried over the continuing fighting in Cambodia and encouraged by the weakness of the president, on 30 June voted to cut off funds for all U.S. military activity in and over Indochina, effective 15 August.[34] The enactment on 7 November 1973 of the War Powers Resolution, which formalized congressional oversight over the president's use of American troops abroad, lent further emphasis to the retreat from Southeast Asia. U.S. ability to deter a new North Vietnamese attack on the South with the threat of re-employing U.S. military power had now been eliminated. Nixon's promises to Thieu to enforce the Paris agreements with appropriate American military action had become but a piece of paper.

North Vietnam was not slow in taking advantage of this new situation. Adherence to the Paris agreements had always been considered necessary only as long as it advanced the goal of liberating the South. This position followed from a long-term, basic tenet of communist strategy, stated as early as April 1966 by General Nguyen Van Vinh, chairman of the Lao Dong party's reunification department: "Whether or not the war will resume after the conclusion of agreements depends on the comparative balance of forces. If we are capable of dominating the adversary [without war], the war will not break out again, and conversely."[35] Since the conclusion of the Paris agreement the Communists' "political struggle" was not making any headway—negotiations for the establishment of a National Council of National Reconciliation and Concord were deadlocked—while on the military plane the NVA/VC had not been able to score any decisive victories. On the other hand, the overall balance of forces had shifted decidedly in favor of Hanoi as a result of the complete American withdrawal and the congressional prohibition of any reintroduction of American combat forces. Hence in October 1973 the Central Committee of the Lao Dong party decided that the time had come to assume the strategic offensive, and in the spring of 1974 the NVA General Staff, the General Political Department and the General Logistics Department began formulating plans for large-scale offensives to be launched in 1975.[36]

Preparation for a New Offensive

Hanoi's methodical preparations for the resumption of full-scale war in the South are described in a series of articles by North Vietnam's Chief of Staff, General Van Tien Dung, which were published in the Lao Dong party's official newspaper, *Nhan Dan,* from 1 April to 22 May 1976:

> In 1974 army corps were gradually formed and deployed in strategic areas most vital to insuring mobility. . . . Great quantities of materiel such as tanks, armored cars, missiles, long-range artillery pieces and antiaircraft guns . . . were gradually sent to the various battlefields. . . . The construction project of a strategic route east of the Truong mountain chain, which had been started in 1973, was speeded up. . . . This 8-meter-wide, all-weather road permitted two-way passage for rapidly moving large trucks and heavy military vehicles and was used night and day to transport hundreds of thousands of tons of materials of all types to insure powerful attacks. A pipeline running from Quang Tri to the Central Highlands and Loc Ninh was capable of fueling tens of thousands of vehicles of various types moving to and fro along the route. . . . While the people in the South were driving back the enemy almost everywhere to regain their right to mastery, tens of thousands of youths throughout the north . . . enthusiastically joined the armed forces and set out for the battlefront.[37]

At the time of the conclusion of the Paris agreement the U.S. had hoped that the Soviet Union would restrict the flow of war materiel to North Vietnam, but this was not to be. No precise figures on the amount of heavy weapons supplied to Hanoi are available, but they were known to include T-54 tanks, heavy (130-mm) artillery pieces, the latest portable air-defense systems armed with surface-to-air missiles (SAM-2, SAM-3 and SAM-6) and mobile, quadruple-mounted antiaircraft guns, plus large quantities of ammunition for all of the above. In early March 1974, i.e. at a time when the North Vietnamese buildup was just gathering steam, U.S. intelligence estimated that NVA strength in the South had reached 185,000 men (compared with 140,000 in January 1973), 500 to 700 tanks, and 24 regiments of antiaircraft troops.[38] A staff report of the Senate Foreign Relations Committee, submitted in August 1974, concluded that in view of "the improved mobility and anti-aircraft defense of the North Vietnamese, the Communists now have the capability of massing their artillery and attacking fire bases from outside the range of South Vietnamese guns." The antiaircraft buildup had severely reduced the effectiveness of South Vietnam's tactical air support, and, "when coupled with the North's vastly improved interior lines of communication, could pose serious problems for the South Vietnamese in the future."[39]

To be sure, South Vietnam, too, had received massive supplies of weapons. In the final weeks of 1972, the U.S. had spared no effort to provide its ally with additional equipment. An emergency airlift, making use of U.S. military as well as chartered commercial cargo planes, had brought in tanks, armed personnel carriers, artillery pieces, communications equipment and tons of ammunition and spare parts for all of these. DOD announced on 20 November that South Vietnam had received about 600 planes and helicopters, making the South Vietnamese Air Force more than 2,000 planes strong and the fourth largest in the world.[40] Yet while this hardware increased the military might of South Vietnam, it also increased the country's dependence on continuing aid to obtain the spare parts, ammunition and fuel necessary for the operation and maintenance of this equipment. South Vietnam itself could produce none of these, and U.S. willingness to continue to supply these commodities came into question as a war-weary Congress, in the face of a badly weakened executive, became increasingly anxious to liquidate any further American involvement in Southeast Asia.

In fiscal year 1973, America had provided $2.270 billion for the support of RVNAF. In fiscal year 1974, ending on 1 July 1974, this support was less than half that amount—$1.010 billion; and for fiscal year 1975 Congress made another cut by one-third—authorizing $700 million. As never before, Capitol Hill had become one of the crucial battlegrounds for

Vietnam. In vain did Secretary of State Kissinger plead for funding of the administration's proposed sum of $1.485 billion. The North Vietnamese, he told the House Foreign Affairs Committee on 4 June 1974, were continuing to infiltrate on a massive scale and were receiving assistance from both China and the Soviet Union. Without American assistance the South Vietnamese could not defend themselves against this military pressure. "They had reason to suppose at the time of the conclusion of the Paris agreement that the United States would continue to support them in the form of military equipment. I do not believe that there is a formal legal obligation, but there certainly is a strong moral obligation."[41]

A few days later Kissinger told the Senate Foreign Relations Committee that after four years of Vietnamization the South Vietnamese now have "assumed the direct responsibility for their own defense. We owe the Vietnamese people the chance to succeed. Failure to sustain our purposes would have a corrosive effect on interests beyond the confines of Indochina."[42] Cutting the military aid program by half, Ambassador Graham Martin warned the Fulbright committee, would "seriously tempt the north to gamble on an all-out military offensive."[43] But Congress disregarded these admonitions, some indeed quite prophetic and accurate in their forecast of future events, and the authorization of $700 million, half of the administration's request, became law.

Aggravated by the worldwide inflation, which raised the cost of 105-mm shells, for example, by 27 percent and that of oil by 400 percent, the cumulative effect of the aid cuts made by Congress in 1973 and 1974 soon began to make itself felt in serious shortages. Taught by the Americans to make lavish use of firepower and not to stockpile ammunition, ARVN found it difficult to adjust to the new conditions of scarcity. Early in 1974 American officials had ordered a reduction of about 30 percent in the quantity of shells being provided under the military assistance program,[44] yet more ammunition was still being expended than was received. By the fall of 1974 available funds were no longer sufficient to allow the one-for-one replacement of lost aircraft, tanks, or artillery pieces permitted by the Paris agreement, and almost all funds had to be used for fuel, ammunition, medical supplies and technical assistance. The tempo of the war, meanwhile, had increased sharply. South Vietnamese losses in 1974 were higher than in 1968, the year of the great enemy Tet offensive.

The Communists now were beginning to reap the fruits of the congressional cuts. Writes General Dung: "The enemy became passive and utterly weakened. . . . The reduction of U.S. aid made it impossible for the puppet troops to carry out their combat plans and build up their forces. . . . Nguyen Van Thieu was then forced to fight a poor man's war. Enemy firepower had decreased by nearly 60 percent because of bomb and ammunition shortages. Its mobility was also reduced by half due to lack of aircraft, vehicles and fuel."[45] According to American sources, the number of close air support and interdiction sorties flown by the South Vietnamese Air Force (RVNAF) was down by 40 percent. Large quantities of equipment were sitting idle due to a shortage of spare parts. Of 1,277 aircraft only 921 were still combat ready. Ammunition consumption by ARVN and RVNAF was down to a dangerously low level. In 1972, the year of the NVA Easter invasion, ARVN had used up ammunition at the monthly rate of 66,500 tons. During the heavy fighting from July 1974 through March 1975, ARVN ammunition use ran at an average of 18,267 tons a month.[46] It would seem that Dung was correct in concluding that he faced a greatly weakened enemy.

The summer of 1974 saw a well-organized effort in the U.S. to bring about a sharp reduction in American aid to South Vietnam. On 31 July, Ambassador Martin told a House committee that the North Vietnamese hoped for a decrease in American assistance of such magnitude "that it will affect the military morale and effectiveness of the South Vietnamese Armed Forces."[47] Congress and the media scoffed at this warning and dismissed it as the kind of exaggeration they had come to expect from administration spokesmen. Yet this time the situation, if anything, was worse than many American officials realized. The cutbacks in military supplies, coming at a time of mounting NVA/VC pressure, had generated a psychology of accommodation and retreat that sometimes approached despair. With severe rationing of ammunition now in effect—85 rifle bullets per man per month, 4 rounds of artillery shells per howitzer per day, etc.—stocks on hand were held to be sufficient for several months of intensive combat. But the South Vietnamese were justifiably fearful what new disasters the next round of congressional appropriations would bring them—if they lasted that long. "The spectre of that yet undetermined day in the future when stock levels will no longer support a protracted battle continues to loom in the minds of the RVNAF," wrote the U.S. defense attaché in his report for the quarter September–November 1974.[48]

The effect on military morale of the economic hardships experienced by the South Vietnamese people appeared to be as serious as the shortages in supplies. The upward movement of worldwide prices had cut the real value of a greatly reduced American aid package and the dollar spending of American servicemen and contractors was drastically diminished, while the cost of imported commodities was going up steadily. South Vietnam's peasants now used water pumps for irrigation, outboard motors for their sampans, motor bikes, and large quantities of fertilizer for the new "miracle rice," but the "Honda boom" increased the demand for petroleum products at the very time when the price of oil had risen sharply. To make up for the loss of American assistance the GVN resorted to raising taxes and printing more money.

The result of these developments was a dangerously high rate of inflation and vast human suffering. From January 1971 to September 1974 the price of food went up by 313.8 percent, that of all items by 330.0 percent. According to American studies, the South Vietnamese soldier received only about one-third the salary required to support an average family. Men stationed near towns were absent without leave seeking additional sources of income and officers were reluctant to enforce discipline. Estimates of effective RVNAF strength were made difficult by reports that the armed forces included at least 100,000 "flower soldiers" who paid their superiors in order to allow them to work elsewhere, "gold soldiers" who hired others to serve in their place and "phantom soldiers" who existed only on payrolls. Pilfering of military equipment was widespread, as were instances of soldiers exacting rice from farmers and merchants.[49]

By mid-1973, the GVN had been successful in returning to their villages or resettling in new locations most of the more than one million refugees created by the NVA 1972 Easter offensive, but the sharp fighting in 1973 and 1974 resulted in hundreds of thousands of new refugees (estimates ran as high as one and a half million). More than one million persons were unemployed, and these thousands of displaced and jobless people crowding into the cities of South Vietnam constituted one of the most serious and intractable problems facing the GVN. Moreover, the confidence of foreign investors had been gravely damaged by the renewal of fighting.

"ARVN morale," wrote a South Vietnamese intellectual at the beginning of 1975, "is at a new low as a result of US aid cuts, runaway inflation and corruption in high places. . . . There are fears of a U.S. sellout as the South Vietnamese prepare to celebrate the poorest, gloomiest and most uncertain Tet of the long war."[50] At the same time, the U.S. defense attaché gave this assessment of RVNAF morale: "ARVN commanders cite the ammunition reduction and close air support restriction as the most significantly detrimental factors. Additionally, the economic situation has its adverse effects and a serious drop in the soldier's will to fight is imminent if not already a fact." During the quarter in question, 59,862 men had deserted from the South Vietnamese armed forces, 26,234 from ARVN alone. This meant that RVNAF desertions were now running at an all-time high of 239,448 men a year (in 1971 RVNAF gross and net desertations had been 168,997 and 140,177 respectively).[51]

In the eyes of many observers on the scene, the economic crisis of South Vietnam during 1974 was so severe that it seemed Hanoi might be content with applying just enough military pressure to force the GVN to maintain its costly military forces and await the internal collapse of the Thieu regime. But the opportunities presented by the weakened posture of the RVNAF were too good to pass up. The October meeting of the Politburo and Central Military Party Committee concluded that "the puppet troops were militarily, politically and economically weakening every day" and that the balance of forces was shifting steadily towards the cause of the revolution. At this conference, General Dung recalls, "a problem was raised and heatedly discussed: Would the United States be able to send its troops back to the south if we launched large-scale battles that would lead to the collapse of the puppet troops?" The conferees agreed that this was highly unlikely. "The Watergate scandal had seriously affected the entire United States and precipitated the resignation of an extremely reactionary president—Nixon. The United States faced economic recession, mounting inflation, serious unemployment and an oil crisis. . . . Having already withdrawn from the south, the United States could hardly jump back in, and no matter how it might intervene, it would be unable to save the Saigon administration from collapse."[52]

The Fall of the Central Highlands

While the Politburo was meeting for its next conference, lasting from 18 December 1974 to 8 January 1975, word was received that NVA forces had succeeded in overrunning and seizing all of Phuoc Long province (MR 3), the first South Vietnamese province to fall completely since 1954. An American in Saigon noted that the loss of Phuoc Long province caused apprehension and widespread cynicism: "Corruption in the Army was believed by many to be so gross that outpost defenders were having to pay other units for artillery support and air supply."[53] When the U.S. failed to react to this major defeat of its ally, Hanoi had empirical confirmation of its earlier conclusion that America would no longer intervene in Vietnam. In the words of General Dung: "It was obvious that the United States was in this position: Having withdrawn from Vietnam, the United States could hardly return. All the conferees analyzed the enemy's weakness which in itself heralded a new opportunity for us. . . . U.S. troops have withdrawn from the south, and our armed forces are present there." The conference consequently decided to launch offensives earlier than originally planned. A two-year strategic plan was adopted which called for widespread, large surprise attacks in 1975, creating conditions for the general offensive and uprising in 1976. The Politburo added the proviso that "if opportunities present themselves early or late in 1975, South Vietnam had to be liberated that year."[54]

These opportunities soon arose as North Vietnamese forces opened a concerted attack in the central highlands, the chief of staff himself, General Dung, now in overall command. RVNAF units here were stretched out thinly while the attacker had the advantage of being able to concentrate his forces and achieve surprise. According to Dung, in the attack on Ban Me Thuot, the capital of Darlac province, the NVA employed nearly three divisions against the defending one ARVN regiment and three territorial force battalions. In infantry strength this provided them with a favorable ratio of 5.5:1; in heavy artillery it was 2.1:1 and in tanks and armored vehicles 1.2:1. Despite Dung's concern over "inexperience in street combat and large-scale joint operations by various armed branches"—the problems which had plagued the NVA 1972 offensive—Ban Me Thuot fell on 11 March after a battle that lasted just over 24 hours and in which RVNAF forces were badly mauled. Taking advantage of this quick success, Dung decided to drive north toward Pleiku and Kontum. RVNAF morale, he later wrote, "has seriously declined. In face of this situation, it is necessary to adopt a spirit of urgency and forcefulness and to promptly seize the opportunity to win great victories." At this point, Dung hoped to seize the central highlands before the onset of the 1975 rainy season.[55]

On 14 March Thieu convened a council of war at Nha Trang with Major General Phan Van Phu, the commander of MR 2. Three days earlier, the day of the fall of Ban Me Thuot, the U.S. House of Representatives had rejected the $300 million supplementary military appropriation bill which President Ford had attempted to push through Congress. It was now crystal clear that South Vietnam, unlike the invader from the north, was on its own and could count on no further aid from the U.S. The council of war ended with Thieu directing Phu to withdraw from Kontum and Pleiku to provide additional forces for a counterattack to retake Ban Me Thuot. Phu, one of the less capable ARVN officers, turned the withdrawal over to a Ranger officer and, together with his staff, flew off to Nha Trang. The idea of abandoning the highlands had been suggested to Thieu by the Australian advisor, Brigadier F. P. Serong, in early 1975, but no detailed withdrawal plans had ever been drawn up.[56] With all major roads leading out of the highlands interdicted, the evacuation quickly turned into a rout. No rearguard forces were provided to protect the troops retreating eastward towards the lowlands; the many thousands of refugees, who joined the exodus and choked the roads, further complicated the defense. Lack of command and control and general panic led to ARVN units fighting among themselves and to atrocities against the civilian population. Materiel worth $253.5 million was lost and fell intact into the hands of the enemy, for the hasty departure of the corps commander had left nobody there with authority to order the destruction of the logistic installations.[57]

The Final Collapse

By 18 March, Pleiku and Kontum were in enemy hands. Only now, it appears, did Giap and Dung realize that the final battle for South Vietnam was upon them and that complete victory in 1975 was in sight. Three fresh NVA divisions from across the DMZ now joined other NVA/VC forces in Quang Tri province in a drive on Hue.

At this point Thieu decided to withdraw his best division in the north—the First Airborne—to the Saigon area. This second of Thieu's far-reaching and fateful decisions was taken either to build up his dwindling reserves in the south or, as some have suggested, to embarrass General Truong, the extremely able and popular commander of MR 1, whom many influential Vietnamese favored as a replacement for Thieu.[58] Whatever the reasons, the removal of the crack airborne troops, made over Truong's vigorous objections, badly weakened northern defenses and quickly led to the loss of Quang Tri province. Thousands of refugees began to stream south, and as they passed Hue the population of that city joined them, clogging roads and contributing to the sense of panic.

Truong's attempts to organize the defense of Hue and Danang floundered on what the defense attaché later called the "family syndrome." ARVN troops always had their immediate families living close to their areas of operation, and in the developing stampede officers and soldiers now deserted their units in order to get their families to safety. Cut off by the swiftly advancing North Vietnamese from further retreat south, almost one million refugees and thousands of soldiers crowded into Danang. Only a small part managed to escape on the ships and barges available. In the afternoon of 28 March the defense attaché's office urged the evacuation of the nearly 200 aircraft at the Danang air base, but no crews could be found for them and shortly thereafter the airfield was overrun by refugees. Pandemonium overtook reason. "The experience was shattering to all who participated."[59] On 30 March, slightly more than 10 years after the marines had landed on the beaches of Danang, the city fell to the enemy. Three ARVN divisions had ceased to exist and vast amounts of equipment and ammunition had again been lost.

Dung now threw all remaining troops in the North into the battle. "Hundreds and thousands of vehicles sped southward—bumper to bumper day and night," he writes, to move troops and supplies to the front lines. Others were flown in by air or transported by sea to land at the newly seized ports.[60] According to U.S. intelligence estimates, between 1 September 1974 and 30 April 1975, the North Vietnamese sent 178,000 combat troops south, over 58,000 in April alone.[61] Here and there Dung makes mention of the contribution of VC forces, but most of the credit is given to "the great strength of the socialist North Vietnamese rear base. The rear base is a factor deciding victory in a revolutionary war. Undergoing sacrifices and hardships, our heroic people did all they could and sent everything necessary in support of the frontlines, including their most beloved sons and husbands."[62]

The disaster that had overtaken Hue and Danang repeated itself farther south. The stream of refugees frustrated any rearguard defense; the "family syndrome" again led to the complete collapse of RVNAF as a fighting force. Rumors, many probably spread by enemy agents, contributed to the feeling that all was lost and few officers were around to attempt to rally the fleeing troops. Writes the defense attaché: "As the bits and pieces of ARVN elements streamed southward to Nha Trang, the MR 2 commander, MG Phu, and LTG Thuan, former commander of MR 3 and then commanding the NCO Academy at Nha Trang, took off for parts unknown." The city fell not as a result of enemy action but because of "panic on the part of ARVN, probably generated by the sudden departure of MG Phu. As late as several days later, enemy troops had not entered the city."[63]

The only effective, organized resistance took place at Xuan Loc, in the final battle for Saigon, where, as Dung grudgingly admits, NVA forces encountered "a desperate, diehard enemy" who for almost two weeks put up a stubborn and fierce defense.[64] But this last demonstration of RVNAF courage could no longer save the day. By 23 April, it was estimated, the North Vietnamese had assembled 120,000 troops in an ever-tightening circle around Saigon. Hundreds of cadres meanwhile had infiltrated the city and contributed to the further demoralization of the weary garrison of about 30,000 RVNAF troops. The spirit of these forces was not helped by the evacuation of the Americans from the besieged city, which was now in full swing.

On 21 April, the day of the fall of Xuan Loc, President Thieu resigned and it was hoped that a cease-fire could be arranged, preventing a bloody battle in the streets of Saigon. Members of the Provisional Revolutionary Government (PRG) in Paris had earlier indicated communist readiness to negotiate with General Duong Van Minh, known to Americans as "Big Minh," and during the last days of April Ambassador Martin directed aides to make contact with the communist delegation, stationed at Tan San Nhut air base under the terms of the Paris agreement. The details of these secret talks, which apparently also involved French diplomats and Polish and Hungarian members of the International Commission on Control and Supervision, are not known. But it is clear now that the constantly escalating communist demands, like the original offer to negotiate, were simply a ploy to further unsettle the South Vietnamese and their American backers. The puppets, writes Dung, "hoped that they could buy time to strengthen their position to enable them to negotiate a cease-fire with us, thereby making it possible for them to maintain their administrative structure and their armed forces."[65] Minh, who was sworn in as president on 28 April, to the last hoped to be able to negotiate a coalition government with the PRG as provided under the Paris accords, but the North Vietnamese had no intention of sharing power with anyone, including the PRG, whose propagandistic usefulness had now come to an end. On 30 April 1975, as North Vietnamese tanks entered Saigon, Minh announced the unconditional surrender of the government of the Republic of Vietnam.

The final defeat of South Vietnam had been brought about by a vast North Vietnamese army, equipped with the most modern heavy weapons, and not by a revolutionary uprising of the people. The "masses," an American scholar notes correctly, had played a largely negative role in the sense that the panic of the South Vietnamese population had contributed to the collapse of the RVNAF.[66] The preponderant role of the North Vietnamese army is emphasized in General Dung's account of the 1975 campaign, even as Hanoi's friends in the U.S. continue to praise the victories scored by the People's Liberation Armed Forces, the military arm of the PRG.[67] That Saigon had fallen to North Vietnamese tanks was certainly obvious to the people of the capital, who recognized the Northerners by their accent and height. In the haste of the advance, writes a European journalist who was on the scene, "many had forgotten their Front badges, with a yellow star on a red and blue background, which at least in those first days were supposed to confirm the claim that they were all soldiers from the South and not from Hanoi."[68] But why had this army triumphed so completely over the RVNAF? Did this victory prove the failure of Vietnamization? Was it inevitable? These questions, difficult as they are, demand our attention.

Why Did South Vietnam Collapse?

It has been suggested that Hanoi launched the 1972 and 1975 invasions because the VC had been defeated in the guerilla phase of the war. This probably is only a half-truth, for the VC in many parts of the country were far from destroyed and the internal weaknesses of the GVN were blatant. It could therefore be argued with equal justice that greater allied success in the years prior to these conventional invasions, when the struggle was still for the allegiance of the people of South Vietnam, might have dissuaded Hanoi from launching these attacks. A stronger and more cohesive national community in the South thus could have brought about a different denouement to this tragic conflict. Weapons alone, after all, are never decisive. It is fighting morale, resolution and the able leadership of an army which make possible the effective use of weapons and which win wars.

There is general agreement that shortages in materiel and ammunition during the last two years of the war forced the RVNAF to substitute higher casualties for the decline in firepower. A disproportionately large number of junior officers and senior NCOs were killed, worsening a chronic leadership problem. Moreover, while these shortages did not endanger the successful conduct of military operations during the NVA offensive, they did have a highly damaging impact on morale. The feeling on the part of many South Vietnamese that they were being abandoned had been growing ever since the Paris agreement, especially after the U.S. had ignored the North Vietnamese violations of the accords, and this feeling had become even more pronounced as a result of the successive cuts in aid. As we have seen, the effect of these reductions had been aggravated by the worldwide rise in prices which had led to inflation and serious difficulties for soldiers and civil servants in making ends meet. The constant criticizing by the U.S. Congress and press of South Vietnamese corruption, implying that South Vietnam did not really deserve U.S. support, appeared to add insult to injury. As one Vietnamese put it to this writer, "Not only did the U.S. not provide us with the assistance they had promised, but they did not even allow us to save face and dignity, the only assets of a poor country. It seemed better to be America's enemy than ally, for the enemy at least had America's respect." All this caused a strong sense of betrayal and weakened the will to fight.

Would the RVNAF have withstood the NVA onslaught if U.S. aid had not been cut and supplies had been plentiful? No conclusive answer to this question is, of course, possible, but there is reason to believe that, everything else being equal, internal weaknesses on the part of the South Vietnamese armed forces alone might have been sufficient to cause defeat in 1975. During the years of Vietnamization and again in late 1972, the U.S. had provided RVNAF with large quantities of sophisticated equipment which the South Vietnamese proved as yet unable to maintain properly. There were not enough skilled managers and technicians; technical manuals translated into Vietnamese were in short supply; the importance of routine and preventive maintenance was poorly understood. Weather-proof storage, the keeping of accurate inventories and the distribution of spare parts were handled badly, and transportation, like the entire logistics system, suffered from bureaucratic inertia and excessive red tape. As a result, much expensive equipment was sitting around rusting or could not be utilized for want of spare parts buried in mountains of crates in some faraway warehouse. Planes were grounded not only because of a shortage of fuel but also because they had not been properly maintained and therefore could no longer fly. RVNAF, concluded the defense attaché in his final assessment, had not achieved "sufficient maturity, technical expertise and managerial capabilities to completely maintain, operate and logistically support their communications systems and equipment resources."[69]

Just as equipment suffered from lack of adequate maintenance, the performance of the troops was impaired by insufficient attention to the value of training and continuous drilling in combat techniques. Training exercises by units in the field were rare. More fundamentally, leadership in many RVNAF units was still woefully inadequate. While there had been improvement in the quality of the lower-ranking ARVN officers, division and corps commanders all too often were still weak leaders. Critical combat and staff assignments were given to incapable or outright corrupt officers. To please the Americans, Thieu occasionally would fire one of the more notorious offenders, but usually the culprit would merely be transferred to some other important post. Some of the 116 Vietnamese generals evacuated from Vietnam arrived in the U.S. with nothing because they had nothing, but others live a life of leisure made possible by illicitly gained wealth.[70] Colonel Nguyen Be, a maverick figure who for a long time headed the pacification training center at Vung Tau, probably summed it up well when he told the *New York Times*'s Fox Butterfield: "Under our system, the generals amassed riches for their families, but the soldiers got nothing and saw no moral sanction in their leadership. In the end they took their revenge."[71]

The building of an effective combat force requires "leadership, weapons, and training, and in that order of importance, for without leadership from the top down the other two factors will be nullified."[72] In Vietnam, the significance of the abundance of equipment owned by RVNAF was negated by inadequate training and leadership.

The German army in World War II could survive tremendous setbacks, losses and long retreats and still remain until the end a functioning combat instrument, thanks in large measure to the quality of its leadership. The state of Israel occupies an extremely unfavorable geographical position, surrounded on three sides by hostile neighbors, and the Arab-Israeli conflict since its inception has been highly asymmetrical in human resources and military equipment.[73] Yet such weaknesses can be compensated for by superiority in leadership. The armed forces of the Republic of Vietnam in 1975, on the other hand, were outgunned *and* lacked effective leadership. The incompetence demonstrated by Thieu and his high command in the final days of the war, prominently including the ill-prepared evacuation of the central highlands and the removal of the First Airborne Division from the northern front, might have been enough to destroy the survival of even a well-disciplined and well-led army. Given the fragility of the RVNAF, it is hardly surprising that these tragic mistakes proved irreversible and that they led to the quick unraveling of any remaining discipline in the officer corps and the rank and file.

The failure of RVNAF morale was linked to certain weaknesses of South Vietnamese society whose contribution to the final collapse is difficult to assess in precise terms, but which undoubtedly played a significant role. In addition to leadership and a sense of comradeship, a soldier's effectiveness and combat morale are sustained by his belief in the basic legitimacy of the society of which he is a member and for which he is asked to risk his life. The South Vietnamese soldier, in the end, did not feel that he was part of a political community worth the supreme sacrifice; he saw no reason to die for the GVN. The country lacked political leadership which could inspire a sense of trust, purpose and self-confidence. It remained a society divided by geographic regionalism, ethnic variety and religious differences, and governed by cliques of politicians and generals. Thieu himself assuredly was not the kind of person who, like in some ways Diem before him, could function as a widely respected leader, a symbol of national unity. While the Communists were fighting for the unification of Vietnam, the GVN suffered from the charge that it favored the partition of the country.

The South Vietnamese government, despite belated reforms like the Land-to-the-Tiller program, had been unable to mobilize mass support in the countryside. In a series of moves in 1972 and 1973, Thieu once again seriously weakened local self-government by abolishing authority for the election of hamlet chiefs, authorizing district chiefs to appoint members of the village and hamlet administration committees and putting the PF and PSDF under the control of military officers instead of village chiefs. This removal of local officials from public accountability was bound to reduce the credibility of government decisions and programs and probably further weakened popular acceptance of the legitimacy of the national government in Saigon. It certainly ran counter to the spirit of the much-heralded "administrative revolution" of 1973 which sought to decentralize the functions of government and provide local and provincial governments with more control over the flow of government benefits. Furthermore, many members of the educated urban elite also looked with disdain upon Thieu and his officers who were serving as province and district chiefs, and regarded them as mere military men who did not merit support and loyalty.

The inability of the Thieu regime to generate popular commitment was reinforced by widespread corruption. Revulsion at this corruption created a feeling on the part of the populace that the government lacked "virtue" and the "mandate of heaven" necessary in order legitimately to govern the country. As long as the Americans were there, corruption had been seen by many as tolerable, for the fat often came off Uncle Sam; now, on the other hand, it affected the dwindling income of ordinary Vietnamese and increased the unpopularity of the GVN. In April 1974, the country was said to have 95,371 disabled veterans, 168,472 widows and 231,808 orphans entitled to social welfare benefits,[74] but corruption often made it difficult for these war victims to receive their meager allowances.

Corruption also worked direct benefits for the VC, thus further increasing popular disgust. VC purchasing agents could obtain supplies in the cities of South Vietnam, GVN officials and officers sold war materiel and food to the enemy, and members of the VCI could buy positions as hamlet and village chiefs, as they did in Vinh Binh province (MR 4).[75] It was well known that VC agents had infiltrated the highest levels of government and of the armed forces, creating an atmosphere of suspicion and distrust.

In July 1974, 300 Catholic priests had organized the People's Front Against Corruption, which quickly attracted support from other political opposition elements. In response to demands from this anticorruption movement, Thieu fired or reassigned a large number of officials accused of corruption—10 cabinet ministers, 14 generals, 151 senior province or district officials, 870 village and hamlet officials, some 1,000 national policemen and 550 military officers. But people had witnessed periodic purges of corrupt officials many times before and therefore had developed a strong cynicism about the real improvements that could be expected from such reshuffles. Moreover, serious charges had also been leveled against President Thieu and his family, and many agreed with the statement of a leader of the Buddhist Reconciliation Force: "If Thieu wants to eliminate corruption in the army he must fire himself first."[76] At a time when the enemy stood at the gates and threatened the very survival of a noncommunist political order, these opposition forces hesitated to press their attack on Thieu too forcefully, but the corrosive effect of such charges, nevertheless, was undoubtedly pronounced.

The emergence of the anticorruption movement was a healthy sign in that it indicated the widespread desire for an honest noncommunist political system free of domination by the disliked Northerners. "A majority of South Vietnamese," wrote a South Vietnamese opposition figure in early 1975, "strongly support a noncommunist regime regardless of how they feel about Thieu. This support explains why the South has not collapsed so far."[77] Many American critics of the Thieu regime consistently ignored the strength of this anticommunist and antinorthern sentiment, just as they exaggerated the dictatorial character of the Thieu government. In the final days of the war, the people of South Vietnam demonstrated their awareness of the difference between a corrupt authoritarian regime, which left them considerable freedom in their private lives, and an efficient, repressive communist state.

During earlier years of the Vietnam conflict, when U.S. and ARVN forces caused much destruction through the lavish use of their great firepower, it was possible and correct to argue that the flow of refugees toward Saigon-controlled areas was due largely to the desire of the rural population to escape allied bombing and shelling. But how explain the flight of hundreds of thousands of people during the last sixty days of the war away from their communist "liberators"? This time people were not fleeing any battles. This time the GVN not only was not generating refugees, but the evacuation of the central highlands was supposed to have been kept a secret from the population of this huge area. People were abandoning their homes and ancestral graves in the highlands and the northern provinces, which the RVNAF were giving up without a fight, and, like the Dutch, Belgians and French in 1940, were fleeing along routes heavily shelled by the advancing enemy forces toward the lowlands and the Saigon area where further battle was likely. To be sure, there was panic, and rumors that the country would be divided, and many of the refugees were members of the GVN administration and territorial forces who, accompanied by their families, were seeking to escape communist "revolutionary justice." In a survey carried out in early April 1975, fear of VC reprisals was cited by 41.4 percent of the refugees as affecting their decision to flee south. Unwillingness to live under communist control was given as the reason by 28.6 percent. The refugees could cite more than one reason, but the survey shows that more than 60 percent of them in effect had been voting with their feet for life in a noncommunist system.[78]

And yet the pathetic flight of the refugees in those tragic days was still only a vote for the lesser evil. As the veteran Vietnam correspondent Robert Shaplen had noted correctly several years earlier, the people who flee toward GVN-held areas "may not love the government more but they seem to be loving the Communists less."[79] This relative or negative preference for the GVN just could not create the strong commitment and popular support that would have been necessary to turn the tide of defeat. One must beware of reading history backward: to regard the collapse of the GVN, plagued earlier by internal weaknesses, as proof that the GVN was not viable is surely to commit the fallacy of *post hoc, ergo propter hoc.* Yet there are good reasons for concluding that this collapse was related to the kinds of problems which I analyzed earlier in my discussion of Vietnamization.

Was this collapse therefore inevitable? Probably not. We know now that South Vietnam in 1973–74 was not as strong as officials in Washington, on the basis of reports received from Saigon, had come to believe. American advisers with RVNAF, as we have seen, tended to exaggerate the progress of Vietnamization. The American embassy in Saigon, as a member of the Defense Attaché Office in Saigon told a congressional committee in 1975, was anxious not to provide ammunition to a hostile press and therefore failed to forward to Washington "even routine reports that indicated the operational readiness, the morale or the general capability of the armed forces [of South Vietnam] was not what it should be."[80] Washington thus was lulled into a false sense of security, and the awakening came late. "It is obvious in retrospect," Secretary of Defense Schlesinger declared at a Pentagon news conference on 2 April 1975, "that the strength, resiliency and steadfastness of those forces were more highly valued than they should have been. . . ."[81]

But if the RVNAF were not as capable as official Washington had assumed, neither were they so weak as to render their defeat a foregone conclusion. The odds were undoubtedly against them, but history, full of contingencies and the unintended consequences of human action, has been known to take unexpected turns. A combination of all or even some of the following events in the two years following the Paris agreement could have prevented the debacle: President Nixon dissociating himself from the Watergate burglars and therefore retaining a credible ability to reintroduce American military power as he had promised Thieu; Congress being persuaded by a strong executive or by some other external factors to provide South Vietnam with an adequate level of military supplies and economic aid; an early breakup of OPEC and a continuation of a cheap supply of oil; a few major mistakes by NVA forces of the kind they committed in 1972; a coup by supporters of General Truong with South Vietnamese nationalists and anticommunist sects like the Hoa Hao rallying to his banner. None of these events was impossible, and if their occurrence in combination was unlikely, this was no more so than the combination of opposite events which did in fact take place.[82]

7

American Military Tactics
and the Law of War

Every war causes large-scale death and suffering, to the soldiers fighting it as well as to the civilian population on whose territory it is fought. But the moral outrages inherent in war are often ignored when the fighting is crowned with success and when the moral justification of the conflict is seen as sufficiently strong. Thus, despite the fact that the Allies in World War II engaged in terror-bombing of the enemy's civilian population and generally paid only minimal attention to the prevention of civilian casualties—even during the liberation of Italy and France—hardly anyone on the Allied side objected to these tactics. The war against nazism and fascism was regarded as a moral crusade in which the Allies could do no wrong, and the fact that it ended in victory further vindicated the use of means that were questionable on both legal and moral grounds.

The Vietnam war, on the other hand, dragged on for years without a real decision and was never perceived as a clear-cut struggle between good and evil. Moreover, while the Communists barred all observers except those known to be supportive of their cause, the war on the allied side took place in a fishbowl. Every mistake, failure or wrongdoing was sooner or later exposed to view and was widely reported by generally critical press and television reporters.

This is not to say that allied military tactics in Vietnam were beyond reproach. However, a situation gradually developed in which the Americans and South Vietnamese could do hardly anything right. The Communists made skillful use of their worldwide propaganda apparatus to disseminate charges of American war crimes and they found many Western intellectuals only too willing to accept every conceivable allegation of wrongdoing at face value. Repeated unceasingly, these accusations eventually came to be widely believed. Among rational people, maintained Noam Chomsky, it was not in dispute that the "United States command is responsible for major crimes in the layman's sense of this term."[1] "The fact is," declared the Committee of Concerned Asian Scholars, "that U.S. war crimes are an accepted and regularly used method of waging war in Indochina."[2]

There soon emerged a veritable industry publicizing alleged war crimes. American servicemen stepped forward with articles and books dealing with their experience in Vietnam and became star witnesses before self-styled war crimes tribunals. Some of these proceedings concentrated on atrocities allegedly committed by individual soldiers or officers, a class of charges we will examine in another chapter. Others, like the International War Crimes Tribunal organized by Bertrand Russell, dealt with American military tactics like the creation of free-fire zones, the use of herbicides, fragmentation bombs, napalm, riot gas and the like.

The Russell tribunal, in large measure, relied on evidence supplied by VC/NVA sources or collected in North Vietnam by persons closely aligned politically with the communist camp; the imprecision and slanted nature of these reports was obvious to most. As against the propagandistic information emanating from Hanoi, more careful observers of the Vietnam war acknowledged that legal judgment was made arduous because of the difficulty of establishing the facts about the conduct of allied military operations. Today the factual record is generally clear. On the other hand, the application of the law of war to battlefield practices remains a thorny task because many of the relevant provisions and rules are vague, were created for very different weapons in a very different world, and therefore are open to different interpretations. Hence acts branded as unlawful by the war crimes publicists are acts which, on a different reading of the law of war, can be considered perfectly legal.

The international law of war, aiming at mitigating the ravages of war, consists first of all of international treaties such as the Hague and Geneva conventions, binding the states which have ratified these treaties, and secondly of customary rules which are considered binding on all states, the proviso being that these rules coincide with general and regular practice on the part of the great majority of states. In addition, tactics or weapons may be deemed forbidden if they violate certain general principles of the law of war such as military necessity, humanity and chivalry. Finally, some lawyers invoke the so-called Martens clause, first appearing in

Hague Convention IV of 1907 and named for the international lawyer George Frederick de Martens, as an additional law-creating source. This clause, included in the four Geneva conventions of 1949, lays down that states have obligations they are "bound to fulfill by virtue of the principles of the law of nations, as they result from the usages established among civilized nations, from the laws of humanity and the dictates of the public conscience."[3] Yet if it is sometimes difficult to establish the correct application of certain clauses of treaty law or to ascertain the constancy of practice required for the binding character of customary law, these difficulties are magnified manifold in regard to the basic principles of the law of war. In particular, to derive specific prohibitions from "the laws of humanity and the dictates of the public conscience" becomes rather hazardous and can easily lead to confusing the law as it is and what it might or should be.

The legal situation in Vietnam was further complicated by the fact that international treaties like the Geneva conventions for the protection of the wounded, prisoners of war and the civilian population are treaties between states that have ratified these conventions and are applicable only to armed international conflicts between two or more of the contracting parties. The U.S. as well as South and North Vietnam had ratified the Geneva conventions; the U.S. and the GVN stated as early as 1965 that they regarded the hostilities an international conflict to which the Geneva conventions applied in full. However, many of the problematic tactics in Vietnam involved relations between the U.S. and GVN on one side and the VC and the civilian population of South Vietnam on the other, and here the various provisions of the Geneva conventions, as we will see soon, frequently were just not applicable. Even Article 3, common to all four conventions and designed to lay down certain minimal humanitarian principles to be observed in conflicts not of an international character, does not really fit the special conditions of modern insurgency warfare in which, for example, the distinction between "members of the armed forces" and "persons taking no active part in the hostilities" is distinctly hazy.

North Vietnam argued that the war was an internal domestic dispute and not an international conflict and denied that any of its armed forces were present in the South. The VC, for their part, announced that they did not regard themselves bound to international treaties to which the other belligerents subscribed though they promised to follow a humane and charitable policy toward prisoners who fell into their hands. Needless to say, all this created a host of legal ambiguities in this "international civil war" which greatly complicated the resolution of various rival claims.[4] In this kind of situation, it will serve the cause of intellectual honesty to admit that the issues are indeed far from simple and that disagreements are possible on account of legal intricacies and not because some men are moral and others insensitive or corrupt.

The discussion that follows attempts to analyze the legal status of certain controversial authorized battlefield practices in Vietnam. I will not be concerned here with the advisability of these practices from the point of view of pacification or their contribution to the overall war effort; these questions have been dealt with in chapter 3. Legal questions concerning the bombing of North Vietnam will be taken up in chapter 11.

Population Relocations
and Free-Fire Zones

The U.S. and GVN throughout the war, but especially during the years 1966–70, engaged in extensive relocations of population, clearing areas of civilians and making them free-fire zones (after December 1965, specified strike zones). This practice appears to have originated in connection with the so-called free areas established in 1958 for the jettisoning before landing of unexpended aircraft ordnance. In 1962 the commander of ARVN began to designate "open zones" which were subjected to bombardment by artillery and air strikes in order to drive the population into the strategic hamlets (see p. 25). By November 1962 there were 105 such zones—14 in I CTZ, 32 in II CTZ and 59 in III CTZ. Requests for air strikes in these areas had to be approved by corps commanders. Forward air controllers were used wherever available.[5]

Relocations of the civilian population and the generating of refugees picked up momentum in 1967 and included big operations such as CEDAR FALLS and HICKORY, involving 6,000 and 13,000 people respectively (see p. 110). These relocations had several aims: (1) to deny the enemy manpower, food and revenue; (2) to clear the battlefield of innocent civilians, establish SSZs and make possible the freer use of firepower; (3) to score a political victory by making people vote with their feet for the GVN. Though there exist no MACV directives specifically authorizing the generating of refugees, the practice appears to have been widespread. Command guidance with regard to the creation of SSZs, requiring that these zones "be configured to eliminate populated areas,"[6] may have indirectly encouraged the relocation of people. Were these population transfers legal under the international law of war?

"One of the most flagrant violations of civilian rights is the forcible relocation of large units of people, in specific violation of Article 49 of the Civilians Convention of 1949, an article framed to avert repetition of the forcible relocations that took place in World War II."[7] This was the finding in 1967 of a group of well-known American theologians, including Martin Luther King, Jr., Harvey G. Cox, Robert F. Drinan, Abraham Heschel, Martin Marty and others. However, it appears that these religious figures were mistaken in their interpretation of the law. Strictly speaking, in the absence of a recognition of belligerency—and today there no longer exists even agreement on the criteria for determining when insurgents should be granted the status of belligerents—we are not dealing with an armed international conflict to which the entire law of war is applicable; in strict law, therefore, the hostilities in South Vietnam should have been subject only to Article 3 of the Geneva conventions of 1949, which specifically applies to conflicts not of an international character. This article contains no prohibition of relocation and limits itself to the protection of certain basic humanitarian principles, forbidding "outrages upon personal dignity" or "violence to life and person." From these general principles few lawyers would venture to deduce a prohibition of population relocation.

On the other hand, if we regard the Vietnam war as an international conflict, then the question of relocation can indeed be considered governed by Article 49 of the Geneva Convention Relative to the Protection of the Civilian Persons in Time of War. However, that article not only *allows* the evacuation of civilians from a combat zone but can be read to impose a *duty* of carrying out such relocations.

Relevant parts of Article 49 read as follows:

Individual or mass forcible transfers, as well as deportations of protected persons from occupied territory to the territory of the Occupying Power or to that of any other country, occupied or not, are prohibited, regardless of their motive.

Nevertheless, the Occupying Power may undertake total or partial evacuation of a given area if the security of the population or imperative military reasons so demand. . . . Persons thus evacuated shall be transferred back to their homes as soon as hostilities in the area in question have ceased.

The Occupying Power undertaking such transfers or evacuations shall ensure, to the greatest practicable extent, that proper accommodation is provided to receive the protected persons, that the removals are effected in satisfactory conditions of hygiene, health, safety and nutrition and that members of the same family are not separated.[8]

The references to "occupying power" show that one of the main intents of this article was to prevent the deportation of people for purposes of subjecting them to forced labor as the Germans did in World War II. The U.S. in Vietnam was, of course, not an occupying power but a co-belligerent, there with the approval of the GVN. But even if we were to regard the U.S. as an occupying power, Article 49 specifically recognizes that "the Occupying Power may undertake total or partial evacuation of a given area if the security of the population or imperative military reasons so demand." It certainly seems reasonable to suggest that the relocations carried out in Vietnam qualified on both of these counts. While it is true that the American command was not merely unselfishly concerned with the "security of the population" in the sense of protecting people against war's harm, but also sought to enhance the efficacy of its firepower, nevertheless the relocation of civilians did in fact provide the population with greater security than if it had remained in the combat zone. Conditions in the refugee camps were generally dismal, but the state of hygiene, health and nutrition, on the whole, was not out of line with the local standard of living and with what one could expect in a wartime situation. Efforts to return evacuees to their homes as soon as hostilities had ceased were made. Some of the relocations of Montagnards carried out by the South Vietnamese probably did not live up to the standards laid down in Article 49, but a country's authority to move its own inhabitants is surely not covered by the Geneva conventions.

As to "imperative military reasons," the principle of military necessity allows a belligerent to take all measures not forbidden by international law that are necessary for the defeat of the opponent in the least possible time and at the least cost to himself. Applying this principle, the relocation of Vietnamese civilians in order to deprive the VC of their support does not seem unreasonable. An eminent British juristic authority, Prof. Hersh Lauterpacht, grants the occupying power even the right to "general devastation" in cases "when, after the defeat of his main forces and occupation of his territory, an enemy disperses his remaining forces into small bands which carry on guerrilla tactics and receive food and information, so that there is no hope of ending the war except by general devastation which cuts the supplies of every kind from the guerrilla bands."[9]

It is clear that MACV really believed, however mistaken its judgment may have been, that forcible relocation of the civilian population would hasten the end of the war and was the most effective way of depriving the VC of supplies and manpower—the water in which they swam. The question as to what in such a situation constitutes "imperative military reasons" must be answered not by hindsight but in terms of what the military commanders at the time believed to be militarily necessary. As the Nuremberg tribunal ruled in the *Hostages* case: "It is our considered opinion that the conditions, as they appeared to the defendant at the time, were sufficient upon which he could honestly conclude that urgent military necessity warranted the decision made. This being true, the defendant may have erred in the exercise of his judgment but he was guilty of no criminal act."[10]

There is other evidence which points toward a duty to remove civilians from a combat zone. In 1956 the International Committee of the Red Cross suggested that belligerents be required "to protect the civilian population subject to their authority from the dangers to which they would be exposed in an attack—in particular by removing them from the vicinity of military objectives and from the threatened areas."[11] In 1970 the secretary general of the United Nations argued similarly that civilians would be best protected if they did not remain in areas of danger, and he proposed that the General Assembly "consider the usefulness of an appropriate resolution—a call on all authorities involved in armed conflicts of all types to do their utmost to insure that civilians are removed from, or kept out of, areas where conditions would be likely to place them in jeopardy or expose them to the hazards of warfare."[12]

Unhappy with life in the refugee camps or out of sympathy with the VC, many villagers drifted back into or remained in areas declared SSZs. Hence, when allied troops carried out ground operations or air strikes in these zones, civilians were still being killed or wounded. However unfortunate on humanitarian grounds and counterproductive from the point of view of pacification, it is not likely that these civilian casualties raise an issue of criminal liability as long as adequate notice of the designation of an area as an SSZ was given. Applicable rules of engagement did require such notice—after February 1969, a minimum of 72 hours notification in advance.[13] If individual officers occasionally violated these ROE, as they undoubtedly did, this involves not an authorized practice but a transgression of military regulations, a problem of a different order. Nor can the American command be held responsible for those instances when the VC forcefully prevented villagers from leaving areas under their control. Lastly, while the Americans for a short time counted the large number of refugees as a political bonus, this consideration was never a decisive reason for generating refugees and more prudent minds soon realized that refugees were indeed a heavy liability.

Bombardment and Destruction of Populated Areas

It is incontrovertible that the allied military effort in Vietnam was characterized by the lavish use of firepower and caused much destruction of property and a large number of civilian casualties. From this many critics of American policy in Vietnam have concluded that American combat practices violated the law of war and that the U.S. therefore was guilty of war crimes. U.S. battlefield tactics, charged Prof. Richard A. Falk in 1971, involved "the massive use of cruel tactics directed indiscriminately against the civilian population in flagrant violation of the minimum rules of war."[14] The above-cited American theologians concluded: "When we measure American actions in Vietnam against the minimal standards of constraint established by the Hague Convention of 1907 and the Geneva Conventions of 1929 and 1949, our nation must be judged guilty of having broken almost every established agreement for standards of human decency in time of war."[15]

An analysis of the applicable law of war suggests a somewhat different conclusion. It first should be recognized that the VC's practice, described above, of "clutching the people to their breast" and of converting hamlets into fortified strongholds was one of the main reasons for the occurrence of combat in populated areas. The existing law of war was not written to encompass this kind of warfare; to the extent that it does apply to insurgency warfare it prohibits such tactics, for it seeks to achieve maximum distinction between combatants and innocent civilians. Resistance fighters must carry arms openly and have "a fixed distinctive sign recognizable at a distance";[16] the civilian population may not be used as a shield—"the presence of a protected person may not be used to render certain points or areas immune from military operations."[17] Whether the VC were justified in disregarding these internationally accepted legal norms, as some writers have argued, is a question to which I shall return. The fact remains that by carrying the war into the hamlets and by failing properly to identify their combatants, the VC exposed the civilian population to grave harm.

Hague Convention IV (1907) prohibits "the attack or bombardment, by whatever means, of towns, villages, dwellings, or buildings which are undefended."[18] "Firing on localities which are undefended and without military significance," stated a 1966 MACV directive, "is a war crime."[19] However, according to the general practice of states, once a village or town is occupied by a military force or is fortified, it becomes a defended place and is subject to attack. The same holds true for civilian homes used to store war materiel. Such places become legitimate military objectives and injuries suffered by the civilian population are considered incidental and unavoidable. Indeed, even hospitals lose their immunity if "they are used to commit, outside their humanitarian duties, acts harmful to the enemy" and due warning has been given to cease such use.[20] One can question the wisdom of attacking the VC once they had holed up in a hamlet and regard such a response as counterproductive in a counterinsurgency setting, but the practice is surely not a violation of the law of war.

Even when attacking a defended place, the rule of proportionality must be observed—"loss of life and damage to property must not be out of proportion to the military advantage to be gained."[21] In the context of Vietnam, this meant, for example, that an American unit drawing a single sniper shot from a village was not justified in obliterating the entire village by using artillery and air strikes. But what if there are five snipers blocking an important bridge situated in a hamlet? How can a commander make a precise estimate of the size of the enemy unit which is firing upon his men? One sniper using an automatic weapon can sound like a platoon. These were the kinds of difficult situations faced by American officers in Vietnam who, as always in combat, had to act on incomplete information.

There is no question that some military men panicked and overreacted to provocation. But, as with regard to the policy of relocation, the question of whether a certain action was or was not justified by military necessity must be decided in terms of the way a commander judged the specific circumstances of the situation at the time. "If the facts were such," declared the Nuremberg tribunal in the *Hostages* case, "as would justify the action by the exercise of judgment, after giving consideration to all the factors and existing possibilities, even though the conclusion reached may have been faulty, it cannot be said to be criminal."[22] If a commander in Vietnam employed artillery and air strikes against a village—whether because he overestimated the size of the enemy force faced or because he sought to avoid excessive casualties to his own men—and his action caused the loss of civilian life, he may have hurt the cause of pacification but his action probably was not illegal.[23] Illegal conduct could arise if the commander was negligent—if he *could* or *should* have known that the use of overwhelming firepower was not really necessary to overcome enemy resistance—but the determination of such wrongdoing in a fluid battle-field situation is extremely difficult.

Another source of confusion in judging the matter of civilian casualties was the designation by many critics of all villagers as innocent civilians. We know that on occasion in Vietnam women and children placed mines and booby traps, and that villagers of all ages and sexes, willingly or under duress, served as porters, built fortifications, or engaged in other acts helping the communist armed forces. It is well established that once civilians act as support personnel they cease to be noncombatants and are subject to attack. Allied troops usually counted all dead persons found after battle in a defended hamlet as VC,[24] and there existed, of course, no way in which they could have distinguished willing helpers of the VC from those pressed into service. They also could not tell who had been engaged in such support and who had been a mere innocent bystander caught in the battle. Here again we see the unfortunate consequence of the fact that the VC chose to fight from within villages and hamlets which provided useful cover, avenues of escape and a source of labor for the building of fortifications. Inevitably, the civilian population was involved in the fighting.

The law of war forbids the destruction of personal property "except where such destruction is rendered absolutely necessary by military operations."[25] It does allow the destruction of fortifications. Since in Vietnam the VC often built their trenches, bunkers and escape tunnels right in the middle of hamlets—if not in, around and underneath huts and houses—the destruction of fortifications usually amounted to the destruction of homes or even entire hamlets. This is what happened in the widely publicized case of Cam Ne (4) in 1965 (see p. 53), as well as in numerous other instances, and critics soon started accusing U.S. forces of conducting a scorched-earth policy. In response to one such complaint, involving the burning of two villages in Binh Dinh province (II CTZ), the Army's assistant judge advocate general explained that "the two Vietnamese villages were not burned as a reprisal for the hostile fire that came from the houses in the village. They were destroyed because the houses and tunnel networks connecting them constituted enemy fortified positions."[26] In actual practice it often was difficult to distinguish an enemy bunker, constructed right under a hut, from a shelter built by a villager for his protection, and there undoubtedly were many cases where houses were destroyed without compelling justification.

The Rules of Engagement

The ROE issued by the American command sought to incorporate the relevant law of war and apply it to the concrete conditions of the Vietnam war. Based on the directives issued by MACV, subordinate commands down to the brigade level promulgated their own ROE or standing operating procedures (SOPs). MACV directives sought to strike a balance between the force necessary to accomplish the mission of U.S. forces in Vietnam and the need to reduce to the minimum the casualties and damage inflicted on the civilian population. They laid down procedures for the control of tactical air power, B-52 strikes, the establishment of specific strike zones, the use of tanks, naval gunfire, artillery and mortar fire, and the like.[27] I have had occasion to refer to specific provisions of the ROE in earlier chapters. Although South Vietnamese forces were not formally bound by these rules, American advisers were under orders to make every effort to obtain compliance therewith. Prof. Telford Taylor, formerly chief counsel for the prosecution at the Nuremberg war crimes trials and a critic of many facets of U.S. Vietnam policy, has called the MACV rules of engagement "virtually impeccable."[28]

Directives were frequently changed to assure their currency and relevancy to the different phases of the war. For example, during the 1968 February and May offensives enemy forces had entrenched themselves in densely populated urban areas, and in the process of dislodging them allied firepower caused much destruction. In Saigon alone, 9,580 dwellings were destroyed and many civilians were killed or wounded. Most of the casualties and damage, an investigation conducted in May 1968 found, were attributable to allied air strikes.[29] The board of inquiry recommended the adoption of special ROE for the employment of air strikes in urban areas, and such new rules were issued in order to prevent a recurrence of the devastation wrought in 1968. Leaflets and loudspeakers were to be used to warn the civilian population of impending air strikes even if fire was received from the area to be attacked, incendiary ammunition was to be avoided if at all possible, riot control agents were to be employed to flush out enemy forces so as to reduce the need to destroy civilian property, and so forth.[30]

Impeccable as MAVC rules of engagement were, their implementation ran into numerous problems. Even though the ROE were republished every six months to insure maximum visibility to all U.S. personnel during their tours of duty, the distribution of the rules to lower levels was often inadequate. Only the Air Force, it appears, made a systematic effort to test the actual knowledge of the ROE by its personnel. Pilots and all men in the fire control structure had to pass an examination based on the ROE before assuming operational duty and every three months thereafter. In the other services, familiarity with the ROE was often spotty. A senior embassy official, ordered to check out allegations of disregard for civilian life and property made by Jonathan Schell against the Americal Division, reported in December 1967 that while all officers interviewed had at least heard of the ROE, "subordinate commanders, Bn [battalion] and Co [company], have varying notions as to what the rules really are and their exact application. One Bn CO [commanding officer] quite readily admitted that he had never read any such rules and wasn't certain that there were copies of written instructions on the subject at his headquarters."[31] Most officers, he said, relied upon their common sense.

The previously cited inquiry into the destruction of civilian life and property resulting from the 1968 Tet offensive found similarly that a majority of the officers interviewed reflected vagueness and unfamiliarity with the ROE.[32] In December 1969 the commanding general, U.S. Army Vietnam, stated his view that reports of accidents and incidents involving death or injury to allied forces and civilians indicated that "some personnel do not have complete knowledge of the ROE" or misunderstand them.[33] These findings are confirmed by a survey of 173 U.S. Army general officers with service in Vietnam conducted in 1974, in which 28.7 percent of respondents stated that the ROE were "well understood" throughout the chain of command, 49.1 percent thought that they were "fairly well understood," and 16.7 percent stated that they were "frequently misunderstood."[34] In a situation where anything but a clear understanding of the ROE could result in the loss of innocent life this level of familiarity was obviously less than satisfactory.

There is evidence indicating that the ROE were applied inconsistently, one reason being the fact that MACV directives were often couched in language which allowed for multiple interpretations. Some subordinate commands, it appears, therefore followed practices which at times caused unnecessary civilian casualties. For example, one brigade of the Americal Division in 1967 permitted fire upon anyone taking evasive action, while another required positive identification of combatant status—the sighting of weapons or uniforms—before engaging evading personnel.[35] Different practices also prevailed with regard to air strikes on hamlets. In accordance with Article 26 of Hague Convention IV (1907), which requires notice of an impending bombardment "except in cases of assault," the applicable MACV directive stated that "if the attack on a village or hamlet is not in conjunction with any immediate ground operation, the inhabitants must be warned by leaflets and/or loudspeaker system prior to the attack and must be given sufficient time to evacuate the area." After obtaining GVN approval and once the inhabitants had been adequately warned and given time to evacuate, "the hamlet/village may then be struck without further warning."[36] In the absence of greater specificity, some FACs went by the rule "once warned, always warned," and since villagers often returned to their homes after a battle had ended, this reading of the ROE resulted in the generation of refugees or civilian casualties.[37]

In an attempt to prevent unauthorized interpretations of MACV rules, the consolidated ROE for all types of supporting fire issued in March 1969 stated: "This directive will not be modified by subordinate commands nor will directives modifying or interpreting substantive rules in the directive be published by subordinate commands."[38] Yet this order did not, of course, eliminate problems caused by lack of precise guidance in some MACV directives.

The tendency to take maximum license within the ROE appears to have been especially pronounced in the case of Army helicopter gunship crews who, unlike the predominantly professional Air Force pilots, were mostly inexperienced and often trigger-happy young men. When not operating in support of helicopter landing operations, these gunship crews tended to want to become fighter pilots and circumvented the ROE.[39] Mission data were often inadequate, which made it difficult to ascertain what the gunships had been doing when hunting "targets of opportunity." Officers in command of Army aviation units were concerned about this situation, as can be seen from the following command memorandum, dated 4 August 1965:

> We have had incidents in all CTZ's in which friendlies have been killed by fire from our weapons. In some cases this is part of the game and well-nigh unavoidable but in other cases we have not exercised good judgment or adequate restraint. We cannot afford to be criticized as indiscriminate killers. The argument for our weaponry has always been that we have the capability to be very selective; that at the ranges we use we can more readily identify and separate friend from foe. We must not permit a hidden sniper or a suspected shot in our direction to trigger a burst of haphazard and wanton fire into a general area from which the shot *may* have come. We cannot fire into a group of non-combatants which may harbor several VC. It is better to go home. If we are to have a populace which will join actively in our common struggle, we cannot alienate them by these actions. I admit that the problem is not clear cut. If we are directed to "zap" an area and we have doubts as to the advisability, we must inform those who have ordered the mission before we become executioners. It is often true that the order would be rescinded if the real situation were known. . . . I also expect each commander to have a soul-searching session with his aviators and gunners. Army aviation units have no unilateral hunting license and will not take these decisions onto themselves. There will be no tolerance of "zap happy" aviators or gunners in this command.[40]

And yet, incidents continued. "There have been far too many instances of reported indiscriminate firing of our gun birds which have resulted in needless friendly casualties," complained the new commanding officer of the Army helicopter unit addressed in the above memo on 18 April 1966.[41] The problem, the officer said, resulted in part from divergent interpretations of the ROE, and he therefore urged better training in the rules. "There is a tremendous amount of command interest in this field from higher levels. Each time we have an unfortunate incident or shoot up some friendlies we come under a tremendous amount of fire. I want commanders at all levels to continually review procedures, regulations and training to make sure that each crew member knows and understands the rules. This is still a judgment area on the part of the crew, so they must be knowledgeable."[42]

In the final analysis, of course, no set of rules, no matter how precisely worded, could substitute for the special restraint, discrimination and good judgment required in the Vietnam environment. This kind of calm judgment was not always in evidence, but, understandably, commanders were hesitant to impose severe punishment on their men for not being as mature, deliberate and judicious as they might have been. Such action, they feared, could damage morale and impede the aggressive carrying out of assigned missions. Thus, for example, when on 1 July 1969 two helicopters of the Americal Division on a visual reconnaissance mission shot up two hamlets in Quang Tin province (I CTZ), killing 10 villagers and wounding 15, the crews were merely reprimanded for not having been completely conversant with the division's ROE and having used unnecessary force. In the investigation of the incident, one of the pilots maintained that he had heard his helicopter being fired upon by about 15 rounds, and this defense was accepted. As the officer in charge of the investigation subsequently put it: "I think the pilots at Ky Chanh overreacted, but we have to give them the benefit of the doubt. If a man says he got fired on, and the investigation can neither prove nor disprove it, he's got something." The pilots had used too much ammunition, but "I just didn't think that they should be brought to trial because of their lack of judgment and their lack of understanding of the rules of engagement."[43]

To be sure, failure correctly to understand the ROE could and did cost the lives of innocent people. In the incident just discussed, the crews had disregarded the recently promulgated rule that pilots of planes or helicopters fired upon were allowed to return fire only if "the source of fire can be visually identified."[44] They testified that they had merely *heard* the rounds. But in a situation where young and often inexperienced junior officers were called upon to make quick judgments while under fire, there was obviously room for error. A commander's main concern was the successful completion of his mission and the protection of his men. Considerations of operational efficiency and self-defense had to be balanced against the likely destruction of property and the infliction of casualties on persons he often had good reason to consider unfriendly. There was no formula that could guarantee a perfect judgment; everything depended on good training and a high caliber of leadership.

The Question of Command Responsibility

The requirements of the law of war could be considered satisfied if there existed ROE incorporating applicable provisions of the law of war and the

American command made a credible effort to make known and enforce these rules. It is in the areas of dissemination and enforcement of the ROE that the record of MACV and subordinate commands is open to serious criticism. Until the exposure of the My Lai massacre American combat units in Vietnam not only failed to receive adequate instruction in the Geneva conventions (a subject to which we will return in the next chapter), but, as we have seen, commanding officers often lacked meaningful familiarity with the ROE. Such deficiencies had serious consequences. The December 1967 report on the Americal Division noted that officers were not sufficiently versed in the ROE; it was a unit of this same division which less than three months later committed the My Lai outrage (see pp. 325–26). The Army's review of this atrocity noted that marginal training in the ROE "played a significant part in the Son My* operation."[45]

The fact that MACV had issued impeccable ROE which, if observed, would have prevented this war crime is not sufficient to clear MACV of all collateral responsibility for it. A commander must not only issue correct directives, he must also make sure that his orders are followed—through proper training and enforcement by way of discipline. The disregard of applicable ROE by Americal Division personnel at My Lai, stated the House Armed Services Committee investigating the incident, "could be due to the negligence of the particular officers involved, or it could mean that the MACV directives were merely regarded as window dressing by subordinate units. Issuance of directives, alone, is insufficient; those directives must be followed through and implemented in order to convince subordinate commanders that they are to be observed."[46]

Charges that Lieutenant Calley was a scapegoat and that the real culprits of the My Lai massacre were his superiors in the military chain of command at least up to COMUSMACV, General Westmoreland, began to be heard soon after the story of the massacre broke in the fall of 1969. Accusations that the conduct of allied military operations violated the law of war and that, under the principles applied to the military commanders of the Axis powers after World War II, members of the U.S. command in Vietnam should be punished as war criminals had been made almost from the beginning of the American involvement. But these charges received new currency from the My Lai incident; responsible critics like Telford

* My Lai was one of four hamlets in the village of Son My.

Taylor now argued that the leaders of the Army had to face the question of command responsibility for violations of the law of war in Vietnam in order to recover the Army's "moral health."[47]

With former COMUSMACV Westmoreland now Army chief of staff, the Army took the accusations seriously. In early 1971 it established a task force of eight Army staff officers who spent approximately 14 weeks composing a lengthy report which dealt with the allegation that General Westmoreland had personal culpability for war crimes in Vietnam—because he was responsible for noncombatant casualties and destruction of property not required by military necessity and because he had failed to exercise adequate command supervision to insure adherence to the laws of war.[48]

The task force for the research project "Conduct of the War in Vietnam" (short title: COWIN) was under instructions to examine how effectively the ROE were carried out, whether violations were reported, and what disciplinary action was taken. "If the facts to be subsequently developed support them," several conclusions were held to be "desirable," among them that "no basis whatsoever exists for concluding that General Westmoreland could be found guilty of being responsible for war crimes."[49] This conclusion was duly reached. Yet despite the considerable legal learning displayed in the task force report, especially its legal annex, the issue does not seem to present such an open-and-shut case. Even though the task force was charged to look into the way the ROE were enforced, there is little evidence in the report bearing on this question. Whatever evidence is available from other sources shows that knowledge and full understanding of the ROE were generally inadequate and that this deficiency led to avoidable civilian casualties and, as in the My Lai incident, was a contributory cause of war crimes. What, under applicable case law, is the responsibility of General Westmoreland for this state of affairs?

A commander who orders the commission of a war crime can, of course, be punished as a war criminal. He can also be liable for offenses committed by his troops, which he did not order, if he failed to take all possible measures to prevent such crimes. That was the conclusion in the case of Gen. Tomoyuki Yamashita, who was convicted in October 1945 of condoning widespread atrocities by Japanese troops under his command in the Philippines even though he denied knowledge of these crimes. The opinion of the military commission which convicted Yamashita did not address the question of whether the commission believed Yamashita's protestations of innocence, but the board of review which confirmed the death sentence concluded that he did know of these offenses and had not, as he alleged, lost tactical control of his troops. The atrocities, the board found, were so numerous and widespread that the accused's professed ignorance was implausible. There also was evidence in the record linking Yamashita more directly with some of the atrocities, evidence that he knew of the atrocities and either gave his tacit consent or failed to do anything to prevent them or punish their perpetrators. The board concluded: "Taken all together, the court was fully warranted in finding that accused failed to discharge his responsibility to control his troops thereby permitting the atrocities alleged and was thus guilty as charged."[50]

The U.S. Supreme Court in upholding the conviction of Yamashita stated that, with regard to the law of war, a higher commander has "an affirmative duty to take such measures" as are "within his power and appropriate in the circumstances. . . ."[51] Contrary to popular accounts of the Yamashita case, neither the decision of the military commission nor that of the Supreme Court established that knowledge of or personal responsibility for war crimes on the part of the commander can be ignored in assessing guilt. The dissenting opinions of Judges Rutledge and Murphy were probably occasioned primarily by other serious procedural questions raised by the case and the judges therefore somewhat uncritically accepted all arguments by counsel for the accused.[52]

The decision of the Nuremberg tribunal in the *High Command* case further clarifies the matter of knowledge. The decision suggests that a commander's liability is not absolute and must involve a deliberate and reckless disregard of his duty to control his subordinates:

> A high commander cannot keep completely informed of the details of military operations of subordinates and most assuredly not of every administrative measure. He has the right to assume that details entrusted to responsible subordinates will be legally executed. The President of the United States is Commander in Chief of its military forces. Criminal acts committed by those forces cannot in themselves be charged to him on the theory of subordination. The same is true of other high commanders in the chain of command. Criminality does not attach to every individual in this chain of command from that fact alone. There must be a personal dereliction. That can occur only where the act is directly traceable to him or where his failure to properly supervise his subordinates constitutes criminal negligence on his part. In the latter case it

must be personal neglect amounting to a wanton, immoral disregard of the action of his subordinates amounting to acquiescence. Any other interpretation of international law would go far beyond the basic principles of criminal law as known to civilized nations.[53]

Based on these decisions the Army's manual on the law of land warfare states that a commander can be held criminally liable "if he has actual knowledge, or should have knowledge, through reports received by him or through other means, that troops or other persons subject to his control are about to commit or have committed a war crime and he fails to take the necessary and reasonable steps to insure compliance with the law of war or to punish violators thereof."[54]

The question of whether Westmoreland *should* have known that in the Vietnam environment inadequate understanding of the ROE could and would lead to violations of the law of war must be answered in the affirmative. There is no evidence that MACV knew of the My Lai massacre, but MACV was undoubtedly aware of the high civilian casualties resulting from fighting in and around hamlets and villages, of the existence of command pressure for a high body count and of the belief of many soldiers in the "mere-gook rule"—that the lives of Vietnamese were cheap and not protected by the law of war. Indeed, the constantly repeated expressions of intense concern of MACV with the question of civilian casualties can be read as an acknowledgment that rules aimed at protecting civilian life and property were, for a variety of reasons, not applied and enforced as they should have been.

New training manuals issued by the Army after the My Lai incident explicitly addressed these and related problems. Military personnel now were put on notice that "if you disobey the rules of engagement, you can be tried and punished for disobedience of orders. The disobedience may also be a war crime for which you can be tried and punished."[55] Such instructions should, of course, have been issued earlier, and the fact that such corrective measures were not taken until a major incident had revealed the existing disregard of the ROE indicates at least dereliction of duty or perhaps even criminal negligence on the part of MACV and General Westmoreland as COMUSMACV.

According to the *Manual for Courts-Martial* "a person is derelict in the performance of his duties if he willfully or negligently fails to perform them, or when he performs them in a culpably inefficient manner. When the failure is with full knowledge of the duty and an intention not to perform it, the omission is willful. When the nonperformance is the result of a lack of ordinary care, the omission is negligent. Culpable inefficiency is inefficiency for which there is no reasonable or just excuse." Culpable negligence is defined as "a negligent act or omission accompanied by a culpable disregard for the foreseeable consequences to others of that act or omission."[56] The determination of which of these degrees of wrongdoing is applicable to the case at hand would have to be made by a legal tribunal taking into account all relevant aspects of the situation and is beyond the scope of this discussion. It is clear, however, that knowledge and intent are not the only standards of criminal responsibility.[57] This is recognized in the Army's new training manual on the law of war, which states that a commander has legal responsibilty for the commission of war crimes "if he should have known, through reports or by other means, that those under his command are about to commit or have committed war crimes, and he fails to take reasonable steps to prevent such crimes or to punish those guilty of a violation. As a minimum, such a commander is guilty of dereliction of duty."[58] The fact that Westmoreland's responsibility here was one step removed from the actual commission of war crimes—it involved failure adequately to enforce ROE, a dereliction which in turn led to war crimes—would be a mitigating element, but it is unlikely to constitute a defense.

Incendiary Weapons

Hague Convention IV forbids employment of "arms, projectiles, or material calculated to cause unnecessary suffering,"[59] and the American law of land warfare accepts this prohibition.[60] The rule is an expression of the general principles of proportionality and humanity which reflect the intent of the law of war to avoid needless suffering. Yet in practice states have drawn the line between necessary and unnecessary suffering in a way hardly suggested by the humanitarian spirit of the Hague Convention. The criterion has normally been whether a weapon inflicts suffering disproportionate to the military advantage to be gained by its use, and this has meant that no militarily decisive and effective weapon has ever been regarded as causing "unnecessary suffering," no matter how painful the resultant suffering. Suggestions that humanitarian factors such as the nature of the injury, long-term medical effects, the risk of death, etc., be given greater weight have so far not been accepted, and the test has remained that of actual practice. "What weapons cause 'unnecessary injury' can only be determined in light of the practice of States in refraining from the use of a given weapon because it is believed to have that effect."[61]

The use of fire as a weapon of war has a long history and so has man's fear of fire. That is one reason why incendiary weapons continue to be used despite the great suffering which they inflict on their victims. In this century petroleum fuels have been used in flamethrowers, bombs, shells and mines, but it was the discovery of the thickener napalm in World War II that greatly increased the effectiveness of incendiary weapons, especially against equipment and fortified positions. It is estimated that during World War II about 14,000 tons of napalm bombs were used, two-thirds of them in the Pacific area; in the Korean War the U.S. Far East Air Force dropped a total of 32,557 tons of napalm. But the most extensive use of incendiary weapons took place in Indochina. Napalm bombs there constituted about 10 percent of all fighter-bomber munitions, reaching an estimated total of close to 400,000 tons during the course of the war.[62]

Incendiary munitions proved particularly important against enemy forces holed up in caves, bunkers and tunnel complexes and against targets in such close proximity to allied troops that high-explosive fragmentation bombs could not be used. White phosphorus munitions were utilized for marking targets and providing smoke screens but also against inflammable objects such as houses and huts, often in conjunction with napalm, since the spontaneously igniting white phosphorus helps to ensure the ignition of napalm.

The ROE provided that in attacks on villages and hamlets "the use of incendiary type ammunition will be avoided unless absolutely necessary in the accomplishment of the commander's mission,"[63] but in practice this rule does not appear to have restricted the use of such weapons. A marine captain told the House Armed Services Committee in September 1965 that napalm at first was denied in some instances. "This was subsequently rectified and now we can have napalm whenever we want it."[64] Air strikes with napalm bombs are indeed mentioned routinely in most after-action reports. During Operation CEDAR FALLS in January 1967 flamethrowers were employed "to assist in the capture of VC located in bunkers and tunnels. The flamethrowers reduced the amount of oxygen in the tunnels, to say nothing of producing a significantly adverse psychological effect on the enemy."[65] White phosphorus marking rockets were not classified as incendiary munitions and were popular with Army aviation crews. White phosphorus rockets, one helicopter pilot recalls, were "our favorite ammunition. With them you could see what you were hitting, and it was no problem to burn an enemy ville."[66]

Protests against the use of incendiary weapons were heard early on in the war. Critics charged the indiscriminate use of napalm against civilian targets and they argued that it was an illegal weapon because it maximized suffering by killing its victims slowly and maiming permanently. In January 1967 *Ramparts* magazine published an article which included large color photographs of burnt children; the author stated that he personally had seen thousands of infants and small children burnt by napalm in Vietnamese hospitals.[67] The International Commission of Enquiry into U.S. Crimes in Indochina, meeting in Oslo in 1971, concluded that the use of napalm and phosphorus bombs constituted a prohibited method of warfare because it was "designed to cause 'unnecessary suffering' as defined in Article 23 of the Fourth Hague Convention of 1907."[68] During the fighting near An Loc in the spring of 1972 a girl was hit by napalm and the picture of this naked little girl running in terror along a road in order to escape the battle shocked the world.

There is no question that the use in Vietnam of incendiary munitions caused civilian casualties, including children, but the exact number of burn victims is impossible to establish. The impression created by critics of the war that many thousands of villagers and children were burnt by napalm is undoubtedly false. A team of physicians representing the Committee of Responsibility to Save War-Burnt and War-Injured Vietnamese Children (COR) in the spring of 1967 visited 35 of the 45 government hospitals in South Vietnam and reported that they had seen 105 burn victims, 29 of whom were children. Thirty-eight of these 105 burns (36 percent) were war-caused; the rest were so-called household burns. The total number of war-burnt children seen was 16.[69]

Another medical team, organized by AID and visiting Vietnamese hospitals at the suggestion of President Johnson in the summer of 1967, reported similarly: "Throughout our visit, individual teams paid particular attention to burns. The cases were relatively limited in number in relation to other injuries and illnesses, and we saw no justification for the undue emphasis which had been placed by the press upon civilian burns caused by napalm."[70] In a separate account, Dr. John H. Knowles of the Massachusetts General Hospital, a member of the AID-sponsored team, wrote that, in all, "burns due to napalm are very few and far between. . . ."[71]

Both medical teams agreed that the majority of burns were due to the explosion of gasoline used in lanterns and for cooking in place of kerosene or mixed with it as well as from the spillage of hot boiling water from rice pots. Other observers on the scene, including non-American physicians who worked as volunteers in Vietnamese hospitals, have confirmed this finding. An Australian doctor reported in 1968 that exploding petrol lanterns were "probably a more frequent cause of serious burns in Vietnam than napalm or white phosphorus," and the wife of an English doctor who served on a medical team at Saigon's Children's Hospital wrote that they looked for positive evidence of napalm burns "without seeing a case about which we could be certain. Most of the burns had been caused by domestic accidents. . . ."[72] A radio campaign to alert the Vietnamese to the danger involved in using mixtures containing the highly combustible jet fuel had had some success by 1973, though accidents continued to happen. Two fires in refugee camps, which resulted in the loss of life, were traced to this source.[73]

Another cause of burn wounds which received even less attention outside Vietnam was the use of napalm-fueled Russian-made flamethrowers by VC/NVA forces. One incident that did receive publicity because of the scope and enormity of the atrocity was the attack in December 1967 on the Montagnard hamlet of Dak Son in Phuoc Long province (III CTZ), some 75 miles northeast of Saigon, which contained a large number of refugees. Seeking to drive home the point that the GVN could not protect refugees, some 600 VC, armed with an estimated 60 flamethrowers, attacked the hamlet at midnight. The ensuing massacre left 252 of the Montagnards dead and nearly 50 wounded, 33 of them with severe burns.[74] Bad burns also resulted from the explosion of gas tanks when automobiles hit VC-planted mines.

The fact that hospitals in Vietnam had relatively few civilian patients with napalm-caused burn wounds does not in and of itself prove that few civilians were hurt by napalm. Medical studies have shown that napalm burns are deep and that mortality from respiratory embarrassment, shock, fluid loss and sepsis is high in proportion to the total body surface area involved, especially in the case of children.[75] According to some observers, this meant that under wartime conditions relatively few napalm burn victims were able to reach a hospital alive or, if they did reach medical help, died soon after admission. In conformity with Vietnamese custom, many moribund patients were taken by their relatives to die at home.[76] Napalm, writes the leader of an Australian surgical team which spent three months in 1967 in a Vietnamese hospital, is "an all-or-nothing weapon and just as it was not usual to be called upon to treat bayonet wounds in World War I or II . . . it is rare to see napalm burns; in 3 months we did not encounter a single instance.[77] But the evidence for napalm's unusually high mortality rate is fragmentary and inconclusive and, if true, would bolster the argument made by the military that napalm is a highly effective weapon.

There is general agreement that while many patients with third-degree burns will die without feeling much pain, those who survive or those with less severe burns will experience excruciating pain over a long period of time. But the question whether the suffering caused by incendiary weapons is worse than that resulting from the crush and blast effects of high explosives is debatable, and the claim that this suffering is disproportionate to the military advantage derived from their use is even more doubtful. Because these munitions are grimly effective against underground bunkers and fortified positions and because their area of effectiveness is more limited than that of high explosives, they are not easily replaceable by other weapons. The consensus of legal opinion therefore is that as the law of war stands today incendiary weapons employed against targets necessitating their use do not violate Article 23 of the Fourth Hague Convention because the suffering they cause is not unnecessary.[78] The actual practice of states in resorting to flamethrowers and fire bombs in most military conflicts since World War I further demonstrates that no customary rule of international law exists which forbids resort to these weapons.[79]

Communist protests against the use of napalm in Vietnam in large measure undoubtedly derived, as earlier in Korea, from the fact that the communist side was unable to use napalm as extensively as could the Americans with their great advantage in air power. That is, of course, another reason why the U.S. is unlikely to agree to a ban on napalm, for nations are reluctant to place limits on weapons which give them an advantage over their enemies. "Cobras would advocate the banning of hooves, claws, and cutting teeth but would denounce in the strongest terms a proposal to outlaw venom."[80] Nevertheless, a strong humanitarian argument can be made for a total prohibition of napalm which would go beyond the limitations on the use of incendiary weapons which the U.S. followed in Vietnam.

As we have seen, the ROE in Vietnam urged the avoidance of incendiary munitions in inhabited and urban areas unless the survival of allied troops was at stake or their use was necessary for the accomplishment of the commander's mission. However, this limitation, in practice, did not prevent the very wide use of napalm; in addition, white phosphorus marking rockets were explicitly excluded from the restriction.[81] The Army's *Law of Land Warfare* states that "the use of weapons which employ fire, such as tracer ammunition, flamethrowers, napalm and other incendiary agents against targets requiring their use is not violative of international law,"[82] and the unpublished annotation to this manual explains that "the words 'against targets requiring their use' have been inserted in order to preclude such conduct as the wanton use of tracer ammunition against personnel when such use is not militarily necessary."[83] Yet this intent never found its way into the applicable ROE in Vietnam, and white phosphorus rockets consequently were used rather freely to set fire to houses and huts when neither survival nor essential mission objectives were at stake.

In the absence of a showing of military necessity, and in view of the fact that wounds caused by white phosphorus will smolder long after the initial trauma, it is doubtful that the suffering inflicted upon the human victims of this ammunition can be considered necessary and justified. The issue, of course, transcends purely legal considerations. While the use of white phosphorus rockets to set fire to abandoned huts would probably be perfectly legal, their employment against inhabited villages and hamlets, even when under VC control, raises legal and moral issues as well as considerations of counterproductive conduct in an insurgency environment. In such a conflict it is not enough for government forces to carry out the literal meaning of the law of war.

Incendiary weapons have been the subject of discussion at several conferences convened by the International Committee of the Red Cross aimed at updating the Geneva conventions of 1949. The United Nations General Assembly in 1972, following a recommendation of the secretary general, and again in 1974, passed resolutions condemning the use of napalm and other incendiary weapons. Passage of these resolutions without any negative votes—both the U.S. and USSR were among the abstaining nations in 1974—indicates a widespread aversion to the use of incendiary weapons. However, it remains to write such an aversion into international law.[84]

Tear Gas

The best known of the various types of tear gas, and one figuring prominently in the Vietnam debate, is CS, sometimes called a super tear gas, which is based on a compound developed by the American chemists B. B. Corson and R. W. Stoughton in 1928. First used by the British in the 1950s, CS was standardized by the U.S. Army Chemical Corps as the riot control agent of choice in 1959 and was called CS after the first letters of the names of its discoverers. Strictly speaking, CS is not a gas but a solid used in finely divided particles as a dust cloud. Unlike other types of tear gas, CS causes almost instantaneous reactions in those exposed to it—irritated eyes, nose and respiratory tract, and chest pains, choking and vomiting.[85] CS is used by federal, state and local law enforcement agencies to control civil disturbances. It is believed that about 30 other nations stock CS as a riot control agent.

In mid-1962 the South Vietnamese were supplied with three types of tear gas—CS, CN and DM—which were subsequently used a few times as riot control agents (RCA). In June 1963 CS was tested for battlefield use at Fort Campbell, Kentucky. The first employment of CS by U.S. forces in Vietnam came on 23 December 1964, when CS grenades were air-dropped as part of an attempt to rescue U.S. prisoners held at a location in An Xuyen province in the Delta, though no contact with enemy forces was actually made in that operation. In February 1965 Westmoreland informed the senior advisers of the four CTZs that U.S. policy permitted the use of riot control munitions in self-defense. Kits containing gas masks and CS grenades were issued to each advisory team.[86]

The controversy over the employment of gas in Vietnam began in March 1965 when Associated Press correspondent Peter Arnett described the use of RCA by ARVN forces. At a news conference on 24 March 1965, Secretary of State Rusk explained that there was no question of "embarking upon gas warfare in Vietnam" or of the use of "gas in contravention of established conventions." Involved in these incidents were riot control agents currently in the hands of police forces in many parts of the world, which were employed in Vietnam in such situations as use by the VC of villagers as a protective shield. The desire was "to use the minimum force required to deal with the situation to avoid death or injury to innocent people." This did not represent a new departure of policy. "We do not expect that gas will be used in ordinary military operations."[87]

There followed an examination by both military and political agencies of the pros and cons of the use of CS in Vietnam. Before a decision had been reached, on 5 September 1965, a marine unit in northern Binh Dinh province (II CTZ) commanded by Col. Leon N. Utter encountered an enemy force entrenched in tunnels and bunkers. In order to spare the women and children who were reported to be among this force, and supposedly unaware of any restrictions, Utter ordered the use of CS to clear the complex. This purpose was accomplished, but his action was disapproved by higher echelons and all senior commanders were reminded that "MACV policy clearly prohibits the operational use of riot control agents."[88]

On 9 September Westmoreland asked CINCPAC for authority to use RCA for the specific purpose of clearing tunnels, caves and underground shelters encountered in tactical operations. Past experience, he said, had shown that the destruction of underground fortifications by explosives deprived U.S. forces of potential prisoners and intelligence and caused unnecessary casualties among women and children mixed in with the VC. "I am utterly convinced that the use of RCA is both militarily and morally preferable to the use of high explosive or flame weapons in circumstances where non-combatants are habitually encountered."[89]

Westmoreland first obtained authorization to use CS in one specific operation by the 173rd Airborne Brigade which began on 8 October in the Iron Triangle. The operation was preceded by considerable publicity stressing that the use of CS was designed to reduce casualties to both friend and foe. On 3 November 1965 the JCS informed Westmoreland that he was authorized to employ CS and CN at his discretion to support military operations in South Vietnam, and this authority was further delegated to the major subordinate commanders. The decision to allow the use of RCA was made by the president. The State Department had urged that the somewhat stronger gas DM, known to have caused fatalities, not be authorized, and this recommendation became policy. On the other hand, the view of the State Department that the use of RCA should be limited to humanitarian purposes was rejected,[90] and from that point on RCA were treated as routine weapons. It is interesting to note that a more restricted request made by U.S. commanders in the Korean conflict to use RCA in order to flush North Korean and Chinese troops from certain entrenched fortifications was never granted.[91]

Officers in the field soon began to see many additional ways—not related to the original request to use RCA for the clearance of caves and tunnels—in which the highly effective CS, in particular, could be put to use. The Army's field manual dealing with chemical and biological agents, issued in March 1966, pointed out that in offensive operations CS could "be used to 'flush out' unmasked enemy troops from concealed or protected positions, to reduce their ability to maneuver or use their weapons, and to facilitate their capture or their neutralization by other weapons."[92] Used in this way, CS, instead of promoting humanitarian aims, could become a weapon indirectly bringing about lethal effects. To be sure, CS continued to be employed to rescue airmen downed in enemy territory or in defense of ambushed convoys or to get civilians mixed in with enemy troops out of caves and bunkers. But whenever wind conditions and the availability of masks allowed it, CS was now also used as an offensive weapon to increase enemy casualties. Thus, for example, the commander of Operation MASHER/WHITE WING in the densely populated northeastern part of Binh Dinh province in the spring of 1966 reported that CS was used extensively in the search of houses and tunnels and that it reduced noncombatant casualties. At other times, the commander related, CS was employed to dislodge the VC from their entrenched positions, thereby increasing the effectiveness of artillery.[93] Or again, in the battle of Tam Quan on 8 December 1967, fought in the same general area of Binh Dinh province, CS was used to drive enemy forces from their trenches and bunkers into an artillery barrage which killed 23 of them.[94]

RCA, in the words of a MACV directive regulating their use, thus had become "normal components of combat power extending the range of measured force available to the commander."[95] Between fiscal year 1965 and fiscal year 1969, procurement of CS for Southeast Asia underwent a 24-fold increase (see Table 7-1). By 30 June 1969, some 13.7 million pounds of CS had been used and, as the House Foreign Affairs Committee put it in 1970: "The situation is clearly one in which practice has determined policy."[96] Testifying before that same committee in December 1969, Rear Admiral William E. Lemos of the Office of the Assistant Secretary of Defense for International Security Affairs tried to convince the committee that CS was "a lifesaving part of military operations. . . . The

Table 7-1 Procurement of CS for Southeast Asia, FY 1964–69
(Thousands of Pounds)

1964	1965	1966	1967	1968	1969
367	253	1,595	1,207	4,251	6,063

SOURCE: *Congressional Record*, House, 12 June 1969, p. 4775.

use of CS in combat operations clearly reduces casualties among friendly troops, permits extraction of civilians who may be under enemy control often without casualties, and frequently allows the enemy the option of capture rather than casualties."[97] This was true, but only part of the truth, and when Congressman Fraser pressed Lemos on the question of the use of CS to flush enemy troops out of fortified positions to increase casualties, Lemos became downright evasive: "It is just not possible to answer your question in a definitive way. I would simply state that I know of no deliberate effort to use CS in a way that would insure increased casualties." He admitted: "I do not normally see field reports."[98]

The VC/NVA on several occasions also employed tear gas, making use of captured American stock and, perhaps, also of Chinese-made tear gas grenades.[99] But this did not prevent the Communists from launching an aggressive worldwide campaign charging that the U.S. was resorting to poison gas in Vietnam. During Operation CEDAR FALLS and other campaigns, contended the *Vietnam Courier* in Hanoi in February 1967, the Americans had "used toxic gas to massacre civilians";[100] at a conference held in Paris in December 1969 and chaired by Jean-Paul Sartre, testimony was given about 20 cases of "death from poison gas, the bio-chemical and pathological action of which resembled the deadly 'nerve gas.'"[101] At another international conference dealing with U.S. chemical warfare convened in Paris a year later the North Vietnamese jurist Pham Van Bach called U.S. use of "poison gas" in Vietnam illegal and criminal, and the editor of the *Vietnam Courier* concluded: "In World War II, millions of civilians were victims of toxic gases used by Hitlerite fascist troops. The present war conducted by the USA in South Viet Nam is no different either in its nature or its effects."[102]

At the second session of the Russell International War Crimes Tribunal held in Copenhagen in late 1967, an American soldier, David Kenneth Tuck, testified about the pumping of tear gas into tunnels: "The tear gas does not kill anyone as long as they can get out to the fresh air, it just irritates them. Uh—as far as I know, tear gas was the only chemical agent being used to bring these people out of the tunnels." One of the judges, surprised at this turn of the testimony, made Tuck concede that he knew very little chemistry and he argued that Tuck, therefore, "would not be able to distinguish between various reagents." But the American soldier stuck to his story: "Yes, but on the other hand, we were given training in detecting such as mustard gas, chlorine gas and so forth. So, the only gas that I saw being used was tear gas." Despite this inconvenient testimony, the tribunal, relying on a more dependable "commission of experts," concluded "that the gases used in Vietnam, in particular CS, CN and DM, are used under such conditions which make them always toxic and often deadly."[103] Not to be outdone, the American Committee of Concerned Asian Scholars charged that American troops used "poison gases, and other weapons generally considered illegal in 'civilized' warfare."[104]

The charge that CS was toxic and therefore a lethal poison gas like those which killed many thousands of soldiers in World War I or like that used in the Nazi gas chambers rests on a *non sequitur.* An international committee of experts appointed by the UN secretary general, which included Russian, Polish and Czech scientists, submitted a unanimous report in June 1969 which stated that tear gases are called "incapacitating because the ratio between the lethal and incapacitating doses is very high." CS was found to be "the least toxic of the tear gases"; the report acknowledged that "human beings vary in their sensitivity to, and tolerance of, tear and harassing gases" and that the toxicity of these gases varies "in different environmental conditions."[105] Yet, as Dr. Ivan L. Bennett, a member of this committee, pointed out, this does not mean that one cannot distinguish between lethal and nonlethal agents "on the basis of the statistical probability of their effects if disseminated in a specific amount among a given target population."[106] Evidence from animal experimentation extrapolated to humans, two other American scientists have written, indicates "that for CS the difference between an incapacitating exposure and one that might produce serious lasting effects is quite large, a factor of many thousands."[107]

A Canadian physician working at the Tuberculosis Hospital at Quang Ngai from May 1965 to August 1968 has reported the occurrence of death from exposure to gas in nine cases of women and children who either had an already diseased lung or were in a generally debilitated state because of other diseases or malnutrition,[108] but no independent confirmation of this report is available. The Stockholm International Peace Research Institute, after a careful review of all reports about CS casualties in Vietnam, concluded that while these allegations should not be dismissed out of hand, there could be no certainty about their truth, for "all are unsubstantiated."[109] This coincides with the official American position, which holds that "there is no known verified instance of lethality by CS, either in Vietnam or anywhere else in the world where it has been used to control disturbances by many governments."[110]

There is no assurance, of course, that even in situations of riot control some of those exposed to RCA will not feel the effects of these agents more seriously than others, but a large number of nations continue to use them. It would seem, a political scientist has written, that opposition to the use of CS in Vietnam became "merely another stick with which to beat U.S. Southeast Asia policy over its head." If Britain in 1940, on the point of being overrun by Hitler's panzers, had used such gas on its beaches, the whole world would probably have applauded.[111] This is not to say that the legality of the use of RCA in military operations is perfectly established. Questions can be raised, though the issues are more complex than most critics have allowed.

Several international conventions adopted before World War I attempted to regulate the use of gas in war, but their wording was highly restrictive and so was their application among states. Thus when gas was used on a large scale in World War I, causing close to 100,000 deaths and over 1,000,000 injuries, it could be argued that this practice was not illegal. The Hague Gas Declaration of 1899, for example, prohibited merely "the use of projectiles the *sole* object of which is the diffusion of asphyxiating or deleterious gases" (my italics), while many of the gas projectiles used in World War I also projected shrapnel.[112] The most significant international agreement dealing with gas and bacteriological methods of warfare is the Geneva protocol of 1925 which bans "the use in war of asphyxiating, poisonous or other gases, and of all analogous liquids, materials or devices." The protocol went into effect in 1928 and by 1973 had been ratified or acceded to by 104 states.[113]

By the time of the Vietnam war, the U.S. was among the few big nations of the world which had not accepted the Geneva gas protocol, for the Senate in 1926 had failed to ratify the treaty. The Army's manual of land warfare then in force therefore stated: "The United States is not a party to any treaty, now in force, that prohibits the use in warfare of toxic or nontoxic gases."[114] But the manual did not affirm the absence of a customary rule of international law restricting the employment of gas, as it did in regard to atomic weapons, and the acceptance of such a binding customary norm prohibiting at least the first use of lethal gases could be inferred from a number of American pronouncements. For example, at the beginning of World War II, President Roosevelt had called poisonous gases inhumane and barbarous and "outlawed by the general opinion of civilized mankind. . . . I state categorically that we shall under no circumstances resort to the use of such weapons unless they are first used by our enemies."[115] On the other hand, there was no agreement on the existence of either a customary or conventional rule prohibiting the use of nonlethal gases.

The controversy over whether the 1925 Geneva protocol outlaws the use in warfare of RCA is based in part on a difference between the English and French texts of the convention, both of which are accepted as authentic. Whereas the English version bans the use of "asphyxiating, *poisonous or other gases*," the French text forbids the use in warfare of "gas asphyxiants, *toxiques ou similaires*" (my italics). The English text seems to suggest a broad interpretation, banning *poisonous and all other gases*, while the French text appears to prohibit merely *toxic and similar gases*. But such a narrow reading is by no means conclusive because even incapacitating, nonlethal gases can be considered toxic, though, of course to a lesser degree. On the other hand, one must also take into account the circumstances surrounding the adoption of the Geneva protocol. The framers of the 1925 convention lifted the texts of both the English and French versions verbatim from the Versailles treaty of 1919, which was concerned with prohibiting Germany from manufacturing or employing the lethal gases used in World War I. From this one can conclude that the Geneva protocol was meant to apply only to the kinds of gases which caused such horrendous casualties in the first world war. Resolution of this dispute is not helped by the disagreements which surfaced at various disarmament conferences held between the two world wars, by the varying practices of states or by the fact that a large number of nations ratified the Geneva protocol with reservations.[116]

At the time that the U.S. was using RCA in support of military operations in Vietnam there thus existed considerable uncertainty regarding the legality of this practice. When the UN General Assembly in 1966 called for strict observance of the Geneva gas protocol and invited all states to accede to it, the United States and other governments again denied that this convention applied to RCA, and these same disagreements surfaced again during another UN debate on chemical and biological weapons in 1969.[117] The French jurist Henri Meyrowitz, generally critical of U.S. policies and practices in Vietnam, probably expresses the consensus of legal opinion when he writes: "In the current state of positive law, it is thus impossible to affirm with certainty that, in a general fashion, the use by the United States of incapacitating agents or irritants is illegal."[118]

A legal objection could perhaps be framed not against all use of RCA in military operations but against their routine use. As we have seen, the U.S. State Department unsuccessfully argued against the approval of this practice in 1965, and the legal argument against such routine use draws strength from the position taken by the U.S. at various international conferences dealing with the legality of RCA. In all of these discussions the U.S. stressed the humane character of RCA and implied that it would or was employing them only to minimize the suffering caused by war. Thus the U.S. delegate to the First Committee of the UN General Assembly in 1966 declared: "It would be unreasonable to contend that any rule of international law prohibits the use in combat against an enemy, *for humanitarian purposes,* of agents that Governments around the world commonly use to control riots of their own people" (my italics).[119] It could be argued that the employment of RCA in combat for humanitarian purposes such as the recovery of wounded personnel or the separation of combatants and noncombatants is in line with the humane goals of the Geneva protocol, but that their routine use—which, in effect, often increases casualties— violates that underlying humanitarian spirit. Yet enemy combatants are, of course, a legitimate military target; hence the practice of using RCA to help bring about the death of enemy soldiers flushed out of protective positions while claiming that RCA were being used for lifesaving and humanitarian purposes raises an issue of disingenuousness, if not outright duplicity, but not of illegality.

It has also been argued that once combatants have been incapacitated by RCA, they are thereby placed out of combat within the meaning of Article 3 of the 1949 Geneva conventions and, like combatants wounded by other weapons, must be "treated humanely" and "collected and cared for."[120] But, of course, soldiers incapacitated by RCA are not entirely *hors de combat;* they can still use their weapons, even if in a less effective manner, and they cannot just be "collected" like other wounded who are indeed out of combat. Two well-known legal authorities, Professors Thomas and Thomas, therefore maintain: "Since they are disabled by the tear gas for a short time only and can quickly return to battle, the killing by bombing would appear to be justified by military necessity as a proportionate measure necessary to bring about the submission of the enemy as soon as possible."[121]

With criticism of U.S. military tactics in Vietnam mounting, President Nixon on 25 November 1969 renounced the first use of lethal and incapacitating chemical weapons, except for RCA, and stated that he would resubmit the Geneva protocol to the Senate. The formal submission came in August 1970; both Britain and Japan by then were on record as supporting the U.S. view that the protocol did not apply to RCA. But the Senate Foreign Relations Committee argued that it would be in the interest of the U.S. to ratify the protocol without restrictive understandings and therefore failed to take action.[122]

Meanwhile American participation in the war in Vietnam was winding down, and many supporters of U.S. objectives in Vietnam argued that the benefits the U.S. had derived there from the use of RCA were not worth the cost. "The United States has isolated itself politically in this case," argued Prof. Howard S. Levie, formerly in the U.S. Judge Advocate General Corps. Just as CS in Vietnam had come into use for limited, humanitarian reasons but had quickly turned into a major combat weapon, so the danger existed that the unrestricted employment of RCA could in some future conflict gradually escalate into full-fledged gas warfare.[123] In other words, the only sure protection against such a dangerous escalation of violence—the only reliable firebreak—was the principle of "no gas."

This all-or-nothing argument, which in effect demanded that war remain destructive in order to remain controllable, did not carry the day. In the latter part of 1974, the Ford administration launched a new initiative to obtain Senate ratification of the Geneva protocol. The new proposal put before the Foreign Relations Committee on 10 December by Fred Ikle, director of the Arms Control and Disarmament Agency, in effect embraced the position taken by the State Department in 1965. The U.S., said Ikle, was prepared to renounce as a matter of national policy the first use of RCA except in defensive military modes to save lives—to control rioting prisoners of war, to protect civilians used to mask or screen attacks, to rescue remotely isolated personnel such as downed aircrews, to protect convoys in rear-echelon areas. Under an earlier directive still in force, any such use would have to be approved in advance by the president himself. Two days later the Foreign Relations Committee unanimously approved the Geneva gas protocol of 1925; on 16 December the Senate voted its approval, also unanimously. President Ford approved ratification on 22 January 1975,[124] and on 8 April 1975 he signed Executive Order No. 11850 formally renouncing first use of RCA except in the defensive circumstances mentioned. This now is national policy.

Defoliation and Crop Destruction

During the late 1940s British forces in Malaya employed chemicals to defoliate thick growth along important lines of communications with a fair degree of effectiveness; American tests of defoliation began in 1958–59. In June 1961 a joint American–South Vietnamese Combat Development Test Center was established in Saigon which later that year started experimental tests of dissemination devices and commercially available herbicides for purposes of defoliation and crop destruction. The results were positive, and in early December MAAG informed Washington that the GVN proposed the undertaking of a "crop warfare program" by means of chemicals. Such a program would be merely an extension of the present program of destroying VC crops and food whenever found in the field; the denial of food "would drive VC and their supporters out of their safe haven at last."[125]

Concerned about adverse political repercussions among the South Vietnamese people as well as communist charges of germ warfare, the U.S. decided against the release of chemicals for this purpose. Instead, on 3 January 1962 President Kennedy authorized limited operational testing of defoliation operations, and the first defoliant spray flights flown by U.S. Air Force planes took place on 13–16 January under the code name RANCH HAND, covering a stretch of approximately 16 miles of road west of Saigon.[126]

Pressure from the GVN and MAAG for an extension of the defoliation program and for the beginning of crop destruction continued despite early meager results. In October 1962 the first large-scale defoliation mission was flown by American planes against some 8,000 acres of mangrove forest along rivers and canals in the Ca Mau Peninsula, a long-time VC stronghold in the southern tip of South Vietnam. The planes flew under rules which required a Vietnamese observer aboard. The first crop destruction mission carried out by South Vietnamese personnel and helicopters was undertaken on 21 November 1962. By March 1963 authority to order defoliation missions without submission of each detailed plan to Washington for approval had been delegated to COMUSMACV and the ambassador in Saigon. Crop destruction missions had to be approved by the assistant secretary of state for Far Eastern affairs and DOD. The guidelines laid down that defoliation operations should be few in number; crop destruction was to be "confined to remote areas known to be occupied by VC. It should not be carried out in areas where VC are intermingled with native inhabitants and latter cannot escape."[127]

Once approved in principle, both defoliation and crop destruction programs quickly escalated, reaching a high point in 1967 (see Table 7-2). Between 1965 and 1971, 3.2 percent of South Vietnam's cultivated land and 46.4 percent of the total forest area were sprayed one or more times.[128] Most of these areas were indeed thinly populated. Only about 3 percent of the population lived in defoliated areas, and less than 1 percent in areas where crops were destroyed.[129] Crop destruction was limited to VC-controlled territory in I, II and III CTZ "where food is scarce and where denial of food would create an operational burden on the enemy." Special care was to be taken to prevent damage to rubber and fruit trees.[130] The entire herbicide program was formally directed by the GVN; U.S. person-

Table 7-2 Defoliation and Crop Destruction Coverage, 1962–70 (Acres)

	Defoliation	Crop Destruction	Total
1962	4,940	741	5,681
1963	24,700	247	24,947
1964	83,486	10,374	93,860
1965	155,610	65,949	221,559
1966	741,247	103,987	845,144
1967	1,486,446	221,312	1,706,758
1968	1,267,110	63,726	1,330,836
1969	1,198,444	64,961	1,263,405
1970	220,324	32,604	252,928
Total	4,747,587	481,897	5,229,484

SOURCE: MACV, *Command History 1970*, vol. II, p. XIV-6.

nel assisted in the selection of targets, planning and evaluation. A special Air Force unit flew transport (C-123) planes with spraying equipment in what was known as Operation RANCH HAND. Aircraft participating in the crop destruction program had to be flown under FARMGATE rules which required Vietnamese markings and a Vietnamese observer aboard.[131] Final authority to approve C-123 defoliation and crop destruction operations was in the hands of COMUSMACV and the ambassador.

Approximately 90 percent of the total herbicide effort was devoted to defoliation. Carried out along roads and canals, with emphasis on ambush sites and tax collection points, and in jungle terrain, defoliation was held to be effective in improving aerial observation and inhibiting enemy movement during daylight hours. It also improved the defense of base perimeters by opening fields of fire and facilitating observation from outposts. The crop destruction program, on the other hand, drew a more mixed evaluation. There was general agreement that destruction of their crops made many villagers move to GVN-controlled areas. In 1967, when the generating of refugees was an officially encouraged policy, the resultant increase in the refugee population was chalked up as one of the gains of the crop destruction program. One of the objectives of this program, stated an Air Force analysis, "was to separate the VC from the people by forcing refugee movements into GVN controlled areas. Intelligence reports documented the success in achieving this objective."[132] It was also argued that crop destruction had a serious impact on enemy food supplies and, in some instances, had forced the VC to divert tactical units from combat missions to food procurement tasks. In areas where extensive crop destruction missions had been carried out, the number of VC defectors was said to have increased as a result of low morale resulting primarily from food shortages.[133]

These findings were challenged by a study of the crop destruction program made by the Rand Corporation in 1967. The study maintained that the VC themselves grew only about one percent of their food and obtained the bulk of their food supplies from the indigenous population. Given the close relationship between the VC and the rural population, the major portion of the crops destroyed through aerial spraying was therefore inevitably civilian-owned and cultivated; it was estimated that more than 325,000 villagers were affected by these spraying operations. "Civilian crops are often destroyed (or partially so) incidentally to an operation against VC crops or cover, but they have also been destroyed purposely with the intent, implied if not stated, of cutting off Viet Cong food sources." Chemical crop destruction struck at central values of the peasant's life—his food supply and his handiwork—and it threatened to disrupt his total pattern of existence. Eighty-eight percent of the villagers interviewed blamed the US/GVN for the destruction of their crops and 74 percent expressed outright hatred. Local food shortages were the usual consequence of a spraying operation, with the burden falling not on the VC but on the general population. Since the crop destruction program did not have a significant effect on VC food supplies, while on the other hand it had a definitely adverse effect on the peasants' attitude toward their own government, the Rand study concluded that the program was probably counterproductive and should be discontinued.[134]

There was other evidence that crop destruction was a liability to the pacification program. An Air Force study in October 1967 pointed out that, despite the explaining leaflets dropped, few people in the countryside understood the purpose of the crop destruction program, that VC propaganda effectively exploited the rural population's great fear of these operations, and that some had joined the VC because of the damage they had incurred. The chief sufferers when crops were destroyed were the local people, because the VC compensated for their losses by confiscating a greater portion of the people's food.[135] But MACV resisted these arguments. While empirical data on the effects of herbicide operations on the VC/NVA were lacking, a message to the JCS in late 1967 stated, "current intelligence reports establish the validity of the program." Large numbers of civilians were moving to GVN-controlled areas "and as a result, the VC suffered manpower shortages for support purposes."[136] Several new reviews were commissioned during the next two years by the U.S. mission, COMUSMACV and CINCPAC; but despite some minor criticism of the poorly functioning compensation program for accidental damage and the ineffective psychological warfare operations designed to combat enemy propaganda, these reviews recommended a continuation of crop destruction.

The question whether the crops destroyed belonged to the civilian population or were grown solely for the enemy's armed forces had important consequences for pacification, but it was also of significance in assessing the legality of herbicide operations. There exists general agreement that enemy forces may be deprived of food and water in order to compel them to surrender. But when measures are taken to render stocks of food and water unusable, this intent should be evident to the enemy to avoid offending Article 23(a) of Hague Convention IV which forbids employment of "poison or poisoned weapons"[137] and thus prohibits the deliberate contamination of food and water actually consumed by the enemy.

American acceptance of the legality of the chemical destruction of crops used by enemy forces was based on a memorandum prepared in March 1945 by Maj. Gen. Myron C. Cramer, then judge advocate general, concerning the possible use of chemical anticrop agents against pockets of Japanese on the Pacific islands. Cramer argued that the use of chemical agents to destroy cultivations or retard their growth would not violate international law provided "that such chemicals do not produce poisonous effects upon enemy personnel, either from direct contact, or indirectly from ingestion of plants and vegetables which have been exposed thereto."[138] Following this interpretation, the Army's manual of land warfare states that the prohibition of the employment of poison and poisoned weapons "does not prohibit measures being taken to dry up springs, to divert rivers and aqueducts from their courses, or to destroy, through chemical or bacterial agents harmless to man, crops intended solely for consumption by the armed forces (if that fact can be determined)."[139] But in Vietnam it was impossible to establish with certainty that the crops to be destroyed were intended solely for the enemy's armed forces. Hence crop destruction missions were disguised as a South Vietnamese activity and flown under FARMGATE rules.

In situations where it cannot be determined whether crops are intended solely for consumption by enemy armed forces, crop destruction can still be lawful if such destruction is demanded by the necessities of war and is not disproportionate to the military advantage gained. The property of noncombatants in a war zone does not enjoy complete immunity from attack and the humanitarian principle that noncombatants not be deprived of food is similarly not absolute. It is considered legal to prevent noncombatants from leaving a besieged place in order to worsen the logistical burden of the defenders and hasten their surrender.[140] The 1949 Geneva convention for the protection of civilian persons requires the passage of "essential foodstuffs . . . intended for children under fifteen, expectant mothers and maternity cases," subject to the condition that there are no serious reasons for fearing "that the consignments may be diverted from their destination" or will cause a definite advantage to the enemy's military efforts or economy.[141] While the application of some of these provisions to conflicts not of an international character is questionable, they do show that civilians may in certain circumstances be deprived of food. In the *Hostage* case, the Nuremberg tribunal recognized that in response to guerilla activity it may be lawful to impose "restrictions on food supplies,"[142] and, as we saw earlier, Professor Lauterpacht in extreme cases even grants the right of general devastation in order to deprive guerillas of their sustenance. However, the fact that crop destruction missions in Vietnam were flown under FARMGATE rules suggests that the U.S. did not want to rest its legal case on such an interpretation of the law.

According to most evidence available now, crop destruction primarily hurt the civilian population, and its effects turned Vietnamese opinion against the GVN and its American ally. But MACV at the time believed otherwise. "The crop destruction program," concluded yet another review undertaken with the participation of various civilian agencies in late 1970, "made an effective contribution to the overall resource-denial program. The enemy's combat effectiveness was reduced as a result of the missions."[143] Obtuseness and mistakes in judgment may lose wars, but unless they are the result of culpable negligence they do not constitute war crimes.

There is next the question whether herbicides used for defoliation and crop destruction did have poisonous effects upon humans and therefore violated Hague Convention IV. This, of course, was the charge made by communist propaganda from the time that herbicides were first employed in Vietnam in 1962. By 1963 Hanoi was alleging that allied troops were using chemicals to wage a war of extermination against the people of South Vietnam. But when a Polish member of the International Control Commission, who was supposed to lend his name and position to the propaganda campaign, asked for substantiating details, such as the names and addresses of victims, and suggested an investigation to secure proof, he was put off with a lecture on the decadence of capitalism and the antihumane nature of imperialism.[144] The North Vietnamese allege that between 1961 and 1970 herbicides killed 1,622 and poisoned 1,536,016 people. At a conference held in Paris in December 1970, North Vietnamese scientists charged that the massive and prolonged utilization of herbicides caused permanent ocular lesions, chromosome alterations and congenital malformations.[145]

Criticism of the use of herbicides from the ranks of the American scientific community at first was limited to concern for the ecology of South Vietnam and did not endorse communist charges of poisonous effects on humans. The first intimation of possible harm to man came when a study by the Bionetic Research Laboratories of selected pesticides and industrial chemicals used in the U.S., undertaken for the National Cancer Institute during the period 1965–68, reported teratogenic effects (malformations) in test animals caused by 2,4,5-T, a component of agent Orange (named for the color markings on its shipping container), the principal herbicide used in Vietnam. This study, filed and forgotten, was found accidentally in an office of the Food and Drug Administration in the summer of 1969, and when brought to the attention of the White House led to an announcement on 29 October 1969 that the use of 2,4,5-T was being partially curtailed. When other studies confirmed the teratogenic effects of 2,4,5-T, DOD began to reduce the scope of the herbicide program. On 11 March 1970 it was announced that all defoliation operations in Vietnam were being reduced by 25 percent, and on 15 April 1970 the use of agent Orange was suspended pending a review. At the same time, the Department of Agriculture announced a ban on the domestic use of 2,4,5-T except along rights-of-way and in remote forest and range areas.[146]

The suspension of agent Orange resulted in a further decrease of herbicide operations. Because of a shortage of agent Blue, the other most commonly used herbicide in Vietnam, two brigades of the Americal Division in the summer of 1970 continued to use agent Orange for crop destruction in violation of the suspension order. A subsequent investigation by the MACV inspector general revealed that brigade and division commanders had falsified reports to hide this practice. Disciplinary action was taken against the officers involved and remaining stocks of agent Orange were put under stringent control.[147] Both defoliation and crop destruction were phased out completely by 30 June 1971.

Meanwhile reports were coming out of Vietnam of an increase in the number of stillbirths and birth defects among Vietnamese exposed to herbicide operations. In 1969 the American Association for the Advancement of Science (AAAS) appointed a Herbicide Assessment Commission to be headed by Professor Matthew Meselson of Harvard University. The commission spent several months in preparatory study and in the summer of 1970 went on an inspection tour of about six weeks in South Vietnam. In its report to the AAAS in December 1970 the commission stated that it had found no evidence of the sudden or new appearance of congenital abnormalities, but added that inadequate health statistics and wartime conditions made any firm conclusions impossible.[148]

In October 1970 Congress ordered the secretary of defense to contract with the National Academy of Science (NAS) for a full study of herbicide operations in Vietnam. This assignment was undertaken by a committee headed by Dr. Anton Lang, director of the Michigan State University/Atomic Energy Commission Plant Research Laboratory, and a lengthy report was completed by January 1974. The committee had received reports of serious illness and death allegedly caused by herbicide operations, especially among children of the Montagnard people heavily affected by the crop destruction program, but it could not visit the central highlands and concluded that, in the absence of medical studies of the exposed populations, these reports could be neither confirmed nor refuted. The committee urged that these reports not be dismissed out of hand and be followed up once peace was restored in these areas. With regard to congenital malformations, the committee studied the records of several hospitals but could find no conclusive evidence of an association between herbicides and birth defects. The committee recommended further studies of the effects of dioxin, an ingredient of agent Orange known to have teratogenic effects in mice and rats, which could be found in the Vietnamese food chain.[149]

As of now, therefore, we have no firm scientific evidence of any direct danger to human health caused by herbicides. The reported increase in the incidence of birth defects may simply be a result of the fact that in the late 1960s more people in Vietnam were receiving medical care which would lead to more reporting of such cases. The damage to the ecology of South Vietnam has no doubt been substantial, though the NAS study shows that the fertility of the soil has not suffered any permanent damage, and the loss of timber stocks has also been somewhat less than originally feared.[150] The charge of "ecocide" has been a politically effective slogan, though its precise meaning is not clear and no evidence whatever of any lasting damage to the economic sustenance of South Vietnam has so far been produced. In any event, the issue of ecological damage is irrelevant to the question whether herbicides violate the Hague Convention, which is concerned only with the effect of weapons upon humans. In a situation where defoliation could prevent casualties, the preoccupation with environmental issues also demonstrated a certain callousness and indifference to the value of human life.

It is possible to argue that the military should have been more alert and sensitive to the possible biological consequences of herbicide operations, but it must be remembered that the herbicides in question had been used worldwide for the control of weeds and unwanted vegetation without causing serious hazards. The record of the military in this respect is probably no worse than that of civilian policy-makers with regard to various domestically used pesticides and herbicides. Here, too, use continued for a long time despite considerable controversy over long-range effects. Soon after serious questions about the teratogenic effects of agent Orange had been raised, its use was suspended, and the entire herbicide effort was finally halted. The charge of a deliberate violation of article 23(a) of Hague Convention IV, forbidding the employment of poison or poisoned weapons, would therefore appear to be baseless.

Another legal challenge to the use of herbicides in war has been based on the Geneva gas protocol of 1925 which, in addition to poisonous gases, forbids the use of "all analogous liquids, materials or devices" and "bacteriological methods of warfare."[151] Even though the U.S. at the time of the war in Vietnam was not a party to this treaty, it has been argued that the treaty had become declaratory of customary law and therefore was binding on all states irrespective of their adherence to the protocol. But there is some question whether the Geneva protocol really applies to herbicides, for both the text and the legislative history are ambiguous on this point. The State Department in 1969 took the position that the U.S., although not a party to the agreement, was "pledged to observe strictly the principles and objectives of the Protocol," but that chemical antiplant agents like those used domestically in many countries, unlike living organisms causing plant diseases, were not prohibited by the protocol.[152] Moreover, even if the protocol is held to outlaw herbicides, it is not at all clear that the use of such weapons has been absorbed in customary law. The fact that little resort has so far been made to them is not in itself decisive. Professors Thomas and Thomas therefore conclude: "The split of authority among reputable international jurists makes evidence of the existence of a customary rule doubtful, and, if it is in existence, evidence of its extent equivocal."[153]

In June 1969 the secretary general of the United Nations urged the organization to affirm that the Geneva protocol did apply to all chemical weapons which then existed or might be developed in the future, and on 16 December 1969 the General Assembly voted such a resolution by a vote of 80 to 3 with 36 abstentions. It declared "as contrary to the generally recognized rules of international law, as embodied in the Protocol . . . signed at Geneva on 17 June 1925, the use in international armed conflicts of . . . any chemical agents of warfare—chemical substances, whether gaseous, liquid or solid—which might be employed because of their direct toxic effects on man, animals or plants."[154] Both the United States and Great Britain denied the authority of the United Nations, an organization only about half of whose members were parties to the protocol, to interpret the meaning of ambiguous principles of law.

While the UN debate was still in progress, President Nixon on 25 November 1969 renounced the first use of lethal or incapacitating chemical agents and of all methods of biological warfare. This renunciation did not include herbicides. A treaty prohibiting the development, production and stockpiling of bacteriological (biological) weapons was signed on 10 April 1972 in Washington, Moscow and London and was submitted to the Senate for approval in August of that year. But the Senate Foreign Relations Committee delayed action, because it sought first a resolution of the riot control and herbicide questions involved in the Geneva protocol. By 1974 the Ford administration was prepared to yield on these two issues and agreed to renounce, together with the first use of RCA, the first use of herbicides in war except for their employment, under regulations applicable to domestic use, for control of vegetation within U.S. bases and installations or around their immediate defensive perimeters. As in the case of RCA, the president himself would have to approve any use of herbicides in war.[155] Executive Order No. 11850, issued 8 April 1975, made this renunciation of the first use of herbicides in war national policy. Both defoliation and crop destruction as practiced in Vietnam are therefore now ruled out as acceptable military tactics.

Cluster Bomb Units (CBUs) and the M-16 Rifle

Cluster bomb units are a refinement or special type of fragmentation munition developed during the early 1960s and are usually referred to as improved conventional munitions. They involve a container or dispenser which holds a large number of bomblets or submunitions. Dropped from an aircraft or fired as an artillery round, the dispenser opens to release the bomblets which, depending on the fuse employed, will fragment before, during or after impact. The military utility of the CBU lies in the large area covered by the widely dispersing fragments traveling at high velocity. CBUs proved particularly useful in flak suppression over North Vietnam where they could either knock out the antiaircraft weapons or prevent them from firing by forcing their crews underground. Primarily an antipersonnel weapon, CBUs can also be employed against logistical installations and trucks.[156] They were used extensively over North Vietnam and the trail complexes of Laos. The first use in South Vietnam took place on 12 February 1968 when an American artillery unit fired such a round in I CTZ.[157]

The North Vietnamese have argued that CBUs are ineffective against buildings or military personnel protected by sandbags and that these bombs therefore were intended solely to kill and wound the greatest possible number of civilians in North Vietnam. They maintained, furthermore, that the exploding fragments penetrate deeply and, because of their irregular shapes, cause wounds which can be compared to those caused by dum-dum projectiles and are very difficult to treat medically. Accepting testimony to this effect, the Russell International War Crimes Tribunal in May 1967 condemned the use of CBUs as indiscriminate, inhumane, causing unnecessary suffering and therefore in violation of Hague Convention IV.[158] Prof. Richard Falk has argued that the "widespread use of such prohibited weapons as anti-personnel cluster bombs and delayed action bombs" raises an issue of criminality.[159]

The evidence to back up these charges is extremely weak. CBUs have proved themselves an effective military weapon and their employment, in the absence of an explicit rule forbidding such weapons, would therefore not seem to violate the ban on the infliction of unnecessary suffering. They cannot be considered indiscriminate, for evidence indicates that they are capable of accurate delivery on their targets. Medical and technical data regarding the degree of suffering and damage caused were discussed at several meetings of experts convened by the International Red Cross, but these evaluations remain essentially inconclusive.[160] The practice of states has established the legality of fragment-producing weapons such as hand grenades, artillery projectiles, mines and rockets. Therefore, as the law of war stands today, CBUs cannot be considered illegal per se.

The M-16 rifle cannot be challenged on the grounds that it is inherently indiscriminate, but it has been attacked as being in violation of the 1899 Hague Declaration forbidding the use of expanding bullets. The U.S. is not a party to this agreement but has agreed to abide by the prohibition of so-called dum-dum bullets.[161] It is argued that the small-caliber, high-velocity ammunition fired by the M-16 rifle tumbles end over end upon impact, that the large entry hole thus created is similar to that produced by expanding or exploding missiles and that the weapon thus causes unnecessary suffering.[162] However, tests have shown that the impact of the M-16 does not differ from that of the Russian AK-47 rifle and other similar weapons. The experts also could not agree whether small-caliber, high-velocity wounds differ in kind and degree from those caused by other weapons.[163] With the technical data inconclusive, there is no basis for the charge that the M-16 rifle (or its Russian counterpart) violates existing international law.

Conclusion

The American record in Vietnam with regard to observance of the law of war is not a succession of war crimes and does not support charges of a systematic and willful violation of existing agreements for standards of human decency in time of war, as many critics of the American involvement have alleged. Such charges were based on a distorted picture of the actual battlefield situation, on ignorance of existing rules of engagement, and on a tendency to construe every mistake of judgment as a wanton breach of the law of war. Further, many of these critics had only the most rudimentary understanding of international law and freely indulged in fanciful interpretations of conventions and treaties so as to make the American record look as bad as possible. Finally, there were the communist propagandists who unleashed a torrent of largely unsubstantiated charges with the hope that at least some of the lies would stick. This is indeed what happened.

If the American record is not one of gross illegality, neither has it been a model of observance of the law of war. Impeccable ROE, based on applicable legal provisions, were issued, but their observance was often inadequate and the American command failed to take reasonable steps to make sure that they would be properly enforced. The greatly improved training courses in the law of war, which were started after the My Lai incident had revealed flagrant disregard of the ROE in some units, indicates what kinds of corrective action could and should have been taken years earlier. Moreover, practice often dictated policy. The use of RCA, for example, escalated quickly beyond the original humanitarian purpose for which RCA had been originally authorized. Similarly, the employment of herbicides was begun on the basis of a legal memorandum prepared in 1945 for a very different situation, and this was symptomatic of the lack of adequate legal review of newly introduced weapons and tactics. In both cases, the U.S. was put on the defensive by the pressure of public opinion and eventually had to make adjustments in policy after the fact.

In October 1974 DOD promulgated a new instruction which required the judge advocate general of each military service to conduct a legal review of all weapons in order to insure that their intended use in armed conflict was consistent with the obligations assumed by the U.S. under applicable international law, including both treaties to which the U.S. was a party and customary international law. The instruction also required that a legal review take place before a contract for the production or procurement of new weapons was awarded.[164] Another directive, issued 5 November 1974, obligated the JCS to "insure that rules of engagement issued by unified and specified commands are in consonance with the law of war."[165] Again, one may wish that such instructions had been issued in 1964 rather than in 1974.

There is no way of being certain that human suffering on the part of the civilian population of South Vietnam could have been mitigated by greater attention to legal considerations and by better enforcement of the ROE. Even if these rules had been applied more firmly, there can be little doubt that the American reliance on heavy weapons and the lavish use of firepower would have exacted a heavy toll in lives, injuries and the destruction of property. American commanders applied the motto "Expend Shells Not Men," and while fighting in often heavily populated areas this manner of warfare was bound to lead to heavy casualties among the civilian population. Failure to pursue an alternative strategy, which would have paid more attention to the proverbial "hearts and minds," is probably a contributory cause of the ultimate collapse of South Vietnam, but it cannot be considered a violation of the law of war. As a judicious observer, Prof. William V. O'Brien, has correctly noted: "There is no question that measures justified by military necessity and security have inflicted grave injuries on the society that they were designed to defend. . . . With such lethal military-political-societal dynamics at work it is not surprising that the law of war provides very little protection."[166]

Efforts to update the law of war in the light of new weapons and military tactics have been under way since 1968. Conferences sponsored by the International Committee of the Red Cross and the government of Switzerland have dealt with incendiary weapons, tear gas, small-caliber high-velocity projectiles, fragmentation weapons, booby traps, and other weapons said to cause unnecessary suffering and indiscriminate damage. Progress so far has been slow, though two protocols broadening the humanitarian provisions of the Geneva conventions of 1949 were adopted on 10 June 1977. The conferences have also taken up the vexing problem of the guerilla fighter who is unwilling to carry arms openly and therefore puts into jeopardy the civilian population among which he moves and fights. These deliberations have been complicated by the unwillingness of Third World nations to accept limits on armed struggle for self-determination.[167]

The need for amending the international law of war in order to codify the world's humanitarian concerns is evident. In the final analysis, of course, law alone, no matter how comprehensive and carefully phrased, cannot assure protection of basic human values. Back in the seventeenth century, Hugo Grotius, the father of modern international law, quoted with approval the advice which Euripides in *The Trojan Women* put into the mouth of Agamemnon addressing Pyrrhus: "What the law does not forbid, then let shame forbid." This counsel retains its moral worth. While the law of war is an extremely important means of mitigating the ravages of war, it cannot be considered an adequate and sufficient measure of human decency. There is need to subject international law to constant moral scrutiny and criticism in order to extend the reach of the law of war and upgrade its concern for humanitarian values. Meanwhile, nations dedicated to basic maxims of civilized behavior at times may have to subordinate criteria of military efficiency to considerations of humane conduct. It is to be hoped that the tragic experience of Vietnam will help men of good will to muster the moral commitment necessary to make humanitarian principles a living reality.

8

Terrorism, Counterinsurgency and Genocide

Attempts to apply the law of war to insurgencies like that encountered in Vietnam and thereby, hopefully, to mitigate the suffering of the civilian population have met opposition not only from Third World nations but also from some jurists in the West. The most prominent proponent of this position is Prof. Richard A. Falk of Princeton University. The argument usually has two parts. First, it is maintained "that the insurgent faction in an underdeveloped country has, at the beginning of its struggle for power, no alternative other than terror to mobilize an effective operation."[1] The situation is said to be one of intrinsic inequality, and the guerilla, therefore, has no choice but to engage in terror, stealth and hit-and-run attacks, a type of warfare which makes adherence to the Geneva conventions quite impossible—for example, he cannot openly identify himself as a combatant or take the required care of his opponent's wounded and captured. Second, responsibility for the suffering of the innocents falls on Goliath and not David, for "insurgent terror tends to be discriminating in its application and to involve relatively small numbers of victims. In contrast, the terroristic tactics of the regime and its supporters tend, as the conflict increases, to become increasingly indiscriminate and to affect larger and larger numbers of victims, most of whom must be presumed innocent of belligerent participation."[2]

This quasi-legal position has had an important political function and effect. In the context of the Vietnam conflict, where this argument was developed, it has romanticized and apologized for the VC's tactics of violence. The resistance fighters allegedly had to resort to terror in order to fight successfully against the oppressive and corrupt Ky-Thieu regime and its American imperialist helpers. In a revolutionary war such as that fought by the partisans of the NLF, it has been argued, one could no more regard the violence of the Vietnamese resistance as criminal than one would the rising of the Warsaw ghetto.[3] The actions of the U.S. in fighting this insurgency, on the other hand, came to be seen as inherently criminal and immoral, a necessary result of a large-scale counterinsurgency effort carried out with high-technology weaponry. According to Falk, "the cumulative effect of counterguerilla warfare is necessarily barbaric and inhumane to such an extent as to taint the entire effort with a genocidal quality."[4]

My purpose here, primarily, is not to evaluate the rival political claims of the Vietnamese guerillas and their opponents but rather to describe certain practices and results of this insurgency/counterinsurgency so as to make the moral calculus a more rational enterprise. Specifically, I will examine the nature and scope of VC terrorism and the attempt of the GVN to cope with it through the Phoenix and emergency detention (*an tri*) programs. I will also address the question whether American conduct in Vietnam substantiates the charge of genocide.

VC Terror

The exercise of violence by the VC/NVA was methodical. The primary instrument of repression—the communist term for eliminating, neutralizing, punishing and reforming enemies—was the VC Security Service, a highly professional organization operating in all parts of South Vietnam and an organic part of the DRV Ministry of Public Security. Key posts in this organization, which in 1970 was estimated to be over 25,000 men strong, were held by North Vietnamese officials. It drew up target lists, manned assassination and abduction teams, arrested and interrogated suspects, maintained detention facilities and carried out sentences.[5]

Statistics on the scope of VC terror are not precise. According to figures considered reliable within a margin of error of plus or minus 25 percent, during the years 1957–72 the VC assassinated a total of 36,725 persons and abducted 58,499 for various lengths of time (see Table 8-1, Appendix II, p. 454). Until May 1967 the figures cover assassinations and abductions of government officials only; it is estimated that for every official assassinated and abducted there were at least four nonofficials killed and two abducted. The figures also do not include villagers killed in attacks on hamlets, refugee camps and the like, or as a result of the shelling of cities and towns with mortars and rockets. Lastly, the data collection system broke down during the 1968 Tet offensive and no firm statistics are available for the period 1 February–15 March 1968.

Statistics for the years 1968–72 indicate that about 80 percent of the terrorist victims were ordinary civilians and only about 20 percent were government officials, policemen, members of the self-defense forces or pacification cadres.[6] The VC directed their violence against the best and the worst government officials. By eliminating those especially competent and energetic they weakened the GVN machinery of civil administration and deprived the country of its natural leaders; by killing corrupt officials the VC could claim the halo of Robin Hood. While torture was generally proscribed, it was at times employed during interrogations. Capital punishment occasionally was carried out by disembowelment with the villagers forced to be in attendance. The Austrian journalist Kuno Knoebl was one of the few Westerners to witness such an execution, of which he provided a harrowing description.[7] However, in general such killings took place well hidden from the eyes and cameras of journalists who had a free run in the part of South Vietnam under GVN control, and whose reports on wartime atrocities therefore inevitably lacked an element of balance.

In communist-published statements the word terror did not appear. As Douglas Pike, a close student of this literature, points out, the victim is "seldom shot or decapitated; he is *punished* or the *Front has exercised its power*. The victim is never a civil servant but a *puppet repressor*, or a *cruel element*; never a policeman but a *secret agent* or a *lackey henchman*. . . . One is not a member of a political or religious group opposing the communists but a *key reactionary* or *recalcitrant elements* (when more than one) in an *oppressive organization*. Always *cruel fascists* are *brought to justice* or *criminal acts against patriots avenged* or the *Front has carried out its severe verdict against the aggressors*, not that non-combatants have been slaughtered."[8] Most of the hapless victims were peasants, teachers, social workers and the like who had sided with the GVN, but by dehumanizing them in this way the use of terror could be rationalized.

The statistics on abductions are somewhat less meaningful. In many instances those abducted returned to their villages after less than a week of indoctrination; there also were reports of youths dodging the draft while their families claimed abduction. Yet in numerous cases those abducted never returned—they were pressed into service, died in captivity or were killed outright as class enemies. This last was the fate of a large group of people from Hue during the 1968 Tet offensive, as part of the most extensive and systematic political slaughter of the war.

A VC/NVA force of about 12,000 men seized Hue during the night of 30 January 1968 and held the old imperial city for 26 days. During this time some 5,800 civilians were killed or abducted; most of the missing are considered dead. In the first phase of the purge local communist cadres, following prepared blacklists, rounded up key civil servants, officers, educators and religious figures—the leaders of the community—and executed them after trials before drumhead courts. Radio Hanoi reported on 4 February: "The Revolutionary Armed Forces punished most cruel agents of the enemy and seized control of the streets . . . rounded up and punished dozens of cruel agents and caused the enemy organs of control and oppression to crumble. . . ."[9] The second roundup involved leaders of organizations, professional people and intellectuals, as well as individuals and their families who had worked for the Americans. An American doctor who was in Hue reports the case of a barber who was brought in with both hands cut off, a form of punishment Robert Shaplen witnessed at the same time in Saigon.[10] But the largest number of people were probably eliminated during the cover-the-traces period when the retreating communist troops seized witnesses of the earlier killings and marched them away to be shot and buried in well-concealed places outside the city. These mass graves were discovered gradually during the following 18 months and yielded some 2,800 bodies. The lack of visible wounds on a large number of these victims, who included two Catholic priests, indicated that they had been buried alive.[11]

A captured VC document with the classification "Absolute Secret" states that during the occupation of Hue the Communists "eliminated 1,892 administrative personnel, 38 policemen, 790 tyrants" and an assortment of other enemies of the party. On 27 April 1969 Radio Hanoi ridiculed the search for the burial place of "the hooligan lackeys who had owed blood debts to the Tri-Thien Hue compatriots and who were annihilated by the southern armed forces and people in early Mau Than spring."[12] Some cadres are supposed to have questioned the extent of the killings, while others considered the repression not extensive enough. It appears that the vast majority of the executions were carried out as a result of rational calculation and very few were due to rage or panic during the communist withdrawal from the city.

The magnitude and ruthlessness of the VC terror during the occupation of Hue left a deep feeling of revulsion among the people of South Vietnam, and Hanoi's sympathizers have made a futile effort to explain away the massacre. The killings at first were attributed to the returning GVN police and to allied firepower during the heavy fighting that accompanied the reconquest of the city.[13] There is no doubt that many civilians were killed during the expulsion of the VC/NVA from Hue, but this would hardly account for the very large number of bodies discovered in sand dunes and other well-hidden places, some in the remotest parts of the province.

Another excuse offered is that the mass executions "were not the result of a policy on the part of the victorious government but rather the revenge of an army in retreat." The vast majority of the victims were supposedly first on re-education lists and were killed during the last few days by cadres embittered by defeat and the loss of many of their comrades in battle.[14] Apart from the fact that this kind of mitigating factor is never conceded by these writers to American or South Vietnamese troops under similar pressure, this explanation contradicts the Communists' own bragging about the large number of class enemies eliminated in Hue and again fails to square with the finding of hundreds of bodies a considerable distance from Hue. Soldiers or cadres killing on impulse or out of frustration do not lead their victims many miles from the scene of battle and thereby increase the difficulties of their retreat.

It must be remembered that the executions in Hue of civil servants, community leaders, and policemen, based on permanent blacklists, were essentially no different from the acts of terror the Communists had been waging all over South Vietnam for many years and continued to carry out during the following years. For example, another wave of killings took place during the 1969 post-Tet offensive. On 28 April 1969 the *Vietnam Courier* in Hanoi reported on the uprisings staged by the people of the Delta during this offensive in 6 provincial capitals, 17 district towns and 150 villages under enemy control, and added: "More than 600 notorious agents of the enemy and traitors were liquidated."[15] Such killings, designed to destroy the ability of the GVN to govern, to even scores or to instill docility in the people and teach them not to cooperate with the Saigon regime, unfortunately were a common occurrence throughout the long years of the insurgency.

The Hue massacre, on account of its calculated character and sheer brutality, received considerable publicity, but the deaths daily inflicted, especially on the rural population, as a result of other terror tactics got far less attention. All of these had a similarly well-defined political purpose—to intimidate, sow a feeling of insecurity, and drive home the point that the GVN could not protect the people under its control. The mortaring of refugee camps was a common occurrence[16] and so was the placing of mines on highways frequented by villagers taking their goods to urban markets. Dr. John H. Knowles, a member of a medical team visiting Vietnam in the summer of 1967, saw the victims of one such incident brought to the provincial hospital of Quang Tri (I CTZ) and commented in his diary: "Never have I seen such human slaughter and misery." Two days later, on 8 August 1967, he wrote of another incident when a bus hit a land mine on the way to Danang (I CTZ): "The V.C. set the mines so they go off only with heavy pressure so they will be sure to get a large number of their fellows (never seen such loaded buses!). Here we go again! The second bus-land-mine catastrophe due to the Viet Cong in 3 days. Are the so-called civilian casualties the result of American guns (haven't seen a fresh case yet) or their own people (Viet Cong caused 16 deaths, 24 injured in 3 days!)?"[17]

The VC tactic of imbedding themselves in hamlets so as to provoke allied troops into attacking and causing civilian casualties has been mentioned. At other times, the VC assaulted villages and hamlets directly with the intention of killing men, women and children and thus causing havoc and panic. The attack with flamethrowers on the Montagnard hamlet of Dak Son (III CTZ) in December 1967, which left 252 dead, was related in the last chapter. On 28 June 1968 another such attack with flamethrowers took place against the hamlet of Son Tra in Quang Ngai province (I CTZ). The toll here was 78 civilians killed, many more wounded and 70 percent of the hamlet destroyed.[18] During the night of 14 June 1970, an NVA sapper battalion, led by local VC cadres, invaded the village of Phuthan some 18 miles south of Danang (I CTZ) and, methodically dropping grenades and satchel charges into the mouths of bunkers, killed an estimated 100 civilians "with the precision of a deadly corps de ballet." An American marine told Laurence Stern of the *Washington Post*, who was at the grisly site, to get all the pictures possible "because I am sick and tired of everyone talking about just American atrocities."[19]

Another terror tactic involving the intentional and indiscriminate killing of innocent civilians was the shelling with 122-mm rockets of Saigon, Danang and other major cities, a clear violation, among other things, of an understanding reached at the 1968 peace talks in Paris. The VC sympathizer Edward S. Herman concedes that "one purpose of some of these attacks was to contribute to civilian insecurity,"[20] and Falk agrees that "firing rockets into the civilian neighborhood of cities" represented "an illegal type of insurgent strategy entailing individual criminal responsibility for their perpetrators and planners."[21] Also in violation of Hague Convention IV, prohibiting the use of poisoned weapons, was the placing of traps with punji stakes—wooden poles or bamboo spikes sharpened to a point—covered with human excrement. The unlucky man plunging onto the poles and pierced by them died a slow death or, if rescued, usually contracted a serious infection at least.

In view of all this it is hard to accept Falk's assertion that the NLF by and large conducted its belligerent operations in conformity with the principles of military necessity, discrimination, proportionality and humanity,[22] or the widespread belief among admirers of the VC that communist terror was discriminating and involved only a small number of victims. The record shows that this terror often was deliberately indiscriminate, designed to cause death and injury to whoever might come into the path of VC mines, booby traps and rockets, and that the number of noncombatants killed and wounded, through deliberate targeting or indiscriminate attacks on populated areas, was indeed substantial (see Appendix I, Table 6, p. 449).

Moreover, the use of these terror tactics constituted an integral part of communist strategy. The allied forces had their share of atrocities, but such incidents for them were a definite liability and they tried, with varying measures of success, to minimize and prevent them. To add to the balance scale measuring the infliction of human misery, as does Falk, the civilian casualties caused by American firepower ignores the crucial fact that these casualties were an incidental byproduct of generally legal military tactics. The killing of noncombatants through VC terror, on the other hand, was systematic and intentional, in violation of the most basic principle of humanitarian conduct in time of war forbidding deliberate attacks upon the civilian population.

In the event of a communist victory in South Vietnam, P. J. Honey, a British expert on North Vietnam, predicted in 1971, on the basis of past performance, that "the minimum number of those to be butchered will exceed one million and could rise to several times that figure."[23] Critics of American policy scoffed at what they called the "myth of the bloodbath," and Hanoi's friends to this day maintain that there is no danger of any such occurrence. It is probably too early to determine which prediction will turn out to be correct. Events so far have followed at least in part the scenario laid out by Douglas Pike in 1970. After a communist victory, Pike wrote, first "all foreigners would be cleared out of the South, especially the hundreds of foreign newsmen who are in and about Saigon. A curtain of ignorance would descend. Then would begin a night of long knives. . . . but little of this would be known abroad. The communists in Viet-Nam would create a silence. The world would call it peace."[24] By September 1976 practically all foreigners, including missionaries, had indeed been expelled from the South,[25] and reports about events there have become sporadic at best.

It is believed that between 150,000 and 300,000 former army officers, civilian officials, labor leaders, and members of anticommunist political organizations as well as anticommunist religious groups such as the Hoa Hao Buddhist sect are being detained in so-called re-education camps. Among those imprisoned are former opponents of the Thieu regime such as Tran Ngoc Chau. Many of these people were arrested immediately after the fall of Saigon; when told to report they were advised to bring with them food and clothing for only a few weeks. But so far few have returned, and reports reaching the West speak of hard labor, an absence of medical care, and starvation in these camps.[26] The news trickling out by way of letters and refugees was ominous enough for a group of former antiwar activists in December 1976 to appeal to the government of Vietnam on behalf of these detainees: "We call for a complete public accounting of those detained or imprisoned, indicating, as well, the charges for which they are held. We call on the Government of Vietnam to facilitate on-the-spot inspection by the United Nations, Amnesty International or other independent international agencies in order to assure that those in the Government's charge are treated in accordance with international covenants regarding human rights. We call on you to release any individuals who are held purely because of their religious or political convictions."[27]

Official Vietnamese spokesmen have denied these charges. Those few still being held are said to have committed crimes against the people or engaged in sabotage.[28] A statement issued in January 1977 by a group of long-time Hanoi sympathizers welcomed the moderation of the government of unified Vietnam and the "extraordinary effort to achieve reconciliation among all of its people." The number of persons detained in re-education centers was said to be "surprisingly small," "perhaps 40,000 at present."[29] Unfortunately, the gullible way in which people like Richard Barnet, Dave Dellinger, Don Luce and Cora Weiss, prior to the 1973 revelations of systematic torture of the American POWs in North Vietnam (see chap. 9), accepted Hanoi's pledges of "humane" treatment does not inspire confidence in their most recent assurances that all is well in Vietnam. The passage of time, which has a way of calling to account wishful thinking, will reveal who is correct.

Counterinsurgency: The Phoenix Program

Among the important measures introduced by the new pacification program that began in 1967 was a stepped up attack on the Viet Cong infrastructure in the villages. This was the apparatus—made up of Communist party, NLF and, after 1969, PRG cadres—which directed the insurgency against the GVN. Its members engaged in acts of terrorism, extortion, sabotage and abduction; they also supported the enemy's military operations by recruiting soldiers and collecting taxes and intelligence, as well as by providing guides, food, clothing, weapons, medical supplies and logistical support. As long as this clandestine organization maintained its strength amid the rural population, the victories scored by the allies in the war against VC/NVA main force units were largely irrelevant. The belated realization of the importance of destroying this politico-military apparatus led to the establishment of the Phuong Hoang (Phoenix) program.

In a war not short on misconceptions, misinformation and propagandistic deceptions, the Phoenix program ranks high as the subject of much misunderstanding. Despite repeated attempts by American officials to explain the purpose and mode of operation of the Phoenix program to both the Congress and the American public, these explanations somehow never managed to catch up with sensationalist media reports and the barrage of accusations made by the critics of American policy in Vietnam who called Phoenix an assassination program and an example of the moral depravity of the American involvement. In evaluating these charges it should be borne in mind that since in the eyes of many of these critics the VC were revolutionaries and fighters for national liberation, the insurgents' use of terror was regarded as a necessary and legitimate tactic, while any concerted action against the VC apparatus became, by definition, counterrevolutionary and repressive.

The Phoenix program was an American-inspired effort to pull together all the ongoing, poorly coordinated and ineffective GVN programs against the VCI. Its aim was to improve the collection of information about the VCI, to identify its members and to conduct operations leading to their apprehension. It was a Vietnamese program for which, as in the case of all GVN war-related programs, the U.S. provided advice and financial assistance. Its origin can be traced to the CIA-directed Intelligence Coordination and Exploitation (ICEX) advisory program in 1967 which sought to improve the collection of intelligence and to bring all military and civilian agencies concerned with intelligence into alignment. On 1 July 1968 the GVN accepted formal responsibility for this program, which was now named Phuong Hoang (translated Phoenix). After 1 January 1969, CIA advisory responsibility was gradually phased out and on 1 July 1969 the program was put under the advisory function of CORDS. By 1971, Phoenix had about 600 American military and 40–50 civilian advisers. Most of them served in the District and Province Intelligence and Operation Coordinating Centers (DIOCC and PIOCC) which supervised the collection of information on individual members of the VCI and planned operations against those identified as VC operatives by using appropriate police, military or paramilitary forces.[30] Those arrested were subject to trial by military courts or to administrative detention assessed by Province Security Committees. I will return to this so-called *an tri* procedure a little later.

In earlier years the pressure on the VCI had been erratic at best. Intelligence was poor and corruption often led to quick release of those arrested. "There is reason to believe," concluded a CORDS study in December 1967, "that any individual possessing a sufficient amount of cash can purchase his freedom at any level of the penal system in Vietnam."[31] The new procedures sought to improve the accuracy of information on the VCI and to achieve a more effective and consistent handling of VC suspects. The word "neutralize" was applied to the overall goal of destroying the VCI—whether its members were captured, rallied or were killed.

The charge that Phoenix was an assassination program arose because reported results always included a considerable number listed as killed (see Table 8-2). When administration spokesmen explained that those killed were killed in the course of normal military operations or police actions or

Table 8-2   Phoenix Operations against VCI, 1968–71

	Captured	Rallied	Killed	Total	Percent Killed
1968	11,288	2,229	2,559	15,776	16
1969	8,515	4,832	6,187	19,534	32
	Sentenced[a]				
1970	6,405	7,745	8,191	22,341	37
1971 (May)	2,770	2,911	3,650	9,331	39

SOURCE: U.S. House, Committee on Government Operations, *U.S. Assistance Program in Vietnam*, Hearings, 92nd Cong., 1st sess., 15 July–2 August 1971, p. 183.

[a] Beginning January 1970, captured VCI were no longer considered neutralized until sentenced to a meaningful jail term.

fighting off arrest with the use of armed force, their assertions were met with considerable skepticism. The administration could have strengthened its position by introducing other available data on the Phoenix program which showed, for example, that during 15 months from January 1970 to March 1971 less than 6 percent of those killed (2 percent of all those neutralized) were killed as a result of special targeting. The vast majority of VCI killed (9,827 of 10,443) were killed "anonymously"—i.e. in the course of operations, many of which were not even initiated by government forces—and were only later identified as VCI.[32] Some of those killed may indeed have been members of the VCI, others were probably claimed as VCI in order to meet the annual target quotas for neutralized VCI set for each province. In any event, the fact that so few of those killed were on the Phoenix target list certainly undermines the charge that the Phoenix program was a program of planned assassinations. But providing these data would also have demonstrated the weakness of the entire program: relatively few operations were targeted against known members of the VCI, for despite a large organized intelligence effort the identity and/or whereabouts of most of these men were just not known. The information, consequently, was withheld and the result was a further widening of the credibility gap.

The program had other weaknesses. Most of those neutralized were low-level members of the VCI playing relatively unimportant roles: during the years 1968 to 1971, only 21 percent of them operated above the local level.[33] Phoenix officials, wrote an American province adviser with a good sense of humor in 1971, had been provided "with a complicated organization chart that ran from the Central Committee of South Vietnam down to the 80 year old woman who is a part-time commo-liaison cadre for the hamlet party chapter. When the Government forces were told that all these cadre were dangerous leaders of the insurgency, they went out and arrested the 80 year old woman."[34] Replacement of those neutralized appeared to be no insurmountable problem, for fluctuations in estimated VCI numbers did not correlate with neutralizations, and overall VCI strength was not seriously affected by them.[35] Toward the end of 1969 MACV estimated that 75–90 percent of all captured VCI were released before sentencing or received prison terms of less than one year. In January 1970 it was therefore decided to discontinue as meaningless the count of those captured (see Table 8-2), for most of these men were not neutralized for very long, if at all.

Many of the shortcomings here mentioned were also pointed out and criticized by U.S. advisers. In a memo to the chief of the JCS dated 7 November 1970, Secretary of Defense Laird called Phoenix a "badly fragmented" program which was not performing adequately, and he suggested that General Abrams appoint a special review group. Such a review was undertaken under the chairmanship of CORDS chief William E. Colby, and the report of this task force, delivered on 12 December 1970, included 27 recommendations for the reform of the Phoenix program.[36] As a result of this review and earlier interventions, the program over time experienced some improvement. To eliminate the temptation by local officials to meet quotas by arbitrary arrests, after January 1970 only sentenced members of the VCI could be credited to the Phoenix program. Over the objections of some CORDS officials, the quotas themselves were retained for their incentive effect. Efforts were made to upgrade the quality of intelligence and of the dossiers on the basis of which action against the VCI was taken. The names of VCI members were publicized in order to generate local correction of the information, and village chiefs had to be informed of operations and arrests in their villages. The offer of rewards for the capture of VCI members was limited to carefully identified, important VCI figures so as to minimize the denunciation of personal enemies.[37]

Concern over the increase in the number killed (see Table 8-2) led to instructions to U.S. advisers that stressed the desirability of obtaining targeted individuals alive so that they could be questioned. "US personnel are under the same legal and moral constraints with respect to operations of a Phoenix character as they are with respect to regular military operations against enemy units in the field. They are specifically unauthorized to engage in assassinations or other violations of the rules of land warfare, but they are entitled to use such reasonable military force as is necessary to obtain the goals of rallying, capturing, or eliminating the VCI in the RVN." Advisers encountering actions by Vietnamese personnel not complying with applicable international law were to make their objections known and to report these violations to the next highest U.S. authority.[38]

The rise in the number killed was probably in large part the result of attempts to fill quotas by including in the count enemy killed in regular combat situations, a practice I have mentioned above. It may also have been linked to the counterterror style of operations of some local anti-VCI forces, since these increases were more marked in some provinces than in others.[39] The charge made by some critics of Colby that the CIA-financed Provincial Reconnaissance Units (PRU)—which were operating exclusively against the VCI, excelled in unconventional tactics and had a reputation of fierce aggressiveness—should be held responsible for the higher ratio of killed[40] is without substance. While the PRU were man-for-man the most effective anti-VCI unit, the number killed by this numerically small force (4,454 in early 1970) did not exceed 7 percent of the total.[41] Their role, therefore, could hardly have been decisive.

Most fundamentally, the weakness of the Phoenix program was, of course, related to the general weakness of support for the GVN among the rural population. As one senior province adviser put it succinctly in 1970, "until a significant proportion of the population is really committed to the government no significant breakthrough is likely to be realized."[42] As long as people were sitting on sidelines and waiting to see who would emerge the winner in the struggle for South Vietnam, they hesitated to risk their lives by providing information about the VCI. The Phoenix program, therefore, had to rely largely on paid informants and much of the intelligence provided by these sources was, in the words of one Phoenix adviser, "insignificant or fabricated."[43] The intelligence collected from a variety of disparate sources was collated and evaluated at district or province levels by outsiders who had no organic connection with the villages and hamlets and who therefore had no real way to know the background of the informants and to determine the reliability of the information provided. The American advisers, often without special training in either the

Vietnamese language or intelligence-gathering techniques, here were of little help.

The same problems plagued the operations planned on the basis of this intelligence; they were carried out by reaction forces which lacked the ties of family, friendship and common interests which bound their opponents into the social fabric of the rural communities. The situation in Long An province (III CTZ), described by Jeffrey Race, appears to be quite typical:

> Instead, these forces, recruited from all areas within the district or province, were retained at district or province level and sent on missions—as indicated by the collection effort—one day to one village and the next day to another. Thus these forces operated in the manner characteristic of conventional war combat organization—independent of their environment—and so did not have the enormous advantage enjoyed by the party apparatus of operating continuously in their home area through a personally responsive network of friends and relatives. This in turn severely handicapped their ability to locate intended targets and to recognize fortuitous ones.[44]

Small wonder, then, that the Phoenix program in many instances degenerated into a mere bureaucratic exercise. The Americans, wrote an American province adviser in the Delta in 1971, furnished "buildings, desks, typewriters, file cabinets, index cards, dossiers, etc. It was inevitable that the program would develop a strong clerical slant. Now, the intelligence is often accumulated, cross-indexed, properly analyzed and filed. That is the end of the process."[45] Success was often measured by the number of intelligence reports processed and dossiers compiled. In some places, Vietnamese officials lacked strong interest in the program because they were frightened of reprisals or had been bought off.

During the first half of 1972 responsibility for Phoenix operations was transferred from the Office of the Prime Minister to the National Police. "Although it is too early to assess the full impact of this transfer," a CORDS study in September 1972 stated, "many reports from the field are pessimistic as to whether a new organization will be able to provide better targeting information than its predecessor."[46] In all, while the Phoenix program undoubtedly made some contribution to the weakening of the enemy's strength in the countryside, most knowledgeable observers felt that the program failed to accomplish a decisive attrition of the VCI. In an August 1970 Rand study, Robert Komer called Phoenix a "poorly managed, and largely ineffective effort,"[47] and this can probably serve as an accurate overall appraisal.

Emergency Detention

Individuals found to belong or suspected of belonging to the VCI—seized by the police, territorial forces or in allied military operations—were either tried by military courts or were subject to an emergency detention procedure known as *an tri.* The need for such an administrative procedure arose from the desire not to have to produce valuable intelligence agents in open court and on account of the difficulty of obtaining sufficent evidence or finding witnesses who would dare to testify against VC cadres. These problems have been encountered in many countries having to deal with terrorist organizations, and the establishment of an administrative emergency detention program therefore has not been unique to Vietnam. Moreover, wartime emergencies often require protective measures unprovided for in normal peacetime legal procedures. Here, too, there are many historical precedents.

During the American Civil War, the secretary of war, in an order dated 8 August 1862, informed all U.S. marshals and local chiefs of police that they were "authorized and directed to arrest and imprison any person or persons who may be engaged by act, speech, or writing, in discouraging volunteer enlistments, or in any way giving aid and comfort to the enemy, or for any other disloyal practice against the United States."[48] Since President Lincoln had suspended the writ of *habeus corpus,* those arrested, no matter how flimsy the charges, could find no relief in the courts. It is estimated that the number of known or potentially dangerous or disaffected persons confined in military prisons during the Civil War was as high as 38,000.[49] During World War II, some 70,000 American citizens of Japanese descent were evacuated from the West Coast, and their detention was upheld by the courts as necessary to protect the country against espionage and sabotage.[50] The Internal Security Act of 1950 authorized the president, acting through the attorney general, "to apprehend and by order detain . . . each person as to whom there is reasonable ground to believe that such person probably will engage in, or probably will conspire with others to engage in, acts of espionage or sabotage."[51] These American examples of detention without regular trial are cited here not as models of democratic practice worthy of imitation, but rather to show that even countries with a long tradition of individual liberty at certain times may decide to abridge such liberties.

Another still more recent example of emergency detention is the internment of suspected terrorists in Northern Ireland, which lasted from August 1971 until December 1975. The system here was a means of detaining suspects who could not be dealt with adequately in the ordinary criminal courts, whether by reason of the intimidation of witnesses or the inadmissibility of evidence necessary for a conviction. By the time the program was terminated, 1,981 men and women suspected of terrorist activity had been held without trial for various lengths of time.[52]

In view of the fact that emergency detention generally involves the detention of civilian persons by their own government, such programs are not regulated by international law. The fourth Geneva convention for the protection of civilian persons in time of war applies to persons who "find themselves, in case of a conflict or occupation, in the hands of a Party to the conflict or Occupying Power of which they are not nationals."[53] Hence South Vietnamese civilians detained by the GVN were not "protected persons" within the meaning of this convention. The convention also does not apply to persons who are citizens of a co-belligerent state (as was South Vietnam in regard to the U.S.) if the state holding them has normal diplomatic relations with their own government.[54] This meant that South Vietnamese civilians captured or detained by U.S. forces were similarly not covered by the fourth Geneva convention. Captured members of the VC main or local forces were considered prisoners of war and were not subject to the Phoenix or *an tri* programs.

None of the specific provisions of the 1949 Geneva conventions are applicable to terrorists except that such persons, like all individuals not considered "protected persons," are to be treated humanely, ruling out, presumably, such punishments as shooting without trial. With regard to the VCI, both the U.S. and GVN accepted as binding Article 3, common to the four Geneva conventions, which prescribes minimum standards of humanitarian treatment to be extended to all individuals not considered "protected persons" within the terms of the conventions. This article prohibits "the passing of sentences . . . without previous judgment by a regularly constituted court,"[55] but this provision is generally held to apply only to sentencing for crimes and does not prohibit emergency detention without formal trial as practiced since World War II in Malaya, Kenya, Northern Ireland and Vietnam.[56]

Even though the detention program was a Vietnamese activity based on GVN legislation in the 1950s, it was advised and supported by the U.S., which acknowledged a residual responsibility with respect to all persons, including civilians, captured or detained by U.S. forces who were turned over to the South Vietnamese. In the American view the fact that the Phoenix program and the *an tri* procedure connected to it did not violate international law did not mean that the *an tri* procedure, in particular, satisfied all criteria of due process. The issue of mistreatment of detainees was raised with regard to the Provincial Interrogation Centers (PIC), built by Vietnamese contractors under U.S. funding. These 44 centers, one in each province, were run by the Vietnamese Special Police, which interrogated VC suspects in order to determine whether they should be subject to emergency detention. This special branch of the national police was advised first by the CIA directly and then by the Pacification Security Coordination Division of CORDS, which was a cover for the CIA. In August 1971, 26 CIA operatives worked with the PICs, providing advice on professional techniques of interrogation and observing the treatment of inmates.[57] CORDS advisers attached to the Phoenix program at times also attended these interrogations.

The Vietnamese police, as we have seen earlier, was not a highly professional organization, and the South Vietnamese generally were reputed to have a low regard for human life and suffering. Hence abuses of persons being interrogated did undoubtedly take place. Specific charges of torture have been made against the PIC at Quang Ngai by Dr. Marjorie Nelson, an American physician with the American Friends Service Committee Project in Quang Ngai city from October 1967 to October 1969, who treated patients sent from the PIC to the prison ward of the Quang Ngai hospital. In a letter addressed to Rep. William R. Anderson she told of seeing "dozens of patients with bruises of varying severity. I also examined patients who had coughed up, or urinated blood after being beaten about the chest, back and stomach. On at least two occasions I was able to document by x-rays fractures of bones following beatings." Prisoners complained to her about being tortured by electricity, forced to drink concoctions containing lime, and being suspended for hours by ropes from rafters.[58] Similar charges were made by the Quaker Service directors in Quang Ngai in October 1972.[59] Allegations of torture at PICs, CORDS chief Colby told a congressional committee in July 1971, had been made in the National Assembly and Vietnamese press. "We have looked into these. On occasion we have found abuses, as I say, unjustifiable abuses, and in collaboration with the Vietnamese authorities we have moved to stop that sort of nonsense."[60]

The success achieved by American intervention against the abuse and torture of VC suspects is difficult to assess. A former adviser to the Phoenix program has written: "While the brutalization of prisoners did occur, interested Phoenix personnel could curtail support for the PIC unless such unauthorized activities ceased. Since most advisers were neither intelligence nor interrogation experts, the tendency existed to provide passive support and not to try and improve PIC operations."[61] In the spring of 1971, Rep. Jerome R. Waldie, together with Rep. Paul McCloskey, on an inspection tour of Vietnam, visited several PICs "on no notice whatsoever to those who were running the center or advising them." He reported to the Congress that he found nothing to indicate the existence of abuses, with the exception of the report of one American adviser who had seen a South Vietnamese interrogator with a rubber hose in his hand.[62] Most American advisers, it appears, tried to get across the proposition that the use of force was not productive of reliable intelligence, and even though the South Vietnamese were not always receptive to this advice there is reason to think that, on the whole, American influence helped somewhat to mitigate the cruelties to be encountered in any civil war.

The *an tri* procedure suffered from other serious shortcomings which American pressure gradually helped to correct in some measure. One such problem was the backlog in processing VCI suspects. So-called communist offenders seized by the police in a village search or by allied troops in the course of military operations were brought after interrogation before the Province Security Committee, which referred them to a military court or, more typically, categorized them as A (leader), B (cadre) or C (follower) and sentenced them to emergency detention. Initially, this committee consisted of an ARVN intelligence officer and six province officials—the province chief, the deputy chief for security, the public prosecutor, the chief of the national police, a representative of the military security service and a representative of the elected province council. The committee was supposed to meet once a week, but the workload was so heavy that suspects in most cases had to wait six months or more before being sentenced or released. Table 8-3 gives an idea of the magnitude of this problem. Every few months several hundred suspects were released or transferred to other jurisdictions to keep the backlog in hand, but the difficulties of coping with the constant influx of VCI suspects continued.[63] Inevitably, therefore, innocent persons were often held for an extended time without a hearing—the result of faulty intelligence, gathered by unqualified personnel, and because some officials were using the program against personal enemies or to extort bribes. As of July 1970, 4,181 persons of the 6,111 captured during the preceding seven months (68 percent) were still awaiting disposition of their cases.[64] Rules in force by June 1971 provided that *an tri* processing was to be completed within 46 days at the maximum, but implementation of this provision proved difficult.

Table 8-3 Communist Offenders in GVN Correctional Centers, May 1968–January 1969

	Sentenced	Unsentenced
May 1968	11,351	11,161
August 1968	11,204	8,721
November 1968	11,237	9,386
January 1969	12,042	10,212

SOURCE: CORDS-PSD.

Ironically, while individuals not guilty of any subversive activity were sometimes being detained, dangerous members of the VCI often were quickly set free. A report on the situation in Quang Ngai province (I CTZ) in September 1969 stated: "Indications are that only about one-third of VCI apprehended are actually convicted and sentenced. The general explanation for this disparity is 'lack of evidence' but there is reason to believe that some VCI escape conviction by paying off some official."[65] While critics of the *an tri* procedure in the West saw it as a program which routinely sentenced all VCI suspects brought before the PSC to long terms of detention, figures showed that until mid-1969 75–90 percent of all captured VCI reported neutralized were released within six months. In addition to corruption, this situation was blamed on poorly prepared dossiers and a chronic shortage of detention facilities;[66] it led to the above-mentioned decision from January 1970 on to count as neutralized only those sentenced to a meaningful term of detention. Efforts at rehabilitation were poor and many of those freed presumably rejoined the VCI.

Table 8-4 Review of *An Tri* Cases by Province Security Committees, January–June 1971

Category	Total Reviewed	Extended	Released	Percent Released
A	215	215	0	0
B	1,441	738	703	48.8
C	3,963	1,060	2,903	73.2
Total	5,619	2,013	3,606	64.2

SOURCE: U.S. House, Committee on Government Operations, *U.S. Assistance Programs in Vietnam*, Hearings, 92nd Cong., 1st sess. (1971), p. 196.

Until August 1971 the PSC disposed of cases without the suspect being in attendance or being represented by an attorney. Based on guidelines prepared by U.S. advisers and promulgated by the GVN, the committees were empowered to sentence category A offenders to detention for two years or more and category B for terms of one to two years, while those in category C were either to be released or held for up to one year.[67] These terms could be renewed indefinitely and in fact frequently were extended, the length and frequency of extension varying with the category of offenders (see Table 8-4). There existed no judicial review of the *an tri* procedure, but the Ministry of the Interior had to concur with the sentences pronounced by the PSC and at times modified them (see Table 8-5).

Table 8-5 Review of *An Tri* Sentences by Ministry of the Interior, January–March 1971

Number reviewed	3,489
Number confirmed	2,530 (72%)
Number modified	
Suspect released	302
Sentence reduced	625
Sentence increased	8
Referred to military court	24
Subtotal	959

SOURCE: Memo, n.d., Detainees and Prisons 1970–74 file, CMH.

The PSC acted on the basis of dossiers prepared by Phoenix personnel which frequently included all manner of hearsay evidence about a person's political views or actions. At U.S. instance, reports from at least three different intelligence sources were required to label somebody as a VCI suspect, but because these dossiers were often of very poor quality there was a tendency to rely on the interrogation report. The reliability of the latter was also, of course, uncertain, with the result that the evidence used by the committees to sentence a person to emergency detention was frequently rather slim. Critics of the Thieu regime in the lower house of the National Assembly and the press charged regularly that the an tri procedure was used by the government against its political opponents, and there can be little doubt that—especially until the promulgation of American-proposed reforms in 1971—many innocent persons were regularly caught in the net. On 15 September 1969 Vietnamese prisons held 13,274 sentenced communist offenders and 8,203 suspects who were not yet sentenced, a total of 21,477 detainees.[68] The number of VCI captured during the period 1 January 1968 to 31 December 1969 was given as 19,709;[69] we know that until 1970 the great majority of these were released within less than six months. Hence it is likely that a significant proportion of those held under the an tri procedure in 1969 were not members of the VCI but were detained for other reasons—to extort a bribe or for what the an tri law called "Pro-Communist neutralism," propaganda and incitement for which constituted "acts of jeopardizing public security."[70]

In 1970 the procedure underwent considerable tightening, largely the result of newly promulgated mandatory sentences for category A and B offenders. The percentage of VCI suspects processed by PSCs who were released or sentenced to a term of less than six months was reduced to 19. But the system now suffered from a rigidity which must have led to new injustices; not only did it require mandatory sentences for the different categories of communist offenders, but there existed a quota for each of these—so many suspects processed to be classified A, so many B (see Table 8-6). There was a saying in Vietnam: Give the Vietnamese a quota and they will fill it somehow. While quotas may have had an incentive effect, they quite obviously also encouraged cheating or the filling of quotas with the wrong people. In either case, the results were counterproductive, and this held true for the body count as well as for the Phoenix and an tri programs.

Table 8-6   Province Security Committee Processing,
January–October 1970[a]

	January–July	January–October
Length of initial sentence		
Less than 6 months	199 (9%)	381 (9%)
6 months–1 year	316 (14%)	597 (14%)
1–2 years	1,048 (46%)	2,044 (47%)
2 years or more	710 (31%)	1,363 (31%)
Number sentenced	2,273	4,385
Number released	341	821
Referred to military court	NA	412

SOURCES: OASD (SA), *SEA Analysis Report*, Sept.–Oct. 1970, p. 31; William E.
Colby, "Internal Security in South Viet-Nam—Phoenix," December 1970, Tab 29.

[a] Percentages refer to the total number sentenced.

The U.S. consistently urged the adoption of more equitable procedures. At a meeting with high-level Vietnamese officials on 26 September
1969, Colby proposed that detainees be given the opportunity to be heard
in person by the PSC before being given an *an tri* sentence.[71] On 12 October 1970 Colby forwarded to the prime minister a suggested revised *an
tri* law which added to the procedure such rights as personal appearance
or other hearing, some form of defense counsel, confrontation of evidence
and the right to a speedy and public trial. It also changed the membership
of the PSC to reduce its majority of police and security officials and
enlarged the supervising function of the public prosecutor.[72] The December 1970 study of the Phoenix program chaired by Colby recommended granting the accused the right to a hearing and defense counsel
"and protection against improper methods of interrogation or detention."[73]

On 2 August 1971 the GVN issued a set of new guidelines for the *an tri*
procedure which incorporated most of these reforms. It granted detainees
the right to appear before the PSC and the right to legal counsel (the text
left it unclear whether the attorney could appear with his client before the
committee). The PSC was barred from renewing a term of detention
unless new evidence, such as recalcitrant behavior while in detention, justified an extension. The membership of the committee was reduced to
three—the province chief, the public prosecutor and an elected member
of the province council. Decisions of the committee were to be made in

public. On 8 November 1971 another instruction withdrew the right of the PSC to impose detention on communist offenders whose prison sentence had expired or who had been acquitted by the courts.[74]

These reforms somewhat reduced the arbitrary character of the *an tri* system and strengthened the claim of the GVN to be a government upholding the rule of law. Yet the practical results of these changes are difficult to assess and, as in the case of many reforms instituted as a result of American pressure, implementation of these well-meaning new guidelines left much to be desired. For example, the right to counsel, as one would expect, in the rural areas remained largely academic, though there were reports that in some cases the availability of legal assistance slowed down the drumhead-court-like procedure and reduced the rate of convictions.[75] The low level of terrorist activity in support of the 1972 Easter invasion in the populated lowlands was attributed to the Phoenix and *an tri* programs. The CORDS senior adviser in Thua Thien province (MR 1) reported at the end of May that to forestall help for the invading NVA forces, 1,370 VCI had been arrested during the month, of whom 814 had been transferred out of the province.[76] The American consul in Danang gave the number of those arrested in Hue and Thua Thien province during April and May as 15,000.[77]

During the 1972 invasion from the North, when the fate of South Vietnam hung in a precarious balance, the need for an emergency detention system could hardly be gainsaid. Yet the *an tri* procedure undoubtedly exacted a heavy political price. The conclusions of a careful study of the interrogation and internment policies followed by the British in Northern Ireland after August 1971 may be applicable to the Vietnamese case as well. These policies helped put terrorists behind bars, but the obvious risk that large numbers of innocent persons would be ill-treated or abused in the course of the arrest and questioning process may have been counterproductive "in the sense that it increased the alienation of the civilian population in troubled areas from the security forces, and thus helped to ensure a continuing flow of recruits to terrorist organizations to replace those who were successfully identified and locked up."[78]

A CORDS legal adviser in July 1968 argued against the use of administrative tribunals like the PSC to handle the flow of civilian security suspects and urged the processing of these cases through the military courts. He conceded that it often was difficult to produce enough evidence to convict members of the VCI in open court and he therefore suggested recourse to charges of draft evasion, desertion, and the forgery of ID cards. The GVN, he stated, did not appreciate the potential of these charges because it had never had to convict gangsters of income tax evasion. Such a procedure was fairer and would prevent the premature release of terrorists.[79] In late 1972 the GVN in fact did use this method to keep members of the VCI under lock and key, but whether this method of coping with the VC apparatus, if used exclusively, would have had better overall results is difficult to say.

By 1972–73 the *an tri* procedure had become a favorite target of attack of Hanoi's sympathizers in the U.S., and the existence of such a system of detention was cited as proof of the repressive character of the Thieu regime. The logic of this argument was surely fallacious. As I noted earlier, emergency detention has been used by democratic nations and the practice in and of itself is not necessarily to be regarded as an unacceptable violation of individual liberty. It is also necessary to reject as a fabrication the allegation that the GVN imprisoned hundreds of thousands of political prisoners. This charge had its origin in Hanoi. On 18 January 1971 the *Vietnam Courier* in Hanoi asserted that South Vietnamese prisons held over 200,000 South Vietnamese patriots who were dying there a slow death.[80] Early in 1973 and after the conclusion of the Paris agreements, the editor of this paper, Nguyen Khac Vien, stated in an interview given in Paris that there were 300,000 political prisoners in South Vietnam. "The men in power in Saigon are determined to exterminate them all."[81] From this point on, the issue of the "political prisoners" became part of a worldwide campaign which aimed at discrediting the GVN and bringing about an end of U.S. assistance to the Thieu government.

In the summer of 1973 a Paris-educated Redemptorist priest in Saigon, Father Chan Tin, charged in a mimeographed handout that as of 1 June 1973 the GVN was detaining 202,000 political prisoners. Chan Tin said that he headed an organization called "Committee to Investigate Mistreatment of Political Prisoners." Western newsmen and Americans visiting Vietnam reported him to be a man deeply concerned with human suffering. In September 1973 some of Hanoi's friends in Washington, operating the "Indochina Resource Center," presented Chan Tin's charges and figures to a congressional committee where they appeared to make an impression.[82] After the fall of Saigon in 1975 it turned out that Chan Tin and several other Catholic priests had been part of the VC underground in Saigon. "They presented themselves as exponents of the Third Force," writes a well-informed European journalist with left-wing political leanings, Tiziano Terzani, who stayed in Saigon after the communist takeover, "but in reality they were part of an operation whose purpose was to back up the struggle of the National Liberation Front."[83]

Chan Tin's figure of 202,000 political prisoners, broken down by category of prison and naming a specific number for each of them, was checked in two exhaustive investigations by American embassy officials in Saigon and was found to exceed by far the total prison and detention population in South Vietnam, which in the July–August 1973 period was around 35,000.[84] This figure included all common criminals and *an tri* detainees. The American surveys were based on statistics supplied by the GVN to the approximately 200 CORDS public safety advisers, who were in a good position to check their trustiworthiness, as well as on GVN records meant for internal use, i.e. what the GVN was telling itself on this subject. The broad accuracy of the embassy figures was confirmed after the fall of Saigon. For example, Terzani reports that 7,000 prisoners were freed from the Chi Hoa prison in Saigon;[85] the embassy survey in 1973 had given the number of prisoners there as 7,911.

But the most serious flaw in Chan Tin's charges was his use of the term "political prisoner" applied indiscriminately to all *an tri* detainees. The *an tri* net, as we have seen, at times caught innocents seized to extort a bribe or anticommunist oppositionists to Thieu's autocratic rule, but to maintain that all detainees were political prisoners surely was to take unacceptable liberties with the meaning of this term. The friendly neighborhood Communist who planted bombs under civilian buses or assassinated teachers and hamlet chiefs surely was no more a "political prisoner" when apprehended than Lee Harvey Oswald or Sirhan Sirhan; the political motive that may have operated in these assassinations does not relieve their perpetrators of criminal responsibility. One can understand that the NLF sympathizer Terzani would refer to a "student who in 1971 had organized terrorist operations against American citizens and installations in Saigon," liberated from Con Son prison in 1975, as a freed political prisoner.[86] But Rep. Robert F. Drinan, a former law school dean, should probably have shown more care in his choice of terminology. Drinan, who accepted Chan Tin's allegations as true, told the Senate Armed Services Committee in July 1973 that the GVN held at least 200,000 political prisoners and "virtually none of those 200,000 have committed an overt act."[87] Father Drinan did not tell the committee how he had arrived at this finding, a feat difficult to accomplish short of reading thousands of court and PSC transcripts.

The naïveté with which many congressmen and other Americans approached this entire problem was exemplified by the support extended in this country to one of the best known "political prisoners," Huynh Tan Mam, the president of the Vietnamese National Student Union. Huynh Tan Mam, supposedly a pacifist and neutralist, repeatedly participated in and led demonstrations in Saigon protesting GVN war policy and U.S. involvement in Southeast Asia, for which actions he was arrested many times. As the *Vietnam Courier* in Hanoi reported happily on 15 February 1971, at a demonstration held on 9 February, a day after the incursion into Laos, "a military vehicle was burnt in front of the U.S. Embassy" and Huynh Tan Mam denounced the collusion of Thieu and Nixon who were "sending South Vietnamese youth to a senseless death in Laos in place of GIs to the only interests of the U.S. imperialists."[88] It is possible to argue that on the whole the GVN could have been more tolerant of political dissent, but it is difficult to deny that leading street demonstrations accompanied by violence constitutes an overt act which a country at war fighting for its life may be unwilling to allow. On 1 May 1975, a day after the fall of Saigon, Huynh Tan Mam was honored and rewarded for his services to the communist cause. At the beginning of the first TV broadcast from Saigon, celebrating the liberation of the capital, after the playing of the NLF anthem and with the screen showing a portrait of Ho Chi Minh, came a speech by Huynh Tan Mam.[89] Knowledgeable South Vietnamese refugees refer to him as a known Communist.

Detention as a VC suspect under the *an tri* procedure, and life in South Vietnamese jails generally, were obviously no picnic. As in most developing nations, the guards were poorly paid and were not paragons of enlightened correctional practice. American financial assistance and American advisers, in the face of heavy odds, gradually ameliorated prison conditions somewhat. Housing, sanitation, medical care and food were improved and the death rate was lowered substantially.[90] It is unlikely that the termination of all public safety programs in South Vietnam, mandated by Congress in 1973, contributed to the greater well-being of the inmates of the South Vietnamese correctional system. But Congress was impressed by the horror stories about political prisoners in South Vietnam and was altogether anxious to liquidate all remnants of the American involvement. Another dubious tale that influenced Congress in this regard was that of the prisoners allegedly paralyzed in the tiger cages of Con Son.

It began with the allegation that the GVN at its Con Son Island prison, a former French penal colony, kept inmates in underground "tiger cages"—a form of incarceration fit only for caged animals. Congressmen William Anderson and Augustus Hawkins, accompanied by staff aide Thomas Harkin and Don Luce of the World Council of Churches, who came upon the tiger cages during an inspection tour of the prison in July 1970, did not report that these isolation cells were below ground. But use of the term "pits" by Harkin and the publication of his photographs in *Life* magazine, taken looking down into the cells,[91] created the impression of subterranean, tiny, dark dungeons.

The imaginations of other writers soon enlarged upon this initial report. The tiger cages, wrote Alfred Hassler, director of the Fellowship of Reconciliation, in 1970, "are too short for even the small Vietnamese to lie full-length in them, and the ceilings are so low that the inmates can barely stand."[92] In 1973 Sylvan Fox described the tiger cages in the *New York Times* as "small concrete trenches with bars on top, in which five to seven prisoners were cramped in a space about five feet wide, six feet long and six feet deep."[93] In point of fact, according to the official U.S. description and measurements, which nobody has challenged as inaccurate, the 48 cells were entirely above ground, located in two windowless buildings with bars forming the ceiling but ordinary doors at the front of each cell, with a catwalk on top. The cells were protected from sun and rain by an overhead roof and measured 6'3" in width, 10'6" in length and 10' in height. The tiger cages had been built by the French in 1941 as punishment cells for unruly prisoners, and in 1970 they were still being used for this purpose, usually five prisoners to a cell. This gave each prisoner about 13⅛ square feet of floor space.[94] The distance of 10 feet from the floor to the ceiling bars would have accommodated a standing human giant and the 10'6" length would have enabled him to stretch out as well.

The prisoners in the tiger cages, the visiting congressmen and Don Luce reported, were unable to stand up and claimed to be paralyzed. "Until a few days ago, they said they had been shackled to a bar that went across one end of the cage. . . . 'We will be shackled again in a few days,' one said as he crawled around the cage using his hands to move himself. One of the prisoners pointed to the scars on his useless legs and said, 'We were shackled here for months.' "[95] The facts again were somewhat different. The prisoners were shackled between the hours of 5 P.M. and

6 A.M. because the doors to the old cells were no longer strong enough to withstand pressure. As to the claimed paralysis, there is evidence to indicate that this condition was simulated by hard-core communist prisoners as part of a propaganda scheme.

On 22 December 1970 and on 5–6 January 1971 three military neurologists examined 116 of the prisoners who complained of paralysis of the legs. They reported: "All patients had normal musculature without atrophy or fasciculation. . . . All patients had normal ankle and knee deep tendon reflexes with no pathological reflexes. . . . In addition, the vast majority of the patients exhibited diagnostic findings of malingering or hysteria. For example: when a patient was asked to flex the knee or ankle, the limb would not move but the muscles used to extend the knee or ankle were felt to contract. In addition patients who complained of total paralysis were observed to move the legs when asked to roll over, slide back on the examination table or remove clothing." The three physicians concluded: "There is no objective evidence of organic neurological disease at this time."[96]

The number of Con Son prisoners who claimed paralysis fluctuated between a low of 105 on 19 June 1971 and a high of 216 on 23 May 1971. All of these prisoners were offered therapy for their condition which they refused. Ten allegedly paralyzed prisoners whose terms of confinement had expired were released on 23 December 1971; another 14 were set free on 15 January 1972 and 124 were released on 16 February 1973. Arriving in Saigon, these men, laboriously moving themselves around by their hands, attracted considerable attention from Western newsmen who generally accepted their claims at face value. A former Air Force physician and a critic of American policy in Vietnam, John Camplin, M.D., testified before the House Foreign Affairs Committee in September 1973 that he had examined 20 of these prisoners in February–March 1973 and had found evidence of organic paralysis.[97]

Hard evidence ends here: the medical diagnosis of the three above-mentioned military neurologists stands challenged by that of a former Air Force doctor. An American journalist reported in February 1974 that according to the Saigon government "the paralyzed 'tiger cage' prisoners, portrayed in widely circulated photographs, were actually Saigon street beggars who were rounded up, paid to pose and claim they were victims of the Con Son cages."[98] During a visit to Con Son, the same journalist found the remaining VC prisoners there well organized; this was also reported by two American political scientists who visited the Con Son prison in January 1974. "It was evident that each cell had its internal infrastructure, well-organized, and with internally designated spokesmen, who were usually well-versed in English and/or French."[99] These reports and the fact that this kind of strong organization had also existed in eight POW compounds during the Korean War, where the communist prisoners staged demonstrations and parades and coerced suspected deviants,[100] suggest that the Con Son prisoners certainly had the organizational capability to stage the paralysis as a propaganda effort.

It should finally be noted that many of those who accepted the allegations of paralysis suffered at Con Son also bought the hoax of the underground tiger cages. Tiziano Terzani, for example, wrote: "The 'cages' were small pits dug in the earth and covered with iron gratings. The prisoners could not move, and their legs atrophied and became frightful sticks of skin and bone."[101]

The Question of Genocide

In 1967 the second session of the International War Crimes Tribunal, organized under the sponsorship of Bertrand Russell, adopted a statement formulated by Jean-Paul Sartre on genocide. The U.S. government, Sartre maintained, was engaged in "wiping out a whole people and imposing the Pax Americana on an uninhabited Vietnam." In the South, specifically, American forces were conducting the "massive extermination" of the people of South Vietnam, killing men, women and children merely because they were Vietnamese, and this represented "genocide in the strictest sense."[102]

The Russell tribunal was not alone in charging the U.S. with genocide. The new military technology used by America in Vietnam, wrote the publicist Theodore Draper in 1967, "produces a dehumanized genocide";[103] American policy-makers, argued Father Daniel Berrigan, have "for some time now, legitimated murder and expanded murder into genocide."[104] According to Pulitzer Prize winner Frances FitzGerald, no one in the U.S. government consciously planned a policy of genocide, but in fact the policy of the military commanders "had no other military logic, and their course of action was indistinguishable from it."[105] The specific violations of the law of war, held Prof. Richard Falk, may have "a cumulative impact that can fairly add up to genocide." Scorched-earth tactics and the use of cruel weapons against the civilian population "appears to me to establish a *prima facie* case of genocide against the United States."[106]

The convention against genocide was adopted by a unanimous United Nations General Assembly on 9 December 1948 and it came into force on 12 January 1951. The U.S. signed but so far has not ratified the convention; however, it probably can be assumed that the prohibition of genocide today is part of customary international law. The crime of genocide was defined as committing, "with intent to destroy, in whole or in part, a national, ethnical, racial, or religious group, as such," acts such as "killing members of the group," "causing serious bodily or mental harm," "deliberately inflicting on the group conditions of life calculated to bring about its physical destruction in whole or in part."[107] The convention thus defines genocide as the deliberate destruction of a group of people, in whole or in part, because of what that group as such represents—its national, ethnical, racial or religious identity. The prototype of genocide which inspired the convention was, of course, Hitler's attempted extermination of the Jews of Europe, designed to bring about "the final solution" of the Jewish question.

Some critics of American policy in Vietnam had to conclude—almost regretfully, it seems—that the UN definition of genocide did not quite fit the conduct of American military forces in Vietnam. For example, the American philosopher Hugo A. Bedau noted that although obliteration bombing, free-fire zones and search-and-destroy missions "tended toward genocidal results," these tactics were not employed with the *intent* to destroy the Vietnamese people *as such*. Thus while the charge of genocide, according to Bedau, had "undeniable rhetorical appropriateness," in actual fact the U.S. had not committed the crime of genocide.[108] That the use of the term genocide was premature was also the position of Daniel Ellsberg in 1970. The war in Vietnam, he argued, so far was "no more brutal than other wars in the past," and the indiscriminate use of concepts such as genocide could blind one to the fact that this war could still become far more destructive in the future. He thought that the term genocide might "be applicable, in a strict sense, to some of our activities in Vietnam, in particular the designation of large, semi-permanent, free-fire zones."[109]

If genocide consists of the *destruction* of a people *in whole or in part,* the first thing to do should be to look at population statistics. According to figures compiled by the United Nations, the populations of North and

Table 8-7 Population of the Democratic Republic of Vietnam (North) and Republic of Vietnam (South), 1965–74 (In Millions)

	North Vietnam	South Vietnam
1965	18.71	16.12
1966	19.18	16.54
1967	19.65	16.97
1968	20.14	17.41
1969	20.64	17.87
1970	21.15	18.33
1971	21.66	18.81
1972	22.17	19.37
1973	22.70	19.95
1974	23.24	NA

SOURCE: *United Nations Demographic Yearbook 1974,* p. 130.

South Vietnam increased steadily during and despite the war, at annual rates of change roughly double that of the U.S. (see Table 8-7). This fact makes the charge of genocide a bit grotesque.

In order to establish occurrence of the crime of genocide one must also be able to demonstrate *intent* to destroy a certain group of people in whole or in part. With regard to the bombing of North Vietnam, I will show in a later chapter that this bombing never deliberately aimed at the population of North Vietnam. As concerns the fighting in the South, the evidence available makes it similarly absurd to argue that the U.S. at any time in the war had the intent of destroying the people of South Vietnam. Indeed, quite the contrary can easily be shown to be true.

While the American way of war undoubtedly took the life of many non-combatants, these casualties were never inflicted as a matter of policy. Moreover, American aid programs contributed substantially to the improvement of public health and the availability of medical care. Between the early 1960s and 1972, AID provided funds for the construction of 9 new hospitals, the major renovation of 11 others, the provision of 29 surgical suites and the construction of more than 170 district, 370 village and 400 hamlet maternity-dispensaries. In addition about 15 percent of occupied beds in American military hospitals were used by Vietnamese civilians. These measures gradually alleviated the overcrowded conditions created in the early years of the war by the load of civilian war casualties. Under contract with AID, 774 American physicians each served a 60-day tour of duty in a Vietnamese hospital; under the Military Provincial Health Assistance Program (MILPHAP) medical teams, each including three physicians, assisted Vietnamese provincial hospitals in the application of medical expertise; every American unit had its Medical Civic Action Program (MEDCAP), which provided medical care in the villages and gave immunizations for polio, TB, tetanus, etc.[110] With all this aid, the quality of medical care in an underdeveloped country like Vietnam often still left much to be desired, and much more could and should undoubtedly have been done. But whatever the shortcomings of the American medical aid program, it surely does not fit into any kind of scheme to destroy the Vietnamese people.

If we add to all this the various aid programs aiming at improving the technological and economic development of South Vietnam, it becomes understandable why the cumulative impact of the American presence was a substantial rise in the standard of living and a consequent population increase. The good effects, a South Vietnamese oppositionist to Thieu wrote in late 1974, "were always intentional while the 'bad effects' were unintentional. They were the side-effects, the by-products of the war and the American presence. A mixed blood abandoned child typifies unintentional 'bad' while the Land-to-the-Tiller program typifies the intentional 'good.' "[111]

The concern of the American command with the prevention of death or damage to the civilian population led to the promulgation of the rules of engagement. American advisers, too, were told to "make every effort to convince Vietnamese counterparts of the necessity for preservation of the lives and property of noncombatants. Counterparts must be encouraged to promulgate and implement parallel instruction."[112] In an instruction program established in 1965, newly arrived soldiers were taught that respect for civilian life was not only a matter of basic decency and legality, but was also essential for winning the hearts and minds of the people. The intelligence gained from a population willingly assisting in the war against the communist insurgents, they were told, could save their lives.[113] Knowledge of the ROE until after the My Lai incident often left much to be desired, and MACV can justly be faulted with failing to take all possible measures to enforce these rules, but such negligence is a far cry from having a genocidal intent to destroy the people of South Vietnam.

While enforcement of the ROE in retrospect looks deficient, at the time many servicemen in the field resented these rules, which they considered a handicap to the effective pursuit of the war. "The military," wrote Roger Hillsman in 1966, "fretted under the limitations, citing incidents in which they took casualties that might have been avoided with more thorough preparatory bombing."[114] Another common source of irritation, especially in 1965 and 1966, was the cumbersome and time-consuming clearance procedure, involving both American and Vietnamese echelons, which was necessary before artillery fire or air strikes could be launched. "It sometimes takes the mortars ages to come in when we call for help," complained a young GI in his diary. "There are too damn many channels to go through. Sometimes Charlie is gone before our guys get fire clearance."[115] The clearance procedures were gradually streamlined, but restrictions on the use of firepower to protect noncombatants remained in effect.

All through the war, the ROE were treated as classified information. After finally obtaining several of these directives, Senator Goldwater in June 1975 inserted them into the *Congressional Record* and expressed his anger at what they revealed. "It is absolutely unbelievable that any Secretary of Defense would ever place such restrictions on our forces. It is unbelievable that any President would have allowed this to happen. . . . I am ashamed of my country for . . . such restrictions to have been placed upon men who were trained to fight, men who were trained to make decisions to win war, and men who were risking their lives. I dare say that these restrictions had as much to do with our casualties as the enemy themselves."[116] These views were shared by many commanders in the field, and such resentments demonstrate that official command policy, in the eyes of at least some of the military, was, if anything, too solicitous to prevent civilian casualties.

The existence of genocidal intent is further belied by command concern for short rounds—the inadvertent or accidental delivery of artillery fire or air strikes which fell short of their intended target and caused death or injury to allied troops or Vietnamese civilians. It may be argued that this concern was prompted mainly by the desire to protect American lives. But in point of fact investigations of short round incidents were conducted equally thoroughly for all incidents without regard to who had been the unfortunate victim. Similarly, penalties were imposed upon all those found guilty of negligence whether the error had cost the lives of American personnel or Vietnamese noncombatants.[117] All this undoubtedly involved most basically the maintenance and enforcement of professionalism, which coincided with humanitarian concerns, yet the evenhandedness with which this search for professional conduct was pursued surely does not bear out charges of gross neglect of Vietnamese life, let alone of genocidal aims. Commenting on the employment of American air power, a British military observer stated in 1967: "Taking the overall environment into account, I personally have never seen air power so discriminately applied, or so much care taken to avoid errors, often at great tactical disadvantage. The idea that air ordnance is scattered on hapless friend and foe alike is simply not true—good newspaper copy though it often seems to be."[118]

On the basis of the calculations made in Appendix I, it is reasonable to conclude that the Vietnam war during the years of active American involvement was no more destructive of civilian life, both North and South, than other armed conflicts of this century and a good bit less so than some, such as the Korean War. If we bear in mind that the battle for Korea leveled practically all major population centers, while much of the most severe fighting in Vietnam took place in uninhabited jungle terrain or in sparsely populated areas, this conclusion is hardly surprising. To be sure, civilian casualties are always regrettable, yet they are an inevitable part of modern war and modern military technology. For all but the pacifist, the decision as to whether any particular military conflict is justified therefore has to be made not on the basis of whether innocent civilians are likely to be killed but in terms of a country's national interest. Whether the American involvement in Vietnam was defensible in such terms is a question I will discuss in my last chapter. Here I merely conclude the following: the cost of the Vietnam war in civilian lives does not appear to support the charge, often heard from the war's critics, that the U.S. was engaged in a conflict where an unusually and unacceptably high number of noncombatants was being killed and where the relationship of means and ends therefore was seriously flawed.

Conclusion

Richard A. Falk and other jurists have argued that the Vietnamese Communists fighting a guerilla war could not abide by the law of war and could not successfully operate without the use of terror and without hiding among the civilian population. Moreover, Falk maintains, because of their modest technological capability, VC atrocities and violations of the law of war were not so destructive as the counterinsurgency effort of the U.S. with highly sophisticated modern weaponry. I have tried to show here that VC terror was not a selective political weapon employed against a few corrupt officials but in fact cost the lives of many thousands of innocent people. The American counterinsurgency effort, on the other hand, while often carried out in a self-defeating manner, generally did not violate international law, did not seek to destroy the civilian population as a matter of deliberate policy, and did not cause civilian casualties in proportions uniquely different from other wars of this century.

In discussions designed to update the law of war and, in particular, to apply it to modern guerilla tactics, the International Committee of the Red Cross (ICRC) has rejected the concept of the "poor" guerilla who cannot afford to abandon the weapon of terror. "There are those," the ICRC stated in 1972, "who feel that they cannot do without terrorism, at the beginning of the conflict at least, because of the effective way in which it establishes their hold on the people. The ICRC considers that, as is the case with torture, which is in a way the countermeasure against terrorism, such acts should be explicitly prohibited."[119]

This position of the Red Cross is eminently sensible. Just as in a regular military conflict military necessity is not allowed to override the humanitarian conventions of the law of war, so in a guerilla war certain minimal humane precepts of civilized conduct should be followed. Even if one accepts the moral justification of revolution in certain situations of political oppression where no peaceful redress is available, one should probably insist that insurgents not employ tactics that inflict inordinately cruel suffering on innocent human beings. To disembowel a hamlet chief in front of the assembled population in order to dissuade the villagers from giving their allegiance to the government in power would appear to go beyond the morally acceptable, no matter how unjust the regime which the hamlet chief nominally serves. To blow up buses carrying women and children so as to sow insecurity and prove that the government cannot protect its people is similarly inherently immoral. It is regrettable that those who claim to seek a more humane society have, in effect, chosen a mode of conflict that puts a premium on new savagery and inhumanity.

The ICRC has also recommended that guerillas continue to be required to identify themselves in some recognizable manner as combatants. This requirement, a legal expert has convincingly argued, "is not premised on forcing the patriot out from his cover. It is based on the desire to deny his enemy any justification for waging war on those with whom the *franc tireur* or his contemporary successor would otherwise be confounded."[120] If guerillas live and operate among the people like fish in the water, then, legally, the entire school of fish may become a legitimate military target. In such a case, the moral blame, too, would appear to fall on those who have enlarged the potential area of civilian death and damage. "To draw any other conclusion," correctly notes the Protestant theologian Paul Ramsey, "would be like, at the nuclear level, granting an enemy immunity from attack because he had the shrewdness to locate his missile bases in the heart of his cities."[121]

There was much in the American military effort in Vietnam that was legal but should probably not have happened. The rather free use of napalm and attacks upon fortified hamlets with artillery and air strikes can be criticized on humanitarian grounds and, moreover, were often counterproductive. The important lesson of Vietnam, therefore, is not Falk's legally incorrect assertion that the methods of large-scale counterinsurgency warfare with high technology weapons necessarily "amount to crimes under international law,"[122] but that these tactics in such a setting frequently do not work and do not accomplish their objectives. Technological superiority in such a war, in other words, is not unlawful but it may be irrelevant to victory and indeed may play a positively negative role. The fact that the tactics employed by the allies were not forbidden by the law of war and did not intentionally aim at inflicting casualties upon the civilian population remains morally significant. Yet in any future guerilla conflict in which the U.S. may become embroiled it will be well to remember that the loss of civilian life caused by modern heavy weapons is not just legal and yet regrettable—it is largely unnecessary and self-defeating.

9

Atrocities:
Fiction and Fact

War brings out the best and the worst in man. It encourages solidarity, devotion to duty and heroism, but it also puts a premium on aggressiveness, promotes permissiveness and license for the use of force and loosens the usual constraints on sadism, and all this inevitably leads to brutalities and excesses in violation of the law of war. Every war, therefore, has had its share of atrocities and Vietnam was no exception to this rule. The unusual element in the Vietnam conflict was the close scrutiny which the conduct of American troops received as a result of the war's unpopularity and the strong worldwide criticism it drew.

Every war also creates its atrocity stories which build upon and embellish the mindless disregard of human suffering and the willful cruelties which always accompany the fighting. Soldiers while away hours and days of boredom by writing home accounts of adventures and outrages which never occurred in quite the exaggerated form portrayed. People at home, reading or hearing these stories of prisoners murdered, women ravished and children mutilated, develop strong indignation against the perpetrators of these foul deeds and thereby gratify certain powerful hidden impulses. When the war is supported by strong currents of patriotism these stories of atrocities focus primarily upon the enemy. Government propagandists and journalists further encourage denunciation of the hated foe. In an unsuccessful and unpopular war like Vietnam, on the other hand, atrocities are blamed on one's own nation's army that persists in pursuing an elusive victory. In either case, a single instance of cruelty, told and retold, soon becomes a prevailing habit which happens all the time. Rhetorical indignation helps hide the lack of proof. A vigorous display of humanitarianism silences any show of incredulity on the part of the listener or reader.

In World War I stories of German atrocities in Belgium were circulated day after day in letters, articles and speeches and were widely believed on the Allied side. A British commission of inquiry, under the chairmanship of the reputable Lord Bryce, stated that the Huns were guilty of wholesale murder and pillage on a scale unparalleled in any war during the preceding three centuries. After the end of the war practically all of these atrocity stories were disproven; it was learned that the Bryce commission had personally interviewed no witnesses and had accepted affidavits of Belgian refugees as conclusive proof. One patriotic San Francisco woman, finding it difficult to convince her listeners that the Germans were cutting off the hands of Belgian children, told them that she had seen with her own eyes such Belgian children without hands. To a friend she later remarked in confidence: "Of course, I hadn't, but it was true, and that was the only way I could convince them."[1]

The same invention and exaggeration of outrages was taking place on the German side. Here the stories were of schoolchildren whose fingers had been chopped off by cossacks, of wounded German soldiers mutilated and doctors murdered by Belgians, and of women raped and slaughtered by the Russian hordes. Newspapers and intellectuals joined in the chorus of denunciation. As Bertrand Russell observed at the time, in such a war of propaganda requests for supporting factual evidence "have no power against a belief which stimulates ferocity, and is on that account felt to be useful."[2] There is no question that atrocities in World War I did occur on both sides, but it is certain that they were far less numerous than was almost universally believed at the time.

Since World War II was a war in which the wickedness of the fascist enemy did not have to be invented, atrocity stories were less fanciful. The war on the Allied side was seen as a moral crusade and that meant, among other things, that the behavior of Allied troops was never subjected to any close examination. Yet World War II was not free of disregard of the law of war by individual Allied soldiers and officers. Eric Sevareid, who was a correspondent with American troops in the Italian campaign, wrote of the shooting of German prisoners and Italian civilians felt to be a burden in the midst of the Allied advance. "As weeks went by and this experience was repeated many times, I ceased even to be surprised—only, I could never again bring myself to write or speak with indignation of the Germans' violations of the 'rules of warfare.' " Old cities and irreplaceable treasures of art, some of which had come down from classical Greece, were destroyed "because we did not care what they were, and it required effort to spare them."[3] Indifference to the loss of civilian life and property was said to be equally widespread in the Korean War. American marines after the landing at Inchon, wrote a British correspondent, "seemed good-natured and good-tempered, and less murderous the farther forward one went. But they never spoke of the enemy as though they were people, but as one might speak of apes. If they remarked a dead Korean body of whatever sex, uniformed or ununiformed, it was simply 'dead Gook' or 'good Gook.' "[4]

The Vietnam Environment

The conflict in Vietnam was a guerilla war without fronts, and this created a setting especially conducive to atrocities. Aggressive behavior is often the result of frustration and anxiety, and American servicemen in Vietnam experienced both of these states of mind in abundance. Troops would tramp for days in tropical heat through swamps and irrigated rice paddies, wade through streams and canals, climb hills and fight dense jungle growth without making contact with the evasive foe. Meanwhile they suffered the deadly depredations of enemy activity—ambushes, snipers, mines and booby traps. Buddies were killed and maimed, yet no enemy was in sight on whom one could revenge these losses. Seeming civilians were actually combatants; women and children tossed grenades or planted traps. Gradually the entire Vietnamese population became an object of fear and hatred. As a marine lieutenant told an American doctor: "You walk through the fucking bush for three days and nights without sleep. Watch your men, your buddies, your goddamn kids get booby trapped. Blown apart. Get thrown six feet in the air by a trap laid by an old lady and come down with no legs." Eventually you conclude, he said, that the only thing to do is to "kill them all."[5]

A 1968 study of American casualties showed that between January 1967 and September 1968, 23.7 percent of U.S. deaths were caused by mines and booby traps.[6] In periods of low combat intensity, like July 1969 for example, the marines in I CTZ experienced 41 percent of their KIA from this source.[7] Since many of these casualties occurred during or after passing hamlets, it became the prudent thing to doubt the loyalty of every villager. Feelings of hatred and vengeance were difficult to control, and the hostility toward the unseen enemy was often transferred to the civilian population which in looks, language and dress was indistinguishable from the elusive guerilla. The value of civilian life grew cheaper. Some soldiers began to adopt the so-called mere-gook rule, the attitude that the killing of Vietnamese, regardless of sex, age or combatant status, was of little importance for they were, after all, only gooks.

The use of unflattering epithets to describe enemies in battle is old. In World War I Americans fought "Huns," in World War II enemy soldiers were "krauts" and "Japs," in Korea "gooks." When American soldiers in Vietnam called the Vietnamese "gooks," "dinks," "slopes" and "slants" they were doing what men in situations of rivalry and competition, including soldiers in combat, have always done—describe their opponents in derogatory and degrading terms in order to convince themselves that they are better and deserve to win.[8] We do know that many soldiers developed strong feelings of animosity towards the Vietnamese population. A survey of marines in Quang Ngai province in 1966 showed that 40 percent disliked the Vietnamese and these negative attitudes were especially pronounced among small-unit leaders. Less than one in five of the NCOs had a positive attitude towards the ARVN and PF.[9] This dislike was often racism; it also resulted from the fact that the soldiers, as we have seen, felt engulfed in a sea of enmity, a situation where no Vietnamese could be fully trusted.

Callousness toward the Vietnamese was also caused by the writings and pronouncements of many American journalists and politicians who, while seeking to end the American involvement, for years exaggerated the faults of the South Vietnamese government and nation and gradually created an image of people not worth defending, if not altogether worthless. For all these reasons, some Americans undoubtedly came to regard the South Vietnamese as somewhat less than human, though the acceptance of the "mere-gook" rule has probably been exaggerated. For each misdeed and instance of mistrust and hostility, unbiased observers in Vietnam could see examples of friendship and generosity. Individual American soldiers, and sometimes entire units, adopted orphans and other children and engaged in various aid programs known as "civic action."

The mistreatment of Vietnamese civilians showed a marked increase over the span of the American involvement. During the early years, relations with the Vietnamese were reported as good. John Mecklin, head of the U.S. Information Service in Vietnam during the years 1962 to 1964, noted the absence of deprecating slang terms for the Vietnamese and he added: "I do not recall a single instance of trouble of consequence between U.S. military personnel and Vietnamese civilians."[10] But as the relatively small number of volunteers was replaced by tens of thousands of draftees, problems began to emerge. On 6 September 1965 MACV instituted an indoctrination program which stressed treating women "with politeness and respect," giving "the people the right of way when you drive," respecting Vietnamese soldiers and officers, and the like.[11] By 1966 Westmoreland talked about the need to arrest the spreading attitude of disaffection towards the Vietnamese, a problem that worsened as a result of rising casualties from mines and booby traps and the decline in morale and discipline among U.S. forces in Vietnam during the years of disengagement. Shooting farm animals, molesting women, throwing objects at Vietnamese civilians from moving vehicles and reckless driving were some of the relatively minor incidents which were reported with increasing frequency. During the year 1970 the U.S. command paid 4,467 Vietnamese claims for property damage and personal injury resulting from traffic accidents, including 853 claims for deaths caused by American drivers.[12] To put this last figure in some perspective it should be noted that this number of fatal traffic accidents was higher than the corresponding number in, for example, the state of Maryland in 1967, which had 1¾ million registered automobiles, trucks and buses.[13] The more serious incidents of violence appear to have followed a similar pattern of increase.

The War Crimes Industry

The extent of American atrocities in Vietnam cannot be established with any precision. Attempts to develop a reliable picture were not helped by the sensationalist accounts to be found in many segments of the media and the generally unsubstantiated charges spread by what in an earlier chapter I called the war crimes industry. A closer look at the origin and mode of operation of some of these self-styled war crimes tribunals is instructive.

The idea of organizing a tribunal to pass judgment on American war crimes in Vietnam had been suggested to Bertrand Russell by M. S. Arnoni, the editor of the U.S. journal *Minority of One*, in 1965. Russell at first was skeptical, but he soon changed his mind, probably under the prodding of his young American confidant, Ralph Schoenman.[14] In early

1966 Schoenman was sent to North Vietnam to collect evidence, and after a preliminary meeting in London in November 1966, the first session of the International War Crimes Tribunal opened on 2 May 1967 in Stockholm with Jean-Paul Sartre as executive president. The members of the tribunal were all well-known partisans of North Vietnam such as Vladimir Dedijer, Simone de Beauvoir, Stokeley Carmichael, Dave Dellinger, Carl Oglesby, Isaac Deutscher; the tribunal was described by its secretary-general, Schoenman, as "a partial body of committed men." President Johnson had been invited to appear in his own defense to answer charges that the U.S. was waging a "war like that waged by fascist Japan and Nazi Germany in Southeast Asia and Eastern Europe, respectively," but he declined to participate in a proceeding characterized by an assumption of guilt before trial, a tribunal, as Russell put it, convened "in order to expose . . . barbarous crimes . . . reported daily from Vietnam." [15]

The American antiwar activist Staughton Lynd had been asked to be a member of the tribunal, but he declined because of the refusal of the tribunal to inquire into the war crimes of both sides. As Lynd later explained, this amounted "to judging one side (the N.L.F.) by its ends, the other side (the U.S.) by its means. Precisely the double standard is what I had thought all of us, in this post-Stalin era, wished to avoid." The attitude that all was permitted against the class enemy dehumanized the opponent and represented a throwback to Stalinism. Schoenman replied to Lynd that the crimes of the aggressor were unique and that no equation could be made between the oppression of the aggressor and the resistance of the victim. To regard this resistance as terror was contrary to the convictions of those who had joined the tribunal. [16]

Many potential supporters were disillusioned by this abandonment of any pretense of impartiality. One letter of protest asked whether it was indeed the position of the tribunal that "when a little child is killed by American napalm it is clearly a crime, but that if that same child were killed by an N.L.F. terrorist it would be no crime at all?" [17] Others, on the other hand, were so pleased with the contribution of the tribunal to the antiwar cause that they swallowed their reservations. Professor Falk, who in 1967 had called the Russell tribunal "a juridical farce," by 1968 argued that despite a "one-sided adjudicative machinery and procedure" the tribunal "did turn up a good deal of evidence about the manner in which the war was conducted and developed persuasively some of the legal implications it seems reasonable to draw from that war." In 1971

Falk wrote that the proceedings of the tribunal "stand up well under the test of time and independent scrutiny."[18]

In chapter 7 I have already examined the nature of the evidence and the legal reasoning of the Russell tribunal. Acting as accuser, juror and judge all at once, the tribunal at times found it difficult to make its witnesses perform as expected. For example, Donald Duncan, a member of the American Special Forces who had served in Vietnam until September 1965, testified about some instances of torture during his tour of duty early in the war. He was then asked by one of the judges, the Pakistani lawyer Mahmud Ali Kasuri: "Now if I were to conclude now that there are more numbers of American troops in Vietnam, the evidence which has been given that there are more cases of direct barbarities by American troops should be believed, would you have anything to say against that?" Duncan replied that he was really familiar only with events up to and including September 1965. He had read and heard about developments after that time, "but I have no facts and figures and I certainly have no firsthand knowledge of it." Kasuri continued to press him: "But you wouldn't be in a position to say that this could not be true?" To which Duncan answered: "Oh, no."[19] By way of a final comment on the International War Crimes Tribunal, it should be noted that Bertrand Russell in 1969 completely broke with Schoenman, having concluded that the latter had an "utter incapacity of imparting reliable information" and was suffering from megalomania.[20]

Standards of evidence, decorum and impartiality were no higher at some of the proceedings staged in the U.S. In early 1970 three young American antiwar activists, including a West Point graduate disillusioned after service in Vietnam, dubbed themselves the National Committee for a Citizens' Commission of Inquiry on U.S. War Crimes in Vietnam (CCI) and organized a series of hearings in various locations across the country at which veterans testified about their personal experiences in Vietnam. In the first week of December 1970 they convened a large hearing, lasting three days, at the DuPont Plaza Hotel in the nation's capital.[21]

Some 40 veterans testified in Washington from 1 to 3 December 1970. Among them, and making his first public appearance, was a former military intelligence officer, Kenneth Barton Osborn, an alleged CIA operative, whom one sympathetic reporter called the inquiry's uncontested superstar. Osborn testified about instances of torture, but he refused to give the names of the individuals involved on the grounds that he had signed an agreement with the CIA not to reveal the specifics of secret operations. Such agreements, he explained, "are an attempt on the organization's part to cover their ass," but he had decided to adhere to it "to avoid endangering intelligence operatives who are still active." Osborn several years later became an official of the Organizing Committee for a Fifth Estate, the publisher of the magazine *Counterspy* which freely and frequently exposes CIA operatives. In 1970 he had another reason for not revealing names: "There's no reason to identify them. The thing to do is to attack the thing at its source, which is at the policy-making level."[22] This was in line with the official position of the CCI which, as one of its spokesmen stated at the end of the Washington hearing, sought to show "that war crimes in Vietnam are not isolated, aberrant acts; that war crimes are a way of life in Vietnam; and that they are a logical consequence of our war policies."[23]

The refusal to name names, and thus provide the kind of concrete information that would make possible an official investigation of the charges leveled, at times led to sharp questioning of the witnesses by correspondents covering the hearing. For example, Michael McCusker of the First Marine Division declined to give the name of the commanding officer (CO) of one of the battalions allegedly involved in an atrocity. "The reason for not giving any particular names is once again we're going to lay it back on individuals. And the whole thing for this investigation is to take it away from individuals and not lay the blame back on them and make it as if it were isolated." This led a correspondent to ask: "You're absolving the CO of the battalion as just doing his duty under standing orders, are you?" McCusker replied: "I'm absolving him as, in essence, the same way I'm absolving myself. That he was just as much a victim of the rigid structure in which he was involved. . . . And he was under orders as I was under orders. And I felt a great sense of powerlessness." Another time, a spokesman for the inquiry put it this way: "We're not trying to find out who's guilty on an individual basis. If we did that we'd probably have to draw up a list with 2,500,000 names on it. What we're trying to do is find the responsibility for these actions and we say that the responsibility is at the highest levels of planning. That these tactical field policies emanate from these highest levels of planning and create a strain, a type of atmosphere in Vietnam, where these type of actions have to occur on a very frequent basis." That also meant, as an organizer of the CCI argued, that the trial of Lieutenant Calley had to be stopped. "The attempt, I suppose, is basically to . . . take the monkey off the individual's back, take it off Calley's back, and put it a step higher—let the generals do what they will with the monkey once it's on their back."[24]

The argument that certain "tactical field policies," as for example the stress on body count, created an atmosphere conducive to atrocities was certainly valid. Yet despite the pressure for a high enemy casualty toll most soldiers in Vietnam did not kill prisoners or intentionally shoot unarmed villagers. Violations of the law of war in this regard were committed by individuals in violation of existing policy. With the exception of rare cases, no orders were issued to commit atrocities, and when the plea of superior orders was introduced, as in the Calley case, courts-martial rejected it as a defense for the commission of war crimes. The "tactical field policies" ordered by the generals, which we have examined in an earlier chapter, did not violate the law of war in any clear manner and they did not provide a license for atrocities. At the most it could be argued that the command had been negligent in enforcing policies aimed at preventing atrocities. Like other critics of the American command in Vietnam, the CCI erroneously assumed that the rules of engagement, with which they were not familiar, were in violation of applicable international law, of which they knew even less, and that individual atrocities therefore were committed in execution of standing orders. This charge was without foundation.

The demand that men like Calley should be freed and that no other individual soldiers or officers be brought to trial in effect was a demand that nobody should be held responsible for atrocities. It amounted to a repudiation of individual responsibility not unlike that made with regard to the German people after World War II. Yet while collective guilt, like the notion of original sin, may have a place in theology, it is not part of Anglo-American jurisprudence. Here guilt is always personal, and if all are guilty then in effect nobody is guilty. Perhaps this was indeed the end result which these veterans relating atrocities, often involving them personally, wanted to bring about. As McCusker, quoted earlier, candidly acknowledged: "I'm absolving him [the CO] as, in essence, the same way I'm absolving myself." Another veteran testifying about atrocities admitted that it was less difficult to live with such killings if you could convince yourself that you had been programmed to do these things. "You know, maybe it wasn't 'GI Joe' who pulled the trigger to kill the baby, but in some very real way, it's the military who has made 'GI Joe' what he was then, who—

quite obviously I think we all believe here—bear the responsibility for the act, if not the actual guilt itself."[25] Some individuals, under pressure and sometimes provocation, committed atrocities while others successfully resisted these pressures and maintained their integrity. Instead of facing up to this harsh fact of individual moral failure it was easier to place "the monkey" on the backs of the generals.

Another organization active in airing charges of American atrocities in Vietnam was the Vietnam Veterans Against the War (VVAW), which was founded in 1967; by 1970 it was said to have 600 members. From 31 January to 2 February 1971, the VVAW, with financial backing from actress Jane Fonda, convened a hearing, known as the Winter Soldier Investigation, in the city of Detroit. More than 100 veterans and 16 civilians testified at this hearing about "war crimes which they either committed or witnessed";[26] some of them had given similar testimony at the CCI inquiry in Washington. The allegations included using prisoners for target practice and subjecting them to a variety of grisly tortures to extract information, cutting off the ears of dead VCs, throwing VC suspects out of helicopters, burning villages, gang rapes of women, packing the vagina of a North Vietnamese nurse full of grease with a grease gun, and the like.

Among the persons assisting the VVAW in organizing and preparing this hearing was Mark Lane, author of a book attacking the Warren Commission probe of the Kennedy assassination and more recently of *Conversations with Americans*, a book of interviews with Vietnam veterans about war crimes. On 22 December 1970 Lane's book had received a highly critical review in the *New York Times Book Review* by Neil Sheehan, who was able to show that some of the alleged "witnesses" of Lane's war crimes had never even served in Vietnam while others had not been in the combat situations they described in horrid detail. Writing in the *Saturday Review* a few days later, James Reston, Jr., called *Conversations with Americans* "a hodgepodge of hearsay" which ignored "a soldier's talent for embellishment" and a "disreputable book."[27] To prevent the Detroit hearing from being tainted by such irregularities, all of the veterans testifying fully identified the units in which they had served and provided geographical descriptions of where the alleged atrocities had taken place.

Yet the appearance of exactitude was deceptive. Sen. Mark O. Hatfield of Oregon was impressed by the charges made by the veterans and inserted the transcript of the Detroit hearing into the *Congressional Record*. Furthermore, he asked the commandant of the Marine Corps to investigate the numerous allegations of wrongdoing made against the marines in particular. The results of this investigation, carried out by the Naval Investigative Service, are interesting and revealing. Many of the veterans, though assured that they would not be questioned about atrocities they might have committed personally, refused to be interviewed. One of the active members of the VVAW told investigators that the leadership had directed the entire membership not to cooperate with military authorities. A black marine who agreed to be interviewed was unable to provide details of the outrages he had described at the hearing, but he called the Vietnam war "one huge atrocity" and "a racist plot." He admitted that the question of atrocities had not occurred to him while he was in Vietnam, and that he had been assisted in the preparation of his testimony by a member of the Nation of Islam. But the most damaging finding consisted of the sworn statements of several veterans, corroborated by witnesses, that they had in fact not attended the hearing in Detroit. One of them had never been to Detroit in all his life. He did not know, he stated, who might have used his name.[28]

Incidents similar to some of those described at the VVAW hearing undoubtedly did occur. We know that hamlets were destroyed, prisoners tortured, and corpses mutilated. Yet these incidents either (as in the destruction of hamlets) did not violate the law of war or took place in breach of existing regulations. In either case, they were not, as alleged, part of a "criminal policy." The VVAW's use of fake witnesses and the failure to cooperate with military authorities and to provide crucial details of the incidents further cast serious doubt on the professed desire to serve the causes of justice and humanity. It is more likely that this inquiry, like others earlier and later, had primarily political motives and goals.

In April 1971 several members of Congress provided a platform on Capitol Hill for the airing of atrocity allegations. Rep. Ronald V. Dellums of California chaired an *ad hoc* hearing which lasted four days and took testimony from Vietnam veterans. Some of the witnesses were old-timers. One Peter Norman Martinson had testified before the Russel tribunal, been an interviewee in Mark Lane's book, and appeared before the CCI inquiry. Some new witnesses sounded as if they had memorized North Vietnamese propaganda. Capt. Randy Floyd, a former marine pilot, ended his testimony by telling the committee that he was ashamed to have been "an unwitting pawn of my government's inhuman imperialistic policy in Southeast Asia. . . . And I am revolted by my government which commits genocide because it is good business." For his testimony Floyd drew the praise of Congressman Dellums: "I would like to thank you very much for the courage of your testimony and the preparation and details. We are deeply appreciative of the fact that you came forward today."[29]

The testimony of some other witnesses was more judicious. When Capt. Fred Laughlin, a West Point graduate, was asked by Rep. Patsy T. Mink of Hawaii about the "mere-gook" rule, he replied that the attitude of American servicemen toward the Vietnamese varied from unit to unit. Some had a bad attitude, but "I felt that most of my unit considered the Vietnamese human." Rep. John F. Seiberling of Ohio wanted to know to what extent Laughlin felt qualified to generalize about incidents of mistreatment, and the captain answered: "I certainly don't feel qualified in generalizing. . . . I hope, as you point out, that we do in this exercise get down to the facts, not be guilty of generalizing. . . ."[30]

The detailed facts of particular incidents were not of any great concern to Kenneth B. Osborn, who testified before the House Government Operations Committee in the summer of 1971. The former intelligence officer had told the CCI inquiry of an incident in which a VC suspect had been pushed out of a helicopter in order to scare other detainees into talking. Asked for the name of the marine officer who had given this order, Osborn declined: "In all due respect, I do recall his name, but I am not willing to go into that. You can see that is irrelevant. In fact, the form of the thing is what we are talking about."[31]

Two years later, in July 1973, Osborn appeared before the Senate Armed Services Committee to oppose the confirmation of William E. Colby as head of the CIA. Sen. Stuart Symington of Missouri asked Osborn for the names of those who had committed the atrocities he claimed to have witnessed, but Osborn again refused. When questioned as to whether he had ever submitted an official complaint about these atrocities while in Vietnam, Osborn replied: "No, sir. They seemed to me at the time to be standard operating procedure." And when asked whether he had made any reports since his discharge from the service, he stated: "Only in the form of my testimony, which has been minimally investigated by the Army."[32] In point of fact, the Army's Criminal Investigation Division (CID) had interviewed Osborn soon after he first made his charges, but, like the two congressional committees later on, the CID had been unable to get him to provide specific information about the alleged incidents.[33]

The refusal of men like Osborn to give substantiating factual information in support of their atrocity allegations created a situation in which the accusers continued to reap generous publicity for their sensational charges while the Army in most cases could neither investigate nor refute them. Since the CID is prohibited from divulging any information regarding its investigations, the Army could not even make it known that it was trying to pursue possible leads despite the absence of crucial details withheld by the accusers. As of 11 April 1971, the CID had determined that 7 of 16 allegations made by the CCI which could be investigated were unfounded or unsubstantiated.[34] Most of the allegations were so general as to defy investigation.

There was another reason to be wary of these allegations and confessions. They all were retrospective reports and therefore, as is well known, subject to distortion—in this case created by the veterans' perceptions of the interviewers and organizers of the hearings, by their attitudes toward the military and by their difficulties in adjusting to civilian life after discharge.

Problems of adjustment to civilian society have been faced by all veterans returning from war. They involve the loss of a closely knit peer group and often disappointment that the veterans' sacrifices are not sufficiently valued by the civilians who stayed at home.[35] In the case of the returning Vietnam veterans these problems were increased manifold because of widespread negative sentiments toward the war in American society which left many of the veterans shocked, thinking that they had wasted their time and feeling guilty for having taken human life in an unworthy cause. By joining a group like the VVAW they could recapture some of the security and camaraderie they had enjoyed in the service and missed in civilian life. By speaking out against the war they could hope to improve their rapport with the dominant currents of opinion in the society they were re-entering. Since their acts of killing in the line of duty were not appreciated, it was tempting to convert these killings into atrocities. In this way the veterans gained approval and acceptance, especially among the college population. By confessing to having committed atrocities they achieved an emotional catharsis and relief for their guilt feelings. When they made these confessions at public hearings they became important persons; by sharing their confessions with other veterans they found a new sense of intimacy and belonging.

Some veterans who experienced adjustment problems, including some who felt uneasy over their role in a counterinsurgency war in which civilians were inevitably killed, were persuaded to join informal rap groups conducted by antiwar-oriented mental health practitioners. In these group therapy sessions they could relieve their guilt feelings by telling their war experiences in a supportive environment, and those who were not yet part of the movement were encouraged to take an active share in the antiwar agitation. A psychoanalyst who led some of these groups has written that merely sharing grief and outrage was not enough. "By actively opposing the very war policies they helped to carry out and by throwing away the medals they won, they symbolically shed some of their guilt."[36]

A certain amount of this guilt feeling was probably encouraged by the leaders of these groups, all staunch opponents of the war, and there is reason to think that at least some of the atrocities confessed at these rap sessions (and perhaps later repeated in public) were induced by group expectations and pressures. Some were the product of fantasy on the part of emotionally disturbed individuals. Robert Lifton, another psychiatrist involved in these sessions who believes in the frequent occurrence of atrocities, recalls the case of one veteran who after a year's attendance in the rap group could "confess that he had been much less violent in Vietnam than he had implied. He had previously given the impression that he had killed many people there, whereas in actuality, despite extensive combat experience, he could not be certain he had killed anyone. After overcoming a certain amount of death anxiety and death guilt, that is, he had much less need to call forth his inner beast to lash out at others or himself."[37]

The question whether the atrocity stories were true or not was dismissed as unimportant by some social scientists. Charles J. Levy, a Harvard sociologist, told the Senate Labor Committee in 1970 that the Vietnam combat experience had a highly brutalizing effect on American servicemen and created in them a propensity to become killers. His finding was based on a study of veterans, primarily in the Boston area, who after allegedly engaging in a great deal of violence in Vietnam had drifted into a life of violent crime in this country. When a senator disputed Levy's evidence for this conclusion, Levy replied that he was "primarily concerned with the subjective reality as to what these episodes that were described by them, meant to these men, how they affected them. It seems to me that if these episodes were not true, that in another way is equally telling."[38]

The existence of a killer instinct which Vietnam veterans allegedly were bringing back from combat in Vietnam was challenged at the same hearing by another sociologist as lacking even "one shred of data or evidence." According to Charles C. Moskos, there existed "a marked tendency at elite cultural and intellectual levels to portray soldiers as, variously, wanton perpetrators of atrocities, or proto-fascist automatons. . . ."[39] Atrocity stories out of Vietnam, Moskos has suggested, were the functional equivalent of heroic war stories out of World War II. Both gave the soldiers' participation in these wars a meaning which could resonate with certain elements of the public back home.

Since the end of the American involvement in Vietnam one has not heard much about the brutalization hypothesis. It would appear, as one student of Vietnam returnees has suggested, that the reports of detrimental psychological effects of the Vietnam combat experience were based on uncontrolled studies of highly selected samples and that "some mental health professionals have overstepped their data to support their politics."[40]

The Role of the Media

In the absence of corroborating evidence, the atrocity stories told by some Vietnam veterans should have been treated by the media with far more circumspection than they in fact were. But the tendency on the part of all too many newspaper and television reporters and editors was to see the war in Vietnam as an atrocity writ large, and specific incidents reported therefore were widely accepted as true. Some allegations were repeated so many times that they seemed to supply their own confirmation: where there was so much smoke there just had to be a fire.

One of the stories told and retold was that of prisoners pushed out of helicopters in order to scare others into talking. It is, of course, possible that some American interrogators engaged in this criminal practice, though not a single instance has been confirmed. We do know of at least one case where such an occurrence was staged through the use of a dead body. An investigation by the CID identified the soldier who had taken the photograph; it also identified a second soldier who acquired the picture, made up the story of the interrogation and mailed it and the photograph to his girlfriend. She in turn gave them to her brother, who informed the *Chicago Sun-Times*. On 29–30 November 1969 the picture and the story appeared in the *Chicago Sun-Times* and the *Washington Post* and generated wide media interest. A lengthy investigation by the CID, which began on 8 January 1970, established that a dead NVA soldier had been picked up on 15 February 1969 after an operation in Gia Dinh province (III CTZ) and adduced other details of how the picture had been posed. The commander of the helicopter in question was reprimanded; the two crew members who had pushed the body out of the aircraft had since been discharged and therefore were beyond the Army's disciplinary jurisdiction.[41]

On at least one occasion a reporter contributed to the commission of an atrocity. On 9 October 1967 the CBS evening news with Walter Cronkite showed a young American soldier cutting off the ear of a dead VC soldier as a souvenir of battle. An investigation disclosed that the soldier and another man in the same unit on 7 October 1967 had apparently acted on a "dare" after being given a knife by a CBS cameraman, who then filmed the sequence. The two soldiers were tried and convicted by special court-martial of conduct to the prejudice of good order and discipline and were sentenced to a reduction in grade and a fine.[42] The CBS cameraman admitted that he had provided the knife, but insisted that he had not known what the soldiers asking for it were going to do with it.

The credulity of the media with regard to charges of war crimes and malfeasance on the part of the Army was demonstrated most vividly in the Herbert affair. In 1971 the media gave extensive publicity to the case of Lt. Col. Anthony B. Herbert, who, it was reported, had been driven out of the Army because he had tried to prevent his superiors from covering up war crimes in Vietnam. The *New York Times* on 12 March 1971 described Herbert as "the most decorated American soldier in the Korean war"; according to "reliable sources" the Army's CID had confirmed the veracity of the allegations. *Time, Newsweek* and *Life* picked up the story. Herbert appeared three times on the "Dick Cavett Show"; Holt, Rinehart and Winston eventually published a book under his byline, written in collaboration with *New York Times* reporter James T. Wooten.[43] The latter published an article in the *New York Times Magazine* on 5 September 1971 entitled "How a Super-Soldier was Fired from His Command," which described Herbert as a conscientious career officer hounded by a vindictive Army.

On 4 April 1969 Herbert had been relieved of command of his battalion in Vietnam for unsatisfactory performance of duty. Almost 18 months later, on 28 September 1970, Herbert formally complained to the inspector general of the Third Army about 21 incidents of war crimes alleged to have occurred in 1968 and 1969 in the 173rd Airborne Brigade, in which he had served. The charges were investigated by the CID, which found seven of the allegations to merit action or further investigation. Several of the incidents had already led to disciplinary action. Not content with the Army's response, Herbert on 15 March 1971 filed charges against the brigade commander and deputy commander, Brig. Gen. John W. Barnes and Col. J. Ross Franklin, for failure to report and investigate alleged violations of the law of war and for dereliction of duty. Herbert now claimed that he had reported a particularly horrible incident, involving the killing of four prisoners and the murder of two babies, to Colonel Franklin on the day the killings had taken place—St. Valentine's Day, 14 February 1969. He had also informed General Barnes of this and other crimes, but instead of acting upon these charges, Herbert complained, the leadership had relieved him of his command.

The key issue in the Herbert affair was not whether atrocities had occurred, but whether Herbert had reported them and had had his career ruined by a military establishment intent on concealing war crimes. Coming in the wake of the My Lai cover-up, Herbert's allegations had immediate credibility. His previous distinguished military record gave his charges special weight.

The story of how Herbert's case gradually collapsed until in the eyes of many he was transformed from a hero and martyr into a liar has been told by a CBS television producer, Barry Lando, who contacted the people named by Herbert and interviewed 120 others who had known him throughout his career. The Army, meanwhile, had concluded its extensive investigation,[44] and many of the officers involved in the charges, who earlier had been forbidden to talk about the affair, were now free to tell their side. "One after another," writes Lando, "refuted many of Herbert's claims."[45] Franklin, it turned out, on St. Valentine's Day 1969, when Herbert allegedly had reported a war crime to him, had been on leave in Honolulu. Herbert's book *Soldier*, concluded Lando, was "a melange, a kaleidoscope of truth, half-truth, and fabrication," and that included many of his exploits in Korea. Among the minor myths now exploded was that of Herbert as the "most decorated soldier in the Korean war." Other soldiers had earned more and higher decorations than Herbert. Most importantly, he had been relieved as battalion commander in Vietnam because he was unreliable and had acquired the reputation of a cold-blooded killer. Attempting to salvage his threatened career and seeking revenge against Franklin and Barnes, he apparently had invented the story of the cover-up of war crimes. The media had helped his case by making him into a celebrity.

Herbert's story from the beginning had numerous weaknesses, not least his unexplained wait of 18 months before he finally put his charges in writing. But for a long time nobody in the media bothered to check into Herbert's allegations. Lando himself recalls how he was impressed when interviewing Herbert for the first time. Even after a segment of "60 Minutes," shown on CBS Television on 4 February 1973, had finally taken away Herbert's halo, the media were slow to retract their earlier enthusiastic endorsement of his claims.[46] Those wishing to believe the worst about the Army's handling of war crimes in Vietnam to this day have failed to take notice that Herbert has meanwhile turned out to be a hero with feet of clay. Writes Prof. Richard A. Falk: "The story of Lt. Col. Anthony Herbert provides insight into the pervasiveness of atrocities and into the refusal of the military command to act in such a way as to discourage their commission."[47] A libel suit for $44 million filed by Herbert in January 1974 against CBS, Mike Wallace and Barry Lando may return the affair to the limelight.

The fact that many of the allegations of atrocities in Vietnam do not stand up under critical examination does not warrant the conclusion that no atrocities took place. Such a conclusion would be as one-sided and wrong as the assertion that the conduct of American forces in Vietnam was but an unrelieved record of brutal war crimes. However, the ease with which such allegations were produced and the transparent political motive manifesting itself in many of them does dictate an attitude of caution. Assertion and allegation are not tantamount to fact and proof.

The Court-Martial Record

Between January 1965 and March 1973, 201 Army personnel in Vietnam were convicted by court-martial of serious offenses against Vietnamese.[48] During the period March 1965 to August 1971, 77 marines were convicted of serious crimes against Vietnamese.[49] This record of court-martial cases provides us with an overall picture of the kinds of atrocities which did take place in Vietnam. They involve offenses such as murder, rape, assault with intent to commit murder or rape, mutilation of a corpse and negligent homicide. The figures encompass all crimes against Vietnamese, including traffic incidents resulting in death or the killing of a bargirl in Saigon; they also take in offenses connected with military operations—the kinds of crimes usually referred to as atrocities or war crimes.

The largest single category of serious crimes against Vietnamese was homicide: 95 Army personnel were convicted of murder and manslaughter, 27 marines were convicted of the murder of Vietnamese. About 25 percent of these homicides represented killings during the course of combat not justified by military necessity.[50] The worst incident of this kind and the best known is the My Lai massacre.

On 16 March 1968, Company C (Charlie) of Task Force Barker, a battalion-size unit of the Americal Division, assaulted the hamlet of My Lai (4) (part of Son My village in the Son Tinh district of Quang Ngai province, I CTZ). The assault, part of a larger action by Task Force Barker in the Son My area, was a standard search-and-destroy operation, which MACV directives defined as an operation conducted for the purpose of seeking out and destroying enemy forces, installations, resources and base areas. In cases where hamlets were fortified, this often meant destruction of all houses and removal of the inhabitants. As we have seen earlier, the rules of engagement required warning prior to an attack on a village or hamlet except when such a warning could jeopardize the success of an operation. In the case of the My Lai operation, no such warning was issued, for the hamlet was said to be held by the 48th VC Battalion, which was expected to put up a stiff fight. During a briefing prior to the operation, the commander of Charlie Company, Capt. Ernest L. Medina, ordered the men to burn and destroy My Lai (4). According to the Peers Inquiry, Medina's instructions concerning the inhabitants of the hamlet "left little or no doubt in the minds of a significant number of men in his company that all persons remaining in the My Lai (4) area at the time of combat assault were enemy, and that C Company's mission was to destroy the enemy." The entire Son My area was a VC stronghold and the American units operating there had taken repeated casualties from snipers, mines and booby traps without making any significant contact with the enemy. "In a very real sense, then, it appears that the operation took on the added aspect of a grudge match between C Company and an enemy force in My Lai (4)."[51]

Contrary to expectations, no enemy forces were encountered during the assault on My Lai (4), yet the men of Charlie Company swept through the hamlet and systematically killed all the inhabitants, comprised almost exclusively of old men, women and children. The number of victims killed by Charlie Company in My Lai (4) is given as 175–200. There were several rape-killings and at least one gang rape. The total number of Vietnamese killed by Task Force Barker in the overall area of Son My village may have exceeded 400.[52]

The execution of this operation, and the massacre of the villagers in particular, violated numerous provisions of applicable MACV directives. Standing operating procedures of the Americal Division, based on these directives, required that in missions against enemy forces in hamlets and villages "maximum effort will be made to minimize noncombatant casualties during tactical operations." Even in free-fire zones, personnel were to be identified as NVA or VC forces by their uniforms, gear, pack or weapons before being engaged with small arms and automatic weapons.[53] The killing of nonresisting and unarmed villagers thus clearly constituted an unauthorized and prohibited action and made it an atrocity and war crime. Eventually, 12 officers and enlisted men were charged with murder or assault to commit murder.

The My Lai massacre was successfully concealed within all command levels of the Americal Division until a letter sent on 29 March 1969 by a serviceman not connected with the division, Ronald L. Ridenhour, who had heard stories of a massacre, brought the incident to the attention of the secretary of defense and other government officials. The cover-up of this crime for over a year has lent strength to the argument made by many critics of American tactics in Vietnam that large-scale massacres of civilians were common and that My Lai, therefore, was merely one of numerous such incidents that leaked out. Even a generally balanced reporter like Alexander Kendrick has written: "My Lai was not an aberration, as some would hold, but a typical incident in the war."[54]

The absence of an atrocity of this magnitude from the court-martial record cannot prove that no other such incident took place, yet in view of the openness of the fighting in South Vietnam to journalists and the encouragement which the My Lai affair gave to other servicemen to come forward with reports of atrocities, it is highly unlikely that anything like the My Lai massacre did escape detection. Villagers were regularly killed in combat assaults on defended hamlets, but the cold-blooded rounding up and shooting of civilians was an unusual event. The "reported reaction of some of the soldiers at Son My," writes Telford Taylor, "strongly indicates that they regarded it as out of the ordinary."[55] Even Daniel Ellsberg, not known for his reticence in criticizing American actions in Vietnam, rejects the idea that incidents like My Lai happened all the time. "My Lai was beyond the bounds of permissible behavior, and that is recognizable by virtually every soldier in Vietnam. They know it was wrong. . . . The men who were at My Lai knew there were aspects out of the ordinary. That is why they tried to hide the event, talked about it to no one, discussed it very little even among themselves."[56]

An atrocity similar to the My Lai massacre was committed by Korean troops in Quang Nam province (I CTZ) on 12 February 1968. After a Korean armored troop carrier had struck a mine and a unit of the 2nd ROK Marine Brigade had drawn some sniper fire from Phong Nhi hamlet nearby, the Koreans called artillery fire on the hamlet and then moved through it using grenades and small-arms fire on the villagers. All the homes were burnt and destroyed, and more than 80 civilians, the majority of them women and children, were killed. Some of the dead were found with powder burns, indicating execution at point-blank range.[57] No firm information on disciplinary action taken is available.

A different kind of atrocity killing took place in the hamlet of Son Thang (4) in the Que Son Valley, also in Quang Nam province, during the night of 19 February 1970. A patrol of five marines—called a "killer team" because its job was to ambush and kill any enemy forces encountered— entered a hamlet with the purpose of searching family bunkers for enemy soldiers. The area was dominated by the VC; women and children at times assisted the guerillas by drawing American forces into ambushes or warning the VC of the Americans' approach. A week earlier the marines had lost nine men; another had been killed the day of the patrol by a booby trap detonated by a boy estimated to be no more than ten years old. Before leaving, the five volunteers for the "killer team" were exhorted by their company and platoon commanders to remember what had happened on 12 February and to "get some," which meant to make contact and kill as many of the enemy as possible. Upon reaching the hamlet, the patrol entered a hut and brought out two women and two children. When one of the women ran towards a tree line she was shot, and the leader of the patrol then ordered the killing of the others. The patrol next entered two more huts and again shot and killed whomever they found.

In all, five women and eleven children were thus killed. The five marines were charged with 16 counts of premeditated murder.[58]

The desire to revenge buddies killed appeared as a motive in other similar cases, but sometimes the circumstances were more ordinary. In early 1967, five soldiers of the First Air Cavalry Division abducted a Vietnamese girl to take along on a roving patrol, raped and then killed her. One of the men reported the incident, which led to charges of rape and murder against the other four.[59] There were several cases of rape of captured North Vietnamese nurses and incidents involving the killing of prisoners.

Sometimes the stress of continuous combat and the loss of friends figured in these cases, as when a marine lance corporal with an exemplary record while on a patrol killed four young Vietnamese captured and suspected of alerting enemy troops of the presence of the Americans. He was charged with four counts of premeditated murder.[60]

Pressure for a high body count was apparently a factor in the case of Lt. James B. Duffy of the Ninth Infantry Division, who ordered the execution of a prisoner. The military court of review noted that "because a unit's effectiveness was measured by its body count, there was competition between battalions and companies for the highest monthly count." One officer superior to Duffy was said to have exerted enormous pressure "to get a high body count and not prisoners."[61] Both Duffy and the sergeant who shot the prisoner were charged with murder.

Also on the record are several cases of the mistreatment and torture of prisoners to extract information. In some instances American advisers were present at, or participated in, the abuse of prisoners by South Vietnamese personnel. The latter were known for their bad treatment of captured VC and often subjected them to various methods of torture such as dragging prisoners behind armored personnel carriers, giving them the "water treatment" and applying electric shocks through the use of field telephones. American correspondents at times took pictures of such scenes with Americans standing by. In a letter of 14 August 1965 to the commander of the Third Marine Division, Maj. Gen. Louis Walt, Westmoreland acknowledged the difficulty of the situation "since we have no command authority over Vietnamese troops that accompany U.S. troops on operations but we must try to moderate the conduct of the Vietnamese in their treatment of prisoners so that it conforms to the spirit of the Geneva Conventions, which the GVN has agreed to in principle. In any case we should attempt to avoid photographs being taken of these incidents of torture and most certainly in any case try to keep Americans out of the picture."[62]

On 21 January 1968 the *Washington Post* published a picture showing an American soldier pinning a Vietnamese to the ground while two other Vietnamese placed a towel over his face and poured water into his nose. The incident was investigated by the CID, and on 28 February 1968 the American soldier, a member of the First Air Cavalry Division, was tried for the offense by special court-martial.[63]

At times Americans were directly responsible for acts of torture. The Peers Inquiry established that on 19 March 1968, during the Son My operation, "an American assisted by an ARVN interpreter interrogated detainees held in the company position. A field telephone with leads attached to various parts of the body to produce electric shocks was one technique being employed to obtain information."[64] A report on war crimes allegations made to the White House on 21 May 1971 by Maj. Gen. Kenneth J. Hodson, the Army's judge advocate general, noted that investigation had confirmed that "on occasion" electrical devices were used to torture Vietnamese during intelligence interrogations.[65]

Ears and fingers cut off from the bodies of dead enemy for a time appear to have been a status symbol in Vietnam. In a message to all commanders, dated 13 October 1967, Westmoreland called this practice "subhuman," "contrary to all policy and below the minimum standards of human decency" and demanded immediate steps to make it clear that such actions would not be condoned.[66] In October 1968 a soldier was dared by an NCO to prove his courage and bring back some "gook" ears. He cut off the ears and index finger of a dead VC and was charged with conduct to the prejudice of good order and discipline.[67] Other cases of mutilation involved cutting off the heads of corpses. In June 1967 an Army sergeant decapitated two bodies of enemy soldiers and together with other members of his unit posed for photographs with the corpses. He, too, was court-martialed for conduct to the prejudice of good order and discipline.[68]

The above court-martial cases provide examples of the kinds of American atrocities which did occur in Vietnam. In trying to understand why they took place one must again remember the overall Vietnam environment—the frustrations resulting from fighting an often unseen enemy, the resentments created by casualties from booby traps frequently set by villagers, the decline in discipline during the years of disengagement.

None of these factors justify the atrocities, but they help provide explanations for them. Probably the most important single element, present in almost all incidents, was weak leadership. Strong and effective commanders managed to keep their subordinates under control even in situations of great stress; but such leaders were often in short supply, especially at the platoon and company level. Almost half of the newly commissioned officers in 1967 were the products of officer candidate school (OCS),[69] and it was common knowledge in Vietnam that many of the officers coming from OCS were not of very high caliber. A man like Calley, under normal peacetime circumstances, probably would not have attained officer rank, but the demand was such that the Army could not be very selective. After Calley's conviction for the murders at My Lai, a colonel at Ft. Benning expressed the view: "We have at least two or three thousand more Calleys in the Army just waiting for the next calamity."[70]

Ineffective leadership resulted in weak discipline. According to the Peers Inquiry report, certain battalions of the Americal Division suffered from poor discipline, and this resulted in "scattered incidents involving the mistreatment, rape, and possibly the murder of Vietnamese by 11th Brigade soldiers prior to the Son My operation. . . ."[71] The tendency to conform to prevailing norms of laxness appears to have led to acts of violence in other units as well. A psychiatric study of such behavior showed "that *all* of the soldiers who participated in personal violence reported that others in their units did so too. Group pressures, the examples of superiors, 'old-timers' and other important group figures, and the acceptable limits implicitly and explicitly set by each unit appear to have been important in regulating the appearance and degree of violence. . . . Soldiers who followed the examples of others in violent acts were frequently attempting to gain acceptance in the eyes of comrades they held in esteem, or were attempting to maintain group membership and cohesion."[72] Some of the court-martial cases cited earlier provide examples of the same dynamics at work.

Inferior leadership also meant inadequate planning of operations and loosely issued orders. The My Lai operation, for example, had a poorly defined purpose which resulted in ambiguous and potentially explosive orders. The command to "get some" issued to the marine patrol in the Son Thang tragedy was defective for the same reason. When units operated in free-fire zones or in generally hostile areas, the failure of commanders to define objectives with precision and to make provisions for noncombatants to be encountered could easily lead to lack of discrimination and the killing of innocents.

The manpower demands of the Vietnam conflict led to lower standards not only for officers but also for enlisted men. Since many in the more highly qualified mental groups obtained draft deferments, the services had to fill their ranks with less qualified personnel. Through "Project 100,000" they had to accept men of lower intelligence ratings who were ill-suited for the exacting demands of a counterinsurgency war like Vietnam. The results could have been expected. The typical marine or soldier tried for serious misconduct had less than 10 years of formal education, was mentally below average, often the product of a broken home. Personnel turbulence created by the short tours of duty further weakened *esprit de corps*. Units at times were assembled hastily, and the constant influx of replacements made it difficult to build cohesion. The average marine involved in a serious incident, writes a former Vietnam judge advocate, "was twenty years of age. He was a replacement or new to an incoming unit. He had been in Vietnam less than four months. He had been in the Marine Corps less than fourteen months."[73]

Finally, there was the lack of adequate training, caused in part by the pressure to ready troops for combat in Vietnam. The men of Task Force Barker, for example, had undergone a curtailed training period. Many of the soldiers, noted the Peers Inquiry, were "not adequately trained as to: a. Their responsibilities regarding obedience to orders received from their superiors which they considered palpably illegal. b. Their responsibilities concerning the procedures for the reporting of war crimes. c. The provisions of the Geneva Conventions, the handling and treatment of prisoners of war, and the treatment and safeguarding of noncombatants."[74] But lack of familiarity with such matters involved more than deficiencies created by a quick buildup. Regular instruction in the law of war was often inadequate. The CO of the marine battalion whose men were involved in the Son Thang killings testified at one of the courts-martial resulting from that incident that "in my 20 years of commissioned service, I know of no time period of instruction where an individual Marine was told when he could disobey an order."[75] I will return to this important matter later.

The Treatment of American Prisoners by the Vietnamese Communists

The tendency on the part of many intellectuals and publicists in the West to believe the worst about the conduct of U.S. forces in Vietnam was accompanied by an amazingly naive acceptance of communist propaganda from Hanoi which regularly spoke of the humane treatment extended to Americans captured in South or North Vietnam. The dishonesty of these assertions was revealed after the release of the American prisoners following the 1973 Paris agreement. As of 1 April 1973, 566 U.S. military personnel and 25 civilians had returned alive; the remains of 23 prisoners said to have died in captivity in North Vietnam were also returned. That left 1,284 men who remained unaccounted for and were officially listed as missing. Some 50 of these had been listed by the North Vietnamese news agency as captured alive, others had been seen alive after capture. The subsequent fate of all of them remained unknown.[76] In view of what the returned prisoners related about the conditions of their captivity, it is likely that an undeterminable number were killed some time after capture or died as a result of mistreatment.

In response to an inquiry from the International Committee of the Red Cross, dated 11 June 1965, the National Liberation Front announced that it did not consider itself bound by international treaties to which others besides itself had subscribed. Nevertheless, the NLF affirmed "that the prisoners it held were humanely treated and that above all, enemy wounded were collected and cared for."[77] The generally accepted position appeared to be that the VC were bound by Article 3, common to all four of the Geneva conventions of 1949, which lays down minimum humanitarian standards of conduct in wars not of an international character, or, at the very least, by the customary law of war, which requires that prisoners of war be treated humanely.[78] Whatever the legalities of the situation, the story told by American and other prisoners released in 1973 was one of brutal abuse which made a mockery of the NLF's claims of humane treatment.

A group of German volunteers, who had worked as hospital nurses for the Knights of Malta and were captured by the VC in April 1969 near Danang, were kept in various jungle prisons in the South before they were eventually sent to North Vietnam. Before their transfer, three of the five died of malnutrition and lack of medical care.[79] The experience of

Americans captured in the South was the same. S. Sgt. David M. Harker, taken prisoner in January 1968, after his release told the House Foreign Affairs Committee of being subjected to a starvation diet without sufficient vegetables and proteins. Ten out of 27 Americans held with him in the central highlands died as a result of insufficient food, chronic dysentery, scurvy or malaria.[80]

The accounts of other captives who survived are identical. The men would contract edema and suffer intense pain from swollen testicles, liver and spleen associated with acute malnutrition. The lack of vitamins and oil in the diet led to skin diseases which left them covered with boils and sores. "The epidermis cracked open with water-blister-type sores that first ran clear serum and then pus. Scratching was almost sexual in its relief but only made the disease worse. The pus dried gluing our pajamas to our backsides. The pain was horrible. Eighteen of us were jammed together on the bed. It was excruciatingly hot. But we had to sleep under our blankets to ward off hordes of mosquitoes. Men cried out at night, 'Kill me! I want to die!' Guys began to schiz out in the daytime by pulling blankets over their heads to shut out the world."[81] Some became walking zombies; eventually they would just refuse to get up and die.

Among the few prisoners to survive five and a half years of captivity by the NLF was an Army physician, Maj. F. Harold Kushner. One of the other survivors recalls: "It was especially hard on him watching men die whom he knew he could save if medicines were available. But nothing was available, or if it was the VC waited as usual until it was too late."[82] The overall death rate of American prisoners held in South Vietnam is estimated as 20 percent; practically all these deaths were preventable. The guards at times made a show of eating the same food, but this was a deliberately staged farce. The fact is that they did not die of starvation.

The only way to get better treatment was to agree to write or tape antiwar statements. Most of those who survived eventually broke and agreed to cooperate with their captors. Several times, men known to their fellow prisoners as "progressives" were released after making the required confessions of crimes and atrocities. Among those who refused to give in was Sgt. Kenneth Roraback, one of four Special Forces sergeants captured in November 1963, who was executed in reprisal for the execution of a VC terrorist in Saigon in September 1965. Article 13 of the Geneva Convention Relative to the Treatment of Prisoners of War states unequivocally: "Measures of reprisal against prisoners of war are prohibited."[83]

While the four sergeants were being subjected to "re-education," they were interviewed by the Australian procommunist journalist Wilfred G. Burchett. The sergeants had assured him, he related in a book published shortly thereafter, that they were being well treated.[84] An American VC sympathizer wrote in 1970: "The NLF, less well armed than the ARVN, and fighting a guerilla war, takes few prisoners by the very nature of its operations. When prisoners are taken they are sometimes killed, but torture of prisoners by the NLF is very rarely reported."[85] This denial of torture was untrue in 1970 and is plainly false in view of what we know today. Those with a stomach for the clinical details of slow death by malnutrition and disease may want to read the grim tale told by two AID officials who survived, published in *Nutrition Today* in May/June 1973.[86]

The Democratic Republic of Vietnam ratified the 1949 Geneva conventions in 1957, but with several reservations. One of these relates to Article 85 of the POW Convention, according to which prisoners of war "prosecuted under the laws of the Detaining Power for acts committed prior to capture shall retain, even if convicted, the benefits of the present Convention."[87] The North Vietnamese reservation stated that "prisoners of war prosecuted and convicted for war crimes or for crimes against humanity, in accordance with the principles laid down by the Nuremberg Court of Justice shall not benefit from the present Convention, as specified in Article 85."[88] After the start of the bombing of North Vietnam in 1965, the DRV took the position that the American pilots shot down and captured were war criminals and therefore not entitled to the benefits of the Geneva convention. Threats to try pilots on charges of war crimes were abandoned after widespread international protests in July 1966, but the DRV nevertheless continued to treat all American captives in North Vietnam as convicted war criminals. This denial of the benefits of the Geneva convention was in violation of the North Vietnamese reservation, which requires prosecution and conviction for war crimes before a prisoner can be denied the protection of the humanitarian provisions of the convention.[89]

The ICRC challenged the North Vietnamese position, but to no avail. Just like the NLF in the South, Hanoi assured the world that despite the terrible crimes the U.S. pilots had committed they were being treated decently and indeed better than they deserved. Ever willing to be of service, Wilfred G. Burchett wrote after an interview with North Vietnamese officials in the spring of 1966: "In view of what is going on in the South and in the North, it is indeed a tribute to the discipline and truly civilized outlook of the Vietnamese people that pilots have been humanely treated from the moment of their capture."[90] Gullible Hanoi sympathizers and antiwar activists in this country accepted these assurances at face value. Between 1967 and 1972 the North Vietnamese released 15 prisoners in batches of 3 to various American antiwar groups. Each release provided the North Vietnamese and the antiwar organizations receiving the prisoners with extensive newspaper, television and radio publicity and each was heralded as proof of Hanoi's conciliatory attitude. If the purpose had been truly humanitarian, the North Vietnamese would, of course, have released the seriously wounded and sick prisoners as required by Article 109 of the Geneva convention. Instead they picked prisoners who had been in captivity a relatively short time and were in more or less presentable physical condition.[91]

Information that the treatment of American prisoners in North Vietnam was something less than "humane" became available even before the release of the survivors in 1973, though it was difficult to get media attention for it. On 6 July 1966, the North Vietnamese paraded 48 American prisoners, handcuffed to each other, through the streets of Hanoi, another violation of the Geneva convention. Press releases and photographs of the parade were released by the official North Vietnamese press agency. The purpose of this march apparently was to whip up support for the trial of captured pilots as war criminals, though the full extent of the mob hysteria engendered became known only later. Col. Robinson Risner, one of the participants in the march, has described how the crowd lined up along the two-mile route hit the Americans and threw rocks at them. By the end of the march, "we were a pretty beat-up looking group. Some were bleeding and swollen and others sagging, semiconscious."[92]

Until 1969 the policy of the Johnson administration was not to publicize the abuses and cruelties known to prevail in the North Vietnamese prisons. There was fear that such publicity might endanger the welfare of the prisoners and hope of obtaining lists of the captives and perhaps the release of the wounded. The Nixon administration concluded that this attitude of restraint had not produced the expected results and that a mobilized world public opinion might have more of an impact. On 19 May 1969 Secretary of Defense Laird accused the North Vietnamese of across-the-board inhumane treatment of the American prisoners. On 5 September 1969 Navy Lt. Robert F. Frishman and Seaman Douglas B. Hegdahl, released the preceding month to a group of American antiwar activists led by Rennie Davis, described the brutality and torture they had experienced and witnessed at a news conference held at Bethesda Navy Hospital. Frishman had lost 45 pounds, Hegdahl 60 pounds. Rennie Davis and his friends had praised the humane treatment of the prisoners. A soft-spoken rebuttal now came from Lt. Frishman: "I don't think solitary confinement, forced statements, living in a cage for three years, being put in straps, not being allowed to sleep or eat, removal of finger nails, being hung from the ceiling, having an infected arm almost lost without medical care, being dragged along the ground with a broken leg and not allowing exchange of mail for prisoners are humane."[93] Pulitzer prize–winning reporter Seymour Hersh in February 1971 commented on Frishman's recital of horror: "There is evidence in the public record that Frishman seriously distorted and misrepresented the prison conditions inside North Vietnam."[94]

The extensive publicity and growing concern over the mistreatment of the American captives by late 1969 had produced some improvement in prison conditions in North Vietnam, though the torture of prisoners continued intermittently. The wish to ignore or disbelieve the unpleasant news about prison conditions in North Vietnam persisted among large segments of the articulate American public. In December 1970 Dave Dellinger denounced what he called the "Prisoner of War Hoax"—"the Nixon Administration's creation of the myth of the innocent and mistreated American prisoners held in North Vietnam. . . . The only verified torture associated with American prisoners held by the North Vietnamese is the torture of the prisoners' families by the State Department, the Pentagon and the White House." Back in 1967, wrote Dellinger, he had personally interviewed Comdr. Richard Stratton in Hanoi, who had assured him that he was being well-treated.[95] Stratton, it was revealed in 1973, following his capture on 5 January 1967 had been brutally tortured until he had signed a much-publicized confession just two months before Dellinger's arrival: "Since my capture, I have been led to see the full and true nature of my criminal acts against the people of Vietnam in terms of injury, death and destruction. I sincerely acknowledge my crimes and repent at having committed them."[96] Stratton's deep bow before his captors, we now know, was meant to show the American audience, which, he thought, might view his filmed appearance, that he was not in control of the situation, but this signal was lost on Dellinger.

For Richard A. Falk, writing in *The Progressive* in March 1971, the new concern about the mistreatment of American prisoners in North Vietnam was "the result of a deliberate and cynical effort on the part of the Nixon administration to exploit the plight of the POWs" in order to rally support for the government's policy of "prolonging and expanding the war." Falk referred to reports by American, French and Japanese peace groups who had visited North Vietnam and had determined that no systematic torture or brainwashing was taking place. The most informed and reliable study, Falk wrote, was that of a former State Department official, Jon M. van Dyke, who had concluded that there was no evidence that North Vietnam was pursuing a policy of torture and whose "careful analysis of the most publicized claims of torture by some released prisoners casts considerable doubt on the authenticity of their allegations."[97] Richard J. Barnet of the Institute of Policy Studies told the House Foreign Affairs Committee on 31 March 1971 that "the evidence of mistreatment is itself highly suspect,"[98] and Steward Meacham, peace secretary of the American Friends Service Committee, informed the same committee that his own first-hand observations in Hanoi had convinced him that "the interrogation process, unlike the situation in the prisons of the Republic of Vietnam (Saigon), is not accompanied by torture."[99]

After the last American prisoners had returned from Vietnam in April 1973, the testimony of numerous senior officers, identical in practically every detail, finally put to rest the myth of "humane" treatment. Testifying before Congress, at news conferences and in many books and articles, these men have described how they were tortured into confessions of criminal conduct and in preparation for meeting delegations from Eastern Europe, North Korea, Japan and America, the testimony to be given carefully rehearsed with a tape recorder.[100] Lt. Comdr. David. W. Hoffman has told that he was "persuaded" to meet with former Attorney General Ramsey Clark in August 1972 by being hung by his broken arm. Upon his return from Hanoi, Clark assured a committee of Congress chaired by Senator Kennedy that the prisoners he had met were well-treated, had exercise, got all they wanted to eat and generally were "good, strong Americans. . . . I think when we say those men are 'brainwashed,' and they don't know what they are doing, we do a terrible disservice to them."[101]

The most frequent mode of torture was to put a prisoner into ropes— arms tied tightly behind the back and head and shoulders forced down until the mouth practically touched the feet. As a result of constricted circulation, after a while the pain became so excruciating that the prisoner was prepared to do anything his captors demanded. The German volunteer nurse Bernhard Diehl recalls the case of one American officer who was hung from the ceiling with a rope around his left wrist. He screamed for an hour before the guards took him down, but they had to repeat the torture 18 times before they managed to break him.[102] Col. James Kasler, by the time the interrogators had finally gotten him to surrender, was in such bad physical shape that they could no longer present him to the delegation for which they had sought to prepare him. Col. Kenneth North told the House Foreign Affairs Committee that according to statistics kept by the prisoner organization, approximately 95 percent of the men in the North Vietnamese prisons were tortured to extract military information or propaganda statements.[103] A study undertaken at the Center for Prisoner of War Studies (a joint Army–Navy–Marine Corps activity) found that 60.6 percent of a representative sample of returned prisoners were subjected to torture devices or procedures such as "the ropes."[104] According to Capt. James A. Mulligan, Jr., who himself spent 42 months in solitary confinement, often without food, water or medical care, about 80 percent were finally broken and made some sort of statement for the enemy.[105]

Anthony Lewis of the *New York Times*, who interviewed Captain Mulligan a year after his return from North Vietnam, was shaken up by the tale of horror he heard and rebuked those "critical of the war [who] seem to regard the reports of how the American prisoners were mistreated as a distraction from larger truths." That was a mirror of attitudes on the other side. "We have to learn again and again that no cause can justify inhumanity. More than most American experiences, the Vietnam war has obscured perception of that moral imperative."[106] A long-time associate of the left-wing Paris weekly *Le Nouvel Observateur*, the British-born journalist Oliver Todd, concluded that in a closely knit communist regime like that ruling North Vietnam, there could be no torture "by accident," abuses committed by sadistic subordinates who act outside the supervision and without the knowledge of their superiors. The treatment of the American prisoners, he wrote in an article entitled "How I Let Myself Be Deceived by Hanoi," meant something essential to him—"it exposes the true nature of the Hanoi regime."[107] Kenneth Crawford wrote in the *Washington Post:* "What is most shocking about the repeated torture of U.S. prisoners is that is was inflicted by uniformed military personnel, obviously as a matter of policy emanating from on high."[108]

Back in 1967 Dave Dellinger had interviewed the North Vietnamese official in charge of the prisoners in Hanoi, Major Bui, who told him:

> Of course we give them books like Felix Greene to read and the text of the Geneva Accords and I myself often talk with them for an hour or two. But you can be sure that there are no pressures brought and that we simply explore as fellow human beings the kind of world it is and the kind of world we would like it to be.
>
> I don't know. Perhaps some Americans would consider that brainwashing but we don't, and I don't think the prisoners do either. And they are free not to talk with us and not have such conversations if at any time they find them offensive.[109]

The freedom "not to have such conversations," it now turned out, had to be bought at the price of solitary confinement, deprivation of food and sleep, being put into irons or trussed in ropes and suspended from the ceiling. And yet, some men refused to the end to sign statements denouncing their country and government. A few of these survived the ordeal such resistance entailed; most died of starvation, disease or mistreatment or were executed. Those who refused to give the North Vietnamese anything but name, rank and serial number, writes a survivor, did not come home.[110]

Five Army enlisted men, captured in the South, became willing propagandists for their captors and formed a so-called Peace Committee. After the release of the prisoners in 1973, Col. Ted Guy, the senior officer in charge of the prisoner organization, filed charges of misconduct against these men for having cooperated willingly with the enemy in a variety of propaganda activities in violation of the Code of Conduct. On 3 July 1973 Secretary of the Army Callaway, acting upon a recommendation of Army Chief of Staff Abrams, announced dismissal of these charges. The dismissals, he explained, were recommended by legal counsel because of lack of legally sufficient evidence and because of DOD's policy against holding trials for alleged propaganda statements. He added: "We must not overlook the good behavior of these men during the two to three years each spent under brutal prison conditions in South Vietnam, before they were moved to the north—the lack of food and medical care, the sub-primitive living conditions, and the physical torture."[111] New and similar charges filed later by another officer were also dismissed.

The treatment of the American prisoners by their Vietnamese Communist captors should not have come as a surprise. Systematic abuse and forced confessions fit into a pattern of communist conduct going back decades. There was the experience of Korea, where 107 captured American flyers were deprived of basic physical needs and subjected to prolonged physical and mental torture in order to extract confessions of germ warfare. The extent of the use of these techniques, the American representative told a United Nations committee after the return of the surviving prisoners in 1953, depended on the degree of resistance shown by the individual prisoner. "The total picture presented is one of human beings reduced to a status lower than that of animals: filthy, full of lice, festered wounds full of maggots; their sickness regulated to a point just short of death; unshaven, without haircuts or baths for as much as a year; men in rags, exposed to the elements; fed with carefully measured minimum quantities and lowest qualities of food and unsanitary water, served often in rusty cans; isolated, faced with squads of trained interrogators, bullied incessantly, deprived of sleep, and browbeaten into mental anguish." Of those tortured, thirty-six finally signed some sort of propaganda statement; 6 admitted to detailed charges of germ warfare which they promptly repudiated after their release; 31 fliers did not survive.[112]

The overall treatment of the captives in the Korean War was so atrocious that 38 percent of the captured Americans died in captivity—mainly as a consequence of malnutrition, exposure, disease and untreated wounds. According to official DOD figures, of 7,140 confirmed prisoners only 4,418 returned alive; 2,701 died after capture—during the death marches to the POW camps or while imprisoned. An undetermined percentage of the 5,866 missing in action are believed to have been killed. In all, 5,639 American servicemen of all ranks are listed as dead as a result of war crimes.[113]

According to several accounts, a prominent role in obtaining the confessions of germ warfare was played by two Western journalists—Alan Winnington of the London communist *Daily Worker* and the Australian correspondent of the French communist paper *Ce Soir,* Wilfred Burchett. The two men are said to have put the confessions into literary form and filmed the depositions.[114] In a book published in Peking in 1954, Winnington and Burchett called the charges of bad treatment of American and British captives a "dreadful atrocity campaign."[115] Testimony about Burchett's part in helping to force the confessions from the captives figured prominently in a recent libel suit in Sydney, Australia.[116] The charge of American germ warfare in Korea is so discredited today that the Soviet Union in 1969 signed a UN report which acknowledged that chemical and bacteriological agents had not yet been used as modern military weapons.[117] An English study of chemical and biological warfare, very critical of American tactics in Vietnam, draws attention to the repudiation of the confessions and concludes: "The whole thing has been written off almost unanimously as Communist propaganda."[118]

Even more relevant is the treatment of French Union prisoners by the Viet Minh in the first Indochina war. The 40-day forced march to POW camps of about 7,000 prisoners taken at Dien Bien Phu in May 1954, wrote the well-informed historian of that war, Bernard Fall, "caused more losses than any single battle of the whole Indochina war."[119] Food on the 500-mile trek was cold rice once a day; those who survived lost more than half their normal weight. Men no longer able to march were left on the wayside to die. This was also the fate of about 1,000 seriously wounded who had been abandoned on the battlefield. Conditions in the POW camps were little better. Food was scarce, medical care at times nonexistent, and prisoners died from various diseases in frightful numbers. Not a single prisoner with battle-incurred injuries of the abdomen, chest or skull survived captivity. Of the 10,754 prisoners returned after the exchange of prisoners began on 18 August 1954, 6,132 required immediate hospitalization. Forty-nine of those who died after repatriation had been captured at Dien Bien Phu just a few weeks earlier; their captivity encompassed a time when aid shipments from the Soviet Union and China had alleviated earlier shortages. Most of the survivors of the communist regimen, writes Fall, "were walking skeletons in no way different from those who survived Dachau and Buchenwald."[120]

Mistreatment involved not just starvation diets and lack of medical care. The Communists considered overcoming the minds of their captives part of their overall struggle. Every detail of life in the camps was the subject of discussions and self-criticism sessions. Prisoners had to write confessions of crimes, and recalcitrants were subjected to harsh punishment, including transfer to the feared Lang-Trang reprisal camp. A French paratroop chaplain, Father Paul Jeandel, who spent three years in communist camps, writes in a book about his experiences: "Medieval tortures are nothing in comparison to the atomic-age torture of brainwashing. . . . The victims must approve and justify in their own eyes the measures which crush them. They must recognize themselves guilty and believe in the crimes which they have not committed. . . . I have seen men leave Camp No. 1 who were dead and did not know it, for they had lost their personality and had become slogan-reciting robots."[121]

There was thus ample reason to suspect Hanoi's assurances that American prisoners received humane treatment and to repudiate as worthless reports coming from friends of Hanoi such as Wilfred Burchett. The West's naïveté in understanding communist tactics of deception is matched only by the failure to learn from even the most painful experiences. Back in 1961 Bernard Fall urged that the true facts about the treatment of French prisoners in the first Indochina war be known in the West "since future complications in the area may compel conflict with the same foe once more under similar conditions."[122] His exhortation fell on deaf ears then, and the same indifference and credulity continue today. The atrocities committed by the Communists against American prisoners during the Vietnam war have not received much attention. Most of the books cited here have not been reviewed by prestigious journals. Diehard Hanoi sympathizers continue to disbelieve the accounts of torture, grimly monotonous in their repetition of crucial details. A journalist seeking to break the silence that has engulfed this subject met young people who were convinced that the fractures, bruises and other signs of mistreatment exhibited by the prisoners had actually been caused by American doctors after their return.[123]

When I inquired of the State Department why no official White Paper similar to those put out by Allied governments after the Korean War, had been issued on these atrocities, I was informed by a high official: "Part of the reluctance to produce such a document stems, I suspect, from a general feeling in our country and government that it is time to put the Indochina conflict, with all its problems, behind us."[124] One is left wondering whether putting the war in Vietnam behind us must also mean ignoring unpleasant truths and their lessons.

10

The Punishment of Atrocities and War Crimes

The term "war crime" is the technical expression for a violation of the law of war by any person, military or civilian; every violation of the law of war is a war crime.[1] The term "atrocity" has no technical legal definition. In general usage, atrocities are offenses taking place during the course of military operations which would constitute serious felonies against persons under the criminal law of civilized countries—such as murder, rape or aggravated assault. Since many of the victims of American atrocities in Vietnam were citizens of an allied nation, not protected under applicable international law, and since atrocities and violations of the law of war also violated the Uniform Code of Military Justice (UCMJ), which governed the conduct of all U.S. military personnel, both atrocities and war crimes committed by U.S. forces in Vietnam were prosecuted as violations of the UCMJ.

The Reporting of War Crimes

U.S. personnel in Vietnam were under orders to report war crimes to higher authorities, up to and including MACV. Until 25 March 1966, this obligation extended only to war crimes or prohibited acts "inflicted by hostile forces upon U.S. military or civilian personnel assigned to Vietnam."[2] From 25 March 1966 on, it included all war crimes, whether inflicted upon U.S. forces or by U.S. military personnel upon hostile military or civilian personnel. War crimes were defined as violations of the law of war, including the Geneva conventions of 1949. Examples of war crimes cited were willful killing of noncombatants, torture or inhuman treatment of prisoners, maltreatment of dead bodies, firing on undefended places, pillage or purposeless destruction and the like. It was the responsibility of every military individual "having knowledge or receiving a report of an incident or of an act thought to be a war crime to make such incident known to his commanding officer as soon as practicable."[3]

Until 1970, no provision was made for the possibility that a commander might himself be involved in the commission of a war crime, and failure to provide the individual soldier in such a case with an alternative reporting channel may have facilitated the covering up of the My Lai massacre. Upon the suggestion of the Peers Inquiry, the revised outline for the training of troops in the Hague and Geneva conventions, issued 8 October 1970, stated that "if someone in the chain [of command] above you was involved in the alleged crime," the soldier could report such a crime to the local Office of the Inspector General, the military police, a judge advocate or a chaplain.[4]

MACV also required special reports on incidents causing injury or death to noncombatants (known as BACKLASH reports) and on any incident "involving moral turpitude which may result in damaging public confidence in the U.S. Armed Forces and which, because of the nature or personnel involved, may be reasonably expected to arouse public interest and cause continuous or widespread adverse publicity." This included offenses such as manslaughter, assault, rape, burglary, blackmarketing, mutiny.[5] "Incidents which could be detrimental to US/GVN relations" such as "injury, death or mistreatment of noncombatants or significant damage to Vietnamese property in the course of tactical operations" were also subject to immediate "spot reports" by way of telephone or teletype.[6]

On 21 February 1968, following a large number of press reports and photographs portraying disregard for human life, inhumane treatment and brutality in the handling of prisoners and detainees during the heavy fighting of the Tet offensive, MACV once again announced that atrocities and war crimes "will not be condoned." U.S. advisers with South Vietnamese units were instructed to "make every effort to influence their counterparts to observe humane principles and the Geneva Conventions." Violations of these provisions were to be reported in all detail to "the senior in the chain of command."[7]

In 1967 the President's Commission on Law Enforcement and Administration of Justice concluded that about twice as many major crimes are committed in America as are known to the police; similar findings exist in other countries.[8] There is no reason to assume that the situation was very different with regard to military personnel in Vietnam. Despite many directives requiring the reporting of war crimes and acts causing death, injury or property damage to noncombatants, it is likely that many such incidents escaped detection. Some of this was probably unavoidable. As we have seen, the rules of engagement with regard to firing on populated areas and the issuing of warnings prior to attacks, for example, necessarily had to provide commanders with considerable freedom of action. It would have been completely impossible to ascertain in each instance whether villagers killed were innocent bystanders or porters of ammunition, or whether the silencing of a group of snipers in a hamlet through the use of artillery or air strikes was really necessary. Hence it is not surprising that there are hardly any cases on record of commanders or soldiers being punished for killing noncombatants during the course of military operations in which resistance was encountered. Many of the allegations of war crimes involved incidents where, according to the accusers, villagers were killed without military necessity. Even if such an allegation was substantially correct factually, in many cases the situation may have looked quite different to the officer in charge and, as I have shown earlier, a mistake in judgment is not a war crime.

Yet we know that for a long time the ROE were poorly known and understood, and this undoubtedly, as in the case of the My Lai massacre, contributed to the loss of innocent life. Knowledge of the Geneva conventions and other humanitarian treaties was similarly inadequate. Moreover, the system of reporting war crimes in effect required commanders to report their own deficiencies; there existed no independent check on the adherence of units in the field to the law of war. Let us take the example of a company commander whose men burnt the huts of a hamlet in retaliation for sniper fire received from that hamlet. In order to report this incident as a violation of the ROE and a war crime the commander would have had to acknowledge that he had been unable properly to control his men. In such a situation it was far more likely that the officer would use the existence of family shelters dug by most villagers in Vietnam in order to report the incident as having taken place in a fortified hamlet where the burning of the huts was the unavoidable by-product of destroying enemy bunkers and fortifications. The commander of the battalion, hovering above the scene in his helicopter, would have had to acknowledge that he, too, was not in complete control of the battlefield situation, and so forth up the chain of command.

A typical commander probably reacted much the same way to an incident in which a trigger-happy soldier during a sweep through a hamlet killed a Vietnamese later found to be an innocent villager. Instead of reporting that the poorly-disciplined soldier firing the shots had failed to shout the required warning and had killed without military necessity, it was far more likely that the platoon leader, under pressure for body count and not anxious to demonstrate the absence of good fire discipline in his unit, would report the incident as "1 VC suspect shot while evading." Many VC undoubtedly did attempt to escape and failed to heed warnings to stop, but the regularity with which the phrase "shot while evading" appears in after-combat reports seems to indicate that the expression was used in other instances as well.

The officer covering up for his men at times may have done so not only to hide his own ineffective leadership. In some VC-dominated areas like the coastal lowlands of Quang Nam and Quang Ngai provinces in I CTZ, for example, where the line between combatants and noncombatants was extremely fuzzy, the nature of the war was such that the soldier, in order to survive, often had to shoot first and ask questions later. Junior officers shared the frustrations and anger experienced by their men and therefore tried to help them when they got into trouble. Thus the marine lieutenant who sent out the "killer team" in the Son Thang incident not only instructed them "to pay the little bastards back," but after the patrol came back tried to cover up the killing of noncombatants by reporting the incident as a firefight with a group of VC which resulted in the capture of a weapon. The Article 32 investigation of his role (the pretrial screening procedure used in the military justice system which is similar to the civilian preliminary hearing) brought out that he had been generally aware of what had happened during the patrol but had been motivated to conceal it out of loyalty to his men.[9]

Failure to impose meaningful punishment for not reporting war crimes may have contributed to an attitude of laxness and indifference regarding such crimes. During the night of 2 June 1968, two female nurses captured by a company of the Americal Division were subjected to multiple rapes, sodomy and other mistreatment; the following morning one of the two nurses was killed. The company commander was 60 feet from the scene of the murder and, in the words of the court of review, "if the appellant did not hear the three shots (fired when his troops were not engaged in battle), he must have been intentionally deaf." He also knew what had transpired during the night, as was evident from his remark to one of his men concerning the remaining female detainee: ". . . if she's taken back to the MI [military intelligence] interrogation and she tells what happened in the field we'll all swing for it."[10]

The company commander's conduct and his failure to report this atrocity should probably have led to a charge of being an accessory to the crime of rape and murder of a detainee, a war crime. One of the judges of the court of review cited the words of General MacArthur with regard to the case of Yamashita which he felt were "shamefully applicable here": "Rarely has so cruel and wanton a record been spread to public gaze."[11] At the very least, the captain's disregard of the duty of a commander to properly supervise his men amounted to what the Nuremberg tribunal in the earlier-cited *High Command* case characterized as "criminal negligence"—"personal neglect amounting to a wanton, immoral disregard of the action of his subordinates amounting to acquiescence." Instead he was charged with and convicted of failing to report the nonbattle death of a detainee and dereliction of duty in failing to protect a female Oriental in the custody of his unit, and he was sentenced to a reprimand and fine of $2,500. In view of his good previous record, the court of review reduced the fine to $1,200. It is difficult to believe that such punishment could have a significant deterrent effect and help prevent the cover-up of atrocities.

Whatever the reasons, it is apparent that the rules for reporting war crimes were often violated. Many of the prosecutions for willful killings of noncombatants, for the abuse of prisoners or for the mutilation of corpses were indeed started not as a result of reports filed in accordance with required practices by the officers of the units involved in these incidents but in response to charges made by individuals long since separated and discharged from the service. Of the 241 allegations of war crimes involving Army personnel made between 1965 and 1975, 191 (79 percent) were made after September 1969, when the My Lai incident was initially publicized (see Table 10-1). Forty-seven of these allegations were found to be substantiated, providing probable cause for disciplinary action. In most cases it proved impossible to determine whether commanding officers had known of these incidents. The one case investigated thoroughly because of

Table 10-1 War Crimes Allegations[a] against U.S. Army Personnel, Other than Son My (As of 25 June 1975)

	Pre–Son My (1/1/65– 8/31/69)	Post–Son My (9/1/69– 7/25/75)	Total
Allegations made:			
Unsubstantiated/unfounded	19	144	163
Substantiated (probable cause)	31	47	78
Total	50	191	241
Cases of probable cause referred to court-martial:	22	14	36
Convicted	(15)	(5)	(20)
Acquitted/dismissed	(7)	(9)	(16)
Offenses in cases of court-martial conviction:			
Murder/manslaughter	6	3	9
Rape	3	0	3
Mistreatment of PWs/detainees	3	0	3
Mutilation	3	2	5
Subtotal	15	5	20

SOURCE: U.S. Department of the Army, Office of the Judge Advocate General, International Affairs Division.

[a] Numbers refer to cases (incidents) which may involve more than one individual.

the magnitude of the offense—the My Lai massacre—revealed, in the words of the Peers Inquiry, that within "the Americal Division, at every command level from company to division, actions were taken or omitted which together effectively concealed from higher headquarters the events which transpired in TF Barker's operations of 16–19 March 1968." [12] In fact, it is questionable whether even the revised reporting procedures instituted in 1970 on account of the demonstrated inadequacies of earlier directives would have prevented the cover-up. One of the alternative channels recommended in the new instructions, the chaplains, did receive a report on the widespread killing of noncombatants but they, too, failed to act. [13]

A study of problem areas in Vietnam, prepared for the Army chief of staff after the My Lai affair had surfaced, stated: "The number of allegations regarding tactical excesses not all of which can be discounted as deliberate falsehoods, and the relatively small number of reported investigations of such offenses in the field indicate that there have been some gaps in the effectiveness of supervision and correction."[14] In late 1969 the assistant judge advocate general of the Army suggested to the MACV staff judge advocate that MACV open a war crimes office in order to provide fuller surveillance. The staff judge advocate replied on 11 December 1969 that in his view the present system was adequate. No surveillance, he said, could prevent a My Lai–type incident unless one were to have observers at platoon and company level. No reporting system could be effective unless personnel carried out orders to report such incidents. There thus was no way to prevent individual war crimes and no way to ensure that all were reported. "There are clear directives and adequate instruction extant. It is noted that organized society has exactly the same problems with respect to domestic crimes."[15]

The inspector general system, among other things, was supposed to serve as a check on the implementation of and compliance with MACV directives. Inspectors general evaluated and recommended corrective action on matters concerning mission performance, discipline, efficiency and adherence to directives.[16] However, inspectors general could conduct investigations only at the direction and request of commanders. The House Armed Services Committee investigating the My Lai affair and a series of unauthorized bombings concluded in 1972: "As long as the Inspector General remains the agent of the commander, acting only upon his direction, and limited by his instructions, this system will fail to reveal incidents which might embarrass the chain of command."[17] The record bears out this finding. In July 1968 an inspection was held of the Americal Division, but it failed to learn of the My Lai massacre. The unauthorized use of agent Orange by elements of the Americal Division for crop destruction and the unauthorized bombing of North Vietnam in 1971–72 similarly escaped detection by the inspector general. In each case reports were falsified to cover up the violation of directives.

On 10 July 1970 the MACV chief of staff directed that all reports of the investigation of war crimes be reviewed by the MACV inspector general to ensure that these investigations were complete and correct and that appropriate action had been taken by proper authority. Review revealed that several war crimes incidents had been improperly reported. In June 1970 a private and lieutenant of the 173rd Airborne Brigade had mutilated two enemy bodies; there was a case where a captain of the 101st Airborne

Division had witnessed ears being cut off and had failed to report the crime; and there were several other such incidents.[18] In the nature of the case, there is no way of telling how many other such war crimes were similarly not properly reported.

Prosecutions

Figures are available on the number of war crimes allegations made against Army personnel, the number found to be substantiated and the number of individuals tried by court-martial. These statistics are given in Table 10-1. Figures refer to cases (incidents): the 36 cases leading to court-martial involved 61 men, of whom 31 were convicted.[19] If we add the conviction resulting from the My Lai affair, we get a total of 32 Army personnel who were convicted of war crimes in Vietnam.

There exists no central file for allegations of atrocities and war crimes involving American servicemen in Vietnam and of the disposition of these allegations. After the uproar over the cover-up of the My Lai massacre, Secretary of Defense Laird on 11 December 1969 directed the secretaries of the three military services to provide the assistant secretary of defense for administration "with all pertinent facts pertaining to each investigation [of atrocities] as it begins, progresses and is completed."[20] Such reports were filed regularly thereafter, but each service categorized and charged offenses in a different way, which makes comparisons of the performances of the services difficult, if not impossible. The Navy and Air Force had few reported incidents of crime against Vietnamese. Between 1965 and 1971, the Navy had nine court-martial convictions involving Vietnamese victims, the Air Force had seven.[21] Given the limited ground-combat role of these two services this is, of course, what one would expect. The Air Force did not accept as justified the charge that the bombing of North Vietnam involved violations of the law of war; I will return to this subject in a later chapter.

Only the U.S. Army kept statistics on the number of allegations made and their disposition. Also, while the data compiled by the Army differentiated between war crimes—serious offenses committed against Vietnamese during the course of combat operations (or closely linked to them, as in cases of mistreatment of detainees)—and off-duty crimes, the Marine Corps kept statistics only of courts-martial involving serious crimes against Vietnamese. Few of these constituted violations of international law, i.e.

war crimes: the category "murder," for example, includes the robbery-murder of a South Vietnamese soldier who was a drug pusher; "negligent homicide" includes traffic deaths. Table 10-2 (Appendix II, p. 456) should be examined with this important fact in mind. The number of marines convicted was 77, the number acquitted was 38.

Critics of the operation of the military justice system in Vietnam have charged that MACV not only did not adequately investigate alleged war crimes, but that the courts-martial of offenders resulted in excessively lenient treatment. The "mere-gook" rule—the notion that Vietnamese life is cheap—was usually cited as the reason for such mild punishment. One way of testing this charge is to examine the rate of acquittal or dismissal after arraignment in cases of serious crimes where the victim was Vietnamese. Table 10-3 provides such data for the Army and Marine Corps and compares these with some reported results of American domestic trials. This comparison reveals that the rate of acquittal in the case of Army courts-martial was below that of American domestic cases, while in the case of the Marine Corps the rate was about the same. As far as the acquittal rate is concerned, the conclusion of an Army lawyer would therefore appear to be justified: "If courts-martial behave pretty much like American juries, it seems that the drafters of the Uniform Code of Mili-

Table 10-3 Comparative Acquittal/Dismissal Rates (Percent of Individuals Tried) in Trials for Homicide and Rape

	U.S. Army June 1965– June 1968	USMC March 1965– Aug. 1971	U.S. District Courts FY 1969	Kalven & Zeisel[a] (1966)
Homicide	20%	34%	33%	32%
Murder	23%	37%		19%
Manslaughter	18%	32%		45%
Rape	23%	38%	39%	40%
Average	22%	36%	36%	35%

SOURCES: Waldemar A. Solf, "A Response to Telford Taylor's *Nuremberg and Vietnam*," *University of Akron Law Review* V (1972):67; U.S. Navy, Office of the Judge Advocate General, Military Justice Division; U.S. Department of Commerce, *Statistical Abstract of the United States 1970*, table 136; Harry Kalven, Jr., and Hans Zeisel, *The American Jury* (Boston, 1966), p. 42.

[a] The Kalven-Zeisel study was based on information supplied by a sample of judges and involved a total of 3,576 trials.

tary Justice have achieved at least one of their objectives. I find no corroboration for the existence of a 'mere gook rule' in the performance of American courts-martial."[22]

In the case of war crimes, i.e. combat-related crimes against Vietnamese, the detailed data available for the U.S. Army draw attention to certain other matters (see Table 10-4, Appendix II, p. 457). It should be noted, first, that about one-third of all individuals convicted of war crimes were convicted by special courts-martial, which handle relatively light offenses only and therefore may not impose confinement for more than six months. For example, two incidents where the subjects scalped and cut off the fingers and ears of two dead enemy soldiers were tried by special court-martial and resulted in fines of $100,[23] hardly a punishment likely to have a strong deterrent effect. Other individuals were subjected to nonjudicial punishment under Article 15 of the UCMJ. Such punishment usually consists of a reduction in grade, the assignment of extra duties, partial forfeiture of pay, and the like.[24] Still other cases resulted merely in adverse administrative action, such as a reprimand.

The data in Table 10-4 also show that officers received more lenient treatment than enlisted men. Fifty-two percent of enlisted men with substantiated allegations of war crimes were tried by court-martial, and of these 51 percent were convicted. In the case of officers, only 30 percent were tried by court-martial, and of these only 36 percent were convicted. Altogether, 61 percent of the officers were either acquitted, had their charges dismissed before trial or got off with administrative action only. In the case of enlisted men the corresponding figure was 34 percent. Officers are tried by courts composed of officers, while enlisted men are generally not tried by juries of their peers (they can demand that at least one-third be enlisted men,[25] but usually do not avail themselves of this right because of fear of drawing hard-nosed "lifers"), and this difference in procedure may help explain the disparity. Moreover, the commander authorized to convene a court-martial also wields the unfettered power not to prosecute, which can create a problem known as "reverse command influence."

The sentences for serious crimes adjudged by Army courts-martial in a combat zone like Vietnam have generally been lower than the sentences for the corresponding crimes imposed by courts-martial in Europe or the United States. For example, during the years 1967 to 1969 the average sentence for premeditated and unpremeditated murder adjudged against

Army personnel in Europe and the U.S. was 29 and 12.8 years respectively; during the years 1965 to 1970 in Vietnam, and with regard to Vietnamese victims, it was 16 and 9.7 years respectively.[26] The explanation for this disparity is probably not so much the "mere-gook" rule as the sympathy which many officers in the field sitting on courts-martial had for the stress and frustrations their men were experiencing in the Vietnam combat environment.[27] This meant that the killing of a Vietnamese civilian on occasion, and perhaps justifiably, was seen as a somewhat less grave offense than the unprovoked killing of a German, Frenchman or fellow American in a situation where servicemen did not labor under the severe tension produced by a counterinsurgency war.

The argument that the combat environment of Vietnam should serve as a mitigating factor was usually pressed by defense counsel, but it was just as regularly opposed by the prosecutor, and it was not always accepted by the courts. In a case of rape committed in December 1968 by two soldiers of the Americal Division, 19 and 20 years old, defense counsel argued on appeal: "When young men are suddenly placed in combat, where they observe the violent death of their friends caused by guerillas, who are indistinguishable from the local population. . . . their acts although wrong, are quite different than the same acts committed in a normal society. Their prayer for compassion is based upon the fact that they were not responsible for the brutality of combat, nor can they be condemned for their only too human feelings of hostility." In such a situation rape was not so much an ordinary sex offense as an act of plunder.[28] The court of review rejected this argument and confirmed the sentence of dishonorable discharge, forfeiture of all pay and allowances and confinement at hard labor for three years.

The outcome was somewhat different in the case of three soldiers of the First Cavalry Division who in April 1967 had killed a Vietnamese detainee, allegedly on radioed instructions of the company commander. At the court-martial where one of the three, a 19-year-old private, was tried for unpremeditated murder, defense counsel argued that the environment in which this young man had been placed had made execution of such an order seem an acceptable act: "Let's face it, gentlemen, we glorify killing over here. Damn it, we give medals for it. He has seen his friends killed and wounded. He has had a close friend shot twice in the back. He has seen blood and guts. Killing and people being killed is an everyday fact of life. He's out there slopping around. He has seen dead mutilated bodies and he has seen American soldiers shot in the head. He has seen VC atrocities. Gentlemen, this affects a man, nobody can deny that. His platoon was nearly wiped out and a lot of his friends were killed or wounded."[29] At the trial of another of these men, a medic, a sergeant testified in his defense: "A man that gets out there and he sees his buddy get tore up pretty bad. Have any of you people ever sat and watched a man for three or four hours with half his head blown off and watch him die? Circumstances like this are the kind of sort that get a man a little bit blood thirsty out there. I've been the same way. I've been to the point where I'd kill a woman or child if I had a chance after seeing some of my best buddies die."[30]

The prosecutor in vain tried o counter this kind of testimony:

> What the accused did here violates every principle of international law, all the rules of land warfare, and in addition violates the rules against simple humanity. Gentlemen, if this type of conduct is to be condoned by the United States Army this entire war effort has gone far remote, the billions of dollars we've spent, all the human sacrifice, all the human lives have been to no avail. If we are to condone this we might as well pack up and go home. What the accused did is a blot on the profession of our Army that can never be erased. The soldier by the very nature of his being here is charged with the responsibility of protecting the weak and the unarmed whether he be an enemy or whether he be a friend. Even assuming that this man was a Viet Cong there can be no conceivable justification for taking him out with his hands tied and his head bowed and killing him.[31]

But the officers making up the court were more impressed by defense counsel's marshaling of evidence pointing to widespread brutalization in this unit which made the killing of a defenseless Vietnamese seem an ordinary thing. Two men were found guilty of unpremeditated murder and received a sentence of ten and four years confinement at hard labor respectively. The charge of the third was reduced to voluntary manslaughter and he was sentenced to confinement for one year. The commander who convened the court-martial (the convening authority), empowered by the UCMJ to disapprove a sentence in whole or in part,[32] reduced the two sentences for unpremeditated murder to seven and three years respectively. The board of review, required to review all cases resulting in confinement of one year or more and also empowered to set aside a sentence in whole or in part,[33] reduced confinement to two years each.

The company commander who according to the accused had ordered the killing of the detainee was acquitted. His radioman and an NCO present at the company command post corroborated the officer's denial that he had issued such an order.[34] But even if such an order had been issued it would not have absolved the three soldiers accused in the killing. In reviewing the case of one of the two convicted of firing the fatal shots, the board of review took up the argument of superior orders and confirmed the ruling of the judge at the court-martial that the existence of an order did not constitute a defense to the charge of commission of a war crime:

> A soldier or airman is not an automaton but a reasoning agent who is under a duty to exercise judgment in obeying the orders of a superior officer to the extent, that where such orders are manifestly beyond the scope of the issuing officer's authority and are so palpably illegal on their face that a man of ordinary sense and understanding would know them to be illegal, then the fact of obedience to the order of a superior officer will not protect a soldier for acts committed pursuant to such illegal orders. This is the law in regard to superior orders.[35]

In a case involving a marine lance corporal who in August 1966 had killed an unarmed villager, allegedly for revenge, the courts accepted the "combat environment" argument only to a minimal extent. The accused, charged with premeditated murder, took the stand and testified that he had been in heavy combat for several months, had seen many of his buddies get killed and wounded and finally decided "I had to kill a VC for those guys, I just had to kill one." A psychiatrist who had examined the accused testified that as a result of stress experienced "his ability to adhere to the right was significantly impaired"; another psychiatrist maintained that this ability was "to some degree" impaired. The prosecutor, backed up by the law officer of the court-martial, argued that the accused had known what he was doing and that impairment of the ability to adhere to the right to some extent was not sufficient to exculpate criminal responsibility. "Gentlemen," he told the court, "life is not so cheap even in Vietnam. It is not so cheap that indiscriminate killing of a defenseless Vietnamese without justification whatsoever can be tolerated or condoned."[36] The court found the marine guilty as charged and sentenced him to dishonorable discharge, forfeiture of all pay and allowances, reduction to private and confinement at hard labor for life. The convening authority confirmed the sentence as adjudged; the Navy board of review reduced the period of confinement to 25 years. The accused had been through eight combat operations and seen close friends killed or horribly wounded. The incident, a "serious aberration from his usual good conduct, was due to the stress of combat and mitigated thereby."[37] On 22 December 1970, the secretary of the Navy, exercising his prerogative to remit a court-martial sentence in whole or in part,[38] reduced the confinement to 6 years.

While the position taken by the military courts with regard to the "combat environment" argument thus was not uniform, large segments of the people at home strongly opposed the trial of servicemen for acts of violence against civilians committed during combat operations. After two marines involved in the Son Thang (4) killing of 5 women and 11 children had been convicted of murder in February 1970 and sentenced to confinement at hard labor for life and for five years respectively, 160,000 citizens of Oklahoma signed a petition sent to the commandant of the Marine Corps which requested the release of these "unjustly confined" men.[39] In August 1970 Sen. Henry Bellmon of Oklahoma, a World War II marine combat veteran, proposed a sense-of-the-Senate resolution which would have freed U.S. military personnel under hostile fire from individual responsibility for causing civilian casualties incident to direct ground combat.[40] An even larger outburst of popular sympathy followed the conviction of Lt. William Calley for his share in the My Lai massacre.

The Legal Consequences of the My Lai Incident

On 29 March 1971, after a court-martial spread over more than four months, 1st Lt. William Calley was found guilty of three counts of premeditated murder of not less than 22 Vietnamese and of assault with intent to commit murder of a young Vietnamese child. Two days later he was sentenced to life imprisonment at hard labor. The evidence at the trial had established that Calley had directed and personally participated in the killing of numerous unarmed and unresisting men, women and children. Calley's pleading of innocence on the grounds that he had merely followed the orders of his company commander, Captain Medina, was rejected by the court without resolving the conflicting testimony of Calley and Medina in this regard. The court of review upheld this finding: "If the members found that appellant fabricated his claim of obedience to orders, their finding has abundant support in the record. If they found his claim of acting in obedience to orders to be credible, he would nevertheless not automatically be entitled to acquittal. . . . An order of the type appellant says he received is illegal. Its illegality is apparent upon even cursory evaluation by a man of ordinary sense and understanding." Calley had acted with murderous *mens rea,* including premeditation. His claim that he was not aware of having committed a "wrong act" did not absolve him.[41]

Within two months of Calley's conviction President Nixon had received 15,000 letters, almost all of them critical of the conviction. Entire draft boards resigned in protest; the Veterans of Foreign Wars sold "Free Calley" bumper stickers to defray his legal fees.[42] Calley, it was argued, had merely done his duty, he had done what the American people had wanted him to do—to win the war. He and his men had killed out of frustration, horror and hatred of the Vietnamese who had killed and wounded their buddies. The real failure, argued one of Calley's defenders, lay "with the society that forced these kids to go to die in a foreign land for a cause it refused to defend at home."[43]

Calley's supporters on the right wing of the American political spectrum were joined by those in the antiwar movement who regarded My Lai as merely a particularly horrible example of everyday American military tactics. The My Lai massacre, asserted one spokesman for this view, "represents no major deviation. The massacre was a minor embellishment on established policy and practice. We believe it would be hypocritical self-righteousness to condemn the men who committed a minor embellishment without condemning those who set the criminal policy itself."[44] A former national coordinator of the VVAW asked: "How can we isolate and punish instances of criminality in a war that was totally criminal?"[45] As Paul C. Warnke, formerly general counsel of DOD, has pointed out, it seems to have escaped these defenders of Calley on the left that "if the overall injustice of a nation's cause waives individual and personal responsibility on the part of the members of its fighting forces, then Lidice, Orad[our] and the systematic slaughter of Jewish populations in occupied countries cannot be construed as the acts of war criminals."[46]

The widespread show of sympathy for Calley before, during and after his trial undoubtedly influenced President Nixon's handling of the Calley case. Three days after Calley had been sentenced to life imprisonment the

White House announced that before the sentence went into effect the president would personally review the case. It was also stated that pending the outcome of the normal military review procedure, Calley would be under house arrest. All this, of course, was a highly unusual interference in the legal process. The wife of an enlisted man, whose sentence of seven years confinement at hard labor for the killing of a Vietnamese boy was under appeal, wrote the president on 6 May 1971 and demanded that her husband, too, be released from jail: "Or is this preferential treatment only for officers found guilty of killing 22 civilians and not lowly privates found guilty of a crime which was never proven. I am asking that some action be taken that all soldiers who are being accused of crimes in Viet Nam and all over be treated the same whether they are officers or privates."[47] We do not know the response of the White House.

On 20 August 1971 the commanding general, Third United States Army, the convening authority of the Calley court-martial, approved the finding of guilty but reduced the confinement at hard labor to 20 years. The court of military review, whose opinion I quoted earlier, affirmed the findings of guilty and the sentence on 16 February 1973. The U.S. Court of Military Appeals, the highest military court, on 21 December 1973 similarly rejected Calley's appeal. On 15 April 1974 the secretary of the Army reduced the sentence to 10 years and President Nixon announced shortly thereafter that, having reviewed the case, he had decided that no further action on his part was necessary or appropriate. Calley's lawyers next carried his appeal to the federal courts on the grounds that his right to a fair trial had been compromised by prejudicial publicity, but they failed to obtain a reversal of the conviction.[48] Calley was granted parole effective 19 November 1974.

The Peers Inquiry, completed in March 1970, had listed 30 individuals as implicated in various "commissions and omissions," some constituting criminal offenses, related to the Son My operation. Charges were preferred against 16 of these and 5 were tried by court-martial, but only one individual, Lieutenant Calley, was found guilty. The charges against 12 others were dismissed for lack of sufficient evidence. In December 1974 General Peers, by then retired from active service, was quoted as criticizing the excessive leniency demonstrated in the handling of the My Lai massacre—"a horrible thing, and we find we have only one man finally convicted and he's set free after doing a relatively small part of his sentence."[49] Is Peers' criticism warranted?

The acquittal on 22 September 1971 of Capt. Ernest L. Medina, Calley's company commander, on the major charge was the result of legally flawed instructions given by the military judge to the court-martial jury. The prosecution initially had wanted to charge Medina with commanding an unlawful act, homicide, but, not being sure that the evidence for this charge would be sufficient, it charged Medina with involuntary manslaughter in violation of Article 119 of the UCMJ—failure to exercise proper control over his men engaged in unlawful homicide of at least 100 unidentified Vietnamese. During the trial the prosecution alleged that Medina had been in constant radio contact with his platoons, that he had been aware from the beginning of the operation that his company was receiving no hostile fire, and that he soon realized that his men were improperly killing noncombatants. Medina, it was contended, had declined to exercise the responsibility of a commander to control his troops. His failure to act amounted to criminal, culpable negligence; his unlawful inaction was the proximate cause of unlawful homicide by his men.[50] The defense, led by the well-known civilian trial lawyer, F. Lee Bailey, contended that Medina did order the destruction of the village but that he did not become aware of the misconduct of his men until too late, and that immediately upon suspecting that his orders were being misunderstood he ordered them to cease fire. By that time, unfortunately, the deaths had all occurred.

The military judge presiding over the trial instructed the jury that in order to convict Medina of involuntary manslaughter they had to be convinced beyond a reasonable doubt that the deaths at My Lai (4) had "resulted from the omission of the accused in failing to exercise control over his subordinates subject to his command after having gained knowledge that his subordinates were killing noncombatants. . . ." A military commander, said the judge, is responsible for the proper performance of his troops, but not simply on account of the commander/subordinate relationship. A commander is responsible for the misconduct of his men "if he has *actual knowledge* that troops or other persons subject to his control are in the process of committing or are about to commit a war crime and he wrongfully fails to take the necessary and reasonable steps to insure compliance with the law of war." There must be *actual knowledge plus a wrongful failure to act. . . .* While it is not necessary that a commander actually see an atrocity being committed, it is essential that he know that his subordinates are in the process of committing atrocities or are about to commit atrocities" (my italics).[51] Not convinced beyond a reasonable doubt that Medina did have "actual knowledge" of the killing of noncombatants, the jury found him innocent of the charge.

There is general agreement today that the instructions of the military judge were wrong. As we have seen in an earlier chapter, the Yamashita case and the holding of the Nuremberg tribunal in the *High Command* case stress the importance of personal dereliction on the part of a commander, but at the same time hold him responsible for criminal negligence. Based on these precedents, the Army's *Law of Land Warfare* states that a commander can be held criminally liable "if he has actual knowledge, or *should have knowledge,* through reports received by him or through other means, that troops or other persons subject to his control are about to commit or have committed a war crime and he fails to take the necessary and reasonable steps to insure compliance with the law of war . . ." (my italics).[52] The jury therefore should have been instructed that a commander is responsible for war crimes committed by his subordinates not only if he has "actual knowledge" but also, in some situations, if he "should have knowledge" of the commission of such crimes. The military judge included in his charge some phrases from the Army's legal manual but omitted the crucial words "or should have knowledge." Had the jury been instructed to use the correct test of command responsibility, it might well have convicted Medina. In the circumstances of the operation in My Lai (4) it certainly is difficult to resist the conclusion that Medina *should have known* what his men were doing.

Failure to press and apply the criminal negligence test not only led to the acquittal of Medina, but may explain why few commanders in Vietnam were held to account for war crimes. Relatively few officers did have *actual knowledge* of violations of the law of war, but many more undoubtedly did not exert themselves sufficiently to prevent the commission of war crimes. This failure is all the more serious in view of what the Peers Inquiry called "the unique nature of combat operations in Vietnam"[53]— instant radio communication with units in contact with the enemy and the ability of commanders to hover above these operations in helicopters— and such dereliction of duty may implicate the highest echelons. Was Col. Kenneth A. Howard, the military judge in the Medina trial, concerned that the "should have known" test, once introduced, could set a dangerous precedent and lead to charges against some highly placed officers in the Vietnam chain of command? Had Colonel Howard been made aware of General Westmoreland's apprehensiveness about being held responsible for war crimes? We do not know. Colonel Howard, an able lawyer who has written on the subject of command responsibility for war crimes and who was not likely to have been ignorant of current legal doctrine, does not explain the reasons for his peculiar charge to the Medina jury.[54] Whatever the reasons, it is to be hoped that this precedent will not stand uncorrected. As Prof. Roger S. Clark of the Rutgers School of Law correctly points out: "The actual knowledge test, in a context like My Lai, is an invitation to the commander to see and hear no evil."[55]

Captain Medina was also acquitted of the charge of aggravated assault resulting from his interrogation, with the help of a Vietnamese interpreter, of a VC suspect apprehended in My Khe (2) hamlet. In testimony before the Peers Inquiry, Medina had admitted hitting the suspect "sufficiently hard to cause profuse bleeding from a skin laceration." When the man refused to talk, Medina placed him against a tree and fired two rounds into the tree about eight inches above the captive's head. "After indicating to the individual that the third round would hit 'right between the eyes,' CPT Medina then moved away to fire a third round. Medina testified the man talked before the third round was fired and that he admitted being a 'card carrying member in the Communist party for 13 years.' "[56] Failure to convict here was due to absence in the applicable field manual of an explicit prohibition of such methods of interrogation.

At his trial, Medina again freely admitted that he had sought to scare the suspect into talking by the threat to kill him. There also was agreement that the Geneva Convention Relative to the Treatment of Prisoners of War forbade the infliction of any form of torture or coercion upon captives "to secure from them information of any kind whatever" and that prisoners of war "who refuse to answer may not be threatened, insulted, or exposed to unpleasant or disadvantageous treatment of any kind."[57] This provision had been incorporated into the Army's *Law of Land Warfare*. But defense counsel argued that Medina had relied upon a technique, known as "Mutt and Jeff," authorized by the Army's field manual on intelligence interrogation. This ruse involves the use of two interrogators, one of whom is tough and aggressive while the other is friendly and sympathetic. The interrogation is begun by the first interrogator who, according to the manual, may use harsh and abusive language and threaten violence. At a prearranged signal the second interrogator appears, berates the gruff interrogator for his behavior and orders him out of the room.

The relieved suspect, out of gratitude, will then talk.[58] Bailey maintained that this manual created a license to break the law, license to put a man in fear and threaten violence in a convincing way.[59]

Both the prosecutor and the military judge found themselves in the uncomfortable position where an Army regulation appeared to violate an international convention to which the U.S. was a party. To be legally correct they would have had to point out to the jury that treaties relating to the law of war constitute part of the "supreme law of the land" and, as the Army's *Law of Land Warfare* states, "must be observed by both military and civilian personnel with the same strict regard for both the letter and spirit of the law which is required with respect to the Constitution and statutes enacted in pursuance thereof."[60] Neither prosecutor nor judge was prepared to admit that the field manual on interrogation was of no force and effect because it violated the Geneva convention, which forbade all threats to prisoners. Hence they engaged in verbal gymnastics designed to make the best of an impossible situation.

The manual, declared the prosecutor, provided that an interrogator may "verbally threaten violence" but "may not threaten by violence." By firing his M-16 rifle above the suspect's head Medina had used violence and committed aggravated assault.[61] The military judge at first took the same position. In implementing the Geneva convention the Army had issued a directive on intelligence interrogation which "authorized the interrogator to threaten violence in an attempt to get such information; that is, the interrogator may threaten physical violence only, but may not threaten by use of physical violence against the detainee."[62] When defense counsel responded that Medina had not actually used physical force, "assuming that physical force means force to the person,"[63] the military judge finally agreed to let the jury determine whether the accused had done no more than threaten violence. Predictably, the jury had to give the defendant the benefit of the doubt and acquitted Medina. He also was found not guilty of the charge that he had personally killed a woman and child.

Criminal charges against several other defendants similarly did not lead to convictions. Two sergeants were acquitted of assault with intent to commit murder. Charges against 12 others were dismissed before trial. Evidence developed by the Peers Inquiry that Company B (Bravo) of Task Force Barker had killed between 80 and 90 civilians in the hamlet of My Khe (4) led to criminal charges against Capt. (then 1st Lt.) Thomas K.

Willingham, but these charges, too, were dismissed before trial. Military defense counsel for one of the members of Charlie Company has written: "The complexity of events, the reluctance of witnesses to testify against their former comrades-in-arms or in some instances to incriminate themselves, and the enormous distance from events in My Lai in time and environment undoubtedly hampered prosecution efforts. Finally, the unarticulated public feeling that responsibility for crimes at My Lai somehow fell on shoulders other than those of ordinary soldiers argued against their conviction in any forum." [64] Moreover, the immunity from prosecution of those men who had been discharged from the service (a subject to which I will return) without doubt further hurt the effort at prosecution. The fact that soldiers who had confessed on television or other public forums to their participation in the killings would now appear as prosecution witnesses against those unlucky enough to be still in uniform, Telford Taylor noted correctly, "was bound to cause the jury to feel that this was so grossly unfair that it became hard for them to convict the enlisted men at all." [65]

Several officers were charged with their participation in the cover-up—their failure to investigate reports of the incident at My Lai or to report the occurrence—but no convictions were obtained against them either. The man against whom the incriminating evidence might have been strongest, the commander of the task force, Lt. Col. Frank A. Barker, meanwhile had died in combat. Col. Oran K. Henderson, the commanding officer of the Eleventh Infantry Brigade, was tried by court-martial and acquitted; charges against several other officers, including two generals, were dismissed before trial. A panel of officers from the Office of the Judge Advocate General, convened to review the sufficiency of the evidence, had earlier indicated doubt that the evidence assembled by the Peers Inquiry would be legally sufficient to result in successful prosecutions on criminal charges. The House Armed Services Committee has also complained that in its broad recommendation of charges "the Peers Inquiry overreacted in attempting to compensate for the Army's original failure to act." [66] To resolve this matter, involving complex questions of both fact and law, is beyond the province of this discussion.

In the absence of sufficient evidence to warrant criminal prosecution, administrative action for substandard performance of duty was taken against the commanding general of the Americal Division, Maj. Gen. Samuel W. Koster, and the assistant division commander, Brig. Gen.

George H. Young. On 19 May 1971 Secretary of the Army Stanley R. Resor announced that after dismissal of the criminal charges on 28 January 1971, the Department of the Army had conducted an administrative review of all available evidence. Based on recommendations received, he was now taking the following actions against these two officers: (1) placing letters of censure in their personnel files; (2) withdrawing Distinguished Service Medals; (3) reducing the rank of Koster from major general to brigadier general. Koster, explained the secretary, despite information that his troops might have been guilty of serious misconduct, had been derelict in his duty in failing thoroughly to investigate the incident. "Any other conclusion would render essentially meaningless the concept of command responsibility accompanying senior positions of authority." Young, concluded Resor, "did not exercise the degree of initiative and assume the responsibility which is expected with respect to a general officer serving as an assistant division commander."[67]

The dropping of the criminal charges against Koster led to complaints by a member of the House Armed Services Committee who had participated in the committee's investigation of the My Lai incident that the "mythical WPPA, the West Point Protective Association," had once again demonstrated its influence.[68] Others denied that Koster had escaped justice. One writer pointed out the importance of taking into account what a man like Koster, talked about as a future Army chief of staff, had lost as a result of this censure. For Samuel Koster "his punishment could hardly have been greater."[69] Koster himself, who retired from the Army in late 1973, is still trying to obtain a reversal of the actions taken against him by Army Secretary Resor.

The Prosecution of Discharged Servicemen

On 8 April 1971 the Defense and Justice departments announced jointly that, after an 18-month study of the question whether discharged servicemen could be prosecuted for violations of the law of war in Vietnam such as the My Lai massacre, the U.S had decided not to seek such prosecutions. The decision was said to rest on doubt on the part of legal experts that civilians could be tried for war crimes committed while in the military service. There also was speculation that the administration considered the issue too hot politically.[70]

Both in World War II and in the Korean War former servicemen were prosecuted for offenses committed while in the military. But in 1955 the U.S. Supreme Court ruled in *Toth v. Quarles* that courts-martial had no jurisdiction over discharged servicemen.[71] The effect of this decision was to declare unconstitutional paragraph 803, article 3(a) of the UCMJ which provided for such jurisdiction. This raises the question whether the U.S. is now violating its obligations under the Geneva conventions of 1949 "to provide effective penal sanctions for persons committing or ordering to be committed" grave breaches of or all other acts contrary to the provisions of these conventions. "Each High Contracting Party shall be under the obligation to search for such persons alleged to have committed, or to have ordered to be committed, such grave breaches, and shall bring such persons, regardless of their nationality, before its own courts."[72]

The conclusion that *Toth v. Quarles* prevents the punishment of discharged servicemen for war crimes has been challenged by some legal experts. It has been suggested that such suspected war criminals could be tried by military commissions provided for under Article 21 of the UCMJ and enacted under the power of the Congress to "define and punish . . . offenses against the Law of Nations."[73] Such commissions were used most recently against Japanese war criminals. While their jurisdiction is not free of all doubt, the administration certainly could have let these doubts be resolved in the courts through a test case. Even if the jurisdiction of such military commissions is rejected, it has been argued that the federal district courts have the power to try civilians for offenses against the law of war,[74] or that Congress could confer such jurisdiction upon them by appropriate legislation. The latter was the recommendation of the House Armed Services Committee in 1970 after its investigation of the My Lai incident.[75]

On 3 May 1971 Sen. Sam J. Ervin, Jr., of North Carolina introduced legislation to give federal district courts jurisdiction over discharged soldiers accused of offenses committed while in the service. This bill, like an earlier one introduced by Senator Ervin in December 1969, died without action. Enactment of such legislation would seem to be an urgent necessity, not only because of existing international obligations of the U.S. but also for the sake of living up to basic values of equity and justice. Because of the constitutional prohibition of retrospective (*ex post facto*) legislation, a law providing for trial of discharged servicemen probably would not reach men accused of war crimes in Vietnam. This may help overcome political objections to such legislation on account of widespread public disinclination to revive the agony of Vietnam through trials of alleged war criminals.

The Lessons of Vietnam

When Secretary of the Army Howard H. Callaway released the main portions of the Peers Inquiry report on 13 November 1974 he stated: "The release of this report concludes a dark chapter in the Army's history. It is an incident from which the Army has learned a good deal. The lessons have been acted upon. Army training has been revised to emphasize the personal responsibility of each soldier and officer to obey the laws of land warfare and the provisions of the Geneva and Hague Conventions."[76] These changes are indeed significant.

Prior to the uproar caused by the My Lai incident, training in the Geneva conventions and other provisions of the law of war was often perfunctory. Army Regulation (AR) 350-216 of 28 September 1967 required one hour of instruction during basic training and an annual refresher period. Upon arrival in Vietnam all military personnel received an orientation in the Geneva conventions and were given four information cards— "The Enemy in Your Hands," "Nine Rules," "Code of Conduct" and "Geneva Conventions"—which emphasized humane treatment of prisoners and noncombatants. Yet the instructional materials used paid little if any attention to war crimes or to the problem of illegal orders.[77] An order issued in July 1968 by the commanding general, Fleet Marine Force, stressed the importance of scrupulous and compassionate conduct toward Vietnamese civilians and of firm but humane treatment of VC captives or suspects, but did not deal with the duty to refuse unlawful orders.[78]

The Peers Inquiry found that the training received by the men of Task Force Barker, both during basic training and during in-country orientation, had been deficient with regard to the proper treatment of civilians and responsibility for reporting war crimes and atrocities.[79] Nor was this an isolated case. An inspection of U.S Army Vietnam in May–June 1969 noted that about 50 percent of all personnel had not received their required annual training in the Geneva and Hague conventions.[80] At that time, the pressure for body count and the free use of heavy weapons in populated areas probably made this kind of instruction seem rather academic and irrelevant. The MACV staff judge advocate during the period

July 1966 to July 1967, who was in charge of all legal instruction in Vietnam, recalls that it was "frustrating to attempt to teach and apply the laws of war to the situation which prevailed there."[81]

The final report of the Peers Inquiry, submitted in March 1970, listed marginal training in the law of war as a contributory cause of the My Lai massacre. During a press conference held in December 1969, Army Chief of Staff Westmoreland had denied the need to issue any new instructions to the troops serving in Vietnam as a result of this incident.[82] But the message of the Peers Inquiry was difficult to ignore and a business-as-usual attitude no longer sufficed. A revised edition of AR 350-216, issued 28 May 1970, extends the amount of required time devoted to training in the Geneva and Hague conventions and lays down that such instruction be given by teams of legally qualified and combat-experienced commanders, "preferably combat arms officers with counter-insurgency experience."[83] The Army Judge Advocate General School sponsored such a combined team in preparing a complete revision of the instructional lesson plan for this training.

In the past, a Marine Corps officer lawyer has noted, the law of war often was viewed as "an unnecessary, unrealistic restraining device inhibiting the combat commander in the accomplishment of his mission."[84] Instruction in this subject was generally abstract and theoretical. The revised lesson plan (subject schedule), issued on 8 October 1970, represents a concerted effort to be practical and to relate instruction to specific types of combat situations encountered in Vietnam. Making this instruction a team effort by legally qualified and combat-experienced commanders was intended to demonstrate the compatibility of the law of war and the realities of actual warfare. The central theme was that observance of the humanitarian conventions regulating warfare "is consistent with the effective conduct of hostilities."[85]

Entirely new is a section dealing with illegal orders and the responsibility of the soldier to disobey such orders. Servicemen are to be instructed that acting under superior orders is no defense to criminal charges. "While an American soldier must obey promptly all legal orders, he must also disobey an order which requires him to commit a criminal act in violation of the law of war. . . . An order to execute a prisoner or detainee is clearly illegal. An order to torture or abuse a prisoner to get him to talk is clearly illegal. . . . What about an order to cut ears off the enemy dead to prove a body count? This order is illegal, too." What should a soldier do when given an illegal order such as "Shoot every man, woman and child in sight?" He should first try to get the order rescinded, but if the person giving it persists, then he has to disregard it. "The lack of courage to disregard an illegal order, or a mistaken fear that you could be court-martialed for disobedience of orders is not a defense to a charge of murder, pillage or any other war crime."[86] Soldiers are reminded of their obligation to report all violations of the law of war. If someone in the chain of command above them is involved in the alleged crime, they can use other channels such as the chaplain or staff judge advocate.

A special appendix deals with the obligations of battalion and brigade commanders. They are instructed to insure that their orders are clear and unmistakable in meaning. An order to "take care" of a prisoner might make a soldier think that he was commanded to kill him. As commanding officers they have to take positive steps to keep fully informed of what their men are doing, and an officer who fails to so inform himself is derelict in his duty. "Faulty staff procedures do not excuse you as a commander from ultimate responsibility. . . . In short, the officer who sees no evil and hears no evil may nevertheless be charged with the knowledge of evil."[87] Such was the fate of German and Japanese commanders charged, convicted and executed after World War II. The law of war has to be obeyed as part of the duty of an officer. Moreover, brutalities inflicted upon noncombatants and the wanton and unnecessary burning of their homes generates adverse world opinion and erodes domestic public support for the war effort. Winning over the local population is especially crucial in a counterinsurgency war. "Our purpose is not to lay waste to the country as the Romans did to Carthage, and bury its people forever beneath the salted earth." Commanders have to maintain discipline and control over their troops to be able to deal with the strains of combat. "Your men, scared, tired and having their comrades killed, may not respond entirely rationally unless you, by your bearing and conduct, have previously established the control essential to assure their proper response at the moment of testing."[88]

The new instruction plan states that individuals have been "tried and sentenced for such violations as beating a prisoner or applying electric shocks, dunking his head into a barrel of water, or putting a plastic bag over his head to make him talk." No American soldier can be allowed to commit such brutal acts. Moreover, "combat experience proves that intelligence secured by torture is unreliable."[89] The same point is stressed in the revised manual dealing with intelligence interrogation. The ambiguities which led to the acquittal of Captain Medina are now corrected. The "Mutt and Jeff" technique no longer allows threats against uncooperative sources. The use and enforcement of threats constitute "violations of international law and may result in prosecution under the Uniform Code of Military Justice." The inability to carry out threats of violence renders an interrogator ineffective. Threats of force are useless techniques of interrogation "from both legal and moral viewpoints."[90]

Training in the law of war now also utilizes six color films which portray in a highly vivid and realistic manner the dilemmas faced by men in combat and teach the correct way of handling such situations.[91] Response to these films is reported to be good. The service academies and officer training schools teach the law of war in a new and provocative way that emphasizes the responsibility of the soldier to disobey plainly unlawful orders. As one participant reports, "few classes go by without dissent which often reaches considerable magnitude." It is especially difficult "to get to men who have seen atrocities by the enemy."[92]

All these reforms probably came too late to have much of an impact on the final years of the American combat involvement in Vietnam. The failure to implement and enforce proper training in the humanitarian conventions of the law of war until a major incident like My Lai revealed the inadequate training prevailing until then must be considered the responsibility of MACV and of the military and civilian chiefs of the military services. It certainly should have been realized that a counterinsurgency war in an Asian land would create severe problems of proper conduct toward the insurgents and the civilian population, not unlike those experienced following the annexation of the Philippines in 1899. For two and a half years the Army there encountered a cruel guerilla war in which atrocities against U.S. soldiers led to atrocities on the American side such as the burning of villages and the torture of suspects. A brigadier general, Jacob Smith, was court-martialed for instructing a subordinate officer: "I want no prisoners. The more you kill and burn, the more it will please me. Make the interior of Samar a howling wilderness."[93] Racial slurs were common and the life of Filipinos was cheap. Lack of institutional memory may have contributed to ignoring the lessons of this dreadful experience in counterinsurgency, but it cannot serve as an exculpation. What could be and was done in 1970 should have been done in 1965.

Other lessons of the prosecution of war crimes in Vietnam involve certain basic problems of the system of military justice and of contemporary law enforcement generally. Military courts in the 1960s and early 1970s mirrored the attitudes toward crime and punishment then existing in American society. There prevailed the same tendency to downgrade individual responsibility and to focus instead on underlying causes of crime.[94] Procedural rules made it hard to obtain convictions, and punishment was often excessively lenient. The military justice system, complained the commanding general, U.S. Army Vietnam, in July 1971, was seen by many as too "permissive and over-zealous of the rights of individuals." Some military judges were "overly liberal in findings and sentencing" and there applied an "overly stringent interpretation and application of provisions concerning rules of evidence and probable cause. . . ." Many young leaders feared that they were not being backed up by the judicial system. "As a consequence, not only can there be reluctance on their part to bring violations to the attention of superiors, but a number of these same young leaders are prone to relaxing their standards and condoning serious breaches of discipline in an effort to 'sweep it under the rug.' "[95] While these remarks had special relevance to the problem of drug abuse and the decline in discipline experienced during the last years of disengagement from Vietnam, they also applied to the broader situation.

Sentences adjudged by courts-martial in Vietnam at times were so light as to eliminate any deterrent effect, and the review process mandated by the UCMJ often further undercut this important purpose of punishment. As in the civilian system of justice, prisoners were often released on parole after serving only a small part of their sentences. The secretaries of the military services, just like governors who wield the power of pardon or commutation, used their legal prerogative to grant clemency. The results of this process are depicted in Table 10-5 (Appendix II, p. 458) for the cases of marines, 27 in all, convicted of murder in which the victim was Vietnamese.

These data show that in practically all cases the review process resulted in a major disparity between the sentence initially adjudged by the court-martial and the actual sentence served. For example, the average sentence served by the 12 marines sentenced to confinement at hard labor for life for whom full data are available was 6½ years. In only 4 of the 27 cases, all involving sentences of 5 years or less, was the initially adjudged sentence actually served. Retribution is not the only, and perhaps not even the primary, purpose of legal punishment. Yet in view of the viciousness of some of the crimes, resulting in sentences of 20 years or more in 18 of the 27 cases, the leniency demonstrated in the review process was bound to lead to complaints that such actions amounted to disregard for the rule of law and weakened the deterrent effect of punishment.

However, the tendency of courts-martial to assess relatively severe sentences so that the convening authority during review will have the option and opportunity to cut them down is common. Parole action, too, does not appear to have been handled in any unusual way. As of 21 May 1971, 29 Army personnel had been convicted of war crimes in Vietnam and confinement had been adjudged against 15 of them. Data available for 13 of these men show that, on the average, they served 51.5 percent of their sentences before being released as a result of parole or clemency action.[96] This is a rate very similar to that of military prisoners held in penal institutions of the Federal Bureau of Prisons during the fiscal year ending 30 June 1969—those too difficult to handle in the military prisons—who served 52.6 percent of their sentences before release; all inmates of the Federal Bureau of Prisons served 52.2 percent.[97] It is well known that civilian parole boards often act as much in response to political pressures and the currents of public opinion as on the basis of the severity of the crime or the conduct of the prisoners,[98] and the situation was probably no different in the case of servicemen convicted of atrocities or war crimes in Vietnam. In short, in order to account for light sentences and early release on parole for such men there is no need for the "mere-gook" hypothesis.

During the last few years the climate in this country appears to have shifted toward a desire for more severe punishment of criminals. Work release and early parole are less popular. If this trend persists it, too, will probably in due time be reflected in the system of military justice. A more punitive attitude toward lawbreakers is, of course, not the only change that may be appropriate in the handling of servicemen involved in war crimes. The more fundamental issue is whether the Vietnam experience calls into question the ability of the military by themselves to police observance of the humanitarian provisions of the law of war.

The record of the military in policing themselves is mixed. Investigative agencies like the Army's Criminal Investigation Division and the Naval Investigative Service appear to have performed in a professional manner. So did, by and large, the services' legal officers—members of the Judge Advocate General Corps. The difficulties encountered by the judge advocates in the processing of war crimes were often formidable. Security conditions made travel to the scene of crimes hazardous; the 12-month tour of duty and the reluctance of commanders to relieve men from operations in progress made it extremely complicated to bring together all key persons needed for trial; villagers required as witnesses were hard to locate or were dead as a result of combat; offenses at times did not come to light until long after an incident had occurred and principal suspects or witnesses by then were often no longer subject to military jurisdiction. Yet whatever offenses came to the attention of the judge advocates were generally prosecuted promptly and efficiently.

The real problem for the military system of justice in Vietnam was to get hard evidence of what was going on in the field. As we have seen, the reporting system for war crimes in effect required officers to report on their own deficiencies as combat leaders; enlisted men, too, were not anxious to expose their comrades to legal retribution for having killed Vietnamese civilians who generally were perceived as unfriendly. If officers serving on courts-martial acquitted defendants or adjudged light sentences, their verdicts much of the time were the result of the sympathy they felt for the frustrations experienced by the men. And yet there also prevailed a tendency to close ranks and to protect fellow officers or comrades-in-arms from the enlisted ranks. Convening authorities generally followed the professional counsel of their judge advocates, but sometimes were less than zealous in ordering courts-martial appropriate to the severity of the offense. Higher echelons frequently responded to violations of the rules by issuing new regulations forbidding such practices rather than by aggressive enforcement through disciplinary action. Directives, unless enforced, are, of course, mere pieces of paper.

In 1972 Sen. Edward M. Kennedy proposed the creation of "a permanent Military Practices Review Board to advise the Joint Chiefs of Staff on standards and procedures designed to keep U.S. military policies and practices within the bounds of simple humanitarian and international legal obligations, and to monitor the implementation of the rules of engagement governing U.S armed forces in active combat."[99] The ROE in Vietnam were generally impeccable, but their implementation by subordinate commands was often poor. Kennedy's suggestion therefore represents a much-needed reform. More recently two Yale Law School professors and a graduate of that school have proposed to vest jurisdiction for the trial and punishment of war crimes in the U.S. District Court for the District of Columbia and responsibility for their prosecution in the Department of Justice.[100] This proposal most likely violates constitutional guarantees of trial by an impartial jury of peers and constitutes denial of due process because of the impossibility of compelling the attendance of essential witnesses from other countries. Moreover, it is by no means clear that the record of the system of military justice in dealing with war crimes in Vietnam demonstrates the complete inability of that system to cope with the prosecution of war crimes.

The tension between the exigencies of combat and observance of the law of war has been honestly faced in the revised training materials. Commanders have been put on notice that an attitude of "see no evil and hear no evil" can lead to their prosecution for condoning war crimes. There remains the task of providing an effective supervisory and enforcement mechanism to take the place of the self-policing that worked rather poorly in Vietnam. A small start in this direction was made by the establishment, effective 1 January 1972, of the Defense Investigative Service which operates under the authority of the secretary of defense and can conduct any investigation the secretary may require. Since 1972 the inspectors general of the four services no longer report only to their respective military chiefs but also to the civilian service secretaries. A DOD directive, issued in November 1974, made the civilian heads of the military services responsible for the prompt reporting and investigation of alleged violations of the law of war by or against members of their respective departments and for periodic review of all programs aimed at preventing violations of the law of war. A primary point of contact in the JCS was mandated to handle all actions in regard to war crimes.[101]

But these reforms probably do not go far enough. It may be necessary to establish a truly independent inspection service, outside of the military chain of command and reporting directly and exclusively to the civilian service secretaries, perhaps similar to the Pacification Studies Group (PSG) operated by CORDS in Vietnam. PSG was able to look into any aspect of the pacification effort anywhere, and its reports could be candid and free of bias because it operated outside the regular reporting channels. It should be recognized, of course, that no system of inspection can be foolproof and that, in the final analysis, humane conduct will depend on the recognition on the part of the military leadership that violations of the law of war, especially in a counterinsurgency setting, are not conducive to the achievement of military objectives.

373

11

The Bombing
of North Vietnam

Contingency plans for air strikes against North Vietnam were first prepared in March 1964. The proposed bombing program had three major objectives: (1) to signal to Hanoi the firmness of U.S. resolve to defend South Vietnam against communist subversion and aggression; (2) to boost the sagging morale of the GVN; (3) to impose increased costs and strains upon the DRV if it continued its support of the southern insurgency. From the beginning, President Johnson's advisers differed in their views concerning how such a bombing campaign should be conducted. The JCS favored a forceful and decisive application of military power, which they believed would affect the enemy's will. Most civilian advisers, on the other hand, argued for a more gradual and restrained approach, progressively mounting in scope and intensity, in which the prospect of greater pressure to come would be at least as important as any damage actually inflicted. Unlike the military, the majority of the civilians were not convinced that such a campaign would deter Hanoi from its chosen course, but in view of the deteriorating situation in South Vietnam and the existence of a major air capability it appeared worth a try.[1]

It was the graduated approach which was adopted, designed to preserve the option of escalating or not, depending on North Vietnam's reactions. "The carrot of stopping the bombing," note the authors of the *Pentagon Papers*, "was deemed as important as the stick of continuing it, and bombing pauses were provided for. It was hoped that this track of major military escalation of the war could be accompanied by a parallel diplomatic track to bring the war to an end, and that both tracks could be coordinated."[2] To this day, many of the military, and especially the Air Force, blame the failure of air power to deliver the expected results on the decision to mount a campaign of graduated pressures instead of applying maximum available force from the start.

In June–July 1964 a set of targets in North Vietnam was worked up by the JCS and in December 1964 forces were put on stand-by to carry out strikes on these targets. On 7 February 1965, while the debate over when to start this campaign was still going on, the VC carried out well-coordinated raids on a U.S. advisers' barracks in Pleiku and on a helicopter base some four miles away. As a result of these attacks, 9 Americans died and 76 were seriously wounded; 16 helicopters and 6 fixed-wing aircraft were destroyed or damaged. In a 75-minute meeting of the National Security Council, the decision was reached to strike back.

The reprisal strikes in August 1964, following the Gulf of Tonkin incident, had been presented as a one-time retaliatory action in response to a North Vietnamese attack on U.S. naval power in international waters. The strikes against the Dong Hoi military barracks on 7–8 February 1965, given the operational code name FLAMING DART and conducted jointly by South Vietnamese Air Force (VNAF) and U.S. planes, were also described as reprisals, but were linked not only to the attacks on the American installations but to VC attacks on several Vietnamese villages as well. Press releases and briefings tied the bombing of targets in North Vietnam to the "larger pattern of aggression" and thus served notice on Hanoi that the U.S. from now on was prepared to act as a co-belligerent along with South Vietnam in the fight against the VC and their sponsors in the North. The strikes also were designed to signal a change in the ground rules of the conflict: no longer would North Vietnam be permitted to direct and support the war in the South while remaining immune from counterattack against its own territory. The willingness of Washington to continue these pressures as needed was indicated in the public statement: "As the U.S. Government has frequently stated, we seek no wider war. Whether or not this course can be maintained lies with the North Vietnamese aggressors." Another White House release announced the evacuation of American dependents from South Vietnam—"to clear the decks and make absolutely clear our continued determination to back South Vietnam. . . ."[3]

ROLLING THUNDER

In what some observers regarded as calculated defiance, on 10 February VC sappers blew up a U.S. enlisted men's billet in Qui Nhon; 23 Americans were killed and 21 wounded, the heaviest single loss of American personnel yet. The strikes on the North that followed this attack, FLAMING DART II, were executed by 48 U.S. and VNAF planes and were described as "air operations" rather than "retaliation" or "reprisal" raids. On 13 February the president approved "a program of measured and limited air action jointly with the GVN against selected military targets in the DRV" which was given the code name ROLLING THUNDER. A "semi-coup" in Saigon and bad weather forced postponement of the first series of strikes scheduled for 20 February. On 2 March 1965, 104 USAF and 19 VNAF planes hit the Quang Khe naval base in the first attacks under the new program. Beginning with ROLLING THUNDER VII, on 19 March, air action against the North became a regular and sustained effort.[4]

Political turbulence in Saigon and the weather were not the only reasons for delaying the beginning of the air campaign against the North. On 17 February the British ambassador in Washington informed Secretary Rusk that the Soviet Foreign Office had approached the British about the possibility of reactivating the 1954 Geneva Conference, and the U.S. did not wish to jeopardize this possible opening toward a negotiated settlement. The initiative soon collapsed and the strikes were rescheduled, but this was merely the first of many such breaks in the bombing campaign related to potential peace feelers. In all, there were eight complete halts and five partial cessations ruling out attacks on targets in or around Hanoi and Haiphong; the duration of these pauses ranged from 24 hours to 36 days at a time.[5]

The complicated story of these peace feelers is beyond the scope of this work; they have been ably analyzed by Allan E. Goodman.[6] It will suffice to note here that between 1965 and 1968 the administration was in virtually continuous contact, directly or through intermediaries, with the leaders in Hanoi or their representatives. The public knew very little of these communications, detailed now for all to see in the so-called diplomatic volumes of the *Pentagon Papers*,[7] and many blamed the failure to get into a dialogue with Hanoi on the bombing of North Vietnam. Johnson and his advisers never believed that the bombing constituted a serious impediment to peace negotiations. They shared the view of John P. Roche, stated in a memo to the president in March 1967, that Ho Chi Minh was a dedicated Leninist and "like Lenin at the time of Brest Litovsk—would negotiate in cold blood for whatever goals he considers realistic—even if bombs were coming down his chimney."[8] This position was vindicated when the North Vietnamese finally agreed to talks in April 1968 without a complete halt to the bombing. Still, in order not to miss any possible opening toward peace and as a concession to world opinion, the bombing campaign was interrupted numerous times and the military eventually became distinctly unhappy with what they regarded as futile, unreciprocated concessions and a failure to use military force in a convincing manner.

The target selection for the reprisal actions and the first ROLLING THUNDER strikes was dominated by political considerations—affecting Hanoi's will to support the war in the South. But North Vietnam showed no signs of bending to U.S. pressure, and with the acceptance of a more sustained bombing campaign the need developed for a more coherent target system, one that would lead to tangible damage and results. The most obvious candidate under such a concept was the goal of interdicting the flow of men and supplies into South Vietnam by striking at the lines of communication of the DRV. North Vietnamese aggression, after all, was the principal legal justification for the American bombing raids, and the JCS as well as Westmoreland for some time had urged strikes against the rail system in North Vietnam. Moreover, an interdiction stragegy would make it easier to contain the pressures to escalate the bombing rapidly into the northern heart of the DRV's population and industry and facilitate confining targets to the area of direct military relevance to the campaign in the South—the southern panhandle. Adverse political repercussions at home as well as the danger of Chinese intervention would be minimized.

The acceptance by the president on 1 April 1965 of the interdiction concept thus represented a compromise. National Security Action Memorandum 328, which also approved the employment of the marines in South Vietnam for offensive operations (see chap. 2, p. 46), affirmed that the U.S. "should continue roughly the present slowly ascending tempo of ROLLING THUNDER operations, being prepared to add strikes in response to a higher rate of VC operations, or conceivably to slow the pace in the unlikely event VC slackened off sharply for what appeared to be more than a temporary operational lull." Attacks on LOCs were to be stepped up. "Blockade or aerial mining of North Vietnam's ports needs further study and should be considered for future operations." The dispute between those who thought of the bombing as primarily a political instrument and those who sought genuine military objectives, between those who wanted it speeded up and those who wanted it checked, had been not resolved but shelved. The bombing of North Vietnam during the years 1965 to 1968, which on the surface looked like a carefully thought-out program of slowly escalating pressures, to the end remained a compromise between rival policies and pressures.[9]

At the end of March, the JCS submitted a 12-week bombing program built around the interdiction concept, but neither McNamara nor Johnson was prepared to approve a multi-week program in advance. They preferred to retain personal control over attack concepts and individual target selection. Hence throughout the bombing campaign proposals were approved in individual weekly (later bi-weekly) packages with careful attention to political factors and the risk of collateral damage to the civilian population; before approval at the White House each package had to pass through a chain of approvals within senior levels at DOD and the State Department. As was to be expected, the military became increasingly restive and chafed at these restrictions imposed by civilians who, as they saw it, lacked military understanding. Westmoreland mirrors these sentiments in his memoirs: "Interference from Washington seriously hampered the campaign. . . . This or that target was not to be hit for this or that nebulous nonmilitary reason. Missions for which planning and rehearsal had long proceeded might be canceled at the last minute. President Johnson allegedly boasted on one occasion that 'they can't even bomb an outhouse without my approval.' "[10]

By mid-1965 ROLLING THUNDER had grown in scope and intensity. The geographic coverage of the strikes had been extended in stages northward; the assortment of targets had been widened to include bridges, airfields, railroad yards, oil storage sites and even power plants. Aircraft on armed reconnaissance—seeking out targets of opportunity not individually picked in Washington—could now strike vehicles, locomotives, railroad cars, ferries, barges, etc. The total number of sorties flown (a sortie is one flight by one aircraft) had risen to about 900 per week, several times what it had been at the outset of the campaign. Yet while the bombing of the North at first had provided a significant boost to GVN morale, by the summer of 1965 the ARVN in South Vietnam was near collapse and the president had decided to send in substantial U.S. ground forces to save a desperate situation. Earlier expectations that the selective bombing of North Vietnam would turn the tide had been proven wrong. From this point on, the hope shifted from inflicting pain on the North to proving that the VC and their helpers could not win a military victory in the South.[11]

In the face of the ominous developments in the ground war, the military, as before, continued to press for an intensification of the air campaign against the North. But to the president, too, as well as to most of his civilian advisers, the idea of an escalation of the bombing had its attraction. It was difficult to justify sending large numbers of American troops to slug it out in the jungles and rice paddies of South Vietnam without at least trying to see whether stronger pressure on the North might not alleviate the need to increase American troop commitments. The public and the believers in the omnipotence of air power in the Congress had to be convinced that air power was being utilized to the maximum degree possible. On the other hand, there was concern over creating a crisis atmosphere which could lead to an overreaction on the part of North Vietnam and its allies. The bombing of the North should not look like an effort to soften up the DRV for an invasion.

The result of these cross-pressures was again an incremental stepping up of the pace of the bombing rather than the sharp escalation—including mining the major ports and cutting the rail and highway bridges on the LOCs from China—favored by the JCS. New fixed targets from the JCS list continued to be selected, but few strikes were authorized in the vital northeast quadrant which contained the Hanoi/Haiphong urban complexes, the major port facilities and the main LOCs to China. The boundary of armed reconnaissance was enlarged, but it was still kept away from the northeast quadrant, where only individually approved fixed targets were authorized. By April 1966 this restriction was partially removed, but the prohibition on strikes in the immediate Hanoi/Haiphong areas continued. In late June the president approved strikes on seven POL (petroleum, oil and lubricants) storage areas in the Hanoi/Haiphong complex. At the urging of McNamara, the execution message stressed the importance of avoiding damage to merchant shipping and mandated taking every feasible step to minimize civilian casualties. The most experienced crews were to be employed and the strikes were to be flown only when the weather permitted visual identification of the targets. The strikes were launched on 29 June and were reported as highly successful. In December 1966 the first strikes took place within the 30-mile Hanoi sanctuary against a rail classification yard and a vehicle depot. This led to charges by Hanoi and the Russians that the U.S. was attacking residential areas in Hanoi, and on 23 December attacks against all targets within 10 nautical miles of Hanoi were prohibited without specific presidential authorization.[12]

By the end of 1966, the bombing campaign had reached a very heavy

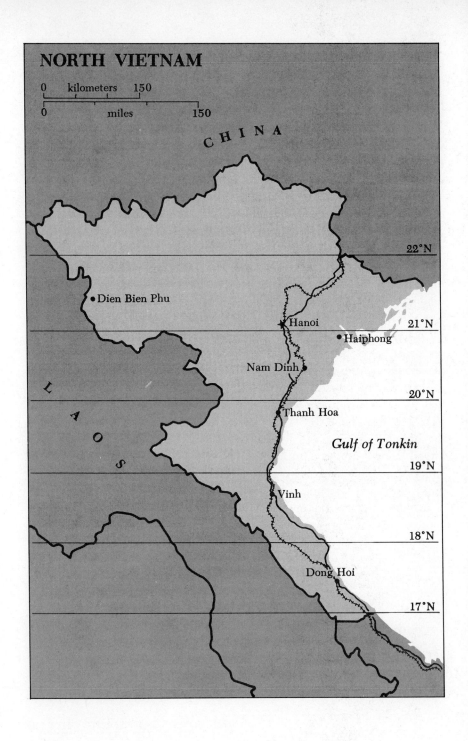

NORTH VIETNAM

0   kilometers   150

0   miles   150

C H I N A

●Dien Bien Phu

Hanoi

●Haiphong

Nam Dinh●

22°N

21°N

20°N

19°N

18°N

17°N

L A O S

Thanh Hoa

Gulf of Tonkin

Vinh

Dong Hoi

Table 11-1 ROLLING THUNDER, 1965–66

	1965	1966
Total sorties flown	55,000	148,000
Tons of bombs dropped	33,000	128,000
Fixed targets struck	158	185
Number of aircraft lost	171	318
Loss rate per 1,000 sorties	3.4	2.1
Estimated economic damage caused	$ 36 million	$ 94 million
Estimated military damage caused	$ 34 million	$ 36 million
Direct operational cost	$460 million	$1,247 million
U.S. cost per $1 of damage	$6.60	$9.60

SOURCE: *Pentagon Papers* IV:136, 232.

volume, several times that of 1965 (see Table 11-1). The results included 4,084 motor vehicles, 2,314 railroad cars and engines, and 9,500 water vehicles destroyed or damaged. Numerous railroad yards, ports and bridges were also reported as put out of commission.[13]

Despite these significant quantitative results the overall accomplishments of the bombing were disappointing. In January 1967 an analysis by the CIA concluded that the attacks had not eliminated any important sector of the DRV's economy or of the military establishment, and that the flow of supplies south had not been significantly impeded. Hundreds of bridges had been knocked down, but virtually all of them had been quickly repaired, replaced or bypassed, and traffic continued. The railroad and highway network had been expanded and improved. Destroyed trucks, freight cars and barges had been replaced through massive imports from China, Russia and Eastern Europe and there was no evidence of equipment shortages. The POL attacks had eliminated 76 percent of JCS-targeted storage capacity, but not until the North Vietnamese had implemented a system of dispersed storage. Tankers continued to arrive, and they unloaded, standing offshore and usually at night, into barges and other boats which transported the POL along internal waterways to hundreds of concealed locations. Thirty-two percent of North Vietnam's power-generating capacity had been put out of action, but the remaining capacity was adequate to supply most of the DRV's small industrial plant. The summary assessment was pessimistic:

The evidence available does not suggest that ROLLING THUNDER to date has contributed materially to the achievement of the two primary objectives of air attack—reduction of the flow of supplies to VC/NVA forces in the South or weakening the will of North Vietnam to continue the insurgency. ROLLING THUNDER no doubt has lessened the capacity of the transport routes to the South—put a low "cap" on the force levels which North Vietnam can support in the South—but the "cap" is well above present logistic supply levels.[14]

By late 1966 McNamara had become convinced that the limited bombing of North Vietnam was a failure. Despite an outlay of at least $250 million per month and mounting losses of aircraft and men, the campaign had been unable to reduce significantly the flow of men and materiel to the South. It is clear, he told the president in a memorandum dated 14 October 1966, that "to bomb the North sufficiently to make a radical impact upon Hanoi's political, economic and social structure, would require an effort which we could make but which would not be stomached either by our own people or by world opinion, and it would involve a serious risk of drawing us into open war with China."[15] Even the present limited bombing carried heavy political costs, both domestic and international, for public opinion identified the bombing as the principal impediment to the opening of negotiations. A well-orchestrated propaganda campaign accused the U.S. of waging a war of obliteration against a small and allegedly defenseless country, and there were all too many, at home and abroad, who believed these charges. Moreover, McNamara felt, the bombing not only complicated the American political posture but distracted attention from the main job of pacification in South Vietnam.[16]

In the fall of 1966, it will be recalled, McNamara had given the go-ahead signal for the construction of a barrier below the DMZ, and this alternative method of impeding infiltration was another reason for his recommendation to the president that the bombing of the North be stabilized. On the other hand, the unprecedented resupply activity during the five-day bombing pause in February 1967 strengthened the position of the JCS and CINCPAC, who maintained that the bombing played an essential role in the war and indeed should be stepped up. They again recommended intensive air strikes against port facilities and aerial mining of the approaches to the major harbors in order to choke off supplies from abroad.

Commenting on these proposals by the military, civilian officials in both

DOD and State warned that mining the ports raised the serious risk of Russia committing its own ships and aircraft to reopening them. A permanent closing of the shipping lanes would mean that all Russian supplies would have tò be sènt to North Vietnam at the sufferance of China, with which the Soviets were having increasing difficulties. In such circumstances, it was believed, the Russians might be compelled to send new forms of military assistance like floating mines that would endanger American ships in the area, and perhaps might even dispatch volunteers. There also could be new Soviet pressures elsewhere, as against Berlin. Last but not least, there was the ever-present fear of a collision with China, which might consider a major escalation of the bombing the Southeast Asian equivalent of the march to the Yalu River in the Korean War.[17]

The president again opted for a compromise. He authorized new bombing targets for ROLLING THUNDER, including some high-value industrial sites, and a mining of rivers and estuaries south of the 20th parallel—all measures which incurred little risk of counterescalation. On 16 May he approved a strike on the Hanoi thermal power plant, but the Hanoi sanctuary as such was preserved. Meanwhile, the internal policy debate was heating up. McNamara suggested examination of a cutback on bombing north of 20°. William Bundy and Walt Rostow were in favor of such a restriction; the JCS opposed it on the grounds that it would reduce the distance over which the flow of men and supplies was subject to attack. In August 1967 the military received support from the powerful Senate Preparedness Subcommittee, chaired by Sen. John C./Stennis of Mississippi, whose members were strong believers in air power and whose patience with a restrained bombing program was wearing thin.

The lead-off witness at hearings which began on 9 August was Admiral Ulysses S. G. Sharp, CINCPAC, who supported the bombing and urged that it be stepped up. The campaign had "reduced the level of infiltration, especially of materiel, well below that which would be possible if traffic was left unimpeded." The bombing, Sharp told the committee some five months before the onset of the countrywide Tet offensive, "has served to limit considerably the enemy's ability to conduct major sustained operations in South Vietnam." Sharp opposed any cutting back of the bombing to the area south of the 20th parallel and instead urged an increase in pressure—making "our air presence felt over the cities of Hanoi and Haiphong."[18] Other military witnesses took the same position.

The final witness was Secretary of Defense McNamara, who defended the limited bombing. The objectives of the air war against the North had been to raise the morale of the South Vietnamese people, to make clear to the leaders in Hanoi that if they continued their aggression in the South they would have to pay a price in the North, and to reduce the flow and/or increase the cost of the infiltration of men and supplies into South Vietnam. These objectives, said McNamara, had been attained, and more could and should not be expected. "The bombing of North Vietnam has always been considered a supplement to and not a substitute for an effective counter-insurgency campaign in South Vietnam." The military services had done a "superb job" in making infiltration more difficult and expensive, but in view of the multiplicity of partially protected routes, involving the terrain of adjoining countries, and the low volume of logistical support required for a guerilla war (estimated at below 100 tons a day), air strikes could not be expected to choke off the flow. The capacity of the LOCs and outside sources of supplies so far exceeded the minimal flow necessary to support the present level of enemy military effort in the South that even heavier attacks against the LOCs within North Vietnam and upon the sea and land importation routes—short of the virtual annihilation of North Vietnam and its people—would not be able to prevent the few truckloads of materiel required daily from getting through.

Those who thought that air attacks could break the will of the North, McNamara explained, ignored the predominantly agricultural character of the country, which had few significant industrial enterprises. The bombing had hurt North Vietnam's war-making capability, forced the diversion of an estimated 300,000 full-time workers and troops to the repair, dispersal and defense of the LOCs and other damaged targets, and strained the limited economic resources of North Vietnam. Yet the people of the country, despite some war-weariness, gave no signs of faltering under the hardships imposed by the bombing. As far as North Vietnam's leaders were concerned, their past reactions provided no evidence that they could be bombed to the conference table. "Their regard for the comfort and even the lives of the people they control does not seem to be sufficiently high to lead them to bargain for settlement in order to stop a heightened level of attack." In all, McNamara testified, strikes had been authorized against 85 percent of the targets recommended by the JCS. The limited importance of the remaining 57 targets, many in heavily defended, populated areas, did not warrant risking the loss of American lives or of a direct confrontation with Communist China or the Soviet Union.[19]

As was to be expected, McNamara's well-prepared testimony did not convince the hawkish committee. Its report, issued on 31 August, castigated the administration's conduct of the bombing campaign and advocated a switch to a program of escalating pressures. "That the air campaign has not achieved its objectives to a greater extent cannot be attributed to inability or impotence of airpower. It attests, rather, to the fragmentation of our air might by overly restrictive controls, limitations and the doctrine of 'gradualism' placed on our aviation forces which prevented them from waging the air campaign in the manner and according to the timetable which was best calculated to achieve maximum results." Civilians had been allowed to overrule the professional judgment of the best military experts. It was time, declared the committee, to allow the military to run the tactical details of military operations and to apply the force required to see the job through.[20]

As long as the military argued that the bombing was necessary to save American lives and indeed, if increased, could shorten the war, and as long as no conciliatory sign was coming out of Hanoi in response to the many pauses in the air campaign, the president was necessarily put on the defensive. Despite much vocal opposition to the bombing, the heaviest pressure in 1967 appeared to come from the hawks. In an attempt to counter the effects of the Stennis committee hearings, and even while the committee was still hearing witnesses, several strikes had been made in the previously prohibited Hanoi circle and in the buffer zone near the Chinese border, and during the remaining months of 1967 Johnson authorized the bombing of 52 of the 57 targets the Stennis report had criticized the administration for failing to hit. These decisions directly overruled McNamara's recommendations. By December 1967 a total of 864,000 tons of bombs had been dropped on North Vietnam, a quantity well above the 635,000 tons dropped during the Korean War and the 503,000 tons dropped in the Pacific theater during World War II.[21] McNamara's resignation at year's end seemed the logical course for someone by then clearly out of line with administration policy.

The Tet offensive, which began on 31 January 1968, demonstrated the failure of the bombing to interdict the flow of men and supplies to the South. Despite heavy bombing of the infiltration routes the Communists had been able to infiltrate the manpower and ammunition necessary for a massive blow. The deliberations of the Clifford task force, set up for a complete review of U.S. strategy in Vietnam (see chap. 4), included the future of the air war, but the group was unable to agree on a clear recommendation to the president. The report sent to the White House on 4 March therefore included papers from both sides. General Wheeler, representing the position of the JCS, advocated a substantial extension of targets in and near Hanoi and Haiphong and a closing of the port of Haiphong through mining or other means. However, a memorandum drafted in the office of Paul C. Warnke, assistant secretary of defense for international security affairs, opposed these steps on the grounds that they ran significant risks of alienating key friendly nations such as Great Britain and forcing the Soviet Union into some form of protective action. The memo advocated a seasonal step-up of the bombing through the spring.[22]

While the Clifford task force limited its recommendations to various kinds of escalation, discussions among the major presidential advisers began to concentrate on the idea of a partial bombing halt, first recommended by McNamara in May 1967. A draft statement announcing such a halt, composed by Secretary of State Rusk, was circulated by Clifford to Wheeler on 5 March. Rusk noted that bad weather in northern North Vietnam in the next few months would severely hamper air operations around Hanoi and Haiphong in any event, and that the proposal to limit the bombing to the area up to and including the city of Vinh, just below the 19th parallel, would therefore not seriously degrade the American military position.[23] It appears that Clifford from the start supported this proposal; it is not clear at what point Johnson embraced the idea of a partial bombing halt. The pessimistic appraisal of the country's mood given him by the "Wise Men" and his endeavor to make a significant conciliatory gesture undoubtedly played a part in his endorsement of the plan. By 28 March the partial bombing halt had found its way into the draft of the speech the president was to make on 31 March, and by 30 March the final version of the announcement had been agreed upon.

In his address to the nation on 31 March the president renewed the offer, first made in his San Antonio speech of 29 September 1967, to stop the bombing of North Vietnam if this would lead promptly to serious peace talks and if during these discussions the Communists would not take advantage of the cessation of the bombing. No response to this offer had been received, but in order to facilitate talks, the president announced that the U.S. was now taking a unilateral step of de-escalation. "Tonight I have ordered our aircraft and our naval vessels to make no attacks on North Vietnam, except in the area north of the Demilitarized

Zone where the continuing enemy build-up directly threatens allied forward positions and where the movements of their troops and supplies are clearly related to that threat."[24]

Information relayed by various diplomatic sources that Hanoi was at last ready for negotiations, Johnson wrote in his memoirs, played a part in the decision to risk a limited bombing halt,[25] but at the time there appears to have been little expectation that the bombing restraint would produce a positive reaction from North Vietnam. A cable sent to U.S. embassies in various friendly nations the night before the president's address, which informed them of the contents of the forthcoming speech, stated: "Insofar as our announcement foreshadows any possibility of a complete bombing stoppage, in the event Hanoi really exercises reciprocal restraints, we regard this as unlikely."[26] Yet three days later, on 3 April, a Hanoi radio broadcast announced the readiness of the DRV "to send its representatives to make contact with U.S. representatives to decide with the U.S. the unconditional cessation of bombing and all other war acts against the DRV so that talks could begin."[27]

After insisting for three years that they would never agree to any talks before the complete end of the bombing, the communist leaders of North Vietnam had now decided that the time had come to open the dialogue. Documents captured in South Vietnam had indicated for some time that Hanoi was getting ready for a period of simultaneous "talking and fighting." That the beginning of negotiations with the U.S. was for the Communists just another front in the war and did not derive from a genuine desire for a settlement became clear gradually.

The president's announcement of the partial bombing halt had been couched in layman's language without a clear demarcation of the line where the bombing would stop. But in describing the halt to other interested governments and the congressional leaders, the U.S. had specified the 20th parallel as the southern limit of the immune area. On 1 April a heavy raid was staged on targets in the town of Thanh Hoa just below 20°. After receiving Hanoi's favorable response and in order to avoid any violation of the bombing restriction, the president on 3 April gave the order not to schedule any attacks north of the 19th parallel. The bombing in the following six months concentrated on the area south of the 19th parallel and was extremely heavy. During this time American fighter-bombers flew 77,081 attack sorties against this limited area, compared with 72,095 sorties flown during the corresponding months in 1967 when all of North

Vietnam had been the target.[28] The military are said to have conceded privately that, just as McNamara and Rusk had predicted, the concentration of the bombing south of the 19th parallel and in Laos was producing more effective results in inhibiting infiltration into South Vietnam than had the full-scale bombing earlier.[29]

On 10 May the representatives of Hanoi and Washington began to meet for preliminary talks in Paris. One of the main problems facing the negotiators was to develop a formula for an end to the bombing acceptable to all parties. The Americans demanded a commitment that the North take "no advantage" of such a halt; the North Vietnamese insisted that the cessation be "unconditional." A reciprocal agreement would enable the U.S. legally to resume the bombing if the conditions agreed upon were violated. The acknowledgement of such conditions would make it more difficult for Hanoi to argue in the future that the bombing of North Vietnam was illegal—a potent political weapon. After several months of wrangling a compromise was finally worked out. The U.S. would end the bombing of North Vietnam on the basis of three "understandings" which Hanoi did not have to confirm publicly: (1) The demilitarized zone would not be used to infiltrate troops, nor would artillery be fired from or across it. (2) There would be no shelling of the major cities of South Vietnam by rockets or artillery. (3) Unarmed American reconnaissance flights over North Vietnam would continue and these planes would not be attacked.[30]

Johnson had reservations about the value that could be attached to such unwritten assurances, but he was under intense political pressure to reach an agreement on the beginning of full-fledged peace talks before the presidential election on 5 November 1968. If Hubert Humphrey was to have a chance at all to defeat Richard Nixon, the start of the peace negotiations had to be assured. Hence after consulting with his military commanders and obtaining the agreement of the GVN, the president announced on 31 October that as of 1 November 1968 all air, naval and artillery bombardment of North Vietnam would stop and that peace talks with representatives of the GVN and NLF in attendance would begin the following week. "We have reached the stage where productive talks can begin. We have made it clear to the other side that such talks cannot continue if they take military advantage of them. We cannot have productive talks in an atmosphere where the cities are being shelled and where the demilitarized zone is being abused."[31]

As it turned out, the plenary talks did not begin until 25 January 1969.

At the last moment the GVN withdrew its consent to the compromise that had been reached. As the chief U.S. negotiator in Paris, W. Averell Harriman, later revealed: "There seems to be little doubt that through one channel or another Thieu was counseled to wait until after the American election. He was evidently told Nixon would be much harder-lined than Humphrey, and he was warned that if negotiations began, Humphrey might be elected."[32] Information about these contacts was apparently developed by the FBI through close surveillance of the Republican vice-presidential candidate, Spiro T. Agnew, and of Mrs. Anna Chennault, the widow of the commander of the Flying Tigers in World War II and the alleged intermediary between the Republicans and the South Vietnamese.[33]

Whether the beginning of full peace negotiations would have saved Humphrey from defeat in the extremely close election cannot, of course, be determined. In any event, the Communists had now finally achieved the cessation of the bombing of North Vietnam, and they promptly proceeded to violate the unacknowledged "understandings." North Vietnamese activities since the bombing halt, the commander of the U.S. Pacific Air Force reported on 18 November 1968, "have been indicative of the degree of good faith that can logically be expected from Hanoi government without significant change in pressures now being exerted upon it."[34] During the following months and years the North Vietnamese intermittently violated the DMZ, shelled the cities of South Vietnam and fired on American reconnaissance flights over North Vietnam. The Paris peace talks, moreover, bogged down in meaningless rhetoric. There thus can be little doubt that North Vietnam had scored a major triumph. The bombing halt, in effect, had become a unilateral concession on the part of the U.S., made necessary by domestic political constraints. Of course, the fact that the North Vietnamese had won something of great importance does not necessarily mean that the bombing campaign between the years 1965 and 1968 had achieved and served American objectives. It is to a consideration of the overall effects of ROLLING THUNDER that I now turn.

ROLLING THUNDER Appraised

There is general agreement that the bombing campaign ROLLING THUNDER caused extensive damage to North Vietnam's military installations and to its small industrial base and transportation network. As of 22 October 1968, American planes striking fixed targets were reported to have destroyed or put out of commission 77 percent of all ammunition depots, 65 percent of all POL storage, 59 percent of the power plants, 55 percent of the major bridges and 39 percent of the railroad shops. North Vietnam had had one plant each for the production of explosives, iron and steel, and cement, and all three of these plants were put out of action. In addition, armed reconnaissance strikes had destroyed 12,521 vessels, 9,821 vehicles and 1,966 railroad cars and engines and damaged many thousands of others.[35] The air campaign had also caused the mobilization of an estimated 475,000–600,000 North Vietnamese for repair, dispersal and transport programs, and of 145,000 for active and passive air defense activities.[36]

Opinions differ with regard to the impact of this damage on North Vietnam's ability to maintain the flow of men and supplies to the South and on the morale of the population. Admiral Sharp mirrored the view of the Air Force and most of the military community when he stated in 1968:

> The cumulative effects of air operations and the demands of the war in South Vietnam resulted in unprecedented stresses and strains on the North Vietnamese economy, production and distribution systems, the life of the people, and the political control apparatus. . . . Hanoi was forced into a defensive posture marked by frustrations and delayed aspirations. . . . Perhaps the most important measure of the effects of the bombing, however, would be the consideration of the situation if there had been no bombing at all. The uninhibited flow of men, weapons, and supplies through North Vietnam to confront our forces in South Vietnam could have had only one result for the United States and its allies—considerably heavier casualties at a smaller cost to the enemy. Since this alternative was unacceptable, the bombing of North Vietnam, as an essential element of the overall strategy, was clearly successful in fulfilling its purposes.[37]

The evaluation of the effects of the bombing by DOD civilians and the CIA was far different, and the correctness of their view appears borne out by the train of events. The theory of either strategic or interdiction bombing, these agencies pointed out, assumed attacks on highly industrialized nations producing large quantities of military goods to sustain armies engaged in intensive warfare. The nature of North Vietnam's economy and the sporadic attacks launched by the VC/NVA in the South did not fit this model, and North Vietnam therefore was an extremely poor target for a sustained air campaign. The country was predominantly agricultural and had little industry and a rudimentary transportation system. North Vietnam's small industrial plant had been built by a poor country over many years and at considerable sacrifice, yet the assumption that destroying or threatening to destroy this industry would pressure Hanoi into abandoning its drive to take over the South had proved mistaken.

The bombing had caused manpower dislocations but apparently had not limited North Vietnam's ability to maintain essential services in the North and to infiltrate ever larger numbers of men into the South. During the years 1965 to 1968 the North was estimated to have sent almost half a million men to the southern battle zones, 227,000 of these between January and October 1968.[38] The bombing of the infiltration routes was believed to have killed about 5 percent of these infiltrators, but the losses had no observable effects on VC/NVA force levels or activity rates in South Vietnam. Between 1965 and 1968 U.S. attack sorties against North Vietnam increased fourfold. Over this same period, communist main force strength increased about 75 percent, enemy attacks fivefold and overall activity levels ninefold.[39] Similarly, while the bombing destroyed about 10 percent of the supplies moving south and undoubtedly complicated the transportation of war materiel, it did not put a ceiling on the volume of supplies the enemy was able to move southward. VC/NVA forces were estimated to depend on external supplies for 24 percent of their food, 30 percent of their weapons and 84 percent of their ammunition. Total supplies coming from outside South Vietnam were no more than 32 percent of total needs and were believed to be below 100 tons a day. The external needs of the enemy's forces were relatively so small that no imaginable interdiction campaign could have reduced their ability to mount offensive military operations in the South. The bombing had failed to reduce support below required levels, even at the increased activity rates of 1968.[40]

Reports from the diplomatic community and observations of travelers in the North indicated shortages of food and consumer goods and widespread economic disruption generally, but there was no evidence that these hardships had reduced North Vietnam's ability or willingness to continue the conflict or had demoralized the population to any appreciable degree. On the contrary, the bombing appeared to have engendered a psychological climate of common danger which aided the government in winning support for its demands of stern sacrifices and facilitated other measures of control. The bombing had also helped the regime to cast the U.S. in the role of a cruel aggressor.[41]

The main reason why the bombing campaign did not destroy North Vietnam's war-making ability was, of course, Soviet and Chinese aid, which more than made up for losses and damage. Imports in 1967 and 1968 prevented any serious food shortages and compensated for shortfalls in the domestic industrial output. Foreign aid also replaced destroyed trucks, railroad stock, watercraft and construction machinery and, most importantly, provided North Vietnam with petroleum products, artillery and small arms and ammunition as well as a highly sophisticated air defense system. The failure to cut off these crucial imports was, therefore, the most outstanding gap in the logic of U.S. coercive strategy.

The JCS, as we have seen, repeatedly urged the destruction of Haiphong harbor and the mining of all major ports, but the administration decided against these steps out of concern over Soviet and/or Chinese retaliation. The benefits that could be expected from such an escalatory course were regarded as not substantial enough to justify the risks. Even though about 80 percent of all imports came through the port of Haiphong, the bulk of military hardware reached North Vietnam by rail from China. It was believed that even in the event of successfully denying all imports by sea—a very difficult undertaking in view of possible offshore unloading into barges—all war-essential imports could be brought into North Vietnam over the rail lines or roads from China.[42] Before the advent of the "smart bomb," a successful choking off of these LOCs was probably beyond the technical ability of American air power, which was also hampered by severe weather problems in North Vietnam, especially during the monsoon season. More importantly, such attacks were precluded by the threat of Chinese intervention.

To emphasize its determination to keep open the rail lines from its border, China by the spring of 1966 had dispatched some 50,000 Chinese military personnel—engineers, railroad construction and antiaircraft divisions—who engaged in combat and served as living proof of the seriousness of China's commitment.[43] The threshhold which U.S. bombing could not pass without precipitating a major Chinese involvement was not known and unfortunately could not be known even within a wide margin of error. As George Ball put it in a memorandum for the president in January 1966 which counseled extreme caution in this regard: "Unhappily we will not find out until after the catastrophe."[44] The miscalculation of Chinese intentions in the Korean War served as a vivid reminder that this was not an irrational and unfounded fear.

In the final analysis, then, Chinese deterrence was the main impediment to a more effective air campaign against North Vietnam. The Chinese border region served as a vast stockpiling area from which supplies were delivered to countless small storage dumps for overland shipment along the Ho Chi Minh Trail and by sea to South Vietnam. Effective attack against these dispersed storage areas was impossible without overflying Chinese territory. American aircraft also never destroyed all DRV airfields, so as not to drive North Vietnamese jets to Chinese bases and thus raise directly the troublesome sanctuary question. Several American jets which strayed across the border in 1967 were shot down by Chinese MIGs. All this reinforced the need to take the Chinese threat seriously.[45]

The military were no doubt right in maintaining that the strategy of gradualism imposed by civilian policy-makers had hampered the effectiveness of the air campaign. "This gradual application of airpower, with frequent bombing halts over the course of time," the former chairman of the JCS, Admiral Thomas H. Moorer, has argued, "was intended to give the enemy pause and motivate him into seeking a political settlement of the war. Instead, gradualism actually granted the enemy time to shore up his air defenses, disperse his military targets, and mobilize his labor force for logistical repair and movement. From a military point of view, gradualism violated the principle of mass and surprise which airpower has employed historically to attain its maximum effectiveness. Gradualism forced airpower into an expanded and inconclusive war of attrition."[46]

Moorer's contentions were no doubt sound military logic, and the North Vietnamese themselves have acknowledged that the slow escalation of the bombing, imposed on the U.S. because of an unfavorable "balance of international forces," helped them to ride out the storm.[47] But the decision for "gradualism" was again made primarily because of fear of Chinese intervention, and whether the likelihood of such an intervention was overrated will never be known. It can be stated with some assurance that even if the military had received permission for a "sharp blow" strategy, this would not have prevented North Vietnam from sending men and supplies to the South or forced Hanoi to sue for peace. Damage initially would have been higher and American losses lower, but after a while North Vietnam most likely would have adjusted. The experience with both interdiction and strategic bombing in World War II and Korea strongly supports this view.

During Operation STRANGLE in the spring of 1944, the U.S. Air Force flew 34,000 sorties and dropped 33,000 tons of bombs on German LOCs in northern Italy, yet while this heavy bombing caused disruption, fuel and supplies were never at a critical level and damage caused was quickly repaired.[48] Results were similar in the Korean War. Between June 1950 and July 1953 the USAF flew 220,168 interdiction and armed reconnaissance sorties, which were reported to have destroyed 827 bridges, 869 locomotives, 14,906 railroad cars and 74,589 vehicles.[49] Yet this massive damage failed to destroy the North Korean supply effort. Helped by the availability of large quantities of both lumber and laborers, they repaired roads and rail lines faster than U.S. planes could destroy them; supplies were secreted in caves and tunnels and then moved at night; extensive and skillful use was made of bypasses and underwater bridges; trucks, oxcarts, horse-drawn wagons and even pack animals provided shuttle service between break points. "The rate of construction and repair of rail and highway bridges by enemy forces in Korea," wrote an American officer at the time of the air campaign, "has been little short of phenomenal."[50] The official history of the American air war in Korea acknowledges that by December 1951 the contest between skilled pilots with expensive aircraft and unskilled coolie laborers armed with picks and shovels had become a stalemate. Air action did delay and diminish the flow of supplies, but it did not stop them or place an intolerable burden on the supply effort.[51]

In his testimony before the Stennis committee, Defense Secretary McNamara drew upon the failure of the interdiction campaign in Korea. He pointed out that the nature of combat in Vietnam, without established battle lines and with sporadic small-scale enemy action, reduced the volume of logistical support needed. The geography of Vietnam, too, was far less favorable to interdiction. In Korea the entire and relatively narrow neck of the peninsula had been subject to naval bombardment from either side and to air strikes across its width. The infiltration routes into South Vietnam, on the other hand, were far more complex and were protected by dense jungle and frequent cloudiness, not to mention the use of the territory of adjoining countries immune, at least in part, to air attack.[52]

In the light of experience with population bombing in World War II, the failure of ROLLING THUNDER to demoralize the people of North

Vietnam and make them rise up against the rulers who exposed them to the hardships of the American bombing should also not have come as a surprise. This is not to say that morale bombing in World War II stiffened the will to resist, as has been claimed by some critics of American policy in Vietnam. Arthur M. Schlesinger, Jr., and David Halberstam are in error in deducing from the U.S. Strategic Bombing Survey the conclusion that the strategic bombing of Germany intensified the determination of the population to resist the Allies.[53] The bombing survey, a careful study of all available evidence carried out in 1945, reported that "the morale of the German people deteriorated under aerial attack." The bombing caused vast suffering among German civilians and "appreciably affected the German will to resist. Its main psychological effects were defeatism, fear, hopelessness, fatalism, and apathy." As a result of the bombing the German people "lost faith in the prospect of victory, in their leaders and in the promises and propaganda to which they were subjected. Most of all, they wanted the war to end."[54]

While the bombing of Germany succeeded in lowering morale, its effect on actual behavior was less decisive. Workers, by and large, continued to work efficiently—out of habit, discipline, the fear of punishment by a powerful police state and the lack of alternative courses of action.[55] The bombing of German cities severely depressed the mood of the people, but it did not stop the war machine. That was accomplished by the precision bombing of essential industries such as oil production and transportation during the last year of the war. In short, the strategic bombing of Germany in World War II demonstrated that bombing focused on the will to resist is unable to accomplish its goal. The far more concentrated and intense bombing of Japan, culminating in the use of two atomic bombs on the cities of Hiroshima and Nagasaki, supports this conclusion. In the words of one expert: "In Japan there was no more tendency than there was in Germany for the low morale to find expression in any organized popular movement to revolt, or in manifest pressure upon the government to surrender."[56]

What about the cost of the bombing? It was estimated that ROLLING THUNDER caused North Vietnam about $600 million worth of damage in terms of destroyed military facilities, loss of capital stock and lost production. However, between 1965 and 1968 North Vietnam received over $2 billion in foreign aid. As for the other side of the ledger, the bombing campaign cost the U.S. about $6 billion in destroyed aircraft alone.[57] This was a rather unfavorable financial balance sheet, to which one had to add heavy political costs. The bombing of North Vietnam strained U.S. relations with other noncommunist nations and greatly exacerbated domestic tensions. The accusations of indiscriminate bombing of civilian targets can now be shown to have been false, but during the years of the air war they were widely believed, and they seriously impaired the moral authority of the U.S. Instead of bringing North Vietnam to the conference table, the bombing helped erode support for the war here at home and thus was counterproductive on still another level. The intensive propaganda campaign against the bombing waged by Hanoi and its friends all over the world therefore was not necessarily a sign that the bombing really threatened the ability of the North to continue the war. Despite discomfort and dislocations, the bombing brought North Vietnam valuable political dividends.

ROLLING THUNDER and the Law of War

Air warfare is not regulated by an authoritative body of law in the same manner as land warfare is by the Hague and Geneva conventions. In 1923 a commission of jurists produced a code of rules, known as the Hague Air Warfare Rules, but it was never ratified and indeed was disregarded by all sides in World War II. The 1954 Hague Convention for the Protection of Cultural Property in the Event of Armed Conflict sets certain implicit limits to aerial bombardment. In 1972 a conference of experts convened by the International Committee of the Red Cross proposed a protocol on air warfare which, while not formally ratified so far, appears to have wide support and today can probably be considered declaratory of international customary law.

According to this draft protocol, aerial attacks are to be limited to military objectives, defined as "objectives which by their nature or use, contribute effectively and directly to the military effort of the adversary, or which are of a generally recognized military interest. . . ."[58] According to the commentary on this draft, military objectives include airfields, railway lines and roads "which are of fundamental military importance," as well as "industries of fundamental importance for the conduct of the war" or installations providing energy "mainly for military consumption."[59] The key factor in defining a military objective is whether it makes an effective contribution to the war effort. The reasonable proportionality which must exist between the damage caused and the military gain produced, writes a French jurist, "constitutes the essential criterion of the legality of bombing directed against targets not having a purely military character."[60]

The ICRC draft protocol forbids direct attacks upon the civilian population, in particular morale bombing and terrorization attacks of the kind that took place in World War II. However, "civilians who are within a military objective run the risks consequent upon any attack launched against this objective."[61] In other words, it is recognized that in the course of attacks on military objectives the civilian population may suffer incidental death or injury and that their property may be destroyed. Such casualties and damage are not violative of international law if they are not disproportionate to the military advantage gained. The draft protocol also rejects the use of the civilian population as a shield: "The civilian population or individual civilians shall never be used in an attempt to shield, by their presence, military objectives from attack."[62] The cities of an adversary do not gain immunity from attack because he has had the shrewdness to locate his military supply depots or missile sites there.

Among legal authorities there is general agreement that the presence of a military force, either in occupation or passing through, deprives an objective of its status as an undefended place. By the same logic, any objective defended by antiaircraft guns or missiles is no longer an undefended place and becomes a legitimate military target. As we have seen in chapter 7, even hospitals lose their immunity if they are used for acts harmful to the enemy (see p. 231). In certain circumstances it may also be permissible to bomb an entire area. Legal justification for such attacks will depend on two factors: "The first must be the fact that the area is so preponderantly used for war industry as to impress that character on the whole of the neighborhood, making it essentially an indivisible whole. The second factor must be that the area is so heavily defended from air attack that the selection of specific targets within the area is impracticable."[63]

Applying these customary rules of air warfare to the American bombing of North Vietnam during the years 1965 to 1968, it appears that the conduct of the U.S. easily passes muster. "Given the state of aerial warfare to which we were brought by the Second World War," writes Telford Taylor, "I can see no sufficient basis for war crimes charges based on the bombing of North Vietnam. Whatever the laws of war in this field *ought* to be, certainly Nuremberg furnishes no basis for these accusations."[64] Indeed, it is clear that the American bombing of North Vietnam during ROLLING THUNDER was decisively more discriminate than the Allied bombardment of Germany and Japan in World War II. There was no bombing directed at the civilian population as such, and attacks either on fixed targets or by armed reconnaissance in fact conformed to the rather strict definition of "military objective" proposed by the ICRC in 1972.

Most of the charges of criminal conduct on closer examination turn out to involve collateral damage which generally appears not to have been disproportionate to the military advantage gained or sought by the destruction of the military objective nearby. The town of Thanh Hoa, for example, which originally had 50,000–60,000 inhabitants, by 1966 had suffered extensive damage and was half deserted. However, Thanh Hoa served as an important transshipment link in the route to the South. The town was also located three miles south of the Ham Rung (Dragon's Jaw) Bridge spanning the Song Ma River, a vital link in the North Vietnamese transportation system. The bridge was heavily defended, and American planes, despite repeated attacks during ROLLING THUNDER, failed to destroy it. Proximity to the Gulf of Tonkin meant that this bridge was covered by low clouds and fog during much of the year. It was finally felled by several "smart bombs" in 1972. The damage suffered by the town of Thanh Hoa and a hospital situated there was an obvious result of the location of the town, in particular its closeness to this important bridge.[65]

Damage inflicted on the Hoan Kiem quarter on the outskirts of Hanoi was related to attacks on the nearby Long Bien (Paul Doumer) Bridge over the Red River, a crucial railroad link with China and the port of Haiphong. *New York Times* correspondent Harrison E. Salisbury called this bridge—5,532 feet long and consisting of 19 spans—"in all probability the single most important military objective in North Vietnam. Without the bridge the movement of traffic from north to south would be radically impeded."[66] The heavily defended bridge was attacked successfully several times in 1966 and 1967. As of January 1967, 52 houses on Nguyen Thiep Street, about 150 yards from the approaches to the bridge, were said to have been destroyed and 54 people killed in these attacks.[67] Needless to say, neither the Long Bien Bridge nor the adjacent area nor, indeed, the city of Hanoi itself could insist on exemption from attack. Reporter David Schoenbrun, who visited Hanoi and toured the surrounding countryside in the summer of 1967, wrote: "Hanoi looks like an armed porcupine, with hundreds, probably thousands, of spiny steel gun snouts sticking out beyond the tops of the trees."[68]

Collateral damage appears to account also for the few confirmed cases of hits on dikes. In January 1966 Assistant Secretary of Defense John Mc-Naughton proposed for consideration attacks on locks and dams in order to cause flooding that could lead to widespread starvation "unless food is provided—which we could offer to do 'at the conference table.' "[69] Successful attacks on irrigation dams and reservoirs had been carried out in the closing days of the Korean War,[70] but this time the idea never even got to the drawing board. Eight of North Vietnam's 94 major locks and dams were on the JCS target list, but only two were approved for strikes and actually hit.[71] In view of the extensive bombing of inland waterways, it is not surprising that here and there incidental damage was done to the dikes and locks connected with them. Certainly if the U.S. had decided to bomb the dikes, the results would have been far more telling, and there would have been extensive flood damage. The continual references to American bombing of the dikes may have been part of a North Vietnamese effort to get the population to step up work on the dikes to prevent natural flooding, an ever-present danger to many of the major cities lying below river levels. "More work was done on the irrigation system during the bombing," writes one student of the subject, "than had been done in the previous years since the Communists came into power, but ironically, no serious flooding occurred until the summer of 1968, after the United States had stopped bombing North Vietnam's delta region."[72]

The communist propaganda onslaught against the bombing of North Vietnam was massive and ceaseless, and after a while many in the West began to accept even some of the more preposterous allegations. For example, witnesses before the Russell International War Crimes Tribunal in May 1967 charged that American flyers systematically and intentionally bombed North Vietnamese medical facilities. Hospitals, it was stated, "are shown *on the maps of targets* in the hands of the U.S. pilots who have been shot down. . . ." (my italics).[73] This testimony, of course, lent itself to a different interpretation: the pilots had to have good maps and hospitals would be marked in order to avoid hitting them. To prevent such a construction, the U.S. Committee of Concerned Asian Scholars reported the testimony in this way: "Maps with hospitals *marked as targets* on them have been found in the possession of U.S. pilots shot down over North Vietnam" (my italics).[74]

One member of an investigating team sent to North Vietnam by the Russell tribunal, a Scottish professor, was bothered by the question of intent. He told Harrison E. Salisbury: "It is easy enough to report that there has been enormous destruction of civilian property and nonmilitary objectives. Anyone who travels in North Vietnam can see this. But is it intentional? This is the difficult question. How can we read the mind of the pilot who dropped the bombs or loosened the rockets? How can we know, for certain, what his orders were? How can we know from the ground what the airman high in the sky really thought he was doing?"[75] But the tribunal preferred to ignore such scruples and did not call the professor as a witness. On 10 May 1967 it concluded unanimously that "the government and armed forces of the United States are guilty of the deliberate, systematic and large-scale bombardment of civilian targets, including civilian populations, dwellings, villages, dams, dykes, medical establishments, leper colonies, schools, churches, pagodas, historical and cultural monuments." By subjecting the civilian population of the DRV to such bombing the U.S. had committed a war crime.[76] Daniel Berrigan was one of many Americans who accepted the truth of these accusations. After his return from a visit to North Vietnam in February 1968, he charged that the U.S. has waged "a monstrous and intentionally genocidal air war" against the North.[77]

More damaging to U.S. prestige than these extreme charges was the reporting of Harrison Salisbury, assistant managing editor of the *New York Times*, who during late 1966 and early 1967 spent two weeks in North Vietnam, the first American correspondent allowed into the country since the beginning of the air campaign. Salisbury's widely discussed dispatches left the impression that the U.S. was willfully bombing nonmilitary targets; newspapers in many countries condemned the duplicity of the American government, which had claimed to bomb only military objectives. An editorial in *Le Monde* on 28 December 1966 stated: "Not a day passes any more but that the most moderate American press catches the President or his collaborators in the flagrant act of lying." And the London *Sun* demanded: "In the name of humanity and of the British people—who know what bombing means—Harold Wilson must warn President Johnson that Britain cannot support the bombing policy."[78]

Only after the articles had appeared and received extensive attention all over the world did a small number of persons learn that Salisbury, in effect, had given the authority of his byline to unverified communist propaganda and that the *New York Times* had printed this information as though Salisbury had established it himself with his own on-the-scene reporting. Two days after the first dispatch from Hanoi, two little-noticed sentences casually pointed out: "It should be noted, incidentally, that all casualty estimates and statistics in these dispatches are those of North Vietnamese officials. However, descriptions of bomb damage are based wholly on visual inspection."[79] Also, when Salisbury's articles were published in book form in April 1967,[80] the author took pains to indicate by the insertion of such phrases as "according to the officials" and "they said" that many of his details were in fact not based on personal observation. By that time, of course, the damage had been done. At no time did either Salisbury or the *New York Times* acknowledge that the dispatches dealing with the bombing of the city of Nam Dinh had borrowed extensively from a North Vietnamese propaganda pamphlet, *Report on U.S. War Crimes in Nam-Dinh City*, which had appeared in October 1966.[81] Failure to name this source is said to have cost Salisbury the Pulitzer Prize for which the *Times* had nominated him.[82]

Salisbury visited Nam Dinh, located some 40 miles southwest of Hanoi and formerly North Vietnam's third largest city, on 25 December 1966 in order to inspect damage caused in earlier bombings. He was shown around by the mayor of the town who, reported Salisbury, "regards her city as essentially a cotton-and-silk textile town containing nothing of military significance. Namdinh has been systematically attacked by American planes since June 28, 1965. The cathedral tower looks out on block after block of utter desolation. . . . No American communique has asserted that Namdinh contains some facility that the United States regards as a military objective." City officials attributed the bombing of their town to an attempt to intimidate the population or to the endeavor to make Nam Dinh an object lesson to Hanoi. "Whatever the explanations," Salisbury wrote, "one can see that United States planes are dropping an enormous weight of explosives on purely civilian targets. Whatever else may be or might have been in Namdinh, it is the civilians who have taken the punishment. A brief tour of Namha province in which Namdinh lies, shows that Namdinh is far from being exceptional."[83]

The impression left with the reader was that the U.S. was deliberately and secretly bombing a harmless textile town without military targets. Yet this was hardly the whole story. Nam Dinh happened to be a major transshipment point for supplies and soldiers moving south who were coming into and through the city by river and the north–south railroad. On at least three prior occasions, American communiques had referred to the bombing of military targets in Nam Dinh—a large railroad yard, a huge storage depot, a POL storage area, and a thermal power plant. The North Vietnamese apparently did not share the view of the mayor of Nam Dinh that the city had no targets of military significance. As a Pentagon statement issued in response to the Salisbury dispatches and printed in the *New York Times* pointed out, the city was ringed by antiaircraft gun batteries and by surface-to-air missile sites.[84] The city's three textile plants had never been targeted for attack, but, being located close to the power plant and the POL storage area, they, like residential buildings, had suffered extensive damage.

Casualty figures and other details on the results of the bombing of Nam Dinh, Salisbury told his readers in another dispatch on 31 December 1966, had come from city officials. When the report on Nam Dinh had first been printed on 27 December it had carried no such qualification and the statistics were given as fact. No mention was ever made of the communist propaganda pamphlet to which Salisbury's dispatch was clearly indebted:

Pamphlet	*Salisbury dispatch of 12/27/66*
During the 33 above said air attacks against Nam Dinh, they caused many losses in lives and property to the City's inhabitants, 89 persons were killed, among them 23 children, 36 women and 405 wounded, among them 61 women, 44 old men and 41 children. Eight hundred and eighty-one dwelling houses (accounting for 13 percent of the city housing), with an area of 86,847 square meters, were destroyed, leaving 12,464 inhabitants homeless.	13 percent of the city's housing, including the homes of 12,464 people, have been destroyed; 89 people have been killed and 405 wounded.

Or again:

The April 14, 1966, air raid over Hang Thao street was one of the biggest deliberate U.S. attacks on human lives. . . . At 6:30 A.M., when those who had just come back from a night shift were still	Street after street in Namdinh has been abandoned and houses stand torn and gaping. One deserted street is Hang Thao or Silk Street, which was the center of the silk industry. Almost every house on

sleeping, those who were about to work were having breakfast, women were getting ready for their shopping or for their housework, and children were getting ready for their kindergartens or infant classes, two U.S. planes came flying at low altitude along Ninh Binh Highway No. 10 and furtively intruded into Hang Thao, Han Cau, Tran Hung Dao streets and Ben Thoe area, dropped 8 MK 84 bombs, killing 49 people . . . wounding 135 people, and destroying 240 houses.

the street was blasted down on April 14 at about 6:30 A.M. just as the factory shifts were changing. Forty-nine people were killed, 135 were wounded on Hang Thao and 240 houses collapsed. Eight bombs—MK-84's—accomplished this.

A last example:

In their bombings and strafings of the city, they have used various ultramodern planes such as the A.4A, A.6A, A.3J, F.105, F.4H, RB.57.[85]

Most strikes have been carried out by F-105's and F-4's but B-57's, A-3's, A-4's and A-6's have also been used.[86]

Department of Defense press releases had always emphasized that the bombing of North Vietnam was limited to military targets and that all possible precautions were being taken to minimize damage to civilian lives and property. As the internal record shows, this was indeed the case, and various spokesmen for the military community repeatedly protested that these protective measures hampered the effectiveness of the bombing. For example, Secretary of the Air Force Harold Brown in a memo of 4 March 1968 urged the lifting of restrictions on the bombing of the North "so as to permit bombing of military targets without the present scrupulous concern for collateral civilian damage and casualties."[87] But these requests were denied, and many pilots were shot down because the rules of engagement required approach angles and other tactics designed to reduce civilian casualties rather than to afford maximum protection to the attacking planes. As a result of this much-publicized concern for noncombatants the impression had been created that the bombing was always perfectly accurate and that no civilian property or lives were being lost.

For reasons to be discussed presently, this was, of course, quite impossible. Hence when the Salisbury articles with their reports of extensive bomb damage to residential areas hit the world's headlines, the U.S. stood accused of being a deceiver and liar.

The North Vietnamese have never released any cumulative civilian casualty figures. According to American estimates, 52,000 civilians were killed during the course of ROLLING THUNDER between 1965 and 1968.[88] Casualties from the bombing were thus *relatively* low—due to the care practiced by American pilots, large-scale evacuations from urban centers and effective civil defense measures. Several factors accounted for the inevitability of collateral damage. First, until the perfection of the "smart bomb" during the last stage of the Vietnam war, bombing was an inherently inaccurate process. Despite sophisticated computer equipment, the precision of the bombing was degraded by errors involving boresight, release mechanisms, bomb dispersion, aiming, and the computational system. Unknown winds at altitudes below the release point further complicated the pilots' task. All this meant that, as one Navy pilot wrote in 1969, "it is impossible to hit a small target with bombs except by sheer luck."[89]

Secondly, the North Vietnamese made it a practice to disperse their storage depots. Salisbury reported seeing oil drums, munitions, and all manner of hardware stacked out in fields, beside rural roads and "cluttering up paths that led to rice paddies—indeed, in all the time I rode about the countryside I think I was never more than two or three minutes out of sight of some kind of supplies and equipment which had come to rest in the most unlikely setting."[90] Supplies placed in "unlikely settings," including inhabited places, of course created the danger of attack and explain the many reports of raids by American aircraft on rural targets. Antiaircraft batteries and SAM sites, too, as reconnaissance photos clearly show, were often located in residential areas. One pilot recalls his difficulties in hitting a railroad yard in the town of Viet Tri northwest of Hanoi because of a nearby complex of buildings off limits as a hospital. "If it was in fact a hospital, it must have been a hospital for sick flak gunners, because every time we looked at it from a run on the railroad, it was a mass of sputtering, flashing gun barrels."[91] When American flyers sought to hit targets placed in the midst of villages and towns or tried to defend themselves against hostile fire coming from such places, civilian lives and property were inevitably lost.

The problem of bombing accuracy was especially acute in the case of armed reconnaissance missions against targets of opportunity along assigned routes or in assigned areas, which constituted about 90 percent of all sorties flown against North Vietnam.[92] In the South, pilots flying fast jet fighter-bombers had the benefit of forward air controllers who marked targets with smoke bombs and guided the jets to them. Without FACs, strike pilots had great difficulty seeing or correcty identifying small objectives.[93] Also, when unable to get to or find lucrative targets, pilots would often go on "hunting" for less important targets until their fuel supply was exhausted. It is possible that these secondary targets on occasion were indeed of limited military significance.

Last but not least, precision in bombing was impaired by the increasingly heavy and sophisticated air defenses of North Vietnam. The number of missiles fired at American planes went up from 200 in 1965 to 3,484 in 1967; the number of antiaircraft guns grew from 700 to 7,400 by March 1968. U.S. losses during ROLLING THUNDER caused by North Vietnam's air defenses, which military observers called the tightest installed anywhere, were 938 planes.[94] As I noted earlier, the variables in the accuracy equation were numerous and created the possibility of error even under perfect flying conditions. In a combat environment, when pilots had to dodge extremely heavy antiaircraft fire and keep an eye on SAMs, accuracy was even more difficult to achieve. Damage also resulted from SAMs which fell back to earth without finding their target, for Russian-made SAMs, unlike American ones, did not have an automatic self-destruct mechanism. American pilots at times had to jettison their bombs in order to be able to enter air battles with enemy jets. In situations where air defenses are intensive, writes one student of the law of air warfare, "it is usually more accurate to recognize that both attacking and defending forces in an air raid cause civilian casualties."[95]

Whatever the wisdom of ROLLING THUNDER on political and other grounds, it is reasonable to conclude that the air campaign against North Vietnam during the years 1965 to 1968 did not violate the law of war and that the extensive damage caused to civilian areas was incidental to the bombing of legitimate military targets. This was also the finding of many critics of American military policy. Telford Taylor noted that Harrison Salisbury's reports had graphically described the extent of the physical damage caused by the American bombing but "fell far short of demonstrating any intent to cause civilian casualties."[96] James Cameron, a British journalist whom *Time* described as of "ban-the-bomb breed," wrote after a visit to North Vietnam in 1966: "It was my impression, and I am not wholly ignorant of the processes of tactical bombing, that United States attacks on North Vietnam had been, as they claimed, aimed generally at what they could define as military objectives. . . . I do not believe that the Americans set out to bomb homes and hospitals; if they had wished to do so it would have been extremely easy to do."[97] An American flyer, Capt. Michael J. Heck, who since 1966 had participated in numerous missions against North Vietnam, in 1972 asked for conscientious objector status and refused to fly any more attacks on the North on the grounds that U.S goals did not justify the destruction and killing caused. Heck told a correspondent of the *New York Times:* "I don't think we intentionally targeted civilian targets. . . ." Nonmilitary objectives were hit because of human error, malfunctioning of equipment or as a result of pilots having to dodge missiles. But "I don't think it was intentional."[98]

The 1969–72 Period

Offensive operations against North Vietnam ended on 31 October 1968, but in accordance with the "understanding" reached in Paris unarmed reconnaissance flights continued. When the North Vietnamese began to shoot occasionally at these planes, armed escorts were provided, and these escort planes retaliated against antiaircraft sites that attacked American aircraft. The ROE limited the authority to strike back to the area south of the 19th parallel. They also required that such strikes be an immediate response to enemy aircraft or SAM/AAA (antiaircraft artillery) sites which had actually taken aggressive action against allied planes.[99] In line with this authorization, during 1969 U.S. fighter-bombers flew a total of 285 attack sorties against targets in North Vietnam. At the same time, the all-time high of 144,323 sorties were flown in 1969 against the Ho Chi Minh Trail in Laos.[100]

In early 1970 the Air Force became imcreasingly concerned about threats to allied aircraft operating against the Ho Chi Minh Trail in Laos that emanated from North Vietnamese SAM units deployed near the Laotian border just below and above 19°. In response to urgent requests for action to meet this threat, CINCPAC on 1 April 1970 authorized the Seventh Air Force to strike SAM/AAA sites up to the 20th parallel. In another important modification of the ROE this order allowed strikes against these sites as soon as enemy radar guidance systems locked in on American aircraft, i.e. even before they actually opened fire.[101] Such strikes became known as protective reaction strikes.

The term "protective reaction" was also used by DOD spokesmen for several missions flown during 1970 against targets in North Vietnam. These strikes were said to be in retaliation for repeated North Vietnamese violations of the Paris understandings—large-scale infiltration across the DMZ, the shelling of major South Vietnamese cities and attacks on unarmed reconnaissance planes. During four days in May 1970, about 500 American fighter-bombers attacked supply dumps, staging areas and other military targets in North Vietnam. On 21 November 1970 approximately 225 strike aircraft repeated what Defense Secretary Laird called "limited duration protective reaction air strikes."[102] In all, 1,113 attack sorties were flown against North Vietnam during 1970. Between the beginning of the bombing halt on 1 November 1968 and November 1970, a total of 10 American planes were lost to the North as a result of enemy action.[103]

The air war over Laos and North Vietnam heated up even more during 1971. North Vietnamese MIGs were increasingly active; by late 1971 the North Vietnamese had installed an integrated and interlocking radar system which enabled their missile sites to launch missiles without alerting U.S. aircraft radar warning gear. Requests from the Seventh Air Force for permission to attack this new electronic guidance system and to engage any MIG operating or seen on the ground south of the 20th parallel were denied by Secretary Laird. Frustration was also created by evidence of an extensive North Vietnamese buildup north of the DMZ and just outside the Laotian trails, which the existing ROE did not permit to be attacked. Several massive "limited duration" strikes were staged in September and December 1971 against POL depots and enemy artillery concentrations, but authority for a more prolonged campaign to smash the enemy's preinvasion buildup continued to be withheld. This, then, was the setting for the secret bombing of North Vietnam carried out by the commanding officer of the Seventh Air Force, General John D. Lavelle, between November 1971 and March 1972, information about which reached the U.S. Senate in early 1972.

A letter written on 25 February 1972 by an Air Force sergeant named Lonni Douglas Franks, in charge of debriefing pilots at the Udorn Air Force base in Thailand, addressed to Sen. Harold E. Hughes of the Senate Armed Services Committee, blew the whistle on this bombing.

According to Sergeant Franks, the practice was to file reports that reconnaissance planes had been shot at and that the SAM/AAA sites involved had been attacked in retaliation by escorting fighters while in fact strikes were preplanned and carried out against truck parks, POL depots, troop concentrations and the like. A second set of reports, listing the actual targets struck, Franks wrote, was filed for the eyes of the Seventh Air Force command only.[104] An investigation by the Air Force inspector general confirmed the main substance of the charges. General Lavelle was relieved of his command, reduced in rank and retired from the service. In all, some 28 missions, involving 147 sorties, were later found to be involved in this bombing of unauthorized targets in violation of existing guidelines.

In June and September 1972 General Lavelle testified about these bombings, and the dual reporting system designed to keep them secret, before the House and Senate Armed Services committees. Lavelle stated that he had decided to attack these targets in order to impede the enemy's preinvasion buildup and thus save American and South Vietnamese lives. On several prior occasions he had been encouraged by higher authorities to use protective reaction strikes to launch attacks against targets other than SAM and AAA sites. He had been told to increase the number of reconnaissance flights over North Vietnam as well as the number of fighter escorts in order to ensure effective results on protective reaction strikes. The "liberal interpretation by higher authority of *what* could be struck, plus the encouragement to be more aggressive and more flexible, influenced my determination to make a similar, though I believe less liberal interpretation of the conditions under which we could strike."[105] Lavelle insisted that all the targets struck were related to the North Vietnamese air defense system—such as airfields, radar sites, missiles on transporters and heavy guns. There was no real difference, he argued, between the Navy's practice known as "trolling," which consisted of sending an aircraft into an area as a bait to provoke enemy fire, thus justifying retaliatory attacks, and his preplanning of strikes on selected targets. Testimony by the Air Force chief of staff, Gen. John D. Ryan, also brought out that changes in the ROE made in January and February 1972—including authority to bomb ground control intercept radars south of 20° when enemy aircraft were airborne and indicated hostile intent—would have permitted many of the strikes for which Lavelle had been disciplined.[106]

General Lavelle accepted responsibility for the secret bombings, though he emphasized that he had acted in response to pressure from the JCS, COMUSMACV and Secretary Laird to be more aggressive and take maximum advantage of existing authority to use protective reaction strikes. Without actually saying so, he implied that he had been assured of the backing of his superiors. In its report on the Lavelle affair the House Armed Services Investigating Subcommittee expressed strong doubt that an officer with a prior record of distinguished service like General Lavelle, who had always lived by the rule book, would jeopardize a brilliant career by unilaterally engaging in actions which could bring him neither honor nor glory and almost certainly could lead to disgrace. This suggested more likely explanations, ranging from "possible tacit approval of General Lavelle's actions by his superiors, to possible civilian direction of the bombings. Vigorous denials by those who possibly were involved could neither be corroborated nor refuted without a review of all relevant documentary evidence." This evidence was refused the committee, leaving it with "an uneasy feeling that someone other than General Lavelle could be receiving the benefits of this secrecy."[107] The question whether President Nixon himself ordered or at least condoned the secret bombings will probably never be answered.

The Lavelle affair, like the My Lai cover-up, demonstrates the weakness of the inspector general system in instances when rules and regulations are violated by highly placed officers. It also points up the difficulty faced by a democratic nation in conducting a war not supported by public opinion. When evidence of methodical enemy preparations for an invasion of South Vietnam was received in late 1971 and early 1972, it probably would have been far better for the moral health of the Air Force and the republic if the U.S. had renounced the 1968 bombing halt and mounted a preemptive air offensive against the buildup. However, the Nixon administration apparently did not feel that Congress and the American public would back up such a decision and therefore opted for the subterfuge of "protective reaction" strikes. The bombing of North Vietnamese supply and staging areas in Cambodia between March 1969 and June 1970, unobjectionable under applicable international law,[108] had to be kept secret so as not to embarrass Cambodia's Prince Sihanouk. He was in favor of putting pressure on the communist sanctuaries on his territory, over which he had lost control, but could not afford openly to acknowledge his support of the American bombing.[109] No such requirement of secrecy existed in the case of North Vietnam; the reason for the use of a stratagem was the lack of domestic support for a forthright challenge to the North Vietnamese invasion plans.

LINEBACKER I and II

The important role played by American airpower in turning back the 1972 Easter invasion of South Vietnam has been detailed in chapter 6. Within three days of the start of this massive attack, American planes were granted authority to bomb military targets in North Vietnam 25 miles above the DMZ. On 9 April this operation, codenamed FREEDOM TRAIN, was extended to the 19th parallel; soon thereafter it was expanded to 20°. On 8 May President Nixon ordered offensive air operations throughout North Vietnam except in the 25–30-mile-wide buffer zone alongside the Chinese border and the restricted areas 10 miles from the centers of Hanoi and Haiphong where specific strike authorization was required. At the same time the president ordered the mining of North Vietnamese harbors and the blockade of the coast, an action for which the JCS had pleaded since 1965.[110] As a result of a new and different international situation, including in prominent place the U.S.-Chinese rapprochement, the communist powers limited their reaction to verbal denunciations of the American actions.

The new full-scale bombing campaign against North Vietnam was called LINEBACKER. In addition to destroying war-related resources and interdicting the movement of men and supplies to the South, LINE-BACKER had the aim of reducing or restricting North Vietnam's receipt of assistance from abroad. Unlike the case of ROLLING THUNDER, the military this time had far more tactical flexibility. Field commanders could pick targets from a validated list and strike them when they wanted. Targets in the key areas around Hanoi and Haiphong were authorized much sooner than during ROLLING THUNDER. By 22 October, when LINEBACKER I ended, 10 MIG bases, 6 major thermal power plants, and almost all fixed POL storage facilities had been hit, which required strikes within 10 miles of the centers of both cities. Most importantly, a new family of "smart bombs," consisting of TV- and laser-guided bombs, had become available that provided pilots with a new and unprecedented bombing accuracy.[111] Several important railroad bridges and tunnels near the Chinese border could now be struck without fear of political complications. The Thanh Hoa Bridge, which had survived numerous attacks dur-

Table 11-2 Number of Sorties, Bomb Tonnage and Plane Losses During ROLLING THUNDER and LINEBACKER I

	1967	April–Oct. 1972
Fighter-bomber and B-52 sorties	106,996	41,653
Bomb tonnage	247,410	155,548
Losses to hostile action per 1,000 sorties[a]	2.38	1.80[b]

SOURCES: U.S. Senate, Committee on Armed Services, *FY Authorization for Military Procurement* . . . , 93rd Cong., 1st sess., March–April 1973; OASD (Comptroller), SEA Statistical Summary, Table 321, 24 October 1973.

[a] Includes reconnaissance and other sorties.
[b] April–September.

ing ROLLING THUNDER, was felled with several laser-guided bombs on 13 May. Aircraft losses were held down through improved electronic countermeasures.

The improved tactical ability of American planes meant that fewer sorties and less bombing tonnage, accompanied by a lower loss rate (see Table 11-2), during seven months of LINEBACKER I in 1972 were able to cause more serious damage to North Vietnam than had been scored during the high point of ROLLING THUNDER in 1967. The shipment of goods through Haiphong and other ports was virtually eliminated; railroad traffic from China was seriously crippled; and most imports were now coming down by truck and on waterways which were under continuous attack. According to estimates, the flow of imports into North Vietnam and the movement of supplies to the South by September 1972 had been reduced to between 35 and 50 percent of what they had been in May of that year.[112]

Once again there were charges of deliberate attacks on hospitals, schools and other civilian targets, charges that were no more substantiated than those made during ROLLING THUNDER. Reconnaissance photos showed bomb craters on several dikes, but these were all in close proximity to other targets of high military value; no major dike was breached or functionally damaged and the high-water season passed without significant flooding. If the U.S. had wished to bomb the dikes, the results quite obviously would have been rather different. At a time when the invasion of South Vietnam had been barely checked and when North Vietnamese air defenses had become among the strongest and most elaborate in the world, the executive secretary of the American Friends Service Committee, Bronson P. Clark, told a congressional committee that "to be raining sophisticated destruction on a relatively defenseless, essentially peasant people who are completely without the means of the slightest attack on our country brings dishonor to American ideals."[113]

Meanwhile a breakthrough had occurred in the long-stalled peace talks in Paris when Hanoi dropped its insistence on a coalition government and the resignation of Thieu. On 23 October 1972 President Nixon, in a gesture of good will, suspended all bombing north of the 20th parallel. On 26 October Secretary of State Kissinger told a news conference that "peace is at hand."[114] But this announcement was premature and by 23 November the negotiations in Paris had reached a new deadlock—the result of sloppy drafting of the text of the projected agreement, new objections from Thieu and a withdrawal of several important concessions by Hanoi. On 19 December Nixon ordered the resumption of full-scale bombing of North Vietnam and there followed the so-called Christmas bombing—LINEBACKER II. Allegations that Kissinger opposed the renewal of the bombing are baseless.[115]

LINEBACKER II lasted 12 days, though the weather was clear enough for visual bombing for only 12 hours. During these 12 days there were 729 B-52 sorties and about 1,000 fighter-bomber attack sorties; 20,370 tons of bombs were dropped over all of Vietnam. A total of 26 planes were lost, including 15 B-52s. The bombing was concentrated on targets in the Hanoi-Haiphong complexes and included transportation terminals, rail yards, warehouses, power plants, airfields and the like. When the bombing halted on 29 December, North Vietnam's electrical power supply was crippled and extensive damage had been caused to all other targets as well. North Vietnamese air defenses were shattered, and during the last few days American planes roamed the skies with virtual impunity.[116]

Bombing accuracy in most cases was almost surgical, but on account of the extensive utilization of B-52 bombers there was some spillage of bomb damage to adjacent residential areas. It was estimated that in 90 percent of all B-52 missions one or more bombs, because of bent or damaged fins, would escape the normal bomb train and land outside the target box.[117] This incidental civilian damage and the overall extremely destructive impact of LINEBACKER II gave rise to predictable outcries of terror-bombing. The December bombing, Hanoi charged, surpassed the atrocities committed by the Hitlerite fascists and represented an "escalation of genocide to an all-time high." In only 12 days "the Nixon administration wrought innumerable Oradours, Lydices, Guernicas, Coventrys. . . ."[118] Antiwar groups in America and many others who should have known better joined in the worldwide chorus of denunciation. One scholar speaks of "unabashed terror tactics" and a "flaunting of established norms of civilized conduct."[119]

These charges are disproven by evidence available then and by later reports from the scene. The North Vietnamese themselves at the time claimed between 1,300 and 1,600 fatalities, and even though both Hanoi and Haiphong were partially evacuated, such a number of victims—regrettable as any civilian casualties always are—is surely not indicative of terror-bombing. Attacks explicitly aimed at the morale of the population took place against Germany and Japan during World War II and killed tens of thousands. According to an East German estimate, 35,000 died in the triple raid on Dresden in February 1945; the official casualty toll of the bombing of Tokyo with incendiaries on 9–10 March 1945, stands at 83,793 dead and 40,918 wounded.[120] The Hanoi death toll, wrote the London *Economist,* "is smaller than the number of civilians killed by the North Vietnamese in their artillery bombardment of An Loc in April or the toll of refugees ambushed when trying to escape from Quang Tri at the beginning of May. That is what makes the denunciation of Mr. Nixon as another Hitler sound so unreal."[121] Part of the death toll was undoubtedly caused by the North Vietnamese themselves, for they launched about 1,000 SAMs, many of which impacted in the cities of Hanoi and Haiphong and took their toll on their own people.

Among the civilian facilities hit was the Bach Mai Hospital in Hanoi. The North Vietnamese cited the extensive damage to this hospital as proof of American criminal intentions, and the charge of deliberate attacks on civilian targets was accepted as true by Dale S. DeHaan, counsel to the Kennedy committee on refugees, who visited Hanoi in March 1973, and by Senator Kennedy himself.[122] However, other observers offered a different explanation. The hospital unfortunately was located about 1,000 yards from the Bach Mai airstrip and the military barracks, which were heavily bombed. The attack, wrote Telford Taylor after visiting the site in January 1973, "was probably directed at the airfield and nearby barracks and oil-storage units."[123] Murray Marder of the *Washington Post* and

Peter Ward of the *Baltimore Sun* concurred in this view, and aerial photographs released by the Defense Department in May 1973 further confirm that the hospital was hit by bombs escaping the normal bomb train. [124]

Damage to residential areas in Hanoi and Haiphong, too, was rather clearly the result of gravity-drop bombs which had fallen short of the railroad sidings, warehouses and industrial plants targeted and destroyed. Malcolm W. Browne of the *New York Times* was greatly surprised by the condition in which he found Hanoi and wrote that "the damage caused by American bombing was grossly overstated by North Vietnamese propaganda. . . ." "Hanoi has certainly been damaged," noted Peter Ward of the *Baltimore Sun* on 25 March 1973 after a visit, "but evidence on the ground disproves charges of indiscriminate bombing. Several bomb loads obviously went astray into civilian residential areas, but damage there is minor, compared to the total destruction of selected targets." [125]

On 30 December 1972 the White House announced at a special press briefing that the president had called a halt to the bombing of the North Vietnamese heartland. "As soon as it was clear," the spokesman declared, "that serious negotiations could be resumed at both the technical level and between the principals, the President ordered that all bombing be discontinued above the twentieth parallel." [126] On New Year's Day the talks in Paris resumed, by 9 January the cease-fire agreement was essentially completed, and on 23 January 1973 it was initialed by Kissinger on behalf of the U.S. and by Le Duc Tho on behalf of North Vietnam. Did the intense bombing of December 1972 bring about this settlement and thus belatedly vindicate the decisiveness of air power?

"I am convinced that Linebacker II served as a catalyst for the negotiations which resulted in the ceasefire," Admiral Moorer has stated. "Airpower, given its day in court after almost a decade of frustration, confirmed its effectiveness as an instrument of national power—in just 9½ flying days." [127] Two Air Force legal officers have argued the same position: LINEBACKER II "was designed to coerce a negotiated settlement by threatening further weakening of the enemy's military effort to maintain and support his armed forces. It is our firm belief that this threat of continued and further destruction of military objectives produced the political settlement." [128]

It may well be that the heavy bombing of targets in the Hanoi and Haiphong complexes, the threat of more such punishing attacks and the unwillingness or inability of the Soviet Union and Communist China to prevent these bombings induced Hanoi finally to sign a cease-fire agreement, just as the intensive bombings during LINEBACKER I may have contributed to the breakthrough in the negotiations in October. However, in order to consider this result as conclusive proof of the decisiveness of air power, one would have to be convinced that North Vietnam, in signing the Paris agreements, put itself at a serious disadvantage, and the evidence for this assumption is lacking. The cease-fire terms—the unanimity principle adopted for the inspection machinery, which virtually guaranteed that supervision of adherence to the agreements would be ineffective, and the legitimation of the presence of NVA forces in the South— hardly represented an American victory. As subsequent events were to demonstrate, the Paris agreements did not impede North Vietnam's military drive to take over the South. Within little more than two years after the signing of the alleged "peace with honor," South Vietnam had fallen to North Vietnamese troops which had never left the South and to massive reinforcements which the meaningless inspection provisions of the Paris agreement could not prevent from entering South Vietnam.

To be sure, as Nixon assured Thieu in November 1972, the administration believed that peace in Vietnam would depend not on the specific clauses of an agreement but on the willingness of the U.S. to enforce a cease-fire. The events of Watergate, which seriously weakened the ability of the U.S. to react to the North Vietnamese violations of the Paris accords, could not have been foreseen. And yet the U.S. quite clearly had had to settle for a compromise; the Nixon administration obviously would have preferred more advantageous terms which did not leave peace in Vietnam dependent solely on the threat of the reintroduction of American air power. LINEBACKER II helped bring about a cease-fire, but it failed to achieve a settlement that could be considered a victory for either South Vietnam or the U.S. By December 1972 there were few military targets left in North Vietnam and, short of the complete obliteration of the country, it is likely that no continuation of the bombing would have induced North Vietnam to withdraw its forces from the South or make other important concessions. In this sense, then, the argument for the decisive effectiveness of strategic air power in the Vietnam conflict—air power within the limits set by international law and Western public opinion— remains unproven.

Conclusion

The bombing of North Vietnam conformed to international law, and the application of American air power was probably the most restrained in modern warfare. At all times, targets, munitions and strike tactics were selected to minimize the risk of collateral damage to the civilian population.

The bombing of the North caused extensive damage to the country's war-making capacity, but at no point did it seriously hamper Hanoi's drive against the South. Neither ROLLING THUNDER nor LINEBACKER was able to wring decisive concessions from the North Vietnamese. The use of a "sharp blow" approach and less regard for civilian casualties might have reduced American losses at the beginning of the air campaign, but, short of the use of nuclear weapons, would have been unlikely to lead to different results.

The costs to America of the air war over North Vietnam were extremely high—both financially and politically. The bombing also helped the communist rulers of North Vietnam to organize their country on a war footing. But probably the most damaging consequence of the bombing of North Vietnam was that it diverted attention from the real hub of the Vietnam problem—the southern battlefield—where the war was going to be won or lost. Back in 1962 President Kennedy told Roger Hilsman, then in the State Department, that communist infiltration from the North was a built-in excuse for failure as well as a built-in argument for escalation. "No matter what goes wrong or whose fault it really is, the argument will be that the Communists have stepped up their infiltration and we can't win unless we hit the North."[129] This is exactly what happened. Frustrated over lack of progress in the war in the South and without searching for the deeper causes of South Vietnam's lagging military fortunes, the decision was taken to bomb North Vietnam. From that point on, the air war developed its own momentum.

Despite much evidence that the bombing was ineffective in decisively curtailing the inflow of men and supplies from the North, or in breaking Hanoi's will to pursue the war, it was continued for over three years and at an ever-increasing pace. The backers of air power until the end of the war—and indeed until today—continued to insist that the application of more force would bring victory. The Air Force and the Navy competed with each other over who could fly more sorties, and the desire of both services to protect their future aircraft procurements probably had an impact on the conduct of the air war, even though the public debate over bombing policy centered on other issues. As stated by one knowledgeable student: "Ultimately the most serious concern of each service was that flying and bombing less than expected would damage its position in long-range planning of roles and missions. . . . The shape of future tactical air capability was at issue."[130]

Presidential adviser John P. Roche wrote in a memorandum for Johnson on 1 May 1967: "What has distressed me is the notion (expressed time and again by the Air Force boys) that air power would provide a *strategic* route to victory; and the parallel assumption that by bombing the North we could get a cut-rate solution in the South and escape from the problems of building a South Vietnamese army."[131] President Johnson finally accepted the logic of this argument, and the bombing of North Vietnam was ended. The Nixon administration belatedly began a program of Vietnamization. The bombing of the North was resumed only in response to the 1972 Easter invasion and under far more favorable international political circumstances, which allowed the imposition of a blockade, a crucial complementary measure to the air war. That this bombing did not bring final victory is no reflection on the true importance of air power, only a refutation of the illusions of air power enthusiasts.

Epilogue:
The Legacy of Vietnam

The growing American involvement in the Vietnam conflict during the years 1950–65 was the result of decisions taken after long and often soul-searching discussions. All four American presidents who presided over the decision-making process during these years—Truman, Eisenhower, Kennedy and Johnson—moved slowly and deliberately and repeatedly turned down recommendations from their advisers which they regarded as too risky and escalatory.

American leaders did consider it vital not to lose Vietnam to a Communist-led insurgency directed and supported by North Vietnam, and this view was widely shared by the Congress, the media and the articulate public. Commitments to the defense of Vietnam like the SEATO treaty of 1954 and the Gulf of Tonkin resolution of 1964 were approved by a practically unanimous legislative branch, and even newsmen critical of U.S. performance in Vietnam, like Neil Sheehan and David Halberstam, by 1964 had concluded that Vietnam was vital to American interests and that the U.S. would dishonor itself by a withdrawal.[1]

With few dissenting voices, American decision-makers considered Vietnam, and indeed all of Southeast Asia, to be of important strategic and economic value to the noncommunist world, but this basic supposition was soon overshadowed by regard for the international and domestic consequences of a loss of Vietnam.[2] Each separate decision on aid—many relatively minor in scope and cost—and each high-level visit to Vietnam seemed to lock U.S. prestige tighter and tighter into the overall commitment to the independence of South Vietnam. Thus the primary consideration soon became not the importance of a noncommunist South Vietnam in itself but the repercussions to be expected from reneging on this commitment. As concerns the impact internationally, the fear was of disillusionment with the worth of the alliances contracted by the U.S. and the encouragement of other Communist-led "wars of national liberation" which might follow a retreat from Southeast Asia. With regard to the domestic scene, the steadfast defense of South Vietnam was to preempt the charge of being soft on communism, an accusation to which Democratic presidents, mindful of Yalta and the "loss of China," were particularly sensitive.

Initially the cost of achieving U.S. goals in Vietnam appeared to be modest. There was the precedent of successful antiguerrilla campaigns in Malaya and the Philippines which proved that communist insurgents were not invincible. Even in 1961, when President Kennedy ordered a rapid increase in the number of American advisers and authorized U.S. military personnel to assume a role of combat support, there was still ground for believing that the situation could be stabilized without a full U.S. involvement and that, as Kennedy told his confidant Arthur M. Schlesinger, Jr., "there was a reasonable chance of making a go of it."[3] And yet, South Vietnamese political and military performance turned out to be far worse and the VC far more determined and enjoying greater local support than expected. Moreover, once American servicemen were committed to combat, the Rubicon was probably crossed and the possibility of a later change of course became remote. Justificatory rhetoric soon helped solidify the commitment made by these actions.

For as long as possible, President Johnson, like Kennedy before him, made minimally necessary decisions and tried to avoid a full U.S. intervention. But the chickens finally came home to roost and Johnson had to decide whether the American stakes were sufficiently high to enter the war as an open co-belligerent. Each of his predecessors had sought to buy time in order to avoid this fateful decision. Johnson had to make the choice, and he ordered the bombing of North Vietnam and eventually the dispatch of U.S. combat forces. The assurances of some of President Kennedy's advisers notwithstanding, it is unlikely that Kennedy, facing the same situation, would have acted differently. He, too, would not have wanted to be saddled with the consequences of failure in Vietnam. Whether the results of failure would indeed have been as disastrous as all four presidents involved in the decision to enter the Vietnam war believed, is a question I want to explore, though the answer is necessarily in some measure speculative.

The American Stake in Vietnam

There can be little doubt that the four presidents dealing with the increasingly intractable Vietnam problem would have acted differently had they been able to foresee what the eventual costs of U.S. intervention would be—in terms of American lives, financial costs and domestic and foreign political repercussions. But what about the original assessment of the importance of Vietnam? Did Vietnam and Southeast Asia represent a vital interest to the United States?

"History is lived forward," the English author C. V. Wedgewood has written, "but it is written in retrospect. We know the end before we consider the beginning and we can never wholly recapture what it was like to know the beginning only."[4] Living in today's world with its bitter conflict between the Soviet Union and China, it is difficult to understand the political atmosphere of the time when the communist bloc was indeed a monolith. During the years following the end of World War II the fear of communism was not an irrational obsession, for the Soviet Union, having absorbed Eastern Europe and even Czechoslovakia in the very center of the continent, did constitute an expansionist force in a highly unstable world. A communist victory anywhere therefore appeared to threaten the U.S. because it represented a further extension of Soviet power. Communist Russia at that time cast a menacing shadow over Western Europe; the American army in Korea had been fought to a standstill and Mao's cry after the launching of the Russian Sputnik in 1957 that "the East Wind is prevailing over the West Wind" reflected the conviction of many that communism represented the wave of the future. The commitment of the U.S. to the independence of South Vietnam was part of the attempt to halt these reverses. Together with American promises to defend Berlin in the grip of a Russian blockade and the show of force in response to the placement of Russian missiles in Cuba in 1962, the decision of the Kennedy administration to prevent the loss of Indochina was meant to demonstrate U.S. resolve and thus discourage Soviet pressures in other areas.

The American endeavor during those years to contain Communist China was similarly not the result of an ideological crusade against communism but was primarily a response to China's attempt to change the status quo in Asia by force. The signing of the Sino-Soviet alliance in 1950 provided a boost to communist revolutionaries throughout Asia and China appeared to be the cutting edge of Soviet influence in that continent.

"China was big, an advocate of revolutionary violence, bellicose and anti-American in its propaganda," recalls the former director of the State Department's Office of Chinese Affairs at that time. "True, after Korea the Chinese were cautious about using their forces outside Chinese territory, but they flexed their military muscles often enough—against the off-shore islands in 1954 and 1958, on the Indian border in 1962, and with nuclear explosions from 1964 on—to remind the United States of their latent military power."[5] During World War II the U.S. had fought to prevent the control of continental Asia and the islands of the Pacific by Japan. The Moscow-Peking axis now once again threatened the domination of Asia by a single power. Preventing the balance of power in Asia from being upset in this manner, it was believed, required the maintenance of independent states in South and Southeast Asia.

The Sino-Indian clash of 1962, argued Sen. Mike Mansfield in February 1963 after his return from the area, "makes clear that it is now necessary for the southeast Asian nations to reckon with the enlargement of the Chinese role at any time to include the use of military power in a full modern revival of the classic pattern of Chinese imperial techniques in southeast Asia." Any sudden U.S. withdrawal from this area, therefore, "would open the region to upheaval and chaos."[6] A communist victory in Vietnam, achieved with Chinese help, would enhance Chinese power and prestige in Asia and vindicate the Chinese revolutionary strategy. When Hans J. Morgenthau argued in 1965 that the U.S. should abandon the military containment of China and that "we must learn to accommodate ourselves to the predominance of China on the Asian mainland,"[7] he was answered by Arthur M. Schlesinger, Jr., that such an alleged geopolitical necessity was no more persuasive in Asia than it had been with regard to the German domination of Europe in the 1930s. "Asia is a very large continent. It has a diversity of cultures, traditions, states, and so on. Nations like their independence in Asia just as much as they do in other parts of the world. To assume that some mystic inevitability has decreed that they are all to be swallowed up in the Chinese empire is not convincing."[8]

Australia and New Zealand, and especially the leaders of Southeast Asia, encouraged the U.S. in the view that a loss of Vietnam would quickly lead to the unraveling of the entire region and that the U.S. stand in Vietnam therefore was crucial to their survival as independent states. The removal of the presence of the U.S. from the region, maintained the Cambodian head of state, Prince Sihanouk, in June 1965, would lead to the victory of communism.[9] Malaysia fully supported U.S. actions in Vietnam, declared Prime Minister Abdul Rahman in the summer of 1965: "In our view it is imperative that the United States does not retire from the scene."[10] The leaders of Singapore and Thailand concurred in this appraisal of the situation. As a result of the broadened American commitment in Vietnam and China's failure to respond to the bombing of North Vietnam, reported Seymour Topping of the *New York Times* in January 1966, the Chinese dragon was considerably deflated.[11] And Tom Wicker, writing from Bangkok in February 1967, noted that the actions of the Johnson administration in Vietnam had provided new confidence in an American umbrella of protection over Asia and enhanced the stability of Southeast Asia.[12] Even Asian leaders publicly critical of U.S. policy in Southeast Asia privately encouraged America to remain in Vietnam; their ranks included Prime Minister Indira Gandhi of India, who told Vice President Humphrey in February 1966 that the continued U.S. presence in Vietnam was important to India.[13]

The fears of the leaders of Southeast Asia that a communist victory in Vietnam would have grave consequences for their own security did not, however, constitute adequate evidence that these repercussions would indeed occur and thus establish the correctness of the domino theory. Still less did it prove that the loss of Southeast Asia would jeopardize essential American interests. Policy-makers often find it convenient to justify important decisions in foreign policy in terms of vital interests affecting the security of their country, yet neither national security nor the national interest represents a fixed point of reference or provides a ready guide for action. Decision-makers see the national interest through the fallible spectacles of their subjective judgment; in making determinations of threats, dangers and interests they are liable to make mistakes such as being unduly influenced by "worst case" calculations or ideological preconceptions. The assessment of the geopolitical importance of Vietnam and Southeast Asia by American leaders from 1950 on was an example of such misjudgment.

American policy-makers were probably justified in fearing the domination of Asia by a single power. Yet only Japan, with its immense physical and industrial resources, was of sufficient economic importance to upset the balance of power in Asia. The facilities and skills of the Japanese added to the economy of Communist China could have constituted a direct threat to U.S. security. However, the assumption that a communist domination of Southeast Asia would force Japan into an accommodation with China was one of the arguments made by American policy-makers that was far from self-evident. Failure of the U.S. to react to a military conquest of Southeast Asia by the Soviet Union or China was bound to damage Japan's confidence in the worth of American commitments to its defense. But the triumph of Chinese-backed insurgencies was not necessarily going to endanger the U.S.-Japan alliance. The importance of Southeast Asia for Japan's trade was also less than vital. In 1969, for example, Japan's imports from the area were about 9 percent of all Japanese imports; exports to Southeast Asia were 15 percent of all exports. Moreover, a communist Southeast Asia was not necessarily going to stop trading with Japan.[14]

The crucial strategic and economic importance of Indochina and Southeast Asia to the noncommunist world was similarly more an endlessly repeated article of faith than a proven fact. The military occupation of Indochina by Japan in World War II was held to have demonstrated the strategic significance of the region, sitting astride the passageway between the Indian and Pacific oceans. The Strait of Malacca, it was pointed out, was Japan's lifeline for its oil imports from the Middle East. But Japan lost in World War II even though it controlled all of Southeast Asia; a closing of the Malacca strait, forcing the use of detours further east, was bound to create an economic burden but would not cripple the Japanese economy. The commodities produced by the area, such as rubber, tin and coconut oil, though important, similarly were not irreplaceable.

Some members of the New Left shared the belief in the economic importance of Vietnam. Private investment opportunities, both immediate and projected, stated one such writer in 1973, "positively affected the U.S. government's continued military commitment to a succession of Saigon regimes from 1954 to the present."[15] But the evidence for this thesis is hardly convincing. U.S. investments in Vietnam have always been a tiny and insignificant fraction of total American investments overseas. By 1969 South Vietnam accounted for less than one percent of American exports.[16] The stock market showed itself to be an accurate barometer of the drain which the Vietnam war caused the American economy; after 1967 the market reflected the desire of the American financial community to see the conflict brought to a speedy conclusion. Each time either side engaged in some conciliatory step the stocks responded with rising prices.[17] By 1970 the war, with all its ramifications, had turned into a near-disaster for the American economy, a disaster for which even the discovery of potential oil off the shores of South Vietnam that same year could not compensate.[18] Needless to say, this discovery in 1970 can hardly explain decisions taken in the previous 20 years.

American policy-makers not only exaggerated the geopolitical importance of Vietnam and Southeast Asia, thus making the consequences of failure far more critical than the facts warranted, but, more importantly, their decisions were overtaken by important changes in the character of world communism, which gradually undermined the premises on which U.S. policy in Southeast Asia was based. By the mid-1960s, Russia and China were no longer close allies but open enemies. The world communist movement no longer represented a monolith, and the addition of a new communist state did not necessarily contribute to the power of America's adversaries. The Sino-Soviet split created a new balance of power in Asia in which China, constrained by Russian pressure on its northern borders, no longer was an aggressive force exporting revolution. In 1971 China entered the United Nations and an accommodation took place with the United States; Chinese foreign policy now was oriented toward finding allies and creating counterbalances to the Soviet Union. This shift in big-power relationships coincided with the cultural revolution in China, which meant a further turning inward. The model for rapid economic growth in Asia was no longer communism but Japan's capitalist economy. Communism had ceased to be the wave of the future.

But before these changes in the Asian balance of power had fully manifested themselves, American commitment in Vietnam had become solidified with the introduction of ground combat forces in 1965. Both the Communists and the U.S. made the outcome of the struggle in Vietnam a test of strength and prestige. North Vietnam's Defense Minister Giap declared in July 1964 that "South Vietnam is the vanguard fighter of the national liberation movement in the present era . . . and the failure of the special war unleashed by the US imperialists in South Vietnam would mean that this war can be defeated anywhere in the world."[19] China's Marshal Lin Piao, in a much-publicized article in September 1965, called revolutionary warfare the method of encircling the developed capitalist countries; he predicted that the defeat of U.S. imperialism in Vietnam would show the people of the world "that what the Vietnamese people can do, they can do too."[20]

Not surprisingly these bellicose claims stiffened the back of the U.S.

and strengthened the argument that America could not afford to lose in Vietnam. A communist success in South Vietnam, declared McNamara in August 1965,

> would be taken as positive proof that the Chinese Communists' position is correct and they will have made a giant step forward in their efforts to seize control of the world Communist movement. . . . In that event we would then have to be prepared to cope with the same kind of aggression in other parts of the world wherever the existing governments are weak and the social structure fragmented. If Communist armed aggression is not stopped in Viet-Nam as it was in Korea, the confidence of small nations in America's pledge of support will be weakened, and many of them, in widely separated areas of the world, will feel unsafe. Thus the stakes in South Viet-Nam are far greater than the loss of one small country to communism.[21]

After three American presidents had declared that the independence of South Vietnam represented a vital interest of the U.S., it could with much justice be said that the American commitment had in fact created a vital interest, for the prestige and credibility of a major world power cannot be dismissed as unimportant. By early 1966 the U.S. had over 200,000 military personnel in Vietnam; American involvement in the war was a fact that could not be wished away. Vietnam was not a region of major military and industrial importance, the veteran diplomat George F. Kennan explained to the Senate Foreign Relations Committee in February 1966, but American prestige was now irrevocably engaged. "A precipitate and disorderly withdrawal could represent in present circumstances a disservice to our own interests, and even to world peace, greater than any that might have been involved by our failure to engage ourselves there in the first place."[22] Protecting the nation's prestige in such a situation meant not the enhancement of national glory or grandeur but the preservation of the nation's ability to influence events and pursue American interests without the use of force.

A smaller nation like France could withdraw from Indochina and North Africa without a serious loss of prestige, argued George W. Ball, a critic of U.S. policy in Vietnam, in 1968. "But the authority of the United States in world affairs depends, in considerable part, on the confidence of other nations that we can accomplish whatever we undertake."[23] There had been a failure to analyze adequately the importance of Vietnam to

America's national interests, Henry Kissinger suggested in early 1969. "But the commitment of five hundred thousand Americans has settled the issue of the importance of Vietnam. For what is involved now is confidence in American promises. However fashionable it is to ridicule the terms 'credibility' or 'prestige' they are not empty phrases; other nations can gear their actions to ours only if they can count on our steadiness."[24] In agreement with Kissinger's position, the orderly disengagement of America from the defense of South Vietnam became the cornerstone of U.S. policy in Southeast Asia under the Nixon administration.

The validity of the belief of both the Johnson and Nixon administrations that the loss of Vietnam would have worldwide repercussions and that, at the very least, it was important to liquidate the American commitment in Vietnam without a humiliating defeat was put to the test in 1975. The full consequences of the collapse of South Vietnam will not be apparent for some time to come, but enough is known to show that this outcome represents not only a tragedy for millions of South Vietnamese but also an important defeat for the United States. Hanoi's victory inevitably came to be seen as a victory for Hanoi's major allies and supporters. Moreover, the long-drawn-out conflict, culminating in failure to achieve American objectives, has had bruising and traumatic effects on American attitudes toward world affairs in general.

The Impact of the Vietnam Debacle

While the Vietnam war was still in progress it was part of the conventional wisdom to ridicule the domino theory, though some of those who today talk about the foolishness of this metaphor and the dire consequences of American belief in the theory at the time saw in it considerable validity. The domino theory, wrote Tom Wicker in February 1967, had much truth, and a communist victory in Vietnam through internal subversion assisted by a neighboring nation "would greatly encourage the use of the same technique for attempted conquest elsewhere in the world."[25] The real and deeper meaning of the domino theory has always been the idea that a communist victory in Vietnam and a demonstration of American failure to prevent such a triumph would have repercussions elsewhere, especially in Southeast Asia, and events since 1975 bear out this prediction. We find an overall weakening of faith in the worth of American commitments and, on the part of the nations of Southeast Asia, attempts to appease the victorious communist powers. The American intervention in Vietnam probably bought time for these countries to improve their own political and social institutions and thus left them in a stronger position to resist external or internal communist pressures. They have also benefited from the competition of Russia and China for influence in the area and from the re-emergence of the historic animosities between the former allies Vietnam and Cambodia. Still, spirits in the region today are reported to be low.

The consequences of the communist victories in Southeast Asia manifested themselves quickly. The fall of the Cambodian capital of Phnom Penh on 17 April 1975 further demoralized the South Vietnamese army, already fighting a losing battle, and the communist victory in Vietnam was soon followed by a communist takeover in Laos. Communist leadership in Laos was always dominated by ethnic Vietnamese, and the country today appears to be under complete Vietnamese control. The Thais, as was to be expected, asked U.S. troops to leave their country, and they now seek their security in a position of neutrality. The government of the Philippines asked for a review of the future status of U.S. bases in that country, and President Ferdinand E. Marcos declared shortly after the fall of Saigon: "The United States must understand we cannot wait until events overtake us. We reserve the right to make our accommodations with the emerging realities in Asia."[26] Even before the guns had fallen silent in South Vietnam, Foreign Minister Adam Malik of Indonesia, a rigidly anticommunist country ever since the bloody suppression of its own communist movement in 1965, predicted that Indonesia would be able to cooperate with the communist regimes in Indochina. The Saigon government, Malik told a *New York Times* correspondent on 26 March 1975, expected too much of the Americans, but others would not make that mistake. "You always tell us, 'My Seventh Fleet is here,' but if there's trouble, nothing happens."[27]

Back in 1964, Assistant Secretary of Defense John T. McNaughton expressed the hope that if South Vietnam ever disintegrated it would be possible to leave the image of "a patient who died despite the extraordinary efforts of a good doctor."[28] But many of America's allies, in and outside Southeast Asia, are not convinced that the U.S. made "extraordinary efforts" on behalf of its "patient." To the contrary, South Korea and Israel in particular are now concerned about the reliability of the American commitment to their defense. Congressional inaction on Indochina in the face of the North Vietnamese onslaught in the spring of 1975 has raised for them disturbing questions about a similar future congressional reaction on aid to their beleaguered countries and about the value of an American guarantee.[29]

In the wake of the trauma of Vietnam, America is in the grip of a "No more Vietnams" psychology which stands in sharp contrast to the spirit of active involvement in global affairs prevailing in the years following World War II; this fear of becoming entangled has led to a decline in the political influence of the United States. There is no reason to assume that the weakening of America's will to act will make for a better and more peaceful world. Discussing the dangers created by the spread of nuclear weapons, a State Department official pointed out on 30 June 1977 that American "security guarantees, where we are able to make them credible in this post-Vietnam era of public attitudes, are some of the most important instruments of our nonproliferation policy."[30] One of the consequences of the current mood of isolationism appears to be diminished confidence abroad in the security provided by the American defense umbrella, which in turn may encourage nuclear proliferation. The greater the number of states possessing nuclear weapons, the greater, of course, the chances of a nuclear conflict.[31]

The tragic and unsuccessful involvement in Vietnam should teach America lessons on how to prevent a repetition of such a disaster, but overreaction is probably as bad as a refusal to understand and learn the correct lessons. Mark Twain told the story of the cat who, after burning herself on a hot stove lid, never again sat on any stove—hot or cold—and he warned against getting out of an experience more wisdom than was in it.[32] An acceptance of the simplistic slogan "No more Vietnams" not only may encourage international disorder, but could mean abandoning basic American values. As John Stuart Mill pointed out more than 100 years ago, "The doctrine of non-intervention, to be a legitimate principle of morality, must be accepted by all governments. The despots must consent to be bound by it as well as the free States. Unless they do, the profession of it by free countries comes but to this miserable issue, that the wrong side may help the wrong, but the right must not help the right."[33] It is well to remember that the nonintervention of the Western democracies in the Spanish Civil War of 1936–39 represented a crucial factor intervening in favor of Franco's victory and helped prepare the way for World War II. America cannot and should not be the world's policeman, but, it can be argued, the U.S. has a moral obligation to support nations in their endeavor to remain independent when we, and we alone, possess the means to do so. "A wealthy man who watches a poor neighbor starve to death cannot disclaim responsibility for the event; a powerful man who watches a weak neighbor being beaten to death cannot avoid being accused (if only through self-accusation) of culpability."[34] As the case of Spain in the 1930s demonstrates, the fulfillment of the moral obligation to intervene in defense of freedom and independence at times may also coincide with prudential long-term national interests.

The original decision to intervene in South Vietnam probably was based on a misreading of the national interest, but it was not wrong because the government of South Vietnam was not truly democratic. To insist that we support or ally ourselves with only governments whose conduct we approve is another fallacious lesson of the Vietnam tragedy. The shortcomings of the Diem and Thieu regimes—and they were many—did not prove that the U.S. should not help South Vietnam and that communist North Vietnam deserved to win. The Western democracies were right in regarding Mussolini's attack on Ethiopia in 1935 as an act of flagrant aggression even though Ethiopia was ruled by an autocratic emperor and was a backward and dismal country—with slavery to boot. America was right to ally itself in World War II with the Soviet Union even though Russia's paranoid dictator had murdered millions of innocent citizens and kept other millions in slave-labor camps. Our own self-respect and regard for the principles for which this country stands should dictate caution in the support of nondemocratic, let alone truly oppressive regimes, but moral considerations alone should not and cannot be the decisive standard for our foreign alliances.

The current moralizing about covert operations represents another overreaction to Vietnam. There are times when for various reasons a nation must undertake actions that cannot be publicly divulged, and it may even be necessary in some cases to violate norms of international law. It is curious, the theologian Paul Ramsey correctly notes, that many of those favoring civil disobedience and even direct action in the internal life of the nation "can see no warrant for ever going beyond the law in international affairs where the legalities are far more imperfect and where the social due process for significantly changing the legal system is even more wanting."[35]

The preservation of the country, the national interest, and national security are standards of conduct which an unprincipled leader can abuse and distort, but their pre-eminence in the conduct of foreign policy should not on that account be questioned or rejected. National leaders who habitually practice concealment and evasion will erode the trust of their people; President Nixon, in particular, at times carried secrecy to excess and therefore eventually laid himself open to the charge of having created an "imperial presidency." Indeed, even in international politics a reputation for probity carries its own pragmatic rewards. But in the final analysis the statesman cannot be a saint, and the requirements of power and national survival in a world without government will dictate moral compromises.

Could the United States Have Won in Vietnam?

One can begin to answer this difficult question by pointing to certain mistakes made by American leaders in holding together the home front, though this task, for reasons to be discussed below, would probably have presented almost insuperable difficulties even to the most adroit leadership. There was the failure, especially on the part of the Johnson administration, to provide a convincing explanation and justification of the American involvement. Simplistic rhetoric like "fighting for democracy in Vietnam" or halting "communist aggression," though not without some element of truth, was inappropriate to the complex situation faced in Southeast Asia; it also was highly vulnerable to the retort of the critics who pointed to the undemocratic character of the Saigon government and to the extensive involvement of Southerners in the conflict.[36]

The government in its pronouncements spoke of success and light at the end of the tunnel, but continued to dispatch additional troops while casualties mounted steadily. As the director of the *Pentagon Papers* task force, Leslie H. Gelb, has observed, optimism without results could only work so long; after that, it had to produce a credibility gap.[37] To be sure, the Johnson administration had never expected to become engaged in a protracted ground war on such a scale, and even when the involvement deepened it attempted to keep the war limited, a war without full mobilization of the home front and without a hated enemy. President Johnson is said to have rejected the view of some of his advisers that in order to hold the support of the country he would have to engage in some outright chauvinistic rabble-rousing and provide the American people with a vivid foe.[38] Such a mobilization of patriotic sentiments, he apparently concluded, could force him into unduly risky actions such as unrestricted bombing and even an invasion of North Vietnam—which, in turn, could lead to a confrontation with Communist China or Russia. At the very least, a widening of the war would prevent the achievement of his domestic "Great Society" programs.

For the same reasons, Johnson refrained from asking Congress for a declaration of war, which until 1967 he probably could have gotten without much difficulty. It is well to remember that at the time even critics of the president's Vietnam policy did not want to press for a formal declaration of war by Congress on the grounds that it would have undesirable consequences—it might trigger secret treaties between North Vietnam and Russia and China, thus risking a dangerous expansion of the conflict, and it could lead to the enactment of wartime curbs on free speech and press.[39] Only years later did charges of an abuse of the Gulf of Tonkin resolution arise. Even though this resolution, considered by most legal authorities a functional equivalent of a declaration of war, was repealed by Congress in January 1971, the Nixon administration did not rely on it for its policy of withdrawal, and Congress did not end military appropriations for Vietnam until the last U.S. serviceman had left Vietnam and the prisoners of war had returned in 1973. Citing these appropriations, the courts consistently rejected charges of an unconstitutionally conducted war.[40] And yet in retrospect it is apparent that Presidents Johnson and Nixon would have been spared much opposition and grief if Johnson had asked Congress for a declaration of war.

As a result of many different considerations, then, the nation fought a limited war, with the full employment of its military power restricted through elaborate rules of engagement and limitations on operations beyond the borders of South Vietnam, while for its determined opponent the war was total. The U.S. fought a limited war whose rationale was never convincingly explained and which, in any event, even an able leader would have had a most difficult time justifying. How does one tell a young conscript that he should be prepared to die in order to create a balance of power in Asia or in order to improve the American bargaining position at the upcoming negotiations that would lead to a compromise settlement?

If the Vietnam war had occurred in a different age some of these difficulties might have been surmountable. There was a time when the mass of the people were deferential to any official definition of the national interest and of the objectives of the nation's foreign policy. For good or for bad, this situation no longer holds in a modern democracy. Moreover, the war was fought at a time when major social evils had come to light in America and when a social transformation at home, the achievement of the "Great Society," was widely and urgently expected. Attacks on the mounting cost of the war in Asia were given special pertinence by the rioting in the urban black ghettos in 1967 and 1968 and by the deterioration of American cities which these racial explosions held up for all to see.

But the most important reason for the steadily spreading acceptance of the view that the American involvement in Vietnam had been a mistake was probably neither the implausibility of the rationale given for the war nor the preoccupation of both the educated classes and the poor with social reform. The decisive reason for the growing disaffection of the American people was the conviction that the war was not being won and apparently showed little prospect of coming to a successful conclusion. There was a clear correlation between declining support and a mounting casualty toll; the increasing cost in lives, occurring in a war without decisive battles or conquered territory, was the most visible symbol of failure. Hanoi's expectation that the American democracy would not be able to sustain a long and bloody conflict in a faraway land turned out to be more correct than Westmoreland's strategy of attrition, which was supposed to inflict such heavy casualties on the Communists as to force them to cease their aggression.

Had the intervention succeeded, say, by 1967, the public's disaffection probably would not have arisen and President Johnson would have emerged as a highly popular figure. As John F. Kennedy is supposed to have said of the reaction to the Bay of Pigs invasion: Success has a thousand fathers, but failure is an orphan. The capacity of people in a modern democracy to support a limited war is precarious at best. The mixture of propaganda and compulsion which a totalitarian regime can muster in order to extract such support is not available to the leaders of a democratic state. Hence when such a war for limited objectives drags on for a long time it is bound to lose the backing essential for its successful pursuit. It may well be, as an American political scientist has concluded, that "unless it is severely provoked or unless the war succeeds fast, a democracy cannot choose war as an instrument of policy."[41]

That American public opinion, as Leslie Gelb has put it, was "the essential domino" was, of course, recognized by both American policymakers and the Vietnamese Communists. Each geared his "strategy— both the rhetoric and the conduct of the war—to this fact."[42] And yet, given the limited leverage which the leaders of a democracy have on public opinion, and in view of the various liabilities to which the American war effort was subject, the ability of American decision-makers to control this "essential domino" was always precarious. For the Vietnamese Communists, on the other hand, ideological mobilization at home and carrying the propaganda effort to the enemy was relatively easy, and they worked at both objectives relentlessly and with great success. Enormous amounts of effort, manpower and money were devoted to creating the image of the Viet Cong as a highly motivated, honest and noble human being, who was engaged in a just war against an imperialist aggressor and his corrupt puppets. This concerted activity, Douglas Pike stresses, was not just pretense and sham. "The communists worked hard to create their image. They altered policy in its name. They shot looters, purged cadres, refused alliances, ordered military offensives, all for the sake of perception abroad."[43] The outcome of this uneven contest was predictable. The Western observer, essentially unable to check out the claims of the communist camp, was left with the image of a tough and highly effective enemy while at the same time he was daily exposed to the human and bureaucratic errors and shortcomings of his own side. Image was bound to triumph over reality.

The coverage of the war by television was a crucial factor in this one-sided publicity. The VC were notoriously uncooperative in allowing Western cameramen to shoot pictures of the disemboweling of village chiefs or other acts of terror, while scenes of South Vietnamese brutality, such as the mistreatment of prisoners, were often seen on American TV screens. Television stresses the dramatic and contentious, and the Vietnam war offered plenty of both. The result was a one-dimensional coverage of the conflict—apparently meaningless destruction of lives and property in operations which rarely led to visible success. War has always been beastly, but the Vietnam war was the first war exposed to television cameras and seen in practically every home, often in living color. Not surprisingly this close-up view of devastation and suffering, repeated daily, strengthened the growing desire for peace. The events of Tet and the siege of Khe Sanh in 1968, in particular, shook the American public. The nightly portrayal of violence and gore and of American soldiers seemingly on the brink of disaster contributed significantly to disillusionment with the war. Gallup poll data suggest that between early February and the middle of March 1968 nearly one person in five switched from the "hawk" to the "dove" position.[44]

Despite the small percentage of individuals actively involved in organized opposition to the war, the antiwar movement had a significant impact on both the Johnson and Nixon administrations. Not only does a small percentage of a country of 200 million constitute a sizable number of people, but the active and articulate few, often strategically placed, can have an importance well beyond their proportion of the population. The tactics of the antiwar movement were often unpopular, and the association of the drive for peace with other causes and groups regarded as radical by most Americans further contributed to its political isolation.[45] Some of the leaders were old-time or New leftists; others were admirers of the Viet Cong, whose struggle and tactics they romanticized. To politically seasoned Americans it was obvious that many of these men and the organizations and committees they spawned were not so much for peace and against the war as they were partisans of Hanoi, whose victory they sought to hasten through achieving an American withdrawal from Vietnam. But the great majority of those who joined peace demonstrations were ordinary Americans—Democrats, Republicans and independents—simply fed up with the seemingly endless bloodletting.

The impact of the antiwar movement was enhanced by the widely publicized charges of American atrocities and lawlessness. The inability of Washington officials to demonstrate that the Vietnam war was not in fact an indiscriminate bloodbath and did not actually kill more civilians than combatants was a significant factor in the erosion of support for the war, especially among the media and the intellectual community generally. The view held by many of these critics that the war did not involve any important national stakes further contributed to their unwillingness to accept a level of violence that was probably less extreme than in many previous wars fought by this country. To attempt such an effort at explanation without appearing to have a callous disregard for human life would, of course, have been extremely difficult. Moreover, there can be little doubt that while the casualties inflicted on the civilian population of Vietnam were not out of line in comparison with World War II and Korea, they did have a highly detrimental effect in a counterinsurgency setting like Vietnam. The realization on the part of many civilian policy-makers that this was so, combined with the unwillingness of the military to forego the highly destructive tools of heavy weaponry, may be one of the reasons why no meaningful effort at explanation was ever undertaken.

In the absence of a frank and convincing official justification of the high level of violence in Vietnam, speculation and unsupported allegations of wrongdoing held sway. Given respectability by the support of well-known public figures, this agitation eventually had an effect upon the larger educated public. Self-flagellation for the alleged gross immorality of America's conduct in the war and its moral decline as a nation became rampant, and calls for the trial of "Amerika's" leaders for crimes against peace and humanity fell on sympathetic ears. Unable to end the war on their terms, many intellectuals vented their frustration in verbal overkill which probably will not be remembered as their finest hour.[46] Shrill rhetoric created a world of unreality in which the North Vietnamese Communists were the defenders of national self-determination, while U.S. actions designed to prevent the forceful takeover of South Vietnam stood branded as imperialism and aggression. Many of those who complained of the repressive character of the Thieu regime were uncritical of or found nothing but praise for the totalitarian regime in Hanoi. Politically innocent citizens paid hundreds of thousands of dollars for newspaper advertisements which recorded their support of charges concerning American actions and motives which they could not possibly have confirmed by any kind of evidence. Academics lent these ads an aura of authority by signing them with their titles and university affiliations. Everyone—from clergyman and biologist to movie actor and pediatrician—could become an instant expert on international law, Southeast Asia, and foreign policy generally. Professors who would never have dared treat their own disciplines in such a cavalier fashion proclaimed with assurance solutions to the Vietnam problem at "teach-ins," complete with folk singers, mime troupes and other forms of entertainment.

The disaffection of large segments of the country's intellectual leadership—in the media, the professions, on the college campuses, and increasingly in Congress—reinforced the growing war-weariness and disillusionment in the country, often quite unrelated to wider political or humanitarian concerns. The Vietnam war ended up as the longest and most unpopular war in the nation's history.

As was to be expected, North Vietnam sought to make the most of the antiwar movement in America. North Vietnamese officials, at meetings with radical antiwar activists held in Cuba, Hungary, Czechoslovakia and North Vietnam, provided tactical advice and helped coordinate worldwide antiwar demonstrations.[47] Communist propaganda regularly reported peace demonstrations as proof that the American people were weakening in their resolve. The North Vietnamese were convinced that just as the Viet Minh had defeated France not only, or primarily, on the battlefield but rather by outlasting the patience of the French people for the war in Indochina, so North Vietnam and the Viet Cong would eventually triumph over the United States on account of their own determination and the failure of the American people to last the course. As Assistant Secretary of Defense John T. McNaughton put it with considerable understatement in a memorandum in May 1967: "The state of mind in the US generates impatience in the political structure of the United States. It unfortunately also generates patience in Hanoi."[48] Well-meaning as most participants in the peace movement were, James Reston wrote in October 1965, "the truth is that . . . they are not promoting peace but postponing it. They are not persuading the President and the Congress to end the war, but deceiving Ho Chi Minh and General Giap into prolonging it."[49]

The opponents of the war had a constitutional right to express their views, but it was folly to ignore the consequences of this protest. American public opinion indeed turned out to be a crucial "domino"; it influenced military morale in the field, the long-drawn-out negotiations in Paris, the settlement of 1973, and the cuts in aid to South Vietnam in 1974, a prelude to the final abandonment in 1975. A more supportive public opinion in America would probably have led to a slower pace of disengagement, but whether this additional time would have materially changed the fighting ability of the South Vietnamese armed forces and thus could have prevented an ultimate collapse remains, of course, an open question.

Opposition to the war in Vietnam benefited from America's moralistic approach to world affairs which, as the political scientist Lucian Pye has suggested, makes Americans uneasy about being identified with governments striving to suppress rebellions. "We tend to suspect that any government confronted with a violent challenge to its authority is probably basically at fault and that a significant number of rebels can be mobilized only if a people has been grossly mistreated. Often we are inclined to see insurgency and juvenile delinquency in the same light, and we suspect that, as 'there is no such thing as bad boys, only bad parents,' so there are no bad people, only evil and corrupt governments."[50] In point of fact, while the communist insurgency in Vietnam undoubtedly for a long time drew strength from the failure of the government of South Vietnam to address and remedy the social and economic problems of its rural population, the GVN eventually carried out a far-reaching land reform and undertook other successful measures to better relations with its people. Just as the internal strength and cohesion of the Republic of Korea did not save it from attack in 1950 and would not have staved off a communist victory without American military intervention, so the strengthening of the GVN did not prevent the North Vietnamese invasions in 1972 and 1975 which finally led to the collapse of South Vietnam. Indeed, at least in part, it was this very improvement of the GVN and the greatly weakened posture of the VC which led to the decision of Hanoi to abandon the tactic of revolutionary war and to resort to conventional warfare with tanks and heavy artillery.

And yet it is also true that the way in which both the Americans and South Vietnamese carried out the effort to suppress the communist insurgency often alienated the population of the countryside. The record, examined in earlier chapters, does not bear out charges of genocide or indiscriminate killings of civilians and wholesale violations of the law of war. However, the strategy and tactics of the allied counterinsurgency, especially the lavish use of firepower, did undermine the efforts of the GVN to win the allegiance of its people. There is reason to believe that the suffering inflicted upon large segments of South Vietnam's rural population during long years of high-technology warfare contributed to the spread of a feeling of resignation, war-weariness and an unwillingness to go on fighting against the resolute opponent from the North. It is also well to remember that revulsion at the fate of thousands of hapless civilians killed and maimed by the deadly arsenal of a modern army may undercut the willingness of a democratic nation to fight communist insurgents and that reliance upon high-technology weapons in an insurgency setting therefore may be counterproductive on still another level.

Despite much talk about "winning hearts and minds," the U.S. failed to understand the real stakes in a revolutionary war and for all too long ignored the conflicts in Vietnamese society which the VC exploited and used to motivate their forces. The U.S. also never really learned to fight a counterinsurgency war and used force in largely traditional ways, and the South Vietnamese copied our mistakes. The military, like all bureaucracies encountering a new situation for which they are not prepared and in which they do not know what to do, did what they knew to do. That happened to be the inappropriate thing. "The Vietnamese Communist generals," Edward G. Lansdale has written, "saw their armed forces as instruments primarily to gain political goals. The American generals saw their forces primarily as instruments to defeat enemy military forces. One fought battles to influence opinions in Vietnam and in the world, the other fought battles to finish the enemy keeping tabs by body count."[51] As it turned out, the enemy's endurance and supply of manpower proved stronger than American persistence in keeping up the struggle. More importantly, the strategy of attrition downgraded the crucial importance of pacification and ignored the fact that the enemy whom it was essential to defeat was in the hamlets and not in the jungles. American forces, applying classic Army doctrines of aggressively seeking out the enemy and destroying his main-force units, won most of the battles but lost the war.

Many of America's military leaders argue to this day that their ability to conduct a winning strategy was hamstrung not only by overly restrictive rules of engagement, designed to protect civilian life and property, but also by geographical constraints imposed on them for fear of a collision with Communist China and the Soviet Union. This argument is less than persuasive, for the war, in the final analysis, had to be won in South Vietnam. Military action in Laos and Cambodia at an early stage of the war, seeking permanently to block the Ho Chi Minh Trail, would have made the North Vietnamese supply effort far more difficult, but basically an expansion of the conflict would not have achieved the American task. Certainly, an invasion of North Vietnam would only have magnified the difficulties faced.

The war not only had to be won in South Vietnam, but it had to be won by the South Vietnamese. Unfortunately, to the end South Vietnamese performance remained the Achilles' heel of the allied effort. A totalitarian state like Communist North Vietnam, possessing a monopoly of indoctrination and social control, was bound to display greater military morale and unity than a fragmented and barely authoritarian country like South Vietnam. Also, the Republic of Vietnam, under American prodding, gradually did improve its stability and cohesion. But progress in building a viable political community was painfully slow, and it was not far-reaching enough to create the sense of purpose necessary for a successful defense against the communist enemy. The ignominious collapse of ARVN in 1975, as I have tried to show, was due not only to ARVN's inferiority in heavy weapons and the shortage of ammunition but in considerable measure was also the result of lack of will and morale.

All this does not mean that the U.S. could not have succeeded in achieving its objectives in Vietnam. It may well be, as Barbara Tuchman has argued, that the American goal of saving Nationalist China after World War II from communist domination was unachievable. "China was a problem for which there was no American solution."[52] But South Vietnam in the early 1970s was not China in the 1940s, and the U.S. position, too, was incomparably stronger.

The U.S. in the years from 1954 to 1975 could have pursued policies different from those actually followed. What if, instead of making a piecemeal commitment of military resources and adopting a policy of gradualism in their use, America had pursued a strategy of surprise and massed strength at decisive points? What if the mining of North Vietnamese harbors had taken place in 1965 instead of 1972? What if the U.S. from the beginning had implemented a strategy of population security instead of fighting Westmoreland's war of attrition, perhaps utilizing the Marines' CAP concept or the village defense program developed by the Special Forces–trained Civilian Irregular Defense Group? What if Vietnamization had begun in 1965 rather than 1968? While one cannot be sure that these different strategies, singly or in combination, would necessarily have brought about a different outcome, neither can one take their failure for granted.

Relations with the South Vietnamese and Vietnamization, too, could have followed a different course. As a result of anticolonialist inhibitions and for other reasons, the U.S. refrained from pressing for a decisive reorganization of the South Vietnamese armed forces and for a combined command, as America had done in Korea under the mantle of a UN mandate. Similarly, in regard to pacification and matters of social policy generally, America sought to shore up a sovereign South Vietnamese government and therefore, for the most part, limited itself to an advisory and supporting role, always mindful of the saying of Lawrence of Arabia: "Better they do it imperfectly than you do it perfectly, for it is their country, their war, and your time is limited." Western aggressiveness and impatience for results, it was said, ran counter to oriental ways of thinking and doing things and merely created increased resistance to change and reform. But if internal weaknesses in South Vietnamese society and the high level of corruption were as important a factor in the final collapse as the evidence examined in earlier chapters seems to suggest, might a radically different approach perhaps have been indicated?

Should the U.S. initially have accepted full responsibility for both military and political affairs, as suggested by experienced Vietnam hands like John Paul Vann, and only gradually have yielded control over the conduct of the war to a newly created corps of capable military leaders and administrators? Should America have played the role of the "good colonialist" who in this way slowly prepares a new country for viable independence? At the very least, should the U.S. have exerted more systematic leverage on its Vietnamese ally? The long record of American failure to move the GVN in directions which in retrospect would clearly have been desirable—for both the people of South Vietnam and America—writes Robert Komer, suggests "that we would have had little to lose and much to gain by using more vigorously the power over the GVN that our contributions gave us. We became their prisoners rather than they ours—the classic trap into which great powers have so often fallen in their relationships with weak allies."[53]

We will never know, of course, whether any of these different approaches would have yielded better results. However, these alternative policy options must be mentioned in order to challenge facile and unhistorical assumptions of an inevitable collapse of South Vietnam. Just as the success of a policy does not prove that it was the only possible successful course of action, a policy can be correct even if for a variety of reasons it fails. The commitment to aid South Vietnam was made by intelligent and reasonable men who tackled an intractable problem in the face of great uncertainties, including the future performance of an ally and the actions and reactions of an enemy. The fact that some of their judgments in retrospect can be shown to have been flawed and that the outcome has been a fiasco does not make them villains or fools. If Hitler in 1940 had succeeded in conquering Britain, this would not have proven wrong Churchill's belief in the possibility and moral worth of resistance to the Nazis. Policy-makers always have to act on uncertain assumptions and inadequate information, and some of the noblest decisions in history have involved great risks. As long as there exists a reasonable expectation of success, the statesman who fails can perhaps be pitied, but he should not be condemned.

Both critics and defenders of American policy in Vietnam can agree that, as Kissinger put it in June 1975, "outside effort can only supplement, but not create, local efforts and local will to resist. . . . And there is no question that popular will and social justice are, in the last analysis, the essential underpinning of resistance to subversion and external challenge."[54] To bolster local ability, effort and will to resist was, of course, the basic purpose of the American policy of Vietnamization. The fact that South Vietnam, abandoned by its ally, finally succumbed to a powerful and ruthless antagonist does not prove that this policy could not have had a less tragic ending. Neither does it vitiate the moral impulse which played a significant part in the original decision to help protect the independence of South Vietnam. Indeed, the sad fate of the people of Indochina since 1975 lends strength to the view that the American attempt to prevent a communist domination of the area was not without moral justification.

Appendix I
Civilian Casualties:
A Quantitative Assessment

The task of establishing accurate statistics on military casualties is a formidable one in any war, and the difficulties are infinitely greater with regard to civilian losses. There arise problems of classification, such as whether to include casualties attributable to inadequate nourishment or disease caused by war conditions or limit the count to casualties resulting from direct military action. For World War II, for example, estimates of civilian deaths range from 20 to 35 million, and many students of war consequently abandon as hopeless the search for estimates of civilian casualties.[1] Because the question of civilian losses has assumed such an importance in the Vietnam debate an attempt to arrive at some figures must be made.

There exists one set of data generally considered quite hard, and that is the number of civilians admitted to hospitals as a result of military action (civilian war casualties—CWC). During the years 1967 to 1971 statistics on admissions to Vietnamese hospitals were compiled by medical teams from America and other allied nations assigned to Vietnamese province hospitals by USAID. Before January 1967 and beginning in January 1972, the figures are based on reports by the Vietnamese Ministry of Health (MOH). We also have data for CWC admitted to American military hospitals from April 1967 until December 1971, when this program was terminated. The yearly figures for these casualties, given in Table A-1, show that between 1965 and 1974 close to one-half million Vietnamese civilians were admitted to MOH and U.S. hospitals as a result of war-related injuries serious enough to require hospitalization. Some private hospitals and other clinics were outside the reporting system, and investigators of a congressional committee chaired by Sen. Edward M. Kennedy, after spot-

Table A-1 Vietnamese Civilian War-Related Casualties Admitted to Hospitals, 1965–74

	MOH Hospitals	U.S. Hospitals	Total
1965	18,791		18,791
1966	23,663		23,663
1967	46,774	1,951	48,725
1968	80,359	7,790	88,149
1969	59,222	8,544	67,766
1970	46,247	4,635	50,882
1971	38,325	1,077	39,402
1972	53,367		53,367
1973	43,218		43,218
1974	41,525		41,525
Total	451,491	23,997	475,488

SOURCES: Republic of Vietnam, Directorate General of Planning, *Statistical Yearbook 1969*, Table 260, p. 333; data compiled by USAID/Public Health.

checks, reported a certain amount of under-reporting in MOH hospitals. To compensate for these omissions I increase the total figure of 475,500 in Table A-1 by 20 percent, which yields a new total of 570,600 CWC.[2]

If civilians were injured in large numbers, there also must have been many who were killed outright. MACV required so-called backlash reports on the number of civilians killed and wounded in a battle, but these reports were filed mostly for special incidents such as when civilians were hit by short rounds or when a military unit shot up an obviously friendly hamlet. In most cases villagers killed in VC-dominated or contested areas were counted as enemy dead (see chap. 3), while others died without being counted. As the U.S. embassy put it in a message to the State Department in March 1966: "How can you determine whether black-clad corpses found on a battlefield were VC or innocent civilians? (They are inevitably counted as VC). . . . How do you learn whether anyone was inside structures and sampans destroyed by the hundreds every day by air strikes, artillery fire, and naval gunfire?"[3]

One way to arrive at an estimate of the number of civilians killed is to apply a known ratio of wounded to killed. Casualty data for the South Vietnamese armed forces show that during the period 1965 to 1972 there was 1 death for every 2.65 seriously wounded who required hospitalization. Applying this factor of 2.65 to the figure of 570,600 wounded, one gets an estimate of 215,320 civilians killed outright as a result of military operations.

To this figure one would have to add those who died of their wounds after admission to the hospital. Figures for CWC in MOH hospitals available for 1969 and 1970 indicate that 3.05 percent of those admitted succumbed to their wounds,[4] but this figure is undoubtedly incomplete. The Vietnamese believed that unless a person was buried by his family his soul would never find a resting place, and dying patients therefore were commonly removed by their kin to die at home. According to one American physician who served in Vietnam, less than 25 percent of all deaths occurred in the hospital.[5] This would raise the mortality rate to 14 percent. On the other hand, at U.S. military hospitals the mortality rate for battle injuries (available only for all foreign nationals) was 21.7 percent during the years 1968–69,[6] and this rate undoubtedly is equally unrepresentative. U.S. military hospitals concentrated on the most serious cases among CWC and transferred the others to Vietnamese hospitals.[7] It therefore seems reasonable to assume that the average hospital mortality rate for CWC was about 15 percent. (This is somewhat lower than the average of the two rates available because the number of the most seriously injured was surely less than half of all those admitted.) This would mean that in addition to the estimated 215,320 civilians killed outright, another 32,300 died of their wounds after admission to a hospital. This yields a total of 247,600 civilian deaths between the years 1965 to 1974.

Even though various congressional committees all through the war years pressed Washington officials for figures on the number of civilians killed in Vietnam, the administration insisted that the only reliable figures available were those for CWC admitted to hospitals. Strictly speaking, this was of course true, though the kind of calculation undertaken here could have been made by Washington officials as well. However, the latter preferred to work with verifiable data rather than estimates and in any event were probably not interested in providing additional ammunition to the critics of American policy who charged the military with the indiscriminate killing of Vietnamese civilians.

In retrospect, this decision to rely only on verifiable data was probably a mistake, because in the absence of official figures the public had nothing but arbitrary statistics based on mere guesswork. For example, in a speech given in New York on 4 April 1967, Martin Luther King, Jr., charged that there were at least 20 civilian casualties for every casualty inflicted on the VC. "So far we may have killed a million of them—mostly children."[8] The meeting had been sponsored by an antiwar organization named "Clergy and Laity Concerned about Vietnam," which had assisted King in preparing the speech. Other than communist propaganda, which had first come out with such a figure, no data were available to support this charge, yet having been made by a man of Martin Luther King's stature, it was widely reported and believed. A more modest Dr. Spock assumed that only 2 civilians died for every VC killed by American forces, and he charged that the latter caused the death of "at least 100,000 civilians each year."[9] Another antiwar activist started with an estimate made by a French newspaper correspondent of 72,000 civilians killed in 1965 and then calculated casualties for the following years on the basis of statistics available for ordnance expended by American forces. He arrived at a figure of 1,116,000 South Vietnamese civilians killed and 2,232,000 wounded for the years 1965 to 1969.[10]

The Senate committee on refugees chaired by Sen. Edward M. Kennedy deserves praise for prodding the administration in Washington into greater awareness of the refugee and civilian casualty problems; Senator Kennedy probably can take credit for bringing about substantial increases in the American aid budget devoted to the alleviation of human suffering in South Vietnam. Yet some of the figures which his committee has publicized on civilian war casualties appear exaggerated and, especially with regard to civilian deaths, based on speculation unsupported by any data. In Table A-2 I list the official CWC figures and my estimate of deaths derived therefrom next to the Kennedy committee figures.

Table A-2 Vietnamese Civilian War-Related Casualties, 1965–74

	AID Figure	My Estimate	Kennedy Committee Estimate
Hospital admissions	475,500	570,600 ⎫	1,005,000[a]
Estimated lightly wounded		342,400 ⎭	
Estimated deaths		247,600	430,000
Total		1,160,600	1,435,000

SOURCES: USAID/Public Health; U.S. Senate, Committee on the Judiciary, Subcommittee to Investigate Problems Connected with Refugees and Escapees, *Humanitarian Problems in South Vietnam and Cambodia: Two Years After the Cease-Fire*, A Study Mission Report, 94th Cong., 1st sess., 27 January 1975, p. 7.

[a] All wounded.

The Kennedy committee's higher estimate of civilian deaths was apparently derived from the assumption that the pattern of Vietnamese civilian casualties was markedly different from the same pattern for the South Vietnamese military, yet this supposition is unfounded. Civilians wounded in outlying areas at times reached hospitals after long delays, but civilian casualties gradually were incorporated into the helicopter evacuation chain and generally received prompt medical attention. In 1967 a monthly average of 993 sick Vietnamese civilians (not all war casualties) were evacuated by helicopter. Between March 1968 and November 1969 a total of 78,781 were evacuated, an average of 3,734 per month.[11] Reporting on the situation in 1967, an American physician, who was part of a medical team treating CWC, wrote: "We are conscious of the fact that the slower civilian chain of evacuation may result in the more severely injured dying before they reach the team, but the magnitude of the injuries treated does not suggest that this was a frequent event."[12] In any event, the availability of medical help for civilians probably did not differ sharply from that for the RVNAF, whose ratio of wounded and dead I have used in my analysis of the civilian death toll.

The Kennedy committee estimate of CWC included lightly injured civilians who did not require hospitalization. In late 1967 the former director of USAID/Public Health in Saigon estimated that in addition to CWC admitted to hospitals a number equivalent to 60 percent of those hospitalized suffered minor wounds treated either not in hospitals or not at all.[13] Using this ratio, I arrive at an estimate of 342,400 lightly wounded civilians. My estimated total of South Vietnamese civilian war casualties during the years 1965 to 1974 thus would be 1,160,600 (see Table A-2). My total figure is about 20 percent lower than that of the Kennedy committee; my estimate of Vietnamese civilians killed is about 40 percent lower.

Who caused these civilian casualties? Critics of American military tactics in Vietnam argued that because of the allied superiority in heavy weapons, especially artillery and planes, and because of the lavish use of this firepower the great majority of CWC were caused by the allied side. The disparity of firepower and the American monopoly in the air, maintained Telford Taylor, "make it a certainty that we are responsible for the greater part of the civilian casualties.[14] Going a bit further, one antiwar publicist wrote: "A very conservative estimate would be that over 80 percent of civilian casualties were caused by U.S and ARVN military operations."[15]

Until 1971 the official U.S. position was that there existed no reliable statistics on the causes of CWC. In December 1970 USAID learned that the Vietnamese Ministry of Health had been maintaining such statistics since 1967, and since a *Newsweek* reporter was on the verge of discovering them, AID in January 1971 reported them to Senator Kennedy even though AID viewed these statistics with reserve. According to MOH officials, they were based on the appearance of the injury and the questioning of the patient and/or his family. "Both of these procedures," noted an AID official, "may be carried out by hospital personnel below the physician level. This factor plus the obvious inability of the wounded person to know exactly how he was injured in many cases, cast real doubt as to the validity of the figures. At most they might be used to show broad trends."[16]

CORDS chief Colby used these statistics in his appearance before the Kennedy committee in April 1971 (see Table A-3). Injuries caused by mine and mortar were attributed to the enemy, those by guns and grenades to either side, and those by shelling and bombing to U.S. forces and RVNAF. Hence the broad trend appeared to indicate an increase in enemy-inflicted CWC (from 35 to 58 percent) and a decrease in CWC caused by allied forces (from 43 to 22 percent).

The caution advised by AID in viewing these figures is very appropriate. Data on causative agents are notoriously poor, as experience in World War II had already shown. "The nature of the wound," wrote an American physician in 1952, "does not reliably indicate the agent in enough cases, nor does the wounded soldier himself often enough know what hit him, for the entries on routine medical records to have great accuracy."[17]

Table A-3 Civilian Casualties Admitted to MOH Hospitals by Cause of Injury, 1967–70

	Mine/Mortar Number	%	Gun/Grenade Number	%	Shelling/Bombing Number	%	Total
1967	15,253	35	9,785	22	18,811	43	43,849
1968	31,244	42	15,107	20	28,052	38	74,403
1969	24,648	47	11,814	22	16,183	31	52,645
1970	22,049	58	7,650	20	8,607	22	38,306

SOURCE: Data presented by William E. Colby to the Senate Subcommittee to Investigate Problems Connected with Refugees and Escapees, *War-Related Civilian Problems in Indochina, Part I: Vietnam,* Hearing, 92nd Cong., 1st sess., 21 April 1971, p. 62.

Table A-4 Ground Munitions Consumption and Air Strikes in South
Vietnam, 1969–71

	1969	1970	1971	Percent Change
Ground munitions consumption[a]	1,331.3	1,010.4	761.4	− 75
Attack sorties[b]	188,308	104,354	46,909	−301

SOURCE: OASD (Comptroller), SEA Statistical Summary, Table 9, 7 November 1973, and
Table 304, 5 December 1973.

[a] In thousand tons.
[b] Includes VNAF.

Moreover, as noted by AID, "all three categories of injured could result
from VC or friendly forces." The data, therefore, were of "no real value"
in assessing responsibility for them.[18]

Nevertheless, other data support the picture of a decline in allied
bombing and shelling. Between 1969 and 1972 the tempo of the war gradually slowed, and this downward trend in violence, reinforced by fiscal
constraints, was reflected in the decreased expenditure of ground ordnance and the lower number of air strikes (see Table A-4). The number of
artillery rounds expended by American and South Vietnamese forces,
Colby told the Kennedy committee in April 1971, had decreased by about
60 percent during 1969 and 1970.[19] Moreover, combat increasingly occurred farther away from the homes of the rural population. Between
January 1969 and January 1971 the percentage of air attack missions
within 1 km of populated hamlets dropped from 15.2 to 4.1 percent, and
within 2 km from 25.4 to 10.8 percent.[20] The downward trend for shelling
and bombing is supported by data from the Hamlet Evaluation System
which show that a growing percentage of the population reported the absence of artillery fire or air strikes near their village (see Table A-5). None
of these data in and of themselves can be considered conclusive, but taken
together they point toward a broad trend indicating a decrease in the
number of CWC caused by allied bombing and shelling.

There exists yet another set of data which bears on the question of
responsibility for CWC. From 1969 on U.S. provincial advisory teams
compiled statistics of civilian casualties resulting from enemy-initiated
incidents—assassinations, the mining of roads, the shelling of hamlets or
refugee camps, etc. Whereas, as we have seen, it is difficult to pinpoint

Table A-5 Answer to Question: "Were Any Friendly Artillery or Air Strikes Directed in or Near the Inhabited Area of This Village This Month?" (Percentage of Population)

	December 1969	December 1970	December 1971
No	69.8	83.5	89.0
Yes			
Once	(3.1)	(4.7)	(2.7)
Sporadically	(16.2)	(9.4)	(5.8)
Repeatedly	(7.8)	(2.2)	(2.3)
Subtotal	27.1	16.3	10.8

SOURCE: Hamlet Evaluation System Computer Printout.

responsibility for CWC incurred in situations of combat, these casualties were the result of deliberate attacks upon the civilian population. Figures available for the years 1969 and 1970 are given in Table A-6. We do not know how many of the wounded required hospitalization and therefore cannot calculate what percentage they represented of the total number of CWC hospitalized. The number of deaths (16,715) represents 31 percent of the 53,730 civilians estimated killed outright during these two years. Even if we apply a margin of error of plus or minus 25 percent, indicated for all statistics of VC terror, the number of civilians killed deliberately by the VC is appallingly high. No counterpart to this death toll caused by communist terror tactics exists on the allied side.

How does the number of civilian casualties or the ratio of civilian to military casualties in Vietnam compare to other wars? The proportion of direct civilian deaths in World War I was very small. It is estimated that no more than 5,000 civilians died in air raids, and the relatively static

Table A-6 Civilian War Casualties Resulting from Enemy-Initiated Incidents, 1969–70

	Deaths	Woundings	Total
1969	8,227	21,653	29,880
1970	8,488	19,427	27,915
Total	16,715	41,080	57,795

SOURCE: TIRS, Fact Sheet, 8 June 1971, Refugees 1971 file, CMH.

trench warfare similarly involved few noncombatants. In a total military death toll variously estimated as ranging from 8.5 million to 13 million,[21] civilians killed in the course of military action represented an extremely small percentage.

The percentage of civilians killed in World War II was far higher. The number of civilians killed by aerial bombing alone is estimated at 1.5 million;[22] 67,000 civilians are believed to have died in France as a result of German and Allied ground operations,[23] and the number of civilian victims was far higher in Russia, Yugoslavia and China. The Soviet demographer Boris Urlanis estimates the total number of military deaths in World War II as 22 million; the number of civilians who died as a result of military hostilities and starvation as 16 million.[24]

For the Korean War the only hard statistic is that of American military deaths, which included 33,629 battle deaths and 20,617 who died of other causes.[25] The North Korean and Chinese Communists never published statistics of their casualties. The number of South Korean military deaths has been given as in excess of 400,000;[26] the South Korean Ministry of Defense puts the number of killed and missing at 281,257.[27] Estimates of communist troops killed are about one-half million. The total number of Korean civilians who died in the fighting, which left almost every major city in North and South Korea in ruins, has been estimated at between 2 and 3 million.[28] This adds up to almost 1 million military deaths and a possible 2.5 million civilians who were killed or died as a result of this extremely destructive conflict.

The proportion of civilians killed in the major wars of this century (and not only in the major ones) has thus risen steadily. It reached about 40 percent in World War II and may have gone as high as 70 percent in the Korean War. In order to determine this ratio for the Vietnam conflict, one first has to overcome several statistical hurdles. Between 1965 and 1974 communist forces in Vietnam were reported to have suffered 950,765 deaths.[29] These body count figures were believed by DOD officials to be inflated by about 30 percent; deducting this percentage, one gets a more realistic total of 666,000 enemy deaths. (I will return a little later to the question of what part of this figure represented combatants.) Allied military deaths are given in Table A-7 and show a total military death toll of 281,730 men. In all, this yields a total of about 950,000 military deaths during the years 1965 to 1974.

We have earlier estimated South Vietnamese civilian deaths resulting

Table A-7 Allied Military Deaths in Vietnam, 1965–74

United States	
Deaths from hostile action	(46,498)
Deaths from other causes	(10,388)
Missing and presumed dead	(719)
Subtotal	56,146
South Vietnam	220,357
Korea	4,407
Australia–New Zealand	469
Thailand	351
Total	281,730

SOURCE: OASD (Comptroller), SEA Statistical Summary, Table 860B, 18 February 1976; Table 865, 15 April 1976.

from military operations as about 250,000 (see Table A-2). To this one must add the 38,954 civilians reported assassinated by the VC,[30] which yields a South Vietnamese civilian toll of about 300,000. In early 1969 U.S. intelligence estimated that the bombing of North Vietnam had killed approximately 52,000 North Vietnamese civilians.[31] Civilian losses during the renewed bombing in 1972 are not known. Using a prorated figure based on the 1965–68 estimate one would have to add another 13,000, which brings the North Vietnamese civilian death toll to 65,000. In all, then, I get a total of about 365,000 Vietnamese civilians, north and south, who died during the years 1965 to 1974. This would mean that the number of civilian deaths amounted to about 28 percent of the overall casualty toll of 1,313,000 (see Table A-8), substantially lower than the estimated proportion of 40 percent for civilian deaths in World War II and 70 percent in Korea.

There remains the question how many of the 666,000 reported as enemy (VC/NVA) deaths were combatants and auxiliary personnel and how many were true noncombatants—villagers caught in the battle. How many of the 24,819 VCI reported as killed between January 1968 and February 1972 as a result of Phoenix operations were taken from the enemy combat toll in order to fill quotas? How many were truly part of the communist apparatus?

It is impossible to establish with any precision the number of noncombatants included in the enemy casualty toll. The Vietnamese Military Civil Assistance Program (MILCAP), and from 1968 on the Ministry of Social Welfare, with American help paid a special allowance to the next of kin of civilian war victims killed in the course of military operations, irrespective of which side had started a battle or raid. Figures available for the years 1968 through 1974 show a total of 123,100 claims submitted for killed or wounded war victims, with about half of these being claims for deaths,[32] but the data for CWC given in Table A-2 show that these claims figures represented only a small fraction of the total civilian casualties.

The fact that American units always reported more enemy killed than weapons captured indicates that many of those reported as enemy dead were actually not part of the enemy's combat force. American forces captured about 1 weapon for every 3 enemy reported killed, and this ratio was accepted as normal, since the NVA/VC were known to make great efforts to recover weapons from the battlefield, while other weapons could not be found by the Americans or be retrieved. Yet in many operations taking place in densely populated areas the ratio ran far above the average of 1:3. Task Force Barker, the unit involved in the My Lai massacre, operating in early 1968 in Quang Ngai province (I CTZ), reported 1 weapon captured for every 10 enemy killed.[33] During Operation SPEEDY EXPRESS in the Delta in the first half of 1969, the Ninth Infantry Division had a ratio of 1:14.6.[34] This disparity could be due to an exaggerated body count or to the inclusion of noncombatants, or to a combination of these two factors. It should be borne in mind that these ratios would look even worse if one were to deduct the weapons found in arms caches or taken from prisoners. It is thus clear that a steady percentage of those reported as VC dead were in fact villagers not carrying weapons. Among CWC in MOH hospitals about one-third were women and close to a quarter were children under 13.[35] More than half of the CWC thus were women and children, and even if some of them functioned as VC auxiliary personnel many others clearly must have been bona fide noncombatants.

If we assume that one-third of those reported as VC/NVA deaths were in fact just innocent bystanders, i.e. neither arms-carrying VC/NVA, nor auxiliary personnel serving as porters or building fortifications, nor VC cadres, etc., we find that the ratio of civilian to military deaths is not sub-

Table A-8 Ratio of Civilian to Military Deaths in the Vietnam Conflict, 1965–74

	VC/NVA Dead Counted as Military Deaths	VC/NVA Dead Counted as ⅔ Military, ⅓ Civilian Deaths
Allied military deaths	282,000	282,000
Communist military deaths	666,000	444,000
Total military deaths	948,000	727,000
Civilian deaths—north and south	365,000	587,000
Total deaths	1,313,000	1,313,000
Civilian deaths as percent of total	28%	45%

stantially different from that of World War II and is below that of the Korean War (see Table A-8).

It must be emphasized that all the above calculations work with estimates and extrapolations and therefore cannot be expected to yield exact results. On the other hand, the broad picture is probably valid.

Appendix II
Tables and Charts

Table 8-1 VC/NVA Assassinations and Abductions, 1957–72

	Assassinated	Abducted
1957–60	1,700 (est.)	2,000 (est.)
1961	1,300 (est.)	1,318
1962	1,118	1,118
1963	827	1,596
1964	516	1,525
1965	305	1,730
1966	1,732	3,810
1967	3,707	5,357
1968	5,389	8,759
1969	6,202	6,289
1970	5,951	6,872
1971	3,573	5,006
1972	4,405	13,119
Total	36,725	58,499

SOURCES: OASD (PA), Atrocity Fact Sheet; Douglas Pike, *The Viet-Cong Strategy of Terror* (Saigon, 1970), p. 82.

Table 5-3 Republic of Vietnam Armed Forces Strength [a]

	Army	Air Force	Navy	Marine Corps	Total Regular	Regional Forces	Popular Forces	Total Territorial	Grand Total
1954–55	170,000	3,500	2,200	1,500	177,200	54,000 [b]	48,000 [b]	102,000	279,200
1959–60	136,000 [c]	4,600	4,300	2,000	146,000	49,000 [c]	48,000	97,000	243,000
1964	220,000	11,000	12,000	7,000	250,000	96,000	168,000	264,000	514,000
1967	303,000	16,000	16,000	8,000	343,000	151,000	149,000 [c]	300,000	643,000
1968	380,000	19,000	19,000	9,000	427,000	220,000	173,000	393,000	820,000
1969	416,000	36,000	30,000	11,000	493,000	190,000	214,000	404,000	897,000
1970	416,000	46,000	40,000	13,000	515,000	207,000	246,000	453,000	968,000
1971–72	410,000 [c]	50,000	42,000	14,000	516,000	284,000	248,000	532,000	1,048,000

SOURCE: James L. Collins, Jr., *The Development and Training of the South Vietnamese Army, 1950–1972* (Washington, D.C., 1975), p. 151.

[a] All figures are approximate only.
[b] Civil Guard (later Regional Forces) and Self-Defense Corps (later Popular Forces) were officially authorized only in 1956.
[c] Decline due to increased desertions and recruiting shortfalls.

Table 10-2   Serious Offenses[a] Committed by USMC Personnel against Vietnamese Figuring in Courts-Martial, March 1965–August 1971

Offense	Convicted	Acquitted
Murder	27	16
Attempted murder	1	2
Rape	16	10
Attempted rape	2	0
Assault with intent to commit murder, rape or indecent assault	10	8
Indecent acts with a female	8	0
Manslaughter	15	7
Negligent homicide	6	1
Mutilation of a corpse	1	0
Arson	1	0
Kidnapping	1	2
Officer filing false report to cover up murders or failing to report murders	2	0
Total number of offenses	90	46

SOURCE: U.S. Department of the Navy, Office of the Judge Advocate General, Military Justice Division.

[a] Numbers refer to offenses. Since some individuals were found guilty of more than one offense, the number of offenses exceeds the number of individuals tried.

Table 10-4 Disposition of War Crimes Allegations against U.S. Army Personnel, Other than Son My

	Pre–Son My (1/1/65– 8/31/69)	Post–Son My (9/1/69– 7/25/75)	Total
Disposition of cases of probable cause			
Court-martial	22	14	36
Charges dismissed/not tried	3	15	18
Nonjudicial punishment (Article 15)	3	5	8
Adverse administrative action	3	12	15
Command action pending	0	1	1
Total	31	47	78

Status of individuals (as of 21 May 1971)

	Enlisted Men No.	Enlisted Men %	Officers No.	Officers %	Total No.
Tried by court-martial	49	52	11	30	60
Convicted by court-martial	(25)	(51)	(4)	(36)	(29)
General court-martial	(17)		(3)		(20)
Special court-martial	(8)		(1)		(9)
Acquitted/charges dismissed after arraignment	(24)	(49)	(7)	(64)	(31)
Charges dismissed/not tried	6	6	9	25	15
Nonjudicial punishment (Article 15)	14	15	2	5	16
Adverse administrative action	2	2	6	17	8
Found to be insane	1	1	1	3	2
Granted immunity to testify in another case	3	3	0	0	3
Killed in action or died before disposition	2	2	1	3	3
Not tried for various grounds	12	13	3	8	15
Command action pending	5	5	3	8	8
Total	94	99% [a]	36	99% [a]	130

SOURCES: U.S. Army, Office of the Judge Advocate General, International Affairs Division; Report of the U.S. Army judge advocate general to the White House, 21 May 1971.

[a] Column does not add up to 100 because of rounding.

Table 10-5 Review of Confinement Adjudged in Cases of Marines Convicted of Murder in Which Victim Was Vietnamese, 1965–71

Individual	Sentence Adjudged (in years)	Sentence Approved (in years) By CA[a]	By NCMR[b]	Action by USCMA[c]	Sentence Resulting from Parole (P) or Clemency (C) Action[d] (in years)
1	10	10	7	Appeal denied	C: $6^{1}/_{12}$
2	Life	Life	25	Sentence affirmed	C: 6
3	5	5	5	Appeal denied	C: Denied
4	Life	Life	3	Appeal denied	
5	Life	25	5	Appeal denied	C: 2¾
6	4	4	4	Appeal denied	C: Denied
7	Life	Life	Life	Appeal denied	C: 12
8	50	35	10		C: 8
9	Life	35	5	Appeal denied	C: $2^{5}/_{12}$
10	30	30	Dismissed (insanity)		
11	10	5	5	No petition	C: 4
12	Life	30	30	Appeal denied	C: 3
13	Life	Life	Life	Appeal denied	C: 9
14	Life	20	20	Appeal denied	C: $7^{1}/_{12}$
15	Life	20	20	Appeal denied	C: 7
16	2	2	2	Appeal denied	C: Denied
17	2	2	2		C: Denied
18	2	2	2	Appeal denied	
19	Life	Life	3	Appeal denied	
20	Life	30	3	Appeal denied	
21	4	1¼	⅔	Did not petition	C: Denied
22	Life	30	15	10 years	P: 3
23	Life	40	15	Appeal denied	P: 3¾
24	5	1	1	Appeal denied	C: Denied
25	Life	1	1	Did not petition	C: Denied
26	20	20	Dismissed		
27	Life	25	25	Appeal dismissed	C: 19

SOURCES: Data provided by U.S. Marine Corps and Department of the Navy, Offices of the Judge Advocate General, and by Naval Clemency and Parole Board.

[a] Convening authority.
[b] Navy Court of Military Review.
[c] U.S. Court of Military Appeals.
[d] Does not take into account time off earned for good behavior.

Chart 1. Military Assistance Command, Vietnam, 1965

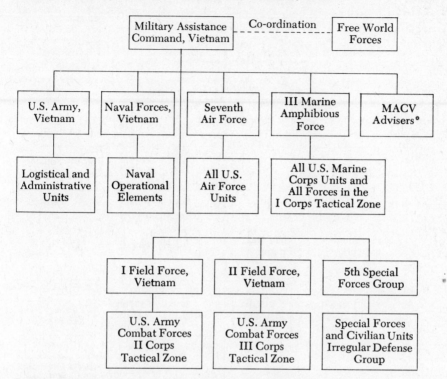

* Except those MACV advisers who double as commanders of U.S. troop units

SOURCE: *Report on the War in Vietnam (as of 30 June 1968)* by Admiral U.S. Grant Sharp, USN, and General William C. Westmoreland, USA (Washington: 1969), Section II, Chapter III, p. 102.

Chart 2. CORDS Field Organization, 1967

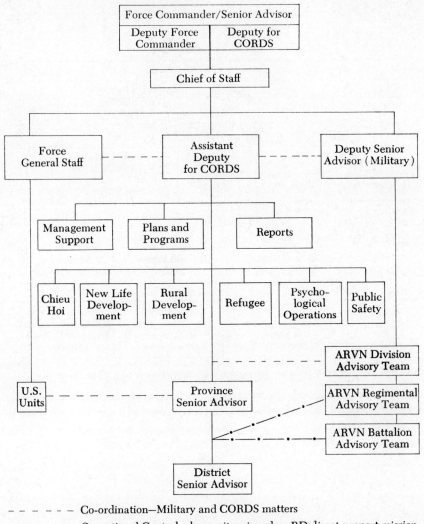

– – – – – – Co-ordination—Military and CORDS matters

—•——•—— Operational Control when unit assigned an RD direct support mission

SOURCE: *USMACV Command History, 1967,* Vol. II, p. 589.

A Note
on Military Records

Most military records are classified. Under Executive Order No. 11652 of 8 March 1972, classified records of the U.S. government, except for 4 categories of especially sensitive information, are subjected to automatic declassification, normally within 10, 8 or 6 years. As a result, many Vietnam records are now declassified and available without special clearance. Also under Executive Order No. 11652, qualified researchers may apply to the secretaries of the military services for permission to have access to military documents which are still classified.*

Documents marked CMH are to be found at the Current History Branch, U.S. Army Center of Military History (CMH), Washington, D.C. Wherever possible, specific files have been cited. Unless otherwise indicated, all other Army-originated records are on deposit at the Washington National Records Center, Suitland, Maryland, the place of retirement for all MACV records. Precise locations can be ascertained by consulting the appropriate indices and inventories at CMH.

U.S. Marine Corps combat records and command histories are at the History and Museums Division of USMC Headquarters in Washington, D.C.

U.S. Air Force–originated records are on deposit at the Albert F. Simpson Historical Research Center, Maxwell Air Force Base, Alabama. A selection from these records has been filmed and is held at the Office of Air Force History, Washington, D.C.

Records of general courts-martial and of special courts-martial resulting in a bad conduct discharge involving U.S. military personnel tried and convicted in Vietnam are held at the Washington National Records Center. Access to Army cases is arranged through the U.S. Army Judiciary,

* New regulations on national security information are currently being drafted by the Carter administration. It is expected that the principle of access for historical researchers will be preserved.

Falls Church, Virginia. Access to Marine Corps cases is through the Military Law Branch, USMC Office of the Judge Advocate General. Published decisions of the military courts of review and of the U.S. Court of Military Appeals are cited from the commercially edited *Court Martial Reports* (CMR). Investigative files on war crimes are held at the respective Offices of the Judge Advocates General, but probably are no longer accessible due to Privacy Act constraints.

Two sources of statistical data cited extensively are the Southeast Asia Statistical Summary, compiled by the Office of the Assistant Secretary of Defense (Comptroller), and the *Southeast Asia Analysis Report*, published by the Office of the Assistant Secretary of Defense (Systems Analysis), now part of the Office of the Assistant Secretary of Defense (Program Analysis and Evaluation). Copies of both publications are on file at the historical offices of the military services and at the originating offices of the Department of Defense.

The following introductions to textual and machine-readable Vietnam records and data will be found useful: G. A. Carter *et al.*, *User's Guide to Southeast Asia Combat Data*, R-1815-ARPA (Santa Monica, Calif.: Rand Corp., 1976); Jack Shulimson, "Vietnam Historical Data Base," *Marine Corps Gazette* LIII, no. 2 (February 1969): 43–45; U.S. Department of the Army, *Contrast: An Annotated Bibliography* (*Lessons Learned in Vietnam*), n.d., classified.

Notes

1. THE ROOTS OF INVOLVEMENT

1. *The Pentagon Papers: The Defense Department History of United States Decisionmaking on Vietnam*, Senator Gravel edition (Boston, 1971), I:66 (hereafter cited as *Pentagon Papers*).
2. *Ibid.*, p. 373.
3. *Ibid.*, p. 77.
4. *Ibid.*, pp. 385–87.
5. *Ibid.*, p. 378.
6. *Ibid.*, p. 203.
7. Cf. Melvin Gurtov, *The First Vietnam Crisis: Chinese Communist Strategy and United States Involvement, 1953–1954* (New York, 1967), p. 44.
8. U.S. Department of State, *American Foreign Policy, 1950–1955: Basic Documents* (Washington, D.C., 1957), II:2375.
9. U.S. President, *Public Papers of the Presidents of the United States: Dwight D. Eisenhower, 1954* (Washington, D.C., 1960), p. 383.
10. On the battle of Dien Bien Phu generally see Bernard B. Fall, *Hell in a Very Small Place: The Siege of Dien Bien Phu* (New York, 1967).
11. *Pentagon Papers* I:100–101.
12. Cf. John S. Hannon, Jr., "A Political Settlement for Vietnam: The 1954 Geneva Conference and Its Current Implications," in Richard A. Falk, ed., *The Vietnam War and International Law* (Princeton, N.J., 1969), II:889–90.
13. Falk, "International Law and the United States Role in Vietnam: A Response to Professor Moore," in *ibid.*, I:467.
14. George McTurnan Kahin and John W. Lewis, *The United States in Vietnam* (New York, 1967), p. 57.
15. Note 9 above, pp. 786–87.
16. Hans J. Morgenthau, "The 1954 Geneva Conference: An Assessment," in American Friends of Vietnam, *America's Stake in Vietnam* (New York, 1956), p. 69.
17. Complete text in Council on Foreign Relations, *Documents on American Foreign Relations, 1954* (New York, 1955), pp. 315–16.
18. Complete text in n. 9 above, pp. 787–88.
19. Robert F. Randle, *Geneva 1954: The Settlement of the Indochinese War* (Princeton, N.J., 1969), p. 410.
20. Note 12 above, p. 552.

21. Cited by John N. Moore *et al.*, "The Lawfulness of United States Assistance to the Republic of Vietnam," *Congressional Record* CXII, part 12 (13 July 1966):15549.

22. Cf. Daniel G. Partan, "Legal Aspects of the Vietnam Conflict," in n. 12 above, p. 210.

23. Jeffrey Race, *War Comes to Long An: Revolutionary Conflict in a Vietnamese Province* (Berkeley, Calif., 1972), pp. 34–35.

24. Note 8 above, I:788.

25. Articles I and IV, Protocol, n. 8 above, I:913–16.

26. Note 8 above, I:936.

27. *Ibid.*, I:913.

28. Edwin Brown Firmage, "International Law and the Response of the United States to 'Internal War,' " in n. 12 above, p. 118.

29. Note 9 above, p. 949.

30. *Pentagon Papers* I:218.

31. Mike Mansfield, "Reprieve in Vietnam," *Harper's*, January 1956, p. 50.

32. Note 16 above, pp. 10–11. Kennedy's address is also reprinted in Wesley R. Fishel, ed., *Vietnam: Anatomy of a Conflict* (Itasca, Ill., 1968), pp. 142–47.

33. Note 16 above, pp. 13, 12.

34. Chester L. Cooper, *The Lost Crusade: America in Vietnam* (Greenwich, Conn., 1972), p. 191.

35. David Halberstam, *The Making of a Quagmire* (New York, 1965), p. 42.

36. Cf. Robert L. Sansom, *The Economics of Insurgency in the Mekong Delta of Vietnam* (Cambridge, Mass., 1970), pp. 57–58; William Bredo, "Agrarian Reform in Vietnam: Vietcong and Government of Vietnam Strategies in Conflict," *Asian Survey* X (1970):742–48.

37. Ellen J. Hammer, *The Struggle for Indochina: 1940–1955* (Stanford, Calif., 1966), p. 359.

38. Joseph Buttinger, *Vietnam: The Dragon Embattled* (New York, 1967), II:940.

39. *Washington Post*, 26 February 1956, reprinted in Hans J. Morgenthau, *Vietnam and the United States* (Washington, D.C., 1965), p. 24.

40. Philippe Devillers, "The Struggle for the Unification of Vietnam," in P. J. Honey, ed., *North Vietnam Today* (New York, 1962), p. 42.

41. Note 14 above, pp. 119–20.

42. Note 23 above, p. 107, n. 5.

43. *Ibid.*, p. 122.

44. Bernard B. Fall, *The Two Viet-Nams: A Political and Military Analysis*, 2nd rev. ed. (New York, 1967), p. 156.

45. Hoang Van Chi, *From Colonialism to Communism: A Case History of North Vietnam* (New York, 1964), p. 72. Attempts by the Hanoi sympathizer D. Gareth Porter to deny the scope of this terror remain unconvincing. See his *The Myth of the Bloodbath: North Vietnam's Land Reform Reconsidered* (Ithaca, N.Y., 1972), and U.S. Senate, Committee on the Judiciary, Subcommittee to Investigate the Administration of the Internal Security Act and other Internal Security Laws, *The Human Cost of Communism in Vietnam—II: The Myth of No Bloodbath*, Hearing, 93rd Cong., 1st sess., 5 January 1973.

46. Ho Chi Minh, *Selected Works,* 4:128, cited by Robert F. Turner, *Vietnamese Communism: Its Origins and Development* (Stanford, Calif., 1975), pp. 168–69.

47. Note 23 above, p. 112.

48. King C. Chen, "Hanoi's Three Decisions and the Escalation of the Vietnam War," *Political Science Quarterly* XC (1975):247, n. 27.

49. *Pentagon Papers* I:264.

50. *Hoc Tap,* January 1960, cited by Douglas Pike, *Viet Cong: The Organization and Techniques of the National Liberation Front of South Vietnam* (Cambridge, Mass., 1966), p. 78.

51. Cited by Turner, n. 46 above, pp. 203–4.

52. Note 23 above, pp. 107, n. 5; 120–21.

53. Cf. George A. Carver, Jr., "The Faceless Viet Cong," *Foreign Affairs* XLIV (1966):372.

54. Note 14 above, p. 132.

55. Jean Lacouture, "A Bittersweet Journey to Vietnam," *New York Times,* 23 August 1976.

56. Note 23 above, p. 123; n. 50 above, pp. 137–42.

57. *Pentagon Papers* I:318.

58. *Ibid.,* II:36.

59. *Ibid.,* II:38–39.

60. *Ibid.,* II:50.

61. *Ibid.,* II:653.

62. *Ibid.,* II:111.

63. Clifford E. Garrett, "A Preliminary Study of the Politically Specified Rules of Engagement for Air Operations in Southeast Asia" (Air War College Research Report no. 3354, May 1967), p. 8.

64. *Pentagon Papers* I:573–83.

65. *Ibid.,* II:438; George S. Eckhardt, *Command and Control: 1950–1969,* Vietnam Studies (Washington, D.C., 1974), pp. 9–15.

66. State to embassy Saigon, 5 October 1961, JFK Library, NSF/V, vol. I(c), Box 192-4; n. 63 above, p. 7.

67. *Pentagon Papers* II:438.

68. U.S. Department of State, *A Threat to the Peace: North Viet-Nam's Effort to Conquer South Viet-Nam* (Washington, D.C., 1961), pp. 27, 32.

69. Memo of 5 October 1961, p. 3, JFK Library, NSF/V, vol. I(c), Box 192–4.

70. Dennis J. Duncanson, *Government and Revolution in Vietnam* (London, 1968), pp. 304–5.

71. U.S. President, *Public Papers of the Presidents of the United States: John F. Kennedy, 1961* (Washington, D.C., 1962), p. 801.

72. *Ibid.,* 1962 (Washington, D.C., 1963), p. 13.

73. OASD (Comptroller), SEA Statistical Summary, Table 103, 26 September 1973.

74. JFK Library, NSF/V, vol. X, Box 196–8; OASD (Comptroller), SEA Statistical Summary, Table 322, 19 April 1972.

75. Cf. Pike, n. 50 above, pp. 66–67.

76. *Pentagon Papers* II:151.
77. Note 70 above, p. 321.
78. Report of 25 February 1963, reprinted in U.S. Senate, Committee on Foreign Relations, *The Vietnam Conflict: The Substance and the Shadow*, 89th Cong., 2nd sess., 6 January 1966, p. 23.
79. John Mecklin, *Mission in Torment: An Intimate Account of the U.S. Role in Vietnam* (Garden City, N.Y., 1965), pp. 90–98.
80. *Ibid.*, pp. 32–33.
81. *Pentagon Papers* II:738–39.
82. *Ibid.*, II:251.
83. *Ibid.*, II:257.
84. *Ibid.*, II:270.
85. *New York Times*, 3 November 1963.
86. Note 37 above, p. v.
87. Note 70 above, pp. 342–43.
88. *Pentagon Papers* III:494.
89. U.S. Embassy, Saigon, "The Viet-Nam Workers' Party's 1963 Decision to Escalate the War in the South," *Viet-Nam Documents and Research Notes*, Doc. no. 96 (July 1971), pp. 15, 29, 40.
90. *Pentagon Papers* III:150–51.
91. *Ibid.*, III:498.
92. *Ibid.*, III:155.
93. Bernard B. Fall, *Viet-Nam Witness: 1953–66* (New York, 1966), p. 114.
94. Roger Hilsman, *To Move a Nation: The Politics of Foreign Policy in the Administration of John F. Kennedy* (Garden City, N.Y., 1967), p. 536; *Pentagon Papers* III:44.
95. For the full text of NSAM 288 see *Pentagon Papers* III:499–510.
96. U.S. President, *Public Papers of the Presidents of the United States: Lyndon B. Johnson, 1963–64* (Washington, D.C., 1965), I:388.
97. *Pentagon Papers* III:292.
98. *Ibid.*, III:180–81. For the text of a draft resolution, dated 25 May 1964, see *ibid.*, V:339–41.
99. Lyndon B. Johnson, *The Vantage Point: Perspectives of the Presidency 1963–1969* (New York, 1971), p. 115.
100. *Pentagon Papers* III:182–83.
101. *Pentagon Papers* V:323–25.
102. U.S. Senate, Committee on Foreign Relations, *The Gulf of Tonkin, the 1964 Incidents*, Hearing, 90th Cong., 2nd sess., 20 February 1968, p. 15. This is confirmed by Chester L. Cooper, who was in the White House situation room when these messages arrived (n. 34 above, p. 296).
103. *Pentagon Papers* V:325–27.
104. Public Law 88-408, reprinted in n. 12 above, I:579.
105. *Congressional Record* CX, part 14 (6–7 August 1964):18403–4.
106. *Ibid.*, p. 18407.
107. *Ibid.*, pp. 18409–10.

108. *Ibid.*, pp. 18415, 18421.
109. Ralph Stavins *et al.*, *Washington Plans an Aggressive War* (New York, 1971), pp. 280–81; Joseph C. Goulden, *Truth Is the First Casualty: The Gulf of Tonkin Affair—Illusion and Reality* (New York, 1969), p. 13.
110. Note 102 above, p. 64.
111. *Ibid.*, p. 81.
112. U.S. Senate, Committee on Foreign Relations, *Legislative Proposals Relating to the War in Southeast Asia*, Hearings, 92nd Cong., 1st sess., 20 April–27 May 1971, p. 571.
113. *Pentagon Papers* V:328–29.
114. Speech at Manchester, N.H., 28 September 1964, n. 96 above, II:1164.
115. Peter A. Poole, *The United States and Indochina: From FDR to Nixon* (Hinsdale, Ill., 1973), p. 121.
116. Maxwell D. Taylor, *Swords and Plowshares* (New York, 1972), p. 327.
117. *Pentagon Papers* III: 110, 562.
118. Ball's memo of 5 October 1964 was put before the president in January 1965. Cf. George W. Ball, "Top Secret: The Prophecy the President Rejected," *The Atlantic* (July 1972): 36–49.
119. U.S. Department of State, *Aggression from the North: The Record of North Viet-nam's Campaign to Conquer South Viet-nam* (Washington, D.C., 1965), pp. 1, 11, 16, 29.
120. I. F. Stone, "A Reply to the White Paper," *I. F. Stone's Weekly*, 8 March 1965, in Marcus G. Raskin and Bernard B. Fall, eds., *The Viet-Nam Reader*, rev. ed. (New York, 1967), pp. 155–62.
121. Note 94 above, p. 578.
122. Theodore Draper, *Abuse of Power* (New York, 1967), pp. 81, 174. This canard is repeated by Frances FitzGerald, *Fire in the Lake: The Vietnamese and the Americans in Vietnam* (New York, 1973), pp. 196–97.
123. U.S. Department of State, "Working Paper on the North Vietnamese Role in the War in South Vietnam," in Falk, n. 12 above, II:1205. This carefully researched and documented report, based on captured documents, intelligence briefs and interrogation reports, issued in May 1968, was a product of an interagency study group convened by McNamara in 1967. A part of the document was published in nos. 36–37 of the *Viet-Nam Documents and Research Notes*, issued by the U.S. Embassy in Saigon, June 1968.
124. U.S. House, Select Committee on Intelligence, *U.S. Intelligence Agencies and Activities: The Performance of the Intelligence Community*, Hearings, 94th Cong., 1st sess., part 2, 11 September–31 October 1975, pp. 717–18.
125. Note 123, above, p. 1204.
126. Committee of Concerned Asian Scholars, *The Indochina Story: A Fully Documented Account* (New York, 1970), p. xx.
127. Note 94 above, p. 458.
128. OASD (SA), *SEA Analysis Report*, May 1968, p. 4.
129. Note 122 above, p. 84.
130. Note 70 above, p. 367.

2. THE BIG-UNIT WAR

1. *Pentagon Papers* III:417.
2. Franz Schurmann *et al.*, *The Politics of Escalation in Vietnam: A Citizen's White Paper* (Boston, 1966), p. 64.
3. *Pentagon Papers* III:417.
4. William C. Westmoreland, *A Soldier Reports* (Garden City, N.Y., 1976), p. 126.
5. *Ibid.*, pp. 128–29.
6. *Pentagon Papers* III:703.
7. *Ibid.*, p. 447.
8. *Pentagon Papers* III:703.
9. *Public Papers of the Presidents of the United States: Lyndon B. Johnson 1965* (Washington, D.C., 1966), I:370.
10. *Pentagon Papers* III:458.
11. *Ibid.*, p. 440.
12. *Ibid.*, p. 461.
13. *Ibid.*, IV:616.
14. *Ibid.*, p. 612.
15. Note 9 above, p. 429.
16. Lyndon B. Johnson, *The Vantage Point: Perspectives of the Presidency 1963–1969* (New York, 1971), p. 149.
17. Chester L. Cooper, *The Lost Crusade: America in Vietnam* (Greenwich, Conn., 1972), p. 345.
18. For the full text of the president's prepared statement see n. 9 above, II:794–98.
19. *Ibid.*, p. 801.
20. See n. 16 above, p. 153.
21. *Pentagon Papers* IV:294.
22. Note 4 above, p. 165.
23. 1st Bn, 9th Marines, AAR 1-65, 8 August 1965, Annex C.
24. 7th Marines (RLT-7), Command Chronology, AAR, STARLIGHT, 5 October 1965.
25. OASD (SA), *SEA Analysis Report*, May 1968, p. 25.
26. RLT-7, Sit Rep #16, 23 August 1965.
27. MACJ2 Fact Sheet, n.d., Body Count file, CMH.
28. 1st Bn, 7th Marines, AAR #1, STARLIGHT, 27 August 1965.
29. U. S. G. Sharp and W. C. Westmoreland, *Report on the War in Vietnam (As of 30 June 1968)* (Washington, D.C., 1969), p. 99.
30. U.S. Joint Logistics Review Board, *Logistics Support in the Vietnam Era* (Washington, D.C., 1970), II:259; U.S. Army Materiel Command Historical Office, *Arsenal for the Brave: A History of the U.S. Army Materiel Command, 1962–1968* (Washington, D.C., 1969), pp. 215–17; U.S. House, Committee on Government Operations, *Military Supply Systems: Lessons from the Vietnam Experience*, 37th Report, 91st Cong., 2d sess., 8 October 1970.

31. *Pentagon Papers* IV:303.
32. *Ibid.*, p. 306.
33. Mike Mansfield, *Two Reports on Vietnam and Southeast Asia to the President of the United States* (Washington, D.C., 1973), pp. 23, 32.
34. *Pentagon Papers* IV:304; John Albright *et al.*, *Seven Firefights in Vietnam* (Washington, D.C.), chap. 1. See also n. 4 above, pp. 156–57.
35. *Pentagon Papers* IV:321; n. 4 above, p. 164.
36. David Ewing Ott, *Field Artillery, 1954–1973*, Vietnam Studies (Washington, D.C., 1975), p. 105.
37. 1st Cavalry Division, AAR, MASHER/WHITE WING, 25 January–6 March 1966, 28 April 1966, p. 23.
38. 1st Cavalry Division, AAR, THAYER I/IRVING, 13 September–24 October 1966, 13 January 1967, Incl. 1.
39. Letter of Assistant Judge Advocate General Kenneth J. Hodson to Lothar H. Belck, Geneva, Switzerland, 20 October 1966, JAGW 1966/1462. International Affairs Division, JAGO, Department of the Army.
40. Note 38 above, p. 32.
41. See n. 37 above, p. 23.
42. MACCORDS-PSG, "Binh Dinh Province—the Challenge 1971," 12 June 1971, p. 7, CMH.
43. Note 37 above, pp. 15, 25.
44. Note 38 above, p. 41.
45. Report of Edward B. Marks, Refugee Coordinator, 17 December 1966, CMH. The figure was taken from unverified Weekly Ministry of Social Welfare reports, which were known to be understated.
46. 1st Cavalry Division (Airmobile), AAR, THAYER II, 25 October 1966–12 February 1967, 25 June 1967, Incl. 6-5.
47. *Ibid.*, pp. 15, 25, 49, 58, Incl. 1, 3.
48. *Ibid.*, Incl. 6-2.
49. Briefing on CINCPAC Operations Security Progress Report, 8 April 1968, p. 20, CMH.
50. Task Force Delta, AAR, DOUBLE EAGLE I & II, 23 March 1966, p. 30.
51. *Pentagon Papers* II:587–88.
52. 4th Bn, 9th Infantry, 25th Infantry Division, AAR, LANIKAI-Pacification, 14 September–5 November 1966, 30 November 1966, Appendices 2, 8, 14.
53. *Ibid.*, pp. 7, 57.
54. OASD (SA), *SEA Analysis Report*, January 1967, p. 15.
55. Bernard W. Rogers, *Cedar Falls—Junction City: A Turning Point*, Vietnam Studies (Washington, D.C., 1974), p. 74.
56. Jonathan Schell, *The Village of Ben Suc* (New York, 1967).
57. SACSA report, 13 December 1967, and draft of memo for secretary of defense, n.d., Refugees 1967 file, CMH.
58. *Pentagon Papers* IV:402.
59. Note 55 above, p. 158.
60. *Pentagon Papers* IV:335–36.

61. Telegram, Embassy Saigon to State, 24 April 1967, CMH.
62. USMC, *U.S. Marine Corps Forces in Vietnam March 1965–September 1967*, I:4–27.
63. USMC, History and Museums Division, *The Marines in Vietnam 1954–1973: An Anthology and Bibliography* (Washington, D.C., 1974), p. 73.
64. Vo Nguyen Giap, "The Big Victory, the Great Task," in Patrick J. McGarvey, *Visions of Victory: Selected Vietnamese Communist Military Writings, 1964–1968* (Stanford, Calif., 1969), p. 215.
65. Note 4 above, p. 313.
66. McGarvey, n. 64 above, p. 43.
67. OASD (SA), *SEA Analysis Report*, January 1968, pp. 19–20.
68. *Pentagon Papers* IV:386.
69. MACCORDS-RE, "Evaluation Report: Task Force Oregon Operations," 13 September 1967, p. 8, U.S. Forces and Pacification 1961–68 file, CMH.
70. Task Force Oregon, "Operational Report for Quarterly Period Ending 31 July 1967," 5 November 1967, CMH.
71. 1st Bde, 101st Airborne Division, AAR, MALHEUR, 2 September 1967, CMH.
72. See, e.g., the after-action reports for Operations HOT SPRING and UTAH, with a great disparity between body count and the number of weapons seized.
73. Note 69 above, p. 7.
74. MACCORDS-RE, "Evaluation of Refugee Handling Operations in Quang Ngai Province," 4 September 1967, Refugees 1967 file, CMH.
75. Binh Son Subsector Adviser to Quang Ngai Sector Adviser, 16 August 1967, PSG files, CMH.
76. Jonathan Schell, *The Military Half: An Account of Destruction in Quang Ngai and Quang Tin* (New York, 1968).
77. Report to the ambassador, 12 December 1967, Civilian Casualties file, CMH.
78. Washington National Records Center, 286-76-084 (2/68:17-1), file POL 27-15.
79. Report of travel, Binh Dinh and Phu Yen province, 5 March 1968, p. 1, Phu Yen province file, CMH.
80. 1st Cavalry Division (Airmobile), AAR, PERSHING—Search and Destroy, 12 February 1967–21 January 1968, 29 June 1968, Tab 2, p. 1.
81. MACCORDS, "A Study of Pacification and Security in Cu Chi District, Hau Nghia Province," 29 May 1968, p. 34, CMH.
82. Note 63 above, p. 71.
83. *Pentagon Papers* IV:428–30.
84. Note 4 above, p. 227.
85. *Pentagon Papers* IV:528.
86. *Ibid.*, p. 538.
87. Fleet Marine Force, Pacific, *U.S. Marine Corps Forces in Vietnam 1967*, vol. II, December, pp. 9–10.
88. Note 4 above, p. 231.
89. Neil Sheehan, "U.S. Undervalued Enemy's Strength Before Offensive," *New*

York Times, 19 March 1968. See also OASD (SA), *SEA Analysis Report*, February 1967, p. 10.

90. Thomas C. Thayer, "War Without Fronts," *Journal of Defense Research*, Series B, Tactical Warfare Analysis of Viet Nam Data, Vol. 7B, no. 3 (Fall 1975):787.

91. U.S. House, Select Committee on Intelligence, *U.S. Intelligence Agencies and Activities: The Performance of the Intelligence Community*, Hearings, 94th Cong., 1st sess., part 2, 11 September–31 October 1975, p. 684.

92. Letter to *New York Times*, 29 September 1975.

93. OASD (Comptroller), SEA Statistical Summary, Table 105, 10 January 1973.

94. *Pentagon Papers* IV:539.

95. Henry A. Kissinger, *American Foreign Policy*, expanded ed. (New York, 1974), pp. 106–7.

3. THE FAILURE OF ATTRITION AND PACIFICATION

1. *Pentagon Papers* IV:380–50.

2. MACV Strategic Objectives Plan, n.d., p. 52, CMH.

3. MACV Directive 381-21, 26 December 1967, Tab B to Appendix 1 to Annex A.

4. MACJ2 Fact Sheet, n.d., Body Count file, CMH.

5. The calculation assumed that for every 100 enemy soldiers KIA there were 150 others wounded seriously enough to require hospitalization; for American forces the corresponding figure was 380. The MACV calculation furthermore assumed a hospital mortality rate of 2 percent; for American wounded, enjoying a system of medical care of very high quality, it was 2.6 percent. To be sure, the American military counted as wounded many whom their opponents probably did not so classify, and the availability of speedy helicopter evacuation meant that mortally wounded American casualties were brought to a hospital where their subsequent death raised the hospital mortality rate. Still, the MACV estimate was basically conservative; the U.S. Intelligence Board in 1966 calculated that for every 100 enemy KIA 50 others died of their wounds or were permanently disabled. Spurgeon Neel, *Medical Support of the U.S. Army in Vietnam: 1965–1970*, Vietnam Studies (Washington, D.C., 1973), p. 51, and *Pentagon Papers* IV:370.

6. MACV, Inspector General, Summaries of Reports and Investigations, and Inquiries 1967–72 (film). The report cited here is dated 7 April 1968.

7. Alain C. Enthoven and K. Wayne Smith, *How Much Is Enough? The Defense Program, 1961–1969* (New York, 1971), p. 296.

8. Bunker to State, 2 November 1967, Body Count file, CMH.

9. Thomas C. Thayer, "War Without Fronts," *Journal of Defense Research*, Series B, Tactical Warfare Analysis of Viet Nam Data, Vol. 7B, no. 3 (Fall 1975):846.

10. *Washington Post*, 6 April 1969, p. 4-F.

11. Memo, 3 September 1969, Body Count File, CMH.

12. The unit was the 2nd bn, 502nd Strike Force Infantry. Cf. HIMS Microfilm Collection, U.S. Army Military History Research Collection, Carlisle Barracks, Pa., film 277.

13. Message, 23 November 1967, Body Count file, CMH.

14. Note 7 above, p. 296.

15. Richard A. McMahon, "Bury the Body Count for Good," *Army* XIX, no. 6 (June 1969):67.

16. Douglas Kinnard, "Vietnam Reconsidered: An Attitudinal Survey of U.S. Army General Officers," *Public Opinion Quarterly* XXXIX (1976):449–50.

17. See the reports on Ewell's commanders' conferences, U.S. Forces and Pacification 1969–72 and Body Count files, CMH.

18. *U.S. v. Duffy*, 47 CMR 658 (ACMR 1973) at 661.

19. William V. O'Brien, "The Law of War, Command Responsibility and Vietnam," *Georgetown Law Journal* LX (1972):636.

20. Memorandum of 17 November 1966, *Pentagon Papers* IV:371.

21. Memorandum of 1 May 1967, *Pentagon Papers* IV:465.

22. NSSM 1 [February 1969], *Congressional Record* CXVIII, part 13 (10 May 1972):16751.

23. *Pentagon Papers* IV:370.

24. Note 22 above.

25. OASD (Comptroller), SEA Statistical Summary, Table 52, 7 November 1973; *Pentagon Papers* IV:370.

26. OASD (Comptroller), SEA Statistical Summary, Table 105, 10 January 1973.

27. OASD (SA), *SEA Analysis Report*, June 1968, p. 31.

28. Memorandum to Wheeler and Sharp, 2 January 1967, *Pentagon Papers* IV:404.

29. *Ibid.*, p. 371.

30. Note 22 above, pp. 16797, 16751.

31. U.S. Department of the Army, Office of the Deputy Chief of Staff for Military Operations, "A Program for the Pacification and Long Term Development of South Vietnam" (short title: PROVN), 1 March 1966, p. 100.

32. Robert Thompson, *No Exit from Vietnam*, rev. ed. (New York, 1970), p. 144.

33. Quoted in Roger Hilsman. *To Move a Nation: The Politics of Foreign Policy in the Administration of John F. Kennedy* (Garden City, N.Y., 1967), p. 426.

34. Lewis W. Walt, *Strange War, Strange Strategy: A General's Report on Vietnam* (New York, 1970), p. 7.

35. Robert W. Komer, *Bureaucracy Does Its Thing: Institutional Constraints on U.S.-GVN Performance in Vietnam*, R-967-ARPA (Santa Monica, Calif., 1973), p. 145.

36. F. J. West, Jr., *Area Security: The Need, the Composition, and the Components*, P-3979 (Santa Monica, Calif., 1968), pp. 1–3.

37. *Pentagon Papers* IV:351.

38. Douglas Pike, *The Viet-Cong Strategy of Terror* (Saigon, 1970), pp. 82–83.

39. *Pentagon Papers* IV:351.
40. MACV, Lessons Learned no. 35, "Clear and Hold Operations," 10 January 1964, CMH.
41. William C. Westmoreland, *A Soldier Reports* (Garden City, N.Y., 1976), p. 147.
42. *Pentagon Papers* IV:351.
43. Note 31 above, p. 53.
44. Note 7 above, p. 294.
45. Robert L. Gallucci, *Neither Peace Nor Honor: The Politics of American Military Policy in Vietnam* (Baltimore, 1975), pp. 129–30.
46. Lawrence E. Grinter, "How They Lost: Doctrines, Strategies and Outcomes of the Vietnam War," *Asian Survey* XV (1975):1116.
47. MACCORDS, Province Report, Quang Ngai province, 3 February 1968, CMH.
48. Nathan Leites, *The Viet Cong Style of Politics* (Santa Monica, Calif., 1969), p. 8.
49. SAAFO, "Statistical Trends: Security Situation," April 1974.
50. OASD (SA), *SEA Analysis Report*, February 1969, p. 30.
51. Maj. Gen. R. Wetherill to COMUSMACV, 28 August 1969.
52. OASD (Comptroller), SEA Statistical Summary, Table 4, 11 February 1972.
53. MACCORDS, Province Report, Quang Nam province, January 1970, CMH.
54. U.S. Senate, Committee on Foreign Relations, *Briefing on Vietnam*, 91st Cong., 1st sess., Hearings, 18–19 November 1969, p. 118.
55. MACCORDS, "Civic Action Statistics for December 1967 and for the Year 1967," 15 February 1968, COWIN Ref. Doc. 40.
56. Jeffrey Race, *War Comes to Long An: Revolutionary Conflict in a Vietnamese Province* (Berkeley, Calif., 1972), p. 201.
57. Edward G. Lansdale, "Vietnam: Do We Understand Revolution?" *Foreign Affairs* XLIII (1964):77.
58. *Pentagon Papers* II:581.
59. Note 56 above, p. 187.
60. Charles A. Joiner, "The Organizational Theory of Revolutionary Warfare: A Review Article," *Vietnam Perspectives* II, no. 3 (February 1967):31.
61. Note 48 above, pp. 87, 114.
62. "Exchanging Advisory Influence," 25 April 1967, Leverage file, CMH.
63. Westmoreland message, "Minimizing Non-Combatant Casualties," 7 July 1965, COWIN Ref. Doc. 8.
64. COWIN Ref. Doc. 20.
65. Robert M. Kipp, "Counterinsurgency from 30,000 Feet: The B-52 in Vietnam," *Air University Review* XIX, no. 2 (January–February 1968):17.
66. Abstract from "Operational Evaluation of Armed Helicopters," Monthly Report no. 3, 16 December 1962–15 January 1963, Annex K, U.S. Forces and Pacification 1961–68 file, CMH.
67. Note 33 above, p. 465.
68. Message of 5 March 1963, JFK Library, NSF/V, vol. X, Box 196–98.

69. Note 41 above, p. 257.
70. Embassy Saigon to State, 3 February 1966, Civilian Casualties file, CMH.
71. David Douglas Duncan, *War Without Heroes* (New York, 1970), p. 113.
72. Ward S. Just, *To What End: Report from Vietnam* (Boston, 1968), pp. 150–51.
73. Edwin H. Simmons, "Marine Corps Operations in Vietnam, 1969–1972," *Naval Review 1973*, p. 207.
74. OASD (SA), *SEA Analysis Report*, August 1969, p. 45.
75. *Ibid.*, February 1967, p. 41.
76. OASD (PA), "Vietnam Fact Book," 17 August 1973.
77. U.S. Joint Logistics Review Board, *Logistics Support in the Vietnam Era* (Washington, D.C., 1970), III:2–3.
78. Note 35 above, p. 53.
79. MACV Directive 525-10, 2 March 1966, p. 2.
80. Note 7 above, p. 305; OASD (SA), *SEA Analysis Report*, November 1967, p. 24.
81. Report to the ambassador, 12 December 1967, Civilian Casualties file, CMH.
82. Memo of James A. Herbert, USAID Quang Nam, to Regional Director I Corps USAID, Danang, 2 April 1966, CMH.
83. OASD (SA), *SEA Analysis Report*, July 1967, p. 19.
84. *Ibid.*, November 1967, p. 28.
85. Nathan Leites and Charles Wolf, Jr., *Rebellion and Authority: An Analytical Essay on Insurgent Conflicts* (Chicago, 1970), p. 109.
86. U.S. Senate, Committee on Armed Services, Preparedness Investigating Subcommittee, *Investigation into Electronic Battlefield Program*, Hearings, 91st Cong., 2nd sess., 18–24 November 1970, p. 92.
87. David Ewing Ott, *Field Artillery, 1954–1973*, Vietnam Studies (Washington, D.C., 1975), p. 187.
88. Note 84 above.
89. Neil Sheehan, "Not a Dove, But No Longer a Hawk," *New York Times Magazine*, 9 October 1966, p. 137.
90. COWIN Ref. Doc. 22.
91. MACV Directive 525-3, 7 September 1965, p. 2.
92. U.S. Department of the Army, *Report of the Department of the Army Review of the Preliminary Investigations into the My Lai Incident*, 14 March 1970, I:10-18 (hereafter cited as Peers Inquiry).
93. 1st Cavalry Division (Airmobile), AAR, PERSHING, 12 February 1967–21 January 1968, 29 June 1968, Tab 2, p. 6.
94. MACV, DOD Intelligence Information Reports, Report no. 1516-0320-69, 28 March 1969.
95. Bunker to McNamara, Katzenbach, Bundy, 30 December 1967, Refugees 1967 file, CMH.
96. Memo, Senior Adviser's Policy for Combat in Populated and/or Built-up Areas, 4 April 1972, CMH.

97. Note 32 above, p. 164.
98. Herman Kahn in Frank E. Armbruster *et al.*, eds., *Can We Win in Vietnam? The American Dilemma* (London, 1968), p. 211.
99. MAVC Directive 525-3, 14 October 1966, p. 1.
100. 1st Bn, 9th Marines, AAR 1-65, 8 August 1965, Annex C.
101. Note 41 above, p. 152.
102. MACV Directive 525-3, 7 September 1965, p. 2.
103. "Guidance for Commanders in Vietnam," n.d., Peers Inquiry, vol. III, bk. 1, p. 26.
104. Message of 23 November 1969, n. 12 above, film 54.
105. Peers Inquiry, I:10-18.
106. Memo of Maj. Gen. C. S. Eckhardt, 4 April 1968, Civilian Casualties file, CMH.
107. Ellsworth Bunker, "The Vietnam Refugee Problem," November 1969, COWIN Ref. Doc. 36.
108. Bob Kelly, Report, Refugees 1967 file, CMH.
109. MACCORDS-RE, "Evaluation of Refugee Handling Operations in Quang Ngai Province," 4 September 1967, Refugees 1967 file, CMH.
110. Note 31 above, p. 4-35.
111. Jerry M. Tinker, *The Refugee Situation in Dinh Tuong Province* (McLean, Va., 1968), p. 14.
112. A. Terry Rambo, *The Causes of Refugee Movement in Viet-Nam: Report of a Survey of Refugees in I and IV Corps* (McLean, Va., 1968), p. 7.
113. Note 22 above, p. 16777.
114. U.S. Department of the Air Force, "Herbicide Operations in South-East Asia: July 1961–June 1967" (CHECO SEA Report), 11 October 1967, pp. 55–56.
115. MACCORDS-RE, "The Refugee Operation: National Overview," December 1967, Refugees 1967 file, CMH.
116. A. Terry Rambo, Jerry M. Tinker and John D. Le Noir, *The Refugee Situation in Phu-Yen Province, Vietnam*, abridged ed., (McLean, Va., 1967), p. 56.
117. State to Embassy Saigon, 3 September 1966, Refugees 1966 file, CMH.
118. USMC, *Operations of Marine Corps Forces: Vietnam 1966*, vol. II, December 1966, p. 58.
119. *Ibid., 1967*, vol. II, October 1967, p. 53.
120. USMC, *Counterinsurgency Operations* (FMFM 8-2), 22 December 1967, p. 171.
121. U. S. G. Sharp and W. C. Westmoreland, *Report on the War in Vietnam (As of 30 June 1968)* (Washington, D.C., 1969), p. 149.
122. Note 116 above, p. 63.
123. *Pentagon Papers* IV: 441, 508.
124. Richard Holdren, End of Tour Report, 24 August 1969, pp. 8–9.
125. Note 115 above.

126. Komer to Westmoreland, 29 December 1967, Civilian Casualties file, CMH.
127. Seymour J. Deitchman, *The Best-Laid Schemes: A Tale of Social Research and Bureaucracy* (Cambridge, Mass., 1976), pp. 341–42.
128. *Pentagon Papers* II:576.
129. Chester L. Cooper, *The Lost Crusade: America in Vietnam* (Greenwich, Conn., 1972), p. 494.
130. Note 7 above, p. 270.
131. *Ibid.*, p. 292.
132. Note 41 above, p. 161.
133. *Ibid.*
134. William F. Long, Jr., "Counterinsurgency Revisited," *Naval War College Review* XXI, no. 3 (November 1968):7.
135. For an excellent account of the life and trials of one such CAP see F. J. West, Jr., *The Village* (New York, 1972).
136. OASD (SA), *SEA Analysis Report,* November 1968, p. 12.
137. Note 36 above, p. 11.
138. Note 41 above, p. 166.
139. Note 35 above, p. 66.
140. Samuel P. Huntington, in Richard M. Pfeffer, ed., *No More Vietnams? The War and the Future of American Foreign Policy* (New York, 1968), p. 111.
141. Note 9 above, p. 854.
142. Harvey Meyerson, *Vinh Long* (Boston, 1970), p. 152.
143. Cf. Anne Karalekas, ed., "Conducting Military Operations," in *Report of the Commission on the Organization of the Government for the Conduct of Foreign Policy* (Robert D. Murphy Commission) (Washington, D.C., 1975), vol. IV, part 6, p. 394.
144. Note 35 above, p. 70.
145. *Ibid.*, p. 76.
146. John Mecklin, *Mission in Torment: An Intimate Account of the U.S. Role in Vietnam* (Garden City, N.Y., 1965), p. 17.
147. *Pentagon Papers* IV:351.
148. *Pentagon Papers* II:289.
149. Bernard Fall, *The Two Viet-Nams: A Political and Military Analysis,* 2nd rev. ed. (New York, 1967), p. 399.
150. MACCORDS, Province Report; Kien Hoa province, 16 February 1968, p. 3, CMH.
151. MACCORDS-RE, Task Force Oregon Operations, 13 September 1967, p. 9, U.S. Forces and Pacification 1961–68 file, CMH.
152. *Pentagon Papers* II:476–77, IV:440.
153. Note 121 above, p. 104.
154. COWIN Ref. Doc. 65, p. 6.
155. Unsigned memo for senior adviser IV CTZ, 29 October 1968.
156. Note 32 above, p. 135.
157. Note 41 above, p. 134.
158. Note 35 above, pp. 121–25.

159. Addendum to Mission Council Action Memorandum 190, 3 May 1967, CMH.
160. Robert W. Komer, "Clear, Hold, and Rebuild," *Army* XX, no. 5 (May 1970): 19.
161. "Year-end Synopsis of 1967 HES Data Changes," COWIN Ref. Doc. 2; Note 9 above, p. 875; *Pentagon Papers* IV:556.
162. Samuel P. Huntington, "Political Stability and Security in South Vietnam," a study prepared for the Policy Planning Council, Department of State, December 1967, pp. 13–21.

4. DISENGAGEMENT

1. MACCORDS, Province Report, Dinh Tuong and Kien Hoa provinces, January and February 1968, CMH.
2. MACCORDS Fact Sheet, Subject: GVN Civilian Casualties, 8 March 1969.
3. William C. Westmoreland, *A Soldier Reports* (Garden City, N.Y., 1976), p. 338.
4. *Ibid.*, p. 353.
5. *Ibid.*, p. 352.
6. *Pentagon Papers* IV:542–43.
7. Note 3 above, pp. 354–56.
8. *Ibid.*, pp. 356–57; John B. Henry II, "February 1968," *Foreign Policy*, no. 4 (Fall 1971):20–23.
9. *Pentagon Papers* IV:555–59.
10. *Ibid.*, pp. 561–68.
11. *Ibid.*, pp. 568–72.
12. *Ibid.*, pp. 575–83.
13. Note 3 above, pp. 358–59.
14. Lyndon B. Johnson, *The Vantage Point: Perspectives of the Presidency 1963–1969* (New York, 1972), pp. 418, 422. The *Pentagon Papers* erroneously date the meeting of the "Wise Men" as March 18–19.
15. Herbert Y. Schandler, *The Unmaking of a President: Lyndon Johnson and Vietnam* (Princeton, N.J., 1977), p. 302.
16. COWIN Ref. Doc. 1.
17. Leslie D. Carter, "Pacification of Quang Dien District: An Integrated Campaign," 1 March 1969, U.S. Forces and Pacification 1969–72 file, CMH.
18. Henry A. Kissinger, *American Foreign Policy*, expanded ed. (New York, 1974), pp. 104, 134.
19. MACV, "Commander's Summary of the MACV Objectives Plan," n.d., pp. 28–29, CMH.
20. MACV, "One War: MACV Command Overview 1968–72," n.d., p. 15, CMH.
21. Note 19 above, pp. 22–28.

22. Brian M. Jenkins, *The Unchangeable War*, RM-6278-1-ARPA (Santa Monica, Calif., 1972), p. 3; Douglas S. Blaufarb, *The Counterinsurgency Era: U.S. Doctrine and Performance 1950 to the Present* (New York, 1977), pp. 207, 269.

23. Martin Blumenson and James L. Stokesbury, *Masters of the Art of Command* (Boston, 1975), pp. 362–73.

24. Task Group 79.5, Special Landing Force Bravo, Command Chronology for Period 1–31 January 1969, 28 February 1969, and AAR, BOLD MARINER/RUSSELL BEACH, part II, 24 January–9 February 1969.

25. MACCORDS-PSG, 1969 Sit Rep #7, Quang Ngai province, 21 September 1969, CMH.

26. 198th Infantry Bde, 23rd Infantry Division (Americal), AAR, NANTUCKET BEACH, 20 July 1969–1 March 1971, 18 March 1971, p. 11.

27. U.S. Department of the Air Force, "Air Support in Quang Ngai Province" (CHECO SEA Report), 25 February 1970, pp. 55–56.

28. Quang Ngai Province Advisory Team 17, Province Monthly Report, 31 March 1969, p. 1.

29. USAID-compiled CWC figures, Washington National Records Center, 286-76-084 (2/68:17-1), file POL 27-15.

30. MACCORDS Refugee Directorate, reports for January, February, March 1969.

31. 19th Military History Detachment, 9th Infantry Division, after-action interview 8-67, 27 October 1967, p. 2.

32. U.S. 9th Infantry Division, AAR, SPEEDY EXPRESS, 1 December 1968—1 June 1969, 30 June 1969.

33. U.S. Department of the Army, Office Chief of Staff, memo for General Bennett, 12 January 1972, SPEEDY EXPRESS file, CMH.

34. Note 32 above, Tab E-1.

35. Julian J. Ewell and Ira A. Hunt, Jr., *Sharpening the Combat Edge: The Use of Analysis to Reinforce Military Judgment*, Vietnam Studies (Washington, D.C., 1974), p. 106.

36. MACCORDS-PSG, "Redeployment Effects of the 9th U.S. Division from Dinh Tuong and Kien Hoa Province," 3 August 1969, p. 2, CMH.

37. "Senior Officer Debriefing Report: LTG Julian J. Ewell, CG, 9th Inf. Div., Period 25 Feb 1968 to 5 April 1969," 17 September 1969, p. 12, CMH.

38. U.S. Department of the Air Force, "Riverine Operations in the Delta" (CHECO SEA Report), 31 August 1969, p. 42.

39. Kevin P. Buckley, "Pacification's Deadly Price," *Newsweek*, 19 June 1972, pp. 42–43.

40. "Letter from Saigon," *New Yorker*, 31 January 1970.

41. Note 36 above, p. 11.

42. OASD (SA), *SEA Analysis Report*, September–October 1970, p. 17 (HES scores). The figures cited are for December 1969 but had been even lower in June 1969, at the conclusion of SPEEDY EXPRESS.

43. U.S. Department of the Air Force, "Operation DELAWARE, 19 April–17 May 1968" (CHECO SEA Report), 2 September 1968; Willard Pearson, *The*

War in the Northern Provinces, Vietnam Studies (Washington, D.C., 1975), pp. 89–92.

44. 22nd Military History Detachment, "Narrative APACHE SNOW, 101st Airborne Division, 10 May–7 June 1969," n.d.

45. David Hoffman, "Hamburger Hill: The Army's Rationale," *Washington Post,* 23 May 1969.

46. Melvin Zais, "Battle at Dong Ap Bia (Hamburger Hill)," 5 January 1971, p. 2, CMH.

47. *Vietnam Courier,* no. 219, 2 June 1969, p. 7.

48. MACCORDS, Province Report, Thua Thien province, March, May, July 1969, CMH.

49. Facts on File, *South Vietnam,* IV (New York, 1973), p. 63.

50. Address to the nation, 3 November 1969, U.S. President, *Public Papers of the Presidents of the United States: Richard Nixon 1969* (Washington, D.C., 1971), p. 906.

51. OASD (Comptroller), SEA Statistical Summary, Table 860B, 18 February 1976.

52. F. J. West, Jr., "U.S. Strategy and Policy: The Da Nang Case," n.d., p. 3, Area Security file, CMH.

53. 2nd Bn, 7th Marines, 1st Marine Division, Command Chronology, 1–31 May 1968; 27th Marines, 1st Marine Division, AAR, ALLENBROOK, 1 September 1968.

54. 1st Marines, 1st Marine Division, AAR, PIPESTONE CANYON, 26 May–7 November 1969, 31 May 1970, p. 52.

55. Edwin H. Simmons, "Marine Corps Operations in Vietnam, 1968," *U.S. Naval Institute Proceedings* XCVI (May 1970):318.

56. *Ibid.*

57. Note 54 above, p. 41.

58. MACCORDS, Province Report, Quang Nam province, January 1970, p. 7, CMH; Edwin H. Simmons, "Marine Corps Operations in Vietnam, 1969–72," *Naval Review, 1973,* p. 211.

59. Marine Task Group 97.4, AAR, DARING REBEL, 8 June 1969; Command Chronology, 1–31 May 1969.

60. III MAF, ROKMC/USMC Operation DEFIANT STAND, 2–19 September 1969; Marine Task Group 79.4, Special Landing Force Alfa, AAR, DEFIANT STAND.

61. Republic of Vietnam, Directorate General of Planning, *Viet Nam Statistical Yearbook 1970,* Table 304, p. 363.

62. *Ibid.*

63. OASD (SA), *SEA Analysis Report,* March–April 1971, p. 32.

64. MACCORDS, Province Report, Quang Nam province, December 1969, p. 6, CMH.

65. MACCORDS, Refugee Division, I CTZ, CORDS Refugee Field Program Report, Period 21 November 1969 through 20 December 1969, Refugees 1970 file, CMH.

66. George J. Klein, "Observations on the Refugee Program in I, II and IV CTZ," 18 June 1969, p. 8.

67. *Ibid.*, p. 19.

68. OASD (Comptroller), SEA Statistical Summary, Table 103, 26 September 1973.

69. Cf. James P. Sterba, "After Dark in Queson Valley: 'If It Moves, Shoot It,' " *New York Times,* 7 March 1970.

70. MACCORDS-PSG, "Quang Nam Province," 29 February 1972, CMH.

71. Robert D. Heinl, "The Collapse of the Armed Forces," *Armed Forces Journal* CVIII, no. 19 (7 June 1971):30.

72. Laird to Hebert, 14 September 1971, reprinted in U.S. House, Committee on Internal Security, *Investigation of Attempts to Subvert the United States Armed Forces,* Hearings, 92nd Cong., 2nd sess., 1972, pp. 7080–81.

73. CG, USARV, to Army Commanders, 19 July 1971, pp. 1–2, CMH.

74. Allan H. Fisher, Jr., *Preliminary Findings from the 1971 DOD Survey of Drug Use* (Alexandria, Va., 1972), p. 23.

75. Martin Luther King, "Declaration of Independence from the War in Vietnam," *Ramparts* V, no. 11 (May 1967):33.

76. U.S. Department of Commerce, *Statistical Abstract of the United States 1970,* Table 388, p. 258; Thomas C. Thayer, "War Without Fronts," *Journal of Defense Research,* Series B, Tactical Warfare Analysis of Viet Nam Data, vol. 7B, no. 3 (Fall 1975):854–55.

77. Cf. Gilbert Badillo and G. David Curry, "The Social Incidence of Vietnam Casualties: Social Class or Race?" *Armed Forces and Society* II (1976): 397–406.

78. Bryan G. Fiman *et al.,* "Black-White and American-Vietnamese Relations Among Soldiers in Vietnam," *Journal of Social Issues* XXXI, no. 4 (Fall 1975): 46.

79. II Field Force Vietnam Commanders' Conference, Talking Paper: Racial Problems, n.d.

80. Staff Judge Advocate 25th Infantry Division, "Civil Rights and Industrial Relations," 29 September 1968.

81. Cf. D. B. Bell and T. J. Houston, *The Vietnam Era Deserter: Characteristics of Unconvicted Army Deserters Participating in the Presidential Clemency Program* (Arlington, Va., 1976), pp. 29, 45.

82. MACCORDS-PSG, "Anti-Americanism and the Viet Cong," 24 December 1970, pp. 1–2, CMH.

83. MACCORDS-PSG, "Anti-American Demonstrations in Qui Nhon," 18 April 1971, pp. 4–5, 14, CMH.

84. Note 72 above, p. 7070.

85. Charles C. Moskos, Jr., "The American Combat Soldier in Vietnam," *Journal of Social Issues* XXXI, no. 4 (Fall 1975):36. An inflated estimate of GI dissent is found in some of the books dealing with this subject: Andy Stapp, *Up Against the Brass* (New York, 1970); Fred Halstead, *GIs Speak Out Against*

the War (New York, 1970); Fred Gardner, *The Unlawful Concert* (New York, 1970).

86. U.S. Senate, Committee on the Judiciary, Subcommittee to Investigate the Administration of the Internal Security Act and Other Internal Security Laws, *Organized Subversion in the U.S. Armed Forces, part 1: The U.S. Navy,* Hearings, 94th Cong., 1st sess., 25 September 1975, pp. 32–33.
87. The USMC desertion and AWOL rates were 105.0 and 300.9 respectively per 1,000 average monthly strength. The Navy's desertion rate, which until FY 1967 had never gone above 11.1, in FY 1976 reached 24.8 per 1,000; data provided by OASD (Manpower and Reserve Affairs).
88. See Moskos, note 85 above, p. 32. See also Robert L. Pettera, "Psychiatric Management of Combat Reactions with Emphasis on a Reaction Unique to Vietnam," *Military Medicine* CXXXIV (1969):673–78.
89. *U.S. News and World Report,* 25 January 1971, pp. 9–10F.
90. Peter G. Bourne, "Military Psychiatry and the Viet Nam Experience," *American Journal of Psychiatry* CXXVII (1970):482.
91. Spurgeon Neel, *Medical Support of the U.S. Army in Vietnam: 1965–1970,* Vietnam Studies (Washington, D.C., 1973), pp. 45–47.
92. Testimony of Gen. Bruce Palmer, Jr., Army Vice Chief of Staff, before U.S. House, Committee on Appropriations, Subcommittee on Department of Defense, *DOD Appropriations for 1972,* Hearings, 92nd Cong., 1st sess., part 9, 23 September 1971, pp. 578–82.
93. Note 83 above, p. 18.
94. Note 73 above, pp. 7–8.
95. *Ibid.,* pp. 6–7.
96. Paul L. Savage and Richard A. Gabriel, "Cohesion and Disintegration in the American Army: An Alternative Perspective," *Armed Forces and Society* II (1976):340–76. See also their book *Crisis in Command: Mismanagement in the United States Army* (New York, 1978).

5. THE TRAVAIL OF VIETNAMIZATION

1. *Public Papers of the Presidents of the United States: John F. Kennedy 1963* (Washington, D.C., 1964), p. 652.
2. *Public Papers of the Presidents of the United States: Lyndon B. Johnson 1968–69* (Washington, D.C., 1970), Bk. I, p. 471.
3. *Pentagon Papers* IV:376, 503.
4. *Ibid.,* p. 376.
5. OASD (SA), *SEA Analysis Report,* September 1968, p. 19, and November 1968, p. 36.
6. William C. Westmoreland, *A Soldier Reports* (Garden City, N.Y., 1976), p. 222.
7. *Pentagon Papers* IV:467.

8. See Lee Ewing, "Exclusive Interview with the Former Premier," *Air Force Times*, 4 June 1975, p. 5.

9. John Paul Roche, in Morton A. Kaplan *et al.*, *Vietnam Settlement: Why 1973, Not 1969?* (Washington, D.C., 1973), p. 156.

10. Don Oberdorfer, *Tet!* (Garden City, N.Y., 1971), p. 105; Lyndon B. Johnson, *The Vantage Point: Perspectives of the Presidency 1963–1969* (New York, 1971), p. 261.

11. Herbert Y. Schandler, *The Unmaking of a President: Lyndon Johnson and Vietnam* (Princeton, N.J., 1977), pp. 179–80.

12. James L. Collins, *The Development and Training of the South Vietnamese Army 1950–1972*, Vietnam Studies (Washington, D.C., 1975), pp. 88–89.

13. OASD (Comptroller), SEA Statistical Summary, Table 7, 9 February 1972, and Table 3, 26 September 1973.

14. Note 12 above, pp. 90–91.

15. Note 13 above, Table 35, 18 April 1973.

16. Norman H. Stutzer, "Vietnamization Progress," *Ordnance* LVI (1971):229.

17. Note 6 above, p. 294.

18. MACV, "Commander's Summary of the MACV Objectives Plan," n.d., p. 30, CMH.

19. Note 12 above, pp. 129–30.

20. See, e.g., his memo of 25 April 1967, Leverage file, CMH.

21. MACCORDS, Province Report, Phu Yen province, 30 September 1970, p. 6, CMH.

22. Note 12 above, p. 75.

23. John Paul Vann memo, "Improvement of Security Within South Vietnam," 13 November 1967, U.S. Forces and Pacification 1961–68 file, CMH.

24. NSSM 1, *Congressional Record* CXVIII, part 13 (May 10, 1972):16803.

25. Thomas C. Thayer, "War Without Fronts," *Journal of Defense Research*, Series B., Tactical Warfare Analysis of Viet Nam Data, Vol. 7B, no. 3 (Fall 1975):812.

26. Note 12 above, p. 100.

27. Note 23 above.

28. Matthew B. Ridgeway, "Indochina: Disengaging," *Foreign Affairs* XLIX (1971):588.

29. MACCORDS-PSG, "Dinh Binh Province—the Challenge, 1971," 12 June 1971, CMH.

30. OASD (SA), *SEA Analysis Report*, August–October 1971, p. 8.

31. MACV, *Command History, 1970*, II: VII-29, CMH; n. 5 above, February 1970, p. 54.

32. Note 25 above, p. 911.

33. Quoted in Edward H. Simmons, "Marine Corps Operations in Vietnam, 1969–1972," *Naval Review 1973*, p. 223.

34. Note 6 above, p. 252.

35. Cf. Erik Castrén, *The Present Law of War and Neutrality* (Helsinki, 1954), pp. 462–63; Morris Greenspan, *The Modern Law of Land Warfare* (Berkeley,

Calif., 1959), p. 538; L. Oppenheim and H. Lauterpacht, *International Law*, 7th ed. (London, 1952), II:695, n. 1.

36. Note 25 above, p. 837.

37. Note 5 above, October 1968, pp. 34–36; n. 25 above, p. 837.

38. COSVN Circular of 1 February 1968, in Patrick J. McGarvey, *Visions of Victory: Selected Vietnamese Communist Military Writings, 1964–1968* (Stanford, Calif., 1969), p. 253.

39. Paul Berman, *Revolutionary Organization: Institution-Building Within the People's Liberation Armed Forces* (Lexington, Mass., 1974), pp. 168–78.

40. *Ibid.*, pp. 69, 77; Douglas Pike, *Viet Cong: The Organization and Techniques of the National Liberation Front of South Vietnam* (Cambridge, Mass., 1966), p. 376.

41. Edward A. Shils and Morris Janowitz, "Cohesion and Disintegration in the German Wehrmacht in World War II," *Public Opinion Quarterly* XII (1948): 280–315.

42. Nathan Leites, *The Viet Cong Style of Politics* (Santa Monica, Calif., 1969), pp. 109, 95.

43. Charles C. Moskos, Jr., *The American Enlisted Man: The Rank and File in Today's Military* (New York, 1970), p. 147.

44. Nathan Leites and Charles Wolf, Jr., *Rebellion and Authority: An Analytical Essay on Insurgent Conflicts* (Chicago, 1970), p. 150.

45. Memo by Robert H. Johnson for Mr. Rostow, 6 October 1961, pp. 1–2, JFK Library, NSF/V, vol. I, Box 192-4.

46. MACV, "A Partial Outline of U.S. Communications with Republic of Vietnam Regarding Compliance with the Law of Land Warfare," n.d.

47. *Pentagon Papers* II:584.

48. MACCORDS, Province Report, Phong Dinh province, February 1968, p. 5, CMH.

49. Note 24 above, pp. 16804, 16819.

50. MACCORDS-PSG, "Trip Report of the Delta," 1 January 1973, p. 4, CMH.

51. MACCORDS-PSG, "RVNAF Depredation," 31 December 1971, p. 8, CMH.

52. Memo by Dennis G. Harter for Ambassador Colby, 31 March 1970; memo by Alexander Firfer for CORDS Refugee Directorate, 14 May 1970; CORDS, Refugee Field Program Report, I CTZ, 20 February 1970; W. E. Colby to Prime Minister Tran Thien Khiem, 2 February 1970.

53. MACCORDS-PSG, "The People of the U-Minh Forest Area: A Survey of Their Attitudes in the Context of Past and Present VC/GVN Activities." 10 June 1971, CMH.

54. MACCORDS-PSG, "Highland Resettlement: Lessons Learned," 12 May 1971, pp. 3, 15, CMH.

55. MACCORDS-PSG, "An Evaluation of the Pacification Program of Cat Hanh Village, Binh Dinh Province," 6 April 1970, pp. 15–16, CMH.

56. CPDC Communiqué 1412, Refugees 1971 file, CMH.

57. MACV Directive 525-3, 14 October 1966, p. 3.

58. Note 46 above, p. 3.

59. Brian M. Jenkins, *A People's Army for South Vietnam: A Vietnamese Solution*, R-897 (Santa Monica, Calif., 1971), p. 9.
60. Lt. Col. Robert E. Wagner, Province Senior Adviser, Quang Tin province, Completion of Tour Report, 10 June 1972, Quang Tin province file, CMH.
61. Note 30 above, p. 8.
62. Lt. Col. Raymond L. Fleigh, Province Senior Adviser, Binh Duong province, Completion of Tour Report, 9 November 1970, p. 5.
63. Note 55 above, p. 15.
64. Col. Nguyen Be, one-time commandant of the National Training Center at Vung Tau, cited by Jeffrey Race, *War Comes to Long An: Revolutionary Conflict in a Vietnamese Province* (Berkeley, Calif., 1972), p. 245.
65. Cf. Donald S. Marshall, memo, Discussions with Col. Do Ngoc Nhan and Col. Nguyen Quoc Quynh, 31 August 1969, CMH.
66. Note 13 above, Table 3, 26 September 1973.
67. George G. Tucker, Jr., Province Senior Adviser, Quang Nam province, Completion of Tour Report, 9 June 1972, Quang Nam province file, CMH.
68. William Bredo, "Agrarian Reform in Vietnam: Vietcong and Government of Vietnam Strategies in Conflict," *Asian Survey* X (1970):738–39; Richard Critchfield, *The Long Charade: Political Subversion in the Vietnam War* (New York, 1968), p. 195.
69. Robert L. Sansom, *The Economics of Insurgency in the Mekong Delta of Vietnam* (Cambridge, Mass., 1970), p. 217.
70. Roy L. Prosterman, "Land-to-the Tiller in South Vietnam: The Tables Turn," *Asian Survey* X (1970):759–60.
71. For the complete text of Law 003/70 see MacDonald Salter, "The Broadening Base of Land Reform in South Vietnam," *Asian Survey* X (1970):734–37.
72. Note 64 above, pp. 273–74.
73. U.S. Senate, Committee on Foreign Relations, *Vietnam: May 1972*, a staff report (Washington, D.C. 1972), p. 29.

6. VIETNAMIZATION ON TRIAL

1. OASD (SA), *SEA Analysis Report*, August–October 1971, pp. 23–24.
2. Allan E. Goodman, "South Vietnam and the New Security," *Asian Survey* XII (1972):123.
3. Robert W. Komer, "Impact of Pacification on Insurgency," *Journal of International Affairs* XXV (1971):55.
4. *Ibid.*, p. 60.
5. Albert G. Bole, Jr., and K. Kobata, *An Evaluation of the Measurements of the Hamlet Evaluation System* (Newport, R.I.: Naval War College, 1975).
6. MACCORDS, Province Report, Phu Yen province, 30 November 1970, p. 5, CMH.
7. Steve Young, "Political Attitudes and Organization in Binh Duong," 1 March 1970, p. 3, Binh Duong province file, CMH.

8. Donald I. Colin, Deputy Province Senior Adviser, Vinh Binh province, End of Tour Report, 19 August 1971, p. 2, Vinh Binh province file, CMH.

9. MACCORDS, Province Report, Binh Dinh province, 1 September 1971, CMH.

10. MACCORDS-PSG, "Binh Dinh Province—the Challenge, 1971," 12 June 1971, pp. 25–27, CMH.

11. *Ibid.*, pp. 34–35, 37.

12. OASD (SA), *SEA Analysis Report*, November 1971–January 1972, p. 9.

13. Cf. Robert Thompson, *Peace Is Not at Hand* (New York, 1974), chap. 6.

14. MACCORDS-PSG, "Impact of the Enemy Offensive on Pacification," 16 September 1972, p. 2, CMH.

15. *Ibid.*, pp. 3–4.

16. Note 13 above, pp. 110–11.

17. *Ibid.*, pp. 111–12.

18. *Ibid.*, pp. 109–10.

19. OASD (Comptroller), SEA Statistical Summary, Table 322, 24 October 1973.

20. *Ibid.*, Table 9, 7 November 1973.

21. Note 13 above, pp. 99, 113–14.

22. *Ibid.*, p. 110.

23. Testimony of Col. Henry A. Shockley before the House Select Committee on Intelligence, *U.S. Intelligence Agencies and Activities: The Performance of the Intelligence Community*, Hearings, 94th Cong., 1st sess., part 5, 4 November–17 December 1975, p. 1657.

24. Lt. Col. Robert E. Wagner, Province Senior Adviser, Quang Tin province, Completion of Tour Report, 10 June 1972, p. 4, Quang Tin province file, CMH.

25. MACCORDS, Military Region 4 Overview, 31 July 1972, p. 2, CMH.

26. MACCORDS, Province Report, Vinh Long province, 31 May 1972, p. 3, CMH.

27. Henry Kissinger, in an interview with Pierre Salinger of *L'Express*, 12 April 1975, Department of State, Bureau of Public Affairs, Office of Media Services release.

28. F. P. Serong, "Vietnam After the Cease-Fire," *Asian Affairs* II, no. 1 (September–October 1974):17; Robert Thompson, "Why Did Hanoi Sign the Cease-Fire Agreement?" *Ordnance* LVIII (July–August 1973):50.

29. The letters were made public on 30 April 1975 by Nguyen Tien Hung, former GVN Minister of Planning and a personal assistant to President Thieu in 1973, and were printed in *The New York Times*, 1 May 1975. There is no reason to doubt their authenticity.

30. Full text in Facts on File, *South Vietnam*, VII (New York, 1973), pp. 235–36.

31. *Ibid.*, p. 280.

32. *Ibid.*, p. 290.

33. See also Kissinger's news conference of 29 April 1975 (State Department PR 220/53), in which the secretary of state indirectly confirmed this account.

34. The vote came on an amendment to a supplemental appropriations bill. A

reluctant Nixon signed it into law on 1 July 1973. See *Congressional Quarterly Weekly Report* XXXI (1973):1854.

35. U.S. Department of State, Working Paper on the North Vietnamese Role in the War in South Viet-Nam, n.d., Appendices, Doc. 303, p. 14.
36. Van Tien Dung, "Great Spring Victory," *Foreign Broadcast Information Service*, Daily Report, Asia and Pacific, vol. IV, no. 110, Supp. 38, 7 June 1976, pp. 1–2.
37. *Ibid.*, p. 3.
38. Drew Middleton, "Pentagon Cites Build-Up by Hanoi," *The New York Times*, 4 March 1974.
39. U.S. Senate, Committee on Foreign Relations, *Vietnam: May 1974*, a staff report, 93rd Cong., 2nd sess., 5 August 1974, p. 6.
40. Note 30 above, p. 202.
41. U.S. House, Committee on Foreign Affairs, *Fiscal Year 1975 Foreign Assistance Request*, Hearings, 93rd Cong. 2nd sess., 4 June–11 July 1974, p. 27.
42. U.S. Senate, Committee on Foreign Relations, *Foreign Assistance Authorization*, Hearings, 93rd Cong., 2nd sess., 7 June–25 July 1974, p. 19.
43. *Ibid.*, p. 406.
44. Note 39 above, p. 22.
45. Note 36 above, p. 5.
46. JCS/J-5, "Vietnam Fact Book," 28 February 1975, p. 12; U.S. Embassy Saigon, Defense Attaché Office, Army Division, Final Report, Vol. III, 18 June 1975, Tab N.
47. U.S. House, Committee on Foreign Affairs, Subcommittee on Asian and Pacific Affairs, *Report on the Situation in the Republic of Vietnam*, Hearings, 93rd Cong., 2nd sess., 31 July 1974, p. 5.
48. U.S. Embassy Saigon, Defense Attaché Office, RVNAF Quarterly Assessment, 1 February 1975, p. 2.
49. Note 39 above, p. 5.
50. Le Hoang Trong (pseud.), "Survival and Self-Reliance: A Vietnamese Viewpoint," *Asian Survey* XV (1975):283.
51. Note 48 above, p. 2-8.
52. Note 36 above, pp. 5–6.
53. John C. Donnell, "South Vietnam in 1975: The Year of Communist Victory," *Asian Survey* XVI (1976):1
54. Note 36 above, pp. 7–8.
55. *Ibid.*, pp. 18, 35–41.
56. Denis Warner, *Not with Guns Alone: How Hanoi Won the War* (London, 1977), pp. 13–14.
57. Defense Attaché Office, n. 46 above, vol. I, 18 June 1975, p. 9.
58. Cf. W. Scott Thompson, "The Indochina Debacle and the United States," *Orbis* XIX (1975):996. See also Jean Lacouture, "Vietnam After the Debacle," *New York Review of Books*, 1 May 1975, p. 34, who speaks of an imminent putsch of officers against Thieu.
59. U.S. Embassy Saigon, Defense Attaché Office, RVNAF Final Assessment, 15 June 1975, pp. 6-30, 16-B-6.

60. Note 36 above, vol. IV, no. 131, Supp. 42, 7 July 1976, pp. 64–65.
61. Note 59 above, p. 1-11.
62. Note 36 above, p. 16.
63. Note 59 above, p. 16-B-7.
64. Note 60 above, p. 80.
65. *Ibid.*, p. 114. See also Frank Snepp, *Decent Interval* (New York, 1977), p. 326.
66. Cf. Thompson, n. 58 above, p. 994.
67. See, e.g., Gareth Porter, *A Peace Denied: The United States, Vietnam and the Paris Agreements* (Bloomington, Ind., 1975).
68. Tiziano Terzani, *Giai Phong: The Fall and Liberation of Saigon.* trans. John Shepley (New York, 1976), p. 111.
69. Note 59 above, p. 10-18.
70. Cf. Peter Arnett, "Once-Ranking Vietnamese Make Way in U.S.," *The New York Times*, 22 November 1975.
71. Fox Butterfield, "How South Vietnam Died—By the Stab in the Front," *New York Times Magazine*, 15 May 1975, p. 35.
72. Matthew B. Ridgeway, "Indochina: Disengaging," *Foreign Affairs* XLIX (1971):588.
73. Michael Curtis, "American Interests in the Middle East," *Middle East Review*, no. 8 (Spring/Summer 1976):15.
74. Special Assistant to the Ambassador for Field Operations, "Statistical Trends: Security Situation, April 1974," CMH.
75. MACCORDS-PSG, "Trip Report Through the Delta by James H. Holl and Lee Braddock," 10 January 1973, p. 5, CMH.
76. Cited by Allan E. Goodman, "South Vietnam: War Without End?" *Asian Survey* XV (1975):82.
77. Note 50 above, p. 289.
78. Le-Thi-Que, A. Terry Rambo and Garry D. Murfin, "Why They Fled: Refugee Movement During the Spring 1975 Communist Offensive in South Vietnam," *Asian Survey* XVI (1976):855–63.
79. Robert Shaplen, *The Road from War: Vietnam 1965–1971*, rev. ed. (New York, 1971), p. 218.
80. Note 23 above, p. 1659.
81. News Conference with Secretary of Defense James R. Schlesinger at the Pentagon, 2 April 1975, typescript, p. 5.
82. This point is well made by W. Scott Thompson, n. 58 above, p. 995.

7. AMERICAN MILITARY TACTICS AND THE LAW OF WAR

1. Noam Chomsky, *For Reasons of State* (New York, 1973), p. 19.
2. Committee of Concerned Asian Scholars, *The Indochina Story: A Fully Documented Account* (New York, 1970), p. 128.
3. For example, Art. 142, Geneva Convention Relative to the Treatment of Prisoners of War, 12 August 1949, U.S. Department of the Air Force, *Treaties*

Governing Land Warfare (Air Force Pamphlet 110-1-3), 21 July 1958, p. 117.

4. Cf. James E. Bond, *The Rules of Riot: Internal Conflict and the Law of War* (Princeton, N.J., 1974); Henri Meyrowitz, "The Law of War in the Vietnamese Conflict," in Richard A. Falk, ed., *The Vietnam War and International Law* (Princeton, N.J., 1969), II:516–49.

5. Verbal Presentation of Col. A. T. Sampson in Gov. Harriman's office, 11 December 1962, Civilian Casualties file, CMH.

6. MACV Directive 525-3, 7 September 1965, p. 2.

7. Clergy and Laymen Concerned About Vietnam, *In the Name of America* (New York, 1968), p. 7.

8. Geneva Convention Relative to the Protection of Civilian Persons in Time of War, 12 August 1949, n. 3 above, p. 150.

9. L. Oppenheim and H. Lauterpacht, *International Law*, 7th ed. (London, 1952), II:415–16.

10. *U.S. v. Wilhelm List et al.*, *Trials of War Criminals Before the Nuremberg Military Tribunals Under Control Council Law no. 10* (Washington, D.C., 1950), XI:1297. See also the discussion by Robert E. Jordan III in Peter D. Trooboff, ed., *Law and Responsibility in Warfare: The Vietnam Experience* (Chapel Hill, N.C., 1975), p. 57.

11. International Committee of the Red Cross, *Draft Rules for the Limitation of Dangers Incurred by the Civilian Population in Time of War* (Geneva, 1956), Art. 11.

12. Report of the Secretary General, "Respect for Human Rights in Armed Conflicts," 18 September 1970, UN Doc. A/8052 (1970), p. 15.

13. MACV Directive 525-13, Change 1, 14 February 1969, p. 1.

14. Richard A. Falk, introduction to Frank Browning and Dorothy Forman, eds., *The Wasted Nations* (New York, 1972).

15. Note 7 above, p. 1.

16. Note 3 above, Art. 4, p. 69.

17. Note 8 above, Art. 28, p. 145.

18. Hague Convention No. IV Respecting the Laws and Customs of War on Land, 18 October 1907, Annex, Art. 25, n. 3 above, p. 13.

19. MACV Directive 20-4, 25 March 1966, p. 1.

20. Note 8 above, Art. 19, p. 141. See also n. 18 above, Art. 27, p. 13.

21. U.S. Department of the Army, *The Law of Land Warfare* (FM 27-10), 18 July 1956, par. 41, p. 19.

22. Note 10 above, p. 1196.

23. See on this also Franklin A. Hart, "Yamashita, Nuremberg and Vietnam: Command Responsibility Reappraised," *Naval War College Review* XXV, no. 1 (September–October 1972):31–32.

24. See my discussion of body count in chapter 3.

25. Note 8 above, Art. 53, p. 152.

26. Kenneth J. Hodson to Lothar H. Belck, 20 October 1966, JAGW 1966/1462, International Affairs Division, JAGO, Department of the Army.

27. MACV Directives 95-2, 95-4, 525-13, 525-18. See also, generally, U.S. De-

partment of the Army, Deputy Chief of Staff for Military Operations, "An Analysis of the Evolution of MACV Rules of Engagement Pertaining to Ground Operations 1965–69," n.d., CMH.

28. "Vietnam and the Nuremberg Principles: A Colloquy on War Crimes," in Falk, n. 4 above, vol. IV (1976), p. 369.

29. MACV, Inspector General, "Summaries of Reports and Investigations, and Inquiries 1967–72" (film), Investigation of Destruction Resulting from VC Offensive, 3 June 1968.

30. MACV Directive 525-13, 9 March 1969 and 27 April 1969, Annex A, p. 3.

31. Report to the Ambassador, 12 December 1967, Civilian Casualties file, CMH.

32. Note 29 above.

33. Memo of 1 December 1969, HIMS Microfilm Collection, film 54, U.S. Army Military History Research Collection, Carlisle Barracks, Pa.

34. Douglas Kinnard, "Vietnam Reconsidered: An Attitudinal Survey of U.S. Army General Officers," *Public Opinion Quarterly* XXXIX (1976):451.

35. James D. Hataway to the ambassador, "Destruction in Quang Ngai and Quang Tin," 26 January 1968, p. 1, Civilian Casualties file, CMH. This memo constitutes observations on the research project cited in n. 31 above.

36. MACV Directive 95-4, 28 June 1966, Annex D, p. 2, and Change 1, 14 February 1967, p. 1.

37. Note 35 above, p. 2.

38. MACV Directive 525-13, 9 March 1969, p. 1.

39. U.S. Department of the Air Force, "Strike Control and Reconnaissance (SCAR) in Southeast Asia" (CHECO SEA Report), 22 January 1969, p. 63.

40. U.S. Army Aviation Group (Provisional), Command Memorandum no. 1, 4 August 1965, p. 3, COWIN Ref. Doc. 27.

41. U.S. Army Aviation Brigade (Provisional), Commander's Notes no. 2, 18 April 1966, p. 1, COWIN Ref. Doc. 28.

42. U.S. Army Aviation Brigade (Provisional), Commander's Notes no. 11, 14 March 1967, p. 3, COWIN Ref. Doc. 30.

43. Seymour M. Hersh, "The Reprimand," *The New Yorker*, 9 October 1971, pp. 114, 116.

44. Note 38 above, Annex A, p. 6.

45. Peers Inquiry, I:8-13.

46. U.S. House, Committee on Armed Services, Armed Services Investigating Subcommittee, *Investigation of the My Lai Incident*, Report, 91st Cong., 2nd sess., 15 July 1970, p. 48.

47. Telford Taylor, *Nuremberg and Vietnam: An American Tragedy* (New York, 1971), p. 182 (my references are to the Bantam ed.).

48. U.S. Department of the Army, Office of the Deputy Chief of Staff for Military Operations, "Final Report of the Research Project: Conduct of the War in Vietnam" (COWIN), May 1971, CMH.

49. "Outline of the Research Project: Conduct of the War in Vietnam," Civilian Casualties file, CMH.

50. U.S. Army Forces, Pacific, Office of the Theatre Judge Advocate, "Review of

the Record of Trial by a Military Commission of Tomoyuki Yamashita, General, Imperial Japanese Army," 26 December 1945, quoted in COWIN, Legal Annex, p. 19.

51. *In re Yamashita*, 327 U.S. 17 (1946).

52. Cf. William H. Parks, "Command Responsibility for War Crimes," *Military Law Review* LXII (1973):36.

53. *U.S. v. Wilhelm von Leeb et al.*, n. 10 above, XI:543–44.

54. Note 21 above, par. 501, pp. 178–79.

55. U.S. Department of the Army, *Army Subject Schedule 27-1, The Geneva Conventions of 1949 and Hague Convention No. IV of 1907*, 8 October 1970, p. 11.

56. *Manual for Courts-Martial, United States 1969*, rev. ed. (Washington, D.C., 1969), par. 171(c), p. 28-22, and par. 198(b), p. 28-46.

57. Cf. Jordan J. Paust, letter to the editor, *Naval War College Review* XXV (1973):103–7.

58. Note 55 above, p. 10.

59. Note 3 above, Art. 23(e), p. 12.

60. Note 21 above, par. 34, p. 18.

61. *Ibid.*

62. Stockholm International Peace Research Institute, *Incendiary Weapons* (Cambridge, Mass., 1975), pp. 40–50.

63. MACV Directive 525-18, 19 October 1966, p. 3.

64. U.S. House, Committee on Armed Services, Special Subcommittee on Tactical Air Support, *Close Air Support*, Hearings, 89th Cong., 1st sess., 22 September–14 October 1965, p. 4738.

65. Bernard W. Rogers, *Cedar Falls—Junction City: A Turning Point*, Vietnam Studies (Washington, D.C., 1974), p. 72.

66. Quoted in Zalin Grant, *Survivors* (New York, 1975), p. 51.

67. William F. Pepper, "The Children of Vietnam," *Ramparts* V, no. 7 (January 1967):59.

68. Note 14 above, p. 295.

69. Testimony of Dr. John D. Constable, 18 May 1967, U.S. Senate, Committee on the Judiciary, Subcommittee to Investigate Problems Connected with Refugees and Escapees, *Civilian Casualty, Social Welfare and Refugee Problems in South Vietnam*, Hearings, 90th Cong., 1st sess., 10 May–16 October 1967, pp. 245–46.

70. USAID, "Report of the Vietnam Medical Appraisal Team," 20 September 1967, p. 83.

71. John H. Knowles, "Vietnam Diary—Medicine and Politics," *The Pharos* XXX (1967):142.

72. Alister Brass, *Bleeding Earth: A Doctor Looks at Vietnam* (London, 1968), p. 26; Barbara Evans, *Caduceus to Saigon: A Medical Mission to South Vietnam* (London, 1968), p. 45.

73. MACCORDS, "Analysis Report of January 1973 Province Reports and Military Region Overviews," n.d., CMH.

74. "The Massacre of Dak Son," *Time*, 15 December 1967, pp. 32–34. See also George E. Cushmac, "Enemy Napalm in Vietnam," *Army* XVIII, no. 8 (August 1968):58–59.
75. Peter Reich and Victor W. Sidel, "Napalm," *New England Journal of Medicine* CCLXXVII (13 July 1967):87.
76. Testimony of Dr. Theodore S. Tapper, n. 69 above, p. 246.
77. H. A. F. Dudley *et al.*, "Civilian Battle Casualties in South Vietnam," *British Journal of Surgery* LV (1968):334.
78. Cf. Tom J. Farer, "The Laws of War 25 Years After Nuremberg," *International Conciliation*, no. 583 (May 1971):22.
79. Ann van Wynen Thomas and A. J. Thomas, Jr., *Legal Limits on the Use of Chemical and Biological Weapons* (Dallas, 1970), p. 155.
80. Joseph W. Bishop, Jr., *Justice Under Fire: A Study of Military Law* (New York, 1974), p. 270.
81. 7th Air Force (PACAF) Regulation 55-49, 3 November 1969, p. 9.
82. Note 21 above, par. 36, p. 18.
83. Cf. U.S. Department of the Army, *International Law*, vol. II (Pamphlet 27-161-2), 23 October 1962, p. 42.
84. Note 62 above, pp. 69–73, 83–86.
85. U.S. Army Munitions Command, "Riot Control Agents for the Vietnam War," Historical Monograph AMC56M (June 1970), p. 3.
86. John H. Hay, Jr., *Tactical and Materiel Innovations*, Vietnam Studies (Washington, D.C., 1974), p. 35.
87. Statement made by Secretary Rusk on 24 March 1965, U.S. Senate, Committee on Foreign Relations, *Background Information Relating to Southeast Asia and Vietnam*, 89th Cong., 1st sess., 16 June 1965, pp. 196–97.
88. Note 86 above, p. 36.
89. Westmoreland to CINCPAC, 9 September 1965, CMH.
90. George H. Aldrich in Trooboff, n. 10 above, p. 175.
91. Note 79 above, p. 147.
92. U.S. Department of the Army, *Employment of Chemical and Biological Agents* (FM 3-10), 31 March 1966, par. 46(a), pp. 25–26.
93. 1st Cavalry Division, AAR, MASHER/WHITE WING, 25 January–6 March 1966, 28 April 1966, p. 22.
94. 1st Cavalry Division, AAR, PERSHING—Search and Destroy, 12 February 1967–21 January 1968, 29 June 1968.
95. MACV Directive 525-11, 28 March 1970, p. 4.
96. U.S. House, Committee on Foreign Affairs, Subcommittee on National Security Policy and Scientific Developments, *Chemical-Biological Warfare: U.S. Policies and International Effects*, 91st Cong., 2nd sess., 16 May 1970, p. 4.
97. *Ibid.*, Hearings, 91st Cong., 1st sess., 19 December 1969, p. 228.
98. *Ibid.*, p. 238.
99. Carnegie Endowment for International Peace, *The Control of Chemical and Biological Weapons* (New York, 1971), pp. 80–81; L. Craig Johnstone, "Ecocide and the Geneva Protocol," *Foreign Affairs* XLIX (1971):714.

100. *Vietnam Courier*, no. 96 (6 February 1967):3.

101. Wilfred Burchett in *Guardian* (New York), 27 December 1969, p. 16.

102. Nguyen Khac Vien, ed., *Chemical Warfare* (Hanoi, 1971), p. 121.

103. John Duffet, ed., *Against the Crime of Silence: Proceedings of the International War Crimes Tribunal* (New York, 1970), pp. 407, 416, 646.

104. Note 2 above, pp. 105–6.

105. "Chemical and Bacteriological (Biological) Weapons," 30 June 1969, n. 97 above, p. 402.

106. *Ibid.*, p. 61.

107. See Carnegie Endowment for International Peace, n. 99 above, p. 69.

108. Alje Vennema, "Medical Aspects of Antipersonnel Gases," in J. B. Neilands *et al.*, *Harvest of Death: Chemical Warfare in Vietnam and Cambodia* (New York, 1972), p. 105.

109. Stockholm International Peace Research Institute, *The Problem of Chemical and Biological Warfare* (Stockholm, 1971), I:205.

110. Letter of John S. Foster, Jr., Director of Defense Research and Engineering, U.S. Department of Defense, 15 April 1969, n. 97 above, p. 356.

111. George H. Quester, "Chemical and Biological Warfare," *American Political Science Review* LXVIII (1974):1286–88.

112. Note 79 above, p. 138.

113. U.S. Arms Control and Disarmament Agency, *Arms Control and Disarmament Agreements: Texts and History of Negotiations* (Washington, D.C., 1975), pp. 14–17.

114. Note 21 above, par. 38, p. 18.

115. Cited by Thomas and Thomas, n. 79 above, p. 164.

116. See on this the careful discussion of *ibid.*, ch. 4.

117. *Ibid.*, pp. 111–13.

118. Meyrowitz, n. 4 above, p. 557.

119. Cited by Thomas and Thomas, n. 79 above, p. 111.

120. Cf. George Bunn, "Banning Poison Gas and Germ Warfare: Should the United States Agree?" *Wisconsin Law Review* CCCLXXV (1969), reprinted in n. 100 above, p. 335.

121. Note 79 above, p. 149.

122. Note 113 above, pp. 11–12.

123. Levie in Trooboff, n. 10 above, p. 156.

124. Note 113 above, pp. 12–13.

125. MAAG to CINCPAC (JCS pass to Vietnam Task Force), 4 December 1961, JFK Library, NSF/V, vol. V, Box 195.

126. McNamara to Kennedy, 2 February 1962, *ibid.*

127. Joint State/Defense message to Embassy Saigon, 7 May 1963, *ibid.*, vol. X. See also Arthur F. McConnell, "Mission: Ranch Hand," *Air University Review* XXI, no. 2 (January–February 1970):89.

128. U.S. House, Committee on Foreign Affairs, Subcommittee on National Security Policy and Scientific Developments, *U.S. Chemical Warfare Policy*, Hearings, 93rd Cong., 2nd sess., 1–14 May 1974, p. 283.

129. OASD (SA), *SEA Analysis Report*, March–April 1971, p. 35.
130. MACV Directive 521-1, 22 November 1967, p. 1.
131. MACV Directive 95-4, 28 June 1966, Annex D, p. 4.
132. U.S. Department of the Air Force, "Ranch Hand: Herbicide Operations in Southeast Asia" (CHECO SEA Report), 13 July 1971, p. 20.
133. Testimony of Admiral Lemos, n. 97 above, p. 232.
134. Russell Betts and Frank Denton, *An Evaluation of Chemical Crop Destruction in Vietnam*, RM-5446-ISA/ARPA (Santa Monica, Calif., 1967), pp. 21–22, 33.
135. U.S. Department of the Air Force, "Herbicide Operations in Southeast Asia: July 1961–June 1967" (CHECO SEA Report), 11 October 1967, pp. 54–55.
136. CINCPAC to JCS, 10 December 1967, quoted in U.S. Department of the Air Force, "The War in Vietnam: July–December 1967" (CHECO SEA Report), 29 November 1968, pp. 73–74.
137. Note 18 above, Art. 23(a), p. 12. See also Morris Greenspan, *The Modern Law of Land Warfare* (Berkeley, Calif., 1959), pp. 316–17.
138. Letter of J. Fred Buzhardt, General Counsel of DOD, to Sen. J. W. Fulbright, *International Legal Materials* X (1971), cited by L. C. Green, "Aftermath of Vietnam: War Law and the Soldier," in Falk, n. 4 above, vol. IV (1976), p. 155.
139. Note 21 above, par. 37, p. 18.
140. Note 21 above, par. 44(a), p. 20. See also Oppenheim and Lauterpacht, n. 9 above, p. 419.
141. Note 3 above, Art. 23, p. 143.
142. Note 10 above, p. 1250.
143. MACV, *Command History 1970*, II:XIV-14.
144. Mieczylaw Maneli, *War of the Vanquished*, trans. Maria de Görgey (New York, 1971), pp. 92–105.
145. Note 102 above, p. 80.
146. U.S. Army Combat Developments Command Civil Affairs Agency, "Civil Affairs Aspects of Chemical and Biological Operations," n.d., pp. 5-8–5-11.
147. Note 143 above, p. XIII-18.
148. Note 86 above, p. 94; letter by Professors John D. Constable and M. S. Meselson, *The Times* (London), 16 June 1971.
149. For the full text of the summary and conclusions of the NAS study see n. 128 above, pp. 251–93.
150. This matter has been the subject of controversy in the NAS committee. See Deborah Shapley, "Herbicides: Academy Finds Damage in Vietnam After a Fight of Its Own," *Science* CLXXXIII (1974):1177–80.
151. See n. 113 above, p. 14.
152. Letter of H. G. Torbert, Jr., assistant secretary of state for congressional relations, to Rep. Richard D. McCarthy in n. 97 above, p. 360.
153. Note 79 above, p. 246.
154. Note 128 above, p. 372.
155. Note 113 above, p. 12.

156. Michael Krepon, "Weapons Potentially Inhumane: The Case of Cluster Bombs," in Falk, n. 4 above, vol. IV (1976), 266–74.
157. David E. Ott, *Field Artillery 1954–1973*, Vietnam Studies (Washington, D.C., 1975), pp. 147–48.
158. Note 103 above, pp. 306–7.
159. Richard A. Falk, "The American POWs in Power Politics," *The Progressive* XXXV, no. 3 (March 1971):15.
160. Paul A. Robblee, Jr., "The Legitimacy of Modern Conventional Weaponry," *Military Law Review* LXXI (Winter 1976):139–42.
161. Note 21 above, par. 34(b), p. 18.
162. Lawrence C. Petrowski, "Law and the Conduct of the Vietnam War," in Falk, n. 4 above, p. 505.
163. Note 160 above, pp. 135–38. See also Arthur W. Rovine, "Contemporary Practice of the United States Relating to International Law," *American Journal of International Law* LXVIII (1974):528–30.
164. DOD Instruction 5500.15, "Review of Legality of Weapons under International Law," 16 October 1974.
165. DOD Directive 5100.77, "DOD Program for the Implementation of the Law of War," 5 November 1974.
166. William V. O'Brien, "The Law of War, Command Responsibility and Vietnam," *Georgetown Law Journal* LX (1972):658.
167. See Richard R. Baxter, "Humanitarian Law or Humanitarian Politics? The 1974 Diplomatic Conference on Humanitarian Law," *Harvard International Law Journal* XVI (1975):1–26, and the same author's "Conventional Weapons Under Legal Prohibition," *International Security* I, no. 3 (Winter 1977):42–61; Sydney D. Bailey, *Prohibitions and Restraints in War* (London, 1972).

8. TERRORISM, COUNTERINSURGENCY AND GENOCIDE

1. Richard A. Falk, ed., *The Vietnam War and International Law* (Princeton, N.J., 1969), II:240.
2. *Ibid.*, pp. 240–41.
3. John Duffet, ed., *Against the Crime of Silence: Proceedings of the International War Crimes Tribunal* (New York, 1970), p. 8.
4. Note 1 above, p. 240.
5. Stephen T. Hosmer, *Viet Cong Repression and Its Implications for the Future*, R-475/1-ARPA (Santa Monica, Calif., 1970).
6. SAAFO, "Statistical Trends: Security Situation, April 1974," Table 10.
7. Kuno Knoebl, *Victor Charlie: The Face of War in Viet-Nam*, trans. Abe Farbstein (New York, 1967), pp. 95–96. See also Malcolm W. Browne, *The New Face of War* (Indianapolis, 1965), p. 103.
8. Douglas Pike, *The Viet-Cong Strategy of Terror* (Saigon, 1970), p. 9.
9. Cited in *ibid.*, p. 34.

10. John A. Parrish, *12, 20 & 5: A Doctor's Year in Vietnam* (New York, 1972), p. 270; Robert Shaplen, *The Road from War: Vietnam 1965–71* (New York, 1971), p. 199.
11. Don Oberdorfer, *Tet!* (Garden City, N.Y., 1971), pp. 201–16.
12. Robert F. Turner, *Vietnamese Communism: Its Origins and Development* (Stanford, Calif., 1975), p. 251, n. 72.
13. Edward S. Herman, *Atrocities in Vietnam: Myths and Realities* (Philadelphia, 1970), p. 40; Noam Chomsky and Edward S. Herman, *Counterrevolutionary Violence: Bloodbaths in Fact and Propaganda* (Andover, Mass., 1973), p. 28.
14. Gareth D. Porter and Len E. Ackland, "Vietnam: The Bloodbath Argument," in Paul T. Menzel, ed., *Moral Argument and the War in Vietnam: A Collection of Essays* (Nashville, Tenn., 1971), pp. 144–46.
15. *Vietnam Courier*, no. 214, 28 April 1969, p. 5.
16. The CORDS Dinh Tuong (IV CTZ) province report for March 1968 listed three such attacks; the report for Quang Ngai (I CTZ) for March 1969 noted that attacks on refugee camps had killed 81, wounded 50 and left 303 houses 50 to 100 percent destroyed; the report for Quang Nam (I CTZ) in January 1970 mentioned 2 attacks which killed 16 and wounded 72. The list could be continued.
17. John H. Knowles, "Vietnam Diary—Medicine and Politics," *The Pharos* XXX (1967):117, 121.
18. MACCORDS, Province Report, Quang Ngai province, June 1968, CMH; F. J. West, Jr., *The Village* (New York, 1972), p. 275.
19. Laurence Stern, "Shock Grips Red Massacre Village," *Washington Post*, 16 June 1970.
20. Note 13 above, p. 60.
21. Falk in Peter D. Trooboff, ed., *Law and Responsibility in Warfare: The Vietnam Experience* (Chapel Hill, N.C., 1975), p. 106.
22. *Ibid.*, pp. 106–7.
23. P. J. Honey, "Vietnam: If the Communists Won," *Southeast Asian Perspectives*, no. 2 (June 1971), p. 26.
24. Note 8 above, p. 42.
25. "Last 215 Foreigners Flown from Vietnam," *New York Times*, 15 September 1976.
26. See the testimony given before the House Committee on International Relations, Subcommittee on International Organizations, *Human Rights in Vietnam*, 95th Cong., 1st sess., 16–26 June 1977; Horst Faas, "Vietnam Is Seeking Full Civil Control," *New York Times*, 13 November 1977.
27. "Antiwar Activists Appeal to Hanoi," *New York Times*, 21 December 1976.
28. "Vietnamese at U.N. Denies Allegations on Human Rights," *New York Times*, 31 December 1976.
29. Advertisement, "Vietnam: A Time for Healing and Compassion," *New York Times*, 30 January 1977.
30. Statement for the record on Phung Hoang Program (Phoenix) by Ambassador W. E. Colby, U.S. Senate, Committee on Foreign Relations, *Vietnam: Policy*

and Prospects, 1970, Hearings, 91st Cong., 2nd sess., 17 February–19 March 1970, pp. 723–27. The figures on U.S. advisory strength were provided to the Senate Armed Services Committee in 1973; see n. 40 below.

31. MACCORDS-RE, "Processing of Viet Cong Suspects," 11 December 1967, Detainees and Prisons 1961–69 file, CMH.

32. OASD (SA), *SEA Analysis Report,* June/July 1971, p. 6.

33. OASD (Comptroller), SEA Statistical Summary, Table 62, 2 June 1972.

34. Donald I. Colin, deputy province senior adviser, Vinh Binh province, End of Tour Report, 19 August 1971, p. 8, Vinh Binh province file, CMH.

35. Note 33 above.

36. MACV, *Command History 1970,* II:VIII-48–54; William E. Colby, "Internal Security in South Viet Nam—Phoenix, December 1970," CMH.

37. Article 23 (b) of Hague Convention IV makes it illegal "to kill or wound treacherously individuals belonging to the hostile nation or army," and this provision has been construed as ruling out assassinations or putting a price on the head of enemy individuals. But the Phoenix program did not involve "individuals belonging to the hostile nation or army," nor was it a program of planned assassinations.

38. MACV Directive 525–36, 18 May 1970. This directive formalized an earlier set of instructions, dated 15 October 1969.

39. Memo of W. E. Colby to assistant chief of staff, CORDS, 7 August 1969.

40. See, e.g., the testimony of David S. Harrington, U.S. Senate, Committee on Armed Services, *Nomination of William E. Colby,* Hearings, 93rd Cong., 1st sess., 2–25 July 1973, pp. 97–98.

41. Note 32 above, p. 6.

42. Lt. Col. Raymond L. Fleigh, senior advisor, Binh Duong province, Completion of Tour Report, 9 November 1970, p. 7.

43. Warren H. Milberg, "The Future Applicability of the Phoenix Program," Air University Command and Staff College Research Study, Maxwell Air Force Base, May 1974.

44. Jeffrey Race, *War Comes to Long An: Revolutionary Conflict in a Vietnamese Province* (Berkeley, Calif., 1972), p. 239.

45. Note 34 above, p. 8.

46. MACCORDS-PSG, "Impact of the Enemy Offensive on Pacification," 16 September 1972, pp. 4–5, CMH.

47. Cited by Robert W. Komer, "Impact of Pacification on Insurgency in South Vietnam," *Journal of International Affairs* XXV (1971):53.

48. Quoted in John A. Marshall, *American Bastille: A History of the Illegal Arrests and Imprisonment of American Citizens During the Late Civil War* (Philadelphia, 1869), p. 721.

49. Thomas I. Emerson and David Haber, *Political and Civil Rights in the United States,* 2nd ed. (Buffalo, 1958), I:281.

50. *Ibid.,* p. 421.

51. *Ibid.,* p. 410.

52. Kevin Boyle *et al.,* *Law and State: The Case of Northern Ireland* (Amherst,

Mass., 1975), p. 59; "Detention Without Trial Ended in Ulster," *New York Times*, 6 December 1975.

53. Geneva Convention Relative to the Protection of Civilian Persons in Time of War, 12 August 1949, Art. 4, in U.S. Department of the Air Force, *Treaties Governing Land Warfare* (Air Force Pamphlet 110-1-3), 21 July 1958, p. 136.
54. *Ibid.*
55. *Ibid.*, Art. 3, par. 1(d), p. 136.
56. See the discussion in the legal memorandum of the Department of State, August 1971, in U.S. House, Committee on Government Operations, Subcommittee on Foreign Operations and Government Information, *U.S. Assistance Programs in Vietnam*, Hearings, 92nd Cong., 1st sess., 15 July–2 August 1971, p. 217.
57. Note 56 above, pp. 197, 226, 335.
58. Letter of 8 July 1970, *Congressional Record* CXVI, part 19 (28 July 1970):26017.
59. *Ibid.*, vol. CXIX, part 14 (4 June 1973):17891.
60. Note 56 above, p. 186.
61. Note 43 above, p. 61.
62. Note 56 above, p. 335.
63. OASD (SA), *SEA Analysis Report*, October 1969, p. 15, and June/July 1971, p. 1.
64. *Ibid.*, September/October 1970, p. 31.
65. MACCORDS-PSG, 1969 Sit Rep #7, Quang Ngai province, 21 September 1969, p. 3.
66. MACCORDS-Phoenix, "Fact Sheet: Legal Processing and Significant Actions," 23 October 1969, Detainees and Prisons 1961–69 file, CMH.
67. George S. Prugh, *Law at War: Vietnam 1964–1973*, Vietnam Studies (Washington, D.C., 1975), p. 25.
68. Deputy for CORDS, memorandum of conversation, 26 September 1969, p. 16.
69. OASD (Comptroller), SEA Statistical Summary, Table 62, 2 June 1972.
70. Note 56 above, p. 205.
71. Note 68 above, p. 19.
72. Colby, n. 36 above, Tab 33.
73. MACV, *Command History 1970*, II:VIII-48–51.
74. Translation in Detainees and Prisons 1970–74 file, CMH.
75. MACCORDS, Province Report, Binh Dinh province, August 1971, p. 3, CMH.
76. MACCORDS, Province Report, Thua Thien province, May 1972, p. 4, CMH.
77. U.S. Senate, Committee on the Judiciary, Subcommittee to Investigate Problems Connected with Refugees and Escapees, *Relief and Rehabilitation of War Victims in Indochina*, part IV, Hearings, 93rd Cong., 1st sess., 1 August 1973, p. 69.
78. Boyle in n. 52 above, p. 53.
79. Memo, n.d., Detainees and Prisons 1961–69 file, CMH.

80. *Vietnam Courier*, 18 January 1971, p. 4.
81. Nguyen Khac Vien, *Tradition and Revolution in Vietnam*, trans. Linda Yarr *et al.* (Washington, D.C., 1974), p. 148.
82. Testimony of Fred Branfman, U.S. House, Committee on Foreign Affairs, Subcommittee on Asian and Pacific Affairs, *The Treatment of Political Prisoners in South Vietnam by the Government of the Republic of South Vietnam*, Hearings, 93rd Cong., 1st sess., 13 September 1973, pp. 32–33. See also the testimony of Don Luce, *ibid.*, pp. 17–19.
83. Tiziano Terzani, *Giai Phong! The Fall and Liberation of Saigon* (New York, 1976), p. 258.
84. Embassy Saigon, "Father Chan Tin's View of 'Political Prisoners,' " 26 December 1973. This document includes Chan Tin's list and is reprinted in U.S. House, Committee on Foreign Affairs, Subcommittee on Asian and Pacific Affairs, *Political Prisoners in South Vietnam and the Philippines*, Hearings, 93rd Cong., 2nd sess., 1 May–5 June 1974.
85. Note 83 above, p. 97.
86. *Ibid.*, p. 151.
87. Note 40 above, p. 44.
88. *Vietnam Courier*, 15 February 1971, p. 4.
89. Note 83 above, p. 116.
90. It was 1.56 per thousand per month in 1967 and became 0.36 per thousand by 1970. Cf. n. 56 above, p. 6.
91. "The Tiger Cages of Con Son," *Life*, 17 July 1970, pp. 26–29.
92. Alfred Hassler, *Saigon, U.S.A.* (New York, 1970), p. 24.
93. Sylvan Fox, "Four South Vietnamese Describe Torture in Prison's Tiger Cage," *New York Times*, 3 March 1973.
94. The description and measurements were given by Marshall Wright, assistant secretary of state, to the House Foreign Affairs Committee in 1973. See n. 82 above, p. 61.
95. Report of Don Luce to the World Council of Churches, *Congressional Record* CXVI, part 19 (28 July 1970):26007.
96. MACCORDS, "Physical Examination of Prisoners Transferred from Con Son to Chi Hoa," 7 January 1971.
97. Note 82 above, p. 20.
98. James Carey, "Political Prisoners: A Matter of Definition," *San Diego Union*, 3 February 1974.
99. U.S. House, Committee on Foreign Affairs, *FY 1975 Foreign Assistance Request*, Hearings, 93rd Cong., 2nd sess. 4 June–11 July 1974, p. 797.
100. Samuel M. Meyers and Albert D. Biderman, eds., *Mass Behavior in Battle and Captivity: The Communist Soldier in the Korean War* (Chicago, 1968), pp. 301–13.
101. Note 82 above, p. 153.
102. Note 3 above, p. 620.
103. Theodore Draper, *Abuse of Power* (New York, 1967), p. 178.
104. Daniel Berrigan, *Night Flight to Hanoi* (New York, 1971), p. 23.

105. Frances FitzGerald, *Fire in the Lake: The Vietnamese and the Americans in Vietnam* (New York, 1973), p. 502.

106. Note 1 above, pp. 251–52.

107. U.S. Department of the Air Force, *Selected International Agreements* (Air Force Pamphlet 110–20), 1 June 1973, pp. 11-30–31.

108. Hugo A. Bedau, "Genocide in Vietnam?" in Virginia Held *et al.*, eds., *Philosophy, Morality and Public Affairs* (New York, 1974), p. 43.

109. Daniel Ellsberg in Erwin Knoll and Judith N. McFadden, eds., *War Crimes and the American Conscience* (New York, 1970), p. 82.

110. See the testimony of Robert H. Nooter of AID before U.S. Senate, Committee on the Judiciary, Subcommittee to Investigate Problems Connected with Refugees and Escapees, *Problems of War Victims in Indochina, Part I: Vietnam*, Hearings, 92nd Cong., 2nd sess., 8 May 1972, pp. 37–38; Gabriel Smilkstein, "Volunteer Physicians for Vietnam: A Six Year Review," *Journal of the American Medical Association* CCXIX (1972):495–99.

111. Le Hoang Trong (pseud.), "Survival and Self-Reliance: A Vietnamese Viewpoint," *Asian Survey* XV (1975):299.

112. MACV Directive 525-5, 7 September 1965, p. 3.

113. COWIN Ref. Doc. 5, p. 12.

114. Roger Hilsman, *To Move a Nation: The Politics of Foreign Policy in the Administration of John F. Kennedy* (Garden City, N.Y., 1967), p. 444.

115. David Parks, *GI Diary* (New York, 1968), p. 107.

116. *Congressional Record* CXXI, part 14 (6 June 1975):17558.

117. See generally U.S. Department of the Air Force, "Short Rounds: Special Report," 28 September 1967, and "Short Rounds: June 1968–May 1969," 15 August 1969, both CHECO SEA Reports; MACV Lessons Learned #70, 17 October 1968.

118. P. W. Helmore, "Air Operations in Vietnam: I," *Royal United Service Institution Journal* CXII (1967):21.

119. International Committee of the Red Cross, *Conference of Government Experts on the Reaffirmation and Development of International Humanitarian Law Applicable to Armed Conflicts*, vol. II, part 2 (Geneva, 1972), p. 14.

120. Goldie in n. 21 above, p. 87.

121. Paul Ramsey, *The Just War: Force and Personal Responsibility* (New York, 1968), p. 437.

122. Falk in n. 21 above, p. 37.

9. ATROCITIES: FICTION AND FACT

1. James Morgan Read, *Atrocity Propaganda 1914–1919* (New Haven, Conn., 1941), p. 36.

2. Bertrand Russell, *Justice in War Time* (Chicago, 1917), p. 6.

3. Eric Sevareid, *Not So Wild a Dream* (New York, 1946), pp. 388–89, 419.

4. Reginald William Thompson, *Cry Korea* (London, 1951), p. 44.

5. John A. Parrish, *12, 20 & 5: A Doctor's Year in Vietnam* (New York, 1972), p. 316. See on this also Philip Caputo, *A Rumor of War* (New York, 1977).

6. OASD (SA), *SEA Analysis Report*, November 1968, p. 29.

7. *Ibid.*, July 1969, p. 11.

8. W. Hays Parks, "Crimes in Hostilities," *Marine Corps Gazette* LX, no. 9 (September 1976):38–39.

9. F. J. West, Jr., *The Village* (New York, 1972), p. 11.

10. John Mecklin, *Mission in Torment: An Intimate Account of the U.S. Role in Vietnam* (Garden City, N.Y., 1965), p. 54.

11. " 'Do's and Don'ts' for the U.S. Soldier, Sailor, Airman and Marine in Vietnam," COWIN Ref. Doc. 4. See also "Nine Rules," a pocket-size card given to every soldier, Ref. Doc. 6.

12. MACCORDS-RAD, memo, 29 March 1971, Civilian Casualties file, CMH.

13. The number of fatal traffic accidents in 1967 was 806; the number of registered motor vehicles in 1969 was 1,795,000. U.S. Department of Commerce, *Statistical Abstract of the United States 1970*, Tables 858 and 841 (Washington, D.C., 1970), pp. 553, 545.

14. Ronald William Clark, *The Life of Bertrand Russell* (New York, 1975), p. 624.

15. Russell to Johnson, 25 August 1966, in John Duffett, ed., *Against the Crime of Silence: Proceedings of the International War Crimes Tribunal* (New York, 1970), pp. 18–19, 49–50.

16. Staughton Lynd, "The War Crimes Tribunal: A Dissent," *Liberation* XII, no. 9–10 (1967–68):77–79.

17. Note 14 above, 625.

18. Richard A. Falk, ed., *The Vietnam War and International Law*, vol. I (Princeton, N.J., 1968), p. 451, n. 12, and vol. II (Princeton, N.J., 1969), p. 252. The 1971 statement is in an article, "The American POWs: Pawns in Power Politics," *The Progressive*, XXXV, no. 3 (March 1971):16.

19. Note 15 above, p. 506.

20. Note 14 above, pp. 635–51.

21. James Simon Kunen, *Standard Operating Procedure: Notes of a Draft-Age American* (New York, 1971), pp. 23–25. This book reproduces the verbatim text of large portions of the CCI hearing in Washington.

22. *Ibid.*, p. 232.

23. *Ibid.*, p. 360.

24. *Ibid.*, pp. 39, 96–97.

25. *Ibid.*, p. 299.

26. Vietnam Veterans Against the War, *The Winter Soldier Investigation: An Inquiry into American War Crimes* (Boston, 1972), p. xiv.

27. *Saturday Review*, 9 January 1971, p. 26.

28. Office of the Director, Judge Advocate Division, Headquarters USMC, Winter Soldier Investigation files.

29. Citizens Commission of Inquiry, *The Dellums Committee Hearings on War Crimes in Vietnam* (New York, 1972), p. 302.

30. *Ibid.*, p. 22.

31. U.S. House, Committee on Government Operations, Subcommittee on Foreign Operations and Government Information, *U.S. Assistance Programs in Vietnam,* Hearings, 92nd Cong., 1st sess., 15 July–2 August 1971, p. 319.

32. U.S. Senate, Committee on Armed Services, *Nomination of William E. Colby,* Hearings, 93rd Cong., 1st sess., 2–25 July 1973, pp. 109–10.

33. *Ibid.,* p. 117.

34. U.S. Department of the Army, Office of the Judge Advocate General, Talking Paper, "Allegations of War Crimes Other Than Son My," 11 April 1971, JAGW 1971/1068.

35. Cf. Roy R. Grinker and John P. Spiegel, *Men Under Stress* (Philadelphia, 1963), p. 451.

36. Chaim F. Shatan, "How Do We Turn Off the Guilt?" *Human Behavior* II, no. 2 (February 1973):61.

37. Robert Jay Lifton, *Home From the War: Vietnam Veterans–Neither Victims nor Executioners* (New York, 1973), p. 140.

38. U.S. Senate, Committee on Labor and Public Welfare, Subcommittee on Veterans Affairs, *Unemployment and Overall Readjustment Problems of Returning Veterans,* Hearings, 91st Cong., 2nd sess., 25 November–3 December 1970, p. 215. See also Levy's book *Spoils of War* (Boston, 1974), p. 42.

39. U.S. Senate, *ibid.,* pp. 342, 345.

40. Jonathan F. Borus, "Incidence of Maladjustment in Vietnam Returnees," *Archives of General Psychiatry* XXX (1974):556.

41. U.S. Department of the Army, Office of the Judge Advocate General, International Affairs Division, files of atrocity allegations.

42. *Ibid.* See also John J. O'Connor, *A Chaplain Looks at Vietnam* (New York, 1968), p. 47.

43. Anthony B. Herbert (with James T. Wooten), *Soldier* (New York, 1973).

44. Cf. "The Herbert Case and the Record," *Army* XXII, no. 2 (February 1972):6–11.

45. Barry Lando, "The Herbert Affair," *The Atlantic* (May 1973):76.

46. Cf. Lee Ewing, "Col. Anthony Herbert: The Unmasking of an Accuser," *Columbia Journalism Review* (September/ October 1973):14.

47. Falk in Peter D. Trooboff, ed., *Law and Responsibility in Warfare: The Vietnam Experience* (Chapel Hill, N.C., 1975), p. 47.

48. List provided by U.S. Army Judiciary.

49. Statistic provided by U.S. Department of the Navy, Office of the Judge Advocate General, Military Justice Division.

50. Estimate based on data provided by U.S. Army Judiciary.

51. Peers Inquiry, I:5-13.

52. *Ibid.,* p. 2-3.

53. *Ibid.,* p. 9-21.

54. Alexander Kendrick, *The Wound Within: America in the Vietnam Years 1945–1974* (Boston, 1974), p. 256.

55. Telford Taylor, *Nuremberg and Vietnam: An American Tragedy* (New York, 1971), p. 139.

56. Daniel Ellsberg in Erwin Knoll and Judith N. McFadden, eds., *War Crimes and the American Conscience* (New York, 1970), p. 130.

57. MACCORDS-RE, "Pacification in Hieu Nhon and Hoa Vang Districts, Quang Nam Province," 25 March 1968, p. 3. See also *New York Times*, 13 February 1972.

58. *U.S. v. Green*, NCM 70-3811; *U.S. v. Schwarz*, NCM 71-0028, 45 CMR 852 (NCMR 1971); *U.S. v. Boyd*, NCM 70-2498; *U.S. v. Herrod*, NCM 70-2970.

59. *U.S. v. Thomas*, CM 416162, 38 CMR 655 (ABMR 1968); *U.S. v. Gervase*, CM 416161; *U.S. v. J. C. Garcia*, CM 416160; *U.S. v. C. Garcia*, CM 416159, 38 CMR 625 (ABMR 1967). See also Daniel Lang, *Casualties of War* (New York, 1969).

60. *U.S. v. Crider*, NCM 69-4114, 45 CMR 815 (1972).

61. *U.S. v. Duffy*, CM 424795, 47 CMR 658 (ACMR 1973), p. 661.

62. Westmoreland to Walt, 14 August 1965, CMH.

63. Eaton Incident, n. 41 above.

64. Note 51 above, p. 7-15.

65. JAGW 1971/1096, 21 May 1971, Incl. 5, case 51.

66. COWIN Ref. Doc. 76.

67. *U.S. v. Williams*, CM 419872.

68. *U.S. v. Hodges*, CM 420341.

69. Roger W. Little, ed., *Handbook of Military Institutions* (Beverly Hills, Calif., 1971), p. 63.

70. Robert D. Heinl, "The Collapse of the Armed Forces," *Armed Forces Journal* CVIII, no. 19 (7 June 1971):38.

71. Note 51 above, p. 8-11.

72. Yoel Yager, "Personal Violence in Infantry Combat," *Archives of General Psychiatry* XXXII (1975):261.

73. Note 8 above, p. 38.

74. Note 51 above, p. 12-8.

75. *U.S. v. Green*, NCM 70-3811, p. 260.

76. U.S. House, Committee on Foreign Affairs, Subcommittee on National Security Policy and Scientific Developments, *American Prisoners of War and Missing in Action in Southeast Asia, 1973*, Hearings, 93rd Cong., 1st sess., 23–31 May 1973, pp. 41, 59. By the summer of 1977, the number of MIA had been reduced to 712 (cf. *New York Times*, 17 August 1977).

77. 5 *International Review of the Red Cross* 636 (1965), cited by Falk, n. 18 above, vol. II (1969), p. 362.

78. Cf. Howard S. Levie in Falk, n. 18 above, vol. II (1969), pp. 374–75, 391.

79. Monika Schwinn and Bernhard Diehl, *We Came To Help*, trans. Jan van Heurck (New York, 1976), p. 78 and *passim*.

80. Note 76 above, pp. 19–20.

81. Zalin Grant, *Survivors* (New York, 1975), p. 159.

82. *Ibid.*, pp. 164–65.

83. U.S. Department of the Air Force, *Treaties Governing Land Warfare* (Air Force Pamphlet 110-1-3), 21 July 1958, p. 73.

84. Wilfred G. Burchett, *Vietnam: Inside Story of the Guerilla War*, 2nd ed. (New York, 1965), p. 103. The story of the interview is also told by one of the captives. Cf. George E. Smith, *P.O.W.: Two Years with the Vietcong* (Berkeley, Calif., 1971), pp. 158–59.

85. Edward S. Herman, *Atrocities in Vietnam: Myths and Realities* (Philadelphia, 1970), p. 32.

86. Reprinted in n. 76 above, pp. 215–33.

87. Note 83 above, p. 98.

88. U.S. House, Committee on Foreign Affairs, Subcommittee on National Security and Scientific Developments, *The Geneva Convention Relative to the Treatment of Prisoners of War with Reservations . . .* , May 1970, p. 81.

89. "The Geneva Convention and the Treatment of Prisoners of War in Vietnam," Note from *Harvard Law Review*, in Falk, n. 18 above, vol. II (1969), pp. 408–10.

90. Wilfred G. Burchett, *Vietnam North* (London, 1966), p. 53.

91. Cf. Howard S. Levie in Falk, n. 18 above, vol. IV (1976), p. 356.

92. Robinson Risner, *The Passing of the Night: My Seven Years as a Prisoner of the North Vietnamese* (New York, 1973), p. 129.

93. U.S. House, Committee on Armed Services, *Problems of Prisoners of War and Their Families*, Hearing, 91st Cong., 2nd sess., 6 March 1970, p. 6052.

94. Seymour M. Hersh, "The Prisoners of War," reprinted in U.S. House, Committee on Foreign Affairs, Subcommittee on National Security Policy and Scientific Developments, *American Prisoners of War in Southeast Asia, 1971*, Hearings, 92nd Cong., 1st sess., 23 March–20 April 1971, p. 501.

95. Dave Dellinger, "The Prisoner of War Hoax," *Liberation* XV, no. 10 (December 1970): 8–9. See also his earlier article "Indomitable Vietnam—A Fresh Look," *ibid.*, XII, no. 3 (May–June 1967): 14–24.

96. "Confession by Richard Allen Stratton," *Vietnam Courier*, nos. 101–2 (13–20 March 1967):7.

97. *The Progressive*, n. 18 above.

98. Note 94 above, p. 218.

99. *Ibid.*, p. 229.

100. In addition to sources cited above and below see John A. Dramesi, *Code of Honor* (New York, 1975); Ralph Gaither and Steve Henry, *With God in a P.O.W. Camp* (Nashville, Tenn., 1973); John G. Hubbell, *P.O.W.* (New York, 1976); and the collective account of eight senior officers, "Torture . . . Solitary . . . Starvation: POWs Tell the Inside Story," *U.S. News and World Report*, 3 April 1973. See also the earlier book by James N. Rowe, *Five Years to Freedom* (Boston, 1971).

101. U.S. Senate, Committee on the Judiciary, Subcommittee to Investigate Problems Connected with Refugees and Escapees, *Problems of War Victims in Indochina. Part III: North Vietnam*, Hearings, 92nd Cong., 2nd sess., 16–17 August 1972, p. 16.

102. Note 79 above, pp. 227–28.

103. Note 76 above, pp. 3–6.

104. Edna J. Hunter, "The Prisoner of War: Coping with the Stress of Isolation," in Rudolf H. Moos, ed., *Human Adaptation: Coping with Life Stresses* (Lexington, Mass., 1976).

105. Note 76 above, p. 197.

106. Anthony Lewis, "Whosoever Destroys a Soul," *New York Times*, 28 February 1974.

107. Oliver Todd, "How I Let Myself Be Deceived by Hanoi," *Réalités*, September 1973, reprinted in U.S. House, Committee on Foreign Affairs, *Fiscal Year 1975 Foreign Assistance Request*, Hearings, 93rd Cong., 2nd sess., 4 June–11 July 1974, p. 804.

108. Kenneth Crawford, "Operation Homecoming: Joy and Outrage," *Washington Post*, 12 April 1973, in n. 76 above, p. 205.

109. Note 95 above, p. 21.

110. Note 81 above, p. 341; Nick Rowe, "A P.O.W.'s Faith," *New York Times*, 12 February 1975.

111. News release cited n. 81 above, pp. 339–40.

112. Charles W. Mayo, "The Role of Forced Confessions in the Communist 'Germ Warfare' Propaganda Campaign," *Department of State Bulletin*, XXIX (1953):643–45.

113. The official DOD figures are given by David Rees, *Korea: The Limited War* (New York, 1964), p. 461. The war crimes statistics are from Albert D. Biderman, *March to Calumny: The Story of the American POWs in the Korean War* (New York, 1963), p. 94. See also Raymond A. Bauer and Edgar H. Schein, eds., "Brainwashing," *Journal of Social Issues* XIII, no. 3 (1957), and William L. White, *The Captives of Korea: An Unofficial White Paper on the Treatment of War Prisoners* (New York, 1957).

114. John C. Clews, *Communist Propaganda Techniques* (New York, 1964), p. 267. See also White, n. 113 above, pp. 168–71.

115. Alan Winnington and Wilfred Burchett, *Plain Perfidy* (Peking, 1954), p. 24.

116. Cf. Denis Warner, "Wilfred Burchett: Australian Lord Haw-Haw," *National Review*, 11 April 1975, pp. 395–97.

117. Stockholm International Peace Research Institute, *The Problem of Chemical and Biological Warfare*, vol. I (Stockholm, 1971), p. 225.

118. John Cookson and Judith Nottingham, *A Survey of Chemical and Biological Warfare* (London, 1969), p. 62.

119. Bernard B. Fall, *Street Without Joy: Indochina at War, 1946–54* (Harrisburg, Pa., 1961), p. 272.

120. *Ibid.*, p. 264.

121. Quoted in *ibid.*, p. 274.

122. *Ibid.*, p. 265.

123. Joan Colebrook, "Prisoners of War," *Commentary* (January 1974):34.

124. Letter dated 10 July 1975.

10. THE PUNISHMENT OF WAR CRIMES

1. U.S. Department of the Army, *The Law of Land Warfare* (FM 27-10), 18 July 1956, par. 499, p. 178.
2. MACV Directive 20-4, 20 April 1965, p. 1.
3. MACV Directive 20-4, 25 March 1966, pp. 1–2.
4. U.S. Department of the Army, Army Subject Schedule 27-1, *The Geneva Conventions of 1949 and Hague Convention No. IV of 1907*, 8 October 1970, p. 12.
5. MACV Directive 335–18, 18 September 1965; MACV Directive 335-1, 5 January 1966.
6. MACV Directive 335-12, 29 November 1967, pp. 1–3.
7. Peers Inquiry, vol. III, Bk. 1, exhibit M-48.
8. Roger Hood and Richard Sparks, *Key Issues in Criminology* (New York, 1970), pp. 23, 15.
9. *U.S. v. Herrod*, NCM 70-2970, pp. 621ff.
10. *U.S. v. Goldman*, 43 CMR 77 (ACMR 1970), p. 715.
11. *Ibid.*, p. 716.
12. Note 7 above, I:11-1.
13. *Ibid.*, I:10-40.
14. U.S. Department of the Army, "Contrast: An Annotated Bibliography (Lessons Learned in Vietnam)," n.d., Problem Area: Laws of War, sub-area: War Crimes (Deterrence, detection and investigation).
15. Assistant Judge Advocate General Lawrence J. Fuller to MACV Staff Judge Advocate Lawrence H. Williams, 5 December 1969, and reply of the latter to the former, 11 December 1969, HIMS Microfilm Collection, U.S. Army Military History Research Collection, Carlisle Barracks, Pa., film 276.
16. COWIN, p. 88.
17. U.S. House, Committee on Armed Services, Armed Services Investigating Subcommittee, *Unauthorized Bombing of Military Targets in North Vietnam*, Report, 15 December 1972, p. 11.
18. MACV, Inspector General, "Summaries of Reports of Investigations and Inquiries 1967–72" (film).
19. George S. Prugh, *Law at War: Vietnam 1964–1973*, Vietnam Studies (Washington, D.C., 1975), p. 74.
20. USMC, Office of the Judge Advocate General, Winter Soldier Investigation files.
21. W. Hays Parks, "Crimes in Hostilities," *Marine Corps Gazette* LX, no. 9 (September 1976):18.
22. Waldemar A. Solf, "A Response to Telford Taylor's *Nuremberg and Vietnam: An American Tragedy*," *University of Akron Law Review* V (1972):67.
23. See, e.g., case 49, report of the U.S. Army judge advocate general to the White House, 21 May 1971, incl. 4, U.S. Army Judiciary.
24. *Manual for Courts-Martial, United States 1969*, rev. ed. (Washington, D.C., 1969), p. A2-6.

25. *Ibid.*, par. 4c, p. 2-2.
26. Data supplied by U.S. Army Judiciary.
27. The existence of this feeling of sympathy has been attested to by several officers who served on such courts-martial in Vietnam.
28. *U.S. v. Lund, U.S. v. Francis,* CM 420181, argument before Board of Review, 28 May 1969, p. 2.
29. *U.S. v. Woods,* CM 416803, p. 108.
30. *U.S. v. Garcia,* CM 416804, p. 174.
31. *Ibid.*, p. 157.
32. Note 24 above, par. 88, p. 17-7.
33. *Ibid.*, par. 100, p. 20-2.
34. *U.S. v. Ogg,* CM 416896, p. 5.
35. *U.S. v. Griffin,* CM 416805, 39 CMR 586 (ABMR 1968), p. 588.
36. *U.S. v. Schultz,* NCM 66-2846, p. 100.
37. *Ibid.*, p. 9.
38. U.S. Department of the Navy, SECNAV Instruction 5815.3C, 31 August 1973, par. 3(a).
39. Note 20 above.
40. Robert B. Rigg, "Where Does Killing End and Murder Begin in War?" *Military Review* LI, no. 3 (March 1971):6.
41. *U.S. v. Calley,* 46 CMR 1131 (ACMR 1973), pp. 1182–84.
42. Note 21 above, pp. 16–17.
43. Martin Gershen, *Destroy or Die: The True Story of Mylai* (New Rochelle, N.Y., 1971), p. 11.
44. Edward M. Opton, Jr., in Erwin Knoll and Judith N. McFadden, eds., *War Crimes and the American Conscience* (New York, 1970), p. 116.
45. Peter P. Mahoney, "Calley and the Old Bitterness," *New York Times,* 9 January 1974, Op-Ed page.
46. Paul C. Warnke in Peter D. Trooboff, ed., *Law and Responsibility in Warfare: The Vietnam Experience* (Chapel Hill, N.C., 1975), p. 190.
47. Letters of Mrs. Phyllis Gearity to President Nixon, 6 May 1971, *U.S. v. Gearity,* CM 423359.
48. A federal district court in *Calley v. Callaway,* 382 F. Supp. 650 (1974), accepted Calley's plea that his rights had been violated by prejudicial publicity, but this judgment was overturned on 10 September 1975 by the U.S. Fifth Circuit Court of Appeals. On 5 April 1976 the U.S. Supreme Court in *Calley v. Hoffmann,* 425 U.S. 911 (1976), denied certiorari.
49. *Washington Post,* 2 December 1974, n. 46 above, p. 266, n. 11.
50. *U.S. v. Medina,* CM 427162, p. 3440.
51. *Ibid.*, pp. 3520–23. Portions of this charge are reprinted in Leon Friedman, ed., *The Law of War: A Documentary History* (New York, 1972), II:1731–32, and in Joseph Goldstein *et al.*, eds., *The My Lai Massacre and Its Cover-Up* (New York, 1976), pp. 465–68.
52. Note 1 above, par. 501, pp. 178–79.
53. Note 7 above, I:10-26.

54. Cf. Kenneth A. Howard, "Command Responsibility for War Crimes," *Journal of Public Law* XXI (1972):7–22.
55. Roger S. Clark, "Medina: An Essay on the Principles of Criminal Liability for Homicide," *Rutgers-Camden Law Journal* V (1973):78.
56. Note 7 above, I:7-15.
57. Geneva Convention Relative to the Treatment of Prisoners of War, 12 August 1949, art. 17, U.S. Department of the Air Force, *Treaties Governing Land Warfare* (Air Force Pamphlet 110-1-3), 21 July 1958, p. 74. See also n. 1 above, par. 93, p. 37.
58. U.S. Department of the Army, *Intelligence Interrogation* (FM 30-15), 7 March 1969, p. 2-6.
59. Note 50 above, p. 3279.
60. Note 1 above, par. 7(b), p. 7.
61. Note 50 above, p. 3454.
62. *Ibid.*, p. 3316.
63. *Ibid.*, p. 3368.
64. Norman G. Cooper, "My Lai and Military Justice—To What Effect?" *Military Law Review* LIX (1973):102.
65. Telford Taylor in "Vietnam and the Nuremberg Principles: A Colloquy on War Crimes," *Rutgers-Camden Law Journal* V (Fall 1973):9. The colloquy is reprinted in Richard A. Falk, ed., *The Vietnam War and International Law*, vol. IV (Princeton, N.J., 1976), pp. 363–420.
66. U.S. House, Committee on Armed Services, Armed Services Investigating Subcommittee, *Investigation of the My Lai Incident*, Report, 91st Cong., 2nd sess., 15 July 1970, p. 43.
67. Statement of Secretary of the Army Stanley R. Resor, 19 May 1971, DOD press release.
68. Statement of Rep. Samuel S. Stratton in the House, 4 February 1971, quoted in Goldstein, n. 51 above, p. 469.
69. Maureen Mylander, *The Generals* (New York, 1974), p. 12.
70. Jordan J. Paust, "After My Lai: The Case for War Crimes Jurisdiction Over Civilians in Federal District Courts," in Falk, n. 65 above, p. 447.
71. *Toth v. Quarles*, 350 U.S. 11 (1955). Once before, in *U.S. ex rel. Hirschberg v. Cook*, 336 U.S. 210 (1949), the Supreme Court had ruled against such trials.
72. This identical language appears in all four conventions—arts. 49, 50, 129 and 146 respectively.
73. U.S. Constitution, art. 1, sec. 8, cl. 10; Charles W. Corddry, "Jurisdiction To Try Discharged Servicemen for Violations of the Laws of War," *JAG Journal* XXVI (1971):64. See also Cooper, n. 64 above, and the literature cited by him under n. 53.
74. Note 70 above.
75. Note 66 above, p. 7.
76. The statement is reproduced in Goldstein, n. 51 above, pp. 20–23.
77. Cf. U.S. Department of the Army, Army Subject Schedule 21-18, *The Geneva*

Conventions, and 27-1, *The Hague and Geneva Conventions,* both dated 20 April 1967.

78. Fleet Marine Force Pacific Order 1610.2A, "Individual Responsibility," 2 July 1968.
79. Note 7 above, I:4-8, 12-8.
80. *Ibid.,* vol. III, Bk. 1, p. 317.
81. Letter of Col. Edward W. Haughney to Capt. Robert E. Deso, 22 January 1973, Department of the Army, Office of the Judge Advocate General, International Affairs Division, Prugh volume back-up.
82. Press conference at Charlotte, N.C., 9 December 1969, cited in n. 41 above, p. 1159.
83. U.S. Department of the Army, Army Regulation 350-216, Training. The Geneva Conventions of 1949 and Hague Convention No. IV of 1907, 28 May 1970, p. 3.
84. Note 21 above, p. 21.
85. Note 4 above, p. 18.
86. *Ibid.,* pp. 10–11.
87. *Ibid.,* pp. 15–16.
88. *Ibid.,* pp. 17–18.
89. *Ibid.,* p. 7.
90. U.S. Department of the Army, *Intelligence Interrogation* (FM 30-15), 1 June 1973, p. 4.
91. TF 21-4228, *The Geneva Conventions and the Soldier;* TF 21-4229, *When the Enemy Is in My Hands;* TF 21-4249, *The Geneva Conventions and the Military Policeman;* TF 21-4719, *The Geneva Conventions and the Medic;* TF 21-4720, *The Geneva Conventions and the Civilian;* TF 27-3616, *The Geneva Conventions and Counterinsurgency.* This writer has seen two of these films and found them to be of impressive quality.
92. Tom Buckley, "The Rules of Land Warfare," *Soldiers* XXVI, no. 8 (August 1971):6–7.
93. Quoted in n. 4 above, p. 16.
94. Cf. Ernest van den Haag, "Vietnam Journal," *National Review,* 22 October 1971, p. 1176.
95. CGUSARV to Army Commands, 19 July 1971, CMH.
96. Note 23 above.
97. U.S. Department of Justice, Federal Bureau of Prisons, *Statistical Report: Fiscal Years 1969 and 1970,* Table C-2A, pp. 142–43.
98. David T. Stanley, *Prisoners Among Us: The Problem of Parole* (Washington, D.C., 1976), p. 68; Marvin E. Frankel, *Criminal Sentences: Law Without Order* (New York, 1973), p. 94.
99. U.S. Senate, Committee on the Judiciary, Subcommittee to Investigate Problems Connected with Refugees and Escapees, *Problems of War Victims in Indochina. Part I: Vietnam,* Hearing, 92nd Cong., 2nd sess., 8 May 1972, p. 91.
100. Goldstein, n. 51 above, p. 11.

101. DOD Directive 5100.77, "DOD Program for the Implementation of the Law of War," 5 November 1974.

11. THE BOMBING OF NORTH VIETNAM

1. *Pentagon Papers* III:270.
2. *Ibid.*, IV:18.
3. *Ibid.*, III:304–6.
4. *Ibid.*, III:271–72.
5. For a list see Lyndon B. Johnson, *The Vantage Point: Perspectives of the Presidency 1963–1969* (New York, 1971), p. 578.
6. Allan E. Goodman, *The Lost Peace: America's Search for a Negotiated Settlement of the Vietnam War* (Stanford, Calif., 1978).
7. U.S. Department of Defense, Vietnam Task Force, *United States–Vietnam Relations 1945–1967*, Vol. VI.C.1–4. These sections of the *Pentagon Papers* were not part of the material leaked in 1971. With some omissions they were declassified and released in the spring of 1975, and they can be purchased from the Department of Defense.
8. Memo of 27 March 1967, reprinted in John P. Roche, *Sentenced to Life* (New York, 1974), p. 112.
9. *Pentagon Papers* III:340–41, IV:20–21; NSAM 328 is reproduced at IV:702–3. See also Robert L. Galluci, *Neither Peace nor Honor: The Politics of American Military Policy in Viet-Nam* (Baltimore, 1975), pp. 54–57.
10. William C. Westmoreland, *A Soldier Reports* (Garden City, N.Y., 1976), p. 119.
11. *Pentagon Papers* IV:18–19.
12. *Ibid.*, IV:29, 105–7, 135.
13. U. S. G. Sharp and W. C. Westmoreland, *Report on the War in Vietnam (As of 30 June 1968)*, (Washington, D.C., 1969), p. 29.
14. *Pentagon Papers* IV:137.
15. *Ibid.*, IV:350.
16. *Ibid.*, IV:126.
17. *Ibid.*, IV:147–48.
18. U.S. Senate, Committee on Armed Services, Preparedness Investigating Subcommittee, *Air War Against North Vietnam*, Hearings, 90th Cong., 1st sess., part 1, 9 August 1967, pp. 6–13.
19. *Ibid.*, part 4, 25 August 1967, pp. 274–82. Excerpts from McNamara's testimony are reprinted in Wesley R. Fishel, ed., *Vietnam: Anatomy of a Conflict* (Itasca, Ill., 1968), pp. 439–45.
20. *Pentagon Papers* IV:203–4.
21. *Ibid.*, IV:216.
22. *Ibid.*, IV:254–58.
23. *Ibid.*, IV:259.

24. *Ibid.*, IV:272.
25. Note 5 above, p. 396.
26. *Pentagon Papers* IV:270.
27. Note 5 above, p. 495.
28. Data submitted to U.S. Senate, Committee on Armed Services, *FY 1974 Authorization for Military Procurement, Research and Development*, Hearings, 93rd Cong., 1st sess., 28 March–2 April 1973, p. 427.
29. Chester L. Cooper, *The Lost Crusade: America in Vietnam* (Greenwich, Conn., 1972), pp. 474–75.
30. The three "understandings" were confirmed by Defense Secretary Clifford on the CBS program "Face the Nation" on 15 December 1968.
31. Note 5 above, p. 528.
32. W. Averell Harriman, *America and Russia in a Changing World: A Half Century of Personal Observation* (Garden City, N.Y., 1971), p. 136.
33. U.S. Senate, Select Committee to Study Governmental Operations with Respect to Intelligence Activities, *Intelligence Activities: Senate Resolution 21*, vol. VI: *FBI*, Hearings, 94th Cong., 1st sess., 18 November–11 December 1975, pp. 483–84. See also Nicholas M. Horrock, "Ex-F.B.I. Official Testified Agnew Was Investigated," *New York Times*, 3 February 1975.
34. U.S. Pacific Air Force, message, 18 November 1968.
35. OASD (Comptroller), SEA Statistical Summary, Table 360, 22 October 1968.
36. Sam B. Barrett (Aerospace Studies Institute), "The Air Campaign Against North Vietnam," October 1969, p. 14.
37. Note 13 above, pp. 53–54.
38. OASD (Comptroller), SEA Statistical Summary, Table 5, 18 January 1972.
39. Alain C. Enthoven and K. Wayne Smith, *How Much Is Enough? Shaping the Defense Program 1961–1969* (New York, 1971), p. 304.
40. NSSM 1 [February 1969], *Congressional Record* CXVIII, part 13 (10 May 1972):16800, 16834.
41. *Ibid.*, pp. 16780, 16833. See also Raymond J. Barrett, "Graduated Response and the Lessons of Vietnam," *Military Review* LII, no. 5 (May 1972): 87, and the Rand Study by Oleg Hoeffding, *Bombing North Vietnam: An Appraisal of Economic and Political Effects*, RM-5213-1-ISA (Santa Monica, Calif., 1966).
42. Note 40 above, p. 16781.
43. Allen S. Whiting, *The Chinese Calculus of Deterrence: India and Indochina* (Ann Arbor, Mich., 1975), pp. 186–87.
44. *Pentagon Papers* IV:52.
45. Note 43 above, pp. 180–81.
46. Thomas H. Moorer, "Recent Bombing in the North," *Air Force Policy Letter for Commanders*, Supp. no. 2 (February 1973):12.
47. "General Van Tien Dung on Some Great Experiences of the People's War," June 1967, in Patrick J. McGarvey, *Visions of Victory: Selected Vietnamese Communist Military Writings, 1964–1968* (Stanford, Calif., 1969), p. 156.
48. Robert E. Schmaltz, "The Uncertainty of Predicting Results of an Interdiction Campaign," *Aerospace Historian* XVII (1970):150–53.

49. Gregory A. Carter, *Some Historical Notes on Air Interdiction in Korea*, P-3452 (Santa Monica, Calif., 1966), p. 2.
50. Felix Kozacza, "Enemy Bridging Techniques in Korea," *Air University Quarterly Review* V, no. 4 (Winter 1952–53):49.
51. Robert Frank Futrell *et al.*, *The United States Air Force in Korea: 1950–1953* (New York, 1961), p. 443.
52. Note 19 above.
53. Louis Menashe and Ronald Radosh, eds., *Teach-Ins: U.S.A.* (New York, 1967), p. 169; David Halberstam, *The Best and the Brightest* (Greenwich, Conn., 1973), p. 200.
54. U.S. Strategic Bombing Survey, *Summary Report (European War)* (Washington, D.C., 1945), p. 4, and *Over-All Report (European War)* (Washington, D.C., 1945), p. 95.
55. *Over-All Report (European War)*, p. 99; Fred Charles Iklé, *The Social Impact of Bomb Destruction* (Norman, Okla., 1958), p. 198.
56. Bernard Brodie, *Strategy in the Missile Age* (Princeton, N.J., 1959), p. 138.
57. Note 39 above, p. 304.
58. Draft of Art. 43, ICRC, *Conference of Government Experts on the Reaffirmation and Development of International Humanitarian Law Applicable in Armed Conflicts* (Geneva, 1972), I:16.
59. *Ibid.*, II:89.
60. Henri Meyrowitz, "The Law of War in the Vietnamese Conflict," in Richard A. Falk, ed., *The Vietnam War and International Law* (Princeton, N.J., 1969), II:551.
61. Draft of Art. 45, n. 58 above, p. 17.
62. Draft of Art. 46, *ibid.*
63. Morris Greenspan, *The Modern Law of Land Warfare* (Berkeley, Calif., 1959), p. 336.
64. Telford Taylor, *Nuremberg and Vietnam: An American Tragedy* (New York, 1971), p. 142.
65. Jon M. van Dyke, *North Vietnam's Strategy for Survival* (Palo Alto, Calif., 1972), p. 153; A. J. C. Lavalle, ed., *The Tale of Two Bridges and the Battle for the Skies over North Vietnam*, USAF SEA Monograph Series (Washington, D.C., 1976), chs. 3–4.
66. Harrison E. Salisbury, *Behind the Lines—Hanoi* (New York, 1967), p. 183.
67. John Gerassi, *North Vietnam: A Documentary* (London, 1968), pp. 51–55; Harry S. Ashmore and William C. Baggs, *Mission to Hanoi: A Chronicle of Double-Dealing in High Places* (New York, 1968), p. 21; Lavalle, n. 65 above, ch. 5.
68. Reprinted in Marvin E. and Susan Gettleman, eds., *Vietnam: History, Documents, and Opinions on a Major World Crisis* (New York, 1970), p. 421.
69. *Pentagon Papers* IV:43.
70. U.S. Air Force Historical Division, "USAF Operations in the Korean Conflict, 1 July 1952–23 July 1953" (Historical Study 127); *Air University Quarterly Review* Staff, "The Attack on the Irrigation Dams in North Korea," *Air Uni-*

versity *Quarterly Review* VI, no. 4 (Winter 1953–54):40–61; Robert Jackson, *Air War over Korea* (New York, 1975), p. 157.

71. Note 35 above.
72. Van Dyke, n. 65 above, p. 186.
73. John Duffett, ed., *Against the Crime of Silence: Proceedings of the International War Crimes Tribunal* (New York, 1970), p. 189.
74. Committee of Concerned Asian Scholars, *The Indochina Story: A Fully Documented Account* (New York, 1970), p. 126.
75. Note 66 above, p. 58.
76. Note 73 above, pp. 308–9.
77. Daniel Berrigan, *Night Flight to Hanoi: War Diary with 11 Poems* (New York, 1971), p. 65.
78. Quoted in *New York Times*, 29 December 1966.
79. *New York Times*, 29 December 1966.
80. Note 66 above.
81. This discussion of the Salisbury affair is indebted to the careful analysis in Phil G. Goulding, *Confirm or Deny: Informing the People on National Security* (New York, 1970). Goulding is a former assistant secretary of defense for public affairs.
82. James Aronson, *The Press and the Cold War* (Indianapolis, 1970), p. 260.
83. *New York Times*, 27 December 1966.
84. *Ibid.*
85. Note 81 above, pp. 64–65.
86. Note 83 above.
87. *Pentagon Papers* IV:261.
88. Note 40 above, p. 16833.
89. C. Holmquist, "Developments and Problems in Carrier-Based Attack Aircraft," *Naval Review 1969*, p. 214. See also Bernard Appel, "Bombing Accuracy in a Combat Environment," *Air University Review* XXV, no. 5 (July/August 1975):40–41.
90. Note 66 above, p. 81.
91. Jack A. Broughton, *Thud Ridge* (Philadelphia, 1969), p. 223.
92. Note 35 above.
93. U.S. Department of the Air Force, "Strike Control and Reconnaissance (SCAR) in Southeast Asia" (CHECO SEA Report), 22 January 1969, p. 42.
94. U.S. Department of the Air Force, "The War in Vietnam: July–December 1967" (CHECO SEA Report), 29 November 1968, p. 102; n. 36 above, p. 11; OASD (Comptroller), SEA Statistical Summary, Table 321, 19 April 1972.
95. Burrus M. Carnahan, "The Law of Air Bombardment in Its Historical Context," *Air Force Law Review* XVII (Summer 1975):60.
96. Note 64 above, p. 141.
97. James Cameron, *Here Is Your Enemy* (New York, 1966), pp. 57–58.
98. George Esper, "B-52 Pilot Who Refused Mission Calls War Not Worth the Killing," *New York Times*, 12 January 1973.

99. U.S. Department of the Air Force, "Rules of Engagement: November 1969–September 1972" (CHECO SEA Report), 1 March 1973, p. 32.
100. OASD (Comptroller), SEA Statistical Summary, Table 304, 5 December 1973.
101. Note 99 above.
102. U.S. Senate, Committee on Foreign Relations, *Bombing Operations and the Prisoner-of-War Rescue Mission in North Vietnam*, Hearing, 91st Cong., 2nd sess., 24 November 1970, p. 2.
103. *Ibid.*, p. 20; n. 100 above.
104. U.S. Senate, Committee on Armed Services, *Nomination of John D. Lavelle, General Creighton W. Abrams, and Admiral John S. McCain*, Hearings, 92nd Cong., 2nd sess., 11–22 September 1972, p. 235.
105. *Ibid.*, p. 51.
106. U.S. House, Committee on Armed Services Investigating Subcommittee, *Unauthorized Bombing of Military Targets in North Vietnam*, Hearings, 92nd Cong., 2nd sess., 12 June 1972, p. 10.
107. *Ibid.*, report, 15 December 1972, p. 7.
108. The legality of attacking neutral territory which is used by a belligerent is defended by the authorities cited in chap. 5, n. 35.
109. Cf. Sheldon W. Simon, *War and Politics in Cambodia: A Communications Analysis* (Durham, N.C., 1974), p. 105.
110. Note 99 above, pp. 46–48.
111. See Lavalle, n. 65 above, pp. 79–83.
112. U.S. Senate, Committee on the Judiciary, Subcommittee to Investigate Problems Connected with Refugees and Escapees, *Problems of War Victims in Indochina*, Part IV: *North Vietnam*, Hearings, 92nd Cong., 2nd sess., 28 September 1972, p. 12.
113. *Ibid.*, Part III, 16–17 August 1972, p. 42.
114. *New York Times*, 27 October 1972.
115. Marvin and Bernard Kalb, *Kissinger* (Boston, 1974), p. 415.
116. Robert N. Ginsburgh, "Strategy and Airpower: The Lessons of Southeast Asia," *Strategic Review* I (Summer 1973):23; U.S. House, Committee on Appropriations, Subcommittee on DOD, *DOD Appropriations: Bombing of North Vietnam*, Hearings, 93rd Cong., 1st sess., 9–18 January 1973, p. 40.
117. U.S. Department of the Air Force, "Short Rounds: June 1968–May 1969" (CHECO SEA Report), 15 August 1969, p. 27.
118. DRVN Commission for Investigation of the US Imperialists' War Crimes in Viet Nam, *The Late December 1972 US Blitz on North Viet Nam* (n.p., n.d.), pp. 7, 25.
119. Peter A. Poole, *The United States and Indochina: From FDR to Nixon* (Hinsdale, Ill., 1973), pp. 226–28.
120. Max Seiderwitz, *Zerstörung und Wiederaufbau von Dresden* (Berlin, 1955), cited by Melden E. Smith, Jr., "The Strategic Bombing Debate: The Second World War and Vietnam," *Journal of Contemporary History* XII (1977):183;

Stockholm International Peace Research Institute, *Incendiary Weapons* (Cambridge, Mass., 1975), p. 36. See also Hans Rumpf, *The Bombing of Germany*, trans. Edward Fitzgerald (New York, 1963).

121. "Use of Air Power," *Economist*, 13 January 1973, p. 15.
122. U.S. Senate, Committee on the Judiciary, Subcommittee to Investigate Problems Connected with Refugees and Escapees, *Relief and Rehabilitation of War Victims in Indochina*, Part III: *North Vietnam and Laos*, Hearing, 93rd Cong., 1st sess., 31 July 1973, p. 72.
123. *New York Times*, 7 January 1973.
124. Quoted in n. 122 above, pp. 78, 88; Drew Middleton, "Hanoi Films Show No 'Carpet Bombing,' " *New York Times*, 2 May 1973.
125. Quoted in n. 122 above, pp. 74, 78.
126. Quoted in n. 115 above, p. 418.
127. T. H. Moorer, "The Decisiveness of Airpower in Vietnam," *Air Force Policy Letter for Commanders*, supp. no. 11 (November 1973):9.
128. Norman R. Thorpe and James R. Miles in Peter D. Trooboff, ed., *Law and Responsibility in Warfare: The Vietnam Experience* (Chapel Hill, N.C., 1975), p. 145.
129. Roger Hilsman, *To Move a Nation: The Politics of Foreign Policy in the Administration of John F. Kennedy* (Garden City, N.Y., 1967), p. 439.
130. Gallucci, n. 9 above, p. 82.
131. Reprinted in Morton A. Kaplan *et al.*, *Vietnam Settlement: Why 1973, not 1969* (Washington, D.C., 1973), p. 153.

EPILOGUE: THE LEGACY OF VIETNAM

1. David Halberstam, *The Making of a Quagmire* (New York, 1965), pp. 33, 315. See also Ian Maitland, "Only the Best and the Brightest?" *Asian Affairs* III (1976):263–72.
2. Cf. Leslie H. Gelb, "Vietnam: The System Worked," *Foreign Policy* no. 3 (Summer 1971):140.
3. Arthur M. Schlesinger, Jr., *A Thousand Days: John F. Kennedy in the White House* (Boston, 1965), p. 997.
4. C. V. Wedgewood, *William the Silent* (London, 1967), p. 35, cited by Dean Acheson, *Present at the Creation: My Years in the State Department* (New York, 1969), p. xvii.
5. Ralph N. Clough, "East Asia," in Henry Owen, ed., *The Next Phase in Foreign Policy* (Washington, D.C., 1973), p. 50.
6. Mike Mansfield *et al.*, *The Vietnam Conflict: The Substance and the Shadow* (Washington, D.C., 1966), pp. 18–19.
7. Hans J. Morgenthau, *Vietnam and the United States* (Washington, D.C., 1965), p. 65.
8. Arthur M. Schlesinger, Jr., in Louis Menashe and Ronald Radosh, eds., *Teach-Ins: U.S.A.* (New York, 1967), pp. 166–67.

9. Letter to the editor, *New York Times*, 4 June 1965.
10. Tunku Abdul Rahman, "Malaysia: Key Area in Southeast Asia," *Foreign Affairs* XLIII (1965):66–68.
11. Seymour Topping, "South East Asia Isn't Scared of the Chinese Dragon," *New York Times Magazine*, 16 January 1966, p. 68.
12. Tom Wicker, "South East Asia: The Hope of Counterweight," *New York Times*, 9 February 1967.
13. Hubert H. Humphrey, *The Education of a Public Man: My Life in Politics* (New York, 1976), p. 333.
14. International Monetary Fund, *Directions of Trade* (1969), pp. 51–53, cited by Robert W. Tucker, *The Radical Left and American Foreign Policy* (Baltimore, 1971), p. 116. See also n. 5 above.
15. Martin J. Murray, "The Post-Colonial State: Investment and Intervention in Vietnam," *Politics and Society* III (1973):437.
16. U.S. Bureau of the Census, *Statistical Abstract of the United States 1970* (Washington, D.C., 1970), Table 1232, p. 791.
17. Betty C. Hanson and Bruce M. Russett, "Testing Some Economic Interpretations of American Intervention: Korea, Indochina and the Stock Market," in Steven Rosen, ed., *Testing the Theory of the Military-Industrial Complex* (Lexington, Mass., 1973), p. 234.
18. Cf. Robert Eisner, "The War and the Economy," in Sam Brown and Len Ackland, eds., *Why Are We Still in Vietnam?* (New York, 1970), pp. 109–23.
19. Cited by Dennis J. Duncanson, *Government and Revolution in Vietnam* (London, 1968), p. 6.
20. "Long Live the Victory of the People's War," 3 September 1965, in Mao Tsetung and Lin Piao, *Post-Revolutionary Writings*, K. Fan, ed. (Garden City, N.Y., 1972), p. 403.
21. *Pentagon Papers* IV:634.
22. U.S. Senate, Committee on Foreign Relations, *Supplemental Foreign Assistance FY 1966—Vietnam*, Hearings, 89th Cong., 2nd sess., 28 January–18 February 1966, p. 332.
23. George W. Ball, *The Discipline of Power: Essentials of a Modern World Structure* (Boston, 1968), p. 334.
24. Henry A. Kissinger, "The Viet Nam Negotiations," *Foreign Affairs* XLVII (1969):219.
25. Tom Wicker, "Southeast Asia: Dominoes and Master Plan," *New York Times*, 12 February 1967.
26. "Marcos Urges Reassessment of Philippine–U.S. Relations," *New York Times*, 24 May 1975.
27. Joseph Lelyveld, "Indonesia Calm on Red Indochina," *New York Times*, 27 March 1975.
28. Draft memo of 3 September 1964, *Pentagon Papers* III:559.
29. Leslie H. Gelb, "Skepticism on Domino Theory," *New York Times*, 27 March 1975.
30. Joseph S. Nye, Jr., deputy to the under secretary of state for security assis-

tance, science and technology, before the Houston Rotary Club, Department of State, Bureau of Public Affairs, Office of Media Services news release.

31. Cf. Walter Laqueur, *Neo-Isolationalism and the World of the Seventies* (New York, 1972), p. 17; Robert W. Tucker, *A New Isolationalism: Threat or Promise?* (New York, 1972), p. 121.
32. Cf. Earl C. Ravenal, "Was Vietnam a Mistake?" *Asian Survey* XIX (1974):592.
33. John Stuart Mill, "A Few Words on Non-Intervention," *Fraser's Magazine* (December 1859), reprinted in Richard A. Falk, ed., *The Vietnam War and International Law* (Princeton, N.J., 1968), I:38.
34. Irving Kristol, "Consensus and Dissent in U.S. Foreign Policy," in Anthony Lake, ed., *The Vietnam Legacy: The War, American Society and the Future of American Foreign Policy* (New York, 1976), pp. 95–96. See also Paul Ramsey, *The Just War: Force and Political Responsibility* (New York, 1968), p. 459.
35. Ramsey, n. 34 above, p. 31.
36. Cf. Anthony Hartley, "Vietnam, American Public Opinion and the Future," *Brassey's Annual*, 1970, p. 121.
37. Leslie H. Gelb, "The Essential Domino: American Politics and Vietnam," *Foreign Affairs* L (1972):466.
38. John P. Roche, "Can a Free Society Fight a Limited War?" *The New Leader*, 21 October 1968, p. 8.
39. Lawrence R. Velvel, *Undeclared War and Civil Disobedience: The American System in Crisis* (New York, 1970), p. 97; Richard A. Falk, "Six Legal Dimensions of the United States Involvement in the Vietnam War," in Falk, n. 34 above, II:245–46.
40. See, e.g., *Berk v. Laird*, 317 F. Supp. 715 (1970); 404 U.S. 869 (1971). On this subject generally see Anthony A. D'Amato and Robert M. O'Neil, *The Judiciary and Vietnam* (New York, 1972).
41. Ithiel de Sola Pool in Richard M. Pfeffer, ed., *No More Vietnams? The War and the Future of American Foreign Policy* (New York, 1968), p. 206.
42. Note 37 above, p. 459.
43. Interdoc Conference, *Guerilla Warfare in Asia* (The Hague, 1971), p. 63.
44. Don Oberdorfer, *Tet!* (Garden City, N.Y., 1971), p. 241. See also the careful study of Peter Braestrup, *Big Story: How the American Press and Television Reported and Interpreted the Crisis of Tet 1968 in Vietnam and Washington* (Boulder, Colo., 1977).
45. Milton J. Rosenberg *et al.*, *Vietnam and the Silent Majority: The Dove's Guide* (New York, 1970), pp. 44 and 69–70.
46. See on this generally Sandy Vogelgesang, *The Long Dark Night of the Soul: The American Intellectual Left and the Vietnam War* (New York, 1974); Eric F. Goldman, *The Tragedy of Lyndon Johnson* (New York, 1969); Arnold Beichman, *Nine Lies About America* (New York, 1972).
47. U.S. Senate, Select Committee to Study Governmental Operations with Respect to Intelligence Activities, *Foreign and Military Intelligence*, Final Report, 94th Cong., 2nd sess., 23–26 April 1976, Bk. 3, p. 692; Chester A. Bain, "Viet Cong Propaganda Abroad," *Foreign Service Journal* XLV, no. 10 (Octo-

ber 1968):18; Georgie Anne Geyer, "Cuba's Contribution to the American Radical Movement," *The Progressive* XXXIV, no. 12 (December 1970):15. See also Nicholas M. Horrock, "Cuba Aided Weather Underground in War Protest Years, F.B.I. Says," *New York Times*, 9 October 1977.

48. *Pentagon Papers* IV:478.
49. James Reston, "Washington: The Stupidity of Intelligence," *New York Times*, 17 October 1965.
50. Lucian W. Pye, *Aspects of Political Development* (Boston, 1966), p. 131.
51. Edward G. Lansdale in W. Scott Thompson and Donaldson D. Frizzell, eds., *The Lessons of the Vietnam War* (New York, 1977), p. 42.
52. Barbara W. Tuchman, *Stilwell and the American Experience in China: 1911–45* (New York, 1970), p. 531.
53. Robert W. Komer, *Bureaucracy Does Its Thing: Institutional Constraints on U.S.-GVN Performance in Vietnam* (Santa Monica, Calif., 1973), p. 35.
54. Henry Kissinger before the Japan Society, New York City, 18 June 1975, *Department of State Bulletin* LXXIII, no. 1880 (7 July 1975):3–4.

APPENDIX I: CIVILIAN CASUALTIES

1. This is the position taken by J. David Singer and Melvin Small, *The Wages of War, 1816–1965: A Statistical Handbook* (New York, 1972), p. 48.
2. The increase of the CWC figures by 20 percent and the calculations that follow are based in part on the methodology developed by Thomas C. Thayer, "War Without Fronts," *Journal of Defense Research*, Series B, Tactical Warfare Analysis of Viet Nam Data, Vol. 7B, no. 3 (Fall 1975):861–62.
3. U.S. Embassy Saigon to Department of State, 30 March 1966, Civilian Casualties file, CMH.
4. USAID Saigon to Department of State, 24 March 1971, Civilian Casualties file, CMH.
5. D. B. White, "Civilian Medical Care in South Vietnam," *Military Medicine* CXXXIII (1968):650.
6. Data supplied by U.S. Department of the Army, Office of the Surgeon General, Patient Administration Office.
7. Testimony of John A. Hannah (AID) before U.S. Senate, Committee on the Judiciary, Subcommittee to Investigate Problems Connected with Refugees and Escapees, *Civilian Casualty, Social Welfare and Refugee Problems in Vietnam*, Hearings, 91st Cong., 1st sess., 24 June 1969, p. 6.
8. Martin Luther King, "Declaration of Independence from the War in Vietnam," *Ramparts* V, no. 11 (May 1967):34–35.
9. Benjamin Spock and Mitchell Zimmerman, *Dr. Spock on Vietnam* (New York, 1968), p. 83.
10. Edward S. Herman, *Atrocities in Vietnam: Myths and Realities* (Philadelphia, 1970), pp. 43–45.
11. Embassy Saigon to Department of State, 14 October 1967, Civilian Casualties

file, CMH; USAID memo, November 1969, Washington National Records Center, 286-76-084 (2/68: 17-1), file POL 27-15.

12. H. A. F. Dudley *et al.*, "Civilian Battle Casualties in South Vietnam," *British Journal of Surgery* LV (1968):335.

13. U.S. Senate, Committee on the Judiciary, Subcommittee to Investigate Problems Connected with Refugees and Escapees, *Civilian Casualty and Refugee Problems in South Vietnam: Findings and Recommendations*, 90th Cong., 2nd sess., 9 May 1968, p. 40.

14. Telford Taylor, *Nuremberg and Vietnam: An American Tragedy* (New York, 1971), p. 172.

15. Note 10 above, p. 43.

16. Memo by A. E. Farwell, AID associate director for social development, 4 April 1971, p. 2, Civilian Casualties file, CMH.

17. Gilbert W. Beebe and Michael E. de Bakey, *Battle Casualties: Incidence, Mortality and Logistic Considerations* (Springfield, Ill., 1952), p. 12.

18. Note 16 above, p. 3.

19. U.S. Senate, Committee on the Judiciary, Subcommittee on Problems Connected with Refugees and Escapees, *War-Related Civilian Problems in Indochina, Part I: Vietnam*, Hearing, 92nd Cong., 1st sess., 21 April 1971, p. 47.

20. OASD (SA), *SEA Analysis Report*, March/April 1971, p. 31.

21. Cf. Quincy Wright, *A Study of War*, 2nd ed. (Chicago, 1965), p. 664, and Boris Urlanis, *Wars and Population*, trans. Leo Lempert (Moscow, 1971), p. 201. I am indebted also to a research memorandum, "Civilian Versus Military Casualties," of 16 November 1972 by the Swedish researcher Malvern Lumsden of the Stockholm International Peace Research Institute.

22. Urlanis, n. 21 above, p. 278.

23. Bernard B. Fall, *Street Without Joy: Indochina at War, 1946–54* (Harrisburg, Pa., 1961), p. 314; a similar figure is given by Robert Aron, *France Reborn: The History of the Liberation*, trans. Humphrey Hare (New York, 1964), p. 465.

24. See Urlanis, n. 21 above, pp. 290–91.

25. OASD (Comptroller), Selected Manpower Statistics, May 1975, p. 64.

26. S. L. A. Marshall, *The Military History of the Korean War* (New York, 1963), p. 84.

27. Letter of first secretary of the Republic of Korea to Prof. Arthur H. Westing, Windham College, 22 December 1975.

28. David Rees, *Korea: The Limited War* (New York, 1964), pp. 460–61; Samuel P. Huntington, "Democracy Fights a Limited War: Korea 1950–1953," in Merrill D. Peterson and Leonard W. Levy, eds., *Major Crises in American History* (New York, 1962), p. 538.

29. OASD (Comptroller), SEA Statistical Summary, Table 860B, 18 February 1976.

30. See my Table 8-1 and n. 29 above.

31. NSSM 1 [1969], *Congressional Record* CXVIII, part 13 (10 May 1972):16833.

32. Data provided by USAID/Social Development Division, Office of Technical Development, Bureau for East Asia.
33. Peers Inquiry, I:10-24.
34. U.S. Department of the Army, Office Chief of Staff, memo, Subject: SPEEDY EXPRESS, 12 January 1972, SPEEDY EXPRESS file, CMH.
35. Derived from CWC data compiled by USAID/Public Health.

Glossary of Terms, Abbreviations and Acronyms

AAA	Anti-aircraft artillery
AAAS	American Association for the Advancement of Science
AAR	After-action report
ABMR	Army Board of Military Review
ACMR	Army Court of Military Review
AF	Air Force
AFM	Air Force Manual
AID	Agency for International Development
AO	Area of operations
APC	Armed personnel carrier
AR	Army Regulation
ARVN	Army of the Republic of Vietnam (South)
Bde	Brigade
BLT	Battalion landing team
Bn	Battalion
Booby trap	Explosive charge hidden in a harmless object which explodes on contact
CAP	Combined action platoon
CAP	Combat air patrol
Cav	Cavalry
CBU	Cluster bomb unit
CCI	National Committee for a Citizens' Commission of Inquiry on U.S. War Crimes in Vietnam
CG	Commanding general
CHECO	Contemporary Historical Examination of Current Operations
Chieu Hoi	South Vietnamese program to encourage defectors (also known as "Open Arms" program)

CIA	Central Intelligence Agency
CID	Criminal Investigation Division
CIDG	Civilian Irregular Defense Group
CINCPAC	Commander-in-Chief, Pacific Command
CM	Court-martial
CMH	Center of Military History
CMR	Court Martial Reports
CN	Type of tear gas
CO	Commanding officer
Co.	Company
COMUSMACV	Commander, U.S. Military Assistance Command, Vietnam
COR	Committee of Responsibility to Save War-Burnt and War-Injured Vietnamese Children
CORDS	Civil Operations and Revolutionary (Rural) Development Support
COSVN	Central Office for South Vietnam
COWIN	Conduct of the War in Vietnam. A report commissioned in 1971 by the U.S. Army Deputy Chief of Staff for Military Operations
CPDC	Central Pacification and Development Council (GVN)
CS	Type of tear gas
CTZ	Corps Tactical Zone
CWC	Civilian war casualties
CY	Calendar year
DEROS	Date eligible for return from overseas
DIA	Defense Intelligence Agency
DIOCC	District Intelligence and Operation Coordinating Center
DMZ	Demilitarized Zone between North and South Vietnam
DOD	Department of Defense
DRV	Democratic Republic of Vietnam (North)
FAC	Forward air controller
FARMGATE	Code name for early U.S. Air Force support of ARVN
FM	Field Manual
FMFM	Fleet Marine Force Manual
FWMAF	Free World Military Assistance Forces
FY	Fiscal year
GAO	General Accounting Office
GVN	Government of Vietnam (South)

H&I	Harassment and interdiction fire
HES	Hamlet Evaluation System
HIMS	Historical Information Management System
Hoi Chanh	Name ("rallier") given to a defector under the Chieu Hoi program
Hq.	Headquarters
ICC	International Control Commission
ICEX	Intelligence Coordination and Exploitation
ICRC	International Committee of the Red Cross
III MAF	Third Marine Amphibious Force
ISA	International Security Affairs (DOD)
JAG	Judge Advocate General
JCS	Joint Chiefs of Staff
JCSM	Joints Chiefs of Staff Memorandum
JFK Library, NSF/V	John F. Kennedy Library, National Security Files, Vietnam
JGS	Joint General Staff (of RVNAF)
JUSPAO	Joint U.S. Public Affairs Office
KIA	Killed in action
Lao Dong Party	See VWP
LOC	Line of communication
Lt.	Lieutenant
LTG	Lieutenant General
LZ	Landing zone
MAAG	Military Assistance Advisory Group
MACCORDS	Civil Operations and Revolutionary Development Support division of MACV
MACJ2	Military Assistance Command J-2 (military intelligence)
MACV	Military Assistance Command, Vietnam
MAF	Marine Amphibious Force
Maj.	Major
MEDCAP	Medical Civic Action Program
MG	Major General
MIA	Missing in action
MIG	Soviet fighter plane (*Mikoyan i Gurevich*)

MILCAP	Military Civil Assistance Program (South Vietnam)
MILPHAP	Military Provincial Health Assistance Program
Mission	An operational flight by several aircraft. Also the embassy or legation
MOH	Ministry of Health (South Vietnam)
MR	Military Region
NA	Not available
NAS	National Academy of Science
NATO	North Atlantic Treaty Organization
NCM	Navy court-martial
NCMR	Navy Court of Military Review
NCO	Noncommissioned officer
NLF	National Liberation Front
NSAM	National Security Action Memorandum
NSC	National Security Council
NSSM	National Security Study Memorandum
NVA	North Vietnamese Army
OASD (PA)	Office of the Assistant Secretary of Defense (Public Affairs)
OASD (SA)	Office of the Assistant Secretary of Defense (Systems Analysis)
OCO	Office of Civil Operations
OCS	Officer candidate school
OPLAN	Operations plan
PACAF	Pacific Air Forces
PAVN	People's Army of Vietnam (North)
Peers Inquiry	*Report of the Department of the Army Review of the Preliminary Investigations into the My Lai Incident*, 14 March 1970. The inquiry was directed by Lt. Gen. W. R. Peers
Pentagon Papers	*The Defense Department History of U.S. Decisionmaking on Vietnam* (Senator Gravel edition published by Beacon Press, 5 vols., Boston, 1971–72). Official title: *United States-Vietnam Relations 1945–1967* (12 vols., Washington, D.C., 1971)
PF	Popular Forces
Phoenix	English name for the Phuong Hoang program
Phuong Hoang	GVN program to neutralize VCI
PIC	Provincial Interrogation Center
PIOCC	Province Intelligence and Operation Coordinating Center
PLAF	People's Liberation Armed Forces

POL	Petroleum, oil, lubricants
POW	Prisoner of war
Prep	Preparatory fire
PRG	Provisional Revolutionary Government
PROVN	"A Program for the Pacification and Long-Term Development of South Vietnam," a report commissioned in 1965 by the U.S. Army Deputy Chief of Staff for Military Operations and completed in March 1966
PRP	People's Revolutionary Party
PRU	Provincial Reconnaissance Unit
PSA	Province senior adviser
PSC	Province Security Committee
PSD	Public Safety Directorate (CORDS)
PSDF	People's Self-Defense Force
PSG	Pacification Studies Group (CORDS)
RAD	Research and Analysis Directorate (CORDS)
RCA	Riot control agents
RD	Revolutionary Developmment
RE	Reports and Evaluation Division (CORDS)
Ref. Doc.	Reference Document
RF	Regional Forces
RLT	Regimental landing team
ROE	Rules of engagement
ROK	Republic of Korea (South)
ROTC	Reserve Officers Training Corps
RVN	Republic of Vietnam (South)
RVNAF	Republic of Vietnam (South) Air or Armed Forces
SAAFO	Special assistant to the ambassador for field operations
SACSA	Special assistant to the JCS for counterinsurgency and special activities
SAM	Surface-to-air missile
SEA	Southeast Asia
SEATO	Southeast Asia Treaty Organization
Sit Rep	Situation Report
SOP	Standing operating procedure
Sortie	An operational flight by one aircraft
SSZ	Specified strike zone (formerly free-fire zone)
State	U.S. Department of State
SVN	South Vietnam

TAOR	Tactical area of responsibility
Tet	Vietnamese lunar New Year holiday
TF	Task force
TIRS	Terrorist Incident Reporting System
UCMJ	Uniform Code of Military Justice
UN	United Nations
USAF	U.S. Air Force
USARV	U.S. Army Vietnam
USCMA	U.S. Court of Military Appeals
USIA	U.S. Information Agency
USMC	U.S. Marine Corps
VC	Viet Cong
VCI	Viet Cong infrastructure
VNAF	Vietnamese (South) Air Force
VVAW	Vietnamese Veterans Against the War
VWP	Vietnamese Workers' Party (Communist party of North Vietnam)
WIA	Wounded in action

Index

Abductions, 201, 272–73

Abrams, Creighton W., 146, 282, 339; appointed COMUSMACV, 133; and change in strategy, 134, 137–39, 145, 148; responsible for RVNAF, 164; and Vietnamization, 165

Accelerated Pacification Campaign of 1968, 134

Adams, Samuel A., 40, 75

Advisers, American, 124, 168–69

Agency for International Development (AID), 185, 301, 442, 447

Agent Blue, 263

Agent Orange, 263–65, 349

Aggression from the North (1965), 38–39

Agnew, Spiro T., 389

Agrovilles, 25, 89

AK-47 rifle, 163, 268

Americal Division: poor discipline in, 330; and ROE, 234–35, 237–38, 326; use of agent Orange, 263, 349; and war crimes, 346, 353. *See also* Divisions, U.S.

American Association for the Advancement of Science (AAAS), 263

American Friends of Vietnam, 12

Americanization of the Vietnam war, 130, 162

American Servicemen's Union, 159

Amnesty International, 278

Amphibious landing operations, 61, 98, 151

Anderson, William, 287, 297

An Loc, 197–98, 200, 413

Antiwar movement, 159, 434–36

An tri. See Emergency detention

APACHE SNOW operation, 144

Appropriations, congressional: and constitutionality of war, 431; cut off for Southeast Asia, 204; for South Vietnam, 207–8, 212

Area security concept, 137, 184

Army of the Republic of Vietnam (ARVN), 43, 48–49, 63; attitude to population, 19, 87, 177–78; combat effectiveness, 26, 163; corruption in, 217; desertion rate, 166, 172; disregard of civilian suffering, 97; leadership of, 170; modernization of, 131; in 1972 offensive, 198–99; in 1975 collapse, 212–14; reduced firepower in 1974–75, 207–8, 216. *See also* Republic of Vietnam Armed Forces

Arnett, Peter, 248

Arnoni, M. S., 311

Artillery, use of, 59, 70–71, 96–97, 99, 103, 141, 306, 448

A Shau Valley, 144–46, 196

Asia, balance of power in, 421, 431

Atrocities: allegations of, 313–18, 434; court-martial record of, 324–29; group pressure, 330; in Korea, 309, 340; and Korean troops, 327; not a legal term, 343; role of media, 321–24; and Vietnam environment, 309–11, 329, 346, 353, 355–56; in World War I, 308; in World War II, 308–9. *See also* Prisoners of War; War Crimes, U.S.; Viet Cong terror

ATTLEBORO operation, 67

Attrition, strategy of, 46, 51–52, 74, 82, 84, 123, 136, 145, 432, 439

Australia, 10, 46, 421

AWOL rates, U.S., 156–59

Bach Mai Hospital, 413

Bach, Pham Van, 251

Backlash reports, 344, 443

Bailey, F. Lee, 359, 362

Ball, George W., 37, 49, 392, 425

Ban Me Thuot, 211

CEDAR FALLS operation, 64–65, 110, 226, 243, 251

Center for Prisoner of War Studies, 338

Central highlands, 48–49, 212

Central Pacification and Development Council, 179, 181

Chaplains, 348, 368

Chau, Tran Ngoc, 278

Chennault, Anna, 389

Chiang Kai-shek, 19

Chieu Hoi program, 91–92, 173

Chi Hoa prison, 295

China, People's Republic of, 22, 38, 383, 392–93, 420–22

Chomsky, Noam, 224

Chu Lai, 52, 54

Church, Frank, 35

CIA, 22–23, 83; assesses bombing of North Vietnam, 381, 390; and Phoenix program, 280, 283, 287

Citizens' Commission of Inquiry on U.S. War Crimes in Vietnam (CCI), 313–14, 318–19

Civic action program, 93, 302

Civilian war casualties, 55, 98, 100, 105, 127, 181, 304; causes of, 446–48; compared to other wars, 452–53; mortality rate, 444; number of, in hospitals, 71, 141, 151, 442–43; and ROE, 233

Clark, Bronson P., 412

Clark, Ramsey, 337

Clark, Roger S., 361

Clear-and-hold strategy, 88

Clemency, 371

Clergy and Laity Concerned about Vietnam, 445

Clifford, Clark, 130–31, 133, 165–66, 386

Clifford task force, 130–32, 165, 385–86

Cluster bomb units (CBUs), 266–67

Code of conduct, 339

Colby, William E., 179, 282, 287, 292, 447

Collins, Jr., James Lawton, 169, 171

Combined Action Platoon (CAP), 116–17, 183, 439

Combined Campaign Plan for 1968, 113

Command, lack of unified, 121–22, 439

Commander-in-Chief, Pacific (CINCPAC), 48, 51, 114, 128, 138; and bombing of North Vietnam, 382–83; and crop destruction, 260; and McNamara Line, 66

Command responsibility for war crimes, 237–42, 359–69

Committee of Concerned Asian Scholars, 40, 224, 252, 399

Committee of Responsibility to Save War-Burnt and War-Injured Vietnamese Children, 244

Committee to Investigate Mistreatment of Political Prisoners, 294

Communism, fear of, 4, 420

Conduct of the War in Vietnam (COWIN), 239

Confessions, forced, 333, 340–41

Con Son Island, 297–99

Constellation, U.S.S., 36

Containment policy, 4, 420

Conversations with Americans, 316

Cooper, John Sherman, 34

CORDS, 123–25, 170, 460

Corps Tactical Zones (CTZ), 54

Corruption in South Vietnam, 90–91, 169, 201, 217, 219, 280

Counterinsurgency, capability for, 85

Counterspy, 314

Coventry, bombing of, 413

Covert operations, moralizing about, 429

COWIN study, 239

Cox, Harvey G., 227

Cramer, Myron C., 261

Crawford, Kenneth, 338

Credibility gap, 47, 430

Criminal Investigation Division (CID), 318–19, 321–22, 329, 371

Cronkite, Walter, 322

Crop destruction, 109; ecological effects, 264; effects on humans, 262–64; extent of, 258; first use of, 258; impact on pacification, 259–60, 262; legality of, 260–62; suspension of, 263; U.S. renunciation of, 266

CS. See Tear gas

Cua Viet River, 196, 199

Cuba, 19, 420

Czechoslovakia, 420

Dachau, 341

Dak Son atrocity, 245, 276

Dak To, 67

Danang, 42, 46, 52, 54, 147, 213

DARING REBEL operation, 150

Davis, Rennie, 336
Dean, John, 204
De Beauvoir, Simone, 312
"Declaration of the Veterans of the Resistance," 17
Dedijer, Vladimir, 312
Defense Investigative Service, 373
DEFIANT STAND operation, 151
Defoliation: ecological effects, 264; effects on humans, 262–64; extent of, 258; first use of, 257; legality of, 260–62; U.S. renunciation of, 266
DeHaan, Dale S., 413
DELAWARE VALLEY operation, 144
Dellinger, Dave, 279, 312, 336, 339
Dellums, Ronald V., 317–18
Demilitarized Zone (DMZ), 66, 110, 117, 196, 386, 389, 407
Democratic Republic of Vietnam (DRV): aid to southern insurgency, 8, 15, 17, 23, 29, 38–41, 391; amphibious landing in, 73, 129; at Geneva Conference of 1954, 7–8; manpower of, 84; and 1975 invasion, 205; regular forces in South Vietnam, 39–40, 56, 75, 206, 213, 415. *See also* Bombing of North Vietnam
DEROS, 159
Desertions: from RVNAF, 166, 172–74, 201, 210; from U.S. forces, 156–59; from VC/NVA, 173–74
DE SOTO patrol, 32
Detention, preventive. *See* Emergency detention
Deutscher, Isaac, 312
Devillers, Philippe, 15
Diehl, Bernhard, 338
Diem, Ngo Dinh, 7, 11–15, 18–20, 23, 26, 218; overthrow of, 27–28; and personalism, 25
Dien Bien Phu, battle of, 6–7, 128, 341
Dioxin, 264
Discipline crisis among U.S. troops, 153–61
District Intelligence and Operation Coordinating Centers, 280
Divisions, U.S.: Americal (Twenty-third Infantry), 139–40, 234; 82nd Airborne, 128; First Cavalry (Airmobile), 56–59, 68, 103, 353; Ninth Infantry, 81, 141–43, 151; 101st Airborne, 80, 135, 144, 349; Twenty-fifth Infantry, 62–63, 72, 141, 155

Domino theory, 6, 426
Dong Ha, 197
Dong Hoi, 375
Dong, Pham Van, 30
DOUBLE EAGLE operation, 61, 98
DRAGON HEAD V operation, 70
Draper, Theodore, 39, 41, 299
Dresden, bombing of, 413
Drinan, Robert F., 227, 295
Drug problem, 154, 160
Duffy, James B., 81, 328
Dulles, John Foster, 6–7, 10
Duncan, Donald, 313
Dung, Van Tien, 205, 207–8, 210–11, 214–15

Easter offensive (1972), 196–201; effect on pacification, 198; importance of air power, 199–200; North Vietnamese mistakes, 199; performance of RVNAF, 198–99
Ecocide, 264
Edap Enang resettlement area, 110
Efficiency reports, 119, 168
Eisenhower, Dwight D., 6–7, 11, 418
Elections in South Vietnam: for local offices, 14, 94, 218; for national legislature, 94; planned for 1956, 7, 10
Electric shocks, use on prisoners of, 287, 328–29
Ellsberg, Daniel, 300, 327
Emergency detention (*an tri*), 285–94; backlog in processing suspects, 288–89; and CIA, 287; and corruption, 289; and Geneva conventions, 286; in Northern Ireland, 286, 293; reforms in 1970–71, 291–93; torture of suspects, 287–88; in U.S., 285. *See also* Political prisoners
Enclave strategy, 46, 48–49, 56
Enthoven, Alain C., 80, 83
Ervin, Sam J., 365
Ethiopia, attack on, 429
European Defense Community (EDC), 3–4, 6–7
Ewell, Julian J., 81, 142–43
Experience, disregard of, 114–19

FAIRFAX operation, 63
Falk, Richard A., 230, 267, 271, 277, 299, 304, 306, 312, 336–37
Fall, Bernard, 30, 120, 341–42
Fallaci, Oriana, 80

"Family syndrome," 213
FARMGATE rules, 22, 259, 261
Federal Bureau of Prisons, 371
Final Solution of the Jewish Question, 300
Firepower, reliance on, 52, 70, 96, 99, 150, 181, 230, 269, 446
FitzGerald, Frances, 299
Flamethrowers, 243, 245, 276
FLAMING DART. *See* Bombing of North Vietnam
Floyd, Randy, 317
Fonda, Jane, 316
Ford, Gerald R., 257
Fort Bragg, 85
Forward air controllers (FAC), 71, 97, 106, 235, 405
Fox, Sylvan, 297
"Fragging" incidents, 155–56, 159
Franco, Francisco, 428
Franklin, J. Ross, 323–24
Franks, Lonni Douglas, 407–8
Fraser, Donald M., 251
Free-fire zones. *See* Specified strike zones
French Foreign Legion, 177
French Union, 3, 11
Frishman, Robert F., 335–36
Fulbright, J. William, 33–35

Galbraith, John Kenneth, 21
Gandhi, Indira, 422
Gelb, Leslie H., 430, 432
General Accounting Office (GAO), 113
Geneva Conference of 1954, 7–10, 22, 38, 376; binding character of accords, 7, 23; elections for unification, 7–10, 13; final declaration, 8–9, 14
Geneva conventions (1949), 230, 343; applicability to civil war, 225; Common Article 3, 225, 227, 255, 286, 332; and guerilla warfare, 270–71, 305; instruction in, 331; knowledge of, 345; punishment for breaches of, 365; updating of, 247, 270
Geneva Convention Relative to the Treatment of Prisoners of War (1949), 334, 361–62; and North Vietnamese reservation, 334
Geneva Convention Relative to the Protection of the Civilian Persons in Time of War (1949): and passage of food, 261; and popu-
lation relocations, 227–28; and preventive detention, 286
Geneva gas protocol (1925), 253; and crop destruction, 265; ratified by U.S., 257; and tear gas, 254–55
Genocide, 299–304; and bombing of North Vietnam, 400, 413; UN convention on, 300–1
German army in World War II, 176, 217
Germ warfare charges, 257, 340–41
Ghetto riots, 432
Giap, Vo Nguyen, 6, 17, 41, 67, 80, 199, 424, 436
GI underground newspapers, 158
GIs United Against the War in Vietnam, 159
Goldwater, Barry, 303
Go Noi Island, 148
Goodman, Allan E., 376
"Gook," 309–10. *See also* "Mere-gook" rule
Gore, Albert, 35
Government of (South) Vietnam (GVN), 4, 11, 134; communist infiltration of, 60, 122, 219; corruption of, 90–91, 169, 201, 219; lack of effectiveness of, 21, 94; social base of, 94; surrender in 1975, 215. *See also* Republic of Vietnam (South)
Great Britain, 7, 10, 440
Green Berets, 85
Greene, Felix, 339
Grotius, Hugo, 270
Guerilla warfare: and international law, 271–72, 304–6; and morality, 305
Guernica, bombing of, 413
Gulf of Tonkin incident (1964), 32–36, 375
Gulf of Tonkin resolution, 33–34, 418, 431
Gunships, helicopter, 235–36
Guy, Ted, 339

Hague Air Warfare Rules, 396
Hague Convention for the Protection of Cultural Property (1954), 396
Hague Convention IV (1907), 225, 230–31, 235, 242, 244, 262, 277
Hague Gas Declaration (1899), 253
Haiphong, bombing of, 30, 197, 379, 383, 392, 410–13
Halberstam, David, 14, 26, 395, 418
"Hamburger Hill," battle for, 144–46
Hamlet Evaluation System (HES), 125, 179, 191–95, 448

Hammer, Ellen J., 28
Ham Rung (Dragon's Jaw) Bridge, 398, 410
Hanoi, bombing of, 379, 383, 385, 398, 410, 412–14
Harassment and interdiction (H&I) fire, 99–101, 110
Harker, David M., 333
Harkin, Thomas, 297
Harkins, Paul D., 31, 97
Harriman, W. Averell, 389
Hassler, Alfred, 297
Hatfield, Mark O., 316
Hawkins, Augustus, 297
Heck, Michael J., 406
Hegdahl, Douglas B., 335–36
Heinl, Robert D., 153
Helicopters, use of, 24, 59, 86; for evacuation of wounded, 446
Henderson, Oran K., 363
Herbert, Anthony B., 322–24
Herbicides. *See* Crop destruction; Defoliation
Herman, Edward S., 277
Hersh, Seymour, 336
Heschel, Abraham Joshua, 227
HICKORY operation, 110, 226
High Command case, 240–41, 347, 360
Hilsman, Roger, 30, 39, 41, 96, 303, 416
Hiroshima and Nagasaki, bombing of, 395
Hitler, Adolf, 300, 440
Hoa Hao sect, 94, 222, 278
Ho Chi Minh, 7, 14, 16, 376, 436, 438
Ho Chi Minh Trail, 40, 110, 128–29, 393, 406
Hodson, Kenneth J., 329
Hoffman, David, 145
Hoffman, David W., 337
Hondas, 190, 209
Honey, P. J., 277
Honolulu conferences: in 1965, 47; in 1966, 123
Hostages case, 229, 232
Howard, Kenneth A., 360–61
Hue, 145, 196, 213; massacre (1968), 274–75
Hughes, Harold E., 407
Humphrey, Hubert H., 136, 388–89, 422
Huntington, Samuel P., 118, 125

Ia Drang Valley, 57
Ikle, Fred, 256

Improved conventional munitions, 266
Incendiary weapons: history of, 243; legality of, 246–47; and ROE, 243, 247. *See also* Napalm; White phosphorus rockets
India, 12, 421
Indochina Resource Center, 294
Indonesia, 38
Infiltration of northerners, 38–40, 66, 84, 391
Inflation in South Vietnam, 209
Inspector general system, 349, 409
Intellectuals and Vietnam war, 435
Intelligence Coordination and Exploitation (ICEX) program, 280
Interdiction bombing, 377, 394. *See also* Bombing of North Vietnam
Internal Security Act (1950), 285
International Commission of Enquiry into U.S. Crimes in Indochina, 244
International Commission on Control and Supervision, 202, 214
International Committee of the Red Cross (ICRC), 229, 247, 267, 270, 305, 331, 334; draft protocol on aerial warfare, 396–97
International Control Commission (ICC), 16, 22
International Security Affairs (DOD), Office of, 115, 130
International War Crimes Tribunal (Russell tribunal), 224, 251, 267, 299, 312–13, 399
Interpreters, 168
Iron Triangle, 64–65, 249
IRVING operation, 57–58
Isolationalism, 408
Israel, 217, 427

Japan, 5, 12, 423
Japanese-Americans, detention of, 285
Jason Committee, 66
Jeandel, Paul, 341
Johnson, Harold K., 43, 121
Johnson, Lyndon Baines, 29–31, 46, 50, 74, 115, 162, 164, 418, 430; and charges of duplicity, 35, 37; concern for "Great Society," 431; decision to bomb North Vietnam, 375; Gulf of Tonkin crisis, 33; introduces ground combat forces, 42, 419; limits/ends bombing of North Vietnam, 386–87, 417; and 1964 election, 36; and Paris peace talks,

388; resignation of, 133; and Tet offensive of 1968, 128

Johnson, Robert, 29–30

Joint Chiefs of Staff (JCS), 12, 43, 47, 51, 114–15, 128, 165; and bombing of North Vietnam, 29, 37, 374–75, 377–79, 382, 386, 392, 399, 409; and crop destruction, 260; and ground strategy, 138; and prevention of war crimes, 372–73; and relations with COMUSMACV, 114; and use of tear gas, 249

Joint General Staff (South Vietnam), 178, 181

Joint Logistics Review Board, 99

Joint U.S. Public Affairs Office (JUSPAO), 119

Jorden, William J., 23

Judge Advocate General Corps, 371

Judge Advocate General School, 367

JUNCTION CITY operation, 67

Just, Ward S., 98

Kahin, George McT., 15, 18

Kahn, Herman, 104–5

Kasler, James, 338

Kasuri, Mahmud Ali, 313

Katzenbach, Nicholas, 113

Kendrick, Alexander, 326

Kennan, George F., 425

Kennedy committee on refugees, 337, 442, 445–46, 448

Kennedy, Edward M., 113, 372, 413

Kennedy, John Fitzgerald, 18–19, 23, 29, 163, 418, 432; authorizes combat role, 22; on bombing of North Vietnam, 416; increases U.S. advisers, 20–21, 419; meeting with Khrushchev in Vienna, 19; as senator, 12–13; and withdrawal from Vietnam, 419

Kennedy, Robert F., 132

Kenya, 286

Khanh, Nguyen, 30–31

Khe Sanh, 117, 127, 146, 203; First Battle of, 67; media coverage of, 434; and nuclear weapons, 128

Khrushchev, Nikita, 19, 37

King, Jr., Martin Luther, 154, 227, 444–45

Kinnard, Douglas, 81

Kipling, Rudyard, 168

Kissinger, Henry A., 202–3, 412, 426, 441; and aid to South Vietnam, 207; concludes

Paris agreement of 1973, 414; and 1972 Christmas bombing of North Vietnam, 412; on 1968 Tet offensive, 76; on Vietnam strategy, 136

Knoebl, Kuno, 273

Knowles, John H., 244, 276

Komer, Robert W., 75, 86, 98–99, 113–14, 117, 122, 124–25, 191, 284, 440

Kontum (city), 197, 200, 212

Korean War, 4, 54, 99, 118, 309, 420, 437; bombing of dikes, 399; civilian casualties, 304, 435, 450; effects of U.S. bombing, 394; treatment of U.S. prisoners in, 340–42; use of napalm, 243; use of tear gas, 250; volume of aerial bombing, 385

Korea, Republic of (South Korea): atrocity by troops of, 327; troops in Vietnam, 46, 58, 97; U.S. assistance to, 427

Koster, Samuel W., 363–64

Kushner, F. Harold, 333

Ky, Nguyen Cao, 49, 122, 187

Lacouture, Jean, 15, 18

Laird, Melvin, 146, 154, 282, 335, 350, 407, 409

Lando, Barry, 323–24

Land reform: Land-to-the-Tiller Law, 188–89, 218, 302; in North Vietnam, 16; in South Vietnam, 14, 186–89, 437

Lane, Mark, 316

Lang, Anton, 264

LANIKAI operation, 62–63

Lansdale, Edward G., 20, 22, 93, 438

Lao Dong party. *See* Vietnamese Workers' party (VWP)

Laos, 3, 12, 21, 438; bombing in, 388, 406–7; communist takeover of, 427; and Geneva Conference, 8; Laos agreement (1962), 24; 1971 incursion, 167, 174, 296; and SEATO, 11

Laughlin, Fred, 318

Lauterpacht, Hersh, 228, 262

Lavelle, John D., 407–9

Law of Land Warfare (1956), 247, 360–62

Law of War: and air warfare, 396–97; and insurgency/counterinsurgency, 230, 306; legal review of weapons, 269; nature of, 224–25; and ROE, 106, 269; training courses in, 331, 366–69; training films in,

Military justice system, 160, 370
Military necessity, principle of, 224, 228, 232, 247, 256
Military objective, definition of, 231, 397
Military Provincial Health Assistance Program (MILPHAP), 302
Mill, John Stuart, 428
Minh, Duong Van ("Big Minh"), 27, 214
Ministry of Public Security (DRV), 272
Mink, Patsy T., 318
Missiles, surface-to-air. *See* SAM missiles
Mobile Riverine Force, 141
Molotov, V. M., 7
M-1 rifle, 163
Montagnards, 110, 178, 180, 245, 264
Moorer, Thomas H., 393, 414
Morale, military, 176
Morgan, Thomas E., 33
Morgenthau, Hans J., 8, 14, 421
Moskos, Charles C., 320
Moscow-Peking axis, 420–21
Movement for a Democratic Military, 159
M-16 rifle, 164–66, 267–68
Mulligan, Jr., James A., 338
Munition expenditures, 99, 448. *See also* Bombing of North Vietnam
Mussolini, Benito, 429
Mutilation of bodies, 329; ear cutting, 322, 329, 352
Mutiny, 156–57
"Mutt and Jeff" technique, 361, 369
My Lai massacre, 103, 241, 330, 347, 349; concealment of, 323, 326, 344, 348; description of, 325–26; frequency of such incidents, 326–27; legal consequences of, 356–64; and ROE, 238, 268, 345; and training in law of war, 367
My Tho, 127

Nam Dinh, bombing of, 401–3
Napalm, 58–59, 70, 306; children burnt by, 244–45, 312; in Korean War, 243; legality of, 246–47; in World War II, 243
National Academy of Science (NAS), 264
National Council of National Reconciliation, 205
National interest, concept of, 422, 429, 432
Nationalism, appeal of, 3, 218
National Liberation Front (NLF), 272, 295, 312; communist domination of, 16, 18;

formation of, 15; and prisoners of war, 332, 334; 10-point program of, 17
National Police Field Forces, 185
National Security Action Memorandum (NSAM) 288, 30
National Security Action Memorandum (NSAM) 328, 46–47, 377
National Security Council (NSC), 5, 33, 43, 116
NATO, 6
Naval gunfire, 54, 150, 200
Naval Investigative Service, 317, 371
Navarre, Henri, 6
Negligence, criminal responsibility for, 241–42
Nelson, Gaylord, 34
Nelson, Marjorie, 287
New Left, 423, 434
New York Times, 28, 36, 133
New Zealand, 10, 46, 421
Nha Trang, 214
Nhu, Ngo Dinh, 26
Nhu, Mme. Ngo Dinh, 26
"Nine Rules," 366
Nixon, Richard M., 116; and Calley case, 357–58; election of 1972, 136, 388; "imperial presidency," 430; orders blockade of North Vietnam, 198, 410; orders reduction of U.S. casualties, 146; reassures Thieu in 1972 and 1973, 202–4; renunciation of chemical weapons, 256, 266; resignation of, 210; resumes bombing of North Vietnam, 197, 410; and unauthorized bombing of North Vietnam, 409; and U.S. withdrawals, 166, 204; and Vietnamization, 166; Watergate scandal, 203–4, 222
Noncombatants: and body count, 79, 82; difficulty of defining, 232, 451–52; killing of, 236, 277. *See also* Civilian war casualties
Northern Ireland, preventive detention in, 286
North, Kenneth, 338
North Vietnam. *See* Democratic Republic of Vietnam (DRV)
Nuclear proliferation, 428
Nuclear weapons, resort to, 128
Nuremberg trials, 368, 397. See also *High Command* case; *Hostages* case

O'Brien, William V., 269
Office of Civil Operations (OCO), 123

Officer Candidate School (OCS), 330
Oglesby, Carl, 312
OPEC, 222
Open Arms program, 91–92, 173
OPLAN 34A, 32, 36
Oradour, 357, 413
Osborn, Kenneth Barton, 313, 318–19
Oswald, Harvey, 295

Pacification: concept of, 52; damage to, 95–114, 177–82; difficulty of, 143; impact of 1972 Easter offensive on, 198; neglect of, 87, 89; progress in, 63
Pacification Security Coordination Division (CORDS), 287
Pacification Studies Group (PSG), 373
Pakistan, 10
Paris agreement of 1973, 147, 202, 222, 414–15, 436
Paris peace talks (1968–73), 134, 201–2, 388–89, 412, 414
Park, Chung Hee, 97
Parole, 371
Parrot's Beak, 62
Peers Inquiry, 103, 325, 329–31, 344, 348, 358, 361–63, 366–67
Pentagon Papers, 5, 36, 46–47, 68, 74, 114, 120, 376, 430
People's Front Against Corruption, 219
People's Liberation Armed Forces (PLAF), 17, 145, 215
People's Revolutionary Party (PRP), 18
People's Self-Defense Force (PSDF), 134, 182–83, 194, 199, 218
PERSHING operation, 71–72
Personnel turbulence, 160
Philippines, 4, 10, 12, 369, 419, 427
Phnom Penh, fall of, 427
Phoenix program, 125, 279–85, 451; American advisers to, 282–83; annual target quotas, 281–82; legality of, 287; numbers killed, 280–81; reform of, 282–83; weaknesses of, 281–84
Phong Nhi atrocity, 327
Phuoc Long province, loss of, 210
Phu, Phan Van, 211–12, 214
Pike, Douglas, 273, 278, 433
PIPESTONE CANYON operation, 148, 150
Pleiku (city), 38, 212, 375

Poison gas, 251, 253–54. *See also* Tear gas
Police, South Vietnamese, 89, 184–86, 287
Politburo of VWP, 210–11
Political prisoners, 294–96. *See also* Emergency detention
Popular Forces (PF), 90, 134–35, 167, 171–73, 175, 182–83, 194–95, 218
Population increase, 301
Population security strategy, 86, 89, 123, 131–32, 137, 439
Porter, William J., 93, 141, 178
Preparatory fire ("prepping"), 60, 103
President's Commission on Law Enforcement and Administration of Justice, 344–45
Prisoners of War: in First Indochina War, 341; killing of, 353; in Korean War, 299, 340–41; numbers of, missing, 332; release of, 203, 332, 335; torture of, by communists, 332–39; torture of, by South Vietnamese and U.S. forces, 328–29
Prisons, South Vietnamese, 289, 296
"Project 100,000," 160, 331
Propeller-driven aircraft, use of, 98
Property, destruction of, 95, 232–33
Proportionality, rule of, 231
Province Intelligence and Operation Coordinating Centers, 280
Province Security Committees (PSC), 280, 288, 292
Provincial Interrogation Centers (PIC), 287–88
Provincial Reconnaissance Units (PRU), 185, 283
Provisional Revolutionary Government (PRG), 214, 279
PROVN study, 85, 89, 109, 114, 133, 153
Psychiatric disease rate, 160
Psychological operations, 85
Public opinion in U.S., 73–74, 76, 126, 137, 418, 432–37
Public Safety (AID), Office of, 185, 295–96
PUEBLO, U.S.S., 128
Punji stakes, 277
Pye, Lucian W., 436

Quang Khe naval base, 376
Quang Nam province, 147–153
Quang Ngai hospital, 141, 287
Quang Ngai province, 70–71, 139

Schell, Jonathan, 64, 71, 234
Schlesinger, Jr., Arthur M., 12, 395, 419, 421
Schlesinger, James, 221
Schoenbrun, David, 398
Schoenman, Ralph, 311–13
Schools in South Vietnam, secondary, 95, 190
Seaborn, Blair, 31
Search-and-destroy operations, 51, 57, 61, 86, 119, 134, 325
SEATO treaty, 10–11, 34, 418
Seiberling, John F., 318
Sensors, electronic, 100
Serong, F. P., 212
Sevareid, Eric, 308
Shaplen, Robert, 143, 221, 274
Sharp, U.S.G., 383, 390
Sheehan, Neil, 26, 102, 316, 418
Short rounds, 303–4, 443
Sihanouk, Norodom, 409, 421
Singapore, 422
Sino-Indian clash (1962), 421
Sino-Soviet rift, 424
Sirhan, Sirhan, 295
"Smart bombs," 200, 404, 410. *See also* Bombing of North Vietnam
Smith, Jacob, 369
Smith, Walter B., 9
Sniping, reaction to, 69, 72, 102, 231, 309
Social mobility in South Vietnam, lack of, 95, 170
Song Ma River, 398
Son My. *See* My Lai massacre
Son Thang (4) atrocity, 327, 330–31, 346, 356
Son Tra atrocity, 276
Southeast Asia Analysis Report, 115
Southeast Asia, importance of, 3, 5–6, 12, 19, 418, 422–23
South Vietnam. *See* Republic of Vietnam (South)
Soviet Union: support of North Vietnam, 6, 196, 205, 392; threat to Europe, 4, 420; war-time alliance with, 429
Spanish Civil War of 1936–39, 428
Spare parts, shortage of, 217
Special Forces, 20, 22, 85, 313, 333, 439
Specified strike zones, 60, 79, 105–7, 150, 226, 229, 326
SPEEDY EXPRESS operation, 142–43, 151, 452
Spock, Benjamin, 445

Sputnik, impact of, 420
Standing operating procedures (SOP), 233
STARLIGHT operation, 54–55
Stennis, John C., 383–85
Stern, Laurence, 276
Stockholm International Peace Research Institute, 253
Stock market and war, 423
Stone, I. F., 39
STRANGLE operation, 394
Strategic hamlet program, 25, 89, 183
Stratton, Richard, 336
Sukarno, Achmed, 37
Superior orders, plea of, 315, 355–57, 367–68
Switzerland, government of, 270
Symington, Stuart, 318
Systems Analysis (DOD), Office of, 115–16, 130

Task Force Barker, 325, 331, 362, 366, 452. *See also* My Lai massacre
Task Force Oregon, 69–71, 121
Tay Ninh province, 147
Taylor, Maxwell D., 20–22, 29, 37, 43, 46–49
Taylor, Telford, 233, 239, 327, 363, 397, 405, 413, 446
Tear gas, 248–257; first use of, 248; in Korean War, 250; legality of, 253–56; quantities used, 251; routine use of, 250; and State Department, 249, 255–56; toxicity of, 252; UN General Assembly on, 254–55; VC use of, 251
Television coverage of war, 433–34
Territorial Forces. *See* Popular Forces; Regional Forces
Terrorism: and Geneva conventions, 286; legality of, 270–71. *See also* Viet Cong terror; Hue massacre
Terzani, Tiziano, 295, 299
Tet offensive (1968), 75, 193, 233, 385; casualties, 127, 134; effect on GVN, 165; impact on U.S. public opinion, 76, 434; strategic review following, 130–31, 146
Thailand, 10, 12, 49, 422, 427
Thanh Hoa, 387, 398
THAYER I/IRVING operation, 57, 59
THAYER II operation, 59–60
Thieu, Nguyen Van, 122, 166, 170; implicated in corruption, 220; and land reform, 187;

leadership ability and reputation, 218; mistakes in 1975, 218; and 1972 Easter offensive, 197, 201; and 1968 peace talks, 388–89; orders withdrawal from central highlands, 212; and Paris agreement of 1973, 202–3; resignation of, 214

Third Party Inducement program, 91–92

Tho, Le Duc, 414

Thomas, Ann Van Wynen and A. J., 256, 265

Thomas, Norman, 12

Thompson, Robert, 85, 104, 123, 186, 194, 200, 202

Threat to the Peace, A (1961), 23

III Marine Amphibious Force, 54

"Ticket punching," 118

Tiger cages, 297–99

Tin, Chan, 294–95

Todd, Oliver, 338

Tokyo, bombing of, 413

Tompkins, R. Mc., 100

Topping, Seymour, 422

Torture, 344, 361; in North Vietnamese jails, 335–39; by South Vietnamese, 287–88, 328–29; by U.S. troops, 329

Toth v. Quarles, 365

Trojan Women, The, 270

Truman, Harry S., 4–5, 418

Truong, Ngo Quang, 197, 212–13, 222

Tuchman, Barbara W., 439

Tuck, David Kenneth, 251–52

Tunnels, 54, 139, 151

TURNER JOY, U.S.S., 32

Twain, Mark, 428

Twelve-month tour of duty, 118, 160

U Minh Forest, 179

Undeclared war, 431

Uniform Code of Military Justice (UCMJ), 343, 351–52, 354, 359, 365, 370

United Nations action: on chemical weapons, 265–66; on genocide, 300; on napalm, 247; on relocations, 229; on tear gas, 252, 254–55

U.S. assistance: for French in Indochina, 4–5; for South Vietnam, 11, 23, 89, 92, 206, 418

U.S. defense attaché, 208, 213, 217, 221

U.S. force levels in Vietnam, 24, 51, 73–74, 129–31, 133, 147

U.S. Marine Corps: battle for Quang Nam province, 147–53; first units in Vietnam, 42; offenses against Vietnamese, 456; strength in Vietnam, 152; and war crimes, 350–51. *See also* Amphibious landing operations; Combined Action Platoon

U.S. Seventh Fleet, 200, 427

U.S. Strategic Bombing Survey, 395

Unnecessary suffering, concept of, 242, 244

Urlanis, Boris, 450

Utter, Leon N., 249

Van Dyke, Jon M., 337

Vann, John Paul, 103–4, 118, 169–70, 440

Van Tuong Peninsula, 54

Versailles treaty, 254

Vien, Nguyen Khac, 294

Vienna conference of 1961, 19

Viet Cong (VC): appeal of, 93; infrastructure, 57, 63, 135, 137, 151, 279, 282, 284; and land reform, 14, 186–87; morale of, 176, 433; recruitment for, 84, 177, 215; strength of, 74–75, 83–84, 134; terror, 88, 191, 272–79, 448–49, 455

Viet Minh, 3, 5, 8, 10, 14, 186, 436

Vietnamese population, relations with, 158, 310–11

Vietnamese Workers' party (VWP), 15, 18, 29, 39, 204–5

Vietnamization, 182, 202, 441; beginning of, 164–65; and Nixon administration, 136, 164–65

Vietnam veterans, adjustment problems of, 319–21

Vietnam Veterans Against the War (VVAW), 316–17, 319, 357

Village councils, 14, 94, 218

Vinh, 386

Vinh, Nguyen Van, 204

Waldie, Jerome R., 288

Wallace, Mike, 324

Walt, Lewis W., 54, 86, 328

War Crimes, U.S.: acquittal rates, 351; allegations of, 345, 347–48, 350, 457; command responsibility for, 239–42, 359–60; communist charges of, 223, 396, 413; and discharged servicemen, 363–65; reporting of, 343–350, 372; sentences for, 352–53, 370–71, 458; and treatment of officers, 352. *See also* Atrocities; Law of war; Parole